Nāgārjuna's *Reason Sixty*
with
Chandrakīrti's *Reason Sixty Commentary*

The American Institute of Buddhist Studies (AIBS), in affiliation with the Columbia University Center for Buddhist Studies (CBS) and Tibet House US (THUS), has established the *Treasury of the Buddhist Sciences* series to provide authoritative English translations, studies, and editions of the texts of the Tibetan Tengyur (*bstan 'gyur*) and its associated literature. The Tibetan Tengyur is a vast collection of over 3,600 classical Indian Buddhist scientific treatises (*śāstra*) written in Sanskrit by over 700 authors from the first millennium CE, now preserved mainly in systematic 7th–12th century Tibetan translation. Its topics span all of India's "outer" arts and sciences, including linguistics, medicine, astronomy, socio-political theory, ethics, art, and so on, as well as all of her "inner" arts and sciences such as philosophy, psychology ("mind science"), meditation, and yoga.

The Publisher gratefully acknowledges the generous support of David Sloss, the National Endowment for the Humanities, Anonymous, the Conanima Foundation, the Infinity Foundation, the Sacharuna Foundation, Wendy Lochner and the Columbia University Press, Thomas and Mary Yarnall, and Robert and Nena Thurman in sponsoring the publication of this series.

Nāgārjuna's *Reason Sixty* with Chandrakīrti's *Reason Sixty Commentary*

Translated from the Tibetan
with Introductory Study and Annotation
by
Joseph John Loizzo
and the AIBS Translation Team

Edited by
Robert A.F. Thurman, Thomas F. Yarnall, and Paul G. Hackett

Critical Editions by
Joseph John Loizzo and Paul G. Hackett

Tengyur Translation Initiative
Treasury of the Buddhist Sciences series

Published by
The American Institute of Buddhist Studies
at Columbia University in New York

Co-published with
Columbia University's Center for Buddhist Studies
and Tibet House US

2007

Tengyur Translation Initiative
Treasury of the Buddhist Sciences series
A refereed series published by:

American Institute of Buddhist Studies
Columbia University
80 Claremont Ave, room 303
New York, NY 10027

http://www.aibs.columbia.edu

Co-published with Columbia University's Center for Buddhist Studies and Tibet House US

Distributed by Columbia University Press

Printed in Canada on acid-free paper.

ISBN 978-0-9753734-2-2 (cloth)

Library of Congress Cataloging-in-Publication Data

Nāgārjuna's reason sixty with Chandrakīrti's reason sixty commentary / translated from the Tibetan with introductory study and annotation by Joseph John Loizzo ; edited by Robert A.F. Thurman ... [et al.]

p. cm. — (Treasury of the Buddhist sciences)

"Co-published with Columbia University's Center for Buddhist Studies and Tibet House US."

ISBN 978-0-9753734-2-2 (alk. paper)

1. Nāgārjuna, 2nd cent. Yuktiṣaṣṭikā—Commentaries. 2. Mahāyāna Buddhism. I. Loizzo, Joseph John, 1955– II. Thurman, Robert A. F.

BQ7479.8.N347N34 2007
294.3'85--dc22

2007060676

Dedication

In Memoriam

Marius Jerome Loizzo (1919–2001)
Scholar, Teacher, Officer, Physician

Kennst du das Land wo die Citrönen bluh'n?
...O meine Vater, lass uns ziehen!

– Goethe

Contents

TRANSLATIONS

CRITICAL EDITIONS
of the Tibetan Texts

APPENDICES

PREFACES AND ACKNOWLEDGEMENTS

Editors' Prefaces

Series' Editor-in-Chief

Nāgārjuna and Chandrakīrti's works have been more and better studied recently, and it is possible perhaps for a dedicated student of Buddhist Centrist Mādhyamika philosophy more or less to understand it through translations available in the English language. But, it is perhaps still not possible for a philosopher conversant with the history of Western philosophy and even professionally competent in current philosophical practice to use the still relevant critical genius of these great authors in their own thought and writings—at least not without the kind of linguistic and comparative philosophical effort for which it is realistically hard for a busy person to have time. So Dr. Joseph Loizzo, in this innovative, philosophically and psychologically sophisticated study and translation, has done a great service in presenting this fine work on Nāgārjuna's *Reason Sixty* and Chandrakīrti's *Commentary*.

As the author mentions below, the translation was done over a long period of years, with the help of many people, all duly acknowledged by him. It was eventually presented as the translation appendix to a doctoral dissertation, a study of the life and works of Chandrakīrti in the context of Nālandā monastic university. Subsequently, it has been highly re-worked by the author, with the help of an assiduous and meticulous team of scholarly editors, with Thomas Yarnall researching and improving numerous fine points in both study and translations, and Paul Hackett taking the lead in refining and further developing the critical edition of the Tibetan translation text. It is for this reason that Dr. Loizzo and we together decided to include "the AIBS team" in the authorial credit. With all the diligent help received in this manner, Dr. Loizzo remains responsible for the primary research in five languages, the introductory study—with its insightful analysis of currents in traditional Chandrakīrti scholarship, its innovative and important delving into the translator's "philosophical reference frame," its courageous entry into domains of contemporary psychology and philosophy which are part of the necessary process of broadening the usefulness of the Centrist works of these authors, and the final translation itself. For any errors that may have worked their way into the work from the efforts of the editors, we beg the reader's indulgence.

Finally, we welcome the reader to the delightful subtlety and clarity of these works of the Second Buddha, Nāgārjuna, and of Chandrakīrti, whom we could perhaps call the "Second Mañjuśrī," as revealed in English translation from the Tibetan, the former in a serious upgrade of previous versions, and the latter now for the first time.

Robert A.F. Thurman (Ari Genyen Tenzin Chotrag)

Jey Tsong Khapa Professor of Indo-Tibetan Buddhist Studies,
Director, Columbia University Center for Buddhist Studies
President, American Institute of Buddhist Studies
President, Tibet House US

Gandendekyi Ling
Woodstock, New York
February 18, 2007

Series' Executive Editor

It is a great personal pleasure to present this marvelous study, translation, and edition of Nāgārjuna's *Reason Sixty* (YṢ) and Chandrakīrti's *Commentary* (YṢV) by my long-time friend and colleague, Dr. Joseph Loizzo. Dr. Loizzo and I have known each other since the late 1970s and early 1980s when we were both privileged to have had Dr. Robert Thurman as our mutual mentor. Thus, over two decades later, and after Dr. Loizzo's many years of dedicated work on the YṢ and YṢV, it has been a very special joy for all three of us to have had the good fortune to come together again, this time to collaborate as colleagues to bring to final fruition the translation and publication of these essential Centrist (*Mādhyamika*) texts.

It was almost a quarter of a century ago that Dr. Thurman published his own important study and translation of a key Centrist text, the *Essence of Eloquence (legs bshad snying po)*, by the 14th–15th century Tibetan scholar Je Tsong Khapa. This text presented Tsong Khapa's own highly influential and celebrated history, analysis, and resolution of key philosophical points central to the texts and traditions of Nāgārjuna and Chandrakīrti. In his introduction to that book Thurman acknowledged his debt to the twentieth-century philosopher L. Wittgenstein for enabling his own understanding and translation of Tsong Khapa's Centrist text (*cf.* especially 89–111), stating that the philosophical topics explored in the Tibetan original "would not be intelligible and could not even have been translated" without reference to the mature Wittgenstein (21). So, for example, with respect to his understanding and translation of the key Centrist topic of *svatantra* (Tib. *rang rgyud*), Thurman explains that "The precise philosophical translation of this term is extremely difficult in English,...[and] is only made possible by the work of L. Wittgenstein, who in the *Philosophical Investigations* refutes for the first time in Western philosophy the concept of a 'private language,' and a concept of a 'private object,' which ordinary people and philosophers have assumed and theorized, respectively, to be the basis of language and experiential reality..." (321–22 n. 99). It was on this basis that Thurman developed and successfully employed the apt translation "logical privacy" for this complex Centrist concept, emphasizing that thus "it was only with the help of Wittgenstein and his insight into this most subtle of subtleties, as Tsong Khapa calls it, that I myself was able to get clear these profound sections of the *Essence*, not to speak of translating them" (103).

Not surprisingly, Dr. Thurman's pioneering reliance on Wittgenstein for understanding and translating Centrist texts exerted an evident and unmistakable influence on Dr. Loizzo's translation style, terminology, methodology, and interpretation. Thus, Dr. Loizzo's own innovative study and translation of the Centrist texts presented herein continue this interpretive approach, while further developing and deepening the connection and debt to Wittgenstein. Loizzo acknowledges that in recent years (thanks in large part to works such as Thurman's), "comparisons of Centrist philosophers with Wittgenstein have been viewed by many as basic to a coherent postmodern reference frame for Centrist studies...." However, he is critical of the forms such comparisons have taken, highlighting various "subtle forms of...[contemporary] dualistic biases that tend to obscure modern views of Nāgārjuna" (14) which have emerged in more recent years. Moreover, he argues that such "misreadings reflect the conflicting positions of objectivist and constructivist camps in the postmodern debate over the objectivity of scientific knowledge and method, a debate sparked by the relativistic turn in modern physics and the linguistic turn in Western philosophy." Thus, in addition to carefully revisiting Wittgenstein's thought in this comparative context, Loizzo explains that he has herein "attempted to show the family resemblance between the nondualism of Chandrakīrti and Wittgenstein by couching my discussion...in the more accessible language of the postmodern debate over objectivity" (19). In particular, he argues that it is Nagel's approach to "objectivity" that presents perhaps the most promising comparative framework for interpreting Buddhist Centrism, for it is Nagel who "seems...to be clearly on the trail of a radical centrist theory of objective knowledge and responsible agency (analogous to Buddhist 'omniscience' and 'omnicompassion')," insisting on "a radical, nondualistic conclusion in striking sympathy with the program of Buddhist human science: not only is the scientific pursuit of objective knowledge inexorably relative to the philosophical pursuit of self-knowledge but at bottom the two are synergistic and inseparable" (20).

Moreover, in addition to developing and strengthening connections to Wittgenstein and updating the context to include the postmodern debate over objectivity, Loizzo necessarily widens the comparative framework to include other important "language-therapeutic" approaches from several other contemporary disciplines. In particular, Dr. Loizzo's own years of experience as a physician and psychotherapist have clearly had an equally important influence on his understanding of Centrism; and it is this unique blend of sustained experience and expertise in both modern philosophical and psychological disciplines that seems to have uniquely shaped and specially qualified Dr. Loizzo to translate and present to a contemporary audience the particular Centrist texts considered herein. Thus, when examining the presentation of Centrist thought herein, the reader will encounter—in addition to the more familiar philosophical language of "absolutism," "reification," "nihilism," and so forth—manifold uses of more intriguing psychological language such as "projection and denial," "the process of obsession and conflict," "cognitive-affective-behavioral self-transcendence," "emotional self-mastery," "the empathic use of conventional constructs," and so forth. Likewise, drawing on yet other disciplines, Loizzo will explain, for example: "I borrow the terms 'evolutionary epistemology' and 'psychosocial construction' from current exploration—in the fields of neurobiology, sociology, linguistics, and the philosophy of science—of the fact that human knowledge and perception is shaped by the constructive activity of the subject, in dependence on a psychosociobiological matrix of conditions" (93 n 64). And so on.

Thus, just as Dr. Thurman before him argued for the indispensability of Wittgenstein for developing a deeper understanding of Buddhist Centrist philosophical thought in general, so Dr. Loizzo persuasively argues that his own widening of the comparative approach is essential to developing a proper understanding and translation of the particular Centrist texts presented herein. This is so, he argues, because Nāgārjuna's *Reason Sixty* and

Chandrakīrti's *Commentary* fill a unique space bridging these authors' more purely philosophical, critical texts (concerned primarily with wisdom), and their more practical, therapeutic texts (concerned primarily with ethics and the practice of compassion). Thus, in the case of Nāgārjuna's text, Loizzo states: "the *Reason Sixty*...stands midway between...[his other] two masterpieces.... Bridging from the rigorous critiques of the *Wisdom* toward the elaboration of the ethos of compassion in the *Jewel Rosary*, it underlines the central thrust of Nāgārjuna's therapeutic philosophy of language, namely, the elimination of cognitive and affective resistances to nondualistic wisdom and compassion" (6); and thus: "While Nāgārjuna's opening and central focus in the *Reason* highlights the dereifying and illusion-like insights of Centrist analysis, his concluding focus is on preparing the practitioner to apply these twin contemplative modes to the final nondual performance of wisdom and compassion formulated in his *Jewel Rosary*" (105). And in the case of Chandrakīrti's text: "the *Commentary*...serves a transitional role..., linking the critical hermeneutical pedagogy of the *Lucid Exposition* with the practical, therapeutic anthropology of the *Introduction*, just as Nāgārjuna's *Reason* links the *Wisdom* and *Jewel Rosary*" (8); and: "Chandrakīrti highlights the linkage between the dereifying mode of transcendent insight and its virtual or conventional mode.... [T]he two insight-modes are mutually indispensable to liberative development, the critical and practical aspects of a single process" (98); and thus: "...as the *Reason* clears the contemplative way to the final nondual practice of the *Jewel Rosary*, Chandrakīrti's *Commentary* offers a transition from the critical hermeneutics of the *Lucid Exposition* to the altruistic anthropology...in...his *Introduction*...." (42) In sum, Loizzo argues: "The key point to be considered here is how the purely negative or 'critical' dereifying insight of voidness translates into the 'practical,' illusion-like, or virtual, relational insight, sustaining the enlightened cultivation of living individuals and their social consensus" (92).

Furthermore, as implied above, Loizzo further explicitly links these two sets of three texts with the Buddhist three "higher disciplines" (*adhiśikṣa*) of wisdom/philosophy, contemplation, and ethics (*prajñā*, *samādhi*, *śīla*), respectively. In so doing, he helps to clarify links between these three disciplines which—while key throughout the Indo-Tibetan traditions—seem to have been less-well explored in contemporary Western scholarship. Moreover, if the *Wisdom* and the *Lucid Exposition* are aligned with the discipline of philosophy, presenting an analysis of the nature of reality, and as such addressing objective matters, then by aligning the *Reason* and its

Commentary with the discipline of contemplation, and by aligning the *Rosary* and the *Introduction* with the discipline of ethics, Loizzo helps to clarify the distinct ways in which these latter four texts address the *subjective* aspect of Centrist studies (which aspect of course then nondually links back to the objective side as well). It is these latter aspects and dimensions of Centrism in particular that Loizzo compellingly argues may have been "systematically overlooked or distorted by Western scholarship" (4). And it is the interrelated linkages between all of these aspects and dimensions—as well as the unique intermediating functions performed by the *Reason* and its *Commentary*—that have informed and, in the end, necessitated and justified Loizzo's multi-disciplinary approach to the study and translation of these particular Centrist texts.

If most will readily agree with Loizzo's observation that "[t]he post-modern problems of understanding the relativity of knowledge and action, self and language, body and mind, are among the most critical in the Western academy," then we—as the editors of this series—would like to add our voices in strong support of his further conviction that with regard to addressing these critical problems, "understanding the Central Philosophy promises to be invaluable to Indology, to modern philosophy of science, and to science of mind" (23). We have every confidence that the present book can begin to fulfill this promise by making a significant contribution to such an understanding, offering, as Loizzo promises, "a fresh look at Buddhism as a spiritual and scientific civilization committed to the pursuit of objective self-knowledge and self-regulation along the non-egocentrist lines Wittgenstein, Nagel, and others prescribe" (23). We invite the reader to explore, critically assess, respond, and contribute to this updated, nuanced approach to Centrist studies, and to consider seriously what contributions these texts and the Indo-Tibetan "spiritual and scientific civilization" from which they spring may yet have to offer to the many interrelated discourses of our emerging global civilization.

Thomas F. Yarnall, Ph.D.
Adjunct Assistant Professor
Columbia University, Department of Religion

Associate Editor (especially Tibetan Critical Edition)

As one of the texts known collectively as the "Sixfold Canon of Reasonings" (*rigs tshogs drug*), Nāgārjuna's *Reason Sixty* (*yuktiṣaṣṭikā*; *rigs pa drug cu pa*) has been identified by later Tibetan scholars as serving a specific function in the context of Nāgārjuna's overall exposition of the Centrist (*mādhyamika*; *dbu ma pa*) philosophy. Discussing the relationship of the different works to each other, the twentieth century Tibetan scholar, Losang Dorjey (*blo bzang rdo rje*) states that, of the works of Nāgārjuna on the Central Way, there are two types: those establishing the object—subtle voidness—through reasoning, and those teaching that the subject—the view realizing that voidness—is the root of liberation and omniscience. Four of these six works—the *Wisdom: The Fundamental Verses of the Central Way*, the *Finely Woven Treatise*, the *Voidness Seventy*, and the *Rebuttal of Objections*—fall into the first category, while the remaining two—the *Reason Sixty* and the *Jewel Rosary*—fall into the latter.[1]

Although often quoted by scholars in works treating various points of Centrist philosophy, of the dozen or so explicit commentaries known to have been written on the *Reason Sixty*,[2] only the commentaries of Chandrakīrti, Tsong Khapa Losang Drakpa[3] and Gyaltsap Darma Rinchen[4] are readily accessible.[5] In these commentaries, the structure of Nāgārjuna's

[1] Losang Dorjay (*blo bzang rdo rje*), *byang chub lam gyi rim pa'i mtha' dpyod gsung rab rgya mtshor 'jug pa'i gru gzings* (*Ship for Entering into the Ocean of Textual Systems, the Decisive Analysis of [Tsong Khapa's] "Stages of the Path to Enlightenment"*).

[2] E. Gene Smith, private communication.

[3] Tsong Khapa Losang Drakpa (*tsong kha pa blo bzang grags pa*, 1357–1419), *rigs pa drug cu pa'i zin bris* (*Notes [of a lecture] on "The Sixty Stanzas of Reasonings"*). Transcribed by Gyaltsap Darma Rinchen (*rgyal tshab dar ma rin chen*). Tōh. 5403 = 5444.

[4] Gyaltsap Darma Rinchen, *Rigs pa drug cu pa'i ṭikka* (*Commentary on [Nāgārjuna's] "Sixty Stanzas of Reasonings"*). Tōh. 5443.

[5] Although a commentary was also written by the late 19th century author, Gzhan-phan Chos-kyi-snang-ba (1871–1927), since it merely re-states the content of Chandrakīrti's own commentary, it has not been used. Gyaltsap mentions also a certain Zhang-thang-sag-pa Ye-shes-'byung-gnas explicitly by name, as the author of a *rigs pa drug cu pa'i ṭikka*, though this text does not appear to be extant; he would appear to be the same author referred to in Lokesh Chandra's *Materials for a History of Tibetan Literature*, Part 3. New Delhi: International Academy of Indian Culture (1963), p.523 (no. 11346), and in E. Gene Smith's *Tibetan Buddhist Resource Center* database (TBRC Resource Code, W16461).

treatise is explicitly laid out along with discussions of the various points of contention addressed by the individual verses.

Following Gyaltsap's lead, the texts can be divided into the traditional three main sections: homage, body of the work, and the dedication of merits. The body of the work, verses 1 through 59, presents Nāgārjuna's reasonings on four major points:

A. Teaching [the Centrists' presentation of] Relativity as Free from the [Two] Extremes (vss. 1–29)
B. Establishing that the Teachings on the Aggregates are of Interpretable Meaning (vss. 30–39)
C. Perceiving the Faults of Adhering to the Aggregates (vss. 40–56)
D. The Benefits of Liberation (vss. 57–59)

Close to half of the body of the work is devoted to the first topic—eliminating the objections to Nāgārjuna's presentation of relativity as indicative of an extreme of nihilism or absolutism—while the bulk of the second half of the text (the second and third topics) is dedicated to demonstrating that just those same charges actually apply to his would-be detractors.

Throughout the text, Chandrakīrti takes the opportunity not only to explicate various points of Centrist philosophy in relation to Nāgārjuna's verses, but also to reveal his incisive analysis of the texts and tenets of both Buddhist and non-Buddhist critics of Nāgārjuna as well, from the Sarvāstivādins to the Saṁkhyā and Vaiśeṣika. Chandrakīrti combines his defense of the Centrist position with pointed attacks on the implications of others' assertions, most notably (in this text) the foundational concepts of Dignāga's epistemology, and in particular, the presentation of validating cognition (*pramāṇa*) and its grounding in the assertion of intrinsic identity. Moreover, Chandrakīrti repeatedly displays his familiarity and facility with Dignāga's epistemological system and its various categories, such as direct perception (*pratyakṣa, mngon sum*) and specifically and generally characterized entities,[6] being a valid source of knowledge,[7] meaning-universals,[8] aspectual percep-

[6] Commentary to v. 8, where Chandrakīrti makes his argument for a Centrist understanding of the direct perception of negative phenomena ("cessations").

[7] Commentary to v. 28.

[8] Commentary to v. 30.

tion,[9] and others, all the while pointing out the flaws in the attacks of their proponents.

Thus, from a close reading of the terms of the different disputes in his *Commentary*, one can begin to paint a richer picture of the inter-religious and inter-sectarian dialogues taking place in 6th century India. Viewed in this light, the text itself is an invitation to revisit the other works attributed to Chandrakīrti in order to examine further the subtle contextual references contained therein and to more greatly appreciate the intellectual might of Chandrakīrti, himself, that has rightly earned him a reputation as one of the greatest minds of the past two millennia.

Paul G. Hackett
Columbia University

[9] Commentary to v. 34; Gyaltsap expands on this point at length in his *ṭīka*, arguing against the validity of such a mediated perception and the existence of a self-knowing consciousness (*rang rig, svasaṃvedana*) required by such an aspectual model of perception.

Editors' Acknowledgements

Although it is not possible to recognize the many individuals who have made this study possible, we wish to acknowledge those scholars who have directly contributed to the understanding of this work beginning with the "param-guru" of 21st century Tibetan Buddhist studies in America, the venerable Geshe Wangyal, who directly taught and facilitated the scholarship of so many scholars in the field today. We would also like to acknowledge the kind help of the venerable Gen. Lozang Jamspal of the Religion Department at Columbia for his assistance and insights into critical points of the text. Although this work is inadequate as even a small gesture of gratitude and effort to repay the kindness shown to us by these teachers and their lineage, we nonetheless offer to them this study and translation of the *Yuktiṣaṣṭikā* and *Yuktiṣaṣṭikāvṛtti*.

Special thanks are due to Bob Chilton of the Asian Classics Input Project (ACIP) for electronic copies of the Tibetan translations of the *Yuktiṣaṣṭikā* and *Yuktiṣaṣṭikāvṛtti*, and to Geshe Thupten Jinpa of the Institute of Tibetan Classics who provided us with their electronic copy of Gyaltsap Darma Rinchen's *Rigs pa drug cu pa'i ṭīkka*.

Author's Acknowledgements

In recognizing the many individuals who have made this study possible, I begin by acknowledging the lineage of teachers by whom the Central Philosophy of Nāgārjuna and Chandrakīrti has been preserved and transmitted down to the present. In the tradition of Tsong Khapa, it is vital to first acknowledge Mañjuśrī, Archetype of Transcendent Wisdom and patron of the lineage of profound view, whose vow is to appear in all universes and epochs to spark the pursuit of transcendent insight into the profound nonduality of voidness and relativity/compassion. Then come the teachers cited by Tsong Khapa as his Central Way lineage (plus intermediaries cited by Tāranātha), beginning with Nāgārjuna (second century), Āryadeva (third century), Buddhapālita (fifth century), Bhāvaviveka (sixth century), (Kamalabuddhi) and Chandrakīrti (seventh century), and coming through (Jayadeva), Śāntideva (eighth century), Vidyakokila senior and junior, Sarahā, Hasumāti, Kanakavarma (early eleventh century), to Patshab Nyi-ma Grags (1055–1145), Tibetan translator of the *Yuktiṣaṣṭikākarikās*, who transmitted the Central Way authority to three abbots of rMabya Monastery including Shakya Seng-ge. From him it continued in Tibet through Kun-mkhyen mChims, sKyo-ston-pa, rGyang-ro Pan-chen, mTsur gZhon-nu Seng-ge, mKhan-chen Zhang-pa, sLob-dpon dGe-'bar (fourteenth century), dbU-tshad-pa Od-zer-grub (fourteenth century), Mog-lo bZhang-po (fourteenth century), Rin-po-che Kun-rgyal, and Red-mda-ba gZhon-nu bLo-gros (1349–1412), the main Centrist teacher of Tsong Khapa (1357–1419). From Tsong Khapa the lineage includes mKhas Grub rJe (1385–1438), Ba-so Chos-kyi rGyal-mtshan (1402–1473), Grub-chen Chos-kyi rDo-rje (late 15th century), rGyal-ba dbEn-sa-ba (1505–1566), Sangs-rgyas Ye-shes (1525–1591), Pan-chen bLo-bzang Chos-kyi rGyal-mtshan (1570–1662), rDo-rje 'Dzin-pa dKon-mchog rGyal-mtshan (1612–1687), 'Jam-dbyangs bZhad-pa Ngag-dbang brTson-'grus (1648–1721), Khri-chen bLo-bZang bsTan-pa'i Nyi-ma (1689–1746), lCang-kya Rol-pa'i rDo-rje (1717–1786), Thu'u-bkvan bLo-bzang Chos-kyi Nyi-ma (1737–1802), dKon-mchog 'Jigs-med dbAng-po (1728–1791), Gun-thang 'Jam-bdyangs bsTan-pa'i sGron-me (1762–1823), dbAl-mang dKon-mchog rGyal-mtshan (19th century), rTsa-ba'i bLa-ma rTa-mgrin bLo-bzangs rTa-dbyangs (1867–1937), and Geshe sByin-pa of the sGo-mang College of Drepung, who transmitted it to the venerable Geshe

Wangyal, who taught Robert Thurman. I express here the profound debt I owe each one of these scholars, without whom the living therapeutic philosophy of Nāgārjuna and Chandrakīrti might have vanished along with the texts studied and translated below.

The seed of this study was planted over thirty years ago, when I had the good fortune to meet Robert Thurman at Amherst College, the year he began his teaching career there. With my Nietzsche and Freud volumes parked on the shelf, the next four years unfolded as an eye-widening tutorial in Buddhist philosophy and psychology that culminated in a year-long senior independent study project and thesis on Wittgenstein and the Mādhyamika. To this day I remain profoundly grateful to the late Ludwig Wittgenstein, whose penetrating genius taught me that the exquisite subtlety of Chandra's Dialecticist Centrist thought is indeed universally human. My budding interest in the Indo-Tibetan stream of therapeutic language philosophy thrived in the glow of Thurman's work on Tsong Khapa's hermeneutical *Essence of True Eloquence Differentiating Interpretable and Definitive* (*Drang Nges Legs bShad sNying po*), invaluable in clarifying Chandrakīrti's Prāsaṅgika critique of less critical schools of Buddhist and non-Buddhist thought. As a senior I made an English rendering of Philipp Schaeffer's German version of the *Yuktiṣaṣṭikā*, then the only European language translation of Nāgārjuna's text. Shortly after graduation, Thurman started me on Pa-tshab Nyi-ma Grags' Tibetan translation, and then, Yeshes sDe's Tibetan version of Chandrakīrti's *Yuktiṣaṣṭikāvrtti*. During my medical studies in New York, I tried to read the *Commentary* in my free time with the kind help of Dr. Losang Jamspal, then a Ph.D. student at Columbia. At one point, I took a leave to continue reading with Thurman—in Amherst, Woodstock, and India—especially trying to decipher the difficult passages in which Chandrakīrti is critiquing the views of Buddhist Logicians, Idealists, and Dogmaticist Centrists being debated at Nālandā in his day. Although the year flew by with precious little time for formal study, it kept my interest "moist," as the Tibetans say, and helped establish contacts that would sustain me through the dry years of medical education and psychiatric training.

Thanks to that leave in 1979 with Thurman, I was privileged to have encountered some of the most eminent teachers of the Tibetan refugee community in India, who would become my direct links to the Tibetan tradition of Indological scholarship. First among these was the late Venerable Tsenshab Serkhong Rinpoche, an authority on the *Legs bshad snying po*. Those of us who received his "mystic textual transmission" of the *Essence* in the summer of 1981 in Woodstock were stunned when he recited Tsong Khapa's entire philosophical masterpiece from memory, in four hours. No less crucial to this work have been my encounters over the years with His Holiness Tenzin Gyatso, the Fourteenth Dalai Lama of Tibet. In his regular visits to America he has exemplified for me the heritage of philosophical insight and empathic art one finds still alive in the Indo-Tibetan Centrist tradition, especially reinforcing the therapeutic meaning of Buddhist philosophy and practice through his inspired teaching on the four noble truths and his interest in the meeting of Buddhist and Western sciences of mind. In another vein, I must express my profound indebtedness to the late Venerable Yongzin Ling Rinpoche, then designated head of the Gelukpa academic tradition as successor to Jey Tsong Khapa's Ganden throne, for an introduction to Mañjuśrī that has never left my mind. Finally, there is Ngawang Gehlek Rinpoche, whose combination of personal teaching and caring friendship has embodied for me the Buddhist tradition of marrying Centrist philosophy, psychology, and ethics, reaching back to Chandrakīrti, Nāgārjuna, and Shākyamuni himself. In addition, during my later studies at Harvard, Masatoshi Nagatomi's precise scholarship helped me appreciate why Buddhist logic so influenced Mahāyāna thought. I am indebted to him for his scholarly example. I must also thank Mādhyamika scholar D.S. Ruegg, and my fellow Chandrakīrti scholar Peter Fenner, who taught me during off-call hours, through their helpful studies and translations. I am especially indebted to Christina Scherrer-Schaub, whose brilliant French translation of the *Yuktiṣaṣṭikāvṛtti* made her a virtual member of my translation team, particularly helping me and my colleagues to cross-check philological questions on the model of our great Indian and Tibetan ancestors.

Inevitably, my green scholarship needed more than just the passage of years to mature. Fortunately, Thurman had moved to Columbia by the time I was ready for the help I needed to bring this project to fruition. In addition to his genius for translation and cheerful perseverance, I met many old and new friends here whose contributions I must acknowledge. I owe a debt to the faculty of the Columbia Department of Religion, for granting me the Mellon fellowship that has allowed me complete this project. I thank Great Brahma for Gary Tubb, who combines the divinity of Sanskrit with a humanity that on many days made saving a syllable feel like the breath of life itself. To him and his fellow Indologists, Jack Hawley and Rachel

McDermott, I am indebted for helping me to see how the Buddhist traditions preserved in Tibetan Indology grew intertwined with their Vedist counterparts, especially in the fertile ground of India's "golden age." Ryūichi Abé has been a guide in many ways, not only in leading me into the new terrain of East Asian Buddhism, but also in offering invaluable criticisms and suggestions on my work, partly in the mirror of his own work on Kukai. On the Western scholarly front, I am also grateful to Wayne Proudfoot and Robert Glick (of the Psychoanalytic Institute) for helping me to locate Chandrakīrti's contribution in the context of current debates in the philosophy of science and of mind, and hopefully to indicate some of its contemporary relevance. As for friends old and new, Laura Harrington, David Gray, and Christian Wedemeyer, for freely sharing their excitement and discoveries with me. And as for my colleagues in the AIBS Translation Team, especially Thomas Yarnall and Paul Hackett, I thank them wholeheartedly for their painstaking, careful scholarship, their time-consuming perseverance, and their unflagging editorial diligence, in bringing the translation and edition finally up to the level these great classics deserve. I of course take full responsibility for all remaining errors and deficiencies.

On a more personal note, my acknowledgements would not be complete without thanking the individuals who, in various ways, helped me make the difficult transition from California back to New York. Thanks to my parents, Marius Jerome and Carmela Paula Napoli Loizzo, whose commitment to Catholic culture gave me a taste for antiquity, and whose own mid-life journey served as my prime example of the value of lifelong education. I am also deeply grateful to Stephanie, Nyla, and Mark for supporting my move at a difficult time. Thanks are also due to former and present colleagues who have encouraged my research and teaching, including Howard Eisenstark, Ann Long, Edwin Brennan, and Murray Eiland in California, and Mary Sciutto and Ellen Stevenson, who welcomed me into the Department of Psychiatry here at Columbia. Last but not least, I want to express my heartfelt gratitude to my wife Gerardine Hearne Loizzo, for her patience as muse and partner, to my sons, Maitreya and Ananda, and to my colleague and friend Robert Rosenthal, for his psychological insights into Western academic rites of passage.

It is finally to Robert Thurman that I must express the greatest thanks and appreciation. For it is thanks to his kindness that I was introduced to the peerless genius of Nāgārjuna and Chandrakīrti. It is as a small gesture of gratitude and effort to repay a fraction of the kindness life has shown me that I offer this study and translation of their *Yuktiṣaṣṭikā* and *Yuktiṣaṣṭikā-vṛtti*. Whatever its merits, may they help cool the minds and open the hearts of living beings to the ends of this earth and the farthest reaches of space.

Technical Notes

For the transliteration of Sanskrit words we have followed standard conventions established by Monier-Williams (with the exception of *ś* instead of *ç*).

Unless explicitly indicated (e.g., ks. 1, 5, 6, 19, 30, 33, 34, 39, 46, 47, 48, 55; Lindtner, *Nāgārjuniana*), all Sanskrit terms given in the footnotes are suggested equivalents based on other parallel Tibetan-Sanskrit sources.

For the transliteration of Tibetan words we have followed the standard conventions established by Turrell Wylie.

While most Sanskrit and Tibetan proper names are given in their conventionally transliterated forms, a select few have been anglicized (e.g., Chandrakīrti, Shākyamuni, Tsong Khapa, Gyaltsap, Jamyang Shepa).

Citations of Tibetan passages from Chandrakīrti's MA are from Fenner, *The Ontology of the Middle Way* (1990). Transliterations have been modified to conform to the Wylie system.

Citations of Sanskrit passages from Nāgārjuna's MMK are from Inada, *Nāgārjuna* (1970).

Bibliographic references in the footnotes are given in the shortened form—following the guidelines set forth in *The Chicago Manual of Style* (14th Edition, 15.248–250)—containing only the author's last name and a shortened form of the title (the publication date is given when relevant to the context). Full citations for all sources are given in the bibliography.

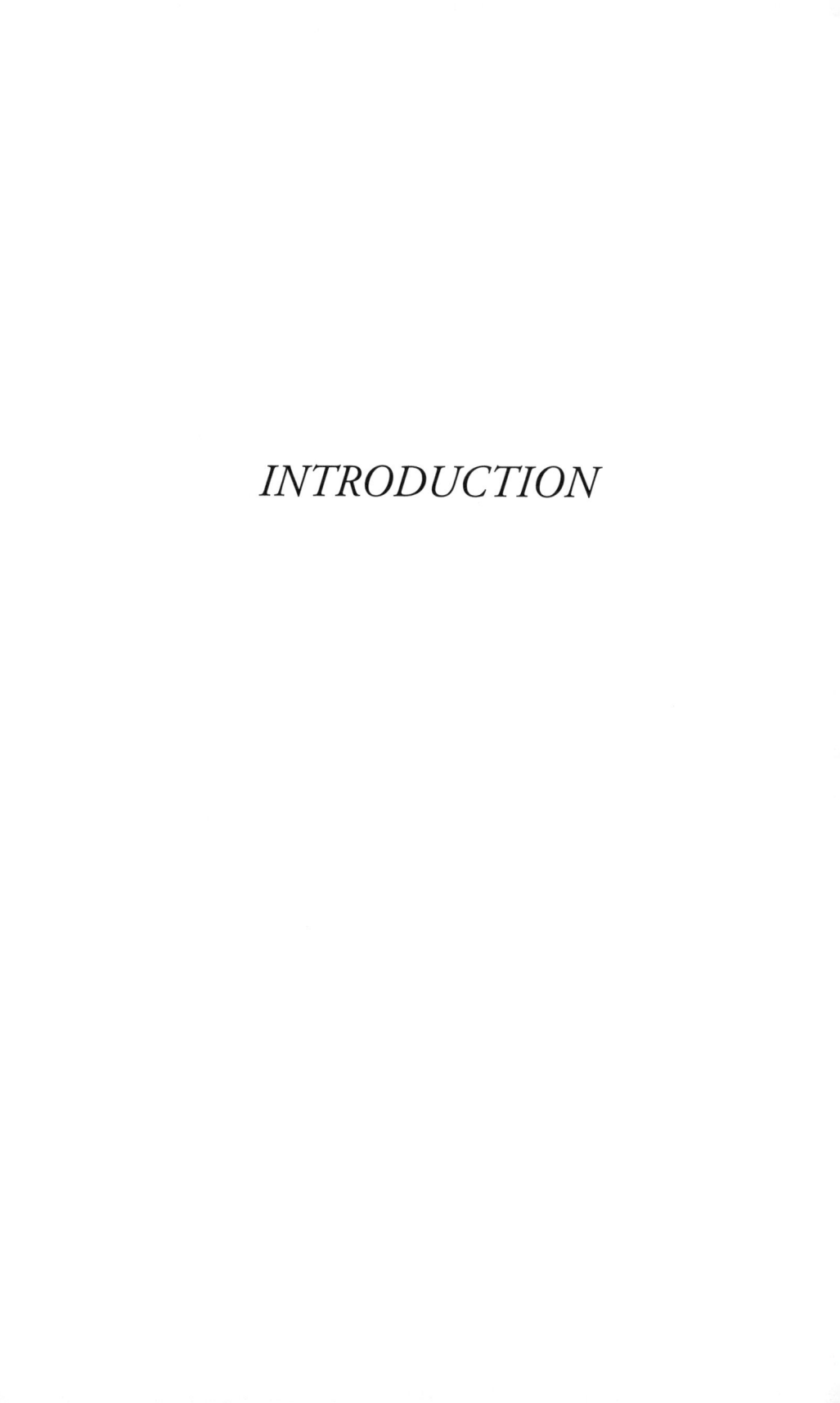

INTRODUCTION

I. The Other Chandrakīrti: A Corrective, Contextual, Textual Study

Chandrakīrti is known to Western scholars primarily for his articulation of the distinction between what Tibetan scholars glossed as the two main schools of Central Philosophy—Dialecticist and Dogmaticist[1]—in his definitive commentary on Nāgārjuna's *Wisdom* (*Prajñā*),[2] the *Lucid Exposition* (*Prasannapadā*). Yet Tibetan scholars know him primarily through another of his works, *Central Way Introduction* (*Madhyamakāvatāra*), still the required text for the introductory Centrist studies course in the core curricula of Nyingma, Kagyu, Sakya, and Geluk orders' monastic colleges. In contrast to the *Lucid Exposition* and its critical, hermeneutical concerns, the *Introduction* concerns itself with the practical application of Centrist thought, as a philosophical language therapy crucial to the Universalist (*Mahāyāna*) ethos of compassion that aims to produce enlightened altruists (*bodhisattva*) and fully enlightened beings (*saṁbuddha*).[3] One would expect the discrepancy between the Chandrakīrtis known to modern Western and Tibetan scholars to have been resolved when, after a decades-long lull since the pioneering work on the *Lucid Exposition*, a recent revival in Chandrakīrti scholarship has yielded several fine translation-studies of others of his texts, including three of the *Introduction*.[4] Not so. The two main *Introduction* studies by Western scholars focused exclusively on the philosophical sixth chapter and Chandrakīrti the Centrist philosopher, while the one

---

[1] Terminology for *madhyamaka*, *mādhyamika*, *prāsaṅgika*, and *svātantrika*, following Thurman, *Essence of Eloquence* (1984). We translate *madhyamaka* with "Central Philosophy," phrases using its derivative *mādhyamika* with "Centrist School," "Centrism," and so forth, rather than with the conventional "Middle Way Philosophy," and so forth, to avoid the latter's connotation—explicitly rejected by Nāgārjuna and his heirs—that the Madhyamaka entails a "doctrine of the mean."

[2] *Prajñā-nāma-mūlamadhyamakakārikā*, nicknamed by Tibetans simply as "Root Wisdom" (*rtsa-ba she-rab*).

[3] On the *Introduction* as a system for cultivating nondual insight and empathy, see Fenner, *The Ontology of the Middle Way* (1990).

[4] These are the recent contributions of Fenner, *Ontology* (1990); Huntington, *The Emptiness of Emptiness* (1992); and Gyatso, *Ocean of Nectar* (1999).

translation study by a Tibetan scholar focused on the entire work and Chandrakīrti the Universalist.

Is this discrepancy simply a reflection of the divergent interests and methods of "modern scientific" (i.e., supposedly "objective," "culture-neutral") scholarship versus "traditional religious" (i.e., supposedly "relative," "culture-bound") scholarship? Or, does it reflect a divergence between two equally objective yet culturally distinct scientific perspectives, which reveal two complementary aspects of Chandrakīrti's lifework? If we entertain the latter alternative, it is possible that a major aspect of a major Buddhist thinker's contribution has been systematically overlooked or distorted by Western scholarship as a result of conceptual biases and methodological limits assumed with the received consensus of modern scientific Indology. Perhaps more importantly, it is also possible that these Euro-ethnocentric biases and limits may be overcome in part by a critical exploration of the received consensus of Indo-Tibetan Buddhological Indology.[5]

Here, I outline the argument that, in fact, such a systematic distortion has occurred, hindering the advancement of Western Chandrakīrti studies. Although some Western academics have begun to reverse the received bias against Tibetan scholars that considers them "native informants," and recognize them as "Indologists *avant la lettre*,"[6] the very idea that "traditional" Buddhist theories and methods may meet some current criteria of "objectivity" or "science" challenges the consensus of Western Indology; challenges the modern use of those terms in any Western language;[7] and, in another direction, challenges the postmodern mania for "deconstructing" the modern scientific ideal that human knowledge can/should be judged by such universal standards.[8] Obviously, I cannot here fully address these complex challenges. Instead, I offer in outline some suggestions of how to meet the three challenges, to provide a philosophical context for understanding my translation.

---

[5] Cf. Wedemeyer, "Vajrayāna and its Doubles" (2000).

[6] Ruegg's phrase, cited in Wedemeyer, "Vajrayāna," ch. III, along with a similar oral communication from L. van der Kuijp.

[7] Kitcher, *The Advancement of Science* (1993).

[8] Lenoir, ed., *Inscribing Science* (1998).

First, I offer a brief sketch of the key works of Nāgārjuna and Chandrakīrti in order to clarify the significance of the *Reason Sixty* and its *Commentary.* I then provide a summary of what I consider to be the problems of interpretation and translation that have marred Western study of these two texts, to illustrate the way in which the dualistic bias of European scholarship has limited Western Centrism (*Mādhyamika*) studies. I also attempt to elaborate briefly both the extent and intent of Chandrakīrti's contribution and to show its broader relevance to modern Indology as well as to current debates in the philosophy of science and objectivity. I introduce Chandrakīrti's *Reason Sixty Commentary* (*Yuktiṣaṣṭikāvṛtti*) as a major work on epistemological agency bridging the critical concerns of the *Lucid Exposition* and the practical concerns of the *Introduction.*

From the standpoint of modern historiography, traditional biographies[9] give us little on which to base a factual account of Nāgārjuna's life. Nāgārjuna is celebrated by Tibetan historians as the Savior (*Nātha*), founding Champion (*Mahāratha*), and Noble Father (*Āryapitā*) of the Universal Vehicle, as well as the Great Master (*Mahācārya*) of its Central Philosophy.[10] As for the *oeuvre* that must serve as frame of reference for reconstructing his life, one recent study gives a conservative list of fifty-two works attributed to Nāgārjuna by traditional sources, crediting thirteen philoso-

---

[9] See Obermiller, trans., *History of Buddhism [by Bu-ston]* (1931–1932); Chattopadhyaya and Chimpa, *Tāranātha's History of Buddhism in India* (1970); Roerich, trans., *The Blue Annals* (1976); Robinson, trans., *Buddha's Lions: The Lives of the Eighty-Four Siddhas [by Abhayadatta]* (1979).

[10] Ruegg, "Purport, Implicature and Presupposition," 317, advises a contemporary hermeneutical stance toward "the elicitation of meaning" in studies of Mādhyamika texts. Lindtner, *Nāgārjuniana*, 21–22 nn. 66–74, implicitly applies the method we suggest in his attempt to clarify Nāgārjuna's "ideas...personality...[and] immense impact" as part of the work of laying "the solid foundation required for real progress in these [Mādhyamika] studies" (9). For modern biographies of Nāgārjuna, see Ramanan, *Nāgārjuna*, 25–30; Murty, *Nāgārjuna*, 38–67; Walleser, *The Life of Nāgārjuna.* For the traditional intent behind Tsong Khapa's usage of these epithets, for example, see Thurman, *Essence*, 22.

phical and religious texts as genuine,[11] and fifteen more, including works on ethics, medicine, and biochemistry, as possibly authentic.[12]

Among the uncontested works, we take three as defining our Nāgārjuna: the *Wisdom*, the *Jewel Rosary*—these two generally acknowledged as his masterpieces on philosophy and religion, respectively—and the *Reason Sixty*, because, as I understand it, it stands midway between those two masterpieces. Bridging from the rigorous critiques of the *Wisdom* toward the elaboration of the ethos of compassion in the *Jewel Rosary*, it underlines the central thrust of Nāgārjuna's therapeutic philosophy of language, namely, the elimination of cognitive and affective resistances to nondualistic wisdom and compassion. Thus, our philosophical sketch of the man who composed the *Reason* presents the product of his prolific genius as an *oeuvre* defined by the intersection of the three spheres of concern he addresses in the *Wisdom*, *Reason*, and *Rosary*, respectively, as follows: 1) applying the methods of Indian linguistics and analytic contemplation to a critique of the self-limiting reifications and habitual misuse of binary conceptuality;[13] 2) applying the dereifying, philosophical, language therapy of voidness to correct the dualistic cognitive and affective resistances to wisdom's attainment of omniscience, or epistemological objectivity; and 3) formulating a communicative ethics of voidness-compassion as a nondualistic standard of enlightened agency. The key point of intersection of these three spheres is the theory and practice of nondualism (*advaya-vāda*), the reconciliation of dichotomies caused by reification of dualistic constructs in the philosophi-

---

[11] Lindtner, *Nāgārjuniana*, 11, lists twelve in addition to the MMK as "genuine": *Śūnyatāsaptati*, *Vigrahavyāvartanī*, *Vaidalyaprakaraṇa*, *Vyavahārasiddhi*, *Yuktiṣaṣṭikā*, *Catuḥstava*, *Ratnāvalī*, *Pratītyasamutpādahṛdayakārikā*, *Sūtrasamuccaya*, *Bodhicittavivaraṇa*, *Suhṛllekha*, and *Bodhisaṁbhāra*.

[12] Lindtner, *Nāgārjuniana*, 12–15. The works on ethics, medicine, and alchemy are, respectively, the *Mūlasarvāstivadādi-śramaṇerakārikā*, the *Yogaśataka*, and the *Rasavaiśeṣikasūtra*, whose authenticity is discussed in Filliozat, *Yogaśataka*, iv–xix. See Dash, *Tibetan Medicine, with Special Reference to Yoga Śataka*; Muthuswami, ed., *Rasavaiśeṣikasūtram*; Lindtner, *Nāgārjuniana*, 14–15, and nn. 25, 28, 30.

[13] Ruegg, in *Literature*, and in "Mathematical and Linguistic Models," 174ff., points out that, although the invention of mathematical zero indeed predates Nāgārjuna, the use of *śūnya* to designate it postdates him. This shift in usage is of great interest, and one possibility must certainly be that the shift reflects a general recognition of the relationship between Nāgārjuna's philosophical formulation of *śūnyata* as a dereifying convention and earlier mathematical and linguistic models.

cal, cognitive-perceptual, and practical domains. Thus, the interpretive key to the biographical legends surrounding Nāgārjuna must be his singular focus as author of the Central Philosophy: to treat therapeutically the reification of dualistic constructs limiting human reason's realization of personal, social, and cultural aims.

The unity and enduring impact of the *Wisdom*, the *Reason*, and the *Jewel Rosary* lie in their formulations of nonduality (*advayatā*) in terms of a series of three equations—voidness = relativity; voidness = omniscience, or epistemological objectivity (*sarvajñatā*); and voidness = compassion—the three designed to guide the dereification of biases and resistances limiting the development of enlightened conceptuality, objective knowledge, and altruistic action. Nāgārjuna's elegant system of formulating and reproducing the relativistic insight of nonduality—in terms of the voidness of intrinsic reality, of intrinsic objectivity, and of intrinsic identity (*svabhāva-svarūpa-svalakṣaṇa-śūnyatā*)—stands as the backbone of the Universal Vehicle, which sustained the Asian Buddhist experiment in civilization. In this sense the legendary longevity and impact of Nāgārjuna *is* the longevity and impact of his Centrist system. It is this system whose critical edge refined the logic of Vedic reflection, inspiring the nondualism of Gauḍapāda and Śaṅkara;[14] it is this system whose nondual formula of transcendent insight reached to East Asia, earning Nāgārjuna recognition as the fourteenth patriarch of the Ch'an/Zen tradition;[15] and it is this system whose art of self-conquering wisdom and compassion helped "tame" the fierce warriors of Tibet and Mongolia. The life of Nāgārjuna's systematization of Indian nondualism in this sense may be as perennial as the network of humanity's binary symbols; its therapeutic impact is as protean as the symbolic mind's self-deceptive demon of reification.[16]

---

[14] Thurman argues, "Śaṅkarācārya tacitly admitted its unassailability by merely dismissing Nāgārjuna as unworthy of consideration, after having just leveled a Nāgārjunian critique against every other opponent in the field" (*Essence*, 26). Cf. Thibault, *Vedāntasūtras of Bādarāṇya*, 344ff.; and Thurman, *Essence*, 48–49.

[15] See Cleary's translation of *The Blue Cliff Record*, Thirteenth Case.

[16] See YṢ, 34, 36, and YṢV, trans. below.

Among Chandrakīrti's uncontested works,[17] we focus here on his *Lucid Exposition* (*PP*),[18] *Central Way Introduction* (*MA*), and the *Reason Sixty Commentary* (*YṢV*) translated below. We rank the *Commentary* with Chandrakīrti's two more well-known masterpieces because it serves a transitional role in his system, linking the critical hermeneutical pedagogy of the *Lucid Exposition* with the practical, therapeutic anthropology of the *Introduction*, just as Nāgārjuna's *Reason* links the *Wisdom* and *Jewel Rosary*. This contextual reference frame is consistent with the modern Western and Tibetan views of Chandrakīrti as the supreme interpreter of Nāgārjuna's system, in the context of the intellectual climate of 6th–7th century Nālandā University. Based on the three works of Nāgārjuna, the concerns of the *Lucid Exposition*, the *Commentary*, and the *Introduction*, respectively, can be defined as follows: 1) to articulate Nāgārjuna's conventionalist method as a therapeutic philosophy of language, in which the ultimate reality of voidness serves as a second-order sign and dereifying reminder of the antifoundationalist, antiessentialist insight that the social consensual reality we construct is based on mere conventional language use (*upādāya-prajñaptimātra*) and is viable only as critically unexamined in ultimate terms (*aparamārthika-vicaryamānasiddha**); 2) to apply his language therapeutic method to define the epistemology of Centrism, based on privileging a de-objectifying (*nirālambana*)[19] rational mode in which the pure non-finding of any essentialist self or world counters cognitive bias in, and affective resistance to, objective self-knowledge and rational action; and 3) to translate this social epistemology into a Centrist anthropology, combining philosophical language therapy and communicative ethics in a self-corrective practice meant to produce enlightened altruists (*bodhisattva*) as ideal epistemological and social agents.

---

[17] These include *Mūlamadhyamakavṛttiprasannapadā*, *Madhyamakāvatāra*, *Madhyamakāvatārabhāṣya*, *Yuktiṣaṣṭikāvṛtti*, *Catuḥśatakaṭīkā*, and *Pañcaskandhaprakaraṇa*. For traditional and modern lists see Chattopadhyaya and Chimpa, *Tāranātha's History*, 401–402; Ruegg, *Literature*, 126, 129–130.

[18] For the purposes of this discussion, I subsume his other major work, the CŚṬ, with the PP, insofar as Āryadeva's *magnum opus*, the CŚ, was traditionally considered inseparable from Nāgārjuna's MMK, the latter critiquing primarily Individualist Buddhist philosophers, the former then taking on the Brahminical philosophers.

[19] For this translation, see below.

The point of intersection of these three concerns is deobjectifying wisdom and compassion (*anopalambha-prajñā-karuṇā**), the self-critical, communicative competence at the heart of Centrist method, which aims to free the practitioner to see through and artfully master the spell of linguistic convention" on which the cooperative construction of all human life-cycles depends.[20] Hence, the hermeneutical reference point in the following discussion and translation will be Chandrakīrti's deobjectifying method, his therapy for the disease of the reification of philosophical, scientific, and mundane conventions of language that limits human reason's realization of personal, social, and cultural aims.[21]

Previous Studies of the *Reason Sixty*

It has long been a commonplace of cross-cultural research in intellectual history that the methods of philology cannot convey the truth of a work independent of the hermeneutical reference frame of the translation. Yet there are few areas in Indology or Buddhology where the interdependence of philological method and philosophical clarity are as critical as in Centrist studies. Christian Lindtner's 1982 study of Nāgārjuna's works seeks "the solid foundation required for real progress in these studies" in the objective tools of philology, rightly pointing out that modern translations suffer from their "insufficient philological outfit."[22] Yet the translations

---

[20] See the *Commentary* to verses 10 and 18 for Chandrakīrti's discussion of the two aspects of deobjectifying insight, with the famous similes of the mirage river and magician's illusion, respectively.

[21] This focus gave Chandrakīrti the critical tool he needed to break through subtle reifications like Bhāvaviveka's, since it showed that the positive subjects, reasons and examples Bhāvaviveka sought in his Dogmaticist Centrism could not be "self-sufficient" (*svatantra*) or "self-evident" (*svalakṣaṇasiddha*), even "conventionally" (*vyāvahārika*), but must be based on nothing more than "unexamined" (*avicāramāna*) assent to conventions which are "mere linguistic usages" (*upādāyaprajñaptimātra*). In this, Chandrakīrti anticipated Nietzsche and the mature Wittgenstein, as well modern sociology and linguistics. Cf. Loizzo, "Wittgenstein and the Mādhyamika" (1977); Berger and Luckman, *The Social Construction of Reality* (1967); and Chomsky, *Aspects of the Theory of Syntax* (1965).

[22] Lindtner, *Nāgārjuniana*, 9–10, and n. 7. Unfortunately, his own study neglects the hermeneutical foundation required for Mādhyamika studies. Eight pages later in the same work, his preliminary summary of the "ultimate goal" of Nāgārjuna's philosophy seems to me to be inaccurate on three of its four "angles," even though the pertinent references from

(cont'd)

Lindtner mentions[23] suffer equally from inadequate hermeneutical frames of reference, and this remains a fundamental problem limiting progress in the field, despite the philological gains which have so benefited recent efforts. Most recently, another group of scholars, including de Jong, Ruegg, Thurman, Huntington, and Fenner,[24] have argued cogently for a methodology combining philological and hermeneutical rigor in equal measure. The overview below outlines the concepts and methods presupposed as the framework of this translation, in an effort to address remaining critical limitations in recent Centrist studies in general and Chandrakīrti studies in particular.

Previous translations of the *Reason Sixty* exemplify the importance of combining philological with hermeneutical rigor. The first modern language version, Philipp Schaeffer's German translation, suffers equally from its neo-Kantian interpretive framework, as from its reliance on the Chinese text: "Die Madhyamaka-Schule steht auf dem Standpunkt, das man selbst diese *Attribute dem absoluten Wesen, das den dharma zu Grunde liegt, nicht zuschrieben kann*, da sie auf der Empirie basieren."[25] Unlike Stcherbatsky's felicitous comparison of the critical epistemology and logic of Dignāga and Dharmakīrti with those of Kant,[26] Schaeffer's comparative approach to Nāgārjuna obscures rather than clarifies the thrust of Centrist philosophy, whose critique is directed against precisely the kind of reified terms on which Kantian critique is based, especially against dualistic constructs of persons and things "in themselves" (*an sich* = *svabhāvatā*).

---

the early Mādhyamika literature have been duly considered and cited in his notes. I believe that he errs, when: 1) he states that "ultimate truth" is "only an object metaphorically," as if superficial things, by contrast, were established in some other way, as *literally* or *really* objects; 2) he states that the passions are to be "abolished," attributing to Nāgārjuna the extreme of annihilationism; and 3) he defines Nāgārjuna's ethical aim as "freedom from the bonds of *karma* but subjection to the altruistic imperatives of compassion," whereas Nāgārjuna's ethos is that there is no freedom outside karmic causality, and compassion is the means to freedom and happiness within karmic causality.

[23] Schaeffer, *Yukti-ṣaṣṭikā: Die 60 Sätze des Negativismus* (1923); Streng, *Emptiness* (1967); Inada, *Nāgārjuna* (1970); and Sprung, *Lucid Exposition* (1979).

[24] de Jong, "The Study of Buddhism," 26; Ruegg, *Literature*, 239; Thurman, *Essence*, 149ff.; Huntington, *Emptiness*, 5–15; Fenner, *Ontology*, 1–3.

[25] My italics. Schaeffer, *Yukti-ṣaṣṭikā: Die 60*, 13, n. 5.

[26] Stcherbatsky, *Buddhist Logic* (1962; originally published 1930–32).

One measure of the depth of this obstacle is how persistently subsequent translations of the *Reason* and its *Commentary* have been marred by similar misunderstandings. Despite their successive gains in philological precision, most of the recent Western language versions of our texts apply a hermeneutical dualism to Nāgārjuna's nondualistic message.[27] These and earlier modern misreadings fall into two basic classes, depending on whether they misidentify the ultimate reality of voidness as an ineffable something, or as a tautological nothing. The former class tacitly assumes an idealist or mystical form of modern foundationalist-essentialist (i.e., neo-Kantian) critique, in which reason dialectically approximates or intuitively leaps toward a direct experience of the ineffable particularity of things in themselves; the latter class tacitly assumes a skeptical, pragmatist, or materialist form of modern critique, in which reason knows its truths and itself as objective non-entities, intrinsically empty constructions devoid of all concrete sense or meaning.[28] Exemplifying the former, we read in the introduction to Scherrer-Schaub's recent translation of the *Commentary*:

---

[27] At the last minute, as we finalized this present work, we discovered Dr. Peter Della Santina's "Reasoning: The Sixty Stanzas"—an excellent translation of the *Reason Sixty* verses, with the author's own commentary—which seems both philologically solid and hermeneutically neutral. This can be found as part 3 of his *Causality and Emptiness: The Wisdom of Nagarjuna* (2002), available as a PDF publication at various online web sites.

[28] Thurman, *Essence*, 149ff., discusses these hermeneutical extremes, following the Indo-Tibetan tradition in defining them in terms of the position of the Jo-nang-pa *Dol-bu-pa Shes-rab rGyal-mtshan* (1292–1361) and the position shared by the Indian *Jayānanda* and the Kadampa *rNgog Lo-tsva-ba bLo-ldan Shes-rab* (1059–1109), respectively. Without linking these explicitly with Kantian critique, he locates four major modern interpreters of Nāgārjuna in relation to these two misreadings, linking Stcherbatsky and Murti with the romantic reading, and Streng and Sprung with the pragmatist. In parallel with this, I add the interpreters of the *Yuktiṣaṣṭikā*, among whom Schaeffer, Tola and Dragonetti, and Scherrer-Schaub fall into the romantic camp, while Lindtner falls into the pragmatist. See Schaeffer, *Yukti-ṣaṣṭikā: Die 60* (1923); Murti, *Central Philosophy of Buddhism* (1955); Streng, *Emptiness* (1967); Sprung, *The Problem of Two Truths* (1973); Stcherbatsky, *The Conception of Buddhist Nirvāṇa* (1927); Lindtner, *Nāgārjuniana* (1980); Tola and Dragonetti, "Yuktiṣaṣṭikā" (1983); and Scherrer-Schaub, *Yuktiṣaṣṭikāvṛtti* (1991). Interestingly, these scholarly misreadings correspond to applied and popular misunderstandings of insight in contemporary Buddhist meditative and Western psychotherapeutic practices. Thus, the mystic view is prevalent in popularized American versions of Zen as an anti-intellectual leap philosophy, as well as the neo-Hegelian/Existentialist view held by Jungian, Gestalt, and Transpersonal psychology in which insight is an irrational intuitive faculty of the unconscious, like the "negative capability" of the romantics or the "unknowing" of the ancients. The pragmatic

(cont'd)

> La connaissance de la réalité (*tattva-jñāna*) est un savoir pratique que la sage réalise par une vue immédiate, un fait d'expérience personnelle. Si les chemins sont divers et représente autant d'instruments d'entrée dans la réalité, cette dernière et sa connaissance sont de nature unique. Pour rendre compte de cet état, le langage utilise des expressions apparemment paradoxales, *ultime recours de l'expression verbale pour sortir d'elle-même.*[29]

Exemplifying the latter, we read in Lindtner's recent "summary" of Nāgārjuna's epistemology, "The ultimate truth (*tattva*) is the object of a cognition without an object (*advayajñāna*), thus only an object metaphorically speaking (*upādāya-prajñapti*)."[30]

Reflecting two views of the same dualistic framework, the pervasiveness of these misreadings is no accident, but a historical consequence of the tacit assumption of nineteenth century neo-Kantian epistemology as the philosophical foundation of modern text-critical disciplines and their methods.[31] Not until the (antifoundationalist) perspectival relativism of Nietzsche and the (antiessentialist) linguistic conventionalism of the later

---

view corresponds to popularized American versions of *vipassana* as simple mindfulness, as well as the neo-Kantian/Empiricist view of insight and its object held by Freudian schools, including Kohut's Self-Psychology and the derivative psychodynamic therapies.

[29] Scherrer-Schaub, *Yuktiṣaṣṭikāvṛtti*, xlii (italics mine). In effect, this misinterpretation yields a Yogācāra-Svātantrika misreading of Chandrakīrti's Prāsaṅgika system. Although this reading is analyzed in the comparative interpretation below in terms of the explicit hermeneutic of Fenner's *Ontology*, it applies equally to Scherrer-Schaub's translation. This is evident in statements such as: "Nāgārjuna et Candrakīrti admettent l'existence des *samskṛta-lakṣaṇa* (*utpāda, stithi, nirodha*) en *saṁvṛtti-satya*...En vérité absolue (*paramārtha-satya*), leur existence est semblable a celle d'un mirage" (*Yuktiṣaṣṭikāvṛtti*, 192, n. 303). Such statements inadvertently overlook Chandrakīrti's critique of Bhāvaviveka's way of establishing *saṁvṛti* by appeal to a superficial *svalakṣaṇa*, as well as Chandrakīrti's distinctive Prāsaṅgika presentation of *saṁvṛti* as viable only in an illusory way, that is, as established by the mere suspension of analysis (*avicāryamanasiddha*).

[30] Lindtner, *Nāgārjuniana*, 19.

[31] de Jong, "The Study of Buddhism," 13–26, alludes to the influence of "the historical tradition of the nineteenth century." See Huntington, *Emptiness*, 5–15, for a more thorough discussion of the Western intellectual historical context of this problem; and Ricoeur, *Hermeneutics and the Human Sciences* (1982), for a critical treatment of nineteenth century hermeneutics.

Wittgenstein has the West produced nondualistic conceptual frameworks and critical methods adequate to translate Buddhist Centrist insight and method accurately.

Given this comparative philosophical reference frame, discussed at length elsewhere,[32] the present textual study assumes a hermeneutic based on the antifoundationalist, antiessentialist (i.e., post-Kantian) critique of knowledge and language in Nietzsche and Wittgenstein. The cross-cultural validity of this comparative framework is supported by the basic structure and argument of Nāgārjuna's *Reason Sixty* root text and Chandrakīrti's *Commentary*, especially when these are viewed in the context of these authors' main works. This thesis is threefold: 1) the dualistic readings of voidness that have obscured modern translations are precisely those already critiqued as the "(absolutized) view of voidness" (*śūnyatādṛṣṭi*) by Centrists from Nāgārjuna and Chandrakīrti to Tsong Khapa; 2) the prime intent of the *Reason* and its *Commentary*, and the social-epistemological pivot of Nāgārjuna's and Chandrakīrti's systems, is to prescribe a method to treat the reifying mental habit (*gro 'dogs pa'i 'dzin stang, adhyāropa-grahabandha**) that underlies both absolutistic and nihilistic malignant views; and 3) that the insight and method of social-epistemological self-correction (*buddhiviśodhana*) these texts prescribe are best understood as part of a linguistic anthropology whose closest analogues in the West are the language-therapeutic philosophies of Nietzsche, Freud, Lacan, and especially Wittgenstein and certain of his heirs.

Some may object that translation of an ancient Sanskrit/Tibetan philosophical text should not use any contemporary philosophical method as a comparative lens through which to understand and articulate the original philosophy. I certainly see merit in such an objection, and I would recommend that those who hold such views should limit themselves to restoring Tibetan translations such as the YṢ and YṢV back into facsimiles of Nāgārjuna's and Chandrakīrti's original Sanskrit texts.[33] If translation into

---

[32] Loizzo, "Wittgenstein and the Mādhyamika"; Thurman, *Essence*; Huntington, *Emptiness*, 5–15; and Fenner, *Ontology*, 3ff., who refers to Wittgenstein, while relying more on Gangadean's Neitzschean-Heideggerian comparative framework.

[33] This extremely worthwhile effort to restore numerous Tengyur texts back into Sanskrit from their Tibetan translations is currently being conducted at the Central Institute of Higher Tibetan Studies (Deemed University) in Saranath, India, by Tibeto-Indian teams of scholars, funded by the Government of India.

English or another modern language is the object, however, we have no choice but to be as self-conscious and self-critical as possible in weighing the philosophical reference frames that influence our choices of translation terminologies.

Given my view that the *Reason* and its *Commentary* formulate the self-corrective heart of Centrism as a human scientific method, and acknowledging that the choice of hermeneutical framework is key in any attempt to understand and translate that method, I offer here a comparative reference frame from which I believe its intent may be more clearly interpreted and expressed. The reference frame in chapter three of this introduction centers on the comparative matching between the nondualism of Nāgārjuna as refined by Chandrakīrti, and the critical philology of Nietzsche as refined in the language philosophy of Wittgenstein. Given the above critique of the Kantian comparative reference frame of modern Indology, comparisons of Centrist philosophers with Wittgenstein have been viewed by many as basic to a coherent post-modern reference frame for Centrist studies.[34] The challenge posed by such comparisons, however, is that, unlike Kant, whose critique of reason the West has had centuries to assimilate, Wittgenstein is newer to modern scholarship than Nāgārjuna. One response to this challenge has been a recent tendency to avoid an in-depth comparative study of Wittgenstein, and to rely primarily on more familiar or recent Western thinkers.[35] The problem with this is that the more familiar or recent thinkers are typically less critical of the reifying habit than Wittgenstein, and so translating through their reference frame perpetuates subtle forms of the dualistic biases that tend to obscure modern views of Nāgārjuna. Two

---

[34] See Loizzo, "Wittgenstein and the Mādhyamika"; Gudmunsen, *Wittgenstein and Buddhism* (1977); Thurman, "Non-egocentrism in Chandrakīrti and Wittgenstein" (1980); Thurman, *Essence* (1984), 89ff.; Huntington, *Emptiness*, 5–15; Fenner, *Ontology*, 3ff.; Tillemans, *Materials* (1990).

[35] Huntington, *Emptiness*, relies on Rorty, *Philosophy and the Mirror of Nature* (1979), who in turn uses Wittgenstein to call for an "end" to the modern philosophical framework of dualism, in an effort to reconcile idealistic and pragmatic revisers of Kant like Heidegger and James. Fenner, *Ontology*, relies on Gangadean, "Formal Ontology and the Dialectical Transformation of Consciousness" (1979), who in turn uses Aristotelian logic to define Centrism as a critique of language meant "to move consciousness beyond any and all conceptual structures" (22), apparently in an effort to reconcile the phenomenological and empiricist versions of neo-Kantian tradition and their dissociation of deductive from inductive methods.

thoughtful recent efforts in Centrist studies, both based on Chandrakīrti's *Introduction*, illustrate this problem.

Relying on Richard Rorty's view of Wittgenstein, Huntington's excellent study makes a sophisticated attempt to offer a Dialecticist reading of Nāgārjuna, which yet seems to turn out to be closer to Bhāvaviveka's Dogmaticism than Chandrakīrti's Dialecticism.[36] He assumes Rorty's claim that Wittgenstein maintained a pragmatic contextualism of language, and so reads Nāgārjuna as holding things to lack "existence grounded outside the context of everyday experience" but to have "an intrinsic nature which accounts for their existence in the world," that is, within the "context" or "nexus of cause and effect which defines our shared sociolinguistic experience."[37] As in Bhāvaviveka, this appears to be a clear reification of a relative or conventional "intrinsic nature" (*svalakṣaṇa*), which is posited as a pragmatic ground of shared knowledge and language. This move of course consigns "ultimate reality" to the status of an empty abstraction absolutely devoid of experiential sense or linguistic reference.[38] Given this doubly misplaced comparative rationale, Huntington asserts that Nāgārjuna and Chandrakīrti join Wittgenstein in avoiding what Rorty critiques as the "ocular metaphor" (i.e., the image of the mind as a giant "mirror of nature" filled with representations of the world). Though this insight of Rorty, followed by Huntington, is certainly a striking way of expressing the three philosophers' avoidance of a naïvely absolutist metaphysic, it should be reconciled with the fact that all three do subscribe to a conventionalist metaphysic, and routinely describe the effect of their therapeutic philosophies with analogies between dereifying insight and key conventions of visual perception.[39] Finally, comparing Rorty's view of Wittgenstein's "edifying"

---

[36] Following the later Tibetan tradition of so characterizing their interpretive systems.

[37] Huntington, *Emptiness*, 48–49.

[38] Hence Huntington admits "my own reluctance to call Murti's concept of a 'subjacent ground' wrong" (207, n. 66), which reluctance seems to reflect a subtle dichotomization of the two realities, and an attendant impulse to "fill the vacuum" left by a shift in reification from an ineffable "absolute" to an absolutized "relative."

[39] Especially in the *Reason*, Nāgārjuna reserves the language of vision, "transcendent insight" (*vipaśyanā*), "seeing reality" (*tattvadarśana*) (YṢ, 5, 11), "seeing relativity" (*pratītyotpāda-darśana**) (YṢ, 48), or simply "seeing" (*darśana*) (YṢ, 25, 55) for the nondualistic negative faculty of insight, also called "genuine insight" (*samyagjñāna*) (YṢ, 10) as opposed to conventional dualistic knowledge or understanding (*parijñāna*, Tib. *yongs su shes pa*), or wisdom

(cont'd)

philosophy with a Dogmaticist reading of Nāgārjuna, Huntington describes Centrism as "propaganda" for a Buddhist form of life,[40] without grounding his argument in any direct interpretation of Wittgenstein's major works, where he distances himself from pragmatism and rhetorical persuasion[41] and offers his method as "therapy" for compulsive habits of mind[42] and illnesses of language.[43] In sum, Huntington's use of Rorty's interpretation of Wittgenstein leads him to interpret Centrism as more consistent with Bhāvaviveka's Dogmaticism than Chandrakīrti's Dialecticism.[44]

(*prajñā*); he also develops the metaphor of "seeing with the intellect" (*blo yis mthong ba*) for the illusion-like insight (YṢ, 17) and of "seeing with the insight eye" (*ye shes kyi mig gis mthong*) (YṢ, 54). Cf. VV, 11. Chandrakīrti, in the *Commentary*, ad k. 17 and 54, below, and *Lucid Exposition*, PPMMV, ed. La Vallée Poussin, 373, refines the analogy further, defining the organ of transcendent insight as the "intellect" (*buddhi*) whose disease of misknowledge or reification is healed by "the eye-ointment of the voidness insight" (*śūnyatādarśanāñjana*); the analogy is sustained through much of *Introduction* 6, MABh 6.2, where he compares the leadership of the "intellect" (*blo*) to that of a sighted person (*mig ldan*) among the blind; 23, 27, 29, 105, 108, 120, where he speaks of "seeing with the intellect" (*blo yis mthong ba*); and in 213, "we assert that insight has the character of a direct perception" (*ye shes ni mngon sum msthan nyid du 'dod*). In the West, Wittgenstein speaks in his *Philosophical Investigations* (PI) of gaining "a *clear view* or *perspicuous representation* (*einsichtliche darstellung*) of our use of words...which produces that understanding which consists in 'seeing connexions'," adding that this visual metaphor "earmarks...the way we look at things" (PI, §122). He repeatedly compares the aim of his philosophy to "seeing what is always before one's eyes" in a new light (PI, §129), and describes as the result of this method a "*complete* clarity" in which "philosophical problems...*completely* disappear" (PI, §133). His method of "therapy" aims at producing a gestalt-switch in perception, a process which is the main focus of Part II of the *Investigations*. The analogy of his insight to the negative insight of Centrist reason is clear in his description of seeing through the egocentric illusion of self-evident objects, subjects, and experience, "there is here no question of a 'seeing'...nor of a subject, nor therefore of 'I' either" (PI, §398).

40 Huntington, *Emptiness*, 127 ff., decontextualizes a reference to "propaganda" which Wittgenstein made in an informal critique of Freud's use of "persuasion," and his own "pragmatic-deconstructionist" reading of Nāgārjuna's statement that "voidness" has a "usage" (*prayojana*) (MMK, 24.7) as the comparative grounds for this reading. See Wittgenstein, *Lectures and Conversations* (LC), 18–29, especially 28.

41 PI, §118, 127–128, 309, 342, 413, 599, 610; PI, II, 219; *On Certainty* (OC), 422.

42 PI, §109, 115, 140, 309.

43 PI, §254–255, 119, 123, 133, 593.

44 Chandrakīrti's critique of Bhāvaviveka's style of "private reasoning" (*svātantrānumāna*) in *Lucid Exposition I* and elsewhere applies to this misreading. The gist is that Bhāvaviveka wrongly attributes to the conventional a kind of contextual logical consistency, leading him

(cont'd)

Fenner's fine recent study of Chandrakīrti also seems to arrive at an equally subtle misreading, albeit opposite in sense, by assuming Gangadean's comparative critique of language. Interestingly, the study abandons the insight of Fenner's own previous work on the "therapeutic contextualization"[45] of Centrist philosophy, presumably in the conviction that Gangadean's logical formalism, reminiscent of the early rather than late Wittgenstein, explicitly defines the "structural foundations"[46] of Centrist method. Following Gangadean's account of Centrist analysis as a "transformational dialectic" meant "to move consciousness beyond any and all conceptual structures,"[47] Fenner reads Nāgārjuna and Chandrakīrti as offering a deconstructive training for a "realization of voidness" defined as "like most mystical experiences...ineffable...inconceivable...inexpressible"[48] and "indefinable."[49]

In contrast to Huntington's subtly skeptical pragmatist view (à la Bhāvaviveka), this subtly mystical study arrives at an Idealist-Dogmaticist reading of Nāgārjuna, like that of Śāntarakṣita and Kamalaśīla, whose integration of the systems of Sthiramati, Bhāvaviveka, and Dharmakīrti so influenced Tibet. After offering a cogent account of how and why Centrist "bi-negations" confront the mind with the relativity of language's "predicate structure," Fenner obscures the therapeutic point of the consequent "destructuring of conceptuality," defining the aim of dereifying insight as a

---

to overanalyze and overpolemicize the fictive world of consensual experience. In response, in PPMMV and MABh we find Chandrakīrti arguing that the conventional cannot withstand analysis and stands only as long as "critically unexamined" (*avicāryamana*), and issuing repeated challenges designed to take the realistic wind from the sails of rationalism, much less propaganda: "What's the use of applying such fine analysis to mundane conventions? The superficial is found to have its self-existence merely by erroneous cognition" (PPMMV, 7, ad k. 32; as quoted by Tsong Khapa in Thurman, *Essence*, 338).

45 Fenner, "A Therapeutic Contextualization of Buddhist Mādhyamika Consequential Analysis" (1988).

46 Fenner, *Ontology*, 104.

47 Gangadean, "Formal Ontology," 22.

48 Fenner, *Ontology*, 38.

49 Fenner, *Ontology*, 115.

voidness "necessar[il]y...beyond conventions" of language.[50] As a consequence of the dichotomous way in which he dissociates the conventional realm of "predicate structure" from the "ineffable" realm of "*śūnya* consciousness,"[51] Fenner has problems explaining the subtle therapeutics of the voidness insight which are very similar to the problems encountered by the proponents of Idealist-Dogmaticist Centrism.[52] The first problem is that of how realization of a "necessarily" non-linguistic voidness results from the Centrist system of "bi-negative" rational analysis, a problem only compounded by the Idealist-Dogmaticist strategy of locating the "dialectical transformation" from linguistic to non-linguistic experience within "consciousness," linguistically reified as a subtly ineffable something outside the conventions of speech. The second problem is the inverse of the first: explaining how the non-linguistic content of that negative insight can ever "translate" into the new freedom brought about by illusion-like insight (*māyopama-jñāna**) into the usage of conventions of language. If, in Gangadean's terms, the content of the negative insight is "an unintelligible flux," how are "the utterances of natural language...seen to be figurative and metaphorical"[53] in the subsequent virtuality insight where "the world is regained by reconstituting the predicative structure?"[54] A final, more serious

---

50 Fenner, *Ontology*, 38. Fenner's discussion of space-like "holy equipoise insight" (*ārya-samāhitajñāna*) and illusion-like "holy aftermath insight" (*āryapṛṣṭhalabdhajñāna*) in terms of Gangadean's "formal ontology" overlooks the fact that "what lies outside the predicative structure of language" is not a language-independent referent labeled "voidness" or "consciousness"; "what lies outside..." is a conventional expression whose usage, sense, and referent exists only within that predicative structure (Fenner, *Ontology*, 88–89, especially n. 111). Consider Nāgārjuna, MMK, 18.7: *nivṛttamabhidhātavyam nivṛtte cittagocare* / The range of mind ends where the verbalizable ends; and MMK, 24.7: *atra brūmaḥ śūnyatāyāṁ na tvaṁ vetsi prayojanaṁ // śūnyatāṁ śūnyatārthaṁ ca tata evaṁ vihanyase //* "Here, let us explain. You do not know either the sense, usage, or referent of 'voidness' and so do yourself such injury." Compare the later Wittgenstein: "Thinking is essentially the activity of operating with signs" (BBB, 6; PI, §327); "No sign leads us beyond itself, and no argument either" (1975, 71).

51 Fenner, *Ontology*, 100.

52 Tsong Khapa viewed the faults of the Idealist-Dogmaticist view as equivalent to those of Bhāvaviveka, and so treated them in light of Chandrakīrti's critique of Bhāvaviveka in *Lucid Exposition* 1. We follow his procedure here. See Thurman, *Essence*, 288ff.

53 Gangadean, "Formal Ontology," 39, as quoted in Fenner, *Ontology*, n. 111.

54 Fenner, *Ontology*, 100.

problem with locating voidness outside the world of everyday communication is explaining how the voidness insight opens the way to developing empathy rather than fostering withdrawal into "*śūnya* consciousness." Hence this study's "more tentative...conclusions"[55] about the linkage between wisdom and compassion are limited to speculations about how voidness can buffer rather than heighten empathic sensitivity, "nullify[ing] the potential for the problems of others to *personally* affect and disturb" the practitioner by exposing them as "creatures of fiction...nothing more than a verbal denotation."[56]

While these, in my opinion, subtly dualistic misreadings of Chandrakīrti are analogous to Traditionist-Centrist and Idealist-Centrist[57] readings of Nāgārjuna, their currency in Western scholarship is not a random event occurring within an intellectual-historical vacuum. In fact, these misreadings reflect the conflicting positions of objectivist and constructivist camps in the postmodern debate over the objectivity of scientific knowledge and method, a debate sparked by the relativistic turn in modern physics and the linguistic turn in Western philosophy. Although such subtly dualistic camps are evident in the current schools of thought on the radical nondualism of Wittgenstein, their positions are more widely known in connection with the debate between the objectivist and constructivist approaches to knowledge advocated by the physical and social scientific communities of the Western academy. Therefore I have attempted to show the family resemblance between the nondualism of Chandrakīrti and Wittgenstein by couching my discussion of the Traditionist-Idealist-Centrist debate that took place in the classical Buddhist academy in the more accessible language of the postmodern debate over objectivity. In this context, the closest match to the nondualism of Wittgenstein and Chandrakīrti I have found is the approach to "objectivity" developed by legal philosopher Thomas Nagel.[58] While he admits to many of the doubts which plague the essentialist *alter*

---

[55] Fenner, *Ontology*, 205.

[56] Fenner, *Ontology*, 190–191.

[57] Sautrāntika-Mādhyamika and Yogācāra-Mādhyamika.

[58] Nagel, *The View From Nowhere* (1986). Now that I have critiqued my esteemed colleagues' uses of Rorty and Gangadean, I am offering them back the opportunity to critique my use of Nagel!

ego in Wittgenstein's *Investigations*, Nagel seems to me to be clearly on the trail of a radical centrist theory of objective knowledge and responsible agency (analogous to Buddhist "omniscience" and "omnicompassion"). Critiquing the prevalent objectivist defense of objective knowledge as "scientistic," he also unequivocally breaks with the subjectivist, antiscientific conclusions of constructivism and historicism. Instead he insists on a radical, nondualistic conclusion in striking sympathy with the program of Buddhist human science: not only is the scientific pursuit of objective knowledge inexorably relative to the philosophical pursuit of self-knowledge but at bottom the two are synergistic and inseparable. Avoiding both modern dualistic extremes—scientistic objectivism and antiscientific subjectivism—Nagel insists in *The View From Nowhere*:

> These errors are connected; they both stem from an insufficiently robust sense of reality and of its independence of any particular form of human understanding. (5)
>
> ...What really happens in the pursuit of objectivity is that a certain element of oneself, the impersonal or objective self, which can escape from the specific contingencies of one's creaturely point of view, is allowed to predominate. Withdrawing into this element one detaches from the rest and develops an impersonal conception of the world and, so far as possible, of the elements of the self from which one has detached. (9)
>
> ...We are in a sense trying to climb outside of our own minds, an effort that some would regard as insane and that I regard as philosophically fundamental. (11)

Given this radical centrist approach, Nagel can effectively link objectivity with intersubjective agreement and the pursuit of objective knowledge with a rigorous process of epistemological self-correction:

> Because a centerless view of the world is one on which different persons can converge, there is a close connection between objectivity and intersubjectivity.... The pursuit of objectivity requires the cultivation of a rather austere universal objective self. (63)

This linkage finally compels him to explore the post-Cartesian connection between epistemological self-correction and ethical self-development, which he describes in terms of the cultivation of an increasingly impartial and altruistic "objective will," dependent in part on the development of self-regulation:

> This involves the idea of an unlimited hypothetical development on the path of self-knowledge and self-criticism.... We assume that our own advances in objectivity are steps along a path that extends beyond them and beyond all our capacities. But even allowing unlimited time, or an unlimited number of generations, to take as many successive steps as we like, the process can never be completed, short of omniscience.... What is wanted is some way of making the most objective standpoint the basis of action. (128–129)
>
> ...In a sense, I am agreeing with Kant's view that there is an internal connection between ethics and freedom.... We cannot act on the world from outside, but we can in a sense act from both inside and outside our particular position in it. Ethics increases the range of what it is about ourselves that we can will—extending it from our actions to the motives and character traits and dispositions from which they arise. We want to be able to will the sources of our actions down to the very bottom, reducing the gap between explanation and justification. (135)

Nagel's vision of a gradual, nondualistic path toward embodied cognitive-practical objectivity bears a striking resemblance to Nāgārjuna and Chandrakīrti's gradualism, aimed at "the enlightened performance whose essence is voidness-compassion" (*bodhisādhanaṁ śūnyatākaruṇāgarbhaṁ*). In particular, his centrist ethics, like theirs, involves marrying a linguistic analysis of self with a pragmatic discipline of self-regulation. Hence, like Wittgenstein and Chandrakīrti, Nagel subordinates objectivist standards of objectivity to a nondualistic cognitive-practical ideal of objectivity as the self-transcendent potential natural to all humans as social-epistemological agents; and like them, he aligns that potential with the nondualistic attitude of non-egocentrism:

> Our objectivity is simply a development of our humanity and doesn't allow us to break free of it. It must serve our humanity and to the extent that it does not we can forget about it.... The objective self is a vital part of us, and to ignore its quasi-independent operation is to be cut off from oneself as much as of one were to abandon one's subjective individuality.... Finally, there is an attitude which cuts through the opposition between transcendent universality and parochial self-absorption, and that is the attitude of non-egocentric respect for the particular. (221–222)

These brief excerpts should suffice to illustrate the family resemblance between Nagel's Wittgensteinian approach to objectivity and Chandrakīrti's approach to transcendent wisdom. This resemblance serves to introduce the comparative philosophical framework presented below, based on matching the contexts of non-egocentrist thinkers in classical Buddhist India and the postmodern scientific West. It should come as no surprise that Nagel is unaware of the existence of a twenty-five century tradition of non-egocentrist philosophy and self-corrective anthropology, despite his reading of Parfit. While he is to be congratulated on his challenge to "the bizarre view that we, at this point in history, are in possession of the basic forms of understanding needed to comprehend anything," the findings of our study of the *Reason Sixty* and its Dialecticist elaboration pose a similar challenge to his belief "that the methods needed to understand ourselves do not yet exist" (10). Leaving aside his blanket dismissal of the modern West's human scientific tradition from psychoanalysis to cognitive science, Nagel is representative of the Western academic consensus that all religious approaches to human life are dismissible as "precritical," "premodern," or "prescientific," because they are all theistic and hence "antihumanist." Indeed, such dismissal is quite correct when "religious" is defined as attitudes derived from "non-rational," "blind" faith:

> The wish to live so far as possible in full recognition of the fact that one's position in the universe is not central has an element of the religious impulse about it, or at least an acknowledgement of the question to which religion purports to supply an answer. A religious solution gives us a borrowed centrality through the concern of a supreme being. (210)

However, the intellectual history of Buddhism suggests that Nagel's common conception of "religious" does not apply to the Buddhist tradition. To the contrary, this study offers a fresh look at Buddhism as a spiritual and scientific civilization committed to the pursuit of objective self-knowledge and self-regulation along the non-egocentrist lines Wittgenstein, Nagel, and others prescribe. Not surprisingly, the self-corrective insights and methods of Buddhism stubbornly defy categorization in terms of the mechanistic-science-versus-theistic-religion dichotomy that has polarized the discourse of the modern West and continues to split the Western academy into objectivist and constructivist camps. Instead, I will argue that the self-corrective insights and methods explored below reflect a religious tradition of scientific humanism that not only anticipated problems only now coming to our attention but also charted the central human scientific road-not-taken by the objectivist physical science and constructivist social science of the West.[59]

Although it poses some of the most difficult challenges facing contemporary Buddhologists, understanding the Central Philosophy promises to be invaluable to Indology, to modern philosophy of science, and to science of mind. The postmodern problems of understanding the relativity of knowledge and action, self and language, body and mind, are among the most critical in the Western academy. The very idea that these human science problems might have been recognized, debated, and resolved by the Buddhist academy, in centuries of open dialogue, demands our attention, however inconceivable it seems to the ethnocentric. If Nagel is right that our future as a civilization critically depends on developing the self-understanding and self-mastery that can help us avoid the extremes of scientism and antiscientism, then the human-scientific Centrism of Nāgārjuna and Chandrakīrti can help us save vital time and avoid grave errors.

Under the pressure of these larger challenges, this brief study of Chandrakīrti's text of therapeutic philosophy may help us to begin the work needed to resolve some of the stubborn problems facing modern Buddhology. The prevailing misreadings of Chandrakīrti's thought, however subtle, underscore the indispensability of hermeneutical research to the advancement of Centrist studies. Moreover, they are clear signposts warning us of the structural faults in Western Buddhology and reminding us of the need

---

[59] Cf. Jacobson, *Buddhism and the Contemporary World* (1983).

to correct our received Orientalist bias against the only extant modern tradition of nondualistic Centrist studies: Tibetan Indological scholarship.

II. Materials for the Study of the Reason Sixty and its Commentary

1. Nāgārjuna's *Reason Sixty* (*Yuktiṣaṣṭikākārikā*)

Modern scholars are in unanimous agreement with the traditional attribution of the *Reason Sixty* (*Yuktiṣaṣṭikā*) to Nāgārjuna,[1] known as the founder of the Central Way or Centrist school of Buddhist philosophy. The original Sanskrit is lost, although twelve verses preserved through citation in other works have been identified,[2] and an additional twenty-five reconstructed from the Tibetan.[3] With sixty-one verses including the opening stanza of dedication, the *Reason* is the briefest of Nāgārjuna's philosophical works, numbered by traditional and modern scholars at six to eight.[4] The preservation of some portion of its Sanskrit verses reflects the fact that it is among the works of Nāgārjuna most often cited by Centrist commentators. Chandrakīrti measures its importance in Nāgārjuna's eyes by the fact that "the Master" composed an opening dedication for the *Reason*, unlike such

---

[1] Cf. Schaeffer, *Yukti-ṣaṣṭikā: Die 60*, 2–3; Murti, *Central Philosophy*, 88–89; Ruegg, *Literature*, 19–20; Lindtner, *Nāgārjuniana*, 10–11; Tola and Dragonetti, "Yuktiṣaṣṭikā," 94–95; Scherrer-Schaub, *Yuktiṣaṣṭikāvṛtti*, xxiii. Traditional attributions to Nāgārjuna include those by Chandrakīrti, *Madhyamakaśāstrastuti* (cf. de Jong, "Madhyamakaśāstrastuti," 47–56); Bu-ston, *History of Buddhism I*, 50–51; and the colophons of the Tibetan translations in the *sDe-dGe* and Peking editions of the *bsTan-'gyur*.

[2] Lindtner has collected the twelve Sanskrit verses of the *Yuktiṣaṣṭikā* preserved through citation in other works, and presents them in critically edited versions in *Nāgārjuniana*, 102–119. Cf. Yamaguchi, *Chūgan Bukkyō Ronkō*, 29–110; Ruegg, *Literature*, 19 n. 43; Tola and Dragonetti, "Yuktiṣaṣṭikā," 96–97; and Scherrer-Schaub, *Yuktiṣaṣṭikāvṛtti*, 101–114. These verses are cited in the notes to the translations, below.

[3] Twelve of those reconstructed by Uryūzu Ryūshin, "Nāgārjuna Kenkyū" 1–2 (1973–74), have been collected by Tola and Dragonetti, "Yuktiṣaṣṭikā," 97–98, and the ten which do not duplicate preserved verses are cited in the notes to the translations, below.

[4] Chandrakīrti, in his *Madhyamakaśāstrastuti* (cf. de Jong, "Madhyamakaśāstrastuti"), and at the end of the Tibetan translation of his *Prasannapadā*, includes YṢ among his list of eight works attributed to Nāgārjuna. Bu-ston, *History of Buddhism I*, 50–51, lists five in addition to MMK: *Śūnyatāsaptati*, *Vigrahavyāvartanī*, *Vaidalyaprakaraṇa*, *Yuktiṣaṣṭikā*, and *Ratnāvalī*. Lindtner, *Nāgārjuniana*, 11, lists six philosophical works in addition to the MMK as "genuine": *Śūnyatāsaptati*, *Vigrahavyāvartanī*, *Vaidalyaprakaraṇa*, *Vyavahārasiddhi*, *Yuktiṣaṣṭikā*, and *Pratītyasamutpādahṛdayakārikā*.

works as the *Rebuttal of Objections* (*VV*) and *Voidness Seventy* (*ŚS*). Chandrakīrti's own assessment of the *Reason*'s importance is reflected in his decision to single it out as the only text of Nāgārjuna's beside the *Wisdom* (*MMK*) and its companion texts to receive direct commentary. The text's place in the Tibetan tradition is also clear from its inclusion in the Sixfold Canon of Reason (*Rigs tshogs drug*), recognized by historian-scholar Bu-ston Rin-chen-grub (1290–1364) as the textual basis for the Centrist studies (*dBu-ma*) portion of the monastic philosophy curriculum.[5] This may explain why there are two Tibetan commentaries on the *Reason*, both written after the time of Bu-ston.

The *Reason* appears to have been among the first Centrist works translated into Tibetan during the early dissemination (*snga dar*) of Buddhism under Srong-btsan sGam-po (r. 627–651) and Khri-srong lDe-btsan (754–797). With no Sanskrit title or mention of any member of its translation team, this early version dates to no later than the start of the ninth century, when it was included in the lDan-dkar Catalogue (824) of works translated into Tibetan.[6] This version comes to us preserved in two of the Dunhuang manuscripts, and is thought to have influenced the version of the root text embedded in Ye-she-sDe's eventual translation of the *Commentary*.[7] The canonical version of the text was translated approximately three centuries later by a team including the Indian Abbot Muditāśrī and the Tibetan Translator (*Lo-tsa-ba*) Pa-tshab Nyi-ma Grags (1055–1145). While this text differs markedly from the earlier version in its syntax and translation of technical terms, the differences are mostly simple inversions and substitutions that do little to alter the sense of the translation. Additionally, an extra-canonical version attributed to Pa-tshab and edited at Zhol Par-khang has also been preserved, although this version is essentially identical to the canonical one. The only other translation is the Chinese version attributed to Dānapāla (Ch. Shīhu'), an Indian master who reportedly emigrated to Kaifeng, China, from his native Uḍḍiyāna in 982.[8]

---

[5] On Bu-ston, see Ruegg, *The Life of Bu ston Rin po che* (1966).

[6] Lalou, "Les Textes Bouddhiques au Temps de Khri-sroṅ-lde-bcan" (1953), 333 n. 591. Cf. Scherrer-Schaub, *Yuktiṣaṣṭikāvṛtti*, xxiii n. 5.

[7] P nos. 795–796. Cf. Scherrer-Schaub, *Yuktiṣaṣṭikāvṛtti*, xxiii.

[8] *Lieou che song jou li louen*, Taisho, XXX, no. 1575, 254b–265a. Cf. Ruegg, "Le Dharmadhātustava," 463 n. 67; Scherrer-Schaub, *Yuktiṣaṣṭikāvṛtti*, xxvi and n. 8.

The first modern translation of the *Yuktiṣaṣṭikā*, Philipp Schaeffer's 1923 German version, *Yukti-ṣaṣṭikā: Die 60 Sätze des Negativismus*, was based primarily on the Chinese.[9] Subject to the limitations of that translation, Schaeffer's early effort is acknowledged as marred by philological inaccuracy.[10] Equally flawed is its hermeneutical strategy of reading Nāgārjuna's nondualism as a critique of reason essentially equivalent to the standard Kantian critique of reason.[11] As already elaborated above, this problem is only beginning to come to the attention of modern Buddhologists and Indologists, with the consequence that hermeneutical inaccuracies have not been eliminated from subsequent translations as easily and completely as have philological ones.

Early philological inaccuracies were effectively corrected by translations relying on critical editions of the characteristically systematic canonical Tibetan versions of Pa-tshab and Ye-shes sDe. Yamaguchi's 1944 critical edition of the Tibetan with Chinese was the basis of his 1965 Japanese version,[12] the first of six philologically critical modern language translations. Lindtner's 1980 Danish and 1982 English translations[13] benefit from the critical edition offered with the latter, enhanced by twelve recovered Sanskrit verses as compared with the one and one-half available to Yamaguchi. Tola and Dragonetti's 1983 English version[14] has the added benefit of ten reconstructed Sanskrit verses from the first two of Uryūzu Ryūshin's four studies on the *Yuktiṣaṣṭikā*.[15] And finally, there is the invaluable 1991 French version embedded in Scherrer-Schaub's French translation of the *Yuktisaṣṭikavṛtti*, solidly informed by a critical edition of the Tibetan translation of the *Yuktiṣaṣṭikā* that compares four canonical versions with the extra-canonical version of Pa-tshab's translation and with the anonymous

---

9 *Yukti-ṣaṣṭikā: Die 60 Sätze des Negativismus nach der Chinesischen Version Übersetzt.*

10 Cf. Lindtner, *Nāgārjuniana*, 100, n. 138.

11 See the discussion of hermeneutics in the sections, above, and in the following text.

12 Yamaguchi, *Chūgan Bukkyō Ronkō*, 29–110, offers the critically edited text with Japanese translation.

13 Lindtner, "Den rette laeres tres vers" (1980), 85–92; and *Nāgārjuniana* (1982), 100–199.

14 Tola and C. Dragonetti, "Yuktiṣaṣṭikā" (1983).

15 Uryūzu Ryūshin, "Nāgārjuna kenkyū" 1–3 (1973, 1974, 1981), and "Rokujūju Nyoriron ni okeru Nāgārjuna no shiso" (1981).

translation of the Dunhuang manuscripts. Drawing on the recent studies of Ruegg,[16] Scherrer-Schaub is also the first translator to deploy a post-Kantian hermeneutic, and hence the first to clearly translate the critical thrust of Nāgārjuna's relativism.[17]

As for the traditional commentarial literature, some scholars assume the existence of an autocommentary by Nāgārjuna, listed in Catalogues of the Tibetan Canon as *Rigs pa drug cu pa'i rang 'grel.*[18] Although this reference appears to be spurious, it suggests the possibility that such a commentary was written and even translated, but that both the Sanskrit and Tibetan versions were lost. That Nāgārjuna would have written such a commentary is plausible in itself, given the existence of autocommentaries on works such as the *Rebuttal of Objections* and *Voidness Seventy*, which Chandrakīrti tells us he considered less important. Yet the fact that we find no reference to an autocommentary in Chandrakīrti's *Commentary* makes this unlikely and suggests that the *Reason Sixty Commentary* of Chandrakīrti translated here is the only Indian commentary on Nāgārjuna's *Reason.*[19] The fact that the two known Tibetan commentaries both post-date Bu-ston suggests the continued importance of this text in the Indo-Tibetan teaching and practice lineage of the Central Philosophy, especially in the tradition of the Gelukpa founder Tsong Khapa (1357–1419). They are the *Zin Bris*, comprising Gyaltsap's (1364–1432) notes of Tsong Khapa's oral teachings on the text; and the recent *mChan 'Grel* of gZhan-phan Chos-kyi sNang-ba (1871–1926).[20]

---

[16] Ruegg, "The Uses of the Four Positions" (1977); "Mathematical and Linguistic Models" (1978); and *Literature* (1981).

[17] Even if not, in my opinion, quite capturing the full thrust of its evolutionary view of causality or its subtle conventionalism.

A more recent English translation of the *Reason Sixty* verses by Dr. Peter Della Santina was discovered too late to consider herein. This philologically solid and hermeneutically neutral translation was published on the web in 2002. See above, p. 11 n. 27.

[18] Vaidya, *Études sur Āryadeva*, 49, presumes the existence of such a commentary and its preservation in Tibetan, giving as reference *Tibetan Canon, mDo* XXVII, 7, *Cordier* III, 292. Cf. Lalou, *Répertoire du Tanjur*, 3:122, who lists the title as *Rigs pa drug cu pa'i* (*rang 'grel*); Tola and Dragonetti, "Yuktiṣaṣṭikā," 95, 117 n. 1.

[19] Cf. Scherrer-Schaub, *Yuktiṣaṣṭikāvṛtti*, xxvii.

[20] *Rigs pa drug cu pa'i zin bris rJe'i gsung bzhin rGyal tshab chos rjes bkod pa*, TKSB, v. 15 (ba) (New Delhi, 1979), 595–617; and *Rigs pa drug cu pa'i tshig le'ur byas pa zhes bya ba'i mchan*

(cont'd)

2. Chandrakīrti's *Reason Sixty Commentary* (*Yuktiṣaṣṭikāvṛtti*)

The attribution of the *Commentary* to Chandrakīrti is uncontested.[21] The original Sanskrit of the text has been lost, except for the opening dedication and a few following lines identified by V.V. Gokhale on the back of the manuscript of Bhāvaviveka's *Heart of the Central Way* (*MH*) found at Zha-lu Monastery in 1936.[22] Chandrakīrti's *Reason Sixty Commentary* was preserved only in the Tibetan translation found in various versions in editions of the *Tengyur*. According to its colophon, this was the work of a ninth century team including the Indian scholars Jinamitra, Dānaśīla and Śīlendrabodhi,[23] and the Tibetan translator Ye-shes sDe.[24]

The *Commentary* has been translated from the Tibetan in two recent modern language versions. The first is an annotated translation into Japanese by Uryūzu, which appeared in 1974.[25] The second is Scherrer-Schaub's 1991 French translation, accompanied by a critical edition of the Tibetan text.[26] Other studies include a brief analysis of Chandrakīrti's comments on

---

'grel, The Collected Works of gZhan-phan (New Delhi: Jayyed Press, 1978), 459–495. The topic outline inserted in the translation and edition below was taken from the former text.

[21] There is general agreement that Chandrakīrti lived in the latter half of the seventh century. Cf. Ruegg, *Literature*, 71 n. 288; and "Towards a Chronology of the Madhyamaka School," 513–514. See also appendix, below.

[22] The manuscript was discovered by Rāhula Sāṁkṛtyāyana, and its YṢV fragment presented in Gokhale, "The Vedānta-Philosophy described by Bhavya" (1958), 165 n. 1. Cf. Scherrer-Schaub, *Yuktiṣaṣṭikāvṛtti*, xxix.

[23] On this Indian team, see Simonsson, *Indo-Tibetische Studien*, 228–229, 241–242; Naudou, *Les Bouddhistes*, 86–87; de Jong, "Notes à propos des colophons," 507; Hoffmann, *Tibet*, 132–133.

[24] See the critical editions below. On Ye-shes sDe, see Roerich, BA, I, 345; Simonsson, *Indo-Tibetische Studien*, 242; Ruegg, *Literature*, 210–211, and 211 n. 16; and Ruegg, "Autour du lTa ba'i khyad par de Ye shes sde," 207–229.

[25] Uryūzu Ryūshin, *Rokujūju Nyoriron* (1974), 5–88, nn. 364–372.

[26] Scherrer-Schaub, *Yuktiṣaṣṭikāvṛtti* (1991).

verse thirty by Lindtner,[27] and a résumé of the *Commentary*'s contents by Scherrer-Schaub.[28]

3. Central Philosophy as a Method of Self-Correction

I understand Nāgārjuna's Central Philosophy as an application of the Indian linguistic-mathematical placeholder zero (*śūnya*) to critically redefine the formula of relativistic origination (*pratītyasamutpāda*), traditionally known as the epitome of Buddhist teaching.[29] Thus, before presenting the concept of voidness (*śūnyatā*) and its therapeutic use, Nāgārjuna begins both his *Wisdom* and his *Reason* by praising the Buddha for his insight and teaching of relativity. Likewise, having introduced Nāgārjuna's celebrated formula equating the relativity of things with their voidness with respect to intrinsic reality (*svabhāvaśūnyatā*), Chandrakīrti opens his *Commentary* by describing the *Reason* as "a primary study of the principle of relativity, like the *Wisdom*" (YṢV, ad k. 0).

Considering the fact that Nāgārjuna uses the term "relativity" variously in various contexts, with senses ranging from philosophical contingency and psychobiological causality to the ethical sense of a natural law of psychosociocultural development, his formula that relativity equals intrinsic realitylessness (*niḥsvabhāvatā*) supports various senses for the term voidness, as well. Thus, he speaks of voidness as "the cure for worldviews" (MMK, 8.8); as the vessel in which we "cross the ocean of intolerable existence" (YṢ, 59); and as "essentially compassion" (RA, 4.96). So, to resolve the various senses of this equation, we need a parallel equation of the voidness-relativity

---

[27] YṢV, P23a2–23b1; in Lindtner, "Atīśa's Introduction" (1981), 167–168. The root verse is among those for which the Sanskrit is preserved.

[28] Scherrer-Schaub, "*Yuktiṣaṣṭikāvṛtti* of Candrakīrti" (1995), in the *Encyclopedia of Indian Philosophies*, ed. by K. Potter.

[29] Ruegg, "Mathematical and Linguistic Models in Indian Thought: The Case of Zero and Śūnyatā." The formula which scholars call "the Buddhist creed," traditionally known as the heart of relativity (*pratītyasamutapādahṛdayā*), presents the basic four truths' framework as a system of rational self-knowledge and liberative practice that was considered general enough to have been applied to Indian medicine. / *oṁ ye dharma hetū prabhava, hetun teṣām tathāgata hy 'vādat / teṣām cayo' nirodha evam vādi mahāśramaniya svāhā /*. Thurman's translation of the term in the Centrist context with "relativity" presupposes the traditional glosses, *pratītyasamutpāda = idaṁpratyāyamātra*, and *parasparāpekṣa*.

nonduality with the Central Way, which Nāgārjuna links to his primary formula in the final dedicatory verse of the *Rebuttal of Objections*: "I salute that incomparable Buddha who taught the equivalence in meaning of voidness, relativity, and the Central Way."[30]

This second equation links Nāgārjuna's critical use of voidness as a nondualistic alternative to binary (positive or negative) symbolic constructs with his practical use of relativity as a Centrist alternative to the dualistic extremes of thought and action which result when such binary constructions are reified in self-deceptive projection or denial. Since this reifying habit is the cognitive root of dualistic extremisms, known philosophically as absolutism and nihilism (*asti-nāsti-vāda*), psychologically as projection and denial (*samāropa-apavāda*), and ethically as eternalism and nihilism (*śāśvata-ucchedavāda*), the therapeutic rationale for Nāgārjuna's Central Philosophy is to apply voidness as an allopathic remedy to that self-limiting mental habit, much as zero is used to overcome the limits of mechanical counting systems.

To do its work, Nāgārjuna's voidness must keep the mind open despite its habit of closing prematurely or rigidly on its own binary constructs; it must free the symbolic mind from its own demon (*māra*), the instinctive misknowledge that takes the medium of signs for the message of reality, placing self-imposed limits on the development of cognitive objectivity and universal altruism. This interpretation of Nāgārjuna's system explains why, of all conceivable views, the only view said to block the Centrist philosophy's therapeutic effect is one which reifies voidness as a presence or absence independent of the constructs it critiques. "Since the Victors teach voidness as the cure for all worldviews, whomsoever takes voidness as a worldview they pronounce incurable" (MMK, 8.8).[31] Whether such a worldview reifies voidness as an ineffable something or an absolute nothing, it is called "the view of voidness" because it conceives its ultimate reality

[30] *yaḥ śūnyatāṁ pratītyasamutpādaṁ madhyamāṁ pratipadaṁ ca / ekārthāṁ nijagāda praṇamāmi tam apratimasaṁbuddham //*. This equation is implicit in the famous affirmative consequence in MMK 24.10 sq., which, Tsong Khapa commented in his *Rigs-pa'i rgya-mtsho*, should be appended to every critique in MMK as a safeguard against a skeptical misunderstanding of voidness. Cf. Thurman, *Essence*, Introduction.

[31] *śūnyatā sarvadṛṣṭīnaṁ proktā niḥsaraṇaṁ jinaiḥ // yeṣāṁ tu śūnyatādṛṣṭānasādhyān babhāṣire* //. Compare YṢ, 31, and YṢV, below.

dualistically, as somehow distinct from the fabric of causal relations and symbolic conventions Nāgārjuna calls "superficial reality." When misused in this way, the potent medicine of voidness can be toxic, confirming either the mystic illusion of an ultimate somewhere beyond the relative, or the pragmatic illusion that there is no ultimate truth, no cure for the ills of human self-deception. Thus, Nāgārjuna issues his famous warning, "Voidness wrongly viewed may bring the slow-witted to ruin, like a poorly caught snake or a misapplied formula" (MMK, 24.11).[32] And, elsewhere he directly critiques the binary alternatives of mystic projection and pragmatic denial that result from reifying voidness, reminding the mystic that "voidness...is defined in a conventional sense" (MMK, 22.11), and the pragmatist that "without relying on convention, the ultimate cannot be taught" (MMK, 24.10).[33]

Thus, from its inception, the Central Philosophy confronted dualistic misreadings of Buddha's teaching of voidness clearly analogous to the neo-Kantian views that obscure modern translations of Nāgārjuna. In fact, Nāgārjuna considered such views the most serious obstacles to the understanding and use of Centrist philosophy, anticipating the hermeneutical problems that modern scholars and translators have had with his works. This significant cross-cultural finding supports Nāgārjuna's premise that such dualistic distortions are universal symptoms of the symbolic mind's self-limiting illness of reifying its own fabrications (*prapañca*). Thus, modern studies and translations of Nāgārjuna suffer from the same critical weaknesses that Centrist philosophy was designed to treat among Indian Buddhist and non-Buddhist scholar-practitioners.

The dualistic views of voidness Nāgārjuna addressed continued to be of critical concern to masters of the Indo-Tibetan Centrist tradition down to the modern era, as evidenced by the Dialecticist systems of Chandrakīrti and Tsong Khapa. The misunderstandings Chandrakīrti takes most pains to critique in his *Lucid Exposition* and *Introduction* fall into the two same classes Nāgārjuna addressed. His critique of Bhāvaviveka's Dogmaticist for-

---

[32] MMK, 24.11: *vināśayati durdṛṣtā śūnyatā maṇḍamedhasaṁ // sarpo yathā durgṛhīto vidyā vā duṣprasādhitā//.*

[33] MMK, 22.11: *śūnyam iti na vaktavyam aśūnyam iti vā bhavet / ubhayaṁ nobhayaṁ ceti prajñapty arthaṁ tu kathyate //*. MMK, 24.10: *vyavahāram anāśritya paramārtho na deśyate / paramārtham anāgamya nirvāṇaṁ nādhigamyate //.*

malism in *Lucid Exposition* 1 takes Bhāvaviveka to task for reifying the dichotomy between conventional and ultimate by insisting that mundane perception and language must work by conventionally identifying objects or referents via some kind of self-evident given that is not, however, ultimately identifiable by philosophical analysis. Chandrakīrti argues that this requirement is excessive, violating the superficial reality of unexamined social consensus and constraining the profound therapeutic insight of voidness that overrides the reifying habit limiting human knowledge and communication: "Otherwise, the superficial would not be the superficial, and would either lack validity entirely or become [ultimate] reality."[34] Chandrakīrti returns to this point in discussing the view of voidness explicitly in *Lucid Exposition* 13: "How can those who insist upon [intrinsic] being even in voidness ever cease such insistence on being? Since they do not recognize even such a universal medicine [as voidness], the supreme doctors, the transcendent buddhas, must turn away from such individuals."[35] Finally, in his discussion of the sixteen voidnesses in *Introduction* 6.179–223, he addresses the problem of understanding voidness as an entity (*bhāva*) in his definitions of the voidness of voidness (k. 186), voidness of the ultimate (ks. 189–190), voidness of absence (k. 217), and voidness of nothingness (k. 220).

As for the view which reifies voidness as an absolute nothing, a tautology devoid of sense or reference, Chandrakīrti takes great pains to critique it in the *locus classicus* of his defense of the Dialecticist stance of positionlessness in *Introduction* 6.171–178, as we see from *Introduction Commentary* (ad k. 172): "Although negation and negated do not exist [analytically]... one should know that negation negates the negated conventionally. Negation devoid of intrinsic reality negates the negated, and a reason, even without [analytic] validation...proves what is to be proven."[36] Furthermore, Chandrakīrti makes it clear in the *Reason Commentary* that this negation is no empty abstraction, but has a sense and reference like any other conventional cognition:

---

[34] PPMMV 1, ed. Vaidya, 23: *anyathā hi saṁvṛttir upapattyā na viyujyate tad eva tattvam eva syāt na saṁvṛttiḥ* /.

[35] PPMMV 13, ed. Vaidya, 108: *evaṁ yeṣāṁ śūnyatāyām api bhāvābhiniveśaḥ kenedānīṁ sa teṣāṁ tasyāṁ bhāvābhiniveśo niṣidhyatāmiti / ato mahābhaiṣajye 'pi doṣasaṁjñitvāt parama-cikitsakairmahāvaidyaistathāgataih pratyākhyātā eva te* /.

[36] MABh, ad k. 173.

> Even in mundane [parlance], one calls such types [of cognition], "direct experience." For instance, when surveying from a great distance the country in the region before him, a traveler sees something as if filled with abundant, pure [water], and wants to cross it. Yet from his experience, [thinking] he will not be able to, and being afraid, he asks a farmer who comes from the region, "Just how [expansive] is this water?" That [farmer] may say to him, "Where is this water? This resembles water but it is a mirage. If you don't believe my words about it, go there and look—*you will directly experience [the truth of] my words.*" Just as, by indicating the absence of water, one says "directly experience" to the traveler, likewise the world also conventionally designates absences and non-perceptions as "directly experienced." Because of this, there is no contradiction with the truth of worldly conventions in calling the cognition of non-perceptions [such as cessations] a "direct experience." (YṢV, ad k. 8)[37]

This negative perception is in fact the realistic intuition (*samyag-jñāna*) Chandrakīrti aligns with ultimate truth, because of its ultimate therapeutic import and effect: "Reality is the domain of those with realistic intuition; what is falsely perceived is declared superficial reality."[38] Thus, Chandrakīrti's understanding of the proper use of the therapeutic convention and transcendent insight of voidness is consistent with Nāgārjuna's definition of voidness as a treatment for the reifying mental habit, the root of misknowledge:

> Misknowledge, whose nature is the obscuration of the understanding of the real nature (of things) through reification (of

---

[37] Chandrakīrti borrows the same simile Nāgārjuna used in *Jewel Rosary* (RA, 1.55–57) to clarify the scope of the pure negation involved in self-analysis, but with a slightly different emphasis: stressing the truth value of the negative finding it yields, rather than reminding us not to reify that nominal finding into a substantial nothingness. See Tsong Khapa's *Legs-bshad snying-po* (LSNP), VII, 3 (Thurman, *Essence*, 376ff.).

[38] MA 6.23: *dngos kun yang dag rdzun pa mthong pa yis / dngos rnyed ngo po gnyis ni 'dzin par 'gyur / yang dag mthong yul gang de de nyid de / mthong ba brdzun pa kun rdzob bden par gsungs //.*

> [intrinsic] reality) in things without intrinsic reality, is utterly false.... Thus, the superficial truth is established under the influence of the addictive misknowledge included among the (twelve) factors of existence.[39]

In the modern era, dualistic misreadings of voidness as an ineffable something or an absolute nothing are clear targets in Tsong Khapa's hermeneutical treatment of Centrist philosophy in the *Essence*. Thurman, in introducing his translation of the *Essence*, identifies the advocates of these misreadings in Tsong Khapa's era.[40] The great Tibetan was concerned to critique the overly mystic readings advocated by Chinese Ch'an master, Hoshang Mahāyāna (8th CE)[41] and Dol-bu-pa Shes-rab rGyal-mthsan of the Jonangpa school (1292–1361). And he was equally concerned to critique the overly skeptical reading represented by the legacy of Jayānanda (11th–12th CE) and rNgog Lo-tsva-ba bLo-ldan Shes-rab of the Kadampa school (1059–1109), translator of the *Lucid Exposition* and *Introduction*. That Tsong Khapa's concern to critique these overly mystical and skeptical misreadings of voidness is consistent with Nāgārjuna's and Chandrakīrti's is evident from the "false views" he addresses in this formulation of the therapeutic effect of Central Philosophy, from the *Essence*:

> In regard to (phenomena) such as a sprout, there are three perceptual habits: one holding it to be objectively existent; one holding it to be objectively inexistent; and one holding it without qualifying it in either way. If the distinction is clearly understood that all three of these habit-patterns exist in the mental process of one in whom the realistic view is generated, but that only the first and last are present in the mental process of one in whom no realistic view has been generated, then one will put a stop to the following false views: (the view) that rationality does not put a stop to all

---

[39] This passage from MABh 6, ad k. 28, is cited in Tsong Khapa's LSNP and quoted as translated in Thurman, *Essence*, 309 (parentheses in original).

[40] Thurman, *Essence*, 49ff.

[41] For an account of the debate between Hoshang Mahāyāna and Kamalaśīla, organized by King Khri-srong lDe-btsan (r. 754–797), see Tucci, *Minor Buddhist Texts* (1958); and Demiéville, *Le Concile de Lhasa* (1963).

> perception (controlled) by mental constructions (such as) "this is it"; (the view) that all practices before the generation of the realistic view, such as cultivation of the will to enlightenment, are but truth-habits, or sign-habits; and (the view) that after one lays claim to having generated in mind the realistic view, there will be no intentionality in all one's acts.[42]

In the first two false views we recognize the idealistic and mystical misunderstandings which reify voidness as an ineffable something that can only be known approximately, by constructions of reason, or intuitively, by leaping beyond reason; while in the third false view we recognize the materialist or pragmatic misunderstandings which reify voidness as an absolute nothingness, whose knowledge is supposed to dispel the "illusion" that there is any ultimate truth or aim to strive for. In place of these views, Tsong Khapa defines the realistic view in terms of the cultivation of a habit of deobjectifying, dereifying insight that adds a new degree of freedom from the learned conditioning of perception and the instinctive cognitive bias of reification. This liberative, dereifying habit builds a negative faculty of transcendent insight that counteracts what Tsong Khapa calls the objectifying mental habit (*yul gyi 'dzin stangs*), freeing the mind from the self-deceptive grip of reified constructs and self-deceptive instincts.[43] Because the therapeutic convention and insight of voidness works to counteract the reifying habit at the root of misknowledge, views which reify voidness block the therapeutic effect of Centrist philosophy. As Tsong Khapa sees it:

---

[42] Tsong Khapa, LSNP, trans. in Thurman, *Essence*, 342–343 (parentheses in original).

[43] *Lam gtso rnam gsum: snang ba rten 'brel bslu ba med pa dang // stong pa khas len bral ba'i go ba gnyis // ji srid so sor snang ba de srid du // da dung thub pa'i dgongs pa rtogs pa med // nam zhig res 'jog med par cig car du // rten 'brel mi bslur mthong ba tsam nyid nas // nges shes yul gyi 'dzin stangs kun 'jig na // de tshe lta ba'i dpyad pa rdzogs pa lags //.* The psychological formulation follows a discussion in the *lhag mthong* section of Tsong Khapa's *Lam rim chung ngu*, where he cites the *Elucidation of the Intention* quote: "He who practices quiescence and transcendent insight will be freed from the bondages of negative conditionings and of signs," then comments: "'Negative conditionings' here refers to instincts underlying mental processes, which instincts increasingly generate a distorted subjectivity. 'Signs' refers to the continuous habitual adherence to mistaken objects which reinforce those instincts. The former are abandoned by transcendent insight, and the latter by peaceful quiescence." Tsong Khapa's *Collected Works* (TKSB), pha, f. 132a–b, as quoted in Thurman, *Essence*, 131–132. A full translation of the section is available in Thurman, *Life and Teachings of Tsong Khapa*, 108–185.

> All the reasonings of the central way are factors of the eradication of the habit-pattern of misknowledge, the root of the life-cycle. Hence, having identified how our own unconscious misknowledge maintains its hold, we should strive to terminate it, and should not amuse ourselves with expertise in mere hair-splitting with other philosophers![44]

Thus, those who assume the objectivist framework of modern critical scholarship are ill-equipped to interpret and translate Centrist works, since the dualistic reference frame they assume contains a hermeneutical bias toward mystical and skeptical misreadings, malignant views known to traditional scholars as the prime intellectual obstacles to a clear view of the Central Philosophy's intent and use.

4. A Nondualistic Hermeneutic for the *Reason Sixty Commentary*

Given the general need for a nondualistic comparative framework for interpreting Nāgārjuna and Chandrakīrti's texts, we turn now to consider the particular importance of such a framework for translating the *Reason* and its *Commentary*. The special importance of a nondual reference frame for these texts follows from the key role they play in their authors' systems: formulating the Central Philosophy's critical nondualism as a self-corrective therapy for the reifying mental habit. Chandrakīrti's *Commentary* explains that this briefest of Nāgārjuna's works was of special interest to its author and tradition because of its technical focus on the "Centrist way" that "clears away dualistic extremes" that block the insight of relativity. Chandrakīrti starts his work by citing the liberative primacy of that insight to explain why the *Reason* is among the few works beside the *Wisdom* and *Jewel Rosary* for which Nāgārjuna wrote a dedication. Presumably, that technical primacy also explains why the *Reason* is the only text beside the *Wisdom* and its companions to receive Chandrakīrti's direct commentary, and why it is among the works of Nāgārjuna most often cited by other Centrist commentators. Given the tradition that Chandrakīrti's own *Introduction* is an indirect commentary on the *Jewel Rosary*,[45] Chandrakīrti's decision to

[44] Thurman, *Essence*, 310.

[45] As elaborated in Gyatso, *Ocean of Nectar*.

comment on the *Reason* suggests he viewed it as occupying a key role alongside the masterpieces of wisdom and compassion, *Wisdom* and *Jewel Rosary*, as one of Nāgārjuna's three main works. But what precisely is the *Reason*'s role, and how does it relate to those of the *Wisdom* and *Jewel Rosary*? The *Reason*'s dedication suggests that its intent is methodological:

> I bow to the Lord of Sages,
> Who proclaimed relativity,
> The way by which he abandoned
> [Real] creation and destruction! (YṢ, 0)

Given this image of Shākyamuni Buddha as a master sage and the traditional praise of his message of relativity (*rten 'brel*), Nāgārjuna's precise focus on liberative method might be anything from philosophical or psychological to anthropological. Comparing this with the dedicatory verses of the *Wisdom* and *Jewel Rosary* helps pinpoint Nāgārjuna's intent here, by defining the *Reason*'s precise technical focus. First, consider this abridged version of the first two *Wisdom* verses:

> I salute the Completely Enlightened One,
> That supreme philosopher,
> Who taught relativity,
> The quieting of fabrications that is peace![46]

Here, in line with an image of Buddha as Completely Enlightened (*saṁbuddha*) and the epithet "supreme philosopher" (*vadatāṁ varaṁ*), relativity figures as the royal reason (*yukti-rājā**) proving voidness, the critical means to that perfect clarity of mind that can only come from transcending the fabrications arising from reifying one's own binary mental constructs into intrinsic realities. In this light, the *Reason*'s "Lord of Sages" is a relatively contemplative image, and the sense of relativity it embodies is that of a system of insight which frees one from the double-edged alienation

---

[46] I omit the four line list of dualistic extremes whose exclusion defines the ultimate nature of relativity, "Free of extinction and creation; without annihilation and permanence; with no coming and no going; not a unity, nor a plurality" (MMK, 1.1–2), representing the main philosophical alternatives which will be targets of Nāgārjuna's critique in the *Wisdom*: *anirodhamanutpādam-anuchedam-aśāśvataṁ anekārtham anānārtham-anāgamamanirgamaṁ / yaḥ pratītyasamutpādaṁ prapañcopaśamaṁ śivaṁ / deśayāmāsa saṁbuddhastaṁ vande vadatāṁ varaṁ //.*

of reifying one's self and world as either a divine creation or a material accident. In this sense, the division of labor between the two texts may be viewed as one of theory versus practice, with the *Wisdom* covering the phase of cognitive enlightenment with its analytic therapy for worldviews (MMK, 8.8), and the *Reason* covering the second phase, the practical application of that analytic method to the contemplative task of developing enlightened self-knowledge. Thus, the *Reason*'s aim is to apply Nāgārjuna's critical method as a cure for the misknowing human condition; its means is to use the nondual equation of relativity and voidness to revise the dualistic epistemologies of theism and materialism, as well as any subtly dualistic reification of the disease-cure dichotomy between the self-enclosed life-cycle (*saṁsāra*) and its extinction (*nirvāṇa*).

So, the role of the *Reason* among Nāgārjuna's major works can be understood as one of practical versus critical method. Its dedication is appropriate to this role. Another parameter of the *Reason*'s focus on Centrist method emerges when we look further on the praxis side and compare its dedication with the opening dedication of Nāgārjuna's masterpiece on bodhisattva practice, the *Jewel Rosary*:

> I bow to the Omniscient One,
> Who is free from all faults,
> And adorned with all qualities,
> The sole friend of all living beings![47]

While this verse seems more soteriological than methodological, a closer look reveals the anthropology behind Nāgārjuna's buddhology. The traditional image of Buddha as omniscient, or perfectly objective (*sarvajñā*), condenses the praise due his person and his teaching, celebrating him for embodying the ideal of simultaneous realization of both the cognitive ideal of objectivity and the practical ideal of altruism. With it, Nāgārjuna introduces the *Jewel Rosary* as his treatment of that nondual practice of combined transcendence and ascendance (*niḥśreyasa-abhyudaya*) whose fruit is integration of a mind "faultless" in ultimate wisdom of voidness with a body fully "adorned" with conventional mastery of communicative art. This buddhological image of human evolutionary perfection is well suited to the third and last phase in the nondual methodology of Nāgārjuna's system, the

---

[47] RA, 1.1.

enlightened performance (*bodhisādhana*) of voidness and compassion (*śūnyatā-karuṇā-garbha*), based on the therapeutic anthropology of internalizing an ideal model of enlightened agency via the art of relying on a healing guide (RA, 5.92). So, the *Jewel Rosary*'s role is to formulate the nondual performance that reproduces the agency of enlightened altruism, based on the nondual capacity to transcend the egocentric life-cycle while rising to divine heights as a God Beyond Gods (*Devātideva*), Sole Friend and Healer to all living beings (RA, 5.97).

Thus, a reading of the *Reason*'s dedication in the context of those of two of Nāgārjuna's other major works suggests that our text is located between his masterpieces on critical philosophy and practical methodology. The *Reason*'s place in his *oeuvre* is central since it puts the critique of the *Wisdom* into practice, reframing it as a self-analytic or self-corrective practice that clears the way for the nondual performance of objectivity and altruism formulated in the *Jewel Rosary*. In terms of the traditional threefold cultivation of wisdom—through learning, critical reflection, and meditation (*śruta-cintā-bhāvanā-mayī-prajñā*)—the practice of transcendent insight outlined in the *Reason* describes the reflective link between the *Wisdom*'s cognitive "solution" and the *Jewel Rosary*'s practical "performance" of wisdom and compassion.

Just as the *Reason* holds a pivotal place among Nāgārjuna's major texts, the *Commentary* is pivotal in relation to Chandrakīrti's theoretical and practical masterpieces, the *Lucid Exposition* and the *Introduction*. We can see this from the introductory verse to the *Commentary*:

> Bowing to the author of the *Reason Sixty*
> Which dispels the two extremes,
> Following the Victor's path of reasoning,
> I will elucidate it with the Central Way. (YṢ, ad k. 0)

Chandrakīrti's dedication demonstrates his view of the *Reason*'s intent in four respects. First, it salutes Nāgārjuna for his liberative use of language, traditionally viewed as the ultimate tool for cultivating and communicating transcendent insight. Second, its substitution of "Victor" (*jina*) for Nāgārjuna's "Lord of Sages," highlights the text's tone of confidence in the perfectibility of reason (*yukti*) in nondual objectivity, the mind's ultimate victory over cognitive bias and affective resistance. Third, the dedication places the *Reason* and its author as "following the Victor's path of reasoning," defining the thrust of Nāgārjuna's text as a demonstration of the Centrist method "which dispels the two extremes" by treating the reifying habit underlying them. Finally, its structure models the production of altruistic agency from the insight of nondual, immediate nirvāṇa, the aim of the contemplative path mapped in the text. Thus, Chandrakīrti's verse presents the *Reason*'s author as embodying "the Victor's path of reasoning," just as Nāgārjuna's verse praises "that Lord of Sages," who for him personifies "the method that frees." In fact, Chandrakīrti not only mirrors but extends the reproductive structure of the path to the objective knowledge of buddhahood, by offering himself to the reader as a product of the living tradition of Centrist philosophy, "I will elucidate it with the Central Way."

By contrast, Chandrakīrti's dedication to the *Lucid Exposition* depicts Nāgārjuna not as a model for those who seek to emulate the Victor's path of selflessness (*anātmavāda*), but as a warrior champion (*mahāratha*) who clears the way by vanquishing the self-reifying views (*satkāyadṛṣṭi*) that block the path to self-transcendent wisdom:[48]

> I bow to that Nāgārjuna,
> Who took birth in the ocean of the genius of buddhas,
> And lived to extinguish dualistic extremes,
> Empathically sharing his own realization
> From the depths of the treasury of Excellent Teaching;
> Whose blaze of vision consumes others' views
> Burning away the gloom from their minds.
> Matchless in wisdom, the showering arrows of his words
> Vanquish the whole hostile army of [egocentric] existence,

---

[48] Chandrakīrti's *Commentary* identifies the six main schools of Indian thought whose dualistic extremes Nāgārjuna critiqued, suggesting that a critical familiarity with these is part of the intellectual culture assumed by the author of the *Reason*. "Those who wish to travel to the city of nirvāṇa by abandoning all the claims of realists, theists and others as to the creation and destruction of life through intrinsic reality, a Creator, nature, spirit, time, God, and so on, yet are handicapped by error through misperceiving the two realities [ultimate and superficial], will not be able for a very long time to reach that city of nirvāṇa whose nature is the termination of cyclic life" (YṢV, ad k. 0). For a treatment of India's orthodox six perspectives (*ṣaḍdarśana*), see Raju's *Philosophical Traditions of India* (1971); for the perspective of Tibetan traditions on these views, see Thurman, *Essence*, 13–17.

And win him glorious dominion over all three realms
Of this world to be civilized, along with its gods.[49]

There is no mistaking this brilliant icon of the triumph of complete philosophical clarity. Chandrakīrti depicts his master's insight into relativity as the sun rising from the ocean of Buddha's genius, burning the self-drawn veils from the minds of those who take their own objectivist or subjectivist constructs for reality itself, "civilizing" with his words the self-limiting narcissism both of humans and their gods, as the sun's rays dispel all shadows from the face of the planet. By comparison, the *Reason Sixty Commentary*'s dedication portrays Nāgārjuna not as Champion in the war with the gods of egocentric resistance, "the hostile army of existence," but as the paragon of Centrist method, a model for the sustenance and guidance of all those who would follow in the footsteps of the Victor's self-analysis. In this, it is consistent with Nāgārjuna's dedication to the *Reason*, which gives us Buddha not as Supreme Philosopher, but as that Lord of Sages who personifies the relativity insight.

Thus, as the *Reason* clears the contemplative way to the final nondual practice of the *Jewel Rosary*, Chandrakīrti's *Commentary* offers a transition from the critical hermeneutics of the *Lucid Exposition* to the altruistic anthropology celebrated in the dedication to his *Introduction*:

I salute those who develop compassion for beings
Who revolve helpless as buckets in a water-wheel,
Coming to insist on a self, once they say "I,"
Growing addicted to things, saying "This is mine."[50]

Once the *Reason* and its *Commentary* are placed in the context of their authors' main works, their focus can be suggestively defined as follows:

---

[49] PPMMV, ed. Vaidya, 1: *yo antadvayāvāsavidhūtavāsaḥ saṁbuddhadhīsāgaralabhdajanma / saddharmatoyasya gambhīrabhāvaṁ yathānubuddhaṁ kṛpāyā jagāda / yasya darśanatejāṁsi paravādimatendhāngaṁ / dahantyadhyāpi lokasya manasāni tamāṁsi ca // yasya asamajñā-vacaḥ-śaraughā nighnanti niḥśeṣabhāvārisenaṁ / tridhāturājyaśriyam adadhāna vineyalokasya sadevakasya // Nāgārjunāya praṇipatya tasmai //.*

[50] MA, 1.3: *dang por nga zhes bdag la zhen gyur zhing // bdag gi 'di zhes dngos la chags bskyed pa // zo chun 'phyan ltar rang dbang med pa yi // 'gro la snying rjer gyur gang de la 'dud //.*

Discipline	Philosophy	Contemplation	Ethics
Canon	Abhidharma	Sūtra	Vinaya
Root Text	MMK	YṢ	RA
Comments	PPMMV	YṢV	MA

Table 1: Nāgārjuna's and Chandrakīrti's Works in Context

Since the *Reason*'s focus is on the self-corrective "path of reason" that leads from the intellectual analysis of worldview to the nondual performance of enlightened altruism, its internal structure can be mapped into three steps, corresponding to the three developmental stages of cognitive-affective-behavioral self-transcendence. The three steps on this core path of relativistic self-correction are intellectual, reflective, and meditative. First, relativistic reason is linked with cognitive self-correction, aligned with the purely negative, dereifying insight of voidness that overcomes cognitive biases that block objectivity or omniscience. Next, relativistic reason is linked with affective self-correction, aligned with the deobjectifying insight that overcomes emotional resistances to objective self-knowledge. Third, relativistic reason is linked with behavioral self-correction, emerging from meditative integration of the nondual, dereifying insight that culminates in unbiased objectivity and unconditional altruism, the cognitive-practical ideal of enlightened altruistic agency. In what follows, I will briefly survey the argument of the *Reason* and its *Commentary* in light of these three self-corrective steps toward an enlightened social epistemological agency.

1) The *Reason* begins by introducing relativity, the epitome of Buddhist teaching, as transcending the grasp of dualistic constructs (*astināsti-vyatikrānta*) (YṢ, 1). With its subject clear, it defines as its audience the overly-realistic adherents of the Buddhist Analyst and Traditionist (*Vaibhāṣika* and *Sautrāntika*) schools, who reject nihilism but are still prone to absolutism (*astitā*) (YṢ, 2). In the following verses, Nāgārjuna defines the thrust of his *Reason* (*yukti*) in terms of a rational insight (*darśana*) which penetrates reified views of creation or destruction, *saṁsāra* or *nirvāṇa*, as absolute "being or nothingness" (YṢ, 3–9). Such realistic insight or precise intuition (*samyagjñāna*), the cure for misknowledge (*avidyā*) (YṢ, 10) and [extremist] worldviews (*dṛṣṭi*) (YṢ, 17), is then defined as the immediate nirvāṇa state (*dṛṣṭadharmanirvāṇa*), that purely negative finding (YṢ, 11–12; 25–27) which frees the noble (*ārya*) and the skilled (*paṇḍita*) (YṢ, 28–29).

2) Having defined the ultimate, dereifying mode of transcendent insight, Nāgārjuna turns to define its relative, virtual mode as the source of emotional self-mastery (YṢ, 29); of the empathic use of conventional constructs (*vyāvahārikavikalpa*) to communicate insight (YṢ, 30–38); and of freedom from self-deceptive views (*dṛṣṭi*) and biases (*doṣa*) that come of reifying illusory social constructs (YṢ, 40–45).

3) Finally, the author goes on to define these nondual insight modes as the cure for the process of obsession and conflict (*parigrahavivādādikrama*) (YṢ, 49), the door to the impartial, great soul (*apakṣika-mahātma**) (YṢ, 50), and the wisdom-insight eye (*jñāna-cakṣuḥ*) (YṢ, 54) which frees individuals from the trap of [false] objects (*viṣaya-pañjara*) (YṢ, 53–56), allowing them to transcend dualistic constructs (YṢ, 57–58) and so cross the ocean of intolerable existence (*tīvrabhāvārṇava*) (YṢ, 59).

As for Chandrakīrti's *Commentary*, its argument faithfully follows the threefold structure of the *Reason*, critiquing the subtle epistemological rationalizations of the reifying habit current among his contemporaries. It elucidates the intermediate steps in Nāgārjuna's argument and refines his conventionalist methodology, appealing to everyday language to arrive at distinctive Dialecticist formulations of the key points. The following celebrated passages formulate each of the three steps.

First, Chandrakīrti describes the pure non-finding of ultimate dereifying insight as an intuitive non-perception, as already mentioned above.[51]

Second, Chandrakīrti describes transcendent insight by expanding on Nāgārjuna's simile of the virtual person (*māyā-puruṣa**) in YṢ, 16:

> Conditioned by a magician's spell, young women appear as well trained performers, exquisite in form and movement, with an elegant manner. Captivating with their consummate skill in seduction, they will be a source of intense pleasure like a real mate for those who are addicted to desire and ignorant of their nature. But the magician, who knows that their nature lacks any intrinsic reality that corresponds to the fantasies of the ignorant, will recognize their appearance as

---

[51] See p. 34 n. 37 above, and YṢV, ad k. 8.

> an unreal illusion and hence have no such confused conception of it.[52]

Third, Chandrakīrti describes how the nondual practice of transcendent insight empowers the liberated self to develop the unbiased agency of an enlightened altruist:

> A child, not understanding mundane activities, his awareness stupefied with intrinsic realities, sees a mirror image, holds it to be a real thing, and can fall in love with it and play with it however he can. In just that way, naïve persons, endowed with misknowledge created by the force of their delusions, are mentally, verbally, and physically obsessed with arguing about [intrinsically] real things, insisting on "this" or "that." They are helplessly seduced by desire, anger, pride, and the other [addictions]. And, not knowing the nature of cyclic life, they are completely trapped in its thicket, whatever they try to do. Such people are objects of loving concern for the noble ones. For they, having opened their wisdom eyes, can see reality as it truly is. (YṢV, ad k. 53)

An intriguing parallel to this threefold argument of the *Reason* and its *Commentary* can be found in the opposites of the three false views about transcendent insight addressed by Tsong Khapa: 1) rational insight does put a stop to perceptions controlled by reified verbal constructs in forms like "this is it"; 2) before one perfects actual insight one may use simulated negative and illusion-like insights to break egocentric mental habits and cultivate altruistic ones;[53] 3) the realization of genuine insight frees one to develop genuine empathy and maintain an altruistic intentionality through all one's acts.[54]

---

[52] See YṢV, ad k. 16.

[53] This distinction between simulated (*rjes su mthun pa*) and actual (*dngos*) forms of transcendent insight (*lhag mthong*) may be traced to Prajñākaramati's distinction between causal wisdom (*hetubhūtaprajñā*) and fruitional wisdom (*phalabhūtaprajña*). See Vaidya, ed., *Bodhicaryāvatāra[pañjikā]*, 349.

[54] See Thurman, *Essence*, 168–172, 342–43.

III. Self-Correction in the Reason Sixty Commentary

1. A Comparative Philosophical Framework for Therapeutic Self-Correction

A therapeutic philosophy is a philosophy meant to define and treat ignorance as an illness, rather than to advance one worldview against opposing views. From the Buddha's first teaching of four noble truths, the basic framework of Buddhist thought and practice was to expose and end the misknowledge that conditions human suffering, by diagnosing the delusional self-habit (*ātmagraha*) it supports, and extinguishing it with the philosophy of selflessness (*anātmavāda*). The Central Philosophy of Nāgārjuna and Chandrakīrti is no exception to the Buddha's therapeutic teaching; its basic framework of two realities, resolved in the equation of relativity (*pratītyasamutpāda*) with voidness (*śūnyatā*), must be understood not as a formula of causality or deconstruction, but as further clarifying the symptoms, origin, treatment and cure of the self-habit. The essence of its clarification is the Dialecticist definition of delusions of "self" as any concepts or percepts of intrinsic reality (*svabhāva*), intrinsic identity (*svalakṣaṇa*) or intrinsic objectivity (*svarūpa*). For Nāgārjuna, according to Chandrakīrti, it is the instinctive reification (*adhyāropa*) of such delusive "selfhood" in persons or things which is the root of misknowledge; and it is this addictive, compulsive self-habit that must gradually be exposed and corrected by the self-analytic wisdom of voidness. Thus, Nāgārjuna's *Reason* says:

> Those who insist on a non-relative
> "Self" or "world"—Alas!
> They are deprived by addictive views
> Such as absolutism and nihilism. (YṢ, 43)

And his "Analysis of Self" in the *Wisdom* concludes: "Since what exists in relation to anything can in no way be identical to that thing nor distinct from it, any such [self which relates to mind-body aggregates] is neither eternal nor annihilated" (MMK, 18.10).[1] Chandrakīrti refines the equation in a famous formulation of the voidness of self in persons and things:

---

[1] MMK, 18.10: *pratītya yad yadbhavati na hi tāvattadeva tat // na cānyadapi tasmānnocchinnaṁ nāpi śāśvataṁ //.*

> As for "self," it is a reality or substance of things that does not relate to anything else. As it does not exist, there is selflessness. That again is understood as twofold because of the distinction between persons and things; namely personal selflessness and objective selflessness.[2]

Although modern Western philosophy after Descartes became increasingly critical of the permanent, substantial matter and soul (*anima*) of scholastic thought, from the Centrist perspective it remained uncritically tied to egocentrist notions of non-relational subjects and objects. Thus, Kant's residual reification of a transcendent ego and things in themselves was replaced only by Nietzsche with a critical relativism comparable to Nāgārjuna's: "That the world is a unity neither as spirit nor as sensorium, that alone is the great liberation!"[3] Given Nietzsche's philological methods and insights, Kant's egocentrist categories of experience could finally be exposed and treated as delusions of ego-substance (*ich-substanz = svabhāva*) traced to reified linguistic constructions:

> We are constantly led astray by words and concepts, and are induced to think of things as other than they are: as autonomous, indivisible, existing in the absolute. A philosophical mythology lies hidden in language.... It is language which sees everywhere deed and doer; this which believes in the "ego" as being, in the "ego" as substance, and which projects its belief in ego substance on to all things—only thus does it create the concept "thing." Being is everywhere foisted on us as cause; it is only from the conception "ego" that there follows derivatively the concept "being."... Today we know it is merely a word.[4]

Although Nietzsche's philosophy is generally associated with his ideas of transcendence (*ubergangung*) and cultivation (*erzeugung*), its therapeutic thrust is clear in his prophecy that psychology will displace metaphysics as "Queen of the Sciences," a prophecy partly fulfilled in the "talking therapy"

---

[2] CŚṬ, 12, ad k.13; C, ya, 29a6ff. Translation from Thurman, *Essence*, 298.

[3] Nietzsche, *Twilight of the Idols*, 37–38.

[4] Nietzsche, *Twilight of the Idols*, 38, elisions mine.

which his and Goethe's philosophies inspired in Freud. A philosophically educated neurobiologist who sought "a middle way between philosophy and medicine," Freud saw his prime contribution as the analytic insight that stopped egocentric delusions of a fixed, independent self:

> Normally there is nothing we are more certain of than the feeling of our self, our own ego. It seems to us an independent and unitary thing, clearly distinguished from everything else. That this is a deceptive appearance, that on the contrary the ego...serves as a kind of facade...was first discovered by psychoanalysis. The universal narcissism of men...has suffered three blows from...science; and this [after Copernicus and Darwin's]...was probably the most wounding.[5]

Yet despite this basic non-egocentrist thrust, Freud's reliance on a neo-Kantian philosophical method left the "metapsychological" framework of his insight therapy burdened with reifications, especially of the key concept of an unconscious mind, later identified with the structural agency he fashioned after Nietzsche's "It."[6] While subsequent schools have done much to dereify and critically revise Freud's framework, much as the later therapeutic philosophies of Buddhism, the Traditionist, Idealist, and Centrist schools, dereified and revised the scientific teaching of the classical Analysts, psychoanalytic thought has not yet reached the level of critical refinement of Nietzsche and Wittgenstein.[7] Thus, while the non-egocentrist philoso-

---

[5] Freud, *Standard Edition*, 21: 74; *Standard Edition*, 17: 137, brackets added.

[6] The *loci classici* for Freud's development of these concepts, drawn from the philosophies of German Idealism, are his *Interpreteation of Dreams* (1900, *Standard Edition*, V), his paper on "The Unconscious" (1915), and *The Ego and the Id* (1923). For a review of their origins and development from a contemporary hermeneutical-phenomenological perspective, see Ricoeur, *Freud and Philosophy* (1970).

[7] Considering the cultural-historical distance involved, the parallels are remarkable in a comparison of the false "self-object constructs" analyzed by various schools of psychoanalytic and Buddhist insight. Although the Analysts (*Vaibhāṣika*) assert no "subconscious mind" (*ālaya-vijñāna*), they use their "table of elements" (*dharmasaṁketa*) as a grid for self-analytic insight much as classical Freudian analysts use the structural model; Traditionists (*Sautrāntika*) use the same grid, but dereify the elements and stress their relationality, much as object-relations theorists do with the metapsychology; the Idealists (*Cittamātra*), or Experientialists (*Yogācāra*) accept a subconscious mind, and focus on its "transformation" (*parāvṛtti*) by analyzing the reified dichotomy of inner self and outer object, much as do the Jungian, gestalt and humanis-

(cont'd)

phies of Nietzsche and Freud provide a matching context for cross-cultural comparison with the therapeutic philosophy of Nāgārjuna and Chandrakīrti, they do not provide a complete comparative framework. What Nietzsche lacks in therapeutic methodology, Freud and his heirs lack in philosophical methodology. Since Wittgenstein's later philosophy of language refines both Nietzsche's language-based philosophical method and Freud's language-based therapeutic method, the non-egocentrist ideas and techniques presented in his later works are well suited to a comparative framework for Dialecticist Centrism. Before outlining such a framework, however, it is important to realize that it does not stop with comparing the language-therapies of Chandrakīrti and Wittgenstein, but rather uses that comparison as a frame of cross-cultural reference from which the full range of applications of Dialecticist thought can be compared with the analogous applications of ordinary language philosophy in the West. We have already alluded to some of these by implicitly comparing the application of Centrist methods in Buddhist anthropology and scientific method with Thomas Nagel's general theory of objective self-knowledge. It is also possible to extend the analogy to compare the role Centrist self-corrective methods played in the Buddhist traditions of human science of mind (*adhyātma-vidyā*) with the role language philosophy has played in the cognitive therapies and cognitive sciences.

I will here present the basic comparative framework. That presentation must be threefold, since in order to effectively translate the *Reason* and

---

tic schools; the Dogmaticist Centrists (*Svātantrika-Mādhyamika*) are divided in their stance on the subconscious mind but all the more critical of the reification of self-object constructs as having any non-relational, non-socially-constructed status, much as the most recent Kohutian hermeneutical and intersubjective schools; the Dialecticist Centrists (*Prāsaṅgika-Mādhyamika*), including Nāgārjuna as understood by Chandrakīrti, reject the subconscious as equivalent to a reified soul or God that evolves, and reject any construct of an intrinsically real or identifiable self or element, accepting persons and things only as "mere linguistic usages" (*upādāya-prajñāptimātra*) "based only on unexamined assent" (*avicāryamānasiddha*) to linguistic "conventions" (*vyavahāra*). Since no modern Western philosophical psychology but Wittgenstein's defines the false and true self in a comparable way, our comparative framework must center on Wittgenstein.

For critical views of the schools of psychoanalysis, see Greenberg and Mitchell, *Object Relations in Psychoanalytic Theory* (1983); Hillman, *Revisioning Psychology* (1977); Stolorow and Atwood, *Contexts of Being: The Intersubjective Foundations of Psychological Life* (1992); and Spence, *Narrative Truth and Historical Truth* (1982).

its *Commentary*, our comparative framework will need to relate the concepts and terminology of Nāgārjuna, Chandrakīrti, and Wittgenstein in three key areas, corresponding to the three main aspects of Dialecticist contemplative method and the three perceptual habits defined by Tsong Khapa. The three aspects are: 1) defining relativity as the reason for negating intrinsically real, identifiable, or objective subjects and objects, and hence, as the conventional ground for a form of self-corrective analysis, the ultimate logical conclusion of which is the dereifying voidness insight; 2) defining relativity as the psycholinguistic process sustaining human subjects and objects as working consensual fictions, and hence, as the conventional ground for a form of self-corrective thinking and acting whose unexamined premise is the voidness-relativity insight; and 3) defining these nondual modes of self-transcendent insight as the critical and practical conditions for responsible social knowledge and communication, and hence, as the conventional ground for a self-corrective anthropology aimed at reproducing free and responsible social agents.

2. Dereification and Self-Correction in Chandrakīrti and Wittgenstein

Although the self-habit in its natural (*sahaja*), instinctive form is the root of misknowledge and all its ills, the first step in its treatment in most human beings must be the analysis of the self-reifying views (*satkāyadṛṣṭi*) that are its highest level of defense, and the worldview-habit (*dṛṣṭigraha*) or reality-habit (*satyagraha*) of objectification (*ālambanagraha*) or reification (*adhyāropa*) underlying them. Since the crux of these views and the resistance to objective truth they maintain consists in reified subjective constructs of identity and reality, non-egocentrist philosophers are especially concerned with treating the reification of such constructs. Thus, the *Reason* is concerned with egocentrist views that stem from the habit of absolutism (*astivāda*) (YṢ, 2–3, 40), which Nāgārjuna defines as the presumptive commitment to intrinsic things (*bhāvābhyupagama*) (YṢ, 46–47) that reifies the forms of language into substances:

> When "this" or "that" [appears a fact],
> Yet when analyzed is not perceived,
> What wise person would advocate with arguments
> That "this" or "that" is [really] true? (YṢ, 42)

Once they commit to [intrinsic] things,
They are trapped in painful malignant views
Which produce attachment and aversion,
And the disputes that spring from them. (YṢ, 46)

Chandrakīrti's *Commentary* elsewhere underscores the point:

> Thus, alienated beings are deceived by their own minds from their insistence upon [a being in] things. Since this insistence on [a being in] things is constructed by their own minds, even though such things are not established with intrinsic objectivity, their insight into the suchness of things is obstructed, and through mistaken reification [of intrinsic realities in things], their own minds deceive them, that is to say, [they become] deluded. (YṢV, ad k. 24)[8]

And Wittgenstein: "We are up against one of the great sources of philosophical bewilderment: a substantive makes us look for a thing that corresponds to it." (BBB, 1)

These philosophers' critique of the habit of reifying language has led some to compare them with contemporary deconstructionists.[9] But unlike some deconstructionists, they prove themselves to be non-subjectivist, or rather non-egocentrist, by their therapeutic focus on the reification of the language of personal identity and reality, centered on the substantive pronouns "I" and "mine." Thus, the *Reason* narrows its focus on reification to highlight self-centered views that come from reifying constructs of "myself" and "my world":

Those who insist on a non-relative
"Self" or "world"—Alas!
They are deprived by views
Such as absolutism and nihilism. (YṢ, 43)

Chandrakīrti's *Commentary* explains:

---

[8] Cp. MA, 6.117: *so so'i skye bo rnams ni rtog pas bcing // mi rtog rnal 'byor pa ni grol 'gyur bas //* "Egocentric individuals are bound by their own constructions; non-conceptual practitioners are freed."

[9] See Fenner, *Ontology*; and especially Huntington, *Emptiness*.

> Those who do not designate "the self" in dependence on the five aggregates—which are devoid of intrinsic reality just like mirror reflections—but rather, locate "the self" in an intrinsically identifiable mind, will no doubt be swept far from the road to nirvāṇa and carried away by the stream of worldviews.
>
> Why is that? Now, if one asserts the objectively real status of mind, it must be either permanent or impermanent. If it is permanent, then one is an eternalist. Alternatively, if [one asserts] its impermanence, then one is a nihilist, since the nihilistic view is that something [once] emerged can [then] become a nothing. Thus, "Alas! They are deprived by views." The word "alas" should be known as an exclamation of either regret or certainty. Likewise, if [instead of an intrinsically identifiable mind] one claims the five aggregates—known as "the world"—to be intrinsically identifiably established, similar problems apply. (YṢV, ad k. 43)[10]

In the modern West, most Wittgenstein scholars agree that the prime focus and contribution of Wittgenstein's later philosophy is the treatment of solipsism offered in his critique of the language of private experience, especially in his *Investigations*:[11]

> The problems arising through a misinterpretation of our forms of language...are deep disquietudes.... (PI, §111)
>
> The philosopher's treatment of a question is like the treatment of an illness.... (PI, §255)
>
> You have a new conception and interpreted it as seeing a new object. You interpret a grammatical movement made by

---

[10] Cp. MA, 6.120: *nyon mongs skyon rnams ma lus 'jig tshogs la // lta bas byung bar blo yis mthong gyur zhing // bdag ni 'di yi yul du rtogs byas nas // rnal 'byor pa yis bdag ni 'gog par byed //.* "Having come to the intellectual insight that the illnesses of addictions develop from egocentric views, and since the self is constructed as the object of these [views], practitioners [of insight] work to negate [reified constructs of] the self."

[11] Cf. Morick, *Wittgenstein and the Problem of Other Minds* (1967); Kenny, *Wittgenstein and his Times* (1982); Hacker, "The Refutation of Solipsism" (1986).

> yourself as a quasi-physical object which you are observing.... (PI, §401)
>
> "I" is not the name of a person, nor "here" the name of a place, and "this" is not a name.... (PI, §410)
>
> [A] whole cloud of philosophy condensed into a drop of grammar. (PI, II, 222)

Given the clear cross-cultural parallel in our non-egocentrists' diagnoses of the linguistic self-habit and its underlying structure of reification, we turn to examine whether that parallel extends to the aims and methods of their therapeutic analysis. First, one finds a clear parallel between the general statements of aim and method in the *Reason* and *Commentary* and those in Wittgenstein's later work. The essence of non-egocentrist therapeutic strategy is to communicate a rational insight that remedies the habit of reifying the language of experience, by exposing the relativity of words and their referents, especially of "I" and "mine," and the persons and things they designate. The *Reason* uses the metaphor of visual perception to define the aim of realistic insight (*samyagjñāna*) (YṢ, 10), and the method of seeing relativity (*pratītyasamutpāda-darśana**) (YṢ, 48), or of simply seeing (*darśana*) (YṢ, 5, 11, 25, 54). It develops the metaphor by defining intelligence or mind (*buddhi*, Tib. *blo gros*) as the organ of insight, speaking of seeing with the intellect (*blo yis mthong ba*) (YṢ, 17) and seeing with the eye of intuitive wisdom (*ye shes kyi mig gis mthong*) (YṢ, 54). Chandrakīrti's *Commentary* defines genuine insight as the remedy for "whose intellectual eye is blinded having been covered by the cataract of misknowledge" (ad k. 29), and, as often in his *Lucid Exposition* and *Introduction*, also speaks of the intellectual eye as diseased by egocentric views, and healed only by the salve of the voidness insight applied with the method of the reason of relativity.[12] By showing the pervasive relatedness of things, this method trains realistic insight to see through things' deceptive superficial reality (*mṛṣasaṁvṛtisatya*)

---

[12] MA, 6.115: *gang phyir dngos po rten nas rab 'byung nas // rtog pa 'di dag rtag par mi nus pa // de'i phyir rten 'byung rigs pa 'di yis ni // lta ngan dra ba mtha' dag gcod par byed //.*

to their profound ultimate reality (*tattva*).[13] In the West, Wittgenstein defines his therapeutic aim and method in similar terms:

> A main source of our failure to understand is that we do not *command a clear view* of the use of our words.... A perspicuous representation produces just that understanding which consists in 'seeing connexions'.... It earmarks the form of account we give, the way we look at things. (PI, §122)

> The aspects of things which are most important for us are hidden.... (One is unable to notice something—because it is always before one's eyes.)... [W]e fail to be struck by what, once seen, is most striking and most powerful. (PI, §129)

> For the clarity that we are aiming at is indeed *complete* clarity. But this simply means that the philosophical problems should *completely* disappear. The real discovery is the one that makes me capable of stopping doing philosophy when I want to.—The one that gives philosophy peace, so that it is no longer tormented by questions which bring *itself* in question.—Instead, we now demonstrate a method, by examples.... There is not *a* philosophical method, though there are indeed methods, like different therapies. (PI, §133)

The cross-cultural parallel in diagnoses we saw in comparing these three non-egocentrist philosophers extends to their general aims and methods, as well. Remarkably enough, the parallel remains consistent with more detailed comparison of the means and ultimate end of their respective de-reifying insights. When we compare the style of these philosophers' critical analyses of the reified "I" and "mine," we find a striking similarity in the line of reasoning they prescribe, as well as in the negative insight that is their logical conclusion. One way to further the comparison is to follow the concise fourfold logical structure in which the contemplative practice of ultimacy-analysis (*paramārthavicāra**) is framed to this day in the Tibetan

---

[13] Cf. MA, 6.23: *dngos kun yang dag rdzun pa mthong pa yis // dngos rnyed ngo bo gnyis ni 'dzin par 'gyur // yang dag mthong yul gang la de nyid du // mthong ba brdzun pa kun rdzob bden par gsungs //.*

tradition. This structure is that of a pure or exclusion negation (*prasajya-pratiṣedha*) proving things' voidness of intrinsically identifiable reality without implying anything else. In contrast to an implicative negation (*paryudāsa-pratiṣedha*), such an exclusion negation implies no other thesis, but simply rules out the logical possibility that things are intrinsically identifiable or intrinsically real, as they appear to the reifying and objectifying mental habits.[14] In the Gelukpa tradition, this concise mode of analysis is taught in four steps or "keys" (*gnad bzhi*), although it may be abbreviated further to three, as we shall see below. Since the expanded modes—from the six-key tetralemma of Nāgārjuna's *Wisdom* 1, to the nine-key chariot-like analysis in Chandrakīrti's *Introduction* 6—assume the same basic logical form, we refer the reader to more extensive treatments elsewhere.[15] For the purposes of this comparison, the four keys may be defined as follows: 1) identifying the false self-habit to be analyzed; 2) committing oneself to the binary linguistic conventions of rational analysis; 3) seeing the absurdity of absolute unity; 4) seeing the absurdity of absolute diversity.

3. The Language of Objective Self-Correction: Mapping the Four Keys onto the *Reason Sixty*

3a. Targeting the False Self

The first step in the investigations of non-egocentrist philosophers is the clear identification of what is to be analyzed, comparable to the precise diagnosis of the illness to be treated. Thus, the analyses themselves begin by simply focusing on objectified constructs of subject or object as self-sufficient or self-evident, with the aim of exposing these as forms of self-deception, the result of reification of linguistic constructs of "I" and "mine." After defining the *Reason*'s larger focus on absolutistic views of the self-enclosed life-cycle (*saṁsāra*) and its extinction (*nirvāṇa*), Nāgārjuna

---

[14] Traditional examples of the implicative and exclusion negation, respectively, are "This man is not a Brahmin," which implies that he belongs to another caste, and "Brahmins should not drink beer," which indicates what they should not drink (thereby "excluding" beer) but does not imply what they should drink.

[15] For a detailed discussion of these and other reasoning patterns, see Hopkins, *Meditation on Emptiness*, and Thurman, *Essence*.

highlights the target of his analysis, the way such views subtly obstruct the contemplative insight of relativity:

> If, after that insight into the truth,
> One discovers any particular here,
>
> Imagining any sort of creation,
> In anything, however subtle,
> Such an unwise individual
> Does not see the meaning of "conditioned arisal." (YṢ, 11cd–12)

Later, he identifies the objectified constructs he is targeting as reifications of the technical terms that frame the Buddhist analysis of selflessness, comparing the psychophysical aggregates (*skandha*), experiential media (*āyātana*) and elements (*dhātu*) to the mundane conventional expressions "I" and "mine":

> Just as the Victors say "I"
> And "mine" for a useful purpose,
> So they speak of "aggregates," "media,"
> And "elements" for a useful purpose. (YṢ, 33).

Finally, Nāgārjuna pinpoints the egocentrist habit of reifying "I" and "mine," "self" and "world," highlighting such linguistic truth-habits as the target for non-egocentrist analysis, the cognitive crux of maladaptive views, and hence all the addictions and conflicts they foster. To quote again:

> Those who insist on a non-relative
> "Self" or "world"—Alas!
> They are deprived by views
> Such as absolutism and nihilism. (YṢ, 43).

Chandrakīrti's elucidation of this verse in the *Commentary* defines the subject to be analyzed in terms quite consistent with Nāgārjuna's. Chandrakīrti's comment on another verse (YṢ, 24) is also relevant in this context:

> Those who insist upon an enduring self in things, whether they maintain a real [personal] self or a self in things, are those "who hold self [as] real," since, by maintaining a self, they perceive it. Alternatively, by being conceptually attached to things, they hold things as selves; and since they conceptually develop the failing of being mistaken with regard to

> being and nothingness, they fall under the influence of addictions. (YṢV, ad k. 24)

Later, Chandrakīrti will return to describe the illness of reification to be treated again, making more explicit the fact that the target of contemplative analysis is in fact reified linguistic convention: "A child, not understanding mundane conventions, his awareness stupefied with intrinsic realities, sees a mirror image, holds it to be a real thing, and can fall in love with it and play with it however he can" (YṢV, ad k. 53). The linguistic nature of the reified conventional constructs he targets is underlined by the following key verse from his *Introduction*: "The referent of beings' constantly arising mental habit of 'I,' in relation to which they develop the mental habit of 'mine,' is the 'self'; it comes from delusion, which designates it without examination."[16]

As for Wittgenstein, the analysis of language-independent facts or "simple objects" (PI, §46) in the opening of the *Investigations* only serves to introduce the subject that is the main target of the analysis of his later work: the egocentrist conception of logically "private" subjects and objects, the supposedly self-sufficient and self-evident "givens" of personal experience, of which the identity and reality are assumed prior to the mundane conventions of language. Wittgenstein gradually sharpens the focus of his *Investigations* to highlight the mental habit which insists on reifying such egocentrist constructions, expressed by the anonymous opponent many consider the ghost of his own early philosophy:

> A *picture* held us captive. And we could not get outside it, for it lay in our language and language seemed to repeat it to us inexorably. (PI, §115)

> When philosophers use a word—"knowledge", "being", "object", "I", "proposition", "name"—and try to grasp the *essence* of the thing, one must always ask oneself: is the word ever actually used in this way in the language-game which is its original home? (PI, §116)

---

[16] MA, 6.164: *gang la rtag tu 'gro rnams ngar 'dzin blo // rab tu 'byung zhing de yi gang yin der // nga yir 'dzin blo 'byung ba'i bdag de ni // ma brtags brtags par gti mug las yin no //.*

> "But when I imagine something, or even actually *see* objects, I have *got* something which my neighbour has not."—I understand you. You want to look about you and say: "At any rate only I have got THIS."—What are these words for? They serve no purpose. (PI, §398)
>
> You interpret a grammatical movement made by yourself as a quasi-physical phenomenon you are perceiving. (PI, §401)
>
> You think that after all you must be weaving a piece of cloth: because you are sitting at a loom—even if it is empty—and going through the motions of weaving. (PI, §414)

The similarity in critical texture and intent here is all the more remarkable given our preconception that vast cultural and historical gulfs separate Nāgārjuna, Chandrakīrti, and Wittgenstein. In this sense, the inevitable differences that earmark their writings as belonging to distinct intellectual historical milieus serve only to emphasize a resemblance that marks the universality of their therapeutic purpose. As therapeutic non-egocentrists, these three philosophers concern themselves less with the differentia of cultural conventions than with the generic variety of self-deception that makes any convention limiting to individuals in any world: the reification of linguistic constructs that lets the naïve (*bāla*) rationalize the innate habit of egocentrism. Thus, for the non-egocentrist, philosophy begins with the recognition of a problem that is endemic to the life-cycle (*saṁsāra*), in any form of life (PI, §241); and its precise recognition is as crucial to the outcome of analysis as a proper diagnosis is to medical treatment. For if the kind or degree of reality falsely attributed to "the self" is either understated or overstated, the result of the analysis will be to leave unanalyzed a residual resistance to treatment, an absolutistic or nihilistic obstruction to the insight of relativity, to "seeing connexions."

As for the precise measure of their subject, the fact that these three philosophers agree in recognizing all habits of mind and action consistent with concepts of unrelated being or essence as forms of the solipsistic or subjectivist habit makes it clear that their prime target is nothing less than the illness of self-deception at the core of all egocentric life. The fact that they agree in targeting their analyses at the use of pronouns like "I" and "mine" makes it clear that the subject they examine is nothing more mysterious than the misuse of the everyday language of personal experience.

3b. Committing to Commonsense

The second key aspect of the language of self-correction in Nāgārjuna, Chandrakīrti, and Wittgenstein raises the complex issue of the place of discursive reason in their philosophies. Despite the persistence and refinement of the skeptical and mystical readings of these philosophers, their mature work is characterized by the clear conviction that the rational conventions of everyday language are the gold standard by which all knowledge and communication, mundane and transcendent, must be judged. Thus, these philosophers unequivocally state that the linguistic conventions of reason (*yukti*) are a perfectly adequate means to realize and convey relative and ultimate truths; and they also can be articulated as the formal validating cognitions (*pramāṇa*) that include perception, tradition, and inference.

In the *Reason*, Nāgārjuna's therapeutic alignment of insight with voidness, and self-deception with reified constructs, is supported by a methodological alignment of insight with critical intellect, and method with all other sources of knowledge:

> One whose intellect sees existence
> As similar to an illusion or mirage,
> Is not deceived by [extremist] views
> Of an ultimate beginning or end. (YṢ, 17)

Critical intellect sees through the authority of tradition and consensus:

> What is proclaimed as the truth in this world
> By Brahmā [the Creator] and the others,
> Was declared "false" for the noble ones.
> What else remains that is otherwise? (YṢ, 28)

And critical intellect is also definitive in interpreting received tradition:

> [The Victors] speak of "aggregates," "media,"
> And "elements" for a useful purpose.
>
> [Things first] proclaimed, such as primary elements,
> Then are incorporated into consciousness.
> Since knowing that, you break free [of them],
> Are they not unreal constructions? (YṢ, 33cd–34)

What is it about intellectual insight that makes it definitive and unequivocal in Nāgārjuna's eyes? Nāgārjuna makes his views on this complex issue clear in three of the key methodological pronouncements of the *Wisdom*. The first of these is the often misunderstood statement that the ultimate scope of mind is determined by the medium of language: "The range of mind ends where the verbalizable (*abhidhātavya*) ends." (MMK, 18.7)[17] That Nāgārjuna defines the scope of the mental faculty in terms of language shows the traditional Centrist stance, contra that of Buddhist logicians, that nondiscursive perception (*pratyakṣa*) and discursive inference (*anumāna*) may share the same object, and is consistent with Chandrakīrti's claim that they may be conflated (*samplava*). This is especially clear in modes of mental perception (*mānasapratyakṣa*) like realistic insight (*samyagjñāna*), in which reason breaks free of "unreal constructions" (*mithyāvikalpa*) and corrects falsely objectified, dualistic intuitions of the senses. In this sense, the intellectual eye (*buddhicakṣu*) or faculty of thought is not intrinsically inferior to the faculties of sense, insofar as it relies on the objective medium (*viṣayāyātana*) of language.

This brings us to a second point: the kind of language Nāgārjuna means when he speaks of "the verbalizable" is not some special language of pure logic or mystic paradox, but the common language of everyday linguistic convention (*vyavahāra*). Thus, the celebrated methodological statement: "Without relying on convention, the ultimate import cannot be taught." (MMK, 24.10)[18] While this reliance on mere convention would seem to be a disadvantage, the great strength of everyday language is that it is a common possession, a medium of exchange shared by all trained speakers, and that the conventional signs (*nimitta*) and usages (*upādaya*) of language are not founded (*anāśrita*) in any being, essence, or objectivity intrinsic to persons or things. That they are mere fabrications (*prapañca*), based on a recursive logic of mutually defining binary constructs (*vikalpa*), is precisely what makes them viable, in Nāgārjuna's view. What constricts

---

[17] MMK, 18.7: *nivṛttamabhidhātavyam nivṛtte cittagocare* /. I say "medium" here since the word translated as "range" or "scope" (*gocara*) is the familiar technical term distinguishing the objective fields or "media" (*āyatana*) of the "faculties" (*indriya*), in this case the "ideational objects" (*manoviṣaya*) of the sixth or "mental faculty" (*mānendriya*), from their subjective field, the medium of consciousness.

[18] MMK, 24.10: *vyavahāramanāśritya paramārtho na deśyate* //.

their use is the reifying habit that would bind the selfless and empty reference frame of language to an egocentrically fixed perspective (*dṛṣṭi*) or position (*pakṣa*). Voidness is the ultimate therapeutic convention because it counteracts the habit that perverts all linguistic conventions into forms of self-deception: "Everything is coherent which coheres with voidness; nothing is coherent which does not cohere with voidness" (MMK, 24.14).[19]

Nāgārjuna's third point is that voidness must be understood as a critical linguistic convention before it can serve as a signpost or placeholder for transcendent insight: "Here, let us explain. You do not know either the sense, usage, or referent of 'voidness' and so do yourself such injury" (MMK, 24.7).[20]

Given these three intervening steps, we can pick up the *Reason*'s methodological argument and follow it to conclusion. Critical intellect is not to be freed *from* conventions of language but *with* those conventions; hence, the only means by which it can treat its self-limiting "demon" of reification is to commit itself without vacillation to the relative, binary constructs of language: "As long as the mind vacillates, it remains under the dominion of Māra" (YṢ, 36ab). The only alternative to the ambivalence of the mystic or skeptic is to accept as practically binding the binary structure which frames Centrist analysis: 1) if this self truly exists as objectively as it appears, 2) *then it must ultimately be found to exist in logical conformity with one or another alternative in an exhaustive dichotomy*; for instance, it must ultimately be found to exist *either* 3) as an absolute unity identical with its parts, causes, aspects, or designation, *or* 4) as an absolute plurality unrelated to its parts, causes, aspects, or designation. Only given the crucial second key, does the finding that absurd consequences follow from examining both alternatives serve as a reason for negating the reality of the unrelated self identified as assumed in key one, just as only committing to an exhaustive search of the house makes the non-finding of the spider I thought I saw a decisive way of ruling out its presence. This binary analysis, which exclusively negates the false self of persons or things by exposing its logical

---

[19] MMK, 24.14: *sarvaṁ ca yujyate tasya śūnyatā yasya yujyate // sarvam na yujyate tasya śūnyaṁ na yujyate //.*

[20] MMK, 24.7: *atra brūmaḥ śūnyatāyāṁ na tvaṁ vetsi prayojanaṁ // śūnyatāṁ śūnyatārthaṁ ca tata evaṁ vihanyase //.*

absurdity, is what Nāgārjuna reminds his readers of in the much quoted statement:

> When "this" or "that" [appears a fact],
> Yet when analyzed is not perceived,
> What wise person would advocate with arguments
> That "this" or "that" is [really] true? (YṢ, 42).

Only after this pivotal key of commitment to a binding language of analysis does Nāgārjuna bring his argument home to target the objectified constructs of self and world that hinge on the habit of reifying expressions like "I" and "mine": "Those who insist on a non-relative 'self' or 'world'—Alas! They are deprived by views" (YṢ, 43a–c), and "Once they commit to [intrinsic] things, they are trapped in painful malignant views" (YṢ, 46ab).

Of course, when binary analysis of the referents of pronouns like "I" and "mine" finds neither being nor essence, persons nor things, it does not thereby "demonstrate" something "beyond language," or confirm that there is nothing to know beyond egocentrist conventions.[21] Instead, it tells us

---

[21] Fenner, *Ontology*, 166ff., following Gangadean, "Formal Ontology," points out that Nāgārjuna's system is designed to train its user to conform his critical intellect *more* exclusively to the conventions assumed as canons of realistic logic: the laws of contradiction, identity, and excluded middle. The added "insight" Fenner calls "the principle of definition through logical opposites," if not classically recognized as a convention, has certainly been recognized by most modern linguists as fundamental to "natural language." Puzzling is why Fenner views Nāgārjuna's system as "reasoning into reality" by moving outside of language, rather than by moving more radically *into language*. Despite the sophistication of their readings, which we cannot do justice to here, Fenner and Huntington exemplify the persistence of the tendency to over-dichotomize language and reality. While Huntington's pragmatic skepticism and Fenner's dialectical mysticism both abandon the naïve realistic correspondence theory that words mirror reality, they also both maintain the residual theory that language is substantially or clearly distinct from the ultimate reality of things. The skeptical view holds that that reality is in principle unknowable by language and hence by the human mind; the mystical view holds that that reality is unknowable by language but can be known by a mind that goes beyond language. Both views continue a legacy of critical thought that dates to the neo-Platonic *via negativa* and continues through Kant to contemporary deconstructionist and inductivist views. The essence of this ancient tradition is the Dionysian dictum that the best name for reality is no name; its obviously problematic implications are that reality is either nothing at all or a unity beyond linguistic differentiation. In contrast to this tradition, Nāgārjuna's voidness theory has an advantage like that enjoyed by the Indian ("Arabic") numerical system over the Roman numerical system. By defining the critical linguistic convention of voidness in binary opposition to all the binary oppositions of ordinary linguistic convention, Nāgārjuna can represent within language the relativity of signifier and

(cont'd)

something ultimately freeing about the pronouns "I" and "mine," namely, that their relative use lies in their absolute voidness, as part of a family of words modern linguists call "indexicals" or "shifters," including "this" and "that," "here" and "now." This family of words, typically seized on by realistic epistemologists as the ostensive pointers that "hook" language onto a public or private world of self-evident referents, in fact shows that language works only because empty referents are uncritically designated by the empty conventions governing the usage of such verbal tools. Like the zero of a measure, these mere designations (*prajñaptimātra*) allow language to be universal and flexible, by relativistically centering its anonymous, contentless reference frame on particular persons and things, or particular aspects of persons and things, while conventionally defining the particularity of those very designative bases in the process.[22] By incorporating zero

---

signified which is the "groundless ground" for the workings of language. This step frees the user of language to represent in language the subject and object of its use without any further binary determination that would unnecessarily limit their range of action, including such determinations as identical/diverse, unitary/multiple, absolute/relative, self/other. Cf. Yates, *Giordano Bruno and the Hermetic Tradition* (1964); Rotman, *Signifying Nothing: The Semiotics of Zero* (1987).

[22] It is important here to distinguish the subtlety of this Dialecticist reading of Nāgārjuna's stance on the conventional reality of linguistic usage from what has been called the "linguistic interpretation" of Centrist thought (cf. Huntington, *Emptiness*). In the eyes of Dialecticists from Chandrakīrti to Tsong Khapa, the voidness of linguistic and conceptual signs is not opposed to any sort of self-evidence or identity intrinsic to their referents, whether conceived as the unconsciously constructed impressions of preverbal intuition or the pragmatically functional particulars of perception. While only the latter particulars (*svalakṣaṇa*)—held as distinctly characterized and efficient things-in-themselves by Traditionist thinkers—were explicitly critiqued by Nāgārjuna as empty, the former psychosocially constructed impressions—the "differential bases" (*āśrayavyāvṛtti*), "conceptual bases" (*abhiniveśyādhāra*), and conventional "intrinsically identifiable perceptual bases" (*svalakṣaṇasiddhālambanaviṣaya*) of conceptuality held in the successively subtler systems of Buddhist Logicians, Idealists, and Dogmaticists—would have been equally critiqued by Nāgārjuna, according to Chandrakīrti and his Dialecticist descendants. The thrust of the Dialecticist reading here is that, for Nāgārjuna, the apparent self-evidence of particular perceptual objects is no less empty than that of the abstract concepts that refer to them; for not only must the ultimate validity of such objects be determined by means of critical reason, in dependence on linguistic conventions, but also their actuality is part of the constructive, evolutionary process of dependent origination (*pratītyasamutpāda*), the factors of which include "name-and-form" (*nama-rūpa*), the words and referents of language. For an in depth treatment of the Dialecticist critique of the realistic epistemology of other schools, see Thurman, *Essence*, 231ff. and 238ff., especially 232 n. 68; 234 n. 72; 304 n. 51.

(*śūnya*) as a special, dereifying convention of language, Nāgārjuna has given the ordinary language user a new degree of freedom, a constant reminder of the relativity and conventionality on which the usefulness of words depends, and a new unrestricted (*apratiṣṭhita*) space for keeping the mind open to master its most universal medium for knowledge and communication. While most modern readings present Nāgārjuna as a critic of discursive reason, forced to rely on it as a means to an end, in this reading he is a critical therapist of reason, who views language as both the means and the end; the space in which the mind is ultimately free from self-habits, and the method of clearing that space of the self-imposed limits of reified language. By reducing "constructions," "fabrications," "consciousness," "insight," and "intellect" to the public conventions of speech that define them, Nāgārjuna frees the self-critical mind to unravel misuses of language constricting its space of intersubjective exchange.[23] For him, what dereifying insight achieves is a decentering of the thought process from any delusion of non-relative "I" and "mine." This closely relates to the famous Dialecticist stance known as "positionlessness" (*nirapakṣatva*), which doesn't mean the Dialecticist is not there to argue with his opponent, but means that his vantage point is purely relational, standing in a free space of equal communication with the opponent:

> [Those] overwhelmed by mistaken knowledge,
> Are trapped by attachment in a process
> Of obsession and conflict,
> Clutching to truth in the [intrinsically] untrue.
>
> Great souls are beyond disputes,
> [For,] they assume no [fixated] position.
> For those who have no position,
> How can there be opposition? (YṢ, 49–50)

Here, Nāgārjuna finally refers to the Centrist methodological stance of being positionless (*apakṣa*) or without thesis (*apratijñā*), a stance that historically has been misread as a skeptical or mystical rejection of the place

---

[23] Compare Ricoeur, *Hermeneutics*: "everything happens as if, in order to enter the symbolic universe, the speaking subject must have at his disposal an 'empty space' from which the use of signs can begin...[a space which] could also be expressed as a distantiation of self from itself...the ruin of the ego's pretension to constitute itself as ultimate origin" (116, 113).

of linguistic reason and logic in developing and communicating insight. His preceding reference to the reality-habit (*satyagraha*), however, makes clear what Chandrakīrti would further elucidate: that the position or thesis he means to reject is one which presumes that logic has some intrinsically real foundation or identifiable essence. As Nāgārjuna would state in other works,[24] one who reasons with voidness makes no such presumption, but advocates the logical stance that logic has and needs no ground other than ungrounded convention and its metaphysically unexamined use. In its structural commitment to convention as method, Nāgārjuna's grammatically based philosophy advocates a specifically human ontology, epistemology, hermeneutic, and therapeutics, based on the position that human forms of life revolve around the empty conventionality of language. Thus, his analytic method is meant to turn the ordinary human condition of self-reification toward the performance of enlightened altruists, whose liberative speech is the conventional expression of their self-transcendence.

Chandrakīrti is acknowledged by traditional and modern scholars alike for his key role in clarifying the Dialecticist view of Nāgārjuna's conventionalist methodology presented above. Chandrakīrti's extensive treatment of the use of linguistic conventions of analysis in *Lucid Exposition* 1 and *Introduction* 6 are applied in the *Commentary* to the contemplative practice of deobjectifying insight. Here, we need only touch on its three main points as condensed in the *Commentary.*

First, Chandrakīrti follows Nāgārjuna by arguing that all determinate sense perception and intellectual formulas depend on mental constructs, and that these in turn depend on the conventional signs of everyday language:

> [T]he primary elements and what arises from the primary elements, the mind and mental factors, as well as things not associated [with the mind]—because of being causal components of consciousness—all of these things howsoever

---

[24] Cf. MMK, 4.8: "When one argues by means of voidness and an opponent tries to answer, none of his statements serve as answers, since his proofs always remain to be proven"; VV, 29: "If I were to have any thesis whatsoever, I would be liable to that fault; but I am completely faultless, because I have no thesis"; CŚ, 16.25: "Whoever takes no position at all, either 'existence,' 'non-existence,' or 'both existence and non-existence,' cannot be refuted even if [one tries] for a long, long time."

> feasibly explained as this and that primary element, and so forth, are subsumed and understood within consciousness.
>
> Now, a yogin/ī sees that pure consciousness, which superimposes [on things] the meanings of being existent and being non-existent, as the possessor of an object that is false and deceptive and, at the time of seeing it as lacking intrinsic production, knows that [insight] to be definitive. (YṢV, ad k. 34)

The dereifying insight Chandrakīrti prescribes here to free the intellect from uncritical adherence to constructs is predicated on its ability to use the fictive conventions of reason to prove the voidness of all conventional signs and referents with respect to intrinsic identity:

> Such full understanding does not perceive any [real] absence of the intrinsically objective creation of existence, as the reality of existence; it just has the nature of the complete eradication of all signs. It is called "nirvāṇa" in accordance with conventional truth, and must be understood as lacking any intrinsically objective status whatsoever. (YṢV, ad k. 6cd)[25]

The second main point in Chandrakīrti's argument is to apply his distinctive Dialecticist view—that language works *only* in the absence of intrinsic identity or self-evidence—to explain how ultimacy-analytic reason (*don dam pa'i dpyod pa'i rigs pa, paramārtha-vicārayukti**) draws the logical conclusion that is the ultimate therapeutic insight of voidness. Essential to Chandrakīrti's refinement of Centrist conventionalism, this pivotal point is one traditional scholars consider the subtlest in his Dialecticist system.[26] Where Nāgārjuna urged the naïve reifying minds of his day to embrace the voidness of linguistic conventions in terms of their lack of any ground in

---

[25] Thurman notes how Tsong Khapa clarifies the sense in which Chandrakīrti here and later in the *Commentary* speaks of nirvāṇa as ultimate *by convention*. According to Tsong Khapa, Chandrakīrti means that its ultimacy is established by its therapeutic non-deceptiveness in relation to superficial cognition, not that it is a conventional reality. Cf. Thurman, *Essence*, 368 n. 9.

[26] Tsong Khapa states this in Thurman, *Essence*, 288ff.

intrinsic reality, Chandrakīrti urged the subtle reifying minds of his day to embrace the voidness of linguistic conventions in terms of their lack of any essential ground in intrinsic identity, referentiality, or self-evidence. Thus, where the *Reason* critiques the self-habit displaced by Analysts and Traditionists from naïve egocentrism into reifying the life-cycle and its extinction as realities outside mere conventions of language, the *Commentary* critiques the subtler self-habit displaced by Idealists and Dogmaticists into reifying the relative and its voidness into intrinsic identities outside empty conventions of language. According to Tsong Khapa, Chandrakīrti supports his critique with four imperative, absurd consequences that follow from the assumption of intrinsic identity or self-evidence, no matter how "relative" or "conventional." The order of consequences in Chandrakīrti's classic statement in *Introduction* 6.34–36 and its *Commentary* (ad k. 34) differs in his *Reason Commentary*.[27] Chandrakīrti's use of these consequences here is less explicit than in the MABh. They may be paraphrased as follows:

> If relative or conventional things depended on any kind of intrinsic identity or self-evidence:
>
> 1) it would contradict the scriptural statements that all things are devoid of intrinsic reality;[28]
>
> 2) it would mean that they would have to withstand analysis, since what is intrinsically identifiable or self-evident by definition has its identity ultimately, unrelated to anything else;[29]

---

[27] What I order as 1, 2, 3, 4, corresponds to Chandrakīrti's 2, 3, 1, 4 in the MA and MABh, and to Tsong Khapa's 4, 2, 1, 3 in the *Essence*.

[28] YṢV, ad k. 3; see trans. below, where the consequence parallels the argument that if saṁsāra was a "real" something and nirvāṇa a real "nothing," that would contradict the statement of the natural voidness of things made in the *Saddharma-puṇḍarīka*, 13.19c, ed. Wogihara-Tsuchida, 239: *śūnya nirīhā sthita nityakālaṁ//*. Cp. MABh, 6, ad k. 34, where the reference is to the famous statement in the *Kaśyapa Chapter* of the *Jewel-Heap Scripture*: "Kashyapa, furthermore, the central way is the genuine insight into things; it does not make things empty by means of emptiness, but [realizes that] the very things themselves are emptiness," quoted as translated in Thurman, *Essence*, 165.

[29] YṢV, ad k. 10. Cp. MA, 6.35: *gang phyir dngos po 'di dag rnam dpyad na // de nyid bdag can dngos las thsu rol tu // gnas rnyed ma yin de phyir 'jig rten gyi // tha snyad bden la rnam bar dpyad mi bya //*.

3) it would mean that they would be destroyed when their intrinsic identity or self-evidence was repudiated by the rational insight of voidness, and voidness would be the destructive cause;[30]

4) it would mean that the reasons negating the objective reality of cause and effect would not accomplish that negation, since these reasons apply equally to the intrinsic identifiability of cause and effect, even when these are qualified as "relative" or "conventional."[31]

The aim of Chandrakīrti's argument is to expose and critique the subtle realistic premise that the apparent self-evidence of the referents of everyday language is not a form of self-deception, but is quasi-logically or pragmatically necessary as a relative anchor for conventions of communication. His argument makes it logically imperative to accept the conventions of language as mere linguistic usages (*prajñaptimātra*), because it negates the premise of self-evidence even conventionally, when he shows that self-evidence does not underlie the mundane conventions of language or even the critical convention of voidness. For example, as follows:

> [T]he noble ones—those who are distinguished by realizing things without perceiving an intrinsic reality—neither construct nor perceive that dichotomy [of the life-cycle and nirvāṇa].... Since "cyclic life" is a construction, "nirvāṇa" is also a construction, because they both exist as mundane expressions. (YṢV, ad k. 5)

And this pivotal point brings us to Chandrakīrti's third main point: the distinctive Dialecticist stance that conventional reality, including the logical means of establishing the ultimate therapeutic reality of voidness, has only non-analytic or critically unexamined status (*avicāryamānasiddha*); it exists only insofar as we use it without grounding it in any ultimacy-seeking analysis. Thus, conventional constructions of language, when reified, falsely

---

[30] YṢV, ad k. 13. Cp. MA, 6.34: *gal te rang gi mtshan nyid rten 'gyur na // de la skur bas dngos po 'jig pa'i phyir // stong nyid dngos po 'jig pa'i rgyur 'gyur na // de ni rigs min de phyir dngos yod min //.*

[31] YṢV, ad k. 18–19 (P16b8–17b3). Cp. MA, 6.36: *de nyid skabs su rigs pa gang zhig gis // bdag dang gzhan las skye ba rigs min pa'i // rigs des tha nyad du yang rigs min pas // khyod kyi skye ba gang gis yin par 'gyur //.*

appear as intrinsically identifiable subjects and objects, but once their referents are subjected to binary analysis which seeks their identity as identical with or distinct from their parts, and so on, no such subjects or objects are rationally found to correspond to that appearance. In this way, "self" and "world," "I" and "mine," are shown to be empty fictions, "uncreated" with respect to any intrinsic identity or self-evidence; their reification is thus conclusively logically negated, to be thereafter seen through and treated as a form of self-deception. Although the means and end of that analysis—the conventions of negation and the insight of voidness—are in turn unable to withstand analysis seeking intrinsic identity, this in no way impairs but rather confirms the validity of the analysis. For when simply assumed as unexamined, those conventions do conclusively dispel the illusion of self-evidence, without implying the existence of any intrinsically objective lack of self-evidence.[32] In this sense, the two realities are two perspectives on the uses and referents of language: the superficial, in which their deceptive self-evidence remains unexamined; and the ultimate, in which analysis dispels the illusory self-evidence, and rational insight confronts the voidness of conventions and the voidness of voidness. Thus, the means and end of Centrist analysis are to free the language user to master language's anonymous, groundless frame of reference, without the lingering egocentrist bias that blocks critical intellect from fully inhabiting its fictive medium. The self-critical "I," freed by a new dereifying habit, is the "positionless" subject of Chandrakīrti's Dialecticist methodology. This enlightened "self" is a fictive linguistic agent[33] in full mastery of its communicative medium and object,[34] not trapped in any reified transcendence, but

---

[32] Cf. MA, 6.175: *mi bden bzhin du'ang rnag gi byad bzhin mdzes par bsgrub bya'i phyir / de ni yod pa ji ltar de bzhin 'dir yang shes rab gdong / sbyang bar bya la nus pa mthong bar gyur pa'i gtan tshigs ni / 'thad pa dang bral las kyang bsgrub bya rtogs shes shes par bya //.*

[33] Cf. MA, 6.158: *de ni de nyid du'am 'jig rten du / rnam pa bdun gyis 'grub 'gyur min mod kyi / rnam pyad med par 'jig rten nyid las 'dir / rang gi yan lag brten nas 'dogs pa yin //.*

[34] Cf. MA, 6.177: *dngos rnam mtha' dag dngos po med par rtogs su gzhugs par ni / nus pa ches sla ji lta de ltar rang bzhin gzhan dag la / khong du chud par bde blag tu ni nus pa ma yin no / rtog ge ngan pa'i dra bas 'jig rten ci ste 'dir bcol byed //.*

omniscient in its access to all viewpoints on the culture-medium of verbal convention.[35] As Chandrakīrti's *Commentary* states:

> Such beings who develop such a view by turning their backs on cyclic life, and who generate an aspiration to overcome it, are able to easily realize—*via* the teaching of relativity—the uncreatedness of what is to be abandoned. (YṢV, ad k. 5ab)
>
> Furthermore, since nirvāṇa is established in dependence on that [life-cycle] which is glossed as "like a magician's illusion," it is established, as is impermanence, by worldly convention. (YṢV, ad k. 7)[36]
>
> Just as, by indicating the absence of water, one says "[you will] directly experience" to the traveler, likewise the world also conventionally designates absences and non-perceptions as "directly experienced." (YṢV, ad k. 8)
>
> [I]t is irrational to say that the absence [of action and addiction] is unable to cause [termination]. If [someone] further objects, "[Such] a cause is impossible [because it is not found] under rational investigation," [we reply that] it is not so, for the things of the world cannot be accepted as [critically] examined, but just [presented] according to social convention.... As the absence of such things as water is [conventionally] known as a cause of losses, consequently, it is established that one may speak of "peace through exhausting the cause [of suffering]." (YṢV, ad k. 20)[37]
>
> Since there is no perceivable sign for what is objectively uncreated, none of these aspects—"that form is this," "that sensation is this," "that consciousness is this," or "those other

---

[35] Cf. MA, 6.119: *rang gi lta ba chags dang de bzhin du / gzhan gi lta la 'khug gang rtog pa nyid / de'i phyir 'dod chags khong khro rnam bsal te / rnam dpyod pa na myur du grol bar 'gyur //.*

[36] Cp. MA, 6.23: *dngos kun yang dag rdzun pa mthong pa yis / dngos rnyed ngo bo gnyis ni 'dzin par 'gyur / yang dag mthong yul gang de de nyid de / mthong ba brdzun pa kun rdzob bden par gsungs //.*

[37] Cp. MA, 6.35; cited above, p. 67 n. 29.

> created things are this"—appear in the mind. Hence, those who do not have anything that appears as a concrete particular cannot prove to others, "'that' or 'this.'" It is irrational for the wise to argue about that which is undemonstrable. (YṢV, ad k. 42)

As for Wittgenstein, even a cursory review of the divergent readings that dominate the debate over his mature therapeutic method would require a volume. Among the moderating voices, the two centrist readings of Rorty and Cavell are of interest for their complementary efforts to grapple with what Wittgenstein presented as the "bedrock" of his later philosophy, the conventionalism obvious in statements like: "When we reach conventions, we reach rock bottom," (BBB, 26) and, "this language, like any other, is founded on convention" (PI, §335). A comparison of the Wittgensteinian and Centrist literature on this topic suggests a parallel between the subtly dualistic views on convention expressed by Rorty and Cavell and those expressed by various Dogmaticists. Thus, pragmatist Rorty[38] reads conventions as linked to contextual "criteria" or cues anchoring language use, much as Bhāvaviveka assumed that some relative "intrinsic identity" in things was needed to make conventions of perception and language consensually valid. Alternatively, existentialist Cavell[39] reads conventions as superimposed on the natural self-evidence of personal experience, much as Śāntarakṣita saw them as social constructions veiling the evolving relative, intersubjective nature of the subconscious mind. Our reading of Wittgenstein's conventionalism is that its method and aim are to critique the premise of self-evidence shared by such subtle reifying views, much as Chandrakīrti's Dialecticist system critiqued the Dogmaticist premise of relative or conventional referents that are intrinsically identifiable (*svalakṣaṇasiddha*).[40]

The first point in our reading of Wittgenstein's conventionalist method is that it is meant to analyze the subtle reification of the subjects

---

[38] See Rorty, "Wittgenstein, Privileged Access, and Incommunicability" (1970); "Criteria and Necessity" (1973); and *Philosophy and the Mirror of Nature* (1979).

[39] See Cavell, "The Availability of Wittgenstein's Later Philosophy" (1962); and "Criteria and Judgement" (1979).

[40] For Tsong Khapa's detailed account of the Dialecticist critique of the Dogmaticist thought of Bhāvaviveka, Śāntarakṣita, and Kamalaśīla, see Thurman, *Essence*, 265–344.

and objects of language which are symptomatic of the residual realism of his own early philosophy. His early reifications of the "metaphysical subject" and "simple objects" may be viewed as versions of Kant's transcendent ego and things-in-themselves, redefined in terms of their limiting role in the "grammatical framework" of language, as opposed to Kant's "categorical framework" of knowledge. From this vantage, Wittgenstein's later philosophical method appears as an attempt to complete a partial reframing of Kant's objectivist critique of knowledge, as a *critique of language*. And in this light, conventionalism of language figures as the key advance that allows Wittgenstein to eliminate the last vestige of naïve realism in Kant.

Like Nāgārjuna and Chandrakīrti, Wittgenstein seeks to free the critical intellect from its self-deceptive habit of reification. Thus, following Kant, he argues that logic reveals the mental constructs on which perceptual and conceptual knowledge depend; then, like his Centrist counterparts, he argues that the essence of logic lies in the conventions of language-use he calls "grammar," following Nietzsche. The aim of Wittgenstein's mature *Philosophical Investigations*, then, is to expose the supposedly self-evident objects and subjects of his earlier views as reified forms of the empty conventions of grammar:

> What looks as if it *had* to exist is part of the language. (PI, §50)
>
> We predicate of the thing what lies in the method of representing it. (PI, §104)
>
> *Essence* is expressed by grammar. (PI, §371)
>
> The only correlate in language to an intrinsic necessity is an arbitrary rule. (PI, §372)
>
> Grammar tells us what kind of object anything is. (Theology as grammar). (PI, §373)

The thrust of Wittgenstein's linguistic conventionalism, like Nāgārjuna and Chandrakīrti's, is to free critical intellect from its own self-limiting "demon"—the projection of any "mind" or "world" outside language:

> Philosophy is a battle against the bewitchment of our intelligence by means of language. (PI, §109)

> Thinking is essentially the activity of operating with signs. (BBB, 6)[41]

> No sign leads us beyond itself, and no argument either. (1975, 71)

The second point in our reading of Wittgenstein's method is that this linguistic conventionalism is basic to his critique of the false premise of reified intrinsic identity in persons or things. The structure of his arguments, like the consequential "bi-negations" of his Centrist counterparts, is that of an exclusive negation supported by *reductio ad absurdum* type reasonings against the alternative ways a binary conventional construct can be reified as self-evident. The method he employs to show the absurdity of these alternative philosophical usages is a conventionalist "method by examples" (PI, §133) meant to "bring words back from their metaphysical to their everyday use" (PI, §116) by comparing them with scenarios of conventional usage called "language-games." Like conventional "measuring-rods" (PI, §131), these language-games expose the origin of metaphysical views in reifying one side of binary conventional constructs. Like his Buddhist counterparts, Wittgenstein methodically exposes and negates the premise of self-evidence, by serial analyses of the exhaustive alternatives that follow from reifying any binary construct of an essential subject or object:

> Where does our investigation get its importance from, since it seems only to destroy everything interesting, that is, all that is great and important?... What we are destroying is nothing but houses of cards and we are clearing up the ground of language on which they stand. (PI, §118)

> The great difficulty here is not to represent the matter as if...there really were an object, from which I derive its description, but I were unable to shew it to anyone. And the best that I can propose is that we yield to the temptation to use this picture, but then investigate how the *application* of the picture goes. (PI, §374)

---

[41] Cp. PI, §327.

> It is not a *something* but not a *nothing* either!... We have only rejected the grammar which forces itself on us here. (PI, §304)
>
> The law of the excluded middle says here: It must either look like this, or like that. So it really...gives us a picture. And the problem ought now to be: does reality accord with the picture or not? (PI, §352)
>
> There is here no question of a "seeing"—and therefore none of a "having"—nor of a subject, nor therefore of "I".... [For] if as a matter of logic you exclude other people's having something, it loses its sense to say that you have it.... (PI, §398)
>
> [Despite]...feeling...as if the negation of a proposition had to make it true in a certain sense, in order to negate it,... (PI, §447)
>
> ...[n]egation, one might say, is a gesture of exclusion.... (PI, §550)

These comments outline the means and end of Wittgenstein's conventionalist logic in terms clearly parallel to our authors'. His innovative negation of self-evident ("logically private") subjects and objects has as its logical conclusion the purely critical intellectual insight that "shews the fly the way out of the fly-bottle," as he put it. This critical insight frees the nominal subject from any "bewitchment" of its medium of language, by training the user of language to have "complete clarity" about the empty conventional uses of "I" and "mine," whose reification is the prime egocentric block to "a clear view of our use of language."

The final point in our reading of Wittgenstein's method is that the conventional "ground of language" on which all his arguments stand is not itself grounded in any self-evident reality or identity, but is perfectly valid as long as it is used without ultimacy-seeking analysis. This stance leads Wittgenstein to a series of formulations parallel to the distinctive Dialecticist positions of Chandrakīrti's Centrism. These include formulations of: everyday language as perfectly adequate to philosophical analysis; the experiencing subject as a working "fiction" of conventional language use; a binary opposition between the ultimate voidness of conventions and their relative, unanalyzed use; and the "positionless" stance of therapeutic philosophy. So Wittgenstein states:

> When I talk about language...I must speak the language of every day. Is this language somehow too coarse and material for what we want to say? Then how is another one to be constructed?—And how strange that we should be able to do anything at all with the one we have! (PI, §120)

> The meaning of a word is its use in the language. (PI, §43)

> "Aren't you at bottom really saying that everything except human behavior is a fiction?"—If I do speak of a fiction, then it is of a *grammatical* fiction. (PI, §307)

> At the foundation of well founded belief lies belief that is not founded. (OC, 253)

> Even a proposition like this one, that I am now living in England, has these two sides: it is not a *mistake*—but on the other hand, what do I know of England? (OC, 420)

> The fact that I use the word "hand" and all the other words in my sentence without a second thought, indeed that I would stand before the void if I so much as try doubting their meanings—shows that absence of doubt belongs to the essence of the language-game, that the question "How do I know..." either prolongs the language-game [i.e., is part of it], or else dispels it. (OC, 370)[42]

> Philosophy may in no way interfere with the actual use of language;...it cannot give it any foundation either. It leaves everything as it is. (PI, §124)

> If one tried to advance *theses* in philosophy, it would be impossible to debate them, because everyone would agree to them. (PI, §128)

---

[42] Retranslated from facing German for terminological consistency.

Despite any historicist sense of the vast distance between Wittgenstein, Nāgārjuna, and Chandrakīrti, these comments define in detail a distinctive non-egocentrist method of therapeutic philosophy, of which the clear resemblance to the Dialecticist method speaks to the universality of human language, and the special problems and competence it entails.

3c. Dereifying Reductive Usage

Given the methodological foundation of the first two keys, which explicitly or implicitly define the logical premise, structure, and conclusion of all Centrist analysis, the supporting arguments exemplified in what follows by the third and fourth keys are relatively straightforward. I say "exemplified" because the binary alternatives "identity or diversity" are often expanded by second-order alternatives like "identity-and-diversity or neither-identity-nor-diversity," as in the six-key tetralemma (*catuskoṭi*) of Nāgārjuna's *Wisdom* 1; or further by third-order alternatives like "possessor," "container or contained," "conglomerate," or "configuration," as in the nine-key sevenfold chariot (*saptāṅgaratha*) analysis of Chandrakīrti's *Introduction* 6.151–167. On the other hand, there is the condensed three-key analysis said to be especially useful for advanced practitioners, in which the royal reason of relativity (*pratītyasamutpādayuktirāja*) alone serves to conclusively negate the premise of any intrinsically real, identifiable, or objective self or object.[43] Interestingly, while the *Reason* and its *Commentary*

---

[43] Implicitly presupposing the first two keys, Nāgārjuna's classic tetralemma or "diamond smithereens" argument in MMK, 1.1, is formulated as a negation of production of an effect from a cause which is identical, other, both, or neither. His reasons are that identical reproduction would be senseless and endless; other-production would be unpredictable and uncontrollable; combined production would have combined flaws; production from neither would be uncaused, hence non-production. Chandrakīrti's sevenfold chariot-like argument also presupposes the first two keys, and is formulated as a negation of the possibility of an intrinsically identifiable self which is identical or different from its parts, contained in them, their container, their possessor, their conglomerate, or their configuration. His reasons are that intrinsic identity would obviate the need for the separate designation "self"; difference would preclude the self's having the character of its parts; either form of containment would make agent and act identical; possession entails the faults of difference; conglomeration would entail the faults of identity; and configuration would exclude any immaterial parts. For the royal reason, see MA, 6.115: *gang phyir dngos po rten nas rab 'byung bas / rtog pa 'di dag brtag par mi nus pa / de phyir rten 'byung rigs pa 'di yis ni / lta ngan dra ba mtha' dag gcod par byed //*; Thurman, *Essence*, translation, chs. III, VII. See Hopkins, *Meditation on*

(cont'd)

present this most powerful and elegant form of reasoning as their prime subject, they exemplify the traditional Centrist reliance on the serial negation of binary alternatives like "creation and destruction," the basic training required for proper use of the "relativity…way" (YṢ, 0).

The Centrist procedure advocated in Buddha's philosophy of non-egocentrism is traditionally defined as the remedy for that self-deceptive condition whose symptoms are self-enclosing extremes like ontological absolutism and nihilism, epistemological mysticism and skepticism, metaphysical idealism and materialism, and psychological projection and denial. Of these, the third key's negation of the identity of the self with its constituents is essential to the treatment of nihilism, skepticism, materialism, and denial. Self-enclosing views which reify a construct of self as intrinsically identical with one or more of its constituents imply nihilism since those constituents decay; skepticism, since knowledge is limited to what is sensible to those constituents; materialism, since the effects of actions are limited to pleasure and pain in those constituents; and denial, since any reality beside those constituents is repudiated.

While the *Reason* addresses its audience of Buddhist Analysts and Traditionists as those "who have eliminated nihilism" and so "should attend to the reasons why absolutism must be rejected as well" (YṢ, 2), the *Commentary* clarifies that Nāgārjuna's concern is with the absolutistic habit that reifies dualistic concepts of Buddha's teaching of relativity, yielding subtle forms of absolutism *and* nihilism *about relativity* (YṢV, ad k. 0). In the *Reason*, he also critiques subtle nihilistic views of nirvāṇa and voidness that derive from paralleling the subtle absolutistic reification of the saṁsāric life-cycle by reducing it to the self's supposedly intrinsically real and identifiable constituents. Nāgārjuna's prime argument negating such views exposes the absurdity that reducing the subject to its constituents—here defined in the classical terms of five psychophysical aggregates (*skandha*)—reduces the range of the subject's experience to a point that precludes transcendent insight:

> If cessation happens through annihilation [of the aggregates],
> Not by fully understanding creations,

Emptiness, Ch. 5, 7, and 8, for a detailed treatment of the six, three, and nine key analyses following their presentation in 'Jam-dbyangs bZhad-pa's *Grub mtha' chen mo*.

> Who would be there to experience it?
> How could there be such a destroyed [subject]? (YṢ, 8)[44]

The *Reason*'s intended audience would likely have recognized in this argument the two main absurdities Nāgārjuna cites in the *Wisdom* against the identification of self with its constituent aggregates of matter (*rūpa*), sensation (*vedanā*), conception (*saṁjñā*), emotion (*saṁskāra*), and consciousness (*vijñāna*). The first, the famous opening consequence of the "Analysis of Self Chapter," hinges on the grammar of "self" as a performative designation of continuity through change: "If the self were the aggregates, then it would have [their properties of] creation and destruction" (MMK 18.1).[45] He gives a further elaboration of this consequence in the "Analysis of Worldviews Chapter," where reducing the "self" to its present aggregates is shown to preclude the use of "self" to designate the continuity of subjective experience through evolutionary transformations: "If human and divine [embodiments] were [intrinsically] other, they could not properly constitute [successive forms of] a continuous process" (MMK 27.16).[46] Nāgārjuna's second main consequence, also from the "Worldview Chapter," hinges on the grammar of "self" as a performative designation of agency, as distinct from activity: "When you assert that there is no self except for the appropriation [of aggregates], then, as [the act of] appropriation itself is the self, your self does not exist [as agent]" (MMK 27.5).[47] The thrust of these consequences is to expose any move to identify the "self" with the aggregates as contradicting the conventional use of "self" to distinguish the nominal continuity and agency of evolving beings from the transformations of their constituents.

In the *Reason*, Nāgārjuna is especially concerned with the implications for the process of transcendent insight of the Analysts' and Traditionists' reductive definition of self. By reifying the constituents of the self, these

---

[44] Chandrakīrti repeats the consequence in MA, 6.128: *mya ngan 'das tshe nges par bdag chad 'gyur / mya ngan 'das ngon skad cig dag la ni / skye 'jig byed po med pas de 'bras med / gzhan gyis bsags la gzhan gyis za bar 'gyur //.*

[45] MMK, 18.1: *ātmā skandhā yadi bhavedudayavyaya-bhāgbhavet /.*

[46] MMK, 27.16: *devādanyo manuṣyashcetasaṁtatir nopadyate //.*

[47] MMK, 27.5: *upādānavinirmukto nāstyātmeti kṛte sati / syādupādānamevātmā nāsti cātmeti vaḥ punaḥ //.*

realists tended to displace their self-habit onto those constituents, with the consequence that they also reified the process and goal of transcendent insight as a substantial annihilation (*uccheda*) rather than an altruistic participation in the evolutionary process. This tendency expressed itself in reified views of the life-cycle as an intrinsically real or identifiable being (*bhāva*), and in complementary reifications of nirvāṇa or voidness as an intrinsic nothingness (*abhāva*). To counter this tendency, the *Reason* forces the premise of true identity to logical absurdities in metaphysics, ethics, epistemology, and psychology, and exposes its contradiction of the Buddha's authoritative statements in these domains. Thus, Nāgārjuna targets the materialist view that the subject's evolutionary agency and continuity are not conserved (YṢ, 7, 9); the skeptical view that the evidence of the senses is not deceptive (YṢ, 28); the psychological denial that genuine insight can guide self-transcendence and altruistic open-mindedness (47, 55); and the contradiction of Buddha's injunctions to avoid idle metaphysical speculation (YṢ, 13),[48] to cultivate virtue (YṢ, 31), and to view one's mundane life and world as illusory, constructed processes to be transcended (YṢ, 34, 35, 37).

Chandrakīrti's critique of the premise of identity in the *Commentary* refines and extends Nāgārjuna's two main consequences, including arguments familiar from the extensive analysis of self in *Introduction* 6. While the *Commentary* targets subtler empiricist views of the constituents as self-evident processes, the basic logic of its argument parallels the *Reason*'s, as we see from Chandrakīrti's comment on verse eight:

> [I]f those who see reality necessarily directly experience cessation, when the aggregates have not ceased, [from your

---

[48] YṢ, 13, referring to the Buddha's refusal to speculate about a beginning of the universe, touches on the fourteen areas of non-speculation (*avyākṛtavastunī*) which the Buddha declined to comment on, not out of any conviction that the truth lies beyond reason, but out of the therapeutic insight that the perplexities are symptoms of the self-deceptive reification of language that would be exacerbated by any positive response. The fourteen are that: 1) a Buddha survives death, 2) does not, 3) both, 4) neither; 5) the world is finite, 6) infinite, 7) both, 8) neither; 9) the world has a beginning, 10) does not, 11) both, 12) neither; and 13) the self and the body are the same, and 14) are different. Cf. RA, 1.72: "Ultimately, the world cannot disappear through *nirvāṇa*; asked whether it had an end, the Victor remained silent"; MMK, 25.9: "The fact of life and future, however driven and dependent, is seen to be *nirvāṇa*, without addiction or dependence."

> perspective] just such a cessation could not exist. [Alternatively,] when [the aggregates] have ceased, since there would be no one there at all, who would directly experience that cessation? (YṢV, ad k. 8)

Thus, Chandrakīrti proceeds to show the absurdity of any reductive identification of "self" with its constituents by exposing its contradiction of the conventions of "transcendent insight," as Nāgārjuna did. As for the first consequence, that an identical "self" would be subject to the creation and destruction of its constituents, Chandrakīrti restates Nāgārjuna's argument that this premise contradicts the grammar of insight because it entails the absurdity that negating such a self would annihilate the empirical subject.[49] Extending the argument to its contrapositive, Chandrakīrti shows that if critical insight verified the identity of the constituents it would contradict their deceptiveness,[50] as well as the scriptural reports that such insight is a non-finding.[51] He then proceeds to refine Nāgārjuna's original consequence further by critiquing the common non-Dialecticist view that the constituents themselves form a continuum of intrinsically identifiable causes and effects.

The premise of self-evident constituents not only contradicts reports of their non-findability through objective self-analysis, but also renders incoherent any account of how that non-findability has causes and effects within a continuum of self-evident psychobiological processes. Here Chandrakīrti brings to bear arguments familiar from *Introduction* 6,[52] countering

---

[49] Cf. MA, 6.34; PPMMV, ed. La Vallée Poussin, 342: *ātmacchedo nivṛtau syād avaśyaṁ / nāśotpādau nivṛteḥ prāk kṣaṇeṣu / kartur nāśāt tatphalābhāva eva bhuñjītānyenārjitaṁ karma cānyaḥ//.*

[50] YṢV, ad k. 8, 10. Cf. MA, 6.127cd: *bdag ni rdzas su 'gyur zhing der lta ba / rdzas la 'jug pas phyin ci log mi 'gyur //*; PPMMV, ed. La Vallée Poussin, 342: *skandhā ātmā ced atas tad bahutvād ātmānaḥ syus te 'pi bhūyāṁ sa eva / dravyaṁ cātmā prāpnuyāt tādṛśaś ca dravye vṛttau vaiparitātyaṁ ca na syāt //.*

[51] YṢV, ad k. 10.

[52] Cf. MA, 6.17: *myu gu sa bon dang ni dus mnyam yod pa ma yin te / gzhan nyid med par sa bon gzhan pa nyid du ga la 'gyur / des na myu gu sa bon las skye 'grub par 'gyur min las / gzhan las skyes ba yin zhes bya ba'i phyogs 'di btang bar bya //*; and MA. 6.61: *byams pa nyer sbas la rten chos rnams ni / gzhan nyid phyir na rgyud gcig gtogs min te / gang dag rang mtshan nyid kyis so so ba / da dag rgyud gcig gtogs par rigs ma yin //.*

the non-Dialecticist opponent's objection to accepting such non-discovery as a cause, by showing the absurdity of any continuity between supposedly intrinsically identifiable cause and effect:

> [The Traditionist] objects: "How can you apply the term 'cause' to an absence?"
>
> [Let me reply.] How can you apply the term "cause," even to something [intrinsically] present? At such time as when the seed is present, it cannot be recognized as the material cause of the sprout; it has served as a cause when it has become absent. For instance, compare [your] assumption that the very [moment of] consciousness which has come to pass is the antecedent condition of another [moment of] consciousness. As long as the consciousness persists, it cannot be defined as being the cause of another consciousness, since two [moments of] consciousness cannot occur simultaneously; another consciousness conceived as other than either existing or not existing is [logically] impossible. (YṢV, ad k. 20)

Chandrakīrti's other line of argument against the premise of identity follows Nāgārjuna's second consequence that a self identical with the appropriation of constituents would contradict conventions of agency. Thus, Chandrakīrti reasons that a self identified with intrinsically real constituents could not serve as an agent of transcendent insight in this life, extending the argument also to a self reduced to intrinsically identifiable constituents. In a final parallel to Nāgārjuna's critiques of skepticism and denial, Chandrakīrti goes on to argue that unless the constituents are as much "uncreated" fictions as the self, it would be impossible for the subject's analytic insight to cause delusion to end or to effect self-transcendence and objective self-knowledge in this life (YṢV, ad k. 19); and, as long as the constituents are imagined to be intrinsically existent, their absence in an overconcretized nirvāṇa ("expressed as termination") will be imagined to be intrinsically existent (YṢV, ad k. 20). This distinctive Dialecticist line of argument is more extensively developed in *Introduction* 6, where Chandrakīrti exposes the absurdity of moves to logically ground the linguistic convention of the subject in any supposedly self-evident referential base, however qualified as "relative" or "conventional." There, he cites as consequences of reducing the self to its constituents, their conglomerate or their configuration, namely the respective absurdities that there would be multiple selves (MA, 6.127);[53] that the self would not be a master, controller or agent (MA, 6.134, 137);[54] and that only the gross material constituents would be the self (MA, 6.136).[55] These consequences expose the contradiction between any reductionist view of the subject and the conventional use of "self" to distinguish the nominally unifying subject of linguistic agency in human beings from their psychobiological constituents. Thus, they support the line of argument that concludes in Chandrakīrti's distinctive formulation of "self" as "designated in dependence on its constituents, according to mere unexamined social consensus" (MA, 6.158). And it is this formulation that supports the *Commentary*'s account of the subject, its constituents, and their transformation through insight, as so many "uncreated" fictions of linguistic convention.

Although Wittgenstein has been read by some as a behaviorist[56] and by others as a phenomenologist,[57] his critique of egocentrist views in the *Investigations* in fact proceeds by reducing both the empiricist and transcendentalist modern accounts of the self to absurdity. Thus, while he openly adopts the empiricist and transcendentalist lines of argument used by behaviorists and phenomenologists against each other's positions, he just as openly rejects the binary egocentrist alternatives they advance as formulations of the self. The continued debate over Wittgenstein's psychology reflects the fact that he advanced a non-egocentrist view by negating modern dualistic reifications of the linguistic subject and its referents, and

---

[53] MA, 6.127ab: *gal te phung po bdag na de phyir de / mang bas bdag de dag kyang mang por 'gyur //*; PPMMV, ed. La Vallée Poussin, 342: *skandhā ātmā ced atas tad bahutvād ātmānaḥ syus te 'pi bhūyāṁ sa eva / dravyaṁ cātmā prāpnuyāt tādṛśaś ca dravye vṛttau vaiparitātyaṁ ca na syāt //*.

[54] MA, 6.134: *mgon min 'dul ba'am dbang po kyang min / de med phyir de tshogs pa ma yin no //*; MA, 6.137: *len po rang nyer len gcig rigs ngos min / de lta na las byed pa gcig nyid 'gyur / byed po med las yod snyam blo yin na / ma yin gang phyir byed po med las med //*.

[55] MA, 6.136: *dbyibs she na de gzugs can la yod phyir / khyod la de dag nyid bdag ces 'gyur gyi / sems sogs tshogs ni bdag nyid 'gyur min te / gang phyir de dag la dbyibs yod ma yin //*.

[56] See Chihara and Fodor, "Operationalism and Ordinary Language" (1965).

[57] See Gier, *Wittgenstein and Phenomenology* (1981); Dweyer, *Sense and Subjectivity: A Study of Wittgenstein and Merleau-Ponty* (1990).

did so by a conventionalist method typically mistaken for either a brand of behaviorist "verificationism" or of phenomenological "transcendentalism."

Wittgenstein's critique of an empiricist or behaviorist reduction of the linguistic subject to its psychophysical constituents proceeds by exposing any such reduction's absurd contradiction of the linguistic conventions of self. He is especially concerned with showing how these modern forms of the identity-premise contradict the usage of "self" to designate the human speaker's subjective continuity and intentional agency. He begins by examining the behaviorist reduction of subjective experience to psychophysical states:

> But isn't it absurd to say of a *body* that it has pain?—And why does one feel an absurdity in that? In what sense is it true that my hand does not feel pain, but I in my hand?... Well, something like this: if someone has pain in his hand, then the hand does not say so (unless it writes it) and one does not comfort the hand, but the sufferer: one looks into his face. (PI, §286)

Having outlined the contradiction, Wittgenstein, like Chandrakīrti, traces the identity premise to a reified construct of supposedly self-evident psychophysical processes and states, showing that these lead to an eventual denial of the subject's conventional reality:

> How does the philosophical problem...about behaviourism arise?... We talk of processes and states.... Sometime perhaps we shall know more about them—we think. But that is just what commits us to a particular way of looking at the matter. For we have a definite conception of what it means to know a process better. (The decisive move in the conjuring trick has been made, and it was the very one that we thought quite innocent.)—And now the analogy which was to make us comprehend our thoughts falls to pieces. So we have to deny the yet uncomprehended process in the yet unexplored medium. And now it looks as if we had denied mental processes. And naturally we don't want to deny them. (PI, §308)

Wittgenstein proceeds to expose the self-deceptive habit underlying the identity-premise, by showing the absurdity of supposing that the conventional "self" must be logically grounded in some self-evident referent:

"The chair is thinking to itself…WHERE? In one of its parts?… But then how is it with man: where does *he* say things to himself?" (PI, §361) The argument given here in elliptical form recalls those used against the common target of his analyses of metaphysical language in the phenomenal and personal realm—the intrinsically identifiable "simple" or "private" object which the epistemological realist assumes must underlie all valid knowledge and language:

> But what are the simple constituent parts of which reality is composed?—What are the simple constituent parts of a chair? —The bits of wood of which it is made? Or the molecules, or the atoms?—"Simple" means: not composite. And here the point is: in what sense "composite?" It makes no sense to speak absolutely of the "simple parts of a chair." (PI, §47)

> The great difficulty here is not to represent the matter as if there were something one couldn't do. As if there really were a [simple] object, from which I derive its description, but I were unable to shew it to anyone. (PI, §374)

Thus, the identity-premise contradicts the language of the subject, by reifying the relative conventions of language whose unexamined use is the only ground for the "grammatical fiction" of self (PI, §413). Like Chandrakīrti, Wittgenstein forced reductive empiricism to the point where its premise contradicts the use of "self" to distinguish the nominal continuity and agency of the human speaker; and, like Chandrakīrti, he did so as a way to clear up the "groundless ground" of unexamined usage on which all human language, knowledge, and insight stands:

> A misleading analogy lies at the root of this idea; the causal nexus seems to be established by a mechanism connecting two parts of a machine. (PI, §613)

> When I raise my arm "voluntarily" I do not use any instrument to bring the movement about. My wish is not such an instrument either. (PI, §614)

> Our mistake is to look for an explanation where we ought to look at what happens as a "proto-phenomenon". That is, where we ought to have said: *this language-game is played.* (PI, §654)

3d. Dereifying Abstractive Usage

The final step in the four key framework—the critique of the diversity-premise that the self is intrinsically different from its constituents—concludes the bi-negation that clears the Central Way by dereifying both dualistic extremes of conventional usage. Since it views the true "self" as an independent spirit or soul, substantially and/or essentially different from its empirical constituents, the diversity-premise entails some degree of ontological absolutism, metaphysical idealism, epistemological mysticism, and psychological projection. Although such views, unlike their reductive opposites, give rise to the individual and social evolutionary benefits of "ascendance" (*abhyudaya*) in evolutionary state, they are rigorously critiqued by Centrists as obstacles to "transcendence" (*niḥśreyasa*).[58]

When, at the outset of the *Reason*, Nāgārjuna expresses his intention to critique absolutism (YṢ, 2), one of his main concerns is the tendency of realistic Analysts and Traditionists to project their subtle self-habit onto nirvāṇa, reified as a static "extinction" or anesthetic "nothingness" (*abhāva*) (YṢ, 3–4) absolutely divorced from the constituents of the life-cycle (*saṁsāra*). In the verses immediately following, he clearly targets this form of the diversity-premise as incompatible with "seeing reality" (*tattvadarśana*) (YṢ, 5), instead equating nirvāṇa with the "full understanding of existence" (YṢ, 6) which makes possible the achievement of "immediate nirvāṇa" (*dṛṣṭa-dharmanirvāṇa*) (YṢ, 11) in this life. Nāgārjuna supports his argument with the same consequence he employed against the identity-premise, compelling in this context because it exposes the absurdity of a subject intrinsically divorced from its empirical constituents:

> If cessation happens through annihilation,
> Not by fully understanding creations,
> Who would be there to experience it?
> How could there be such a destroyed [subject]? (YṢ, 8)

Here again, the *Reason*'s intended audience may well have recognized as implicit in this argument the two main consequences against the diversity-premise from Nāgārjuna's *Wisdom*. The first of these is the second hemistich of the opening verse from the "Analysis of Self Chapter": "If the self

[58] Cf. RA, 1.3–4, 57.

were [intrinsically] other than the aggregates, then it could not have the character of the aggregates" (MMK, 18.1).[59] The second is from the "Analysis of Worldviews Chapter": "Nor can the self possibly be other than the appropriation [of aggregates]; for something other without appropriation would be perceived, but nothing is perceived" (MMK, 27.7).[60] Thus, Nāgārjuna's argument against the diversity-premise hinges on exposing its contradiction of the conventional usage of "self" to locate the nominal subject of thought and speech in relation to one set of constituents as opposed to another.

The rational analysis of the diversity-premise completes a bi-negation that conclusively rules out the major premise to be negated by transcendent analysis: the false presumption of an intrinsically real or identifiable "subject" or "object" underlying conventional uses like "I" and "mine," "this" and "that." Thus, Nāgārjuna's *Reason* defines the binary analysis of the referents of such expressions as the conclusive means of dispelling the reification of binary constructs on which self-deception depends:

> When "this" or "that" [appears a fact],
> Yet when analyzed is not perceived,
> What wise person would advocate with arguments
> That "this" or "that" is [really] true? (YṢ, 42)

This new habit of analysis is what frees the linguistic intellect from its own "demon," the reifying habit that gives addictive self-deception a home:

> If any sort of hold is found,
> The cunning poisonous snake of addiction
> Will seize it; but those whose minds
> Have no [such] hold, will not be seized. (YṢ, 51)

Thus, the psychological correlate of the exclusive negation of transcendent analysis is the dereifying insight that frees the intellect to master its definitive communicative medium, the empty and selfless conventions of speech. The purely negative insight of voidness conclusively stops self-deceptive reifications, reminding the symbolic intellect that it cannot find itself

---

[59] MMK, 18.1: *skandhebhyo 'anyo yadi bhavedbhaved-askandhalakṣaṇaḥ //.*

[60] MMK, 27.7: *anyaḥ punarūpādānād ātmā naivopapadyate / gṛhyeta hyanupādāno yadyanyo na ca gṛhyate //.*

among its signs or outside them, any more than the eye can see itself among or apart from its objects. Hence these verses from *Jewel Rosary*:

> As no reflection appears independent of a mirror, so there is no perception of any "I," independent of the aggregates. (RA, 33)
>
> All these beings and things are seen to be fuel for the fire of consciousness; they are consumed in the brilliance of genuine discernment. (RA, 97)

Chandrakīrti's argument against the diversity-premise closely parallels Nāgārjuna's. In the *Commentary*, Chandrakīrti also first targets any projection of the self-habit onto a transcendent subjectivity intrinsically other than the empirical constituents of the life-cycle, citing the two familiar consequences that an absolutely different self would be distinctly perceptible apart from those constituents and would be absolutely incompatible with their empirical character:

> [In the Centrist view] it is taught that "the wise also cannot conceive of anything whatsoever called 'nirvāṇa,' that has an intrinsically real status, without referring to [conventional] things—which are like a magician's illusion." (YṢV, ad k. 6cd)
>
> If [a created thing]...were to have such [intrinsically objective status], it would be seen as an intrinsic reality independent of [any created] thing. (YṢV, ad k. 7)

Readers of the *Commentary* may well have been familiar with Chandrakīrti's more extensive exposition of these consequences in *Introduction* 6.123–124.[61] They may also have recognized other *Introduction* consequences in Chandrakīrti's comments on Nāgārjuna's verse 43:

---

[61] Cf. Chandrakīrti's consequence against the diversity-premise in MA, 6.123–124: *gang phyir bstan bcos las de'i khyad / mu stegs rnams kyis gang bstan de kun la / rang grags ma skyes gtan tshigs kyis gnod pa / de phyir de khyad kun kyang yod ma yin // de'i phyir phung po las gzhan dbag med de / phung po ma gtogs de 'dzin ma grub phyir / 'jig rten ngar 'dzin blo yi rten de yang / mi 'dod de rig min pa 'ang bdag lta'i phyir //.*

> Those who do not designate "the self" in dependence on the five aggregates—which are devoid of intrinsic reality just like mirror reflections—but rather, locate "the self" in an intrinsically identifiable mind, will no doubt be swept far from the road to nirvāṇa and carried away by the stream of addictive views.
>
> Why is that? Now, if one asserts the intrinsically real status of mind, it must be either permanent or impermanent. If it is permanent, then one is an eternalist. Alternatively, if it is impermanent, then one is a nihilist, since [the view that mind] having emerged becomes nothing is the nihilist view. Thus, "Indeed! They are deprived by views." The word "indeed" should be known as an exclamation of either regret or certainty. Likewise, if [instead of an intrinsically identifiable mind] one claims the five aggregates—known as "the world"—to be intrinsically identifiably established, similar problems apply. (YṢV, ad k. 43)

The gist of Chandrakīrti's argument against the diversity-premise in the *Commentary* and elsewhere parallels Nāgārjuna's: to show its contradiction of the conventional use of "self" to zero the grammatical subject on a particular speaking subject, designated in relation to a particular set of psychophysical constituents. Thus, Chandrakīrti argues in the *Introduction* that the "self" cannot possess its constituents, since "self" is neither the name of a person nor something other than a person, as the grammar of possession requires (MA, 6.143); that the "self" cannot relate to its constituents as container or contained, since by convention these must be two different things (MA, 6.165); and that the "self" is not an ineffable private object beyond identity and difference, since it must be as expressible as "mind" in order to be anything at all (MA, 6.147).

With the bi-negation complete, Chandrakīrti has conclusively negated the major premise of any intrinsically real or identifiable self, thus clearing the way for the *Introduction*'s distinctive conventionalist formulation of "self":

> As the referents of [conventional expressions] like these cannot be found in [any of] seven [logical] modes when chariot-like analysis is performed, yet otherwise are [when

> unexamined], they must exist by way of [mere] mundane consensus. (MA, 6.167)[62]

So it is that, simply by freeing the mind from the monopoly of the reifying habit, transcendent analysis and the new habit of rational intuition (*yuktijñāna**) it develops completely frees its practitioner from the ills of self-deceptive activity: "Therefore, by viewing 'myself' and 'my property' as void, the practitioner is completely free of that" (MA, 6.165).[63] And, with Nāgārjuna, he concludes in the *Commentary*:

> Since those who burn all the nesting grounds of the snakes of addictions by not perceiving [an intrinsic reality] in anything, and block the caves of the senses with mindfulness and awareness, thus leave no hold for the snake of the addictions to seize. "Those whose minds have no hold are not seized," because once the mind does not perceive [an intrinsic reality] in things, there is no place in it to hold onto. (YṢV, ad k. 51)

Wittgenstein targets the diversity-premise in his critique of any phenomenological reduction of the self to a subjectivity that transcends all empirical constituents. His analysis of the premise proceeds by exposing its absurd contradiction of the linguistic conventions of self. He is especially concerned with showing how modern forms of the diversity-premise contradict the usage of "self" to zero the grammatical subject onto a particular empirical speaker within a community of similar speakers. To begin, he shows the absurdity of the phenomenologist's location of the subject in a transcendent realm of immediate self-evidence divorced from the "mechanism" of everyday speech, citing the consequence that such diversity contradicts the subject's conventional relation to a set of empirical constituents:

---

[62] MA, 6.167: *yon tan yan lag 'dod chags mtshan nyid dang ni bud shing la sogs dang / yon tan can yan lag can dang mtshan gzhi me la sogs dag / de rnams shing rta'i rnam dpyad byas pas rnam bdun yod pa ma yin zhing / de las gzhan du gyur par 'jig rten grags pa'i sgo nas yod pa yin //.*

[63] MA, 6.165: *gang phyir byed po med can las med can / de phyir bdag gi bdag med par yod min / de phyir bdag dang bdag gi stong lta zhing / rnal 'byor pa de rnam par grol bar 'gyur //.*

> A wheel that can be turned though nothing else moves with it, is not part of the mechanism. (PI, §271)
>
> "But doesn't what you say come down to this: that there is no pain, for example, without *pain-behavior*?"—It comes to this: only of a living human being and what resembles (behaves like) a living human being can one say: it has sensations; it sees; is blind; hears; is deaf; is conscious or unconscious. (PI, §281)
>
> "But in the fairy tale the pot too can see and hear!" Certainly; but it *can* also talk. (PI, §282)
>
> Thinking is not an incorporeal process which lends life and sense to speaking, and which it would be possible to detach from speaking, rather as the Devil took the shadow of Schlemiehl from the ground. (PI, §339)
>
> An inner process stands in need of outward criteria. (PI, §580)
>
> Forget this transcendent certainty which is connected with your concept of spirit. (OC, 47)

If this first aspect of Wittgenstein's critique parallels the first consequence of his Buddhist counterparts, that the diversity-premise precludes the self's having the empirical character of its constituents, the second aspect parallels the second consequence that the self would have to be discoverable apart from its constituents. The gist of his argument is to show that the phenomenologist's location of the subject in an intrinsically private realm of incommunicable self-evidence contradicts the conventional use of "self" or "I" to distinguish the "inner experience" of one empirical speaker from the comparable experience of others:

> Suppose everyone had a box with something in it: we call it a 'beetle'. No one can look into anyone else's box, and everyone says he knows what a beetle is only by looking at *his* beetle.... The thing in the box has no place in the language-game at all; not even as a *something*: for the box might even be empty. (PI, §293)
>
> The sensation...is not a *something*, but not a *nothing* either! The conclusion was only that a nothing would serve just as

> well as a something about which nothing could be said. (PI, §304)
>
> There is here no question of a 'seeing'—and therefore none of a 'having'—nor of a subject, nor therefore of 'I' either.... [For] if as a matter of logic you exclude other people's having something, it loses its sense to say that you have it. (PI, §398)

Thus, by rejecting both dualistic alternatives of self-evident identity and diversity, Wittgenstein exclusively negates the major premise that conventional expressions like "self," "this," "I," and "mine" must refer to some intrinsically grounded or essential referent. Although he has "only rejected the grammar which tries to force itself on us here"—the reifying habit he calls "a main source of our philosophical bewilderment" (BBB, 52)—Wittgenstein nonetheless has made "the real discovery...the one that makes me capable of stopping doing philosophy when I want to.—The one that gives philosophy peace..." (PI, §133). For his non-egocentrist method of examples retrains the language user to stop the self-deceptive habit of egocentrist reifications of grammar, especially by exposing the "I" and "mine" as "grammatical fictions," conventions of which the life lies in their unexamined use. Thus, the therapeutic effect of his method is to free the speaker to selflessly master the empty conventions of language:

> Philosophy is a battle against the bewitchment of the intelligence by means of language. (PI, §109)
>
> The problems arising through the misinterpretation of our forms of language...are deep disquietudes; their roots are as deep in us as the forms of our language and their significance is as great as the importance of our language. (PI, §111)
>
> What we are destroying is nothing but houses of cards and we are clearing up the ground of language on which they stand. (PI, §118)
>
> "What is your aim in philosophy?" To shew the fly the way out of the fly-bottle. (PI, §309)
>
> ...to teach you to pass from a piece of disguised nonsense to something that is patent nonsense. (PI, §464)

> For the clarity we are aiming at is indeed *complete clarity*. But that simply means that the philosophical problems should *completely* disappear.... Problems are solved (obstructions cleared), not a *single* problem. (PI, §133)

4. The Social Epistemology of Self-Correction: Virtual Insight and Agency

Now that the first part of our comparative overview of the *Reason* and its *Commentary* has defined a parallel structure linking their dereifying analysis with the language therapy of Wittgenstein's *Investigations*, the remaining two parts of our comparative framework will be relatively simple. In the three part overview of the critical-contemplative practice of non-egocentrist philosophy, we took the second task to be: defining relativity as the psycholinguistic process sustaining human subjects and objects as working consensual fictions, and hence, as the conventional ground for a form of self-corrective thinking and acting whose unexamined premise is the virtual insight of voidness. The key point to be considered here is how the purely negative or "critical" dereifying insight of voidness translates into the "practical," illusion-like, or virtual, relational insight, sustaining the enlightened cultivation of living individuals and their social consensus. We turn now to compare the treatment of this practical aspect of non-egocentrist contemplation in Nāgārjuna, Chandrakīrti, and Wittgenstein.

Since Nāgārjuna's focus in the *Reason* is to present the voidness insight as the door to nondual transcendence in and through relativity, it is only reasonable that his text highlights the illusion-like virtual insight, the relative reflex of dereifying analysis. Thus, the *Reason*'s initial critique of dualistic constructs of transcendence clears the way for its core practical thrust: presenting a nondual formula of "immediately experienced transcendence" (*dṛṣṭadharmanirvāṇa*), including a contemplative framework in which dereifying (critical) and deobjectifying (virtual) insights are equated as complementary aspects of one nondual practice of corrective self-transcendence. So, the *Reason*'s practical task requires a nondualistic reframing of the Buddha's therapeutic insight of selflessness, and hence of the classical paradigm of human science structured around the easily reified disease/cure dichotomy of cyclic life versus extinction. The crux of this reframing is

Nāgārjuna's evolutionary epistemology of psychosocial construction (*laukika-vikalpanā*),[64] which defines the intersubjective experience of life by a nondual formula whose critical constant is the voidness of all signs, and whose practical constant is that all constructed knowledge, conceptual and perceptual, is relative to its matrix of evolutionary development (*karmavipāka*):

> Those who are expert in things
> See them as impermanent,
> Deceptive in nature, hollow,
> Empty, selfless, and vacant.
>
> With no basis and no perceptual object,
> With no root and no foundation,
> Totally arisen from the cause—misknowledge—
> Bereft of beginning, middle, and end,
>
> Essenceless—like a plantain [tree]—
> Resembling a fairy city,
> And an unbearable city of confusion,
> Life appears like an illusion. (YṢ, 25–27)

The intended audience of the *Reason* would likely have recognized in these verses key statements from the *Wisdom*, including the famous formula from the "Analysis of Evolutionary Causality Chapter": "The Buddha proclaimed the truth of the conservation of evolutionary actions: as voidness, they are not annihilated; as cyclic life, they are not permanent" (MMK, 17.20).[65] This formula's reframing of classical Buddhist psychobiology is nondualistic in that it allows Nāgārjuna to include the subjects and objects

---

[64] I borrow the terms "evolutionary epistemology" and "psychosocial construction" from current exploration—in the fields of neurobiology, sociology, linguistics, and the philosophy of science—of the fact that human knowledge and perception is shaped by the constructive activity of the subject, in dependence on a psychosociobiological matrix of conditions. In this, I am extending Stcherbatsky's comparison between Buddhist and Kantian epistemology to the present day, while recognizing that the comparison between Centrist and contemporary Western constructivism is limited by the residual epistemological dualism of constructivists in the West. Cf. Popper, *The Logic of Scientific Discovery* (1965); Berger and Luckman, *The Social Construction of Reality* (1967); Pribram, *Languages of the Brain* (1971); Piaget, *Genetic Epistemology* (1970).

[65] MMK, 17.20: *śūnyatā ca na cocchedaḥ saṁsāraśca na śāśvatam / karmaṇo 'vipraṇāśaśca dharmo buddhena deśitaḥ //*.

of perception and language within an evolutionary epistemology, as functions of evolution's illusion-like conservative and transformative laws. Since, for Nāgārjuna, all knowledge and truth are relative to life's evolutionary-developmental process, the unaided sense faculties yield deceptive knowledge at best, and must be corrected with the less self-enclosed mental faculties trained in conventional social symbols and signs; while the truth of social consensus is also relative and deceptive, and must in turn be corrected by the intellect that critically appropriates and renews the definitive culture-medium of linguistic convention. Thus, the ultimate truth is the truth that frees the mind from the self-limiting habit of reifying its constructions, while relative truth is what frees the mind to override the innate egocentric bias of sensation and instinct, as one overrides the deceptive evidence of an illusion. These practical themes from the *Reason* also echo formulations from the "Evolutionary Causality Chapter" and the "Misperception Chapter" of the *Wisdom*:

> Freedom comes from ending compulsive activity;
> Compulsive activity comes from constructions,
> Which come from fabrications;
> And fabrications terminate in voidness. (MMK, 17.5)
>
> The forms, sounds, tastes, textures,
> Scents, and [mental] phenomena
> Constructed as the six kinds of objects
> Of desire, anger, and delusion
>
> ...Resemble a fairy city,
> A dream, or a mirage. (MMK, 23.7–8)[66]

This critical nondual anthropology provides the context within which Nāgārjuna's formula of nondual self-corrective insights must be understood. Evolution is not a mechanism to be escaped or a disease to be terminated, but the open matrix within which all illusion-like causes and effects, diseases and cures, must take place. To be truly transcendent, life must be "fully

---

[66] MMK, 17.5: *karmakleśakṣayānmokṣa karmakleśā vikalpataḥ / te prapañcātprapañcastu śūnyatāyāṁ nirudhyate //*; MMK, 23.7–8: *rūpaśabdarasasparśā gandhā dharmāśca ṣaḍvidhaṁ / vastu rāgasya dveṣasya mohasya ca vikalpyate // rūpaśabdarasasparśā gandhā dharmāśca kevalāḥ / gandharva nagarākārā marīcisvapnasaṁnibhāḥ //*.

understood" (YṢ, 6); and the self-corrective insight of voidness is the door to its understanding (YṢ, 54).[67] This is not because the voidness insight leads one "beyond" conceptuality or language into "reality," "nature," or "consciousness," but because it frees the mind to fully inhabit the evolutionary reality of linguistic convention, the definitive culture-medium of enlightened selflessness. If the dereifying insight is corrective because it frees the language user *from* the delusion of an intrinsically real "I" or "mine," the illusion-like insight is corrective because it frees the language user *to* selflessly employ conventional fictions like "I" and "mine." While the insight that "I" is an empty convention displaces the speaker from habitual self-enclosed reference frames, the insight that "I" is a communicative fiction re-centers the speaker within the relatively omniscient inter-subjective reference frame of conventions of speech.

In Nāgārjuna's self-corrective practice, then, these two insights are equated, as are ultimate and superficial in the two-reality theory, and as the voidness of signs and the deception of senses in his nondual anthropology. Specifically, the critical dereifying insight is aligned with the ultimate reality of the voidness of linguistic signs, while the practical, virtual insight is aligned with the superficial reality of perceptual relativity and unexamined convention. The discovery defined by their nondualistic equation is the rational insight of relativity, confirmed by complementary findings under two distinct experiential conditions. When persons, things, or signs are subjected to ultimacy analysis, no shred of logical or perceptual evidence is found to confirm that they have the non-relative reality, identity, or objectivity they appear to have; when persons, things, or signs are *not* subjected to ultimacy analysis, they live and work perfectly well as sheer relativities while still appearing to have non-relative reality, identity, and objectivity, confirming that their non-relative appearance is a psychosocial construction which neither underpins nor undermines their viability.

---

[67] Nāgārjuna's concern with defining the process of "relativity" or "conditioned development" (*pratītyasamutpāda*), like the Buddha's, is not a scientistic concern with defining "causality" objectified as an "empirical" or "inductive law," as some have suggested (Cf. Kalupahana, *Nāgārjuna*, 29ff.; Scherrer-Schaub, *Yuktiṣaṣṭikāvṛtti*, xxxix ff.). Rather, it is a therapeutic concern with defining a conventional model of evolution that helps humans cultivate self-transcendent insight, and hence its liberative and transformative influence on psychosocial development.

The critical linkage and practical complementarity joining these conditions and insights are clear. Without the dereification of habitual self-centered constructs, critical intellect could not be free to override their illusory self-evidence or see and use alternate constructions, such as those others prefer. Without the virtual insight that practically applies dereifying insight to everyday interactions, critical intellect would be limited in its ability to transcend the inertia of biosociocultural patterns and guide the formation of more enlightened ones. In this light, the virtual insight shows the practical intent and use of the convention of voidness: to define a social epistemology and self-corrective anthropology appropriate to humans as cultural agents who speak. And it also shows the intent and use of the *Reason*'s nondual framework of self-corrective insight modes: to advance the *Wisdom*'s analysis of worldviews one step nearer its final application to the *Jewel Rosary*'s enlightened altruism, by training the thinking and speaking agent to dereify and reconstruct itself as a freer, more objective fiction of language:

> One whose intellect sees existence
> As similar to an illusion or mirage,
> Is not deceived by [extremist] views
> Of an ultimate beginning or end. (YṢ, 17)
>
> Seeing things to be like mirror images
> With their eye of intuitive wisdom,
> Great souls do not get stuck
> In the quicksand of "objects." (YṢ, 54)
>
> Those who cherish beauty become attached;
> Those who turn away from it become detached.
> But those who see it as empty,
> Like an illusory person, reach nirvāṇa. (YṢ, 56)

Thus, the self-corrective social epistemology of Nāgārjuna's nondual insight modes is meant to empower its user to override and reform the archaic misknowledge of egocentrist worldviews and perceptions, and so to ascend to inhabit the open and selfless evolutionary stage of objective linguistic intelligence and agency. It is with the anonymous "eye" of speech that living beings are most free to release the reified self-enclosed views that make the life-cycle an "unbearable city of confusion." The complementary voidness insights are two sides of the door leading the verbal subject out of the trap of self-deceit: one cutting through the reification of "I" and "mine" that locks the mind in self-centered constructs; the other cultivating the free and equal exchange of "I"s and "mine"s that turns the illusory fictions of everyday life into increasingly objective selves and worlds. Nāgārjuna describes this virtual process of evolving fictions in the "Evolutionary Causality Chapter" of the *Wisdom*: "As a master may artfully fashion a fiction, which fiction in turn fashions another fiction, so likewise, the agent is a fiction who fashions another fiction, and his action is the fiction he fashions" (MMK, 17.31–32).[68]

Chandrakīrti's anthropological framework for the nondual practice of self-corrective insight closely parallels Nāgārjuna's. Drawing on more extensive treatments in the *Lucid Exposition* and *Introduction*, Chandrakīrti in the *Commentary* clearly describes the illusion-like nature of evolution and its transcendence:

> Regarding the nature of such things, since they lack reality, like illusions, they deceive the naïve by appearing to have reality; such things in fact are "deceptive in nature." In lacking the strength to endure, they are naturally feeble, hence "hollow." Because they lack intrinsic substantiality, they are "empty." Because they are empty of a self, they are "selfless." (YṢV, ad k. 25)
>
> The noble do not perceive the variety of forms of the world, since for them, the world has the singular taste of voidness, and there is no variety of forms in voidness....
>
> Thus, to indicate how it lacks intrinsically objective status, [Nāgārjuna] taught, "bereft of beginning, middle, and end," meaning that [the world] is free from creation, duration, and destruction. Furthermore, that [the world] originates from the seed of misknowledge [is reflected in] this [statement], "Essenceless—like a plantain [tree]." If [the world] did not originate from the seed of misknowledge, then when analyzed, it is reasonable to expect that one would perceive

---

[68] MMK, 17.31–32: *yathā nirmitakaṁ śāstā nirmimīta ṛddhisaṁpadā / nirmito nirmimītānyaṁ sa ca nirmitakaḥ punaḥ // tathā nirmitakākāraḥ kartā yatkarma tatkṛtaṁ / tadyathā nirmitenānyo nirmito nirmitastathā //.*

> its core essence. However, when examined, created things have no core essence, like the trunk of a plantain [tree]. Anything that lacks any essence yet appears to have an essence, must arise through the force of delusion; such being the case, the world originates from the seed of misknowledge....
>
> Therefore, the unmistaken see this [world] as like an illusion. What is a city of confusion for the naïve is seen by the noble as like an illusion, because they are free from the darkness of misknowledge. (YṢV, ad k. 26–27)

As with Nāgārjuna, with Chandrakīrti the pure negations of dereifying analysis translate into the illusion-like transformational laws of the relativity insight:

> Thus, abandoning permanence and annihilation, a dependently arisen form, like a reflection, is not incompatible with the sphere of activity of a mistaken awareness, so the various migrant beings that were spoken of are not impossible.
>
> The noble, as well, abandon such errors and do not reify false [things]; thus, their liberation is not impossible. Since relativity is not objectively created, those who, through this reasoning,[69] accept dependent things as resembling the moon in water and reflections in a mirror, [understand them as] neither intrinsically objectively true nor false. (YṢV, ad k. 45)[70]

Chandrakīrti highlights the linkage between the dereifying mode of transcendent insight and its virtual or conventional mode, as well as defining them in terms of different perspectives on the linguistic usages of mundane convention. As for their linkage, the two insight-modes are mutually indispensable to liberative development, the critical and practical aspects of a single process. Without the freedom from reified constructs of "I" and

---

[69] The "royal reasoning of relativity" (*pratītyasamutpāda-yukti-rāja*).

[70] Cf. MA, 6.37–38: *dngos po stong pa gzugs brnyan la sogs pa / tshogs la ltos rnams ma grags pa yang min / ji ltar der ni gzugs brnyan sogs stong las / shes pa de yi rnam par skye 'gyur ltar // de bzhin dngos po thams cad stong na yang / stong nyid dag las rab tu skye bar 'gyur / bden pa gnyid su 'ang rang bzhin med pa'i phyir / de dag rtag pa ma yin chad pa 'ang min //.*

"mine," the virtual transformation from self-enclosed life-cycle to liberated life-cycle is logically inconceivable; without artful mastery of the intersubjective use of "I" and "mine" in the illusion-like world, their dereification is therapeutically ineffective, if not ruinous:

> For if one does not accept the reality of the non-creation of suffering at that moment as nirvāṇa, then, even though one may be free from addictions—since bonds of desire, and so forth, have been interrupted—still, one would see that the cause of the futile view of the impermanent aggregates [as "I" and "mine"] exists. Because seeing that gives rise to [the addictions] of desire, and so forth, therefore there would be no attainment of any such liberation at all. (YṢV, ad k. 9ab)

> When not taught in this manner, students may succumb to error through the teaching of voidness, since they may come to confound the principle of the two realities, superficial and ultimate. In such cases, they would be unable to avoid non-virtue, since the intellectually inept might cling to the idea, "this world is void." Hence, [thinking,] "If this is voidness, what use is it all," they may not be inspired [to cultivate] the virtuous actions that will make success certain. Consequently, they may be destroyed, like a bird with undeveloped wing feathers thrown from its nest. (YṢV, ad k. 30)[71]

Chandrakīrti also distinguishes the nondual insight modes in social, epistemological terms. While equally therapeutic and mutually indispensable, the dereifying and illusion-like insights are respectively aligned with the ultimate and superficial truths by the fact that the former applies ultimacy-analysis to the referents of linguistic conventions, while the latter simply accepts and employs conventions without such analysis, as unexamined usages:

> Similarly, the noble, as well, do not perceive anything whatsoever established in an intrinsically real way that can be called "cessation," for when analyzed with wisdom, that which is unproduced in any intrinsically real way and lacking

---

[71] Cf. MA, 6.80; Tib. cited below, p. 101 n. 74.

> in objectivity—like a magically fabricated elephant—is [called] "nirvāṇa." Furthermore, since nirvāṇa is established in dependence on that [life-cycle] which is glossed as "like a magician's illusion," it is established, as is impermanence, by worldly convention. Thereby, so-called "cyclic life" and "transcendent nirvāṇa" both lack intrinsically objective status. Therefore, the thorough knowledge of the reality of things, by just that lack of objective perception, should be recognized, without a doubt, as "nirvāṇa." (YṢV, ad k. 7)

> [E]ven the commonsense things in the world must be established by social convention, not by [analytic] validation. (YṢV, ad k. 20)[72]

Yet the logical and epistemological distinction between these two modes does not imply a therapeutic inequality. The illusion-like virtual insight is no more deceived by the apparent self-evidence of perception than the insight in which such false evidence is simply not found. In fact, the virtual insight enjoys a technical primacy in Chandrakīrti's self-corrective framework, as in Nāgārjuna's, by virtue of its practical application to the virtual self and world. This is only reasonable given Chandrakīrti's formulation of that self and world as mere linguistic usages whose reality depends on unexamined assent to conventions, like working fictions. The technical primacy of the virtual insight lies in its role in the art of transforming a deceptively factual, self-enclosed life, into a non-deceptive life of omniscient objectivity and altruism, as one might revise an artless fiction into an artful one:

> Those who see the world as like an illusion completely understand being and nothingness by not perceiving an intrinsically identifiable being or nothingness. Since they do not imagine [an intrinsic identity] in these two, they are not constructed. For those who know the [true] meaning [of reality], having dissolved being and nothingness, desire and the other addictions undoubtedly will no longer function as causes of cyclic life. (YṢV, ad k. 57)

---

[72] Cp. MA, 6.35; Tib. cited above, p. 67 n. 29.

Thus, while illusion-like insight presupposes a suspension of ultimacy-analysis, it does not thereby entail a suspension of conventions of reason, conceptuality, or language. It is not some merely aesthetic "negative capability" or "unknowing." For the premise of virtual insight is the ultimately rational pure negation of dereifying analysis; and it is no less rational for its unanalyzed affirmation that the negative findings of such ultimacy-analysis are indeed decisive grounds for thinking and acting in disregard of the illusion that things have intrinsically real, identifiable, or objective status. Chandrakīrti elaborates on virtual insight's decisive role as the conventional rationale guiding the therapeutic art of self-transcendence, in *Introduction* 6.41 and 80:

> As the type of hair-like [floater] seen by one with eye disease does not assume the form of some other visual object, however equal in lacking objective existence, so one must recognize that the developmental effect of actions is not a gratuitous effect.[73]

> Conventional truth constitutes the art, while ultimate truth is what evolves from the art; those who are ignorant of the distinction between the two, enter through false constructs the path of misfortune.[74]

As for Wittgenstein, Part II of the *Investigations* defines the practical aspect of his method for gaining "a clear view of the use of our words" in terms of the optical-illusion metaphor of gestalt-shifts in perception. This modern account of gestalt-insight, like the ancient Centrist account of illusion-like insight, is set within a language-centered picture of the evolution of human knowledge and forms of life drawn in terms of relativistic "language-games" founded only on "unfounded" convention:

> What we are supplying are really remarks on the natural history of human beings. (PI, §415)

---

[73] MA, 6.41: *ji ltar yul ni yod nyid min mtshungs kyang / rab rib can gyis skra shad rnam par ni / mthong gi dngos gzhan rnam par ma yin ltar / de bzhin smin las slar smin min shes kyis //.*

[74] MA, 6.80: *tha snyad bden pa thabs su gyur pa dang / don dam bden pa thabs byung gyur pa te / de nyis rnam dbye gang gis mi shes pa / de ni rnam rtog log pas lam ngan zhugs //.*

> I shall call the whole consisting of language and the actions into which it is woven the "language-game"...(PI, §7)

> ...and to imagine a language means to imagine a *form of life*.... (PI, §19)

> The evolution of the higher mammals and of man.... The picture...must be explored if we want to understand the sense of what we are saying.... (PI, II, 184)

> [W]hat has to be accepted, the given, is—so one could say—*forms of life*.... (PI, II, 226)

> [W]hat looks as if it *had* to exist is part of the language.... (PI, §50)

> The only correlate in language to an intrinsic necessity is an arbitrary rule.... (PI, §372)

> The truth of certain empirical propositions belongs to our frame of reference.... (OC, 83)

> If the true is what is grounded, then the ground is not *true*, nor yet false.... (OC, 206)

> Here *once again* there is needed a step like the one taken in relativity theory. (OC, 305)

Wittgenstein's method for exploring and correcting egocentric distortions of consensual reality presumes his analogy between the interpretation of unfounded language-games and the deceptive optics of perceptual gestalts, which he refers to as "aspect vision" or "seeing as":

> The aspects of things that are most important for us are hidden...because [they are] always before one's eyes.... (PI, §129)

> Our mistake is to look for an explanation where we ought to...have said: *this language-game is played*.... (PI, §654)

> Look on the language-game as the *primary* thing. And on the feelings, etc.,...as interpretation. (PI, §656)

> Do I really see something different each time, or do I only interpret what I see in a different way?... "I am seeing this figure as a..." can be as little verified as..."I am seeing bright red."... We find certain things about seeing puzzling, because we do not find the whole business of seeing puzzling enough. (PI, II, 212)

> Call it a dream. It does not change anything. (PI, II, 216)

Remarkably, the parallel between Wittgenstein's dream-like insight and the illusion-like insight of his Buddhist counterparts becomes clearer still when we examine the relation between its practical affirmation of the conventional language-games that form human life and the critique that exposes them as devoid of any intrinsically necessary or self-evident ground:

> The meaning of the word "to derive" stood out clearly. But we...wanted to see the essence of deriving. So we stripped those particular coverings off; but then deriving itself disappeared. (PI, §164)

> Any interpretation still hangs in the air along with what it interprets. (PI, §198)

> If language is to be a means of communication there must be agreement not only in definitions, but also (queer as this may sound) in judgements. This seems to abolish logic, but does not do so. (PI, §242)

> Would it not be possible for us...to have a feeling of being guided by the rules as by a spell? (PI, §234)

> This merely shows what goes to make up what we call "obeying a rule" in everyday life. (PI, §235)

> The fact that I use the word "hand" and all the other words in my sentence without a second thought, indeed that I would stand before the void if I wanted so much as to try doubting their meanings—shows that absence of doubt belongs to the essence of the language-game; that the question, "How do I know..." prolongs the language-game or else dispels it. (OC, 370)

> My life consists in being content to accept many things. (OC, 344)

Like Chandrakīrti, then, Wittgenstein links the negative insight that dereifies conventions with the affirmative insight that uncritically accepts them, as perspectives showing two logically consistent aspects or "sides" of every language-game (OC, 420). Also, like Chandrakīrti, he aligns the insight that conventions are devoid of any intrinsic ground with ultimately critical analysis, and the insight that they work effectively in the absence of any such ground with superficially practical, non-analytic acceptance. The parallel is complete when we compare Chandrakīrti's view of the evolutionary efficacy of illusion-like insight with Wittgenstein's view of the efficacy of his dream-like insight to artfully shape a fictive human form of life:

> "Aren't you at bottom really saying that everything except human behavior is a fiction?" If I do speak of a fiction, it is of a grammatical fiction. (OC, 307)

> One says that these sense-impressions can deceive us. But here one fails to reflect that the fact that the false appearance was precisely one of rain is founded on a definition. (OC, 354)

> The game, one would like to say, has not only rules but also a *point*. (PI, §564)

> Compare a concept with a style of painting. For is even our style of painting arbitrary? Can we chose one at pleasure? (PI, II, 230)

> Words are also deeds. (PI, §546)

> Even here,…[c]orrecter prognoses will generally issue from the judgements of those with better knowledge of humankind. Can one learn this knowledge? Yes; some can.… Can someone else be a man's teacher in this? Certainly. (PI, II, 227)

5. The Anthropology of Self-Correction: Objectivity and Altruism

Given the similarity in the modes of therapeutic insight prescribed by our three non-egocentrist philosophers, the final task in our comparative exploration is to see whether this parallel in self-corrective practice carries over into the final application of philosophy to human practice in general. In the outline of our exploration, this last task is: defining these nondual modes of self-transcendent insight as the critical and practical conditions for objective social knowledge and communication, and hence, as the conventional ground for a self-corrective anthropology aimed at reproducing free and responsible social agents.

While Nāgārjuna's opening and central focus in the *Reason* highlights the dereifying and illusion-like insights of Centrist analysis, his concluding focus is on preparing the practitioner to apply these twin contemplative modes to the final nondual performance of wisdom and compassion formulated in his *Jewel Rosary*. Nāgārjuna's closing focus in the *Reason* reframes Buddhist contemplative analysis in three steps that link the practice of transcendent insight to the art of cultivating objective compassion. These three link dereifying insight, illusion-like insight, and their integrated mastery to cultivating impartiality, empathy, and altruism, respectively. With these steps, then, the *Reason* reframes the practice of transcendent insight as the foundation of the non-egocentrist discipline of self-correction (*blo byang ba, buddhiviśodhana*) mentioned in Chandrakīrti's *Commentary* and elaborated in the *Introduction*.[75]

As for the most basic of these, impartiality is linked with the analytic insight that dereifies habitual constructs of "I" and "mine," de-centering the defensive structure of self-enclosed worldviews and egocentric instincts. While philosophically we recognize this de-centering at work in the "positionlessness" of non-egocentrist thought, it is also generally recognized as "objectivity," the key feature in any intellectual open-mindedness, the door to any genuine understanding of unfamiliar views and perspectives. Here, Nāgārjuna reframes this cognitive breakthrough psychologically, as the impartiality which redresses the egocentric bias *for self as opposed to other*, and

---

[75] Cf. Hopkins, *Compassion in Tibetan Buddhism* (1980) for a translation of Tsong Khapa's commentary, *dbu ma la 'jug pa'i rgya cher bshad pa dgongs pa rab gsal.*

so acts as the door to any empathic openness or sensitivity to the experience of others:

> [Those] overwhelmed by mistaken knowledge,
> Are trapped by attachment in a process
> Of obsession and conflict,
> Clutching to truth in the [intrinsically] untrue.
>
> Great souls are beyond disputes,
> [For,] they assume no [fixated] position.
> For those who have no position,
> How can there be opposition? (YṢ, 49–50)

Thus, the insight that dereifies "I" and "mine" is not only the logical precondition for the transcendence of any false self, but also the psychological precondition of self-transcendence in relation to others. In making this linkage, Nāgārjuna aligns the dereifying insight of his contemplative framework with the goal of transcendence (*niḥśreyasa*) in the nondual practice framework of the *Jewel Rosary*, where it is cultivated as the ultimate realization of self-interest in perfect freedom of mind and expression.

The second step in Nāgārjuna's linkage connects the illusion-like insight that cultivates "self" and "world" as cooperative fictions with the recentering of "I" and "mine" within the relational reference frame of linguistic convention. While philosophically we recognize this re-centering in the consensualism of non-egocentrist method, it is also generally recognized as "empathy," a key feature of any technical mastery, the way to the acquisition and renewal of any art embedded in the intersubjective mastery of language. Here, Nāgārjuna reframes this communicative mastery psychologically, as the openness to empathic involvement that redresses the bias *for self before other*, and so acts as the door to an empathic concern and responsiveness that puts others first:

> When one has a place [for reified things],
> One experiences attachment and detachment;
> But the great souls, having no [such] place,
> Are neither attached nor detached. (YṢ, 58).

Thus, the insight that affirms the empty convention of "I" and "mine" is not only the practical precondition for the illusion-like development of a "great soul," but also the psychological precondition for the altruistic cultivation of others' selves. In making this linkage, Nāgārjuna aligns the virtual insight of his contemplative framework with the goal of ascendance (*abhyudaya*) in the nondual practice framework of the *Jewel Rosary*, where it is cultivated as the ultimate realization of public interest in a perfect environment of mutual cooperation and unlimited communicative art.

The third step in Nāgārjuna's reframing is his linkage of the mastery of insight's complementary dereifying and virtual modes with the enlightened performance of nondualistic wisdom and compassion. While philosophically we recognize this performance as the integrated mastery of liberative insight and therapeutic art in non-egocentrist philosophy, it is also generally recognized as "altruism," a key feature of any artful mentorship, the means of personifying any cultural tradition whose aim is to edify or heal. Here, Nāgārjuna reframes this cultural mastery psychosocially, as the unwavering commitment that transforms the self-enclosed life-cycle into a culture arena for the altruistic embodiment of liberative science and art:

> Whoever contemplates freedom,
> And is not moved by the wavering mind,
> Crosses the ocean of intolerable existence,
> Which seethes with the snakes of addiction.
>
> By the virtue [of writing this,] may all beings
> Gather the stores of merit and wisdom,
> And attain the two supreme [buddha bodies]
> Arisen from merit and wisdom! (YṢ, 59–60)

In making this linkage, Nāgārjuna not only places the *Reason*'s self-corrective practice within the classical context of the interdisciplinary curriculum (*adhiśikṣā*),[76] but specifically aligns its nondual contemplative

---

[76] In effect, YṢ 59 prescribes combining transcendent insight with concentrative quiescence (*vipaśyanā-shamatha*), a technique traditionally used for the mutually indispensable cultivation of wisdom (*prajñā*) and concentration (*samadhi*). In his review of this tradition as evidenced in Tsong Khapa's *Middle Transcendent Insight*, Thurman shows how Tsong Khapa derives the therapeutic necessity of joining insight with quiescence. Tsong Khapa first quotes a famous passage from the *Elucidation of Intention Sutra*: "He who practices quiescence and transcendent insight will be freed from the bondages of negative conditionings and of signs." Tsong Khapa then comments: "'Negative conditionings' here refers to instincts underlying mental processes, which instincts increasingly generate a distorted subjectivity. 'Signs' refers to the continuous habitual adherence to mistaken [self] objects which reinforce those

(cont'd)

framework with the goal of "cultivating transcendence with ascendance" (*niḥśreyasa-abhyudayaśca-vardhana*) in the Mahāyāna anthropological framework of the *Jewel Rosary*, where it figures as the path to the integrated realization of self interest and public interest, personified in the inseparable truth and form bodies of buddhahood. So, when viewed in the larger context of Nāgārjuna's work, the *Reason*'s ideal of the great soul (*mahātma**) who masters "contemplation of the void" figures as a transitional goal meant to open the practitioner to the enlightened altruist's resolve to consciously evolve toward full enlightenment. This is why the hermeneutical hierarchy of the *Reason* anticipates the *Jewel Rosary*'s, helping the objective mind see the human body as the empty culture-medium for empathy:

> The naïve are attached to forms;
> The mediocre are detached from them.
> Those with the highest intelligence understand
> The nature of forms, and thus are freed. (YṢ, 55)

Compare the famous *Jewel Rosary* verses:

> To some, [Buddha] teaches doctrines
> That counteract vice;
> To some, [doctrines] that help achieve virtues....
>
> ...[Finally, he teaches] some the profound,
> Awe-inspiring practice of enlightenment
> Whose essence is the voidness that is compassion. (RA 4.95–96)[77]

As for Chandrakīrti, his own formulation of Dialecticist Centrist practice in the *Introduction* is essentially a reframing of the science of objective self-knowledge and the art of objective self-correction within the non-

---

instincts. The former are abandoned by transcendent insight, and the latter by peaceful quiescence." (TKSB, pha, f. 132a–b; Thurman, *Essence*, 131–132, bracket added)

[77] Both YṢ 55 and RA, 4.95–96 describe the three vehicles (*triyāna*) of disciples, hermit buddhas, and bodhisattvas, as forming a single continuum or vehicle (*ekayāna*) leading to the realization of buddhahood. The constant uniting this continuum is the progressive development of transcendent insight which gives all Buddhist practice its "singular flavor of freedom." The progressive meditative and ethical techniques for its development range through progressive degrees of renunciation and empathy.

dual practice-paradigm presented in Nāgārjuna's *Jewel Rosary*. In the *Introduction*'s first verse, Chandrakīrti spells out this threefold reframing:

> While disciples and hermit sages arise from lords of sages, buddhas evolve from enlightened altruists (bodhisattvas); and the causes of these heirs of the victors are nondual intelligence, the compassionate attitude, and the spirit of enlightenment.[78]

In these three "causes," further expanded in the three-verse closing summary of *Introduction* 6, we can recognize Nāgārjuna's threefold framing of the dereifying insight, illusion-like insight, and their nondual mastery, as impartiality, empathy, and altruistic commitment, respectively. Thus, in his *Commentary* on YṢ 50, Chandrakīrti links the contemplation of dereifying insight—which releases all dogmatic perspectives—to the nondual intellect which opens the door to both personal freedom of mind and unconditional or de-objectifying compassion (*dmigs med snying rje*) for others:

> When one assumes a [righteous] position of one's own, one then enters into disputes with others because it has been fixed upon. Consequently those without any such [position]—the great souls—are free from conflict. Moreover, for those who already are free from any [fixated] position, it is no longer possible for another's position to be unassailable. For when you have no [fixed] position, it is impossible to see others as maintaining a [fixed] opposition. Now, even if there were such a thing as a position, without it being one's own position or another's position, it would be utterly irrelevant! (YṢV, ad k. 50ab)[79]

---

[78] MA, 1.1: *nyan thos sangs rgyas 'bring thub dbang las skyes / sangs rgyas byang chub sems dpa' las 'khrungs shing / snying rje'i sems dang gnyis su med blo dang / byang chub sems ni rgyal sras rnams kyi rgyu //*.

[79] Cf. MA, 6.119: *rang gi lta ba chags dang de bzhin du / gzhan gyi lta la 'khrug gang rtog pa nyid / de'i phyir 'dod chags khong khro rnam bsal te / rnam dpyod pa na myur du grol bar 'gyur //*; and MA, 6.224: *de ltar blos gros zer gyis snang ba gsal byas pa'i / rang gi lag na gnas pa'i skyu ru ra bzhin du / srid gsum 'di dag ma lus gdod nas skye med par / rtogs de tha snyad bden pa'i stobs kyis 'gog par 'gro //*.

Chandrakīrti makes explicit the linkage implied by Nāgārjuna's closing verse between mastery of the two self-corrective insight modes and the practice of cultivating the ultimate and conventional spirits of enlightenment (*bodhicitta*) which mature in the twofold embodiment of enlightenment:

> The "store of merit" consists of all the immeasurable virtues achieved—except for wisdom itself and its causes—in order that countless realms of beings may come to understand. And the store of wisdom is all wisdom and the cause of wisdom totally dedicated to the achievement of buddhahood.
>
> May all living beings who succeed in accumulating these two stores attain the unexcelled supreme [buddha-embodiments]. "Arisen" means created. That which has arisen from merit and wisdom [is what is meant by] "arisen from merit and wisdom." What are those two? They are the form body and truth body. (YṢV, ad k. 60)

For Wittgenstein, as for Nāgārjuna and Chandrakīrti, the therapeutic work of philosophy is not done until it results in a changed form of life. Thus, Wittgenstein's repeated statements that philosophy "leaves everything as it is" (PI, §124) and does not "advance theses" (PI, §128) must be understood in the larger context of his mature work to mean that its dereifying insight frees the human speaker from false constructions, self-imposed obstacles to change, by "clearing the ground of language on which they stand" (PI, §118). The life work of non-egocentrist philosophy has only begun when egocentrist philosophy comes to an end:

> The civil status of a contradiction, or its status in civil life: there is the philosophical problem. (PI, §125)
>
> The confusions which occupy us arise when language is like an engine idling, not when it is doing work. (PI, §132)
>
> The real discovery is the one that makes me capable of stopping doing philosophy when I want to. The one that gives philosophy peace, so that it is no longer tormented by questions which bring *itself* in question. (PI, §133)

> The way to solve the problem you see in life is to live your life in a way that will make the problem disappear. (CV, 27)
>
> All good teachings are of no avail. One must change *life*. (Or rather life's direction.) (CV, 53)

If the theoretical problem addressed by Wittgenstein's mature philosophy is reification, its practical concern is with the contradiction of conventions of subjective experience caused by modern egocentrist philosophy's reification of "I" and "my private impressions." Thus, Wittgenstein's dereifying critical insight targets the ideas of intrinsically "private" experience rationalizing the "egocentric predicament"[80] as a prelude to his equalizing practice of bringing philosophy back to everyday "human agreement in language." His complementary dream-like insight accepts the illusory "language-game" as a means to train the empathic exchange on which the "natural history of human beings" depends. And, his aim of a "complete clarity" that uses both insights to master "the two sides of every language-game" is a transitional goal to prepare his reader to aspire to the greatness of genius by conscious cultivation of the critical and technical mastery of communication. Thus, Wittgenstein's contemplative philosophy of language finally translates into a philosophical practice of non-egocentrism; a practice whose end and means is to cultivate a form of life based on the communicative ground of human agreement in language, especially the fundamental language-games of equality, sympathy, and altruism.

The first aspect of Wittgenstein's philosophical practice reframes the dereifying insight into a practice of self-transcendent impartiality. Thus, his ultimate critical insight into the empty conventions of "I" and "mine" is not to deny the subject but to free it from egocentric misuses of language, to embrace its anonymous role in "civil life":

> "Only I have got THIS."—What are these words for? They serve no purpose. —Can one not add: There is here no question of a "seeing"—and therefore none of a "having"—nor of a subject, nor therefore of "I" either? Might I not ask: in what sense have you *got* what you are talking about and saying that only you have got it? Do you possess it? You do

[80] A term borrowed from Saunders and Henze, *The Private Language Problem* (1976).

> not even *see* it. Must you not really say that no one has got it? And this too is clear: if as a matter of logic you exclude other people's having something, it loses its sense to say that you have it. (PI, §398)

In this passage, Wittgenstein reframes his dereifying insight as a non-egocentrist stance whose aim is not simply critical—to free the thinking subject from self-deception—but also practical—to open the human speaker to the interchangeable equality of "you" and "I," the public convention on which private experience depends. Like the "positionless" stance of Nāgārjuna and Chandrakīrti's enlightened and non-egocentrist self, the selfless dispossession of Wittgenstein's dereified speaker opens the door to a new direction within the old form of life: away from the self-enclosed cycle of bias and conflict, towards the intersubjective "agreement" on which any communicative life depends. The practical premise of this new direction is the insight that privacy is not intrinsic to the subject, but an empty convention basic to the game of intersubjective agreement. This game assumes the grammatical rule that first-person reports are taken as authoritative in the language of personal experience. Thus, for Wittgenstein, the privacy of the "I" exists precisely as a "civil institution," a form of cooperative contract between beings who speak. Privacy is a privilege we are trained to grant one another, the grammatical equivalent of "personal space" in the intersubjective field of language. Thus, any inequality in the use of the word "I" is not only logically incoherent, but practically self-defeating, since it contradicts the intersubjective exchange through which all human subjectivity evolves.

The affirmative insight that accepts the everyday game of "self" and "other," "subject" and "object," as a dream-like fiction of grammar here becomes Wittgenstein's way of cultivating the capacity for the spontaneous empathic exchange of perspectives that is basic to language's role as a medium of intersubjective agreement:

> What is essential for us is, after all, spontaneous agreement, spontaneous sympathy. (1992, 699)

> Anyone in such need who has the gift of opening his heart, rather than contracting it, accepts the means of cure in his heart. (CV, 46)

> How am I filled with pity *for this man*? (PI, §287)

> Seeing a living human being as an automaton is analogous to seeing one figure as a limiting case or variant of another; the cross-pieces of a window as a swastika. (PI, §420)

> Look on the language-game as the *primary* thing. And on the feelings, etc., as you would a way of regarding the language-game, as interpretation. (PI, §656)

> My attitude toward him is an attitude towards a soul. I am not of the *opinion* that he has a soul. (PI, II, 178)

For Wittgenstein, then, perfectly mastering language as a medium of communication means integrating the self-critical insight that dereifies any egocentrist stance on the language-game with the empathic insight that sympathetically embraces its fictional rules, along with the stance others take on the game. And motivating this combined critical and practical mastery is a non-egocentrist commitment to embrace and extend the specifically human form of life on which communication in language is based: the altruism exemplified in human parents' first training of their child in the social conventions of language-use:

> How do words refer to sensations?... A child has hurt himself and he cries; and then adults talk to him and teach him exclamations and, later, sentences. They teach the child a new pain behaviour.... The verbal expression of pain replaces crying and does not describe it. (PI, §244)

> It is a help here to remember that it is a primitive reaction to tend, to treat, the part that hurts when someone else is in pain; and not merely when oneself is—and so to pay attention to other people's pain behaviour, as one does *not* pay attention to one's own. (Ze, 540)

> Get to know a new aspect from this special chapter of human behaviour—from this use of language. (Ze, 542)

> Being sure that someone is in pain...and so on, are so many natural, instinctive kinds of behaviour towards other human beings, and our language is merely an auxiliary to, and further extension of this relation. (Ze, 545)

Finally, for Wittgenstein, philosophy entails an extension of natural altruistic behavior, in which one selflessly masters linguistic convention as the definitive instrument and medium through which human genius contributes to cultural evolution:

> It strikes me that a religious belief could only be something like a passionate commitment to a system of reference. Hence, although it's *belief*, it's really a way of living, a way of assessing life. Instruction in religious faith, therefore, would have to take the form of a portrayal, a description of that system of reference, while at the same time being an appeal to conscience. And this combination would have to result in the pupil himself, of his own accord, passionately taking hold of the system of reference. (CV, 64)
>
> That man will be revolutionary who can revolutionize himself. (CV, 45)
>
> One might say: "Genius is talent exercised with courage." (CV, 38)
>
> You can't be reluctant to give up your lie, and still tell the truth. (CV, 39)
>
> The edifice of your pride has to be dismantled. And that is terribly hard work. (CV, 26)
>
> But industry like that requires humility and an enormous capacity for suffering, hence strength. And someone who, with all this, can also express himself perfectly, simply speaks to us in the language of a great man. (CV, 71)

6. The Self-Corrective Anthropology of Nāgārjuna and Chandrakīrti

This overview of the *Reason* and its *Commentary* supports the thesis that the self-corrective procedure these texts prescribe is pivotal to their authors' philosophical systems, in that it links the complementary frameworks of objective self-knowledge and altruistic social agency assumed as foundational by the Universalist traditions of "profound view" and "magnificent deeds." Moreover, it helps overcome the hermeneutical obstacles we found limiting modern Centrist studies, such as the common misreadings we traced above to the implicit or explicit assumption of nineteenth century neo-Kantian epistemology as the philosophical foundation of modern text-critical disciplines and their methods. The alternate reference frame I proposed is based on comparing the therapeutic philosophy of non-egocentrism in Nietzsche, Freud, and Wittgenstein with the Centrist refinement of Shākyamuni's philosophy of selflessness (*anātmavāda*) by Nāgārjuna and Chandrakīrti. The gist of this framework is a reading of Centrist philosophy as a method of correcting the reifying mental habit underlying self-enclosed worldviews and self-defeating forms of life, including both main types of malignant "views of voidness" and the mystical and pragmatic excesses they rationalize. The traditional interpretive context of the *Reason* and its *Commentary* helps reveal the special role these texts play in relation to their authors' other major works as formulating Centrism as a philosophical language therapy and rational self-corrective procedure for reproducing psychologically objective self-knowledge and responsible social agency. A close reading comparing the *Reason* and its *Commentary* with the *Philosophical Investigations* of Wittgenstein, supplemented by references to other major works of the authors, reveals clear and consistent parallels between their respective language therapies and self-corrective procedures. I believe that these point by point parallels show that the comparative framework presented above provides a coherent reference frame for understanding and translating the technical concepts and language of Centrism in general and our texts in particular. If this conclusion strains common preconceptions of the historical and cultural relativity of philosophy, the findings supporting it speak all the more clearly for the relative universality of the condition which non-egocentrist philosophy treats.

In addition to straining our postmodern sense of cultural relativity, this comparative framework also conflicts quite directly with a main modern Indological consensus on Mahāyāna Buddhist history and thought. Far from the nihilistic skepticism or deconstructive mysticism modern and postmodern scholars have projected into Centrist thought, this comparative framework aligns Nāgārjuna and Chandrakīrti with some of the most liberating critical thought and effective therapeutic practices developed in the modern scientific West. Moreover, this post-critical, therapeutic aspect of Nāgārjuna and Chandrakīrti's contribution, largely overlooked by Western scholars, shows us a face of Buddhism that has been quite obscured by the scholarly caricatures of Theravāda rationalism and Mahāyāna decadence. Instead, it matches more closely with decidedly postmodern concepts of science as a human practice of cultivating objective knowledge by optimizing our capacity for epistemological and historical self-correction. The challenge to our preconceived notions of absolute cultural and historical relativity emerges into focus when we consider that the condition diagnosed by therapeutic philosophers like Nāgārjuna, Chandrakīrti, and Wittgenstein is the very reification of evolving and conventional forms of life that breeds egocentric individuals and ethnocentric cultures. Far from being limited to any civilization or species, that condition is sadly universal. Yet in both the modern Western and ancient Buddhist scientific traditions, we humans beings are seen as well equipped to heal ourselves, owing to our highly evolved competence for altruistic life centered around communication. It is this very competence which makes the habit of reifying the convention of "I" seem all the more unnecessary. Hence, Nāgārjuna and Chandrakīrti, like their modern peers, Nietzsche and Wittgenstein, take as the ultimate refinement of non-egocentrist philosophy a method which shows that human life has no reality beyond empty conventions of language, and that the living fiction of our evolution hangs on nothing more than the magnanimous use of such conventions. Of course, the final argument for the truth of this comparative interpretation of our texts is to be found in the cogency of our translation, to the study of which we now invite you.

TRANSLATIONS

The Reason Sixty

by Ācārya Nāgārjuna

In Sanskrit, *Yuktiṣaṣṭikākārikānāma*
In Tibetan, *Rigs pa drug cu ba tshigs le'ur byas pa zhes bya ba*

Reverence to the Insight Hero, Mañjuśrī!

0. I bow to the Lord of Sages,
Who proclaimed relativity,
The way by which he abandoned
[Real] creation and destruction!

1. Those whose intellect transcends
Being and nothing, and does not dwell [between],
Realize the meaning of "condition,"
Which is profound and non-perceived.

2. [You] who have eliminated nihilism,
The source of all ills,
Should attend to the reasons why
Absolutism must be rejected as well.

3. If things were [really] true,
As the naïve construe them,
Then why not accept
Their nothing[ness] as liberation?

4. [You] cannot be liberated through absolutism,
Nor escape this existence through nihilism.
Great souls are liberated
By fully understanding being and nothing.

5. Those who do not see reality presume
The [duality of] life-cycle and nirvāṇa;
Those who do see reality do not presume
Either a life-cycle or a nirvāṇa.

**6. Of the two, existence and nirvāṇa,
Neither is known to exist [intrinsically];
The full understanding of existence
Is what is called "nirvāṇa."**

**7. [The naïve] imagine cessation
As the annihilation of an originated being;
While the wise understand it
As like the ceasing of a magical illusion.**

**8. If cessation happens through annihilation,
Not by fully understanding creations,
Who would be there to experience it?
How could a destroyed [subject] come to be?**

**9. [You claim:] "If the aggregates have not ceased,
Though addictions cease, there is no nirvāṇa."
When here [you] have [intrinsically] ceased,
Only then, [absurdly,] will [you] be freed.**

**10. When one discerns with precise intuition
What occurs conditioned by misknowledge,
One does not experience anything,
Whether created or ceased.**

**11. That is immediate nirvāṇa,
And that very thing is "attaining the goal."
If, after that insight into the truth,
One discovers any particular here,**

**12. Imagining any sort of creation,
In anything, however subtle,
Such an unwise individual
Does not see the meaning of "conditioned arisal."**

**13. If the monk who exhausts his addictions
Completely eliminates cyclic life,
Then why do the perfect buddhas
Not teach the beginning of such [cyclic life]?**

**14. If [you claim] a beginning, then, definitely,
You are embracing an [addictive] view.**

What beginning or end could there be
To that which arises interdependently?

15. How could something primordially created,
Subsequently be eliminated?
Free from initial and terminal limits,
Beings appear like illusions.

16. When an illusion manifests
Or when it is dispelled,
One who knows the illusion is not confused;
One ignorant of the illusion is entranced by it.

17. One whose intellect sees existence
As similar to an illusion or mirage,
Is not deceived by [extremist] views
Of an ultimate beginning or end.

18. Those who imagine that created things
Are [intrinsically] produced and destroyed,
Utterly fail to understand
The turning of the wheel of relativity.

19. What arises, dependent upon this and that,
Is not intrinsically created;
How can you call the intrinsically
Uncreated, "created?"

20. Peace through exhausting the cause
Manifests as so-called "termination";
How can you call the intrinsically
Unterminated, "terminated"?

21. Thus, nothing whatsoever is created,
And nothing whatsoever will cease.
The path of creation and destruction
Was taught for a useful purpose:

22. By knowing creation, you know destruction;
By knowing destruction, you know impermanence.
Through knowing how to enter impermanence,
You eventually come to realize the truth.

23. Those who develop understanding
Of [profound] relativity,
Abandoning creation and destruction,
Cross the ocean of existence with its views.

24. Alienated beings, who hold self [as] real,
Mistake existence and non-existence.
Thus flawed, they are driven by addictions,
And [hence] are deceived by their own minds.

25. Those who are expert in things
See them as impermanent,
Deceptive in nature, hollow,
Empty, selfless, and vacant.

26. With no basis and no perceptual object,
With no root and no foundation,
Totally arisen from the cause—misknowledge—
Bereft of beginning, middle, and end,

27. Essenceless—like a plantain [tree]—
Resembling a fairy city,
And an unbearable city of confusion,
Life appears like an illusion.

28. What is proclaimed as the truth in this world
By Brahmā [the Creator] and the others,
Was declared "false" for the noble ones.
What else remains that is otherwise?

29. How can the worldly, blinded by misknowledge,
Who follow the flow of their cravings,
And the virtuous, who are skilled and
Free of craving, be viewed as equal?

30. To seekers of reality, at first,
You should declare, "Everything exists!"
Once they understand things and grow detached,
Then, [you may teach] them freedom.

31. Ignorant of the meaning of freedom,
Just acting on what they have heard,

They neglect the exercise of virtue—
Such pitiful creatures are lost.

32. [Buddha] declared the effectiveness of actions,
As well as the forms of life [they create];
[Then] taught his full understanding of their nature,
Including their uncreatedness.

33. Just as the Victors say "I"
And "mine" for a useful purpose,
So they speak of "aggregates," "media,"
And "elements" for a useful purpose.

34. [Things first] proclaimed, such as primary elements,
Then are incorporated into consciousness.
Since knowing that, you break free [of them],
Are they not unreal constructions?

35. "Nirvāṇa is the sole truth,"
Is what the Victors declared;
Then, what wise person would suppose,
"Everything else is not false"?

36. As long as the mind vacillates,
It remains under the dominion of Māra.
Such being the case, why not validate
That there is no fault in this?

37. "The world is conditioned by misknowledge!"
Thus spoke the perfect Buddha.
Hence, what's invalid about saying that
"This world is [mere] construction"?

38. When misknowledge ceases,
Since those things misknowledge imagines
Will [also] come to cease,
Why wouldn't [the world] be cleared away?

39. Whatever originates having a cause,
Does not endure without conditions,
And, without conditions, is destroyed.
How can you understand such things as "existent"?

40. When those who advocate [objective] existence
Still hold things as [intrinsically real],
And remain on that very same path,
It is not surprising in the least.

41. But for those who rely on the path of the Buddha,
And advocate the impermanence of all things,
To persist in hanging on to [intrinsic] things
With arguments—they really are amazing!

42. When "this" or "that" [appears a fact],
Yet when analyzed is not perceived,
What wise person would advocate with arguments
That "this" or "that" is [really] true?

43. Those who insist on a non-relative
"Self" or "world"—Alas!
They are deprived by views
Such as absolutism and nihilism.

44. Claiming that dependent things
Are established in reality,
How could they not develop flawed views,
Such as absolutism, about those [things]?

45. Those who accept dependent things
As being like the moon in water,
Neither [intrinsically] real nor unreal,
Are not deprived by addictive views.

46. Once they commit to [intrinsic] things,
They are trapped in painful malignant views
Which produce attachment and aversion,
And the disputes that spring from them.

47. That [reality-habit] is the cause of all views;
Without it, addictions do not develop.
So when its [falsity] is fully understood,
Views and addictions are fully cured.

48. One asks, "How can this be understood?"
[It is understood] by seeing relativity.

"The dependently created is uncreated!"
Thus spoke the supreme knower of reality.

49. [Those] overwhelmed by mistaken knowledge,
Are trapped by attachment in a process
Of obsession and conflict,
Clutching to truth in the [intrinsically] untrue.

50. Great souls are beyond disputes,
[For,] they assume no [fixated] position.
For those who have no position,
How can there be opposition?

51. If any sort of hold is found,
The cunning poisonous snake of addiction
Will seize it; but those whose minds
Have no [such] hold, will not be seized.

52. How could the addictions not poison
Those whose minds keep the place for them?
Even when [ascetics] stay neutral,
The snake of addiction will seize them.

53. As a child with his notion of truth
Falls in love with a mirror image,
Worldly people, due to delusion,
Are trapped in a thicket of objects.

54. Seeing things to be like mirror images
With their eye of intuitive wisdom,
Great souls do not get stuck
In the quicksand of "objects."

55. The naïve are attached to forms;
The mediocre are detached from them.
Those with the highest intelligence understand
The nature of forms, and thus are freed.

56. Those who cherish beauty become attached;
Those who turn away from it become detached.
But those who see it as empty,
Like an illusory person, reach nirvāṇa.

57. Those disturbed by false knowledge
Suffer all the faults of addiction;
But those who come to know the [true] meaning
Have no [false] constructs of being or nothingness.

58. When one has a place [for reified things],
One experiences attachment and detachment;
But the great souls, having no [such] place,
Are neither attached nor detached.

59. Whoever contemplates freedom,
And is not moved by the wavering mind,
Crosses the ocean of intolerable existence,
Which seethes with the snakes of addiction.

60. By the virtue [of writing this,] may all beings
Gather the stores of merit and wisdom,
And attain the two supreme [buddha bodies]
Arisen from merit and wisdom!

So ends the *Reason Sixty* composed by the Master, Ārya Nāgārjuna. This version was prepared by the Tibetan translator Pa-tshab Nyi-ma-grags under the direction of the Indian Abbot Muditaśrī.

The Reason Sixty Commentary

by Āchārya Chandrakīrti

In Sanskrit, *Yuktiṣaṣṭikāvṛtti*
In Tibetan, *Rigs pa drug cu pa'i 'grel pa*

Reverence to the Wisdom Hero,[1] *Mañjuśrī!*

Bowing to the author of the *Reason Sixty*
Which dispels the two extremes,
Following the Victor's path of reasoning,
I will elucidate it with the Central Way.

In this [manner], the Master [Nāgārjuna] gained distinctive joy by seeing the reality of relativity[2] exactly as it is. Knowing that realization to be the source of supreme faith, and also that the whole store of mundane and transcendent virtues—all noble individuals without exception, and even the perfect enlightenment about all aspects of reality which is the unobscured intuition[3] of the victorious buddhas—all arise from seeing relativity, he was moved to explain that relativity. He proclaimed its immunity from the taints of extremist notions of creation and destruction, and being and nothingness, because of its not being intrinsically produced, the magnificence[4] of relativity being its freedom from any intrinsic reality.

---

[1] Tib. *ye shes sems dpa'*, Skt. **jñānasattva.*

[2] Tib. *rten cing 'brel par 'byung ba*, Skt. *pratītyasamutpāda*. It refers to both the classical Buddhist model of causality governing the psychobiology of development ("dependent origination"), and Nāgārjuna's extension of this model into a principle governing all causal systems ("relativity").

[3] Tib. *ye shes*, Skt. *jñāna*, has been translated with "intuition" here since it refers not simply to the initial development of rational insight analyzing the ultimate, but to its complete integration at all levels of the mind-body.

[4] Tib. *che ba nyid kyis*.

I. Author's preliminary homage[5]

Feeling devotion for that Transcendent Lord[6] who taught relativity, himself having become indistinguishable from its actuality, [Nāgārjuna] composed this homage to him:

> **0. I bow to the Lord of Sages[7]**
> **Who proclaimed relativity,[8]**
> **The way by which he abandoned**
> **[Real] creation and destruction![9]**

A. Purpose [of the homage]

Why did the Master compose an homage expressly for this Centrist [teaching],[10] when he expressed no such praise in the *Voidness Seventy* or *Rebuttal of Objections*?

The answer is that since the *Voidness Seventy* and *Rebuttal of Objections* are both elaborations on the [*Fundamental Verses of the*] *Central Way*; they are not independent works, and therefore he composed no separate dedicatory verses in them.

Thus, with regard to the *Rebuttal of Objections* [from the verse in the *Fundamental Verses of the Central Way* (k. 1.3)]:[11]

---

[5] Gray topical outline headings, incorporated throughout the English and Tibetan versions of Chandrakīrti's *Commentary*, are from Gyaltsap's *Commentary* (*rigs pa drug cu pa'i ṭīkka*). The full outline has also been extracted and presented independently in both English and Tibetan in the Appendices.

[6] Tib. *de bzhin gshegs pa*, Skt. *tathāgata.*

[7] Skt. *munīndra*, Tib. *thub pa'i dbang po*, Nāgārjuna's first of three epithets of Buddha in this text.

[8] Skt. *proktaṁ*, Tib. *gsungs pa*.

[9] This verse quoted in Tsong Khapa's *legs bshad snying po* (Thurman, *Essence*, 260), who takes the teaching of relativity (or dependent origination) as the distinguishing feature of the Buddha's teachings above and beyond those of other teachers.

[10] Tib. *dbu ma 'di*, i.e., the YṢ.

[11] The Tibetan text reads *'di ltar rtsod pa bzlog pa ni*, despite the fact that the quote is from Nāgārjuna's *Central Way*.

There is no intrinsic reality in things
Such as [causes and] conditions;
[And] where there is no intrinsic reality
There is no extrinsic reality [either].

—it is evident that the *Rebuttal of Objections* is an elaboration drawn from that [*Central Way* verse], since it treats objections and responses to that verse.

[Similarly, with regard to the *Voidness Seventy*, from the verse in the *Central Way* (k. 7.34)]:

Like illusion, like a dream,
Like a fairy city;
Such is birth, such is life,
Such is death, he proclaimed.

—it is evident that the *Voidness Seventy* is [likewise] an elaboration drawn from that [*Central Way* verse], since it treats objections and responses to that verse.[12]

Since [Nāgārjuna] composed this *Reason Sixty*—just like his *Central Way*—primarily as an investigation of relativity, it is not comparable to those [texts that are] elaborations [of verses] from within the *Central Way*.

B. The concise meaning [of the homage]

Those who wish to travel to the city of nirvāṇa by abandoning all the claims of realists, theists and others as to the creation and destruction of life through intrinsic reality, a Creator, nature, spirit, time, God, and so on,[13] yet are handicapped by error through misperceiving the two realities [ultimate and superficial], will not be able for a very long time to reach that city

---

[12] The Tibetan scholar, Blo-bzang rdo-rje, unpacks these assertions by explaining that the *Rebuttal of Objections* (*vigrahavyāvartanī*) expands on the first chapter of the *Fundamental Verses* by presenting arguments establishing the manner in which proof and refutation are feasible within the context of asserting voidness, while the *Voidness Seventy* (*śūnyatāsaptatikārikā*) expands on the seventh chapter of the *Fundamental Verses*, presenting additional arguments for the efficacy of actions.

[13] Scherrer-Schaub (*Yuktiṣaṣṭikāvṛtti*, 108 n. 18) gives this sequence as: *svabhāva-īśvara-prakṛti-puruṣa-kāla-nārāyaṇa*, which may serve as a list of principles correlated with the Nyāya-Vaiśeṣika, Vedānta, Yoga, Sāṁkhya, Carvāka, and Mīṁāṁsa schools, respectively.

of nirvāṇa whose nature is the termination of cyclic life.[14] And since the mere fact of this teaching of relativity itself serves as the cause of undistorted insight into the two realities, it is the prime, peerless journey all noble individuals have traveled, the universal path that is dedicated exclusively to the city of nirvāṇa, freeing one completely from all creations.[15] Consequently, the unexcelled Teacher, who taught it with the consummate lordly power of the complete stores of intuition and merit, is not celebrated [by Nāgārjuna] as Lord of Sages [simply] because he is chief among the disciples and hermit buddhas.[16] Rather, he recognized him as the Lord of Sages because [only] he discovered and taught the teaching of relativity, [hence Nāgārjuna] said, "I salute that Lord of Sages who proclaimed relativity."

It doesn't happen that someone who is not a Lord of Sages would proclaim relativity, because proclaiming relativity makes one a Lord of Sages, and so is its cause. Furthermore, becoming a Lord of Sages is the cause of proclaiming relativity, since no one else has the ability to explain it. Even the disciples, hermit buddhas, and enlightened altruists[17] are able to explain it only because of the teaching by the Lord of Sages. If one objects that neither [the Lord nor his teaching] is truly established, since they are mutually dependent, we reply as follows. That which is mutually dependent is neither created nor destroyed with any other [intrinsic] reality and *is* relativity; that is precisely what voidness-advocates claim. For one does not become Lord of Sages simply by proclaiming relativity, but rather by articulating the pattern of the mutually dependent establishment of things and hence by negating things' [intrinsically real] creation and destruction.[18]

---

[14] Tib. *'khor ba*, Skt. *saṁsāra*.

[15] Tib. *'dus byed*, Skt. *saṁskāra*, in this context refers to the addictive instincts which drive *saṁsāra*. Cf. MMK, 26.11.

[16] Tib. *nyen thos dang rang sangs rgyas thub pa rnams*, Skt. reconstructed by Scherrer-Schaub (*Yuktiṣaṣṭikāvṛtti*, 111 n. 24) as: *śrāvaka-pratyeka-buddha-munayo*.

[17] *śrāvaka*, *pratyekabuddha*, *bodhisattva*.

[18] As Scherrer-Schaub, *Yuktiṣaṣṭikāvṛtti*, 112 n. 26, points out, citing a similar formulation in Nāgārjuna's *Lokātīta-stava*, 8, Chandrakīrti's reversal of the objection turns on the Centrist account of agent and act as established by mere interdependence, *parasparāpekṣikī siddiḥ*. Cf. Lindtner, *Nāgārjuniana*, 130, 131 n. 8; MMK, 8.12, and MAV, 6.162.

C. The meaning of the individual words of the homage

1. The actual meaning of the words

"Who," [reading the pronoun *yena* as "since he,"][19] expresses [Nāgārjuna's] reason for seeing the Lord of Sages as the peerless Teacher, namely, *since* only *he* taught nonduality;[20] hence the statement, "I salute that Lord of Sages." Alternatively, [reading *yena* as "by whom," Nāgārjuna sees him as] the Lord of Sages *by whom* relativity was discovered, since this method of relativity is his, and it is by this system that he negated the [intrinsically real] creation and destruction of things; hence "I salute that Lord of Sages." An alternate [reading of *yena*] as "whereby" expresses the sufficient cause *whereby* the Lord of Sages taught the relativity of things, negated things' intrinsically real creation and destruction, and so is saluted [with the praise] "I salute that Lord of Sages," that is: his aim to especially benefit the world. Again, seeing that one can develop one's own mind based on the Lord of Sages' discourse as it occurs in the following [text, taking *yena* as "by which," Nāgārjuna] refers to relativity as "the way *by which* he abandoned creation and destruction," and so said, "I salute that Lord of Sages."

2. Dispelling objections

Here [the Buddhist Realist][21] may object: "This formulation of yours is unprecedented; it is impossible for an advocate of relativity to show the

---

[19] The ambiguity of the instrumental singular pronoun *yena* is preserved in Tibetan by *gang gis*, the placement of which at the opening of the verse translates all four meanings Chandrakīrti reads in the original. The opening pronoun can serve: 1) to subordinate all three dependent clauses as adverbial to the main clause, "I salute that Lord...*since he*"; 2) to subordinate all three dependent clauses as a complex predicate for the main clause, "I salute that Lord...*by whom*," by acting as the subject of the chief adjectival clause "relativity was discovered"; 3) to subordinate the two secondary dependent clauses as adverbial to the main clause, "I salute that Lord...who discovered relativity *whereby*"; or 4) to subordinate the two secondary clauses as adjectival to the predicate clause, "Who discovered relativity, *by which* way he abandoned creation and destruction."

[20] Tib. *gnyis su med pa*, Skt. *advaya*. "Nonduality" refers to the pure negation of dualistic extremes which is the definitive truth (*nithārtha*) of the Centrist method, as opposed to the affirmation of relativity and convention which is the truth of interpretable meaning (*neyārtha*).

[21] Of the four major schools (*siddhānta*) of Buddhist Philosophy, Chandrakīrti, following Nāgārjuna (k.2), begins by addressing the realistic, "lower" two schools associated with the Individual Vehicle (*Hīnayāna*), the Analyst (*Vaibhāṣika*) and Traditionist (*Sautrāntika*)

(cont'd)

non-existence of creation and destruction; this would be as irrational as if one were to say, 'Your son is born' and then say, 'Your son is not born.'"

Let me explain. If one employs the eye of one's intellect[22] impaired by the obscuration of misknowledge,[23] the term "relatively produced" may not translate with "uncreated and undestroyed with intrinsic reality"; [yet] when [clearly] examined, one must recognize that [this reading] entails not the slightest fault. The naïve[24] who insist on intrinsic reality are like children with a mirror image; they are unable to realize that things are in fact devoid of intrinsic reality.

II. The actual text which is the object of composition

A. Teaching relativity as free from the two extremes

1. Refuting the extreme of permanence

a. The realization of relativity as free of elaborations

i. The actual explanation

However, for the purpose of teaching that the wise, like those experienced with mirror images, being able to clearly realize things' lack of intrinsic reality, "are able to understand [this," Nāgārjuna says]:

1. Those whose intellect transcends
Being and nothing,[25] and does not dwell [between],
Realize the meaning of "condition,"[26]
Which is profound and non-perceived.

---

schools, as opposed to the more critical Experientialist (*Yogācāra*) and Centrist (*Mādhyamika*) schools of the Universal Vehicle (*Mahāyāna*).

22 Tib. *blo gros kyi mig*, Skt. *buddhicakṣu*.

23 Skt. *avidyā*, Tib. *ma rigs pa*. "Misknowledge" is any cognition mistaken about its object's ultimate mode of being; it refers not to perceptual errors consensually recognized as illusions, but to the way objects of perception—whose reality is habitually assented to—prove deceptive when critically examined.

24 Tib. *byis pa*, Skt. *bāla*. Literally "children," it is a term used pejoratively to refer to those who espouse a "realist" philosophy that assents to conventional appearances as intrinsically real; they are often contrasted by Nāgārjuna and Chandrakīrti to the "wise" or "adept" (Tib. *mkhas pa*, Skt. *paṇḍita*).

25 Skt. *asti nāsti*, Tib. *yod med*.

26 Tib. *rkyen*, Skt. *pratyaya*. A reference to the analysis of conditions (*pratyaya-parīkṣā*) with which Nāgārjuna opens his *Central Way*. According to Chandrakīrti, this is because, of the

(cont'd)

Those who have meditated on voidness in past lives have great [intellectual] talent because of having the potential for seeing voidness through understanding relativity. Even without any extraordinary practice in their present life, the noble Śāriputra and others seem to realize profound relativity, unsullied by the mud stirred up by extremist constructs of being and nothingness; [although] this is not within the intellectual scope of the naïve.

ii. Advice on the teaching of the profound

(1) Conjoining this with the refutation of nihilism

As actions and addictions[27] serve as its cause,
The world arises causally conditioned,
Just so, the Guide proclaimed the causes
That counteract [such] actions and addictions.

[Hence] that best bull of philosophers,
Who proclaimed the supreme freedom,
In which the sufferings of life, aging, and death,
Definitely do not remain, also declared his realization.

So it was that, by simply listening to this [frequently] quoted verse, the noble Śāriputra realized reality. Therefore, the intelligence of such beings transcends perceiving being and nothingness by the sheer force of former practice. Nor does it dwell [in between], since there is no center apart from the two extremes. Since it produces fear in the naïve and [because] they cannot fathom it, it is "profound." Since it is intrinsically uncreated, it cannot be objectified[28] with mental constructs either of absolutistic and nihilistic extremes of being or nothingness or of a [reified] center, therefore it is "non-perceived." The statement that such noble individuals "realize the

---

ten equalities, the equality of all things with respect to their lack of intrinsic production is the easiest to begin with. Cf. PPMMV ad k. 1.5 (La Vallée Poussin, *Madhyamakavṛttiḥ*, 81–82).

[27] Skt. *kleśa*, Tib. *nyon mongs pa*. Where the term can be taken to refer to desire, hatred, misknowledge, and so forth, less as static "afflictions" (i.e., as effects), and more as dynamic forces in a cycle of addictive impulse and behavior. Hence, we translate this as "addictions."

[28] Tib. *yul du dmigs pa*, Skt. **viṣayālambana*.

meaning of condition" means that [they cultivate] an intuitive realization, in other words, a "direct intuition."[29]

Those other than the noble who have serious misperceptions are unable to realize the meaning of relativity, for they presume that the mere term "relativity" means intrinsically real creation. In their effort to find a reason that proves such [intrinsically real creation] and to contradict the voidness-advocate, these [Buddhist Realists] say to this:

"Since it is a rational [person] who perceives relativity and can examine whether it exists or not, the noble ones who contemplate profound relativity with intellects that transcend constructs of being and nothingness cannot do so without having some sort of perceptual object.[30] For if [relative things] were held to be absent [during realization], then, like the horns of a donkey, they could not be perceived, and [this] would invalidate the theory that [the mental continuum] arrives here from a previous life, and proceeds from this life to another [future] life, as well as the explanation of [relativity as] the twelve links of dependent origination [which extend] over three lifetimes, meant to show that the unbroken continuum of cyclic life involves the conservation of action [patterns across lives]. It would also invalidate explanations from the *[Treasury of] Pure Science*[31] of aggregates, media and elements,[32] with their specific and general properties.[33] But all of these exist precisely as presented; and, since they exist, they are valid. Therefore relativity exists as such."

Let me explain. You

---

[29] *mngon sum du byed* is a gloss of *ye shes* indicated by the standard commentarial device *zhes bya ba'i tha tshig go* (= *ity arthaḥ*).

[30] *ji tsam dngos po dmigs su yod pa dag*. Scherrer-Schaub (*Yuktiṣaṣṭikāvṛtti*, 119 n. 53) identifies Chandrakīrti's opponent here as the Analyst-Realist or Vaibhāṣika-Sarvāstivādin, who can only explain the workings of perception and language in reference to a substantially existent object, *ṣaḍ-viṣayāt* (cf. AK ad k. 5.25: Pradhan, 295; La Vallée Poussin, *L'Abhidharmakośa*, IV, 50–51). She further compares this first of Chandrakīrti's progressively subtler critiques of realistic Buddhist views on the object of transcendent analysis and insight with Vasubandhu's Traditionist argument (cf. AK ad k. 5.26; Pradhan, 300; La Vallée Poussin, *L'Abhidharmakośa*, IV, 62–63) that such realism precludes the false self-evidence of superficial objects which is negated by analysis and insight.

[31] Tib. *chos mngon pa*, Skt. *abhidharma-[kośa]*.

[32] Tib. *phungs po, skye mched, khams*, Skt. *skandha, āyatana, dhātu*.

[33] Tib. *rang gi mtshan nyid / spyi'i mtshan nyid*, Skt. *svalakṣaṇa / sāmānyalakṣaṇa*.

2ab. Who have eliminated nihilism,[34]
The source of all ills,

who have supported the elimination of those [nihilistic views] and countered your addictions, you have served as our allies.

(2) Advice to listen to the refutation of the view of absolutism

[Now] as I [explain them, you]

2cd. Should attend to the reasons[35] why
Absolutism must be rejected as well.[36]

Since [the analysis of] relativity is the context [of this verse], it is [the reason of] relativity that must be understood [as its subject]. Now, since holding that [relativity] not to exist repudiates the conservation of action-patterns, those who assert [such] a nihilistic worldview reject all the roots of mundane and transcendent virtues and eventually cause the origination of all ills, because they lay the ground for the accumulation of all non-virtuous elements; hence [their view] is "the original source of all ills." That [extreme] is eliminated through the *[Treasury of] Pure Science*, since that [work] presents the multi-lifetime[37] [cycle of] dependent origination and the variety of habitats[38] generated by the collective activity[39] of all living

---

[34] Tib. *med nyid* (YṢ) / *med pa* (YṢV).

[35] Tib. *rigs pa*, Skt. *yukti*. Here understood to mean not philosophy in general, but the specific Centrist method of rational analysis that clears away dualistic extremes.

[36] Absolutism (*astivāda*) and nihilism (*nāstivāda*), being the two extremes (*antadvaya*) referred to in Chandrakīrti's dedication. Nāgārjuna here is introducing the traditional nondualist schema for critiquing the two main types of views that obstruct transcendent analysis and insight.

[37] Tib. *tshe rabs gsum pa.*

[38] Tib. *snod kyi 'jig rten*, Skt. *bhājanaloka.* The environment referred to here is a natural habitat, an expression of the interaction of migrant beings with the elements and other migrant beings that surround them through successive lifetimes. Cf. AK ad ks. 3.44–59 (Pradhan, 157–165; tr. La Vallée Poussin, *L'Abhidharmakośa*, II, 135–156).

[39] Tib. *spyi'i las bskyes pa.* This refers to the results of actions that are experienced collectively by groups who engage in communal action, such as shared natural environments. Cf. AK ad k. 2.57 (Pradhan, 95; La Vallée Poussin, *L'Abhidharmakośa*, I, 291).

beings.[40] Consequently, [Nāgārjuna] does not present additional reasons to reject [nihilistic] opponents, as that [text does]. [However,] he does explain the pronouncements the Victor made to eliminate absolutism, such as:

> Thus, O monks, non-deceptive in nature, this nirvāṇa is the sole, supreme truth. False and deceptive in nature are all the world's created things.[41] For alas, created [things] are impermanent.[42]

Although such [pronouncements] are seen, because they were not proclaimed in a single text but widely dispersed, and because the naïve have been habituated to an absolutistic view over an extremely long time, [Nāgārjuna] gathered the explanations presented in this and that discourse of the Lord of Sages and distilled them here. Hence [you Realists] "should attend to the reasons why absolutism must be rejected as well."

b. The reasonings that refute the extreme of absolutism

i. A consequence of the appropriateness of the occasion

What are these reasons? To indicate them, [Nāgārjuna] said:

3. If things were [really] true,
As the naïve construe[43] them,
Then why not accept
Their nothing[ness] as liberation?

It is said by the Lord Buddha:

---

[40] Tib. *sems can*, Skt. *sattva*.

[41] Tib. *'dus byed*, Skt. *saṁskāra*. Translated here with "created things" or "creations," *saṁskāra* is a term with diverse technical senses. As a category of phenomena, it refers to the class of *saṁskṛta-dharma*, the created elements shaped by beings' *karma* into migrant beings and environments. As the second step in the twelvefold process of dependent origination, it refers to the "intentions" which structure actions, and as one of the five psychophysical aggregates of beings, it refers to the aggregate of "motivations" or "emotions" which condition their intentional life. Cf. Scherrer-Schaub, *Yuktiṣaṣṭikāvṛtti*, 204 n. 347.

[42] As noted by Scherrer-Schaub ("Yuktiṣaṣṭikāvṛtti," 122 n. 65–66), the first portion of the passage comes from the *Kātyāyanāvavāda* (which Nāgārjuna paraphrases in MMK, 13.1–3), and which occurs in PPMMV. Similar passages to the final line are found in the *Udānavarga*, 1.3, *Avadānaśataka*, the *Vimalakīrtinirdeśa*, and others.

[43] Tib. *rnam par brtags pa*, Skt. *vikalpa*.

> Through precise knowledge of reality and precise knowledge of the truth, delight develops. With delight, happiness develops. With mental happiness comes physical ecstasy. With physical ecstasy, bliss is experienced. Through bliss, the mind becomes one-pointed. Through one-pointed concentration, one understands reality as it is, and sees reality as it is. Through understanding and seeing reality as it is, one develops transcendent renunciation. Through renunciation, one grows dispassionate. Through dispassion, one is liberated.[44]

Thus, it is presented that through insight into reality as it is, one becomes liberated.

(1) The difference between Dialecticist and Dogmaticist Centrists

Those who have not realized ultimate reality discriminate objects such as blue as having some sort of intrinsic objectivity. If they were not mistaken with respect to [ultimate] reality, then their seeing such things just as they appear would be [seeing] objective reality just as the saints do. Hence, they would be liberated through a nirvāṇa which is [merely] a state of non-grasping due to the non-production [associated] with a [real] nothingness; such as the following:

> Wherein the body dissolves,
> Cognition stops, sensation departs,
> Intentional actions are eradicated,
> And consciousness subsides.[45]

And similarly:

> He, who once had an irrepressible body
> And an addiction to sensation,

---

[44] This passage is also quoted in Yaśomitra's *Explanation*. Although Yaśomitra does not name the *sūtra* source, Scherrer-Schaub cites La Vallée Poussin (*L'Abhidharmakośa*, I, 48 n. 2) and others who identify it as the *Daśottara-sūtra* (or, *Saṁgīti-sūtra*). Cf. Scherrer-Schaub, *Yuktiṣaṣṭikāvṛtti*, 28 n. 101 and 125 n. 70 for a discussion of the AKV and other sources.

[45] Although no identification is given, Scherrer-Schaub (*Yuktiṣaṣṭikāvṛtti*, 29 n. 105) identifies this as a verse from the UV (26.16: Bernhard, *Udānavarga*, I, 322; f. 233a.4–.5), while a variation on this verse is found in Chandrakīrti's PPMMV which, not unsurprisingly, more closely resembles the version cited here.

With the liberation of his mind
Is like a lamp extinguished.[46]

Thus, because [of the assumption that] even the naïve see correctly, one would have to accept that they transcend suffering [by a naïve perception of nothingness] just as the saint does by entirely abandoning [naïve perceptions]. Alternatively, if one does not accept that they are freed [by naïve perception] in the same way as the saint is by the absence [of such perception], then what the naïve misperceive through misknowledge must not be ascertained in reality as it [appears] in their imaginative constructions. Consequently, their absolutistic vision is not insight into reality.

(2) Identifying the correct thesis

Therefore, the Lord said [in the *King of Samādhis Scripture*]:

The eye, ear, and nose [sense consciousnesses] are not
validating cognitions;
The tongue, body, and mental [sense consciousnesses] are
not validating cognitions, either.
If these sense faculties were validating [cognitions],
What would be accomplished by the noble path?

Since these sense faculties are not validating [cognitions],
But naturally stupid and unpredictable,
[You], who desire the path to nirvāṇa—
Accomplish your aim by means of the noble path!

[Moreover, the Buddha] stated [in the *Lotus of the True Dharma Scripture*]:

All these things are wrongly construed notions,
They are not genuine and do not exist as genuine.

---

[46] As Scherrer-Schaub notes (*Yuktiṣaṣṭikāvṛtti*, 129 n. 76) this verse is likewise quoted in PPMMV (La Vallée Poussin, *Madhyamakavṛttiḥ*, 520; f. 173b.6) following Chandrakīrti's citation of the previous quote. While La Vallée Poussin notes the similarity between this verse and passages in the *Theragatha* and *Dīgha Nikāya*, de Jong ("Textcritical Notes," 244) observes that the verse occurs in the *Avadāna-śataka* (Speyer, *Avadānaçataka*, II, 199.8–.9) with some differences. Cf. Scherrer-Schaub, (*Yuktiṣaṣṭikāvṛtti*, 129 n. 76) for Pāli equivalents.

They do not originate and are not produced;
Their reality and origination are wrong constructions.

If one inquires why these [false cognitions] do not see reality as it is, later, in that same [scripture, the *Lotus of the True Dharma Scripture*, the Buddha] explains:

When one is free from engagement with anything at all—
Created or uncreated,
Real or unreal,
Large, small, or intermediate—

Stable, one does not engage with any "female,"
Nor construct any "male";
All things being unproduced,
Though sought will not be found.

All these things are absent,
Uncreated and unoriginated,
Eternally void, inert, and at rest;
Such is the sphere of engagement of the wise.

[Hence, only] those with such insight see reality, but it is lacking in the naïve. Therefore, since they do not see reality, they are not considered liberated.

ii. Addenda

(1) There is no liberation through the two views

While nihilism—the source of all ills—has the effect of unfortunate rebirths and unpleasant experiences, in a similar manner, the absolutism to which the naïve are habituated[47] results in fortunate rebirths and the experience of happiness in all lives.[48] However, insofar as both [types of] worldview have cyclic life as their result, they [both] contradict [liberative] reason. [Hence, Nāgārjuna stated:]

---

[47] Tib. *'dris pa*, Skt. **saṁstuta*.

[48] As noted by Scherrer-Schaub (*Yuktiṣaṣṭikāvṛtti*, 131 n. 80) this follows the view expressed in RA (k.57)—the first two lines of which Gyaltsap quotes in his commentary (*ṭīkka*, f. 10a.4)—which reads: "A follower of non-existence goes to bad transmigrations, and a follower of existence goes to happy transmigrations" (Hopkins, *Buddhist Advice*, 101).

4ab. [You] cannot be liberated through absolutism,
Nor escape this existence through nihilism.

Because impurity is not cleansed by impurity, one cannot attain liberation, whose nature is the transcendence of [compulsive] existence, with these two worldviews, the causes from which the impurity of the life-cycle originates. Since nihilistic and absolutistic worldviews thus do not liberate one from the aggregates, media and elements [that constitute the life-cycle], one might inquire, "By what view do yogin/īs reach liberation?"

(2) Liberation [comes only] from a nondual realization[49]

[To answer this, Nāgārjuna states:]

4cd. Great souls[50] are liberated
By fully understanding being and nothing.[51]

Nothing is not established independent of being; nor is being established independent of nothing. Both being and nothing exist without intrinsically real status. Thus, total understanding[52] of being and nothing is the understanding of them both as unreal, their nature free from notions of intrinsically objective[53] being and nothingness. The liberation of the great beings is established by such understanding. Therefore, these [noble] individuals are called great souls because of their own universality, since they abide in the

---

[49] Following his citation of RA (k.57ab), Gyaltsap quotes k. 57d in his commentary (*tīkka*, f. 10b.1) in support of his interpretation of the second half of this verse; RA k. 57cd reads: "Through correct and true knowledge one does not rely on dualism and becomes liberated" (Hopkins, *Buddhist Advice*, 101).

[50] Tib. *bdag nyid chen po rnams*, Skt. **mahātmanām*.

[51] Tib. *dngos dang dngos med*, Skt. **bhāva abhāvaśca*.

[52] Tib. *yongs su shes pa*, Skt. **parijñā* or **parijñāna*. The term refers to the authentic insight which brings about nirvāṇa—defined as a dissociation (*visaṁyoga*) from the addictions (*kleśa*)—accomplished by means of either the discernment of dharmas (*dharma-pravicaya*) or deconstructive analysis.

[53] Tib. *rang gi ngo bo la sogs pa*, Skt. *svarūpādi*, refers to any constructs such as *bhāva*, *vastutā*, *dravya*, *svabhāva*, *svalakṣaṇa*, *svalakṣaṇasiddhatva*, and so on, which entail non-relative status. Regardless of distinctions of degree, Chandrakīrti glosses these together, as the kind of constructs that presuppose ultimate status (*paramārtha-siddhatva*).

intuition of non-perception[54] which far surpasses the naïve; and therefore they are called "noble."

The naïve are bound because the [addictions] such as desire, which develop through their imaginative construction of signs of "being" and "nothingness," serve as the cause for their not transcending the three realms.[55] Thereby, the naïve who engage in such [constructions] are rendered powerless,[56] and revolve in the cycle of the five migrations.[57] The non-perception of being and nothingness definitely breaks the continuum of [the addictions] such as desire, since [the addictions] are not reproduced because the signs [that act as triggers] for them are not constructed. Since breaking the continuum of such [addictions] yields freedom, this [method of the insight of non-perception] is the technique of liberation.

2. Refuting that [lack of intrinsic identifiability] establishes the two extremes
   a. [Objection:] [Lack of intrinsic identifiability] is not scripturally established
      i. [Objecting to the statement:] The naïve will not ascertain it

To this, [the Buddhist Realist][58] may object: "Being and nothingness do exist, for if you hold them as non-existent, then, for you, the life-cycle

---

[54] Tib. *dmigs pa med pa'i ye shes*, Skt. reconstructed by Scherrer-Schaub (*Yuktiṣaṣṭikāvṛtti*, 133 n. 87) as *nir-ālambana-jñāna*.

[55] Tib. *khams gsum*, Skt. *tridhātu*, refers to the three, desire (*kāma*), form (*rūpa*), and formless (*arūpa*) realms.

[56] Tib. *rang dbang med par byas*. Scherrer-Schaub (*Yuktiṣaṣṭikāvṛtti*, 134 n. 90) notes that Yamaguchi (*Index*) attests Tib. *rang dbang med par byed* = Skt. *asvatantrayati*.

[57] Tib. *'gro ba lngar 'khor ba*, Skt. *pañcagatikasaṁsāra*. As Scherrer-Schaub (*Yuktiṣaṣṭikāvṛtti*, 134 n. 89) notes, Chandrakīrti's enumeration here and in PPMMV, 218, agrees with the AK, 114 (La Vallée Poussin, *L'Abhidharmakośa*, III, 11–12), in defining five migrant beings: hell-beings, ghosts, animals, humans, and gods (*nāraka*, *preta*, *tiryak*, *manuṣya*, *deva*), though differs from his discussion of the same in the context of a citation from the *de kho na nyid nges par bstan pa'i ting nge 'dzin* / **tattvanirdeśasamādhi* in the *Central Way Introduction Commentary* (MABh, 175), in which Chandrakīrti refers to six migrations, including the titan (*asura*) form.

[58] Chandrakīrti here moves from his treatment of the relatively naïve realism of the Analyst (*Vaibhāṣika*) to the more subtle realism of the Traditionist (*Sautrāntika*). As noted by Scherrer-Schaub (*Yuktiṣaṣṭikāvṛtti*, 135 n. 91), if the measure of the Analyst's realism is the insistence that even uncreated noumena (*asaṁskṛta-dharma*) like nirvāṇa have being (*bhāva*), the measure of the Traditionist's critical realism (AK, 93; tr. La Vallée Poussin, *L'Abhidharmakośa*, II, 282) is the subtle formulation that nirvāṇa is not being (*bhāva*), but a sub-

(cont'd)

and its transcendence would also be non-existent. Because it is identical with the five appropriative aggregates,[59] the life-cycle is substantial. Just these five appropriative aggregates, driven by actions and addictions,[60] are called 'the life-cycle' because they proceed from life in its various forms to life in other forms; hence, like them, it exists. [Further,] since that [life-cycle] exists, 'being' in fact exists. [Moreover,] nirvāṇa—liberation—has the nature of the exhaustion of the [addictive] life-cycle and is non-being because suffering is not re-produced. Consequently, nirvāṇa—the fact of the absence of the life-cycle—is as existent as cyclic life."

Let me explain. If the life-cycle and nirvāṇa both existed, then indeed it would follow that being and nothingness also both exist; however, the [former] two do not.

[The Buddhist Realist objects:] "But did the Lord not proclaim these both to exist, and teach the doctrine in order to accomplish the termination of the life-cycle and the attainment of nirvāṇa? If these [two] were non-existent, then the teaching of the Lord Buddhas would hence be pointless indeed! Yet it is not pointless. Consequently, the life-cycle and nirvāṇa exist; and, therefore, both being and nothingness are also established."

Let me explain: For whom were both cyclic life and nirvāṇa taught? [You say that] it was for the noble ones. Assuming that it was, if you think that it was explained for those who had become noble already, by what explanation did they become noble? The alternative to this is that such was taught in order [for the naïve] to become noble. If that is the case, this was [taught] for the sake of those not [yet] noble,[61] since they could become

---

sequent nothingness or absence (*paścād-abhāva*) which—while not literally an existent (*bhāvaḥ*)—nonetheless is deserving of the affirmation "it exists" (*bhavati*).

[59] Tib. *nye bar len pa'i phung po lnga*, Skt. *pañca upadādānaskandhāḥ*. The five aggregates are: body, sensation, perception, motivation, and consciousness (*rūpa, vedanā, saṁjñā, saṁskāra, vijñāna*).

[60] Tib. *las dang nyon mongs pas 'phangs pa*, Skt. *karma-kleśākṣepa*. In the *Abhidharma* classification of psychophysical elements (*dharma-saṁketa*), two of the six classes of mental factors (*caitasika*) are devoted to the addictions (*kleśa*). The primary addictions (*mūlakleśa*) are usually listed as three, delusion, desire, and hatred, (*moha, lobha, dveṣa*), and expanded to six, most frequently by the inclusion of envy, greed, and pride (*īrṣya, matsarya, abhimāna*). The secondary addictions (*upakleśa*) are derivatives, typically numbered at twenty. Cf. AK ks. 3.18–19 (Pradhan, 129; La Vallée Poussin, *L'Abhidharmakośa*, II, 57–58).

[61] Tib. *'phags pa ma yin*, Skt. *an-ārya. As noted by Scherrer-Schaub (*Yuktiṣaṣṭikāvṛtti*, 137 n. 97), this refers not only to those who cling to views and activities, but also to Buddhist

(cont'd)

noble through the process of learning it, contemplating it, and so forth.[62] Since such non-noble individuals have been conditioned to a realistic view[63] over the course of lifetimes without beginning, if they were not taught the excellent doctrine of nirvāṇa—whose nature as an antidote turns one away from [compulsive] cyclic life—they could not overcome their attachment to realism. If those addicted to a world filled with enormous happiness, when this is pointed out[64] to them, are able to overcome [attachment] even to those pleasures, what need is there to mention [its effect on those in the grip of things] such as intense suffering.

Thus nirvāṇa was taught. And to indicate that this was [done] precisely for the sake of naïve individuals, [Nāgārjuna] stated:

5ab. Those who do not see reality[65] presume[66]
The [duality of] life-cycle and nirvāṇa;

Those who lack insight into reality insist on the duality of the life-cycle and nirvāṇa, which they call "cyclic life" and "the elimination of cyclic life"; like a disease and its cure, they think to abandon the former and adopt the latter. Such beings who develop such a view by turning their backs on cyclic life, and who generate an aspiration to overcome it, are able to easily realize[67]—*via* the teaching of relativity—the uncreatedness of what is to be abandoned. Once they realize that things are unproduced, they also are able to easily abandon attachment[68] to nirvāṇa with respect to those things'

practitioners on the Paths of Accumulation (*saṁbhāra-*) and Experience (*prayoga*) prior to the Path of Insight (*darśana-mārga*).

62 Tib. *thos pa dang sems pa la sogs pa*, i.e., *thos sems sgom* = Skt. **śrutacintābhāvanā*. Cf. AK ad k. 1.2, 6.15 (Pradhan, 2, 341; La Vallée Poussin, *L'Abhidharmakośa*, I, 4, IV, 158–159).

63 Tib. *dngos por lta ba*, Skt. *bhāvadṛṣṭi*. Scherrer-Schaub (*Yuktiṣaṣṭikāvṛtti*, 137 n. 99) points out that this Tibetan phrase translates a more explicit compound in the PPMMV (La Vallée Poussin, *Madhyamakavṛttiḥ*, 422): *bhāva-sadbhāva-dṛṣti*.

64 Tib. *nye bar bstan*, Skt. **upadiśati*.

65 Gyaltsap (*ṭīkka*, 10b.5) reads: "Those who do not see reality...."

66 Skt. *manyante*, Tib. *rlom sems*.

67 Tib. *bde bar rtogs pa*, Skt. **sukhādhigama* or **sukhāvabodha*.

68 Tib. *mngon par chags pa*, Skt. **abhiṣvaṅga*. Chandrakīrti here articulates Nāgārjuna's concern that nirvāṇa, when misconstrued as reified nothingness, can reinforce misknowledge just as much as reifications of being.

absence, [thinking,] "What thing's absence is nirvāṇa imagined to be?" and thus, abiding in the insight into reality, they become noble.

ii. [Response:] It is not taught for the noble ones

(1) [The life-cycle and nirvana] are not seen by the noble ones

5cd. Those who do see reality[69] do not presume
Either a life-cycle or a nirvāṇa.

The intent of this statement is that the noble ones—those who are distinguished by realizing things without perceiving an intrinsic reality—neither construct nor perceive that dichotomy. Consequently, through indicating that "both the world and nirvāṇa exist [only] on the strength of the constructions of naïve individuals," any claim that "both being and nothingness exist [because the life-cycle and nirvāṇa exist]" is unreasonable.

[To this, the Buddhist Realists reply:] "If both the world and nirvāṇa were not taught for [the sake of] the noble, how is it possible that these were presented as [the first and third of] the four noble truths? If these [first and third noble truths] are truths for the noble, then it is proper to refer to them as noble truths; but if they apply to those who are not [yet] noble, then it is improper to refer to them as such."

[Let me respond with a question:] If that were so, how could it be proper to speak of the "eight noble expressions?" These expressions are not for the noble *per se*, but are for the worldly since they are tainted. Consequently, even regarding mundane things, which are not presented to change one's nature from its actual [tainted] condition may also be called "noble."[70]

Alternatively, the truths by which one becomes noble [may be called] "noble truths."[71] Anything perceivable is perceived in [one of] two modes: mistaken or unmistaken. Mistaken [perception] is that which grasps [painful]

---

[69] Gyaltsap (*ṭīkka*, 11a.3) reads: "Those who see reality…."

[70] Referring to the "eight noble [verbal] expressions" (Tib. *'phags pa'i tha snyad brgyad*, Skt. *āryā aṣṭau vyavahārāḥ*) that comply with the vow to avoid verbal misconduct; cf. AK, ad k. 4.74 (Pradhan, 245; tr. La Vallée Poussin, *L'Abhidharmakośa*, III, 159–160).

[71] The Peking and Snar-thang redactions of the YṢV contain an extra sentence here: "Alternatively, being truths that are taught by the noble, [they may be called] 'noble truths'."

things as pleasant, and so forth,[72] since even conventionally things do not have such a nature. Unmistaken [perception] is of suffering, and so forth, since things conventionally have such a nature. Just like the expression "noble expressions" was applied in such [a context], just so is the expression "noble truths."

[Here, the Buddhist Realist may object: "Then] is even nirvāṇa a conventional truth?"

It is just so! Since "cyclic life" is a construction, "nirvāṇa" is also a construction, because they both exist as mundane expressions.[73] Thus, it was proclaimed in the *Mother of Buddhas*, [the *Transcendent Wisdom Sūtras*:]

> [Śāriputra said:] "Venerable Subhūti, do you claim that even nirvāṇa is like an illusion, like a dream?" [Subhūti replied:] "Śāriputra, even if there were a truth that surpasses nirvāṇa, I would say of it, 'This too is like an illusion.'"[74]

If that [nirvāṇa] were not dependent upon the mental construction of cyclic life, it would not be like an illusion. Since [it is dependent, however], even nirvāṇa is considered to be a conventional truth.

"If that is so," [the Buddhist Realist might object,] "how do you explain pronouncements [by the Buddha] such as, 'Nirvāṇa is the ultimate truth?'"

My explanation is that it is called "ultimate truth" by worldly convention, because its nature is non-deceptive with respect to the world. Anything created[75] is deceptive and is not ultimate truth. [Hence, the other]

---

[72] Tib. *bde bar la sogs pa = gtsang bde rtag bdag*, that is, the four errors (*viparyāsa*) of mistaking the impure for the pure (*aśuci / śuci*), the painful for the pleasant (*duḥkha / sukha*), the impermanent for the permanent (*anitya / nitya*), and the selfless as having a self (*anātman / ātman*). Cf. Gyaltsap (*ṭīkka*, 11b.1–.3).

[73] Tib. *'jig rten gyi tha snyad*, Skt. **loka-vyavahāra*.

[74] A close parallel to this passage occurs in chapter two of the ASPP:

> Those Devaputras said, "O Noble Subhūti, even nirvāṇa is like an illusion, like a dream!?!"
>
> The Venerable Subhūti responded, "O Devaputras, even if there were another noble truth that was even more exceptional than nirvāṇa, I would say, 'This too is like an illusion, like a dream.'"

[75] Skt. *saṁskṛta*, Tib. *'dus byed*.

three [noble] truths are presented as conventional truths, since a characteristic of created [things] is to deceive the naïve by appearing to exist intrinsically. Otherwise, why would the Lord Buddha have announced, "O monks, non-deceptive in nature, nirvāṇa is the sole, supreme truth?" Thus, nirvāṇa is not like the created [things] that deceive the naïve with false appearances; it never appears to the naïve as created things do—with a created nature—because it remains in its nature of permanent non-creation.[76] Consequently, [the truth of] nirvāṇa is explained as "ultimate truth" through worldly convention, because it always remains in its nature of transcending suffering.

[Hence,] in order to establish that the noble, those who dwell in the vision of the ultimate, do not perceive either a cyclic life or a nirvāṇa, [Nāgārjuna] stated "those who do see reality do not presume either a cyclic life or a nirvāṇa."

(2) The correctness of that

Since [the Buddhist Realist] might inquire, "Why do the noble who dwell in the vision of the ultimate not perceive either cyclic life or the ultimate?" [Nāgārjuna explained] thus:

6ab. Of the two, existence and nirvāṇa,
Neither is known to exist [intrinsically];

[We accept that embodied] existence is the five aggregates. Yet, because of their relativity, these [aggregates themselves] lack intrinsic objectivity, just like reflections. Since they do not [intrinsically] exist, and their nothingness certainly does not [intrinsically] exist; therefore [Nāgārjuna] explains, "Neither of the two exists." Seeing their [intrinsic] non-existence is not seeing reality, because that would entail the absurdity that even persons with eye disease see reality [by not seeing anything at all].[77] The noble do see reality, while those who see [nirvāṇa as] an intrinsic non-existence are [simply] unfit.

---

[76] Nirvāṇa is categorized among the four uncreated elements (*asaṁskṛtadharma*) in the classical Abhidharma scheme.

[77] Tib. *rab rib can*, Skt. *taimirika*. Used by Chandrakīrti to refer to disorders like that of cataract sufferers whose visual defects are projected into the visual field as hairs. The point of the example is that just as "hairs" falling across one's visual field are known to be utterly non-existent, this would absurdly qualify as a comparable realization.

b. It is not correct to posit nirvana with respect to the two [extremes]

i. It is not correct that one obtains nirvana by grasping at it

(1) The brief indication

[To this, the Buddhist Realist] may object: "If nirvāṇa were nothing at all, how can one account for the expression, 'noble individuals attain nirvāṇa?'"

[Anticipating this, Nāgārjuna] stated:

> **6cd. The full understanding[78] of existence**
> **Is what is called "nirvāṇa."**

Such full understanding does not perceive any [real] absence of the intrinsically objective creation of existence, as the reality of existence; it just has the nature of the complete eradication of all signs. It is called "nirvāṇa" in accordance with conventional truth,[79] and must be understood as lacking any intrinsically objective status whatsoever. Just as [in the Traditionist view] one cannot present impermanence—whose insubstantial nature lacks status—as intrinsically objectively established,[80] without referring to [impermanent] things, just so [in the Centrist view] it is taught that "the wise also cannot conceive of anything whatsoever called 'nirvāṇa,' that has an intrinsically real status, without referring to [conventional] things—which are like a magician's illusion."

(2) The extensive explanation

[Hence, Nāgārjuna] stated:

> **7. [The naïve] imagine cessation**
> **As the annihilation of an originated being;[81]**
> **While the wise understand it**
> **As like the ceasing of a magical illusion.[82]**

---

[78] Skt. *parijñāna*, Tib. *yongs su shes pa*.

[79] Cf. Thurman, *Essence*, 368 n. 9.

[80] Tib. *ngo bo nyid kyis yongs su 'grub pa*, Skt. *pariniṣpanna-svabhāva*.

[81] Tib. *dngos po byung ba*, Skt. *utpadabhāva*, refers to the twelve-fold dependent origination (*dvādaśaṅga-pratītyasamutpāda*) of the continuum of aggregates (*skandhasaṁtāna*).

[82] Tib. *sgyu ma byas pa'i 'gog pa*, Skt. *māyākṛtaka nirodha*.

Thus, since the impermanence of a created thing is established [only] by that [thing's] becoming non-existent, it has no intrinsically objective status. If it were to have such [status], it would be seen as an intrinsic reality independent of [any created] thing. Similarly, the noble, as well, do not perceive anything whatsoever established in an intrinsically real way that can be called "cessation," for when analyzed with wisdom, that which is unproduced in any intrinsically real way and lacking in objectivity—like a magically fabricated elephant—is [called] "nirvāṇa." Furthermore, since nirvāṇa is established in dependence on that [life-cycle] which is glossed as "like a magician's illusion," it is established, as is impermanence, by worldly convention. Thereby, so-called "cyclic life" and "transcendent nirvāṇa" both lack intrinsically objective status. Therefore, the thorough knowledge of the reality of things, by just that lack of objective perception, should be recognized, without a doubt, as "nirvāṇa."

ii. It is not correct that one obtains nirvana by any other means

(1) In brief

Therefore likewise [Nāgārjuna stated]:

8. If cessation happens through annihilation,
Not by fully understanding creations,
Who would be there to experience it?
How could there be such a destroyed [subject]?

You think that the non-creation [of suffering], when all things are no longer perceived, like [vanished] magical creations, is not nirvāṇa, but rather that nirvāṇa is the subsequent non-creation of anything whatsoever, once such things as form, and so on, no longer possess substantial intrinsic identities, substantial natures, causes, conditions, actions, and addictions. If that were to be the case, then nirvāṇa would occur through the process of severing the continuum, by destroying an intrinsically natural identity of something, [and] it could not be [something that came about] through thoroughly understanding the created.

[To this, the Buddhist Realist] may object, "Although we accept precisely this [nirvāṇa by destruction], we are without fault," but this [objection] is also incorrect.

It is like this: if those who see reality necessarily directly experience cessation, [from your perspective] without the aggregates having ceased, just such a cessation could not exist. [Alternatively,] when [the aggregates] have ceased, since there would be no one there at all, who would directly experience that cessation? Since some person, such as the noble Śāriputra, exists at the time of seeing reality as long as there is a continuum of aggregates, it is reasonable to say "that cessation is directly experienced."

[Someone may also object:] "At that time, what would that [person] be seeing in order to have a direct experience?"[83]

[Let me] explain. Although [the object of this insight] is grasped non-perceptually, it is [nevertheless] designated as "directly experienced" through the knowledge[84] of that [object obtained] by a consciousness. Others, moreover, [such as the followers of Dignāga,] teach as direct experience even other [mental] consciousnesses perceiving "blue," and so forth, because of their correspondence with the particular characteristics of the object. Here, also, even though [that which is cognized, a cessation, only] corresponds with that [purely negative object, nirvāṇa], there is no contradiction in calling this [experience] a "direct experience."

[To this, the objector might respond:] "Since you claim that the intrinsic identity[85] of a thing [such as its non-creation] in the so-called 'direct experience of the cessation of suffering' is the object of [that] direct experience, then such a non-existent thing can not possibly be known by a directly perceiving consciousness. Furthermore, if you do not claim the cessation of suffering to be [something] directly perceived, then how does the truth of cessation come to be directly perceived through [merely] understanding [that] cessation? For the mere non-creation of suffering is not suitable as the essence of a thing."

---

[83] Tib. *mngon sum du 'gyur*, aligns with the Skt. *pratyakṣa* in the Tibetan translation of Dharmottara's *Nyāyabindu-ṭīka* (ad ks. 2.27–30) in the context of Dharmakīrti's discussion of "non-perception of a nature" (*svabhāvānupalabdhi*). The question being asked here—as in Dharmakīrti's text—the manner in which a mere absence can be said to be "directly perceived," is analogous to similar debates seen in the second chapter (*svārthānumāṇa*) of Dignāga's *Pramāṇasamuccaya*.

[84] Tib. *rnam par rig pa*, Skt. *vijñapti*. As noted by Scherrer-Schaub (*Yuktiṣaṣṭikāvṛtti*, 152 n. 150), this is the definition of a consciousness given by Vasubandhu in the AK ad k. 1.16 (Pradhan, 11; La Vallée Poussin, *L'Abhidharmakośa*, I, 30–31): [The root text reads:] "Consciousness is the discernment of discrete [objects]." The perception and knowledge of objects is what is called "the aggregate of consciousness."

[85] Tib. *rang gi mtshan nyid*, Skt. *svalakṣaṇa*.

[We reply:] Someone who does not accept that the mere non-creation of suffering is cessation, however, is unable to point to an intrinsically identifiable cessation that would be a viable alternative[86] to the mere non-creation of suffering. If, [further, you] claim that an undefiled cognition of cessation is a direct experience, then since this too would be just like that [i.e., a cognition that conforms to its negative object], then [by your own argument] this would not be a direct experience [either]. If the understanding of cessation were a direct experience, then at that moment [of direct experience], the cessation that is determined[87] by that [consciousness] would thereby instantly cease as well. For, according to your own treatises on the nature of direct experience, if the [general] cognition of "pot"[88] is not accepted as direct experience, then, just as [the cognition of such] a "pot" would not be suitable as a direct experience, like [the cognition of characteristics] such as "blue," so would [the cognition of] a cessation also not be. [Hence,] any kind of experience of the mere object—[even] without presumption of being a singular [object], unmixed with any kind of conceptual understanding, and produced from the teaching of the Master of Yogin/īs[89]—even that would not be tenable as cessation.[90]

---

[86] Tib. *don gzhan,* Skt. *arthāntara.*

[87] Tib. *yongs su bcad,* Skt. *paricchinna.* This would appear to be a direct reference to the definition of validating cognitions (*pramāṇa; tshad ma*) reflected in later works such as Dharmakīrti's *Ascertainment of Validating Cognitions* (D 4211, f. 152a.4): *'di dag gis don yongs su bcad nas 'jug pa na don bya ba la bslu ba med pa'i phyir ro //* "[Direct perception and inference are validating cognitions] because when [someone's consciousness] engages [an object], having determined it by means of these, [it] is non-deceptive with respect to its purpose."

[88] Tib. *ko bum pa.*

[89] Tib. *rnal byor pa rnams kyi bla ma,* i.e., the Buddha. We add the feminine option here following the Paninian rule that the masculine stands for both genders, just as "man" in English supposedly includes women.

[90] Gyaltsap summarizes this debate highlighting the objector's confusion of the difference between "explicit realization" (*dngos su rtogs*) and "direct realization" (*mngon sum du rtogs*). He states (f. 13a.5–.6): "[An objector claims] 'There is no fault in our [position], since the noble Śāriputra and others directly realize intrinsically uncreated cessations.' This also is incorrect as the direct perception of cessation, since having directly realized the aggregates—the basis of negation—it is incorrect [to say] that [their] cessation is implicitly realized, since, in this context, the aggregates are not claimed to be such. [Similarly,] it is incorrect [to say] that [they] are explicitly realized, since we assert a directly perceiving consciousness to be that which possesses the actual characterized object."

[Now, someone may] object: "Regarding any existent thing[91] with particular characteristics, it is well known that, when one contemplates its universal characteristics, an intuition born of contemplating[92] [it] gradually develops. And since any thing which is the held object of a non-conceptual intuition[93] is also something free from reification, [it is] only a specifically characterized [thing].[94] Just so, when one understands impermanence, one understands merely that thing devoid of past and future aspects. Consequently, if you say that that [realization of cessation] is itself a direct experience, because that too is a specifically characterized object, just as with a consciousness perceiving mere blue, and so forth, then since specifically and universally characterized [things][95] are claimed to be different when analyzed, [cessation] cannot be posited as a specifically characterized object —being a thing that is achieved through the practice of meditating on a generally characterized aspect. Because it is utterly absurd,[96] your argument lacks any bearing on reality!"

[We respond that] although it is just as [you say], with regard to cessation, since there is not even the slightest thing whose essence *is* the elimination of suffering, how could there ever be a direct experience that was a [specifically characterized] cognition of cessation? Furthermore, given the textual pronouncement, "the cognition that suffering is not being created is a direct experience," it is impossible for the cognition of such an entity that lacks creation to be produced [in the same manner] as [a cognition of something] created. Hence, there can be no doubt [that such a cognition of cessation] would be achieved in the mode of the uncreated. Thus, if, in accordance with its perceived [object], the cognition as well is uncreated, then it is suitable for the cognition to be exactly in accordance with its perceived [object].

---

[91] Tib. *dngos por yod pa*, Skt. **vāstava*.

[92] The hypothetical objector here refers to the meditative practice of developing yogic direct perception through contemplating the universal properties (*sāmānyalakṣaṇa*) of an object.

[93] Tib. *rnam par mi rtog pa'i ye shes*, Skt. *nirvikalpajñāna*.

[94] Tib. *rang gi mtshan nyid*.

[95] Tib. *rang gi msthan nyid dang spyis yi mtshan nyid*, Skt. *svalakṣaṇa sāmānyalakṣaṇaśca*.

[96] Tib. *ha cang thal bar 'gyur pa'i phyir*, Skt. *atiprasaṅgāt*.

Even in mundane [parlance], one calls such types [of cognition], "direct experience." For instance, when surveying from a great distance the country in the region before him, a traveler sees something as if filled with abundant, pure [water], and wants to cross it. Yet from his experience, [thinking] he will not be able to, and being afraid, he asks a farmer who comes from the region, "Just how [expansive] is this water?" That [farmer] may say to him, "Where is this water? This resembles water but it is a mirage. If you don't believe my words about it, go there and look—*you will directly experience [the truth of] my words*." Just as, by indicating the absence of water, one says "[you will] directly experience" to the traveler, likewise the world also conventionally designates absences and non-perceptions[97] as "directly experienced." Because of this, there is no contradiction with the truth of worldly conventions in calling the cognition of non-perceptions [such as cessations] a "direct experience." [Thus,] since such a cognition—that which is determinate in accordance with its object, a functioning thing, through any means whatsoever—is called a "direct experience of that," the scriptural reference [quoted above] is correct.

(2) Extensive explanation

(a) That it is not correct for [nirvana] with remainder

Now, [returning to the experience of cessation, itself,] since, in the event of the severing of the continuum of the aggregates, there would be no one at all, [Nāgārjuna asked,] "Who would there be to experience that cessation directly?" [Moreover,] that [view] would invalidate any such cognition of the end of life in such pronouncements as, "my life is finished; I have attained perfect conduct; I have done what must be done; I will know no existence beyond this one."[98] If there were no creation of anything whatsoever, it would preclude saying "things are now terminated." It would also [preclude] saying, "I will not be born again" since, as long as there is creation of this life in the continuum of aggregates driven by causes and conditions, one could never realize such a cessation.

---

[97] Tib. *mi dmigs*, Skt. *anupalabdhi*.

[98] Scherrer-Schaub (*Yuktiṣaṣṭikāvṛtti*, 160 n. 181) lists other Skt. and Pāli citations, noting that this pronouncement from the night of the Buddha's attainment of enlightenment is often cited as a formula for the Arhat's realization.

To this, [the Buddhist Realist] might object, "The implications of the words of the [Buddha's] pronouncement, 'I will not know another existence than this,' would be that he uttered that statement because he did not see his future births." However, if one holds to this view as well, then [such as] this [would follow]:

9ab. [You claim:] "If the aggregates have not ceased,
Though addictions cease, there is no nirvāṇa."

In scripture it is said, "When the aggregates cease, [that is] nirvāṇa"; this occurs in [the passage]:

> The utter abandonment of these sufferings, [their] complete dispersal, purification, eradication, detachment from desire, cessation, pacification and disappearance, dissociation from any other suffering, and non-production of any further suffering—anything that is these very things—is peace, that is sublime. It is like this: completely dispensing with all aggregates, the eradication of [cyclic] existence, detachment from desire, [and] cessation [are] nirvāṇa.[99]

[To respond:] In this scripture, the words "these sufferings" pertain to the sufferings of the present [life] alone, [and that is also what] is referred to in the words "utter abandonment" up to "disappearance." The passage beginning with "dissociation from any further suffering" up to "nirvāṇa" indicates the suffering in the future. Therefore in this [context] also, the words "my life is finished" indicate the non-creation of [suffering within] this present life; while, the expression "I will not know another birth" refers to the ascertainment of [the non-creation of] suffering in the future. Thus, since at that time [when the Buddha uttered both of those pronounce-

---

[99] Chandrakīrti appears to be quoting a sūtra also cited by Vasubandhu (AK ad k. 2.55; Pradhan, 93–94; La Vallée Poussin, *L'Abhidharmakośa*, I, 284–285) in his presentation of nirvāṇa as "mere non-existence" (*abhāva-mātra*). Scherrer-Schaub (*Yuktiṣaṣṭikāvṛtti*, 162 n. 183) notes that this passage and Chandrakīrti's interpretation of it are cited by Tsong Khapa in his commentary on Chandrakīrti's MA (ad k. 1.8d; *dbu ma 'jug pa rnam bshad dgongs pa rab gsal*, f. 36a.3–.6) and Jamyang Shepa's sub-commentary, which identifies it merely as "a Hīnayāna sūtra" (*theg dman pa'i mdo*). La Vallée Poussin (*L'Abhidharmakośa*, 284–285 n. 4) identifies the sūtra source as *Saṁyukta Nikāya*, 13, 5, though notes that a variation on this quote appears in the *Mahāvastu* (ii, 285).

ments], his aggregates had not ceased, [according to your view,] neither that [cessation] nor even nirvāṇa were seen. [Furthermore,] if, at that moment when he saw the non-creation of suffering, he came to the cessation of suffering through not observing its creation, then because you others do not accept this [perspective, then in your view, the Buddha] would not have been in nirvāṇa!

(b) That it is not correct for [nirvana] without remainder

[To this, the Buddhist Realist might further object:] "Why then did the Lord Buddha proclaim nirvāṇa as twofold—with the remainder of aggregates and without the remainder of aggregates? [Nirvāṇa] with the remainder of one's aggregates is no more than just the aggregates; it is liberation from the bonds of the addictions. [Nirvāṇa] without the remainder of the aggregates is defined as the severing of the continuum of those aggregates. In nirvāṇa with remainder one has abandoned the bonds [of the addictions of] desire, and so forth. Still, if you think that is unacceptable as nirvāṇa, then how do you explain the statement in *The Recitation Scripture*:[100] 'Having directly perceived nirvāṇa, Śāriputra explained it'? Now if you say '[We] are certain that this pronouncement was made in terms of [Śāriputra's] direct experience of the absence of the addictions, but this is not separation from the aggregates,' then if you hold that to be the case, you cannot explain statements such as 'he has dispensed with and utterly abandoned this suffering.'"

[We respond:] The passage from the words "utter abandonment of the addicted [sufferings]" up to "disappearance" are correct. It is clear that the assertion of "suffering" subsumes the five appropriative aggregates. Here, "suffering," "origin [of suffering]," "the world," and so on, are given as formulations[101] of the five appropriative aggregates. Although you hold these words as given, you take the terms of the expression in general to have

---

[100] Tib. *rjes bzlas mdo sde*, Skt. **anujalp[it]a-sūtra*. Scherrer-Schaub (*Yuktiṣaṣṭikāvṛtti*, 163 n. 188) finds this passage in Jamyang Shepa (*dbu ma 'jug pa'i mtha' dpyod*, f. 343.4–.6) who cites the quote and commentary that Chandrakīrti gives, and who identifies it merely as "a Sautrāntika Sūtra." Although Scherrer-Schaub has also identified a Pāli source (*Saṁyutta Nikāya* V, iv, 50; PTS, V, 226.4–.7) close to that quoted here, no exact citation has been found that directly compares with Chandrakīrti's given quote.

[101] Tib. *rnam grangs*.

a usage as in a specific sense.[102] Just so, when you say "suffering" in reference to those very addicted [sufferings], there is no reasonable evidence for connecting it with any [specific] meaning whatsoever; hence, when [you do that], then in the context of [discussing] the experience of the non-creation of the very nature of the five appropriative aggregates, it is inappropriate for you to claim "we are utilizing the general term in a specific sense."

Furthermore, if one does not accept that this [general] sense [applies] in [the case when] dependence on the aggregates is not relinquished, then there could be no nirvāṇa [even with remainder, much less without,] despite the criterion of the non-creation of the addictions. For if one does not accept the reality of the non-creation of suffering at that moment as nirvāṇa, then, even though one may be free from addictions—since bonds of desire, and so forth, have been interrupted—still, one would see that the cause of the futile view of the impermanent aggregates [as "I" and "mine"][103] exists. Because seeing that gives rise to [the addictions] of desire, and so forth, therefore there would be no attainment of any such liberation at all. Consequently, it is irrational to assert that one is liberated under such circumstances.

[And so, regarding] the aggregates, [Nāgārjuna states the absurd consequence that]

9cd. When here [you] have [intrinsically] ceased,
Only then, [absurdly,] will [you] be freed.

[which] is incorrect. Those who perceive the aggregates [as intrinsically real] could not terminate the addictions, which arise from that cause, nor could they possibly terminate their aggregates. Since those addictions would exist, and those actions arisen from that cause would project their evolutionary force, the continuum of births produced from causal addictions and

---

[102] Tib. *phyogs gcig.*

[103] Tib. *'jig tshogs la lta ba,* Skt. *satkāya-dṛsti.* This false view (*log lta = mithyā-dṛṣṭi*) of the decaying mass or body as real, is the reason that a being first attaches itself to a reification of the body. Traditionally, these are enumerated as twenty, since the self may be viewed in four relations to each of the five mind-body aggregates, i.e., as an identical or distinct owner, agent or content, thus, the body may be owned by an identical self (*rūpaṁ ātmā svāmivat*), it may be the ornament of such a self (*rūpavān ātmā alaṁkāravat*), it may be the servant of such a self (*ātmīyaṁ rūpaṁ bhṛtyavat*), or it may be its inhabitant (*rūpe ātmā bhajanavat*). Cf. La Vallée Poussin, *L'Abhidharmakośa*, IV, 15ff.

evolutionary actions would never reach a final limit; and therefore their liberation would not be possible, its nature being the termination of the aggregates.

Consequently, the insight into one's association with future aggregates expressed [in pronouncements such] as "life is over" would also be impossible, hence [Nāgārjuna's] question, "How could there be such a destroyed [subject]?"

iii. Correctness with respect to our own [position]

(1) Why created things are not seen by a noble's meditative equipoise

Having thereby demonstrated the complete impossibility of liberation for the advocate of intrinsically real [things][104] by the reasonings already expressed, [Nāgārjuna] made this statement to demonstrate the possibility of liberation for the advocate of voidness:

10. When one discerns with precise intuition
What occurs conditioned by misknowledge,
One does not experience anything,
Whether created or ceased.

In the phrase "What occurs conditioned by misknowledge," "misknowledge" [refers to] the [prime] condition of the sequence of [relativity seen in] the direct experience of objects such as creations and consciousnesses, and so forth.[105]

If objects such as creations, which arise conditioned by misknowledge, were intrinsically established, they could not depend on [conditions such as] misknowledge, since they would be established in terms of their intrinsic identity. [In that case, for example] intrinsically identifiable things

---

[104] Tib. *ngo bo nyid du smra ba*, Skt. **svarūpāstivādin* or **svabhāvāstivādin*. Scherrer-Schaub (*Yuktiṣaṣṭikāvṛtti*, 167 n. 203) points out that this term refers to the realism of the Analyst and Traditionist, for whom nirvāṇa exists as a reified something (*bhāva*) and nothing (*abhāva*).

[105] Gyaltsap comments: "Since the [other] eleven [links of dependent origination of] creations, and so forth, have misknowledge as a condition in things and [one's own] commitment, [they are said] to possess the condition of ignorance. Hence, in the face of seeing the arisal from this [condition of misknowledge] with a correct, noble intuition, creations are not perceived with any elaboration whatsoever—being beginninglessly created and endlessly ceased." (See critical edition, p. 280 n. 215).

—such as a pot—would be perceived perfectly clearly in terms of their essential nature, when the darkness of the obstructions no longer existed. Something imagined by someone with an eye disease, because of particular conditions, is cognized as [falling] hairs, and so forth, and yet has no essential nature, [and] does not appear to those with perfectly clear vision. Just so, intrinsically established things which are imagined in just such [a manner, like falling hairs], cannot be established as existing like real hairs, and so forth.

Similarly, if these creations, and so forth, were intrinsically established, then even noble individuals, whose correct intuition comes from determining the meaning of truth, would see their intrinsic identity as inviolable, and would perceive things such as a pot [as existing] in accordance with its appearance. If it were reasonable for them to be such objects, there would be no [scriptural] statements like "since misknowledge has ceased, emotions have ceased." Yet since, when perfect insight dawns, like the hairs seen by those with eye disease, an intrinsic identity does not appear, intrinsically identifiable existence cannot be established.

Hence, when things arisen from the condition of misknowledge—creations, and so forth—are analyzed [by those] with accurate intuition, like those with disease-free eyes, at that time of precise intuition, the production and destruction of creations, and so forth, are definitely not seen, just as the hairs seen by those with an eye disease, and so forth, [are not seen by the unafflicted].

(2) Thatness as the referent of the conventional expression "the object of meditation is accomplished"

(a) The actual presentation

Hence, when an intuition that does not perceive the [intrinsically real] creation and destruction of any dependently arisen [things arises]:

11ab. That is immediate nirvāṇa,
And that very thing is "attaining the goal."

In this very life, when the yogin/ī [attains] the intuitive wisdom which does not perceive any [real] things, that reality is immediate nirvāṇa. And just the attainment of that goal is precisely what is referred to as "attaining the goal." The precise occasion of [the arisal of] the wisdom that does not perceive creation and cessation should be known as the "the immediate nirvāṇa," and "the attaining of the goal." Thus, in scripture when it says "O monks, having [attained] immediate nirvāṇa, the noble Śāriputra taught this discourse," you should recognize that to be immediate nirvāṇa [in this life]. [Hence,] the statements "life is over," "the pure life has been led," "the goal has been reached," and "I will know no other life beyond this" should also be understood as this very same "attaining the goal"; that is, [the realization of] the uncreatedness and unceasedness of relativities.

[Moreover,] questioning this[106] forsakes precisely this characteristic of not perceiving the creation and cessation of relativities, for if one imagines[107] that things as perceived have some sort of intrinsically identifiable objectivity,[108] since these things would be mutually distinct entities, being ascertained as such, they would necessarily be determinable[109] [only] as individual particulars.[110] For [in such a view] one cannot determine the actuality of a thing through knowing some other actuality, just as one cannot determine [the color] yellow by knowing something blue.

(b) Showing that the realized truth realm lacks variety of forms

Moreover:

11cd. If, after that insight into the truth,
One discover any particular here,

12. Imagining any sort of creation,
In anything, however subtle,
Such an unwise individual
Does not see the meaning of "conditioned arisal."

---

[106] Tib. *ci ste zhes pa 'di.* Scherrer-Schaub (*Yuktiṣaṣṭikāvṛtti,* 172 n. 225) finds this opening problematic, suggesting the *ci ste* is a copyist's error. It is also possible that it translates a variant of the conditional, such as *yadyapi,* in which case it can be linked with the correlative *na* = *atha* in the subsequent line.

[107] Tib. *yongs su rtogs pa,* Skt. *parikalpa.*

[108] Tib. *rang gi mtshan nyid kyi ngo bo.*

[109] Tib. *yongs su bcad.* This would appear to be yet another direct reference to the definition of validating cognitions (*pramāṇa; tshad ma*).

[110] Tib. *bye brag,* Skt. *viśeṣa.*

Here, the term "truth"[111] refers to nirvāṇa, which is nothing other than the reality of relativity. Hence, in the scriptures one finds the pronouncement, "Whoever sees relativity sees the truth."[112] Insight into the truth is any insight which determines relativity to be indistinguishable[113] in nature from nirvāṇa. One who has [genuine] insight into the truth [by definition] must realize the meaning of relativity. Furthermore, it is stated in the treatise, [the *Fundamental Verses* of Nāgārjuna]:

> Whatever is relatively existent,
> That is naturally at peace;
> Hence, both the being created and
> The creating itself are at peace.[114]

Here, [Nāgārjuna] proclaims the meaning of relativity: whatever is [relatively] created and the creating, [both] are objectively uncreated. Hence, since suffering is also a relativity, it is intrinsically uncreated. That which is objectively uncreated in fact is transcendent nirvāṇa, since both [relativity and nirvāṇa] are equally uncreated. Thus, he explains [later in the *Fundamental Verses*]:

> Nirvāṇa lacks any distinction
> Whatsoever from cyclic life;
> And cyclic life lacks any distinction
> Whatsoever from nirvāṇa.
>
> The limit of nirvāṇa
> Is also the limit of cyclic life;
> Hence, between the two one finds
> Not even the subtlest distinction.[115]

---

[111] Tib. *chos*, Skt. *dharma*, here an abbreviation for *dṛṣṭadharmanirvāṇa*.

[112] As noted by Scherrer-Schaub (*Yuktiṣaṣṭikāvṛtti*, 173 n. 231), this is the first half of a frequently cited passage from the *Śālistambha-sūtra*.

[113] Tib. *tha mi dad pa*.

[114] MMK, 7.16.

[115] MMK, 25.19–.20.

The word "limit" means "ultimate extent"; the term "ultimate extent" means "utmost point." Since both [cyclic life and nirvāṇa] are uncreated, their ultimate nature does not fall within the scope of naïve individuals. [Nāgārjuna states that] cyclic life and nirvāṇa are both one, since both are uncreated because they are [equally] uncreated with respect to intrinsic reality.

Consequently, relativity may also be known as "truth," since it is [ultimately] indistinguishable from transcendent nirvāṇa. Since those who see it experience nirvāṇa, "Who sees relativity sees the truth." Furthermore, since the Lord Buddha is indistinguishable from the actuality of truth, "Who sees that, sees the Buddha."[116]

Thus, because true intuitive wisdom sees uncreatedness,[117] the supporting three truths[118] culminate in a single clear realization,[119] with the insight that the objective uncreatedness of relativity is also the actuality of nirvāṇa. Here, the true insight which perceives relativity is the final insight into [the truth of] suffering whose nature is to determine the [objective] non-creation and non-cessation of suffering. That [true insight] which determines the non-creation and non-cessation of actions and addictions is [final] insight into [the truth of] origination. That [true insight] which determines the non-creation and non-cessation of relativity is [final] insight into [the truth of] cessation. And as for the truth of the path also, since it is a relativity, the determination of its non-creation and non-cessation with respect to intrinsic reality is [final] knowledge of the [truth of the] path. Insofar as through knowing [the nature of] things, one sees relativity in a single instant, it is impossible for there to be any other unprecedented view to hold.

---

[116] The second half of the *Śālistambha-sūtra* quote (above).

[117] The Peking and Snar-thang redactions add "and unceasedness."

[118] Tib. *rten bden pa gsum*, Skt. *āśraya-trisatya*. Chandrakīrti here refers to the reformulation of the four truths in terms of two realities, according to which only *nirodha* = *parmārtha*, while *duḥkha*, *samudaya* and *mārga* = *saṁvṛtti*. Cf. MMK, 24.10.

[119] Tib. *mngon par rtogs gcig*, Skt. **ekābhisamaya*. Scherrer-Schaub (*Yuktiṣaṣṭikāvṛtti*, 175 n. 241) refers to the definition of the term *abhisamaya* in AK ad k. 6.2 (Pradhan, 328; La Vallée Poussin, *L'Abhidharmakośa*, IV, 122): *abhisamaya iti ko 'rthaḥ abhisaṁbodhaiṇo bodhanārthavāt*; "What is the significance of the term 'clear realization'? It means 'clear and accurate realization'."

[Here, some Individualist[120] might object:] "If that is so, why are fifteen [other] moments presented on the path of insight?"

[Let me explain.] Some [Individualist] schools[121] do not accept the fifteen [other] moments on the path of insight,[122] but assert that realization culminates in one [instant];[123] their claim and our explanation are not incompatible. Furthermore, [our explanation] is compatible even with the claim of fifteen [insight] moments, since [we assert that] those fifteen moments are defined by dividing the singular actuality of insight, to serve as an aid in teaching that [actuality] to individual disciples.

[The Individualist retorts:] "If that were the case, then [what of] the sixteenth aspect, the contemplation of [the truth of] the path? How could these other aspects of the path be presented as a [pedagogic] construction to introduce those who desire liberation to insight into reality? For, reality is no more than a single actuality."

[Let me explain.] If its distinctly discerned aspects were different entities grasped by different insights, then any aspects not yet determined would need to be determined [by subsequent insights]. If, however, in the aftermath of true insight [into reality], there were some discernable distinction in the object to be determined, then it must necessarily be determined as objectively distinct, since its experience is understood to be different. Yet if the unwise who imagine that "anything, however subtle" is objectively created do not appreciate that reality whose singular taste[124] is the objective

---

120 Gyaltsap, *ṭīkka*, f. 16a.2.

121 As Scherrer-Schaub (*Yuktiṣaṣṭikāvṛtti*, 176 n. 245) notes, not all of the eighteen Vaibhāṣika schools advocated a gradual path of insight divided into sixteen moments, but some (such as the Mahāsāṁghika) advocated complete insight in a single moment.

122 The normative "Analyst" (*Vaibhāṣika*) position presented by Vasubandhu in the AK (k. 6.26; Pradhan, 350ff.; La Vallée Poussin, *L'Abhidharmakośa*, IV, 183ff.) consists of sixteen moments divided into four moments for each "noble truth," beginning with suffering: a tolerance of the doctrinal knowledge of suffering (*duḥkhe dharmajñānakṣānti*), a tolerance of the knowledge of suffering of the desire realm (*kāmāvacare duḥkhe dharmajñānakṣānti*), a tolerance of the knowledge of the remaining suffering (*rūpārūpyāvacare duḥkhe 'nvayajñānakṣānti*) [of the form and formless realms], and subsequent knowledge of suffering (*duḥkhe 'nvayajñāna*), and so on.

123 Vasubandhu considers this perspective in AK ad k. 6.27 (Pradhan, 351ff.; La Vallée Poussin, *L'Abhidharmakośa*, IV, 185ff.).

124 Tib. *ro gcig pa'i don*, Skt. *eka-rasārtha*.

uncreatedness of relativity, what need is there to mention coarse [constituents of the world] such as earth, and so forth?

Thus, the import of relativity is an insight of singular significance,[125] the practice of gradual meditation [on which] wholly terminates misknowledge. Hence, dwelling in that intuitive wisdom which perceives the actuality of relativity is established as "immediately experienced nirvāṇa" and "having attained one's goal"; and nothing else is [so established].

(c) Others' notions untenable in the functionally conventional realm

(i) That others' positions have faults

(x) The consequence that [the life-cycle] would have a beginning

If [it really were the case] as in your scriptural system, then

13. If the monk who exhausts his addictions
Completely eliminates cyclic life,
Then why do the perfect buddhas
Not teach the beginning of such [cyclic life]?

If addictions are eliminated by intuitive wisdom, actions would [also] be eliminated and, because of the absence of these causes and conditions, there would be an interruption of the continuum of intrinsically identifiable form, and so forth, which has continued from one birth and death to another, immersed in cyclic life from beginningless time. Then in that case, since the perfect buddhas have not spoken of a beginning, one would have to identify something like an ultimate beginning of the continuum of one's aggregates, along with [some rationale like] "For reasons such as this, the victors do not define its beginning."

If you claim that the Victor did not say so because he did not know, or for some other reason, then here, since the Lord Buddha is accepted as being omniscient, it is impossible that he does not know. And as for saying that he did not state it for some other reason, that is also incorrect. For example, if you say that he didn't say so because it is beginningless, like a wheel of a chain of water buckets, then it *is* beginningless, like a wheel of a chain of water buckets and there would also be no end. Such could also be said about any other examples, such as a wheel.

---

[125] Tib. *mtshan nyid gcig shes*, Skt. *eka-lakṣaṇa-jñāna.*

By explaining "[the continuum] comes to an end," if you claim that there is an end [to your continuum], it would follow that the Lord Buddha did not know that. Since it is impossible for him to not know that, you would have to show [a reference to support] such a beginning. Even if you can't show anything, if you adhere to this [line of] reasoning, then [such a reference] remains indispensable.

(y) Establishing clarity with regard to the assertion

Therefore, [Nāgārjuna says:]

14ab. If [you claim] a beginning, then, definitely,
You are embracing an [addictive] view.

When you imagine an [intrinsic] creation, you develop a [view of the] life-cycle as having some [absolute] beginning. For it to have an [absolute] beginning, you must assert an uncaused [origin],[126] and hence adopt the quintessential mistaken view.

(ii) That our own thesis lacks faults

(x) The teaching of relativity as free from the extremes

For the advocate of relativity, there is no such fault. Whoever accepts things as dependently arisen, since they are [also] accepted as non-intrinsically created, [also] accepts that they are without beginning or end. To indicate that [a beginning or end] is unimaginable [Nāgārjuna] stated:

14cd. What beginning or end could there be
To that which arises interdependently?

Doubtless, one must accept such statements precisely as they are.

---

[126] Tib *rgyu med par smra ba*, Skt. *ahetuvāda*. This notion—causeless production and its corollary, effectless actions—is presented as the essential false view, *log par lta ba nyid* = *mithyā-dṛṣṭi*. As Scherrer-Schaub (*Yuktiṣaṣṭikāvṛtti*, 181 n. 264) notes, such is specifically identified by Vasubandhu in AK ad k. 4.78 (Pradhan, 247; La Vallée Poussin, *L'Abhidharmakośa*, III, 168): *śubhe cāśubhe ca karmāṇi yā nāstīti dṛṣṭiḥ...saiṣā sākalyena karmaphalāryāpavādikā mithyā-dṛṣṭir bhavati*; "The false view is that virtuous and non-virtuous actions do not exist...[and] the essential false view of all is that of one who denies actions and their result, the noble [individual] (*ārya*)."

(y) That if [the life-cycle] were intrinsically real it would be permanent

Otherwise, cyclic life would have an [absolute] beginning and hence be interminable. In order to show that if something were intrinsically created, since its transformation is impossible, it could only be eternal, [Nāgārjuna] stated:

15ab. How could something primordially created,
Subsequently be eliminated?

The meaning expressed here is that since it is intrinsically unchanging, it is eternal. If you assert that the nature of created things comes from nothing, then, "If [you claim] a beginning, then, definitely, you are embracing an [addictive] view." If things are created from nothing, they would in fact be created causelessly. And therefore you would develop the view of causelessness, and that also turns into the fault of the view of nihilism.[127] In this instance [Nāgārjuna replied,] "What beginning or end could there be to that which arises interdependently?" Since this [cyclic life] is intrinsically uncreated, it is because it arises interdependently.

(z) Giving examples of a lack of intrinsic reality

(1") In brief, through examples

Thus, without a doubt,

15cd. Free from initial and terminal limits,
Beings[128] appear like illusions.

Just as the elephants, horses, persons and such created by a magician through the use of illusion-performing formulas, being objectively uncreated, are perceived as elephants and such without giving rise to constructs of beginning and ending as real elephants and such, likewise things accepted as real elephants, and so on, being relatively originated, are not

---

[127] Tib. *chad par lta ba*, Skt. **ucched-dṛṣṭi*. As noted by Scherrer-Schaub (*Yuktiṣaṣṭikāvṛtti*, 183 n. 271) this is glossed by Chandrakīrti elsewhere (PPMMV ad k. 17.20; La Vallée Poussin, *Madhyamakavṛttiḥ*, 323) as: *vipākābhāve hi karmaṇa uccheda-darśanaṁ syāt*; "In the event of the non-existence of the effects of actions, the view of nihilism is entailed."

[128] Tib. *'gro ba* is ambiguous. It renders both Skt. *gati*, referring to all five or six migrations which constitute the Buddhist world, as well as Skt. *jagat*, referring to both the migrant beings and their migrations.

suited to constructs of initial and terminal limits. Such being the case, [Nāgārjuna stated,] "Free from initial and terminal limits, beings appear like illusions." Once generated, life progresses without stopping even for an instant. Since its nature is deceptive, it is like illusion; since it appears erroneously to those confused about its objectivity, it is deceptive.

(2") The actual explanation

To indicate its deceptiveness, [Nāgārjuna] stated:

16. When an illusion manifests
Or when it is dispelled,
One who knows the illusion is not confused;
One ignorant of the illusion is entranced by it.

Conditioned by a magician's spell, young women appear as well trained performers, exquisite in form and movement, with an elegant manner. Captivating with their consummate skill in seduction, they will be a source of intense pleasure like a real mate for those who are addicted to desire and ignorant of their nature. But the magician, who knows that their nature lacks any intrinsic reality that corresponds to the fantasies of the ignorant, will recognize their appearance as an unreal illusion and hence have no such confused conception of it.

(3") The explanation of the meaning

Likewise, regarding this [cyclic life], wise yogin/īs resemble the magician. [Hence, Nāgārjuna stated:]

17. One whose intellect sees existence
As similar to an illusion or mirage,
Is not deceived by [extremist] views
Of an ultimate beginning or end.

When yogin/īs see created things entirely like an illusion or a mirage, with the genius of wisdom personally realized through the genuine meditation that views the endless creations of cyclic life as resembling illusions or mirages, they do not perceive any ultimate objectivity whatever, and so are not deceived by [imagining] that things have any sort of intrinsic reality which could have an ultimate beginning or end; hence their intellects do not misperceive [life]. Therefore, regarding the path of objectivitylessness

—the journey followed by all the noble beings—those who stray from that are like people not skilled about the illusory woman.

3. Refuting the reality of the two extremes

a. Stating what is correct

i. Stating the context

18. Those who imagine that created things
Are [intrinsically] produced and destroyed,
Utterly fail to understand
The turning of the wheel of relativity.

Those[129] who make such statements as, "created things are intrinsically identifiably produced and intrinsically identifiably destroyed," and imagine things' creation and destruction in the mode of intrinsically identifiable beginning and end, completely misunderstand the wheel of relativity, which revolves like a whirling firebrand, without beginning, middle, or end.

ii. What is actually correct

(1) The general meaning

Although it is impossible for intrinsically real creations to be produced or be destroyed, those who can conceive [conventional] creation and destruction, are said to understand the wheel of relativity.

(2) The secondary meanings

(a) Refuting the extreme of [intrinsic] creation

[Here, you may inquire:] "Why do [you] say that if [someone] assumes intrinsically identifiable creation that they do not understand the meaning of relativity?" In response to that [Nāgārjuna stated]:

19. What arises, dependent upon this and that,
Is not intrinsically created;
How can you call the intrinsically
Uncreated, "created?"

---

[129] Gyaltsap merely identifies these as "the unskilled," while Scherrer-Schaub (*Yuktiṣaṣṭikāvṛtti*, 186 n. 286) identifies the target of Nāgārjuna and Chandrakīrti's critiques as the Sautrāntikas.

The expression "depending upon this and that" means "created upon this and that [set of causes and conditions]."[130] Since "this and that" in general includes everything that follows, the word "this" refers to the entirety of internal things such as misknowledge, and [the word "that" refers to all] external things such as the wind-elements, which [internal and external things respectively] serve as the causal ground for the creation of things such as [addictive] emotions and water-elements.

What is produced depending on such and such a cause, if it were to have intrinsically objective status, would come to exist absolutely and not depend upon a cause of creation at the time of its objective establishment. Yet if it lacked intrinsic reality prior to its creation, then just like a reflection, it is evident that its creation could not have objective existence. Hence [Nāgārjuna] stated "What arises, dependent upon this and that, is not intrinsically created."

[One might think:] "Why, even if creation lacks intrinsic objectivity [ultimately], that's no problem, for [some sort of conventional intrinsically identifiable] creation obviously still exists, since conventionally [we use expressions like] 'forms are created,' 'feelings are created!'"

[To this we reply:] Alas! you have doubtless strayed onto the wrong path. The wise, who rationally examine things with an impartial intellect, [conclude with Nāgārjuna] "How can you call the intrinsically uncreated, 'created'?"

[To this, some might further object:] "The intrinsic identity of earth is solidity. If one thinks that it is not intrinsically identifiably created, then one could conceive of it as being created with the intrinsic identity of [water,] fluidity. But that is impossible. How can one imagine [earth's] being created as anything else?"

[To this we reply:] Consequently, [intrinsically identifiable] creation from self or other is impossible, hence uncreatedness is established.

(b) Refuting the extreme of destruction

Thus having shown the utter impossibility of [substantial or essential] creation in relativity, now intending to demonstrate the impossibility of cessation, [Nāgārjuna] stated:

---

[130] Following Gyaltsap, *ṭīkka*, f. 22a.1.

**20. Peace through exhausting the cause
Manifests as so-called "termination";
How can you call the intrinsically
Unterminated, "terminated"?**

Once a created thing is produced, it decays; its endurance depends solely on conditions;[131] and, in the absence of sustaining conditions, it perishes. That being the case, what is perceived as "peace" in the world in fact is that nirvāṇa which is peace through terminating the causes [of suffering]. Realizing that [termination] is devoid of intrinsically objective status because it depends on the absence of sustaining conditions, and that anything whatsoever is terminated in the absence of its sustaining conditions, [Nāgārjuna] stated, "How can you call the intrinsically unterminated, 'terminated'?"

If there were to be some intrinsically real termination, it could not depend on conditions, and could not come from the complete termination of the causes of [cyclic life]. Therefore, one could reach nirvāṇa even though the manifestations of action and addiction were not yet gone. And consequently, one could be liberated without the need of effort. Moreover, it would be possible for a [well-shielded] lamp to die out without fully consuming its oil and wick! Since such is not the case, however, there is no cessation with intrinsically real status.

[To this, someone] objects: "How can it be that the complete exhaustion of oil and wick is not the cause of the lamp's dying out?"

[Let me explain.] Since, upon the wick and oil's simultaneous finish, there are no cooperative causes for a future moment of the lamp homogeneous with the lamp's last moment, its productive factors do not come into being. Hence there is no termination, though a future [moment of lamp] is not created because of the absence of productive conditions.

If one thinks in that way, that is, if the lack of conditions for the future serves as the cause of non-production, then if it does not happen that there is a lack of causes, something will doubtlessly be produced. Hence, once one entertains this view, the absence of conditions for future lives becomes the cause of not being reborn; for, if there is no lack of conditions, there will doubtless be rebirth. Thus, even uncreatedness is acceptable as [a form

131 Tib. *rkyen gyi kha na las*. Scherrer-Schaub (*Yuktiṣaṣṭikāvṛtti*, 192 n. 304) suggests that this might be "un equivalent rare de *pratyayādhina*."

of] causality; and if one asserts that there is "peace through exhausting the causes [of suffering]," then whatever that is, is called "termination."

For those who maintain that the cessation of things is causeless, their cessation cannot be dependent on such things, because it is causeless, like a flower in the sky.

[To this, the Traditionist responds:] "If, being unreal, things such as pots were not dependently arisen, then, despite their dependence on [real] things [such as clay], they could not be ascertained as a single [entity]."

[Let me explain.] Since [artifacts] are known in the world to have causes, they are not analogous [to your termination]. Alternatively, your [argument] would entail the fault that those [artifacts] do not depend on real things, like your termination.

[To this, the Traditionist further] objects: "How can you apply the term 'cause' to an absence?"

[Let me reply.] How can you apply the term "cause," even to something [intrinsically] present? At such time as when the seed is present, it cannot be recognized as the material cause of the sprout; it has served as a cause when it has become absent. For instance, compare [your] assumption that the very [moment of] consciousness which has come to pass is the antecedent condition[132] of another [moment of] consciousness. As long as the consciousness persists, it cannot be defined as being the cause of another consciousness, since two [moments of] consciousness cannot occur simultaneously; another consciousness conceived as other than either existing or not existing is [logically] impossible.

There are also some[133] who maintain, "It is incorrect to say that the antecedent cessation of the cause is the productive condition of the effect."

[Let me explain.] Since it is the case that even an absence may be a cause, it is irrational to say that the absence [of action and addiction] is unable to cause [termination].

---

[132] Tib. *de ma thag pa'i rkyen*, Skt. **samanatara-pratyaya*. In the classical Abhidharma presentation (AK ad k. 2.61; Pradhan, 98–100; La Vallée Poussin, *L'Abhidharmakośa*, I, 300–306), the mental faculty (*mana-indriya*) is identified with the antecedent condition of present moment of consciousness, that is, the moment of consciousness immediately preceding the present one within the mental continuum (*citta-saṁtāna*).

[133] Scherrer-Schaub (*Yuktiṣaṣṭikāvṛtti*, 197 n. 329) identifies Chandrakīrti's opponent here as a Traditionist (*sautrāntika*), whose realistic account of causality leads to a denial that the destruction of a cause can be the antecedent condition of its effect.

If [someone] further objects, "[Such] a cause is impossible [because it is not found] under rational investigation," [we reply that] it is not so, for the things of the world cannot be accepted as [critically] examined, but just [as presented] according to social convention. Hence, in mundane [parlance] one does refer to absence as a cause. Statements such as "Since there was no water, my crop was a failure," or "Since we had no food, my son died," refer to the absence of water and food as making the crops and child impossible. Since all social conventions[134] are without [logical] justification,[135] even the commonsense things in the world[136] must be established by social convention, not by [analytic] validation. As the absence of such things as water is [conventionally] known as a cause of losses, consequently, it is established that one may speak of "peace through exhausting the cause [of suffering]."

[Hence, Nāgārjuna] presents "termination" as bound[137] to the mere termination of the cause [of suffering]. Such a termination is impossible in a state prior to the exhaustion of [suffering's] causes; and since it only exists through their exhaustion, it has no self-sufficient objectivity. [Hence, Nāgārjuna speaks of the appropriative aggregates as] "what is not terminated in intrinsic reality." If they are not terminated objectively, independent of [the absence of] their [sustaining] causes, how else could these [aggregates] be established as "terminated?" Something which is objectively not terminated cannot [later] be established as objectively terminated, since it would be incompatible with the actuality of termination.[138]

iii. Conclusion

Therefore, since such [intrinsically identifiable] creation and cessation are not possible [either] for self-produced things or for other-produced things, the yogin/ī who critically examines relativity sees it [as naturally peaceful] just as it is. Hence, if this is rationally analyzed,

---

[134] Tib. *'jig rten pa'i tha snyad*, Skt. **laukika-vyavahāra*.

[135] Tib. *'thad pa*, Skt. **upapatti*.

[136] Tib. *'jig rten na grags pa'i don rnams*, Skt. **loka-prasiddhārthāḥ*.

[137] Tib. *nye bar bzung nas*, Skt. **upādāya*.

[138] Tib. *zad pa'i ngo no nyid*.

21ab. Thus, nothing whatsoever is created;
And nothing whatsoever will cease.

b. Eliminating [charges of] contradiction with scripture

i. [Buddha's] mention of creation and destruction as interpretable meaning

[To this, the Buddhist Realist] objects: "If both the creation and destruction [of relative things] are impossible, then why did the Lord say [the following]?

> Alas! Created things are impermanent;
> Their nature is creation and destruction;
> Once created, they arrive at cessation;
> Their pacification is bliss.[139]

If he held both creation and destruction to be non-existent, then surely he would never have taught the path of creation and destruction as an instruction leading to nirvāṇa! Since he taught that, it follows that both creation and destruction do exist."

[Let me explain.] Although the Lord did indeed make such pronouncements, he never recommended relying on the intrinsically real status of those two. Although those [two] do not exist [with intrinsic reality], he taught in conformity with this world's use of them in a relative way.

[Nāgārjuna stated:]

21cd. The path of creation and destruction
Was taught for a useful purpose.

Since the Lord taught the path of the creation and destruction with the intent of achieving a specific purpose, what was his purpose in teaching the path of creation and destruction?

ii. How to understand intrinsic unreality through creation and destruction

(1) The purpose

To indicate that, [Nāgārjuna] stated:

---

[139] Although similar statements are common in the canonical literature, the precise source of this quote remains unidentified.

**22. By knowing creation, you know destruction;
By knowing destruction, you know impermanence.
By knowing how to enter impermanence,
You eventually come to realize the truth.**[140]

Since attachment to [outer and inner] creations stands as an obstruction on the road that leads to the city of nirvāṇa, the Lord explained the path of creation and destruction to certain individuals as an antidote to that [attachment]. If one asks, "How is it such [an antidote]?" Just so, he stated, "by knowing creation, you know destruction," since creation is the root of destruction; [then] "by knowing destruction" [you] realize that destruction and impermanence are the same thing. Living amid the blaze of impermanence [anywhere] within the three realms[141] as if trapped inside a burning house, one doubtless thirsts for escape. And since understanding the reality of relativity—uncreated and unceased—brings sure release, one who [contemplates that path of creation and destruction] realizes the truth known as "profound, supreme, transcendent nirvāṇa."

Therefore, [regarding] those endowed with the highest intelligence, through following the sequence of creation and destruction in such a manner,

(2) The benefits

**23. Those who develop understanding
Of [profound] relativity,
Abandoning creation and destruction,
Cross the ocean of existence with its views.**

Since [when one knows relativity] there is no [intrinsic] creation, one is free from substantivist views. Since there is no destruction, one is free from nihilistic views. Since, in the absence of creation and destruction, there is no intrinsic identity, one does not develop absolutistic views. Thus, when one does not perceive creation and destruction within relativity, one can "cross the ocean of existence with its views." The absolutist views themselves con-

140 These verses (ks. 21cd–23) are cited by Tsong Khapa (*sngag rim chen mo*, P. 6210, f. 7a.8–b.1) to answer precisely the same hypothetical question.

141 Tib. *sa gsum*, Skt. **tri-bhūmi*. Following Scherrer-Schaub's suggestion (*Yuktiṣaṣṭikāvṛtti*, 205 n. 350) that this should be taken as synonymous with *traidhātuka*.

stitute the ocean of existence, as it is just the streams of views. Those who strive toward voidness doubtless will cross that [ocean] on the great vessel of the vision of voidness.

iii. Showing how the fanatical will not understand [the truth]

Those who are ruined by a [mistaken] view of voidness doubtless will not be able to understand relativity without falling to the two extremes of creation and destruction. [Hence, Nāgārjuna said:]

24. Alienated beings,[142] who hold self [as] real,
Mistake existence and non-existence.
Thus flawed, they are driven by addictions,
And [hence] are deceived by their own minds.

They are "alienated beings" because they are alienated [from reality], due to their addictions and evolutionary actions. Those who insist upon an enduring self in things, whether they maintain a real [personal] self or a self in things, are those "who hold self [as] real," since, by maintaining a self, they perceive it [as being there]. Alternatively, by being conceptually attached to things, they hold things as selves; and since they conceptually develop the failing of being mistaken with regard to being and nothingness, they fall under the influence of addictions. [Hence,] pronouncements such as, "Those who grow dependent on attractive things become addicted; in the absence of such [things], they get angry," apply [to them].

Since they fall under the influence of addictions, they engage [in actions]. Since they are attached to [these compulsive] actions, whether virtuous or non-virtuous, they revolve [in cyclic life].[143] Thus, alienated beings are deceived by their own minds from their insistence upon [a being in] things. Since this insistence on [a being in] things is constructed by their own minds, even though such things are not established with intrinsic objectivity, their insight into the suchness of things is obstructed, and through mistaken reification [of intrinsic realities in things], their own minds deceive them, that is to say, [they become] deluded.

---

142 Tib. *so so skye bo*, Skt. *pṛthagjana.*

143 Peking and Snar-thang add *'khor ba na.*

iv. How the positively oriented can understand

(1) How those who have fulfilled their duties can understand

When those who have been taught voidness by a spiritual guide do not conceive of it as an abyss, they understand it to be the ultimate [nature] of things and conducive to the city of nirvāṇa. They correctly recognize the deceptiveness in their deceived minds and do not depend on that [habitual] mentality even for another instant; they are to be regarded as definitely having become noble.

25. Those who are expert in things[144]
See them as impermanent,
Deceptive in nature, hollow,
Empty, selfless, and [therefore][145] vacant.

Since they occur, they are called "things"; the word "things" [here] refers to created things. Since such [created] things, moreover, have the property of decaying at every moment, they are impermanent. Regarding the nature of such things, since they lack reality, like illusions, they deceive the naïve by appearing to have reality; such things in fact are "deceptive in nature." In lacking the strength to endure, they are naturally feeble, hence "hollow." Because they lack intrinsic substantiality, they are "empty." Because they are empty of a self, they are "selfless." Hence, "impermanent" and the rest [of the terms] describe the actual state of things.

Consequently, experts in seeing such things see them as "vacant." "Vacant" [means] empty. Thus, one calls hermitages that are empty of living beings "vacant,"[146] since they are conducive to [a sense of] vacancy. Similarly, to say here that yogin/īs "see things as vacant" amounts to [saying] that they see them as empty [of intrinsic reality]. Their seeing things as vacant is not to deprecate the things themselves, but rather, is to see the

---

[144] Gyaltsap glosses this as "those who are expert in things which are realized as the path leading to nirvāṇa."

[145] Gyaltsap (*ṭīkka*, 24a.1) comments that the attribution of "vacant" is justified by the five distinctive attributes (*khyad par lnga*) of being impermanent, deceptive, hollow, empty, and selfless.

[146] Tib. *skye pa med pa'i dgon pa rnams la dben pa.*

emptiness in things that *are* empty.[147] The particular [terms] such as "impermanent," and so forth, are mentioned in order to indicate emptiness.

Alternatively, if "vacant"[148] is [taken to mean] "stainless," then alienated beings, since they are contaminated with the stains of their own imagination, even about the natural total purity of things, misunderstand [reality]; but such is not the case for the noble. They see [things] as stainless, as vacant, and without reifying their non-existence.

Alternatively, the meaning of [Nāgārjuna's] statement may be that the noble, having emerged from [their contemplative] intuition into ultimate reality, when they look at things, "see them as vacant." Hence, a noble being's "duties are fulfilled," since they do not exhaust themselves by seeing things in the distorted way [of the alienated beings].

(2) How the master [Nagarjuna] himself saw [things]

As for the master [Nāgārjuna], relying on his own understanding, he truly developed a real appreciation for this teaching through his complete realization of reality through reasoning.

Hence, to show his own reasoning, he stated:

26. With no basis and no perceptual object,
With no root, and no foundation,
Totally arisen from the cause—misknowledge—
Bereft of beginning, middle, and end,

27. Essenceless, like a plantain [tree],[149]
Resembling a fairy city,[150]

---

[147] Scherrer-Schaub notes (*Yuktiṣaṣṭikāvṛtti*, 219 n. 391) that a passage in the *Kāśyapa Chapter Sūtra* of the *Ratnakūṭa* collection—cited in PPMMV (La Vallée Poussin, *Madhyamakavṛttiḥ*, 312 n. 1; Thurman, *Essence*, 374)—reflects this sentiment: "Kashyapa, furthermore, the central way is the genuine insight into things; it does not make things empty by means of emptiness, but [realizes that] the very things themselves are emptiness."

[148] The Sanskrit **vivikta* has both meanings of "vacant" and "pure," and may be the original word being glossed here.

[149] Tib. *chu shing*, Skt. *kadalī*. Scherrer-Schaub (*Yuktiṣaṣṭikāvṛtti*, 222 n. 400) identifies this as an abbreviation of *chu shing sdong po* = *kadalī-stamba*, or °*stambha* in reference to its occurrence in the *Bodhicaryāvatāra*.

[150] Tib. *dri za'i grong khyer*, Skt. *gandharva-nagara*. Literally, "gandharvas' city," the gandharvas being described in some contexts as the celestial musicians in the heavens, and in

(cont'd)

And an unbearable city of confusion,
Life appears like an illusion.

[This indicates the four ways in which this (vision) is correct from the perspective of (the critique of) conditions.[151] 1) Concerning their own empowering condition,][152] because they rely upon it, it is a basis, serving as a ground, like the earth which serves as a cause of the harvest. Since there is no basis for this [intrinsically real life], it is "without basis." [2) Concerning their perceptual object condition,][153] because there are objects of the basic [condition], there is a "perceptual object," which is like a cane that enables those incapable of standing to stand. [However, since their basic condition does not exist,] they have "no perceptual object" condition. [3) Concerning the immediately preceding condition,][154] "root" [means] primary cause,[155] that is, cause of the production, development, and growth of those things which arise from it, as, for example, the roots of trees. Since [things] do not have an [intrinsic] foundation, [Nāgārjuna concludes,] they have "no foundation." There are no foundations, perceptual objects, or productive causes; and because of this non-existent foundation, [Nāgārjuna] speaks of the non-establishment of the world [of the six migrations].[156] If these are the causes for establishing things [intrinsically], then since they do not exist for the world, the world, therefore, is false. Thus, [conventionally] the "foundation" is the six sense media, and the "perceptual object [conditions]" are all things together with everything concordant, while the "root"

others as merely semi-physical beings who subsist on scents (hence the Tibetan etymological rendering of *dri za*, "scent-eaters"). The image of a gandharvas' city is one of the Buddha's ten similes (*daśopamāna*) for the world, given repeatedly in *sūtra*.

[151] Gyaltsap (*ṭīkka*, 24a.4).

[152] Tsong Khapa (*zin bris*, 6b.3–.4). Tib. *bdag rkyen*, Skt. **adhipati-pratyaya*.

[153] Tib. *dmigs rkyen*, Skt. **ālambana-pratyaya*.

[154] Tib. *de ma thag rkyen*, Skt. **samanantara-pratyaya*.

[155] Tib. *rgyu'i gtso bo*, Skt. *pradhāna-hetu*, or *pradhāna-kāraṇa*, here glosses *rtsa ba* = *mūla*. AK ad k. 2.50ab (Pradhan, 83; La Vallée Poussin, *L'Abhidharmakośa*, I, 247) defines the primary productive cause as that which has the capacity to produce [a result] (*pradhānaḥ kāraṇa-hetuḥ sa utpādane*), like a seed serving as the cause of sprout.

[156] Tib. *'gro ba*, Skt. **jagat*, that is, "the world"—glossed by Gyaltsap (*ṭīkka*, 24a.4) as "the environment and its beings" (*snod bcud*). Thus, *'gro ba* can be either a "migration" (*snod* or also *gati*) or the "migrant being" (*bcud*).

is the causal condition in terms of things [functioning as] seeds. Because [all] this acts as a foundation, [there is] a [conventional] foundation, and through this, beings abide. Since all these are dependently arisen however, they lack intrinsic objectivity. This was indicated above in: "What arises, dependent upon this and that, is not intrinsically created."[157] Therefore, a world which is bereft of [intrinsically existent] supporting [conditions], and so forth, cannot [intrinsically] exist.

[To this, the Traditionist might object:] "If the world does not exist in such [an intrinsically real manner], how do its own objects appear in various forms?"

[Let me explain.] The noble do not perceive the variety of forms of the world, since for them, the world has the singular taste of voidness, and there is no variety of forms in voidness. Consequently, [4)] in order to show that the naïve, mistaken, and confused with the sleep of misknowledge, see various things like someone asleep dreaming a dream, [Nāgārjuna] declared [them to be] "arisen from the cause—misknowledge." Since it lacks establishment with [intrinsically] objective status and exists through misknowledge, the world is objectively unfounded, yet certain to come about from its cause—the seed of misknowledge.

Thus, to indicate how it lacks intrinsically objective status, [Nāgārjuna] taught, "bereft of beginning, middle, and end," meaning that [the world] is free from creation, duration, and destruction. Furthermore, that [the world] originates from the seed of misknowledge [is reflected in] this [statement], "Essenceless—like a plantain [tree]." If [the world] did not originate from the seed of misknowledge, then when analyzed, it is reasonable to expect that one would perceive its core essence. However, when examined, created things have no core essence, like the trunk of a plantain [tree]. Anything that lacks any essence yet appears to have an essence, must arise through the force of delusion; such being the case, the world originates from the seed of misknowledge.

In another sense, [the world] arises from the seed of misknowledge in that it is similar to a fairy city. Thus, while a fairy city appears like a real one, it is not a real city since it is not so when examined. Thus, when examined in this way, the world—which originates from the seed of misknowledge—is not objectively established, and thus certainly this [world] is "an

[157] k. 19ab.

unbearable city of confusion, [and] life appears like an illusion." Because its nature is difficult to realize, since it is harmful, difficult to reverse, and obscured by the darkness [of misknowledge], he calls the world "unbearable," meaning "pernicious,"[158] "unalleviated,"[159] and "terrifying." Therefore, the unmistaken see this [world] as like an illusion. What is a city of confusion for the naïve is seen by the noble as like an illusion, because they are free from the darkness of misknowledge.

(3) The reasoning for that

(a) [In accordance with] scriptural statements

For this and similar reasons, this life is unreal. Thus, [he stated:]

28. What is proclaimed as the truth in this world
By Brahmā [the Creator] and the others,
Was declared "false" for the noble ones.
What else remains that is otherwise?

This implies the question, "Is there anything whatsoever that is not like an illusion?"

Regarding the determination of those realities that are beyond the sphere of the senses, in the world, Brahmā [the Creator] is [held to be] an authority. Yet whatever seems to be the essential nature of things proclaimed true by those [considered] authorities[160] was called "false" for the noble ones by the Lord Buddha, who declared, "this nirvāṇa is the only truth."[161] If created things are false and deceptive in nature, how could that which appears to others [as true] not be false? To avoid doubt about precisely what is false, [Nāgārjuna said,] "What else remains that is otherwise?" He meant, "there is nothing whatsoever that is not illusory." This should be accepted without reservation.

---

158 Tib. *ma rungs*, Skt. **raudra*.

159 Tib. *dbugs 'byin pa med pa'i gnas*, Skt. **an-āśvasta-sthāna* (Scherrer-Schaub, *Yuktiṣaṣṭikā-vṛtti*, 229 n. 426).

160 Tib. *tshad mar gyur pa*, Skt. *pramāṇa-bhūta*. For a discussion of this term, see Krasser, "On Dharmakīrti's Understanding"; Silk, "Possible Indian Sources"; and Tillemans, *Persons of Authority*.

161 Also cited above, ad k. 2cd, and in k. 35, below.

(b) [In accordance with] reasoning

Otherwise, if Brahmā and other [reputed authorities] were in agreement with the noble in their views of this world, then the noble and the non-noble would be exactly the same. In order to show the impossibility of equating them, [Nāgārjuna] stated:

> **29. How can the worldly, blinded by misknowledge,**
> **Who follow the flow of their cravings,[162]**
> **And the virtuous, who are skilled and**
> **Free of craving, be viewed as equal?**

All beings including Brahmā [the Creator] and other [reputed authorities]—whose intellectual eyes are blinded by the cataract of misknowledge—are bereft of correct sight. Hence, since from beginningless [time] these helpless beings have been driven all over the life-cycle, and as its [suffering] intensifies, the powerful winds of mistaken [views] sweep them down the vast current of cyclic life like foam on a wave. Alienated beings—who in their agitation, with the ship to the virtuous shore being wrecked—follow the flow of craving, and are blinded to the ultimate fruit which is the maturation of virtuous actions, while the experts whose intellectual eye is clarified by wisdom are contented, drinking the ambrosial stream[163] of the holy teaching. How is it possible to imagine that the virtuous whose ways have as their essence the singular truth are equivalent to the worldly described above? To imagine that illumination and obscurity, cyclic life and nirvāṇa are the same is irrational.

Consequently, whatever is true for those who live in conformity with the worldly cyclic life, such as Brahmā [the Creator] and other [supposed authorities], is no doubt false for the noble. Therefore [Nāgārjuna] made the statement that, for such noble individuals, "[Like] an unbearable city of

---

[162] Tsong Khapa and Gyaltsap both read "craving" (*sred*) for "existence" (*srid*). Tsong Khapa glosses this passage as "Brahmā and the other [reputed authorities] who float down the current of craving," while Gyaltsap expands these two lines as: "the worldly [authorities] such as Brahmā and the others, those whose intellectual eye is blinded by the cataract of misknowledge and who have been refuted, the followers of the current of mistaken craving."

[163] Tib. *bdud rtsi'i khu ba*, Skt. *amṛta-rasa*.

confusion, life appears like an illusion."[164] As the wise have eliminated doubt about what he stated, one must give it credence.

B. Proving that mention of the aggregates, and so forth, is of interpretable meaning

1. The stage of teaching reality

a. The actual stage

To this, [the Analyst] objects: "If the world is like illusion and void of intrinsic reality, why then did the Lord Buddha not teach that to be reality, but rather said, 'There do exist the aggregates, media and elements!' How do you interpret this supposedly untrue statement?"

Let me explain. From whence comes your assumption that he taught the truth itself only, and never anything false? In the world, when the truth is unnecessary, some will not present it. Conversely, some intentionally deploy fictions when they have a purpose. Here, since it was necessary as a means of introducing the ultimate, [the Buddha taught] that the unreal aggregates, elements, and so forth, do exist. While such [a statement] is made as a preliminary teaching, the actual reality—voidness—is not [so employed,] since it would have been pointless to teach it right away. This teaching, [which must be understood] secure from the abyss of the two extremes, cannot be digested if taught right away to persons who are intellectually unprepared. Therefore, the Wise One made this [fabrication] as a method for achieving the aims of beings.

30. To seekers of reality,[165] at first,
You should declare, "Everything exists!"[166]
Once they understand things and grow detached,
Then, [you may teach] them freedom.

When you introduce beings who are intellectually uneducated to the view of reality—voidness—they become utterly confused. Consequently, the noble do not teach them voidness right at first. Those who are seeking truth motivated by their habitual self-preoccupation tend to be attached to things, so

---

164 k. 27cd.

165 Both Tsong Khapa and Gyaltsap read this line as "for [those who] seek reality."

166 Skt. *sarvam asti*, Tib. *thams cad yod*. This is a reference to the Abhidharmist doctrines of the Sarvāstivādins, who held that all things are existent equally across the three times, past, present, and future.

first you must teach them that "everything exists," and then correctly describe [for them] the objects of their desire, since they delight in analyzing the natures of those things.

[For such people,] "the nature of something" is its reality. That [reality is thought by them] to have a connection with something expressible as a meaning-universal.[167] "A thing" [to them] means an intrinsically real [thing], since [they think] that the intrinsic reality of something is the thing itself. This means [for them], reality, intrinsic objectivity, actuality, suchness, and non-alterity.[168]

One whose characteristic manner is to seek [true] reality is a realist.[169] If you ask, "what teaching should be offered by a teacher who wishes to help those who desire [thus] to seek reality?" He should declare "everything exists." It was proclaimed [by the Buddha] thus, "O Brahmin, 'everything' refers to the five aggregates, the twelve sense-media, and the eighteen elements."[170] [It should be] combined with an understanding of this. One should describe this or that aggregate, and so forth, as existent, although these aggregates, and so forth, are dependent; that is, they exist as this and that through dependence, designatively, as in long and short, or as in lamp [and] light, and not otherwise. Thus, it is conclusive that they are [merely] dependent or relative.

[To this, the Buddhist Realist] objects: "How [then] can one speak of 'understanding things'?"[171]

[Let me explain.] Since there is no limit to the effects [of one's actions], since there are also multiple conditions of each effect, and since, when each condition is analyzed, one sees no limit to the continuous series of cumulative causes, as [it is] as beginningless as cyclic life, [therefore,] when initiating an effect, [one] immediately understands, with an awareness of destruction, [that effect's eventual] destruction, [since] it is produced by

---

[167] Tib. *don spyi*, Skt. *artha-samanya.*

[168] Tib. *gzhan ma yin pa nyid*; Skt. **ananyatva.*

[169] Tib. *de kho na tshol ba.*

[170] Scherrer-Schaub identifies this citation from *Tattva-saṁgraha-pañjika* as: *sarvaṁ sarvaṁ iti brāhmaṇa yāvad eva pañca-skandhāḥ dvādaśāyatāni aṣṭādaśa ca dhātavaḥ* //. For other citations and variants, see Scherrer-Schaub, *Yuktiṣaṣṭikāvṛtti*, 239 n. 459.

[171] Referring to k.30c, above.

multiple conditions that are themselves the effect of a continuous cumulative series of causes.[172] Hence, understanding that life is achieved with enormous effort, and that the destruction of what is achieved with such enormous effort happens effortlessly, one grows disillusioned about the nature of created things; one does not idealize the activities of naïve individuals. One is neither ecstatic about birth nor fixed in resistance[173] to death. One aspires to renounce addiction to [future] cyclic lives, and wishes to abandon cyclic life [altogether]. When thus one becomes somewhat relaxed in one's addiction to self, understanding things in this manner, [only then,] "freedom" is appropriate, and not before. Proceeding thus, the master [said] that the teaching of voidness will not be fruitless, and the students will not succumb to error[174] by misunderstanding or abandoning [the teaching].

When not taught in this manner, students may succumb to error through the teaching of voidness, since they may come to confound the principle[175] of the two realities, superficial and ultimate. In such cases, they would be unable to avoid non-virtue, since the intellectually inept might cling to the idea, "this world is void." Hence, [thinking,] "If this is voidness, what use is it all," they may not be inspired [to cultivate] the virtuous actions that will make success certain. Consequently, they may be destroyed, like a bird with undeveloped wing feathers thrown from its nest.[176]

b. Perceiving the faults of transgressing that

Since such individuals lack personal realization, [Nāgārjuna warned:]

---

[172] The Peking and Snar-thang versions amend this to read "a continuous series of cumulative causes," in keeping with the previous phrase.

[173] Tib. *mi 'phrod par 'dzin pa.*

[174] Tib. *log par ltung ba,* Skt. **vinipāta.*

[175] Tib. *rnam par gnas pa dang mi mthun par gyur.*

[176] For this image, see Scherrer-Schaub (*Yuktiṣaṣṭikāvṛtti,* 245 n. 472). Chandrakīrti uses it in MA (6.226), where he compares the bodhisattva to the king of swans, whose two wings are the two realities that permit him to fly on winds of virtue to the far shore of the ocean of the Victor's qualities. In a different usage of the same metaphor by Chandrakīrti (PPMMV, 538), the wings are the two stores of wisdom and merit.

31. Ignorant of the meaning of freedom,
Just acting on what they have heard,
They neglect the exercise of virtue—
Such pitiful creatures are lost.

When one has personally realized the reality of voidness, having perfectly cultivated the unmistaken experience, abiding in the ultimate reality of this very world, it is appropriate to practice neither virtue nor non-virtue. However, those who have merely heard the words "voidness" yet lack personal realization imitate[177] the behavior of those who have done what must be done; they tend to engage in non-virtuous activities, not in virtues, and invariably succumb to compulsive extremes, acting like a young sparrow with unformed wings that mimics[178] one with perfect wings. Thirst is not slaked by merely hearing of water, nor is hunger satiated by merely hearing of food. But using [food and water] properly one does become satisfied. Realizing that such [engaging in actions without realization] is like this example, [Nāgārjuna] said, "Such pitiful creatures are lost." Since they engage exclusively in non-virtue, they are "pitiful creatures."

c. The antidotes to that

Thus, wishing them to completely avoid that error, the Lord Buddha initially [taught] his audience certain [teachings of] interpretable meaning that would not undermine[179] superficial reality.

32ab. [Buddha] declared the effectiveness of actions,
As well as the forms of life [they create];

The Lord Buddha spoke of the five realms of life in which sentient beings are born, perform actions, and experience effects. Thereafter, to remedy their physical bonds[180] and exaggerated attitudes that think, "This is the truth of these [things],"

---

[177] Tib. *ltar rjes su 'chos pa*, Skt. *pratirūpaka* Mvy 6688.

[178] Tib. *tshul*, Skt. **ceṣṭita* Mvy 7251.

[179] Tib. *yongs su ma nyams pa*, Skt. **aparihīṇa*.

[180] Tib. *lus kyi mdud pa*, Skt. **kāya-grantha*. There are four "bonds" (*grantha*), actions which tightly bind the individual to the body, and hence to cyclic life. These are identified by Scherrer-Schaub (*Yuktiṣaṣṭikāvṛtti*, 249 n. 483), in reference to the *Saṅgīti-sūtra*, as: 1) greed

(cont'd)

32cd. [Then] taught his full understanding of their nature,
Including their uncreatedness.

Since migrant beings and the rest [of the world] are dependently arisen, they are objectively uncreated. [The Buddha] taught that one must acquire the intuitions of the path of understanding their nature and of the path of [realizing] the uncreatedness of migrant beings and the rest [of the world].

2. The intention behind the statements on the aggregates

a. Actual intention

[To this, the Buddhist Realist] objects: "In that case, which of these two presentations of his own teaching was taught for a reason?[181] And which was taught in reference to reality?"[182] When one examines this [question], it is appropriate to conclude:

33. Just as the Victors say "I"
And "mine" for a useful purpose,
So they speak of "aggregates," "media,"
And "elements" for a useful purpose.

The Lord Buddha abandoned attachment to "I" and "mine," yet from the perspective of the meaning he wished to convey, for the sake of the world he referred to "I" and "mine." Likewise, for a useful purpose he proclaimed the aggregates, [sense-]media, and elements, because there is no method of introducing someone to the reality of the world without teaching its analysis.

b. How to know the intention

One can know that he explained the aggregates, media, and elements for a useful purpose, and that it was not [intended] as the [ultimate] mean-

---

(*abhidhyā*); 2) violence (*vyāpāda*); 3) compulsive asceticism (*śīlavrata-parāmarśa*); and 4) dogmatic fanaticism (*idaṁsatyâbhiniveśa*).

[181] The Tibetan *dgos pa* can mean both "necessity" and "purpose." Gyaltsap's commentary, (*ṭīkka*, fol.26a.6) glosses the phrase as "through the force of [their] intention" (*dgongs pa'i dbang gis*), although in the Sanskrit of the following verse, *kāryavaśāt* conveys the more specific meaning of "for some reason," which is followed by Tsong Khapa (*zin*, 7b.5–.6); thus we translate it here contextually as "useful purpose."

[182] This second question is omitted in the Peking and Snar-thang redactions; Scherrer-Schaub (*Yuktiṣaṣṭikāvṛtti*, 73, 250) likewise omits it in her edition and translation.

ing of reality, since this can be determined through correct [reasoning] and scripture.

i. [Through] reasoning

Regarding that, some [explanations] have been made through the force of reasoning:

> **34. [Things first] proclaimed, such as primary elements,[183]**
> **Then are incorporated into consciousness.**
> **Since knowing that, you break free [of them],**
> **Are they not unreal constructions?[184]**

A cognition apprehends the aspect of some object of experience, and thus [re-]produces that object. Having obtained its own substance as a form procured in a cognition, one imagines it to be a primary element, and so forth, as if it were an objective entity. When it cannot be represented as any form whatsoever in any cognition, it is not possible for the worldly to posit this as actually existing; because it would [logically] follow that even the son of a barren woman, and other such [non-existent things], would exist! Therefore, the primary elements and what arises from the primary elements, the mind and mental factors, as well as things not associated [with the mind]—because of being causal components of consciousness—all of these things howsoever feasibly explained as this and that primary element, and so forth, are subsumed and understood within consciousness.[185]

---

[183] Skt. *mahābhūta*, Tib. *'byung ba che*.

[184] Tsong Khapa notes, in his *Essence of Eloquence* (Thurman, *Essence*, 276), that this verse is cited as a basis for an Idealistic interpretation of Nāgārjuna's Centrism by Śāntarakṣita and others. As noted by Scherrer-Schaub (*Yuktiṣaṣṭikāvṛtti*, 253 n. 492), Ruegg (*Literature*, 90) identified the explanation of this interpretation found in Śāntarakṣita's *Madhyamakālaṁkāra*. Śāntarakṣita explains: "Relying on Idealism, one should understand the non-existence of external things; relying on this [Centrist] method, one should understand the complete selflessness of that [mind] as well." This point is discussed at length by Scherrer-Schaub (*Yuktiṣaṣṭikāvṛtti*, 252ff.).

[185] Tsong Khapa (*zin bris*, 8a.1–.2) condenses this argument into two consequences stating: "With respect to the subject, the four primary elements, mind, mental factors, and anomalous compositional factors, and so forth, it follows that it [i.e., any one of these] is an erroneous imagination by a mistaken cognition because, through the force of the realization of the lack of intrinsic existence of the cognition—that is, the agent that represents it—[that cognition] becomes free from grasping at [the object's] true [existence]. This follows because it is

(cont'd)

Now, a yogin/ī sees that pure consciousness superimposes [on things] the meanings of being existent and being non-existent, [since those things] are false and deceptive objects; and, at the time of seeing them as lacking intrinsic production, knows that [insight] to be definitive. Because he knows that the mind that abides in such a manner [also] lacks production in terms of its own reality, anything whatsoever produced by that [mind]—[that is,] anything whatsoever such as the primary elements, and so forth—will disappear just as a reflection ceasing when [the reflected] form ceases; thus such [productions of mind] are just mistaken constructions, like reflections, are they not?

Therefore, likewise, since there is no existence as such caused by consciousness, once [something] exists, it only does so [in spite of] lacking objective status; hence it is certain that these aggregates, and so forth, were taught intentionally for those having presumptuous pride,[186] grasping at "I" and grasping at "mine."

ii. [Through] scripture

Thus, having first made known through reasoning that the aggregates were taught for a purpose, now in order to indicate with scripture that [they] were pronouncements made for a purpose [Nāgārjuna cites a pronouncement] teaching the aggregates, and so forth, as utterly false:

> **35. "Nirvāṇa is the sole truth,"**
> **Is what the Victors declared.**
> **Then, what wise person would suppose,**
> **"Everything else is not false"?**

The Lord Buddha declared "Thus, O monks, non-deceptive in nature, this nirvāṇa is the sole, supreme truth." Given the meaning [expressed] by this

---

as the cognition of it that the form is established, and having imagined [it] as something in a cognition, it is so established."

186 Tib. *mngon pa'i nga rgyal can*, Skt. **ābhimānika*. In the AK ad k. 5.10a (Pradhan, 284–285; La Vallée Poussin, *L'Abhidharmakośa*, IV, 27) Vasubandhu gives "manifest pride" (*abhimāna*; *mngon pa'i nga rgyal*) as one of seven forms of pride (*māna*), defining it as "Without [actually] having obtained certain qualities, thinking 'I have obtained [them]'" (*aprāpte viśeṣādhigame prāpto mayetyabhimānaḥ*; *khyad par thob par bya ba ma thob par bdag gis thob ba snyam pa*).

scripture, what wise person would not understand the implication that the aggregates, and so forth, are false?

3. Indicating that statements on non-production are of definitive meaning

a. Intrinsic unreality [of things] present [only] to misknowledge

When the aggregates, media, and elements are investigated with reasoning and scripture, just like the forms [of things, as analyzed above,] they lack objective status; hence, it is certain that

36ab. As long as the mind vacillates,
It remains under the dominion of Māra.

Because it obstructs the life-force of the faculty of the noble ones' exalted wisdom, it is [like the devil,] Māra. Moreover, since it pervades all the levels of the three realms,[187] has the four misperceptions as its main agents, is perpetually surrounded by an entourage of addictions such as desire, and so forth, is not confronted by any beings other than the noble, accompanies those who have engaged in harmful activities, and perpetuates the cyclic life of all sentient beings, it is [the devil] called "misknowledge." Hence, it is evident that there is no transcendence of the realm of misknowledge when things are investigated with an inappropriate [dualistic worldview]. At such times, one [remains] "under the dominion of Māra." Yet once that [vacillating mind] is no longer present, since mental engagement [in inappropriate worldviews] will not arise, there will no longer even be a realm of Māra.[188]

36cd. Such being the case, why not validate
That there is no fault in this?[189]

---

[187] Tib. *khams gsum gyi sa chen po pa*, Skt. **traidhātuka-mahābhūmika* Scherrer-Schaub (*Yukti-ṣaṣṭikāvṛtti*, 265 n. 513) notes that *mahābhūmika* is a traditional gloss of the omnipresent class of mental factors (*sarvatraga-cetasika*), in the AK.

[188] Tsong Khapa (*zin*, fol. 8a.6) summarizes this, saying: "So long as there is vacillation with mental engagement in inappropriate [worldviews], for just that long one will not pass beyond the dominion of Māra, who obstructs the faculty that is the life-force of a noble's exalted wisdom."

[189] Following Gyaltsap (*ṭīkka*, fol. 27a.6–27b.1), who expands these lines as: "When that non-creation has manifested, then why is it irrational that there is no fault in teaching the direct realization of non-creation?"

"This" indicates the complete understanding of the non-creation of anything's intrinsic reality. Since in terms of that [insight], one comes close to [such experience,] the deictic demonstrative word "this" is used in "this [insight]."

Thus, moreover, [he implies that] the complete understanding of the non-creation of any intrinsic reality is not a complete understanding of intrinsic reality itself, [since no such intrinsic reality was ever created].

b. Intrinsic unreality according to the pattern of misknowledge

i. Showing its conformity with misknowledge

When one is mistaken about such [objects], they [seem intrinsically] real, but when one is not, they no longer [seem intrinsically] real. Therefore, to indicate this [Nāgārjuna] stated:

37. "The world is conditioned by misknowledge!"
Thus spoke the perfect Buddha.
Hence, what's invalid about saying that
"This world is [mere] construction"?

That which has misknowledge as its condition—that which arises from the condition of misknowledge—is the "world." The world is the five appropriative aggregates. Thus, because the Lord Buddha taught that "the world is conditioned by misknowledge"—with [statements of the twelve links of dependent origination] such as this, "created things have the condition of misknowledge; consciousness has the condition of created things," and so forth—there is no intrinsically objective status. Darkness is not a condition that is substantial and intrinsically objective, and so on, and therefore, since misknowledge serves as the condition [of the world,] why is it incorrect[190] to say that the world is [merely] construction? It is quite correct that the world is mere construction—that is what [Nāgārjuna] thought.

"Construction" [means] constructed. Since [the world] is exhaustively [shown to be] a mere construction, it is constructed. This is the meaning of "exhaustively a mere construction." Since it lacks intrinsically objective status—just like imagined [apparitions] arising like flames in the darkness of a cave—the world is presented as mere construction.

[190] The Tibetan texts read "correct" here, which cannot be correct.

ii. Stopping misknowledge and eliminating [the life-cycle]

Having shown why the world exists [only] when there is such misperception, now, in order to show its non-existence in the absence of [such] misperception, [Nāgārjuna states]:

38. When misknowledge ceases,
Since those things misknowledge imagines
Will [also] come to cease,
Why wouldn't [the world] be cleared away?

Just as one does not perceive flame-like apparitions in the darkness of a cave once there is light, just so, once one gains knowledge one comes to abide in the lack of objective status [of created things/the world], since such errors are definitely imaginatively created by not knowing.

c. Intrinsic unreality, looking at the causes of birth, duration, and destruction

A further reason for [unreality] is that the world is insubstantial, since it originates from causes and conditions, just like a mirror image. To indicate that fact, [Nāgārjuna] stated:

39. What originates having a cause,
Does not endure without conditions,
And, without conditions, is destroyed.
How do you understand such [a thing] as "existent"?

If the world were objectively established, then, since its objectivity would be established with intrinsic reality, it could not originate in dependence on causes and conditions nor from any other causal thing, because an intrinsic nature cannot be made. Moreover, its duration could not be dependent on [sustaining] conditions. If it were objectively established, it could not possibly be transformed. Just so, since [an objectively established object would] lack transformability, an inquiry into the [supporting] conditions of its endurance would be reasonable. For it is only rational that whatever is dependent upon [sustaining] conditions—like a reflection—must be established without intrinsic reality. And it is irrational for an objectively established thing to be eliminated, even without conditions, since it is intrinsically untransformable. What is eliminated when it lacks [supporting] conditions for its endurance—like a mirror reflection [lacking the object reflected]—is properly devoid of intrinsic reality. So, since there are no causes known to exist in any way other than without intrinsically objective status, [it is Nāgārjuna's] thinking that the very existence of such a [caused thing] is irrational.

C. The problems of clinging to the aggregates

1. Establishing the context

a. No wonder that other philosophers only advocate intrinsic realities

Vedist philosophers reject relativity and advocate the intrinsically objective existence of things, and so will not contradict the principles of their own theories. Therefore, [Nāgārjuna stated:]

> **40. When those who advocate [objective] existence**
> **Still hold things as [intrinsically real],**
> **And remain on that very same path,**
> **It is not surprising in the least.**[191]

Sāṁkhya philosophers are consistently trained [to think in terms of] the three intrinsically established, primordial, essential qualities of clarity, energy and density.[192] Vaiśeṣika philosophers are trained [to think in terms of] the permanent composition of all things without exception—that is, compounds[193] of intrinsically established, primordial, atoms of earth, water, fire and air. [Both Vedist philosophers] advocate absolute things. Hence, when they maintain their insistence on substance or maintain their conviction about intrinsic objectivity, the most intelligent are not surprised in the least, since it is no wonder at all.

Why is that, you ask? [The reason] is that, in the world, relying on impossible things is a cause for surprise, but relying on possible things is not [surprising]; for it is rational. Hence, given that [such naïve people] were

---

[191] This, and the following two verses are cited by Tsong Khapa in his *Legs bshad snying po* (Thurman, *Essence*, 262–263). Tsong Khapa's own enlightenment poem expresses the same ideas in two verses (Thurman, *Essence*, 179–180). Lindtner's reading of this verse, that Sarvāstivādins lack *prajñā*, would seem to conflict with the sense of k. 11–12, and Chandrakīrti's YṢV, where he shows that Nāgārjuna's intent is to equate the insight of relativity with the immediate nirvāṇa state (*nirvāṇadṛṣtadharma*) reached by all noble beings (*āryapudgala*), including Individual Vehicle disciples like Śāriputra. This is one of the distinctive Dialecticist positions of recognizing the Individualist saints' realization of objective selflessness.

[192] Tib. *yon tan snying stobs dang rdul dang mun pa gsum*, Skt. **sattva-rajas-tamaśca-triguṇa*.

[193] Tib. *yan lag can*, Skt. *avayavin*.

taught, and hence understand teachings consistent with their own theories that [things] are [intrinsically] existent, there is no cause for surprise; so there cannot be the least surprise.

However, [when Buddhist] Analysts, Traditionists, and Idealists promulgate what cannot possibly exist within their own theories, that is what creates supreme astonishment in the most intelligent!

b. Buddhist philosophers are highly irrational to advocate intrinsic existence

About those [Buddhist philosophers, Nāgārjuna said]:

41. Those who rely on the path of the Buddha,
And advocate the impermanence of all things,
Yet persist in hanging on to [intrinsic] things
With arguments—they really are amazing!

Relativity is the path of the Buddha, according to which, because all created things are dependently arisen, they are impermanent. Those [Buddhist Analysts, Traditionists, and Idealists] who claim to expound that [path] yet wish to prove the intrinsically real status of things, present arguments against the advocates of voidness. Because their reliance on impossible things is astonishing, "they really are amazing." Since what is a great wonder in mundane [parlance] is also amazing, [Nāgārjuna] calls its occurrence "amazing."

Thus, those who would advocate the impermanence of all things and claim the path of relativity, yet teach the [intrinsic] objectivity of things and maintain their conceited ideas, are as astounding to the wise as a wild stallion that has the behavior of a donkey. The term "amazing" is an expression of praise that here is ironic, like an expression of homage made to one unworthy of homage.

c. The correctness of that

Regarding those who accept relativity and rely on the path of the Buddha, [Nāgārjuna stated:][194]

---

194 Ye-shes-sde's translation of this next verse (42) is noticeably different from Pa-tshab's translation of the root verses. Both Tsong Khapa and Gyaltsap clearly follow Chandrakīrti's lead in commenting on the verse, though do so in reference to Pa-tshab's translation. We have followed the way Gyaltsap corrects the corrupt Tibetan blockprints in both verse and verse embedded in commentary. See critical edition, p. 336 n. 506.

42. When "this" or "that" [appears a fact],
Yet when analyzed is not perceived,
What wise person would advocate with arguments,
That "this" or "that" is [really] true?

Thus, because form, sensation, consciousness, and all other created things are dependently arisen, they are not objectively created. Since there is no perceivable sign[195] for what is objectively uncreated, none of these aspects—"that form is this," "that sensation is this," "that consciousness is this," or "those other created things are this"—appear in the mind. Hence, those who do not have anything that appears as a concrete particular cannot prove to others that anything is "this." It is irrational for the wise to argue about that which is undemonstrable. An "argument" [is defined] as something with which one tries to establish one's own position and refute another's position. Thus, when no thing at all is perceived, how could whatever true thing posited by oneself come to exist even in the slightest, and so be indicated by "this"? And, how could whatever false thing posited by opponents come to exist even in the slightest, and so be indicated by "this"?

2. The actual perception of faults

a. Showing naïve realists swept off the liberation path by streams of views

i. Showing Vedist philosophers being deprived by the addictive view

Thus, those who have not realized the meaning of relativity as the meaning of not being created intrinsically, do not understand [the actual teaching] and become mistaken [in their views]:

43. Those who insist on a non-relative[196]
"Self" or "world"—Alas!
They are deprived by views
Such as absolutism and nihilism.

Those who do not designate "the self" in dependence on the five aggregates—which are devoid of intrinsic reality just like mirror reflections—but

---

[195] Tib. *mtshan ma*, Skt. **nimitta*. In the context of an argument (*rtsod pa*), it is the property of the subject (*chos can*) that pervades the predicate.

[196] Gyaltsap (*ṭīkka*, 28b.6) glosses this as "Those such as the Sāṁkhya who, without any basis of [an understanding of] causes and conditions…" (*grangs can sogs gang dag gis rgyu rkyen la ma brten par…*).

rather, locate "the self" in an intrinsically identifiable mind,[197] will no doubt be swept far from the road to nirvāṇa and carried away by the stream of worldviews.

Why is that? Now, if one asserts the objectively real status of mind, it must be either permanent or impermanent. If [one asserts] its permanence, then one is an eternalist.[198] Alternatively, if [one asserts] its impermanence, then one is a nihilist, since the nihilistic view is that something [once] emerged can [then] become a nothing. Thus, "Alas! They are deprived by views." The word "alas" should be known as an exclamation of either regret or certainty. Likewise, if [instead of an intrinsically identifiable mind] one claims the five aggregates—known as "the world"—to be intrinsically identifiably established, similar problems apply.

Alternatively, another interpretation is [that this verse refers] to the Sāṁkhya and other [Vedist philosophers], who insist on an independent self that is eternal, objectively established, and not relative; or on a world whose nature is intrinsically real[199] and objectively established. Since intrinsic reality cannot change,[200] these claims [all effectively] eliminate the variety of transformations [undergone by individuals and their world]. Others claim different things [with similar consequences].[201] Indeed, without doubt,

---

[197] Scherrer-Schaub (*Yuktiṣaṣṭikāvṛtti*, 277 n. 559) identifies the target of Chandrakīrti's critique as the branch of the Sāṁmitīya school whose tenet of identifying mind (*citta*) as the referent of the "self" that he addressed in the MA (6.126), and while Chandrakīrti acknowledges that the target could run the gamut from Vedists to Idealists and Traditionist-Centrists, Gyaltsap takes them to be exclusively Vedists.

[198] Tib. *ther zug tu smra ba*, Skt. **śāśvata-vāda* (Mvy 7288).

[199] Tib. *rang bzhin gyi bdag nyid*, Skt. *prakṛtyātmaka*. The world-principle in the Sāṁkhya system, Nature, is dualistically opposed to Spirit, and conceived as a primordial substance which is both the creator as prime cause and its creatures as illusory effects. Hence, the Sāṁkhya theory of the identity of cause and effect undermines the plausibility of relative change, which makes it a target of serious critique by all systems of Buddhist thought.

[200] Tib. *'gyur ba med pa*, Skt. **avikāra*. In the Sāṁkhya system, (*Sāṁkhya-Kārikā*, k. 3) *mūla-prakṛtir avikṛtir*, "Primordial Nature is unchanging."

[201] Tib. *gzhan dag ni gzhan du 'dod*, Skt. *anyais tv anyatheṣṭaṁ* Scherrer-Schaub (*Yuktiṣaṣṭikāvṛtti*, 279 n. 569) notes that Śāntarakṣita in the TSG maintains that the "others" here refers to theists, who assert the world's creation by the Lord (*Īśvara*), who similarly undermine causality.

those [who insist on a non-relative self or world] will be deprived by addictive views such as absolutism and nihilism.

ii. Showing some Buddhists to be deprived by the addictive view

Among our own schools, those [Analysts and Traditionists] who, despite accepting the self and [its constituent] aggregates as dependently arisen, insist upon their substantial existence,[202] and those [Idealists] who, while [granting that mind] originates from complex causes and conditions such as misknowledge, creations, and the other [factors of dependent origination], nonetheless advocate the substantial existence of consciousness, [mental factors,] and so on—all are indulging false views just like those [of the Vedists]. To indicate this, [Nāgārjuna] stated:

> **44. Claiming that dependent things[203]**
> **Are established in reality,**
> **How could they not develop flawed views,**
> **Such as absolutism, about those [things]?**

Why? Because claiming the objective existence or non-existence of persons or things is tantamount to incurring the problems of absolutism and nihilism.

iii. Showing the assertion of voidness to be the opposite

Having dispelled the above-mentioned views, when one understands the meaning of relativity precisely as it is, [as Nāgārjuna stated:]

> **45. Those who accept dependent things**
> **As being like the moon in water,**
> **Neither [intrinsically] real nor unreal,**
> **Are not deprived by addictive views.**

If [the aggregates]—form, and so forth—were objectively non-existent, then because of their objective non-existence, their transformation into some other objectively [existent] thing would be impossible; for what is objectively non-existent cannot later come to exist. Even given [objectively]

---

[202] Tib. *rdzas su yod pa*, Skt. **dravya-sat*.

[203] Tib. *de nyid du ni grub*, Skt. *tattvataḥ siddha*.

existent causes and conditions, the creation of anything [intrinsically real] is impossible, and since the causes and conditions themselves are intrinsic as well, they are impossible. Hence such [intrinsic reality] is incompatible with relativity.

Alternatively, one could seek to avoid that problem by claiming [some form of] objective existence. If so, however, like something already arisen, [such an objectively existent thing] could not come about through causes and conditions, since the causes and conditions could not exist [as such] because of being unnecessary. In such a case, this too is incompatible with relativity.

If relativity is contradicted, then the assertion of everything is undermined. Just like such [utter unrealities] as the horns of an donkey, not even migrant beings could be seen. Consequently, migrations with their diversity of realms, migrants, types of birth, clans, families, parentage, color and forms, strengths, intelligence and faculties, as well as the external environment of all migrant beings, with its surrounding atmosphere, and so on,[204] with[205] gold, silver, sapphires, crystals, lotus rubies, and other [precious stones],[206] as well as white lilies, lotuses, trees, mountains, medicines, pots, chariots, and so forth,[207] and [all] the variety of things unseen would be non-existent. Claiming that such [things,] seen to exist, do not exist, is irrational.

Consequently, [one should] abandon [notions of] objective existence and non-existence in things that have arisen and depend on something [else], and should assert that they lack objective status like mirror reflections, since they are established by just such [supporting] conditions. As Āryadeva stated:

---

204 Tib. *rlung gi dkyil 'khor*, Skt. *vāyumaṇḍala*. This refers to the "circle of wind" that is the lowest foundation of a world-system in Buddhist cosmology.

205 Scherrer-Schaub (*Yuktiṣaṣṭikāvṛtti*, 282 n. 586) notes that this list follows the classical sequence describing the environmental world (*bhājana-loka*).

206 *gser* = **suvarṇa*; *dngul* = **rūpya*; *indranīla*; *shel* = **sphaṭika*. These are among the seven precious jewels (*sāpta-ratna*) out of which the palaces in the *Akaniṣṭha* heaven at the top of the form realm are built.

207 *shing* = **vṛkṣa*; *sman* = **oṣadhi*; *bum pa* = **golaḥ*; *shing rta* = **ratha*; and so forth. All are included among the semiprecious valuables listed in *maṇḍala* offering rituals.

> For those who assert that effects pre-exist [in their causes]
> And for those who assert that effects do not pre-exist,
> Things such as supporting pillars are useless,
> For the sake of the house, even as ornaments.[208]

Thus, abandoning permanence and annihilation, a dependently arisen form, like a reflection, is not incompatible with the sphere of activity of a mistaken awareness, so the various migrant beings that were spoken of are not impossible.

The noble, as well, abandon such errors and do not reify false [things]; thus, their liberation is not impossible. Since relativity is not objectively created, those who, through this reasoning,[209] accept dependent things as resembling the moon in water and reflections in a mirror, [understand them as] neither intrinsically objectively true nor false. Therefore, those who think thus regarding dependent things realize that what is dependently arisen cannot be substantially existent, since what is like a reflection is not [substantially] real. If it were real, that would entail [the absurdity] that its transformation would be impossible. Yet neither is it unreal, since it manifests as real within the world. Nevertheless, "It is not real" was said for a [contextual] purpose, and to teach certain individuals. Given that [things] are not [intrinsically] real, one will not advocate absolutism; given that they are not [intrinsically] unreal either, one will not advocate nihilism.

Thus, once one understands that dependently arisen [things] lack intrinsic reality, just like mirror reflections, then with that ship of knowledge of relativity one doubtless will cross over the waters of views such as impermanence, whose high waves toss, stirred by the winds of inappropriate ideas. Hence, one will reach the level shore of the garden of transcendent nirvāṇa, adorned with the grove of the distinctive qualities of the Buddha, captivating with the jewel array of the factors of enlightenment, impeccable with its endowment of ten powers, which leads to the bliss of freedom

---

[208] CŚ, 11.15 (Lang, 106–107, and n. 15): *stambhādīnām alaṁkāro gṛhasyârthe nirarthakaḥ // satkāryam eva yasyeṣṭaṁ yasyâsatkāryam eva ca //*. If the house does not pre-exist in the structurally supporting beams—taking the beams as a cause of the house—then the beams and the house, being intrinsically different as cause and effect, cannot work together; if the house already exists in the pillars, then the implication is: what are the beams good for? Decoration?

[209] The "royal reasoning of relativity" (*pratītyasamutpāda-yukti-rāja*).

through the knowledge of termination and non-production.[210] Since [the Buddha] proclaimed that sublime secret instruction of relativity for others to follow there, even those who, in an effort to establish that proclamation,[211] remain in the ocean of cyclic life, bewildered by the streams of worldviews like absolutism, and so forth, will definitely be freed.

b. Teaching that very view to be the cause of everything useless

i. The actual teaching

Those who do not understand this teaching of relativity will imagine an intrinsic identity of things, and undoubtedly

46. Once they commit to [intrinsic] things,[212]
They are trapped in painful malignant views
Which produce attachment and aversion,
And the disputes[213] that spring from them.

Here, "attachment" is defined as an insistence[214] on one's own perspective [and] "aversion" is defined as turning away from the perspective of others. The sources of attachment and aversion are those [views] "that generate attachment and aversion." Since their consequences are extremely unpleasant and exceedingly difficult to bear, [Nāgārjuna calls such views] "unbearable"; and, since they are hard to escape and harm one's mental continuum, [he calls them] "malignant." What is all this? Being thoroughly trapped in views.

Moreover, this fixation on addictive views grows out of the commitment to this and that as [objectively existent] things. Since, when one is maintaining a view, one seeks to prove the reality of one's claim and to dismiss the claims of others, the disputes that arise from asserting an addictive view grow from the root of addiction to [objectively existent] things, which in turn gives rise to other [disputes].

---

210 Tib. *zad pa dang mi skye pa shes pa*, Skt. **kṣaya-anutpāda-jñāna*. As Scherrer-Schaub notes (*Yuktiṣaṣṭikāvṛtti*, 286 n. 603), these together define the realization of an Arhat.

211 Tib. *bsgo ba*, Skt. **ājñā* Mvy 8433.

212 Skt. *bhāvābhyupagama*, Tib. *dngos por khas len [pa]*.

213 Skt. *vivāda*, Tib. *rtsod pa*.

214 Tib. *rnam par zhen pa*, Skt. *abhiniveśa*.

ii. The procedure for reversing that

(1) The teaching in brief

Because it is like this, for the sake of everyone [Nāgārjuna stated]:

47. That [reality-habit] is the cause of all views;
Without it, addictions do not develop.
So when its [falsity] is fully understood,
Views and addictions are fully cured.

Once one asserts [intrinsically real] things, one will succumb to the view of seeing such [real things] by imagining their beginning, middle, and end; hence, that grasping at [objectively real] things is the cause of all views. Once one has an addictive view, the addictions which arise from that cause will develop. Because one develops attachment to one's own views, and with it, one becomes prideful and develops aversion to opposing views, and because delusions regarding all things come about, addictions arise from views.

Since all views and addictions originate from the cause of perceiving [intrinsic reality in] things, these things must be thoroughly understood [to be empty of intrinsic reality].[215] When one understands the actual nature of things, one eliminates such views through their non-perception. When such views are eliminated, addictions are eliminated.

(2) The extensive explanation

(a) The status of objects of knowledge

(i) Relative creation is not incompatible with intrinsic unreality

If, thinking about this,

48. One asks, "How can this be understood?"
[It is understood] by seeing relativity.
"The dependently created is uncreated!"[216]
Thus spoke the supreme knower of reality.

---

[215] Following Gyaltsap (*ṭīkka*, fol. 30a.2).

[216] A similar quote [*gang zhig rkyen las skyes pa de ma skyes; yaḥ pratyayairjāyati sa hyajāto*] appears in the PPMMV ad k. 13.2 (La Vallée Poussin, *Madhyamakavṛttiḥ*, 239), the *Bodhicaryāvatārapañjikā* ad k. 9.2 (La Vallée Poussin, *Bouddhisme*, 240), and others places, and—

(cont'd)

Having seen relativity, one no longer perceives things as objectively [real], since what is created in dependence upon [causes and conditions] is objectively uncreated, like a mirror reflection.

[Someone might object,] "Something that is dependently created is certainly created, yet what would be designated as 'uncreated'? If that is what [you are] referring to as 'uncreated,' it would be irrational to call it 'dependently created,' since it is internally contradictory, and thus [this interpretation of the words of the Buddha] is not correct."

[Let me explain.] If you say this, then since [in common parlance] one who seeks to reproach himself may [do so] even with [statements such as] "Alas, alack, I have no ears, no heart," and finding fault with himself, may come to say "I am despicable," then what possible way is there for you to try to dispute it when we proclaim, "What is created in dependence upon [causes and conditions] is not intrinsically created, like a mirror reflection"?

When we see the mirror reflection of some form arising dependently, we perceive that [mirror reflection] as false and call it "uncreated" [in its semblance of being the reflected object]. The nature[217] by which its [mirror reflection] is presented as unarisen is the very same [nature] by which we define that [dependent creation] as uncreated.

[To this, someone] objects: "With respect to what nature do you present [the dependently created] as uncreated?"

[Let me explain.] It is accepted [as uncreated] with respect to the [intrinsic] actuality which others claim to be ultimate, but not with respect to that false identity [itself], since we accept that that [illusory] reality is relatively originated. Therefore, if both these characterizations of created and uncreated are not attributed to the same object, where is there a single object [about which you claim our statements are internally contradictory]?

[They respond:] "If you are not proving that what is correctly perceived as relative creation is uncreated, but rather proving that it is uncreated in its actuality, the position you are trying to demonstrate here is something different from what we have heard before."

[Let me explain.] We are not stating anything different in the slightest that you have not heard before, since this treatise was composed for the

---

as Scherrer-Schaub (*Yuktiṣaṣṭikāvṛtti*, 289 n. 617) notes—is attributed to the *Anavatapta-nāga-rāja-paripṛcchā-sūtra* (Tōh. 156).

217 Tib. *bdag nyid*, Skt. **ātmatva*.

primary purpose of showing reality precisely as it is. However, the extremist[218] who follows a misperception of reality as it is may imagine it in other than its pure form, according to his tainted perspective.

Relativity is not objectively created. Yet, although it is not created having such a mistaken character, individuals imagine it as objectively created. Thus, insisting on that, they become totally addicted. In order for disciples, hermit buddhas, and altruistic bodhisattvas to abandon such total addiction, those who understand correctly—the perfectly enlightened buddhas—proclaimed, "What is dependently created is uncreated." While the magician does not become totally addicted through insisting on imagining his female creature to be a real woman, those mistaken ones who have developed presumptuous pride and who fancy her to be a real woman become totally addicted. Likewise, here as well, the Lord Buddha's pronouncement that "What is dependently created is objectively uncreated," is to counteract [their] insistence on objectivity in things.

(ii) Showing all faults arising from holding them to be incompatible

Thus, [Nāgārjuna] stated]:

49. [Those] overwhelmed[219] by mistaken knowledge,
Are trapped by attachment in a process
Of obsession and conflict,
Clutching to truth in the [intrinsically] untrue.[220]

Consequently, in order to eliminate[221] the conception of truth in things that are not true, the Lord Buddha taught relativity. Since dependently arisen things are deceptive, they are not true. When one realizes that they are not true, one eliminates attachment to things. Once attachment to things is stopped, grasping at things is eliminated. As grasping produces obsessiveness,[222] that is likewise dispelled. Once that is stopped, conflicts, which come of attachment to desires and attachment to views, are also

[218] Reading *'gron* (one who travels afar) with Peking, sNar thang, and SS.

[219] Tib. *zil gnon pa*, Skt. **abhibhūya*.

[220] Following Gyaltsap (*ṭīkka*, fol. 30b.5–31a.1).

[221] Tib. *bzlog pa*, Skt. *nivartayati, vyāvartayati*.

[222] Tib. *bdag gir byed pa*, Skt. *svīkaraṇa, svīkāra, svīkriyā*.

eliminated. When conflicts are stopped, disputes, and so forth, are also eliminated.

(b) The procedure for realization by awareness

(i) The actual procedure

Consequently, since they do not perceive anything whatsoever that is truly established [intrinsically, yet] dependent upon [other] things, [Nāgārjuna stated,] undoubtedly

50ab. Great souls are beyond disputes,
[For,] they assume no [fixated] position.[223]

When one assumes a [righteous] position of one's own, one then enters into disputes with others because it has been fixed upon.[224] Consequently those without any such [position]—the great souls—are free from conflict. Moreover, for those who already are free from any [fixated] position, it is no longer possible for another's position to be unassailable. For when you have no [fixed] position, it is impossible to see others as maintaining a [fixed] opposition. Now, even if there were such a thing as a position, without it being one's own position or another's position, it would be utterly irrelevant! Hence,

50cd. For those who have no position,
How can there be any opposition?

Just so, when there is no position of one's own or of another, since there are no [truly existent] things, the addictions of those who see [things] in such a manner will definitely cease.

(ii) The reasoning for that

If someone asks, "How is that?" [Nāgārjuna says the great souls are] like this:

51. If any sort of hold is found,
The cunning[225] **poisonous snake of addiction**

---

[223] Tib. *phyogs*, Skt. **pakṣa*.

[224] Tib. *gzugs pa* (f. of *'dzug pa*), Skt. *ropaṇa*.

[225] Tib. *g.yon can*, Skt. **dhūrtaka*.

Will seize it; but those whose minds
Have no [such] hold, will not be seized.

[The poisonous snakes of] desire and the other [addictions] roam throughout the thick forest of intrinsically [real] creations, choke off the life-force of virtuous inclinations, make their nest in the cave of the visual senses of one's addictive views, and [their] long-range stalking follows one's mental attraction on the wind of objects. They are "cunning" [because] they move about in a deceitful manner. [They are] "snakes" because they strive to catch [their prey]. Finding any ground at all that might be a place to nest, they "seize" anything whatsoever. Since those who burn all the nesting grounds of the snakes of addictions by not perceiving [an intrinsic reality] in anything, and block the caves of the senses with mindfulness and awareness, thus leave no hold for the snake of the addictions to seize. "Those whose minds have no hold are not[226] seized," because once the mind does not perceive [an intrinsic reality] in things, there is no place in it to hold onto.[227] Therefore, through such [methods] as these, those whose minds have no such [reality-]perception, are unharmed even by the cunning, poisonous snakes of the addictions and are not seized by them.

c. Showing that you cannot abandon addictions if you have the reality-habit

i. The actual teaching

[Conversely,] those who believe they can abandon addictions while objectively perceiving the intrinsic [reality] of [the aggregates such as] form, and so forth, will never abandon their addictions. In order to show that, [Nāgārjuna] stated:

52ab. How could the addictions not poison
Those whose minds keep the place for them?

When one sees [an intrinsic existence] in things, the development of desire and other addictions will doubtless not stop but progress.

---

[226] The negative particle (*mi*) is omitted in all four canonical redactions of the text, although the insertion of a negative is justified by Gyaltsap's parallel commentary (*ṭīkka*, 32b.1).

[227] The Peking and Snar-thang redactions read: "...there is no position of self or other for the mind to hold onto."

If someone asks, "How?" If the thing were to correspond with such a mental [image of it], then it would be difficult to reverse one's attachment to such [an intrinsically existent thing]. And even when it does not correspond [with that mental image], it still is difficult to eliminate anger and resentment. Further, even when both of these [addictive] emotions are dispelled in a state of equanimity, it will still be hard to stop the instincts[228] for misknowledge concerning [intrinsic] objects, which [instincts] are reinforced by perceptions and reifications of [those objects'] intrinsic reality. Even when one dwells in an simple state of [contemplative] equanimity, the snakes of the harmful addictions that give rise to the suffering of cyclic life associated with instinctual misknowledge, the origin [of suffering], will still [thrive].

ii. Showing loving concern for those endowed [with the reality-habit]

Having seen [this Nāgārjuna] stated:

52cd. Even when [ascetics] stay neutral,[229]
The snake of addiction will seize them.

While those obscurations are constantly being produced, [ordinary] alienated individuals, whose vision of reality is obstructed by total delusion, [must] not hesitate [to critique their habitual misperception of] the nature of things, established by the force of such delusion. [For as Nāgārjuna states:]

53. As a child with his notion of truth,
Falls in love with a mirror image,
Worldly people, due to delusion,
Are trapped in a thicket of objects.

A child, not understanding mundane conventions, his awareness stupefied with intrinsic realities, sees a mirror image, holds it to be a real thing, and

---

228 Tib. *bag la nyal ba*, Skt. **anuśaya*.

229 Tib. *tha mal [pa]*, Skt. **udāsīna*. Both Tsong Khapa (*legs bshad snying po*, fol. 71b.6) and Gyaltsap (*ṭīkka*, fol. 32b.3–.5) follow Pa-tshab's translation, the latter glossing this as: "while abiding in a state of equanimity in between the absence of attachment and aversion...." Our edition and translation follow this preferable reading, both in the verse and just above in the commentary, as "ordinary" makes no sense here.

can fall in love with it and play with it however he can. In just that way, naïve persons, endowed with misknowledge created by the force of their delusions, are mentally, verbally, and physically obsessed with arguing about [intrinsically] real things, insisting on "this" or "that." They are helplessly seduced by desire, anger, pride, and the other [addictions]. And, not knowing the nature of cyclic life, they are completely trapped in its thicket, whatever they try to do. Such people are objects of loving concern for the noble ones. For they, having opened their wisdom eyes, can see reality as it truly is.

iii. How others are the opposite

Therefore [Nāgārjuna stated]:

54. Seeing things to be like mirror images
With their eye of intuitive wisdom,
Great souls do not get stuck
In the quicksand of "objects."

When there is no attachment, one does not get stuck in the swamp of objects, since there is neither attachment to nor engagement with such an [intrinsically identifiable] nature in things.

d. The difference between being and not being stuck in the object trap

i. Summary

"Noble one" means "anyone who has thus educated his mind about mirror images." Naïve minds are doubtless just like children with mirror images.

55. The naïve are attached to forms;
The mediocre are detached from them.
Those with the highest intelligence understand
The nature of forms, and thus are freed.

Here, those who have the characteristics of children are "the naïve." Hence, they think erroneous thoughts, utter erroneous pronouncements, and engage in erroneous actions. Here, thinking erroneous thoughts is thinking that the body—whose nature is impure, transitory, and perishable—has a pure and indestructible nature.[230] To "utter erroneous pronouncements" is to express praise, through diverse constructions of syllables, words, and phrases, for a body that is unfit for praise, whose nature is to suffer and need constant care. To "engage in erroneous actions" is to take up actions which ripen as suffering—the resultant effect of non-virtuous [activity]. Thus, the "naïve" are those addicted to the body which is like something impure. The "mediocre" are those who, being repulsed by the impurity[231] [of the body] as it really is, see it as a mass of many hundreds of pains, and having been freed from desire for forms, achieve immersion in the contemplations and formless trances,[232] far beyond the realm of desire. [Finally,] those who realize that form, like a mirror image, does not intrinsically exist, no doubt transcend constructions of [intrinsically real] forms and other [aggregates. Hence, Nāgārjuna stated:] "Those with the highest intelligence understand the nature of forms, and thus are freed."

ii. Detailed explanation

In order to show the precise meaning of this [Nāgārjuna stated]:

56. Those who cherish[233] beauty become attached;
Those who turn away from it become detached.
But those who see it as empty,
Like an illusory person, reach nirvāṇa.

---

230 Chandrakīrti refers here to three of the four errors (*viparyāsa*), in which these three and the characteristic of suffering (*sdug bsngal* = *duḥkha*) are mistaken for their opposites.

231 Chandrakīrti here refers to the nine aversive ideas (*aśubha-saṁjñā*) contemplated as part of the basic training (*pūrva-śikṣā*) to extinguish addiction to the realm of desire. Cf. AK, ad k. 6.9 (Pradhan, 337; La Vallée Poussin, *L'Abhidharmakośa*, IV, 148–149), and Scherrer-Schaub, *Yuktiṣaṣṭikāvṛtti*, 301 n. 670.

232 Tib. *bsam gtan dang gzugs med pa'i snyoms par 'jug pa*, Skt. *dhyāna-arūpa-samāpatti*. The four trances of the formless realm are in levels of increasingly pure abstraction, in the spheres of infinite space (*ākāśānanty-āyatana*), infinite consciousness (*vijñānānanty-āyatana*), nothingness (*akiṁcanyāyatana*), and neither consciousness nor unconsciousness (*naiva-samjñā-naivāsamjñāyatana*). The four contemplations combine with the four trances and the final state of cessation in the nine stage progression of mental states (*navānupūrva-vihāra*) that leads to supreme liberation, according to Abhidharmic systems.

233 Gyaltsap (*ṭīkka*, fol. 33b.2) explains this as: Those of the desire realm, without any sort of means of conceiving of the suffering of [the aggregates of] form, and so forth, generate attachment through the activity in their minds.

"Like an illusory person," forms of life are vacant and empty. Those who reach nirvāṇa, having seen nirvāṇa, are those endowed with "the highest intelligence," whether they are to be known as disciples, hermit buddhas, or lord buddhas. "The mediocre" are the mundane [ascetics,] who are free from desire and attachment. The "naïve" should be known as those addicted to desire.

D. The benefits of liberation

1. The individual explanations

a. The good qualities of abandonment

How does one reach nirvāṇa through the insight that migrant beings are vacant like illusory persons? [To explain this, Nāgārjuna] stated:

> **57. Those disturbed by false knowledge**
> **Suffer all the faults of addiction;**
> **But those who come to know the [true] meaning**
> **Have no [false] constructs of being or nothingness.**

Those who see the world as like an illusion completely understand being and nothingness by not perceiving an intrinsically identifiable being or nothingness. Since they do not imagine [an intrinsic identity] in these two, they are not constructed. For those who know the [true] meaning [of reality], having dissolved being and nothingness, desire and the other addictions undoubtedly will no longer function as causes of cyclic life.

Such addictions do arise in those disturbed by false knowledge. They are "disturbed," since they are in a state of being actively disturbed. Since they are actively disturbed by false knowledge, they are [called] "disturbed by false knowledge." When these mistaken individuals perceive an object and hold onto it, they are disturbed by the addictions.

Since such [addictions] do not exist in those who realize the [true] meaning [of reality], they doubtless attain nirvāṇa. As for the naïve, since they are mistaken, nirvāṇa is impossible. Since the [naïve and the average] construct a place for attachment and detachment, they thus come to have attachment or detachment for [their respective] perceived objects.

b. The good qualities of realization

As for the noble, in regard to cyclic life,

58. When one has a place [for reified things]
One experiences attachment and detachment;
But the great souls, having no [such] place,
Are neither attached nor detached.

Whether one perceives something to be attached to or perceives something to be detached from, both attachment and detachment are possible. When one does not reify an objective identity in things, neither desirous attachment nor freedom from desirous attachment will arise. The noble ones, since they do not perceive an intrinsic objectivity of things, have no place for these. Free from such perception, they are definitely in nirvāṇa.

2. The conclusion

Therefore, when analyzed in this way,

59. Whoever contemplates freedom,[234]
And is not moved by the wavering mind,
Crosses the ocean of intolerable existence,
Which seethes with the snakes of addiction.

Whoever dwells in the teaching of this freedom, and experiences that "the world is void," stays free from the monkey-like, naturally wild mind, and crosses the ocean of existence, seeing it seethe with the snakes of addiction.

III. Dedicating the virtues arising from composition

Now, in order to fully dedicate the virtues of writing [this book, Nāgārjuna declared]:

60. By the virtue [of writing this,] may all beings
Gather the stores of merit and wisdom,
And attain the two supreme [buddha bodies]
Arisen from merit and wisdom![235]

---

[234] Following Gyaltsap (*ṭīkka*, fol. 34a.5–.6).

[235] This verse is cited by Bu-ston in his *chos 'byung* (Obermiller, *History*, 111). As explained by Nāgārjuna in his RA (3.12): *sangs rgyas rnams kyi gzugs sku 'dir / bsod nams tshog las byung ba ste / chos kyi sku ni mdor bsdu na / rgyal po ye shes tshogs las byung //* "While the form bodies of buddhas evolve from the store of merit, their truth bodies, in brief, O King, evolve from the store of wisdom."

The "store of merit" consists of all the immeasurable virtues achieved—except for wisdom itself and its causes—in order that countless realms of beings may come to understand. And the store of wisdom is all wisdom and the cause of wisdom totally dedicated to the achievement of buddhahood.

May all living beings who succeed in accumulating these two stores attain the unexcelled supreme [buddha-embodiments]. "Arisen" means created. That which has arisen from merit and wisdom [is what is meant by] "arisen from merit and wisdom." What are those two? They are the form body and truth body.

Through the virtue of this [composition], may [all beings] attain these two [bodies of a buddha]!

Remembering the *dragon* [Nāgārjuna], [I] left fear behind,
And [I,] the *moon* [Chandra], shone with *fame* [-kīrti] for the
unenlightened,
Banishing illusion's shadows,[236] source of all ills,
Making the night-lily of [his] philosophy bloom.

Having entered into non-denial of reality,
I wondered if its meaning could be expressed—
Since Buddha never said it would cause harm,
And in true realization I was free of doubts,

I thus gave up my reticence, and faithfully,
I elucidated this *Reason Sixty*.
By whatever merit comes of my analysis,
May all beings quickly become lords of sages!

Regarding the *Commentary on the Reason Sixty*: The Universalist Centrist teacher known as Chandrakīrti, born in the region of Samata, vanquished the manifold confusions of all the assembled hosts of fundamentalists. Since his wisdom born of learning and contemplation came to illuminate the sky of the speech of the Transcendent Lord, dispelling the

---

236 Tib. *rab rib rnam pa*, Skt. *taimirākāra*, the illusory forms seen by those with eye defects, only here afflicting the eye of intelligence (*buddhi-cakṣu*), hence "illusion."

two extremes, his immeasurable, impeccable fame (*kīrti*) is celebrated as the moon (*candra*), [whose light] cools all the living beings who are suffering from the fever of various misperceptions of things which do not exist in reality. Thus, the *Commentary on the Reason Sixty* he composed is completed.

It was translated and critically edited by the Indian scholars Jinamitra, Dānaśīla, and Śīlendrabodhi, and the great [Tibetan] translator, the Venerable Ye-shes-sde.

CRITICAL EDITIONS OF THE TIBETAN TEXTS

About the Critical Tibetan Editions

The following editions of Nāgārjuna's *Reason Sixty* and Chandrakīrti's *Commentary on the "Reason Sixty"* were produced through the combination of several different sources. The initial electronic files were obtained from the Asian Classics Input Project (ACIP), and proofed against their source, the Derge (*sde dge*) redaction of the texts (Tōkyō, 1977). Text critical annotations were added from the two previously published critical editions:

> Christine Scherrer-Schaub, "Yuktiṣaṣṭikāvṛtti," *Melanges Chinois et Bouddhiques* 25 (1991)
>
> *Bstan 'gyur dpe bsdur ma.* Chengdu: Chengdu Peoples' Publishing House (1998–2005), vols. 57 and 60

as well as the Sanskrit fragments given in:

> Ch. Lindtner, *Nāgārjuniana.* Copenhagen: Akademisk Forlag (1982)

and other sources, where appropriate. The annotations were collated and verified, and integrated into the electronic file prior to typesetting in a pattern reflecting the structure of the translation. When the preferred reading differs from that given in the Derge redaction, all variant readings are recorded in the footnotes, otherwise only differences from the Derge are noted. Whereas Scherrer-Schaub endeavored to note all variations in editions, stylistic and typographic, we have only noted actual stylistic variations (e.g., *bltos* vs. *ltos*) and not blockprint deficiencies (e.g., *mad* for *med*). Furthermore, it should be noted that in producing the edition contained here, we have relied upon the texts of the *Yuktiṣaṣṭikā* and *Yuktiṣaṣṭikā-vṛtti* contained in the following Tripiṭakas: the Peking redaction housed at Ōtani University,[1] the Derge redaction housed at the University of Tokyo,[2] the

[1] Tibetan Tripitaka Research Institute. *The Tibetan Tripiṭaka: Peking Edition.* Tokyo and Kyoto, 1956. Scholars in Chengdu (as documented in the Dpe-bsdur-ma redaction) likewise utilized the reproduction of the Ōtani University ms. Scherrer-Schaub utilized the manuscript version of the Peking redaction housed in the Bibliothèque Nationale (Paris). While Imaeda notes that there are clear differences between the Paris and Ōtani mss. of the Peking

(cont'd)

Co-ne redaction reproduced by IASWR,[3] and the Snar-thang redaction. We have further compared our text with the annotations made by Scherrer-Schaub and with those documented in the Dpe-bsdur-ma[4] redaction.[5]

In the edition of the *Yuktiṣaṣṭikā-vṛtti* that follows, we have left the verses as given in the *Yuktiṣaṣṭikā-vṛtti* without attempting to normalize them to the root text, and have only noted variations between redactions of the *vṛtti* itself, though we have noted readings attested in subsequent Tibetan commentaries in both the root text and the *vṛtti*. In addition, we have integrated the topical outline (*sa bcad*) of Nāgārjuna and Chandrakīrti's texts given by Gyaltsap into the body of the work as section headings (also reflected in the translation).

In producing this edition, we have followed the conventions of the Chengdu *Dpe bsdur ma* redaction. The abbreviations used here are:

«པེ་»	Peking redaction
«སྣར་»	Snar-thang redaction
«སྡེ་»	Sde-dge redaction
«ཅོ་»	Co-ne redaction
«དཔེ་»	Dpe-sdur-ma redaction

Bka'-'gyur ("...l'exemplaire de la Bibliothèque Nationale, qui ne représente pourtant pas le même tirage que celui de l'Université Ōtani"), he dismisses the idea that the two printings of the Bstan-'gyur might be different ("Quant au Tanjur, il n'a été édité qu'une seule fois sur un ordre impérial de 1724. Ainsi le problème des différentes éditions ne se pose pas comme dans le cas du Kanjur..."). Similarly, Ch'en takes the Paris and Ōtani mss. to be the same ("Peking Red"). Based on her work with the *Yuktiṣaṣṭikāvṛtti*, Scherrer-Schaub confirms that this ms. is, in fact, identical to that housed at Ōtani University. Consequently, any discrepancies between annotators of the Peking redaction have been resolved in reference to the Ōtani ms. IMAEDA, "Mise au Point," 32–33; Ch'en, "Tibetan Tripitaka," 61; Christina Scherrer-Schaub, private communication.

[2] *Sde dge Tibetan Tripiṭaka bstan ḥgyur*. Tokyo: University of Tokyo (1977).

[3] *Chone Tanjur Microfiche Edition*. Stony Brook, NY: Institute for Advanced Study of World Religions (1976).

[4] The Dpe-bsdur-ma redaction of the Tibetan Bstan-'gyur (Chengdu, 2000–2005).

[5] Where discrepancies exist between the annotations made by Scherrer-Schaub and the staff of the Dpe-bsdur-ma regarding the Snar-thang redaction of the texts, they have been resolved in reference to the Roerich ms. of the Snar-thang Bstan-'gyur housed at Columbia University.

«ཊཱི་»	Gyaltsap Darma Rinchen, *rigs pa drug cu pa'i ṭīkka*
«ཟིན་»	Tsong Khapa Losang Drakpa, *rigs pa drug cu pa'i zin 'bris*
«ལཾ་»	Tsong Khapa Losang Drakpa pa, *lam rim chen mo* (mtsho sngon: 1985, 1997)
«སྙིང་»	Tsong Khapa Losang Drakpa, *legs bshad snying po* (zhol par khang, n.d.)
{Dh}	Dun-huang mss., Pelliot Tib. 795/796
{SS}	Scherrer-Schaub
{CL}	Lindtner
{Y}	Yamaguchi

Other sources are cited explicitly. In addition, the following conventions were used:

:	[double-tsheg] marks the beginning of the scope of an annotation
+	indicates additional text
-	indicates missing or omitted text
*	used to indicate a Sanskrit reconstruction
( )	used to demarcate topical outline (from Gyaltsap's *ṭīkka*) incorporated into the text by the editors

Since it is presumed that any reader consulting the critical edition will have a working knowledge of Tibetan, we have rendered the texts in Tibetan script; Sanskrit we have left in Romanized form.

Regarding pagination of the various redactions, we have followed the standard convention in labeling folios with 'a' and 'b' sides. In general, our pagination agrees with that adopted by Scherrer-Schaub except with regard to the Co-ne redaction (we consider the text of the *vṛtti* to begin on fol. 1b.1, hence our pagination differs by half a folio from that in Scherrer-Schaub's edition) and the Snar-thang redaction (from fol. 24a onwards).

Critical Edition of the
rigs pa drug cu pa'i tshig le'ur byas pa (*Yuktiṣaṣṭikā*)

རིགས་པ་དྲུག་ཅུ་པའི་ཚིག་ལེའུར་བྱས་པ།

[«ཅོ་» 20b.1][«སྡེ་» 20b.1][«པེ་» 22b.3][«སྣར་ 20b.1»]

༄༅། །རྒྱ་གར་སྐད་དུ། ཡུཀྟི་ཥཥྛི་ཀཱ་ཀཱ་རི་ཀཱ་ནཱ་མ།
བོད་སྐད་དུ། རིགས་པ་དྲུག་ཅུ་པའི་ཚིག་ལེའུར་བྱས་པ་ཞེས་བྱ་བ།

འཇམ་དཔལ་གཞོན་ནུར་གྱུར་པ་ལ་ཕྱག་འཚལ་ལོ།

།གང་གིས་[1] སྐྱེ་དང་འཇིག་པ་དག
།ཚུལ་འདི་ཡིས་ནི་སྤངས་གྱུར་པ།
།རྟེན་ཅིང་འབྱུང་བ་གསུངས་[2] པ་ཡི།
།ཐུབ་དབང་དེ་ལ་ཕྱག་འཚལ་ལོ། || **Homage** ||

---

[1] «པེ་»«སྣར་»«སྡིང་ 46a.5»: གིས་ «སྡེ་»«ཅོ་»: གི་

[2] «སྡིང་ 46a.6»: གསུང་

།གང་གིས་བློ་གྲོས་[3] ཡོད་མེད་ལས།
།རྣམ་པར་འདས་ཤིང་མི་གནས་པ།
།དེ་དག་གིས་ནི་རྐྱེན་གྱི་དོན།
།ཟབ་མོ་དམིགས་མེད་རྣམ་པར་རྟོགས། || **1** ||

།རེ་ཞིག་ཉེས་ཀུན་འབྱུང་བའི་གནས།
།མེད་ཉིད་རྣམ་པར་བཟློག་ཟིན་གྱིས།[4]
།རིགས་པའི་[5] གང་གིས་ཡོད་ཉིད་དང་།
།བཟློག་པར་འགྱུར་བ་མཉན་[6] པར་གྱིས། || **2** ||

།ཇི་ལྟར་བྱིས་པས་རྣམ་བརྟགས་[7] བཞིན།
།དངོས་པོ་གལ་ཏེ་བདེན་འགྱུར་[8] ན།
།དེ་དངོས་མེད་པས་རྣམ་ཐར་དུ།
།གང་གིས་མི་འདོད་རྒྱུ་ཅི་ཞིག || **3** ||

---

[3] «པེ་»«སྣར་»{SS}: དག་གི་བློ་ «སྡེ་»«ཅོ་»: གིས་བློ་གྲོས་

[4] {SS}{Y}: གྱི་

[5] «པེ་»«སྣར་»{SS}{Y}: པ་

[6] «པེ་»: མཉམ་

[7] «པེ་»«སྣར་»: བརྟག

[8] «པེ་»«སྣར་»{SS}{Y}: གྱུར་

།ཡོད་པས་རྣམ་པར་མི་གྲོལ་ཏེ།
།མེད་པས་སྲིད་པ་འདི་ལས་མིན།
།དངོས་དང་དངོས་མེད་ཡོངས་ཤེས་པས།
།བདག་ཉིད་ཆེན་པོ་རྣམ་པར་གྲོལ། **|| 4[9] ||**

།དེ་ཉིད་མ་མཐོང་འཇིག་རྟེན་དང་།
།མྱ་ངན་འདས་པར་རློམ་སེམས་ཏེ།
།དེ་ཉིད་གཟིགས་རྣམས་འཇིག་རྟེན་དང་།
།མྱ་ངན་འདས་པར་རློམ་སེམས་མེད། **|| 5 ||**

།སྲིད་པ་དང་ནི་མྱ་ངན་འདས།
།གཉིས་པོ་འདི་ནི་ཡོད་མ་ཡིན།
།སྲིད་པ་ཡོངས་སུ་ཤེས་པ་ཉིད།
།མྱ་ངན་འདས་ཤེས་[10] བྱ་བར་བརྗོད། **|| 6 ||**

།དངོས་པོ་བྱུང་བ་[11] ཞིག་པ་ལ།
།ཇི་ལྟར་འགོག་ [《པེ་》 23a.1] པར་བརྟགས་[12] པ་བཞིན།

---

9 《སྙིང་ 74b.3》: attests this reading

10 《པེ་》《སྣར་》: ཞེས་

11 {SS}: འབྱུང་བའི་

12 《པེ་》{SS}: བརྟག་

།དེ་བཞིན་དམ་པ་རྣམས་ཀྱིས་ཀྱང་།
།སྒྱུ་མ་བྱས་ལྟའི་[13] འགོག་པ་བཞེད། || 7 ||

།རྣམ་པར་འཇིག་པས་འགོག་འགྱུར་གྱི།
།འདུས་བྱས་ཡོངས་སུ་ཤེས་པས་མིན།
།དེ་ནི་སུ་ལ་མངོན་སུམ་འགྱུར།
།ཞིག་ཤེས་པ་དེར་[14]ཇི་ལྟར་འགྱུར། || 8 ||

།གལ་ཏེ་ཕུང་པོ་མ་འགགས་ན།
།ཉོན་མོངས་ཟད་ཀྱང་འདས་མི་འགྱུར།
།གང་ཚེ་འདིར་ནི་འགགས་གྱུར་པ།
། དེ་ཡི་ཚེ་ན་གྲོལ་བར་འགྱུར། || 9 ||

།མ་རིག་རྐྱེན་གྱིས་བྱུང་བ་ལ།
།ཡང་དག་ཡེ་ཤེས་ཀྱིས་གཟིགས་ན།[15]
།སྐྱེ་བ་དང་ནི་འགགས་པའང་རུང་།
།འགའ་ཡང་དམིགས་པར་མི་འགྱུར་རོ། || 10 ||

13 «པེ་»«སྣར་»: པའི་

14 {SS}{Y}: དེ་

15 «པེ་»«སྣར་»«ཏྲེ་ 14b.2»{SS}{Y}{CL}: ན། «སྡེ་»«ཅོ་»: ནས།

།དེ་ཉིད་མཐོང་ཆོས་མྱ་ངན་ལས།[16]
།འདས་ཤིང་བྱ་བ་བྱས་པའང་ཡིན།
།གལ་ཏེ་ཆོས་ཤེས་མཇུག་[17] ཐོགས་སུ།
།འདི་ལ་བྱེ་བྲག་ཡོད་ན་ནི། || **11** ||

།དངོས་པོ་ཤིན་ [«ཅོ་» 21a.1] ཏུ་ཕྲ་བ་ལའང་།
།གང་ [«སྡེ་» 21a.1] གིས་སྐྱེ་བར་རྣམ་བརྟགས་པ།
།རྣམ་པར་མི་མཁས་དེ་ཡི་[18] ནི།
།རྐྱེན་ལས་བྱུང་བའི་དོན་མ་མཐོང་། || **12** ||

།ཉོན་ [«སྣར་» 21a.1] མོངས་ཟད་པའི་དགེ་སློང་གི།
།གལ་ཏེ་འཁོར་བ་རྣམ་ལྡོག་ན།
།ཅི་ཕྱིར་རྫོགས་སངས་རྒྱས་རྣམས་ཀྱིས།
།དེ་ཡི་རྩོམ་པ་རྣམ་མི་བཤད། || **13** ||

།རྩོམ་[19] པ་ཡོད་ན་ངེས་པར་ཡང་།
།ལྟ་བར་འགྱུར་བ་ཡོངས་སུ་འཛིན།

---

16 «པེ་»«སྣར་»{SS}{Y}{CL}: ལས་ «སྡེ་»«ཅོ་»: འདས་

17 «པེ་»: འཇུག

18 «པེ་»«སྣར་»: ཡིས་

19 «པེ་»«སྣར་»: རྩོན་

།རྟེན་ཅིང་འབྲེལ་པར་འབྱུང་བ་གང་།
།དེ་ལ་སྔོན་དང་ཐ་མ་ཅི། || **14** ||

།སྔོན་སྐྱེས་པ་ནི་ཇི་ལྟར་ན།
།ཕྱི་ནས་སླར་ཡང་བཟློག་པར་འགྱུར།
།སྔོན་དང་ཕྱི་མའི་མཐའ་བྲལ་བ།
།འགྲོ[20] བ་སྒྱུ་མ་བཞིན་དུ་སྣང་། || **15** ||

།གང་ཚེ་སྒྱུ་མ་འབྱུང་ཞེ་འམ།
།གང་ཚེ་འཇིག་པར་འགྱུར་སྙམ་དུ།
།སྒྱུ་མ་ཤེས་པ་དེར་མི་རྨོངས།
།སྒྱུ་མ་མི་ཤེས་ཡོངས་སུ་སྲེད། || **16** ||

།སྲིད་པ་སྨིག་རྒྱུ་སྒྱུ་འདྲ་བར།
།བློ་ཡིས་མཐོང་བར་གྱུར་པ་ནི།
།སྔོན་གྱི་མཐའ་འམ་ཕྱི་མའི་མཐའ།[21]
།ལྟ་བས་ཡོངས་སུ་སླད་མི་འགྱུར། || **17** ||

།གང་དག་གིས་ནི་འདུས་བྱས་ལ།
།སྐྱེ་དང་འཇིག་པ་[22] རྣམ་བརྟགས་པ།

---

[20] «པེ་»«སྣར་»: གྲོལ་

[21] {SS}: མཐར་

[22] {SS}: པར་

།དེ་དག་རྟེན་འབྱུང་འཁོར་ལོ་ཡིས།[23]
༑འཁོར་ལོའི་འགྲོ་བ་རྣམ་མི་རྟོག[24] || **18** ||

།དེ་དང་དེ་བརྟེན་གང་འབྱུང་[25] དེ།
།རང་གི་དངོས་པོར་སྐྱེས་མ་ཡིན།
།རང་གི་དངོས་པོ་[26] གང་མ་སྐྱེས།
།དེ་ནི་སྐྱེ་[27] ཞེས་ཇི་ལྟར་བྱ། || **19** ||

།རྒྱུ་ཟད་ཉིད་ལས་ཞི་བ་ནི།
།ཟད་ཅེས་བྱ་བར་རྟོག་[28] པ་སྟེ།
།རང་བཞིན་གྱིས་ནི་གང་མ་ཟད།
།དེ་ལ་ཟད་ཅེས་ཇི་ལྟར་བརྗོད། || **20** ||

།དེ་ལྟར་ཅི་ཡང་སྐྱེ་བ་མེད།
།ཅི་ཡང་འགག་པར་མི་འགྱུར་རོ།

---

[23] {SS}{Y}{CL}: ཡི་

[24] «པེ་»«སྣར་»«ཏྭི་ 18a.2»{SS}{Y}{CL}: འགྲོ་བ་རྣམ་ [«པེ་» 23b.1] པར་མི་ཤེས་སོ།

[25] «པེ་»«སྣར་»{SS}{CL}: བྱུང་།

[26] «པེ་»«སྣར་»: པོར་

[27] {SS}{CL}: སྐྱེས་

[28] «པེ་»«སྣར་»{SS}{Y}{CL}: རྟོགས་

།སྐྱེ་བ་དང་ནི་འཇིག་པའི་ལམ།[29]
།དགོས་པའི་དོན་དུ་བསྟན་པའོ། ‖ **21** ‖

།སྐྱེ་བ་ཤེས་པས་འཇིག་པ་ཤེས།
།འཇིག་པ་ཤེས་པས་མི་རྟག་ཤེས།
།མི་རྟག་ཉིད་ལ་འཇུག་ཤེས་པས།
།དམ་པའི་ཆོས་ཀྱང་རྟོག་[30] པར་འགྱུར། ‖ **22** ‖

ཿགང་དག་རྟེན་[31] ཅིང་འབྲེལ་འབྱུང་བ།
།སྐྱེ་དང་འཇིག་པ་རྣམ་སྤངས་པར།
།ཤེས་པར་གྱུར་པ་དེ་དག་ནི།
།ལྟར་གྱུར་སྲིད་པའི་རྒྱ་མཚོ་བརྒལ། ‖ **23** ‖

།སོ་སོའི་[32] སྐྱེ་བོ་དངོས་བདག་ཅན།
།ཡོད་དང་མེད་པར་ཕྱིན་ཅི་ལོག
།ཉེས་པས་ཉོན་མོངས་དབང་གྱུར་རྣམས།
།རང་གི་སེམས་ཀྱིས་བསླུས་པར་འགྱུར། ‖ **24** ‖

---

29 «ཏཱཻ་ 22b.5» {SS}{Y}{CL}: ལམ། «པེ་» «སྣར་» «སྡེ་» «ཅོ་»: ལས།

30 «པེ་» «སྣར་» {SS}{Y}{CL}: རྟོགས་

31 «ཟིན་»: གང་ཟག་བསྟེན་

32 «པེ་» «སྣར་» «ཟིན་» {Y}{CL}: སོ་

།དངོས་ལ་མཁས་པ་རྣམས་ཀྱིས་ནི།
།དངོས་པོ་མི་རྟག་བསླུ་བའི་ཆོས།
།གསོག་དང་སྟོང་པ་བདག་མེད་པ།
།རྣམ་པར་དབེན་ཞེས་བྱ་བར་མཐོང་། **།། 25 །།**

།གནས་མེད་དམིགས་པ་ཡོད་མ་ཡིན།
།རྩ་བ་མེད་ཅིང་གནས་པ་མེད།
།མ་རིག་རྒྱུ་ [≪ཅོ་≫ 21b.1] ལས་ཤིན་ཏུ་བྱུང་། [≪སྡེ་≫ 21b.1]
།ཐོག་མ་དབུས་མཐའ་རྣམ་པར་སྤངས། **།། 26 །།**

།ཆུ་ཤིང་བཞིན་དུ་སྙིང་པོ་མེད།
།དྲི་ཟའི་གྲོང་ཁྱེར་འདྲ་བ་སྟེ།
།རྨོངས་[33] པའི་གྲོང་ཁྱེར་མི་བཟད་[34] [≪སྣར་≫ 21b.1] པའི།
།འགྲོ་བ་སྒྱུ་མ་བཞིན་དུ་སྣང་། **།། 27 །།**

།ཚངས་སོགས་འཇིག་རྟེན་འདི་ལ་ནི།
།བདེན་པར་རབ་ཏུ་གང་སྣང་བ།
།དེ་ནི་འཕགས་ལ་བརྟུན་[35] ཞེས་གསུངས།
།འདི་ལས་གཞན་ལྟ་ཅི་ཞིག་ལུས། **།། 28 །།**

---

33 ≪པེ་≫ ≪སྣར་≫ : སྨོངས་

34 ≪པེ་≫ ≪སྣར་≫ : ཟད་

35 ≪པེ་≫ ≪སྣར་≫ : རྟུན་

།འཇིག་རྟེན་མ་རིག་ལྡོངས་གྱུར་པ།

།སྲིད་པ་རྒྱུན་གྱིས་[36] རྗེས་འབྲང་[37] དང་།

།མཁས་པ་སྲིད་པ་དང་བྲལ་བ།

།དགེ་བ་རྣམས་ལྷ་ག་ལ་མཉམ། || **29** ||

།དེ་ཉིད་ཚོལ་ལ་ཐོག་མར་ནི།

།ཐམས་ཅད་ཡོད་ཅེས་བརྗོད་པར་བྱ།

།དོན་རྣམས་རྟོགས་ཤིང་ཆགས་མེད་ལ། [«པེ་» 24a.1]

།ཕྱིས་[38] ནི་རྣམ་པར་དབེན་[39] པའོ། || **30** ||

།རྣམ་པར་དབེན་དོན་མི་ཤེས་ལ།

།ཐོས་པ་ཙམ་ལ་འཇུག་བྱེད་ཅིང་།

།གང་དག་བསོད་ནམས་མི་བྱེད་པ།

།སྐྱེས་བུ་ཐ་ཤལ་དེ་དག་བརླག || **31** ||

།ལས་རྣམས་འབྲས་བུ་བཅས་ཉིད་དང་།

།འགྲོ་བ་དག་ཀྱང་ཡང་དག་བཤད།

---

[36] «པེ་» «སྣར་» {SS}{Y}{CL}: གྱི་

[37] «སྡེ་» «ཅོ་» {SS}: འབྲང་ «པེ་» «སྣར་» {Y}{CL}: འབྲངས་

[38] «པེ་» «སྣར་»: འཕྱིས་

[39] «སྡེ་»: དབན་

།དེ་ཡི་རང་བཞིན་ཡོངས་ཤེས་དང་།
།སྐྱེ་བ་མེད་པ་དག་ཀྱང་བསྟན། || 32 ||

།དགོངས་[40] པའི་དབང་གིས་རྒྱལ་བ་རྣམས།
།ང་དངཿ ང་ཡི་[41] ཞེས་གསུངས་[42] ལྟར།
།ཕུང་པོ་ཁམས་དང་སྐྱེ་མཆེད་རྣམས།
།དེ་བཞིན་དགོས་པའི་དབང་གིས་གསུངས། || 33 ||

།འབྱུང་བ་ཆེ་ལ་སོགས་བཤད་པ།
།རྣམ་པར་ཤེས་སུ་ཡང་དག་འདུ།
།དེ་[43] ཤེས་པས་ནི་འབྲལ་འགྱུར་ན།
།ལོག་པར་[44] རྣམ་བརྟགས་མ་ཡིན་ནམ། || 34 ||

།མྱ་ངན་འདས་པ་བདེན་གཅིག་པུར།[45]
།རྒྱལ་བ་རྣམས་ཀྱིས་གང་གསུངས་པ།

---

[40] «ཏྭི་ 26a.5»: དགོངས་ «སྡེ་» «ཅོ་» «པེ་» «སྣར་» {SS}{Y}{CL}: དགོས་

[41] «པེ་» {Y}{CL}: ངའི་

[42] «པེ་» {Y}{CL}: +པ་

[43] «པེ་» «སྣར་» «སྨིང་»: དེ་ «སྡེ་» «ཅོ་»: ད་

[44] «པེ་» «སྣར་» {CL}: པས་

[45] «སྨིང་ 47b.2, 70b.3» «ཏྭི་ 27a.1»: པུ། Geshe Rabten glosses this briefly as: མྱ་ངན་ལས་འདས་པ་ནི་སྟོང་ཉིད་སྣང་གནས་མཐུན་པའི་ཆོས་ཡིན་པས་བདེན་གཅིག་པུ།, while Tsong Khapa provides a more extensive explanation «སྨིང་ 47b.2ff.»: གཅིག་པུ་བདེན་ཀྱི་འདུ་བྱེད་རྣམས་བརྫུན་བསླུ་བའི་ཆོས་ཅན་ནོ་ཞེས་

(cont'd)

།དེ་ཚེ་ལྷག་མ་ལོག་མིན་ཞེས།
།མཁས་པ་སུ་ཞིག་རྟོག་[46] པར་བྱེད། || **35**[47] ||

།ཇི་སྲིད་ཡིད་ཀྱི་རྣམ་གཡོ་བ།
།དེ་སྲིད་བདུད་ཀྱི་སྤྱོད་ཡུལ་དེ།[48]
།དེ་ལྟ་ཡིན་ན་འདི་ལ་ནི།
།ཉེས་པ་མེད་པར་ཅིས་མི་འཐད། || **36** ||

།འཇིག་རྟེན་མ་རིག་རྐྱེན་ཅན་དུ།
།གང་ཕྱིར་སངས་རྒྱས་རྣམས་གསུངས་པ།
།འདི་ཡི་ཕྱིར་ན་འཇིག་རྟེན་འདི།
།རྣམ་རྟོག་ཡིན་ཞེས་ཅིས་མི་འཐད། || **37** ||

གསུངས་པ་ནི་མི་བདེན་པ་བརྫུན་པའི་དོན་སྐབས་འདིར་སླུ་བ་ལ་གསུངས་པས་དེའི་བཟློག་ཕྱོགས་བདེན་པའི་དོན་ཡང་མི་བསླུ་བ་ཡིན་གྱི་ཡིན་ལུགས་ལ་གྲུབ་མ་གྲུབ་དཔྱད་པའི་ཚེ་རང་གི་མཚན་ཉིད་ཀྱིས་ཡོད་པའི་བདེན་པ་མིན་ནོ། སླུ་བ་ནི་དཔེར་ན་ཕན་འདོགས་པ་ཡིན་ཡང་ཕན་འདོགས་པ་ལྟར་བཅོས་ནས་འདྲིད་པ་ལ་སླུ་ཞེས་བརྗོད་པ་བཞིན་དུ་འདུ་བྱེད་འདི་རྣམས་རང་གི་མཚན་ཉིད་ཀྱིས་མ་གྲུབ་བཞིན་དུ་དེར་སྣང་ནས་བྱིས་པ་སླུ་བས་བརྫུན་པའམ་སླུ་བ་ཟེར་ལ། སྣང་འདས་དོན་དམ་པའི་བདེན་པ་ནི་དེ་མངོན་སུམ་དུ་མཐོང་བའི་ངོར་སྒྱུ་མ་ལྟར་སྣང་ནས་སླུ་བ་མེད་པས་མི་སླུ་བའམ་བདེན་པ་ཞེས་གསུངས་སོ། Geshe Rabten (*dge bshes rta mgrin rab brtan*), *drang nges rnam 'byed legs bshad snying po dka' gnad rnams mchan bur bkod pa gzur gnas blo gsal dga' ston*. (Delhi, 1978), f. 101a.6.

[46] {Y}: རྟོགས་

[47] Commenting on the entire verse, Tsong Khapa states «སྙིང་ 70b.3–.4»: རྫུན་པའི་དོན་ངོ་བོ་ཉིད་ཀྱིས་སྟོང་པའི་རང་བཞིན་མེད་པ་ལས་གཞན་དུ་འདྲེན་པ་ལ་གནོད་པ་བརྗོད་ནས་དོན་དེར་ངེས་པར་རྒྱ་ཤེ་ལས་བསྒྲུབས་པས། ཐེག་དམན་གྱི་སྡེ་སྣོད་དུ་ཡང་ཆོས་ཀྱི་བདག་མེད་ཀྱང་བཤད་པ་ནི་འཕགས་པའི་དགོངས་པར་ངེས་པར་འདོད་པར་བྱའོ།

[48] «པེ་»«སྣར་»«ཏྲི་ 27a.5»: ཏེ།

།མ་རིག་འགགས་པར་གྱུར་པ་ན།
།གང་ཞིག་འགག་པར་འགྱུར་བ་དེ།
།མི་ཤེས་པ་ལས་ཀུན་བརྟགས་པར།
།ཇི་[49] ལྟ་བུར་[50] ན་གསལ་མི་འགྱུར། **|| 38 ||**

།གང་ཞིག་རྒྱུ་དང་བཅས་འབྱུང་ཞིང་།
།རྐྱེན་མེད་པར་ནི་གནས་པ་མེད།
།རྐྱེན་མེད་ཕྱིར་ཡང་འཇིག་འགྱུར་བ།
།དེ་ནི་ཡོད་ཅེས་ཇི་[51] ལྟར་རྟོགས། **|| 39 ||**

།གལ་ཏེ་ཡོད་པར་སྨྲ་བ་རྣམས། [«སྡེ་» 22a.1]
།དངོས་མཆོག་ཞེན་[52] ནས་གནས་པ་ནི།
།ལམ་དེ་ཉིད་ལ་གནས་པ་སྟེ།
།དེ་ལཿ་ངོ་མཚར་ཅུང་ཟད་[53] མེད། **|| 40 ||**

---

49 «ཏཱི་ 27b.3»: ཅི་ «པེ་» «སྣར་» «སྡེ་» «ཅོ་»: ཇི་

50 «པེ་» «སྣར་»: བུ་

51 «ཏཱི་ 27b.6»: ཅི་ «པེ་» «སྣར་» «སྡེ་» «ཅོ་»: ཇི་

52 «སྙིང་ 48b.1»: བཟུང་ «ཏཱི་ 27b.6»: གཟུང་

53 «ཏཱི་ 28a.3» reads as above; «སྙིང་ 48b.1» however, reads: ཡ་མཚན་ཆུང་ངུ་འང་. This appears to be a paraphrase by Tsong Khapa, although no subsequent commentators on «སྙིང་» address the discrepancy. The otherwise observant scholar, 'Jigs-med-dam-chos-rgya-mtsho, for instance, does not even note this reading, but rather places his emphasis on

(cont'd)

།སངས་རྒྱས་ལམ་ལ་བརྟེན་ནས་ནི།

།ཀུན་ལ་མི་རྟག་སྨྲ་བ་རྣམས།

།རྩོད་[54] པས་དངོས་རྣམས་མཆོགཿ བཟུང་བས།[55]

།གནས་པཿ གང་ཡིན་[56] དེ་རྨད་[57] དོ། ॥ **41**[58] ॥

---

the final line of k.41 following Chandrakīrti (ad k. 41): ངོ་མཚར་ཆེ་བས་དེའི་རྨད་དུ་གྱུར་པའོ།. Geshe Rabten, in his treatment of the citation, simply glosses the two verses without noting the difference: གལ་ཏེ་ཡོད་པར་ཏེ་གཞན་སྡེ་རྟག་མཐའ་སྨྲ་བ་རྣམས་ནི། རང་སྡེའི་ལུགས་ལས་ཁོ་རང་གི་སྟོན་པའི་ལུགས་ས་མ། དངོས་པོ་མཆོག་ཏུ་བཟུང་ནས་གནས་པ་ནི། ཁོ་རང་གི་སྟོན་པའི་གསུངས་པའི་ལམ་དེ་ཉིད་ལ་གནས་པ་སྟེ། དེ་ལ་ཡ་མཚན་ཆུང་ངུའང་མེད་ན་ཆེན་པོ་ཅི་ཞིག་ཡོད་དེ་བས། སངས་རྒྱས་ཀྱི་ལམ་ལ་བརྟེན་ནས་ནི། ཀུན་ལ་འདུས་བྱས་ཐམས་ཅད་མི་རྟག་པ་ཞེས་སོགས་ཆོས་ཀྱི་སྡོམ་བཞི་ལ་གནས་ནས་ནང་པའི་གྲུབ་མཐའ་སྨྲ་བ་རྣམས་ཀྱང་ཐལ་འགྱུར་བའི་ལུགས་འདི་ལ། རྩོད་པས་བདེན་དངོས་རྣམས་མཆོག་ཏུ་བཟུང་ནས། གནས་པ་གང་ཡིན་དེ་ནི་གཞན་སྡེ་ལས་ཀྱང་ཆེས་ངོ་མཚར་རྨད་དོ།. Perhaps as an acknowledgement of Tsong Khapa's reading, Gyaltsap uses his phrase in the topical outline (*sa bcad*) to his own commentary («ཏཱཻ་ 28a.3»). Cf. 'Jigs-med-dam-chos-rgya-mtsho, *drang nges legs bshad snying po'i 'jug ngogs*. (mtsho sngon, 1999), p.392; Geshe Rabten (*dge bshes rta mgrin rab brtan*), *drang nges rnam 'byed legs bshad snying po dka' gnad rnams mchan bur bkod pa gzur gnas blo gsal dga' ston*. (Delhi, 1978), f. 103a.3–b.1; also, Tsong Khapa, *rjes tsong kha pa'i gsung dbu ma'i lta ba'i skor*. 2 vols. (n.p., 1975) v.1, p.345.3.

54 «པེ་»: བརྩོད་

55 «ཏཱཻ་ 28a.5»: གཟུང་ནས། «པེ་» «སྣར་» {CL}{Y}: གཟུང་པས།

56 «ཏཱཻ་ 28a.5»: ཡང་ནི་

57 «སྙིང་ 48b.2» «ཏཱཻ་ 28a.6» {SS}{CL}{Y}: རྨད་ «པེ་» «སྣར་» «སྡེ་» «ཅོ་»: སྨད་

58 Tsong Khapa comments on these two verses «སྙིང་ 48b.2»: འདིས་ནི་བདེན་པར་མེད་པ་དང་རང་གི་མཚན་ཉིད་ཀྱིས་མེད་པ་ལ་སྐྱེ་འགག་སོགས་མཚན་ཉིད་པ་གཞག་ཏུ་མེད་པར་འདོད་པ་རྣམས་བཞད་གད་ཀྱི་གནས་སུ་གསུངས་སོ།

།འདི་འམ་དེ་འོ་[59] ཞེས་ [《པེ་》 24b.1] གང་དུ།
།རྣམ་པར་ [《སྣར་》 22a.1] དཔྱད་ནས་མི་དམིགས་ན།
།རྩོད༔པ་འདིའམ་དེ་བདེན་[60] ཞེས།
།མཁས་པ་སུ་ཞིག་སྨྲ་བར་འགྱུར། ॥ **42** ॥

།གང་[61] དག་གིས་ནི་མ་བརྟེན་པར།
།བདག་གམ་[62] འཇིག་རྟེན་མངོན་ཞེན་པ།
།དེ་དག༔ཀྱེ་མ་[63] རྟག་མི་རྟག
།ལ་སོགས་ལྟ་བས་འཕྲོགས་[64] པ་ཡིན། ॥ **43** ॥

།གང་དག་བརྟེན་ནས་དངོས་པོ་རྣམས།
།དེ་ཉིད་དུ་ནི་གྲུབ་འདོད་པ།

---

59 {SS}{CL}: དེ་འོ་

60 《ཏཱི་ 28b.2》: པས་འདིའམ་དེ་བདེན་ {Y}: པ་འམ་དེ་བདེན་པ་ 《པེ་》: པ་འམ་དེ་བདེན་

61 《ལོཾ་ 586.2》《སྟིང་ 47b.6》《ཏཱི་ 28b.5》{SS}{CL}{Y}: གང་ 《པེ་》《སྣར་》《སྡེ་》《ཅོ་》: དེ་

62 《ཏཱི་ 28b.5》: གི་ 《པེ་》《སྣར་》《སྡེ་》《ཅོ་》-གམ་

63 《པེ་》《སྣར་》: སྐྱེ་བ་

64 《སྟིང་ 48a.1》: འཕྲོགས་ 《ལོཾ་ 586.3》: འཕྲོག་ 《ཏཱི་ 28b.6》{CL}: ཕྲོགས་

།དེ་དག་ལ་ཡང་རྟག་[65] སོགས་[66] སྐྱོན།
།དེ་དག་ཇི་ལྟར་འབྱུང་མི་འགྱུར། || **44** ||

།གང་དག་བརྟེན་ནས་དངོས་པོ་རྣམས།
།ཆུ་ཡི་ཟླ་བ་ལྟ་བུར་ནི།
།ཡང་དག་མ་ཡིན་ལོག་མིན་པར།
།འདོད་པ་དེ་དག་ལྟས་མི་འཕྲོགས།[67] || **45**[68] ||

།དངོས་པོར་ཁས་ལེན་ཡོད་ན་ནི།
།འདོད་ཆགས་ཞེ་སྡང་འབྱུང་བ་ཡི།[69]

---

65 《ལོ་ 586.5》《སྒྲིང་ 48a.1》《ཏྟི་ 29a.3》{SS}{CL}{Y}: རྟག་ 《པེ་》《སྣར་》《སྡེ་》《ཅོ་》: རྟགས་

66 《པེ་》《སྣར་》《ལོ་ 586.5》《སྒྲིང་ 48a.1》《ཏྟི་ 29a.3》{SS}{CL}{Y}: སོགས་ 《སྡེ་》《ཅོ་》: སྟོགས་

67 《པེ་》《སྣར་》{CL}: བལྟས་མི་འཕྲོག 《ལོ་ 586.7》《ཏྟི་ 29a.5》: ལྟས་མི་འཕྲོག 《སྒྲིང་ 48a.2》 ལྟས་མི་འཕྲོགས།

68 Tsong Khapa comments on these three verses 《སྒྲིང་ 48a.2–.4》: ཡང་དག་པར་མ་གྲུབ་པས་རྟག་ལྟ་སོགས་ལ་རང་རང་གི་བྱ་བ་བྱེད་ནུས་པས་ཆད་ལྟ་སྤོང་སྟེ་དེ་ལྟར་མི་ནུས་པའི་ལོག་པ་ཡང་མིན་ནོ། དེས་ན་ཕྱི་ནང་གི་དངོས་པོ་འདི་རྣམས་རབ་བཞིན་གྱིས་སྟོང་པར་ཡང་འདོད་ལ་སྟོང་པ་དེ་ཀུན་རྫོབ་ཆད་སྟོང་དོ་ཞེས་སྨྲ་བ་ནི་རྟེན་འབྲེལ་རྟག་ཆད་གཉིས་ཀ་དང་བྲལ་བར་ནན་ཏན་གྱིས་སྒྲུབ་པ་ཤིང་རྟ་ཆེན་པོའི་ལུགས་གཉིས་ཀ་དང་འགལ་བར་སྨྲ་བ་ཡིན།

69 《པེ་》《སྣར་》{Y}: ཡིན།

།ལྟ་བ་མི་བཟད་[70] མ་རུངས་[71] འབྱུང་།[72]
།དེ་ལས་བྱུང་[73] བའི་སྤྱོད་[74] པར་འགྱུར། **|| 46 ||**

།དེ་ནི་ལྟ་བ་ཀུན་གྱི་རྒྱུ།
།དེ་མེད་ཉོན་མོངས་མི་སྐྱེ་[75] སྟེ།
།དེ་ཕྱིར་དེ་ནི་ཡོངས་ཤེས་ན།
།ལྟ་དང་ཉོན་མོངས་ཡོངས་སུ་འབྱང་། **|| 47 ||**

།ཿདངོས་པོར་ཁས་ལེན་ཡོད་ན་ནི།[76]
།གང་གིས་དེ་ཤེས་འགྱུར་སྙམ་ན།
།བརྟེན་ནས་[77] འབྱུང་བ་མཐོང་བ་དེ།[78]

70 《པེ་》《སྣར་》{Y}: ཟད་

71 {Y}: རུང་

72 《ཏྸི་ 29b.4》{CL}: འཛིན།

73 {Y}: འབྱུང་

74 《པེ་》《སྣར་》{SS}{Y}{CL}: རྫོད་

75 《ཏྸི་ 29b.6》: སྐྱེད་

76 《པེ་》《སྣར་》《ཏྸི་ 30a.3》: -དངོས་པོར་ཁས་ལེན་ཡོད་ན་ནི།

77 《ཏྸི་ 30a.3》: ཅིང་

78 {SS}{Y}: སྟེ།

།བརྟེན་ནས་སྐྱེ་[79] བ་མ་སྐྱེས་པས།[80]
།ཿདེ་ཉིད་[81] མཁྱེན་པ་མཆོག་གིས་གསུངས། ‖ **48** ‖

།ལོག་པའི་ཤེས་པ་[82] ཟིལ་གནོན་[83] པ།
།བདེན་པ་མིན་ལ་བདེན་ཧྲུན་[84] པའི།
།ཡོངས་སུ་འཛིན་དང་རྩོད་སྩོགས་[85] ཀྱི།
།རིམ་པ་[86] ཆགས་ལས་འབྱུང་བར་འགྱུར། ‖ **49** ‖

།ཆེ་བའི་བདག་ཉིད་ཅན་དེ་དག
།རྣམས་ལ་ཕྱོགས་མེད་རྩོད་པ་མེད།
།གང་རྣམས་ལ་ནི་ཕྱོགས་མེད་པ།
།དེ་ལ་ གཞན་ཕྱོགས་ག་ལ་ཡོད། ‖ **50** ‖

---

[79] «ཏཱཻ 30a.4»: སྐྱེས་

[80] «པེ་» «སྣར་» «ཏཱཻ 30a.4» {SS}{CL}: པར་ {Y}: བར་

[81] «ཏཱཻ 30a.4»: ཐམས་ཅད་

[82] «ཏཱཻ 30b.5»: པས་

[83] «ཏཱཻ 30b.5»: ནོན་

[84] «པེ་» «སྣར་» «ཏཱཻ 30b.5» {SS}{Y}{CL}: འཛིན་

[85] «པེ་» «སྣར་» «ཏཱཻ 30b.5» {SS}{Y}{CL}: སོགས་

[86] {CL}: པས་

།གང་ཡང་རུང་བའི་གནས་རྙེད་ནས།
།ཉོན་མོངས་སྦྲུལ་[87] གདུག་གཡོ་[88] ཅན་གྱིས།[89]
།ཟིན་པར་འགྱུར་[90] ཏེ་[91] གང་གི་སེམས།
།གནས་མེད་དེ་དག་ཟིན་མི་འགྱུར། || **51** ||

།གནས་བཅས་སེམས་དང་ལྡན་རྣམས་ལ།
།ཉོན་མོངས་དུག་ཆེན་ཅིས་མི་འབྱུར།[92]
།ཿགང་ཚེ་བར་མ་འདུག་པ་ཡང་།[93]
།ཉོན་མོངས་སྦྲུལ་[94] གྱིས་ཟིན་པར་འགྱུར། || **52**[95] ||

---

87 {Y}: སྤྲུལ་

88 {SS}: གཡོན་

89 {Y}: ཀྱིས།

90 «པེ་» «སྣར་» {Y}{CL}: གྱུར་

91 «ཏྲི་ 32a.5»: རོ་

92 «པེ་» «སྣར་» {SS}{Y}{CL}: འབྱུང་། «པེ་ P.»: བྱུན། «པེ་»: འབྱུན།

93 «པེ་» «སྣར་» «སྡེ་» «ཅོ་»: -གང་ཚེ་བར་མ་འདུག་པ་ཡང་། «སྣིང་ 71b.6»: གང་ཚེ་བར་མར་འདུག་པ་ཡང་། «ཞོ་» {SS}: གང་ཚེ་བར་མ་འདུག་པ་ཡང་། «ཏྲི་ 32b.2»: གང་ཚེ་བར་མང་འདུག་པ་ཡང་། {CL}: གང་ཚེ་ཐ་མལ་འདུག་པ་ཡང་།

94 {SS} questions the reading in «སྣར་»: སྦྲུ་ལ་

95 'Jigs-med-dam-chos-rgya-mtsho comments on this verse stating: རིགས་པ་དྲུག་ཅུ་པའི་དོན་ནི། གནས་ཏེ་རང་མཚན་གྱིས་གྲུབ་པ་བདེན་འཛིན་སྐྱེ་བའི་དམིགས་པ་དང་བཅས་པའི་སེམས་དང་ལྡན་པ་རྣམས་ལ་ཉོན་མོངས་འབྱུང་སྟེ། དེ་ཆགས་སྡང་མངོན་གྱུར་པ་དང་བྲལ་བའི་བར་མར་གནས་ཀྱང་། ཉོན་མོངས་པ་མ་རིག་པའི་གཞན་དབང་དུ་འགྱུར་

(cont'd)

།བྱིས་པ་བདེན་པར་འདུ་ཤེས་པས།

།གཟུགས་བརྙན་ལ་ནི་ཆགས་པ་བཞིན། [《ཅོ་》 22b.1]

།དེ་ལྟར་འཇིག་རྟེན་རྨོངས་ [《སྡེ་》 22b.1] པའི་ཕྱིར།

།ཡུལ་གྱི་གཟེབ་ལ་ཐོགས་པར་འགྱུར། || 53 ||

།བདག་ཉིད་ [《པེ་》 25a.1] ཆེ་རྣམས་དངོས་པོ་དག

།གཟུགས་བརྙན་ལྟ་བུར་ཡེ་ཤེས་ཀྱི།[96]

།མིག་གིས་མཐོང་ནས་ཡུལ་ཞེས་ནི།

།བྱ་བའི་འདམ་ལ་མི་ཐོགས་སོ།[97] || 54 ||

།བྱིས་པ་རྣམས་ནི་གཟུགས་ལ་ཆགས།

།བར་མ་དག་ནི་ཆགས་བྲལ་འགྱུར།

།གཟུགས་ཀྱི་རང་བཞིན་ཤེས་པ་ཡི།

།བློ་མཆོག་ལྡན་[98] པ་རྣམ་པར་གྲོལ། || 55 ||

།སྡུག་སྙམ་པ་ལས་[99] ཆགས་པར་འགྱུར། [《སྣར་》 22b.1]

།དེ་ལས་བཟློག་[100] པས་འདོད་ཆགས་བྲལ།

པའི་ཕྱིར། ཞེས་པ་སྔེ་གཞུང་དུ་དྲངས་པའི་སྔ་འགྲེལ་གྱི་དོན་ཡང་དེས་ཤེས་སོ།།. 'Jigs-med-dam-chos-rgya-mtsho, *drang nges legs bshad snying po'i 'jug ngogs*. (mtsho sngon, 1999), p.492.

96 《སྣར་》: ཀྱིས་

97 {SS} questions the reading in 《སྣར་》: ཐོག་

98 {SS} questions the reading in 《སྣར་》: ལྡོན་

99 {SS}: ལ་

།སྒྱུ་མའི་སྐྱེས་བུ་ལྟར་དབེན་པར།
།མཐོང་ནས་མྱ་ངན་འདའ་བར་[101] འགྱུར། **|| 56 ||**

།ལོག་པའི་ཤེས་པས་མངོན་གདུང་བའི།
།ཉོན་མོངས་སྐྱོན་རྣམས་གང་ཡིན་དེ།[102]
།དངོས་དང་དངོས་མེད་རྣམ་རྟོག་པ།
།དོན་ཤེས་འགྱུར་[103] ལ་མི་འབྱུང་ངོ་། **|| 57 ||**

།གནས་ཡོད་ན་ནི་འདོད་ཆགས་དང་།
།འདོད་ཆགས་བྲལ་[104] བར་འགྱུར་ཞིག་ན།
།གནས་མེད་བདག་ཉིད་ཆེན་པོ་རྣམས།
།ཆགས་པ་མེད་ཅིང་ཆགས་བྲལ་མིན། **|| 58 ||**

།གང་དག་རྣམ་པར་དབེན་སྙམ་དུ།
།གཡོ་བའི་ཡིད་ཀྱང་མི་གཡོ་བ།[105]

---

100 «ཏྲི་ 33b.2»: ལྡོག་

101 «ཏྲི་ 33b.2»: འདས་པར་

102 «པེ་» «སྣར་» {SS}{Y}{CL}: ཏེ།

103 «ཏྲི་ 33b.5»: གྱུར་

104 {Y}: བྲ་

105 «ཏྲི་ 34a.4»: སྦེ།

།ཉོན་མོངས་སྦྲུལ་[106] གྱིས་དཀྲུགས་གྱུར་པ།
།མི་ཟད་[107] སྲིད་པའི་རྒྱ་མཚོ་བརྒལ། **།། 59 ।།**

།དགེ་བ་འདི་ཡིས་སྐྱེ་བོ་[108] ཀུན།
།བསོད་ནམས་ཡེ་ཤེས་ཚོགས་བསགས་ཏེ།
།བསོད་ནམས་ཡེ་ཤེས་ལས་བྱུང་བའི།
།དམ་པ་གཉིས་ནི་ཐོབ་པར་ཤོག **།། 60 ।།**

།རིགས་པ་དྲུག་ཅུ་པའི་[109] ཚིག་ལེའུར་བྱས་པ་ཞེས་བྱ་བ་སློབ་དཔོན་འཕགས་པ་ཀླུ་སྒྲུབ་ཀྱི་ཞལ་སྔ་ནས་མཛད་པ་རྫོགས་སོ།། རྒྱ་གར་གྱི་མཁན་པོ་མུ་དི་ཏ་[110] ཤྲཱིའི་ཞལ་སྔ་ནས་དང་། བོད་ཀྱི་ལོ་ཙྪ་[111] བ་པ་ཚབ་ཉི་མ་གྲགས་ཀྱིས་[112] བཅོས་ཏེ་གཏན་ལ་ཕབ་པའོ།།

---

106 {Y}: སྤྲུལ་

107 《ཏྭེ་ 34a.4》{SS}{CL}: བཟད་

108 {Y}: བ་

109 《པེ་》《སྣར་》: ཅུའི་

110 {SS}: དི་ཏཱ་

111 《པེ་》:{SS}: ལོ་ཙཱ་

112 《པེ་》《སྣར་》: ཀྱི་

Critical Edition of the
rigs pa drug cu pa'i 'grel pa (*Yuktiṣaṣṭikāvṛtti*)

རིགས་པ་དྲུག་ཅུ་པའི་འགྲེལ་པ།

[《ཅོ་》 1b.1][《སྡེ་》 1b.1][《པེ་》 1b.1][《སྣར་ 1b.1》]

༄༅། །རྒྱ་གར་སྐད་དུ། ཡུཀྟི་ཥཥྚི་[1] ཀཱ་[2] ཝྲྀ་ཏྟི།
བོད་སྐད་དུ། རིགས་པ་དྲུག་ཅུ་པའི་འགྲེལ་པ།

འཇམ་དཔལ་ཡེ་ཤེས་སེམས་དཔའ་ལ་ཕྱག་འཚལ་ལོ།

།རྒྱལ་བའི་རིགས་པའི་ལམ་གྱི་རྗེས་འབྲང་[3] བ།
།མཐའ་གཉིས་སེལ་བའི་རིགས་པ་དྲུག་ཅུ་པ།
།གང་གིས་མཛད་པ་དེ་ལ་ཕྱག་འཚལ་ཏེ།
།བདག་གིས་དཔྱད་མའི་ཚུལ་གྱིས་དེ་རྣམས་[4] དབྱེ།[5]

---

[1] 《སྡེ་》《ཅོ་》: ཥཥྟི་ 《པེ་》《སྣར་》: ཥཥྚི་

[2] 《སྡེ་》《ཅོ་》《པེ་》《སྣར་》: ཀ་

[3] 《པེ་》《སྣར་》{SS}: འགྲོ་

[4] {SS}: རྣམ་

།དེ་ལ་[6] སློབ་དཔོན་ [《པེ་》 2a.1] འདི་ནི་རྟེན་ཅིང་འབྲེལ་པར་འབྱུང་བ་ཇི་ལྟར་གནས་པ་བཞིན་དུ་དེ་ཁོ་ན་གཟིགས་པས་དགྱེས་པའི་ཁྱད་པར་བརྙེས་པ་སྟེ། །དེ་རྟོགས་པ་ [《སྣར་》 2a.1] ནི་དད་པ་མཆོག་གི་གནས་ཡིན་པར་མཁྱེན་ནས་རྟེན་ཅིང་འབྲེལ་པར་འབྱུང་བ་མཐོང་བ་ལས་འཇིག་རྟེན་དང་འཇིག་རྟེན་ལས་འདས་པའི་དགེ་བའི་ཚོགས་མ་ལུས་པར་འབྱུང་བ་དང་འཕགས་པའི་གང་ཟག་མ་ལུས་པར་འབྱུང་བ་དང་། །སངས་རྒྱས་བཅོམ་ལྡན་འདས་ཡེ་ཤེས་སྒྲིབ་པ་མེད་པ་དང་ལྡན་པ་རྣམས་ཀྱི་རྣམ་པ་ཐམས་ཅད་དུ་དེ་ཁོ་ན་ཉིད་[7] མངོན་པར་རྫོགས་པར་བྱང་ཆུབ་པ་ཡང་ [《སྡེ་》 2a.1] གཟིགས་ནས་རྟེན་ཅིང་འབྲེལ་པར་ [《ཅོ་》 2a.1] འབྱུང་བ་རང་བཞིན་གྱིས་མ་སྐྱེས་པའི་ཕྱིར་སྐྱེ་བ་དང་འཇིག་པ་དང་ཡོད་པ་དང་མེད་པའི་མཐར། །རྟོག་པའི་དྲི་ [《པེ་》 2b.1] མས་ [《སྣར་》 2b.1] མ་གོས་པ་རྟེན་ཅིང་འབྲེལ་པར་འབྱུང་བ་ངོ་བོ་ཉིད་ཀྱིས་སྟོང་པ་ཡིན་པར་ཆེ་བ་ཉིད་ཀྱིས་[8] བརྗོད་ནས་རྟེན་ཅིང་འབྲེལ་པར་འབྱུང་བ་འཆད་པར་བཞེད་དེ།

---

5 As Scherrer-Schaub (*Yuktiṣaṣṭikāvṛtti*, 19 n. 4) notes, the Sanskrit of this verse and subsequent prose are preserved as part of the ms. fragments of Bhāvaviveka's *Tarkajvāla* found by Rāhula Sāṁkṛtyāyana and Gedun Choephel (Sāṁkṛtyāyana, "Second Search," 48), cited by Gokhale ("Vedānta Philosophy," 165) and given by Scherrer-Schaub as: *janasya* (read: *jinasya*) *yo mukti* (read: *yukti*) *-pathānuyāyinīn nirākṛtāntadvaya-yuktiṣaṣṭhi*<sic>*kāṁ | cakāra tasya praṇipatya sā mayā vibhajyate madhyamakānusārataḥ || ihāyam ācāryo yathāvasthita-pratītyasamutpāda-darśana-āsādita-prīti-viśeṣaḥ para-prasādāyatanaṁ tad-adhigama....* Cf. Lindtner, "*Pañcaskandha-prakaraṇa*," 88 n. 5.

6 《པེ་》《སྣར་》: -ལ་

7 《པེ་》《སྣར་》: -ཉིད་

8 《པེ་》《སྣར་》: ཀྱི

(I. །དང་པོ། རྩོམ་པའི་སྔོན་འགྲོ་མཆོད་བརྗོད།)[9]

།དེ་སྟོན་པའི་དེ་བཞིན་གཤེགས་པ་རྟེན་ཅིང་འབྲེལ་པར་འབྱུང་བའི་ངོ་བོ་ཉིད་དང་ཐ་མི་དད་པར་གྱུར་པ་ལ། །གུས་པ་སྐྱེས་ནས་དེ་ལ་ཕྱག་འཚལ་བ་རྩོམ་མོ།

གང་དག་[10] སྐྱེ་དང་འཇིག་པ་དག
།འདི་ཡི་ཚུལ་གྱིས་རབ་སྤངས་པ།
།རྟེན་ཅིང་འབྱུང་བ་[11] གསུངས་[12] པ་ཡི།
།ཐུབ་དབང་དེ་ལ་ཕྱག་འཚལ་ལོ། || **Homage**[13] ||

།ཞེས་ཕྱག་འཚལ་བ་བརྩམ་མོ།

(A. །དང་པོ། དགོས་པའི་དོན།)

།ཅིའི་ཕྱིར་སྟོང་པ་ཉིད་བདུན་ཅུ་པ་དང་། །རྩོད་པ་བཟློག་པ་ལས་སློབ་དཔོན་གྱིས་བསྟོད་པ་མ་བརྗོད་པ་[14] དབུ་མ་འདི་ལས་བརྗོད་ཅེ་ན།

---

[9] Gray parenthetical text represents topical outline (*sa bcad*) headings from Gyaltsap's *ṭīkka*, incorporated into the text by the editors. The full outline has also been extracted and presented independently in both Tibetan and English in the Appendices.

[10] «སྣར་ 46a.5»: གིས་

[11] «པེ་» «སྣར་»: འབྲེལ་པ་

[12] «སྣར་ 46a.6»: གསུང་

[13] Geshe Rabten glosses the last two lines as: རྟེན་འབྱུང་ཡིན་པའི་རྒྱུ་མཚན་གྱིས་འགག་སོགས་བརྒྱད་དང་བྲལ་བར་གསུངས་པའི་ཐུབ་དབང་དེ་ལ་ཕྱག་འཚལ་ལོ།. Geshe Rabten (*dge bshes rta mgrin rab brtan*), *drang nges rnam 'byed legs bshad snying po dka' gnad rnams mchan bur bkod pa gzur gnas blo gsal dga' ston*. (Delhi, 1978), f. 98b.5.

[14] «པེ་» «སྣར་» {SS}: ལ་

།སླས་པ། །སྟོང་པ་ཉིད་བདུན་ཅུ་པ་དང་རྩོད་པ་བཟློག་པ་གཉིས་དབུ་མ་ལས་འཕྲོས་པ་སྟེ། །རང་གི་རྒྱུད་ཀུན་ནས་བྱུང་བ་མེད་པས་ལོགས་ཤིག་ཏུ་བསྟོད་པ་མ་བརྗོད་དེ།

།འདི་ལྟར་རྩོད་པ་བཟློག་པ་ནི།

།དངོས་པོ་རྣམས་ཀྱི་རང [«སྣར་» 3a.1] བཞིན་ནི།
།རྐྱེན་ལ་སོགས་པ[15] མེད་པ་སྟེ།
།རང་གི་དངོས་པོ་ཡོད་མིན [«ཅོ་» 2b.1] ཏེ།[16] [«སྡེ་» 2b.1]
།གཞན་གྱི་དངོས་པོ་ཡོད[17] རེ་སྐན།[18]

།རྩོད་པ་བཟློག་པ་ནི་དེ་ལ་བརྐྱལ་བ་དང་ལན་བཏབ་པར་གྱུར་པའི་ཕྱིར་དེ་ལས་འཕྲོས་པ་ཡིན་པར་མངོན་ནོ།

།ཇི་ལྟར་སྒྱུ་མ་སྨི་ལམ་བཞིན།
།དྲི་ཟའི་གྲོང་ཁྱེར་ཅི་འདྲ་བ།

[15] {SS}: ལ་ following MMK 1.3b.

[16] «པེ་» «སྣར་» {SS}: ན་

[17] {SS}: ཡོང་ based on MMK 1.3d: །གཞན་དངོས་ཡོད་པ་མ་ཡིན་ནོ།

[18] MMK 1.3: *na hi svabhāvo bhāvānāṁ pratyayādiṣu vidyate / avidyamāne svabhāve parabhāvo na vidyate //* །དངོས་པོ་རྣམས་ཀྱི་རང་བཞིན་ནི། །རྐྱེན་ལ་སོགས་ལ་ཡོད་མ་ཡིན། །བདག་གི་དངོས་པོ་ཡོད་མིན་ན། །གཞན་དངོས་ཡོད་པ་མ་ཡིན་ནོ།

།དེ་བཞིན་སྐྱེ་དང་དེ་བཞིན་གནས།
།དེ་བཞིན་དུ་ནི་འཇིག་པར་བཤད།[19]

།སྟོང་པ་ཉིད་བདུན་ཅུ་པ་ནི་དེ་ལ་བརྒྱལ་བ་དང་ལན་བཏབ་པར་གྱུར་པའི་ཕྱིར་དེ་ལས་འཕྲོས་པ་ཡིན་པར་མངོན་ནོ།

།རིགས་པ་དྲུག་ཅུ་པ་འདི་ནི་དབུ་མ་བཞིན་དུ་འདིར་ཡང་གཙོ་བོར་རྟེན་ཅིང་འབྲེལ་པར་འབྱུང་བ་དཔྱད་པ་ལས་བརྩམས་ཏེ། །བྱས་པའི་ཕྱིར་དབུ་མ་ལས་འཕྲོས་པ་ལྟ་བུ་ནི་མ་ཡིན་ནོ།

(B. །གཉིས་པ། བསྡུས་དོན།)

།དེ་ལ་ངོ་བོ་ཉིད་དང་དབང་ཕྱུག་ལ་སོགས་པར་སྨྲ་བ་ངོ་བོ་ཉིད་དང་དབང་ཕྱུག་ [«པེ་» 3a.1] དང་རང་བཞིན་དང་སྐྱེས་བུ་དང་དུས་དང་སྲིད་མེད་ཀྱི་བུ་ལ་སོགས་པ་ལས་འགྲོ་བ་རྣམས་ཀྱི་སྐྱེ་བ་དང་འཇིག་པ་ལ་ [«སྣར་» 3b.1] སོགས་པ་ཁས་ལེན་པ་དག་ཐམས་ཅད་བཏང་བས་མྱ་ངན་ལས་འདས་པའི་གྲོང་ཁྱེར་དུ་འགྲོ་འདོད་ཀྱང་བདེན་པ་གཉིས་ཕྱིན་ཅི་[20] ལོག་པར་མཐོང་བ་ལས་ཉམས་པས་ཕྱིར་ཕྱོགས་པ་བཞིན་དུ་འཁོར་བ་རྣམ་[21] པར་ཆད་པའི་མཚན་ཉིད་མྱ་ངན་ལས་འདས་པའི་གྲོང་ཁྱེར་དུ་ཡུན་རིང་མོར་ཡང་འགྲོ་མི་ནུས་སོ། །རྟེན་ཅིང་འབྲེལ་པར་འབྱུང་བ་བསྟན་པ་རྐྱེན་ཉིད་འདི་པ་ཙམ་འདི་ནི་བདེན་པ་གཉིས་ཕྱིན་ཅི་མ་ལོག་པར་མཐོང་བའི་རྒྱུར་གྱུར་པའི་ཕྱིར་འཕགས་པའི་སྐྱེ་བོ་ཐམས་ཅད་གཤེགས་ཤིང་རྗེས་སུ་གཤེགས་པ་དང་[22] པོ་ཟླ་མེད་པ། །འདུས་བྱས་ཐམས་ཅད་

19 MMK 7.34: *yathā māyā yathā svapno gandharvanagaraṁ yathā / tathotpādastathā sthānaṁ tathā bhaṅga udāhṛtaṁ //* །རྨི་ལམ་ཇི་བཞིན་སྒྱུ་མ་བཞིན། །དྲི་ཟའི་གྲོང་ཁྱེར་ཇི་བཞིན་དུ། །དེ་བཞིན་སྐྱེ་དང་དེ་བཞིན་གནས། །དེ་བཞིན་དུ་ནི་འཇིག་པ་གསུངས།

20 «པེ་» «སྣར་» {SS}: +མ་

21 «པེ་» «སྣར་»: རྣམས་

22 «པེ་» «སྣར་» {SS}: དྲང་།

ཡོངས་སུ་སྤྲངས་པ། །མྱ་ངན་ལས་འདས་པའི་གྲོང་ཁྱེར་དུ་གཅིག་ཏུ་གཞོལ་བར་འགྱུར་བའི་[23] ཆེན་པོའོ། །དེ་བས་ན་དེ་སྟོན་པས་བསོད་ནམས་དང་ཡེ་ཤེས་ཀྱི་ཚོགས་མ་ལུས་པའི་དབང་ཕྱུག་ཕུན་སུམ་ཚོགས་པ་སྟོན་པ་བླ་ན་མེད་པ་ནི་ཉན་ཐོས་དང་རང་སངས་རྒྱས་ཐུབ་པ་རྣམས་ཀྱི་གཙོ་བོ་ཡིན་པས་ཐུབ་པའི་དབང་པོར་དགའ་བ་མ་ཡིན་ཏེ། །རྟེན་ཅིང་འབྲེལ་པར་འབྱུང་བ་སྟོན་པར་གྱུར་པ་ཉིད་ཀྱི་ཕྱིར་ཐུབ་པའི་དབང་པོ་ཡིན་པར་རྟོགས་ནས། །རྟེན་ཅིང་འབྲེལ་འབྱུང་གསུང་བ་ཡི། །ཐུབ་དབང་དེ་ལ་ཕྱག་འཚལ་ལོ། །ཞེས་བྱ་བ་སྨོས་སོ།

།རྟེན་ཅིང་འབྲེལ་པར་འབྱུང་བ་ནི་[24] དབང་པོ་མ་ཡིན་པ་མི་འབྱུང་ངོ་། །རྟེན་ [«སྡེ་» 3a.1] [«ཅོ་» 3a.1] ཅིང་འབྲེལ་པར་འབྱུང་ [«སྣར་» 4a.1] བ་[25] གསུང་བ་ནི་ཐུབ་པའི་དབང་པོར་འགྱུར་བའི་ཕྱིར་རྒྱུའོ། །ཐུབ་པའི་དབང་པོར་གྱུར་པ་ཡང་རྟེན་ཅིང་འབྲེལ་པར་འབྱུང་བ་གསུང་བའི་རྒྱུ་སྟེ། །གཞན་རྟེན་ཅིང་འབྲེལ་པར་འབྱུང་བ་འཆད་ནུས་པ་མེད་པའི་ཕྱིར་རོ། །ཉན་ [«པེ་» 3b.1] ཐོས་དང་རང་སངས་རྒྱས་དང་བྱང་ཆུབ་སེམས་དཔའ་རྣམས་ཀུན་ཐུབ་པའི་དབང་པོས་བསྟན་པ་ཉིད་ཀྱི་ཕྱིར་དེ་འཆད་ནུས་སོ། །གལ་ཏེ་གཅིག་ལ་གཅིག་ལྟོས་[26] པའི་ཕྱིར་གཉིས་ག་མི་འགྲུབ་བོ་ཞེ་ན། །སྨྲས་པ་འདི་ལྟ་སྟེ་གཅིག་ལ་གཅིག་ལྟོས་པ་གཞན་ངོ་བོ་ཉིད་ཀྱིས་མི་སྐྱེ་མི་འགག་ཅེས་བྱ་བ་གང་ཡིན་པ་དེ་རྟེན་ཅིང་འབྲེལ་པར་འབྱུང་བ་སྟེ། དེ་ཉིད་སྟོང་པ་ཉིད་དུ་སྨྲ་བ་རྣམས་འདོད་དོ། །རྟེན་ཅིང་འབྲེལ་པར་འབྱུང་བ་གསུང་བ་འབའ་ཞིག་གི་ཕྱིར་དེ་ཐུབ་པའི་དབང་པོར་གྱུར་པ

---

[23] «པེ་» «སྣར་»: +ལམ་

[24] «པེ་» «སྣར་» {SS}: གསུང་བ་ནི་ཐུབ་པའི་

[25] «པེ་» «སྣར་»: བར་

[26] «པེ་» «སྣར་» {SS}: བལྟོས་ «དཔེ་ 938 n. 1» notes that ཚིག་ཚན་འདིའི་ནང་དུ་ལྟོས་རྣམས་ «པེ་» «སྣར་» ལ་བལྟོས་ཞེས་འཁོད་ཀྱང་བསྒྱུར་མཆན་དུ་བཀོད་མེད།

མ་ཡིན་གྱི། །དངོས་པོ་རྣམས་གཅིག་ལ་གཅིག་ལྟོས་པའི་གྲུབ་པའི་ཚུལ་གསུང་བ་ན་དངོས་པོ་རྣམས་ཀྱི་སྐྱེ་བ་དང་འཇིག་པ་བཀག་པའི་ཕྱིར་རོ།

(C. །གསུམ་པ། ཚིག་དོན།)

(1. །དང་པོ། དངོས།)

།གང་གིས་ཞེས་བྱ་བ་ནི་རྒྱུ་སྟེ། །དེས་ཀྱང་གཉིས་སུ་མེད་པ་སྟོན་པའི་ཕྱིར་སྟོན་པ་བླ་ན་མེད་པ་ཐུབ་པའི་དབང་པོ་མཐོང་ནས། །ཐུབ་དབང་དེ་ལ་ཕྱག་འཚལ་ལོ། །ཞེས་བྱ་བ་སྨོས་སོ། [《སྣར་》 4b.1] །ཡང་ན་ཐུབ་པའི་དབང་པོ་གང་གིས་རྟེན་ཅིང་འབྲེལ་པར་འབྱུང་བ་གསུང་བ་ན། །རྟེན་ཅིང་འབྲེལ་པར་འབྱུང་བའི་ཚུལ་འདི་ཉིད་དོ། །རིམ་པ་འདིས་དངོས་པོཿ་རྣམས་ཀྱི་[27] སྐྱེ་བ་དང་འཇིག་པ་བཀག་པས་ཐུབ་དབང་དེ་ལ་ཕྱག་འཚལ་ལོ། །ཡང་ན་གང་གིས་ཞེས་བྱ་བ་ནི་རྒྱུ་ཁོ་ན་སྟེ[28] ། །གང་གི་ཕྱིར་ཐུབ་པའི་དབང་པོ་དེས་དངོས་པོ་རྣམས་ཀྱི་རྟེན་ཅིང་འབྲེལ་པར་འབྱུང་བ་སྟོན་པ་ན་[29] རང་བཞིན་གྱིས་དངོས་པོ་རྣམས་ཀྱི་སྐྱེ་བ་དང་འཇིག་པ་བཀག་པས་ཐུབ་དབང་དེ་ལ་ཕྱག་འཚལ་ལོ། །འཇིག་རྟེན་རྣམས་ལ་ཤིན་ཏུ་ཕན་འདོགས་པའི་ཕྱིར་ཞེས་བྱ་བའི་ཐ་ཚིག་གོ། །ཡང་ན་འོག་ནས་འབྱུང་བ་ཐུབ་པའི་དབང་པོའི་གསུང་རབ་ལ་[30] བརྟེན་ཏེ། །རང་གི་སེམས་ལ་བཀོད་པ་གྲུབ་པར་མཐོང་ནས། །གང་དག་[31] སྐྱེ་དང་འཇིག་པ་དང་།[32] །འདི་ཡི་ཚུལ་གྱིས་རབ་སྤངས་པ།

---

[27] 《པེ་》《སྣར་》: རྣམ་གྱི་

[28] 《པེ་》《སྣར་》: ཏེ་

[29] 《པེ་》《སྣར་》: -ན་

[30] 《པེ་》《སྣར་》: ལས་

[31] 《པེ་》《སྣར་》: གིས་

[32] 《པེ་》《སྣར་》: དག

།ཞེས་བྱ་བ་སྨོས་ཏེ། །རྟེན་ཅིང་འབྲེལ་པར་འབྱུང་བ་ཡི།[33] [《པེ་》 4a.1] །དེའི་ཕྱིར་ཐུབ་དབང་དེ་ལ་ཕྱག་འཚལ་ལོ། །ཞེས་བྱའོ།

(2. །གཉིས་པ། རྩོད་སྤང་།)

།འདིར་ [《ཅོ་》 3b.1] སྨྲས་པ། །ཁྱོད་ཀྱི་ཚིག་གི་ལུགས་འདི་ནི་སྟོན་མ་བྱུང་བ་སྟེ། །རྟེན་ཅིང་འབྲེལ་པར་འབྱུང་བ་སྨྲ་བ་ནི་སྐྱེ་བ་དང་འགག་པ་མེད་པར་སྟོན་པ་མི་རུང་[34] སྟེ། །ཁྱོད་ཀྱི་བུ་སྐྱེས་སོ་ཞེས་སྨྲ་ན་ཁྱོད་ཀྱི་བུ་མ་སྐྱེས་སོ་ཞེས་སྨྲས་པ་མ་ཡིན་པར་འགྱུར་བ་དེ་བཞིན་དུ་འདི་ཡང་མི་རིགས་སོ།

།ཕལ་པ་གལ་ཏེ་མ་རིག་པའི་རབ་རིབ་ཀྱིས་བློ་གྲོས་ཀྱི་མིག་ཉམས་པ་དང་སྦྱར་ཏེ། །རྟེན་ཅིང་འབྲེལ་པར་འབྱུང་བའི་སྒྲ་ལ་རང་བཞིན་གྱིས་མི་སྐྱེ་བ་དང་མི་འགག་པའི་ཚིག་ཏུ་མི་འགྱུར་བར་བརྟག་ན་ནི་ཉེས་པ་ཅི་ཡང་མེད་ཀྱི་རྟོགས་ཤིག །བྱིས་པ་དོ་བོ་ཉིད་དུ་མངོན་པར་ཞེན་པ་རྣམས་ནི་གཟུགས་བརྙན་ལ་བྱིས་པ་ལྟ་བུར་དངོས་པོ་རྣམས་ཀྱི་རང་བཞིན་མེད་པ་ཉིད་ཡོད་བཞིན་དུ་ཡང་རྟོགས་པར་མི་ནུས་ཀྱི།

---

33 《པེ་》《སྣར་》{SS}: ཡིའོ།

34 《སྣར་》: རུངས་

(II. །གཉིས་པ། བརྩམས་པར་བྱ་བའི་གཞུང་དངོས།)

(A. །དང་པོ། རྟེན་འབྲེལ་མཐའ་བྲལ་དུ་བསྟན་པ།)

(1. །དང་པོ། ཡོད་མཐའ་དགག་པ།)

(a. །དང་པོ། རྟེན་འབྱུང་སྤྲོས་བྲལ་དུ་གང་གིས་རྟོགས་པ།)

(i. །དང་པོ། དངོས།)

།མཁས་པ་རྣམས་ནི་གཟུགས་བརྙན་ལ་མཁས་པ་ལྟ་བུར་དངོས་པོཿ་རྣམས་ཀྱི[35] ངོ་བོ་ཉིད་མེད་པར་གསལ་བར་ཁོང་དུ་ཆུད་པར་ནུས་སོ་ཞེས་བསྟན་པའི་ཕྱིར།

གང་བློ་ཡོད་དང་མེད་པ་ལས།
།རྣམ་པར་འདས་ཤིང་མི་གནས་པ།
།དེ་དག་ཟབ་ [《སྣར་》 5a.1] མོ་དམིགས་མེད་པའི།[36]
།རྐྱེན་གྱི་དོན་ལ་རྣམ་པར་བསྒོམས།[37] || 1 ||

།ཞེས་བྱ་བ་སྨོས་སོ། །གང་དག་འདས་པའི་སྲིད་པ་ན་སྟོང་པ་ཉིད་ལ་གོམས་པ་དེ་དག་རྟེན་ཅིང་འབྲེལ་པར་འབྱུང་བ་རྟོགས་ཤིང་སྟོང་པ་ཉིད་མཐོང་བའི་ས་བོན་ཡོད་པའི་ཕྱིར་མཐུ་ཆེ་བ་ཡིན་ཏེ། །ད་ལྟར་གྱི་དུས་ན་སྐྱེས་པའི་གོམས་པ་མཚར་པོ་ཆེ་མེད་ཀྱང་སྐྱེ་བོ་བྱིས་པའི་བློའི་སྤྱོད་ཡུལ་མ་ཡིན་པ་ཡོད་པ་དང་མེད་པའི་མཐར་རྟོག་པས་རྙོག་པའི་དྲི་མས་མ་སྦགས་པ་རྟེན[38] ཅིང་འབྲེལ་པར་འབྱུང་བ་ཟབ་མོ་འཕགས་པ་ཤཱ་རིའི་བུ་ལ་སོགས་པས་ཁོང་དུ་ཆུད་པར་དམིགས་ཏེ།

---

[35] 《སྣར་》: རྣམ་གྲི་

[36] {SS}: པ་ཡི།

[37] The Skt. preserved in the *Sekoddeśaṭīkā*, as noted by Lindtner (*Nāgārjuniana*, 102ff.), reads: *asti-nāsti-vyatikrāntā buddhir yeṣāṁ nirāśrayā / gambhīras tair nirālambaḥ pratyayārtho vibhāvyate //*

[38] 《སྣར་》: བརྟེན་

(ii. །གཉིས་པ། ཟབ་མོ་བསྟན་པར་གདམས་པ།)

((1) །དང་པོ། མེད་ལྟ་དགག་པ་བཤད་ཟིན་དྲན་པ་ལ་སྦྱར་བ།)

།ཇི་ལྟར་འཇིག་རྟེན་ལས་དང་ཉོན་མོངས་རྒྱུར་བྱས་[39] བྱེད་རྒྱུ་ལྡན་འབྱུང་བ།
།ལས་དང་ཉོན་མོངས་ [《པེ་》 4b.1] པ་དག་ལྡོག་རྒྱུ་དེ་ཡང་འདྲེན་པས་རབ་ཏུ་
གསུངས།

།གང་ན་སྐྱེ་དང་རྒ་དང་རྒུད་པའི་སྡུག་བསྔལ་ངེས་པར་མི་གནས་པ།
།ཐར་པ་མཆོག་དེ་སྨྲ་བའི་ཁྱུ་མཆོག་དེ་ཡིས་རང་གིས་[40] མཁྱེན་དེ་གསུངས།[41]

།ཚིགས་སུ་བཅད་པ་དེ་འཕགས་པ་ཤཱ་རིའི་བུས་ཐོས་པ་ཙམ་གྱིས་དེ་ཁོ་ན་རྟོགས་ཤིང་འབྱུང་སྟེ། །དེ་བས་ན་དེ་ལྟར་[42] སྔོན་གོམས་པའི་མཐུ་ཉིད་ཀྱིས་དེ་དག་གི་བློ་ཡོད་པ་དང་མེད་པར་མཐོང་བ་ལས་འདས་སོ། [《སྣེ་》 4a.1] །མཐའ་གཉིས་དེ་ལས་ལྷག་པའི་དབུས་མེད་པའི་ཕྱིར་དེ་ལ་ཡང་གནས་པ་མེད་པས་མི་གནས་སོ། །སྐྱེ་ [《ཅོ་》 4a.1] བོ་བྱིས་པ་རྣམས་ལ་འཇིགས་པར་བྱེད་པ་དང་། །དེ་དག་འཇུག་མི་ནུས་པའི་ཕྱིར་ཟབ་པའོ། །རང་བཞིན་གྱིས་མི་སྐྱེ་བས་ཡོད་པ་དང་མེད་པའི་མཐའ་དང་དབུས་ཡོངས་སུ་བརྟག་པའི་ཡུལ་དུ་དམིགས་པར་མི་ནུས་པའི་ཕྱིར་དམིགས་སུ་མེད་

---

[39] {SS}: བཅས་ following the *Mahā-saṁnipātaratnaketudhāraṇīsūtra.*

[40] 《པེ་》《སྣར་》: གི་

[41] As noted by Scherrer-Schaub (*Yuktiṣaṣṭikāvṛtti*, 117 n. 48), the Skt. is preserved in the *Mahā-saṁnipāta-ratnaketu-dhāraṇī-sūtra* (Dutt, *Gilgit Manuscripts*, v.3 iii, 3–6): *karma kleśa-sa-hetu-kāraṇa-vatī loka-pravṛttir yathā karma-kleśa-nivṛtti-kāraṇam api provāca tan nāyakaḥ / yasmin janma-jarā-vipatti-niyataṁ duḥkhaṁ na santiṣṭhate taṁ mokṣa-pravaraṁ sa vādi-vṛṣabho jñātvā svayaṁ bhāṣate //*

[42] 《པེ་》《སྣར་》{SS}: +དེ་

དོ། །འཕགས་པ་དེ་དག་ཀྱང་རྐྱེན་གྱི་དོན་ལ་རྣམ་པར་སྒོམ་ཞེས་བྱ་བ་ནི་ཡེ་ཤེས་[43] མངོན་སུམ་དུ་བྱེད་ཅེས་བྱ་བའི་ཐ་ཚིག་གོ།

།འཕགས་པ་མ་ཡིན་པ་ཤིན་ཏུ་ཕྱིན་ཅི་ལོག་པ་དག་གིས་ནི་རྟེན་ཅིང་འབྲེལ་པར་འབྱུང་བའི་དོན་དེ་ལྟར་རྟོགས་པར་མི་ནུས་ཏེ། །རྟེན་ཅིང་འབྲེལ་པར་འབྱུང་བའི་སྒྲ་ཉིད་ཀྱིས་རང་བཞིན་གྱིས་སྐྱེ་བར་མངོན་པར་ཞེན་པས་སྟོང་པ་ [‹‹སྣར་›› 5b.1] ཉིད་དུ་སྨྲ་བ་ལ་ཕྱིར་རྒོལ་བ་དང་དེ་བསྟན་པའི་རིགས་པ་བཙལ་བ་ལ་བརྩོན་པའི་ཕྱིར་འདིར་སྨྲས་པ།

འཐད་པ་གང་གིས་རྟེན་ཅིང་འབྲེལ་པར་འབྱུང་བ་དམིགས་ཤིང་ཡོད་པ་ཡང་མེད་པར་བརྟག་ནུས་པ་[44] གང་གི་ཕྱིར་འཕགས་པ་དག་ཡོད་པ་དང་མེད་པར་རྟོགས་པ་ལས་འདས་པའི་བློས་རྟེན་ཅིང་འབྲེལ་པར་འབྱུང་བ་ཟབ་མོ་ལ་རྣམ་པར་སྒོམ་པ་ཇི་ཙམ་དུ་དངོས་པོ་དམིགས་སུ་ཡོད་པ་དག་མེད་པར་མི་རུང་ངོ་། །གལ་ཏེ་མེད་དུ་ཟིན་ན་དེའི་ཚེ་བོང་བུའི་རྭ་བཞིན་དུ་དེ་ཡང་དམིགས་པར་མི་འགྱུར་རོ། །འཇིག་རྟེན་ཕ་རོལ་ནས་འདིར་འོངས་པ་[45] དང་། །འཇིག་རྟེན་འདི་ནས་འཇིག་རྟེན་ཕ་རོལ་ [‹‹པེ་›› 5a.1] དུ་[46] འགྲོ་བར་བསྟན་པ་ལས་དང་འབྲས་བུ་འབྲེལ་པར་འབྱུང་སྟེ་འཁོར་བའི་རྒྱུད་[47] མི་འཆད་པར་བསྟན་[48] པའི་ཕྱིར་རྟེན་ཅིང་འབྲེལ་པར་འབྱུང་བ་ཡན་ལག་བཅུ་གཉིས་ཚེ་རབས་གསུམ་དུ་ཆ་ཤད་པ་ཡང་མི་རུང་བར་འགྱུར་རོ། །ཆོས་མངོན་པ་ལས་ཕུང་པོ་དང་སྐྱེ་མཆེད་དང་། །ཁམས་རྣམས་

---

43 ‹‹པེ་›› ‹‹སྣར་›› {SS}: +ཀྱིས་

44 ‹‹པེ་›› ‹‹སྣར་››: -པ་

45 ‹‹པེ་›› ‹‹སྣར་›› ‹‹ཅོ་››: འདི་འོང་བ་

46 ‹‹ཅོ་›› {SS}: ཏུ་

47 ‹‹པེ་›› ‹‹སྣར་›› {SS}: རྒྱུན་

48 ‹‹སྣར་››: བརྟན་

ཀྱི་རང་དང་སྤྱིའི་མཚན་ཉིད་བཤད་པ་ཡང་མི་རུང་བར་འགྱུར་རོ། །དེ་དག་ཐམས་ཅད་ཇི་ལྟར་བཤད་པ་བཞིན་དུ་འདུག་སྟེ་ཡོད་ན་རུང་བས་དེའི་ཕྱིར་རྟེན་ཅིང་འབྲེལ་པར་འབྱུང་བ་འདི་ཡོད་པའོ།

།བཤད་པ། །གལ་ཏེ་ཁྱོད་ཀྱིས།[49]

ཉེས་པ་ཐམས་ཅད་འབྱུང་བའི་གནས།
།མེད་པ་རྣམ་པར་བཟློག་ཟིན་གྱིས། **|| 2ab ||**

།དེ་དག་དགག་པར་སྒྲུབ་པའི་ཕོ་བོའི་ཉོན་ [《སྡེ་》 4b.1] མོངས་པ་ཡང་ཁྱོད་ཀྱིས་[50] བཀག་པས་ན་ཁྱོད་ཀྱིས་[51] བྱས་ཏེཿ བསྔངས་སོ།[52]

((2) །གཉིས་པ། ཡོད་ལྟ་དགག་པ་ལ་མཉན་པར་གདམས་པ།)

།ཡང་བདག་གིས།[53]

རིགས་པ་གང་གིས་ཡོད་པ་ཡང་།
།བཟློག་པར་བྱ་བ་མཉན་པར་གྱིས། **|| 2cd ||**

།རྟེན་ཅིང་འབྲེལ་པར་འབྱུང་བའི་ [《ཅོ་》 4b.1] སྐབས་ཡིན་པར་[54] རྟེན་ཅིང་འབྲེལ་པར་འབྱུང་བ་ཡིན་པར་ཤེས་པར་བྱའོ། །ཡངཿ ན་མེད་[55] པ་ཅན་ལས་དང་འབྲས་བུར་འབྲེལ་པ་ལ་སྐྱུར་པ་འདེབས་

---

49 《པེ་》《སྣར་》: ཀྱི་

50 《པེ་》《སྣར་》: ཀྱི་

51 《པེ་》《སྣར་》{SS}: +གྲོགས་

52 《སྣར་》: བསྔོ་

53 《སྣར་》: ག

པས་མེད་པར་ལྟ་བ་ཁས་བླངས་པ་གང་ཡིན་པ་དེ་འཇིག་རྟེན་པ་དང་འཇིག་རྟེན་ལས་འདས་པའི་དགེ་བའི་རྩ་བ་མ་ལུས་པ་སུན་འབྱིན་པར་གྱུར་པས་ཉེས་པ་ཐམས་ཅད་འབྱུང་བའི་རྒྱུར་གྱུར་པ་དང་། །མི་དགེ་བའི་ཆོས་ཐམས་ཅད་སྐོགས་[56] པའི་རྒྱུར་གྱུར་པའི་ཕྱིར་ཉེས་པ་ཐམས་ཅད་ཀྱི་འབྱུང་གནས་ཏེ། [«སྣར་» 6a.1] །རྟེན་ཅིང་འབྲེལ་པར་འབྱུང་བ་ཚེ་རབས་གསུམ་པ་དང་། །སེམས་ཅན་ཐམས་ཅད་ཀྱི་སྐྱིའི་ལས་ཀྱིས་བསྐྱེད་[57] པ་[58] སྣོད་ཀྱི་འཇིག་རྟེན་སྣ་ཚོགས་རྣམ་པར་གཞོག་པ་ན། །དེའི་[59] ཆོས་མངོན་པ་ལས་རྣམ་པར་བཟློག་གོ། །དེ་བས་ན་དེ་ལྟར་ཕ་རོལ་དག་ལ་གསལ་བའི་ཕྱིར་དེ་ཡང་རིགས་[60] པ་མི་ཆཤད་དོ། །ཡོད་པ་བཟློག་པ་ནི་

> དགེ་སློང་དག་འདི་ལྟ་སྟེ། །མི་སླུ་[61] བའི་ཆོས་ཅན་མྱ་ [«པེ་» 5b.1] ངན་ལས་འདས་པ་འདི་ནི་བདེན་པའི་མཆོག་གཅིག་པུའོ།[62] །འདུ་བྱེད་ཐམས་ཅད༔ སྣོད་ཀྱི་འཇིག་རྟེན་[63] ནི་[64] བརྫུན་པ་བསླུ་བའི་ཆོས་ཅན་ནོ།[65] །ཀྱེ་མ་འདུ་བྱེད་རྣམས་མི་རྟག[66]

---

[54] «པེ་» «སྣར་» {SS}: པས་

[55] «སྣར་»: ཞེད་

[56] «པེ་» «སྣར་» {SS}: སོགས་

[57] «སྣར་»: བསྐྱེས་

[58] {SS}: པའི་

[59] «པེ་» «སྣར་»: དེ་

[60] «པེ་» «སྣར་»: རིག

[61] «པེ་» «སྣར་» {SS}: བསླུ་

[62] «པེ་» «སྣར་» «ཅོ་»: བུའོ།

།ཅེས་བྱ་བ་ལ་སོགས་པ་བཤད་པ་ན། །བཅོམ་ལྡན་འདས་ཀྱིས་གསུངས་སོ། །དེ་ལྟ་མོད་ཀྱི་དེ་ཕྱིར་ཞིང་བཏུད་དེ་གཞུང་གཅིག་ཏུ་མ་གསུངས་ལ། །ཁྲིས་པ་དག་ཡུན་རིང་པོ་ནས་ཡོད་པར་ལྟ་བ་ལ་གོམས་པས་དེའི་ཕྱིར་ཐུབ་པའི་དབང་པོའི་གསུང་རབ་དེ་དང་དེ་དག་ལས་བཤད་པའི་གསུང་རབ་ལས་བཏུས་ཏེ། །རབ་ཏུ་བྱེད་པ་འདིར་བསྡུས་པ་ཉིད་ཀྱིས། རིགས་[67] པ་གང་གིས་ཡོད་པ་ཡང་། །བཟློག་པར་བྱ་བ་མཉན་པར་གྱིས།

(b. །གཉིས་པ། ཡོད་མཐའ་འགོག་པའི་རིགས་པ།)

(i. །དང་པོ། སྐབས་སུ་བབས་པའི་ཐལ་བ།)

།རིགས་[68] པ་དེ་དག་གང་ཞེ་ན། །དེ་བསྟན་པའི་ཕྱིར།

ཇི་ལྟར་བྲིས་པས་རྨ་བརྟགས་བཞིན།
།དངོས་པོ་དེ་སྟེ་བདེན་གྱུར་ན།

---

63 {SS}: -སྟོད་ཀྱི་འཇིག་རྟེན་ {SS} justifies the omission following MAV (ad k. 6.34: La Vallée Poussin, *Madhyamakāvatāra*, 119–120; tr. and Skt., La Vallée Poussin, "Madhyamakāvatāra," *Muséon*, 11, 313 n. 1).

64 «པེ་»«སྣར་»{SS}: ནི་ «སྡེ་»«ཅོ་»: མི་

65 As noted by Scherrer-Schaub ("Yuktiṣaṣṭikāvṛtti," 122 n. 65), this portion of the passage comes from the *Kātyāyanāvavāda*, the Sanskrit of which occurs in PPMMV (La Vallée Poussin, *Madhyamakavṛttiḥ*, 41): *etaddhi bhikṣavaḥ paramaṁ satyaṁ yaduta amoṣa-dharma nirvāṇaṁ sarva-saṁskārāś ca mṛṣā moṣa-dharmāṇaḥ //*

66 Similar passages to this final line are found in the *Udānavarga*, 1.3 (Bernhard, *Udānavarga*, v.1, 96; UV fol. 209a.2) and *Avadānaśataka* (Speyer, *Avadānaçataka*, II, 198): *anityā bata saṁskārā*, in the *Vimalakīrtinirdeśa* (KOUDA, *Vimalakīrtinirdeśa*, 50): *kye ma'o 'du byed 'di dag ni mi rtag go / anityā vateme sarvasaṁskārā*, and others. Cf. Scherrer-Schaub, "Yuktiṣaṣṭikāvṛtti," 123 n. 66.

67 «པེ་»«སྣར་»: རིག་

68 «པེ་»«སྣར་»: རིག་

།དེ་དག་དངོས་མེད་རྣམ་ཐར་དུ།
།གང་ཕྱིར་མི་འདོད་རྒྱུ་དེ་ཅི། || 3 ||

།ཞེས་བྱ་བ་སྨོས་སོ། །བཅོམ་ལྡན་འདས་ཀྱིས་

དེ་དོན་སོ་སོ་ཡང་དག་པར་རིག་པ་དང་། །ཆོས་སོ་སོ་ཡང་ [«སྡེ་» 5a.1] དག་པར་རིག་པ་ལས་མཆོག་ཏུ་དགའ་བ་སྐྱེའོ། །རབ་ཏུ་དགའ་བ་ལས་བདེ་བ་སྐྱེའོ། །ཡིད་བདེ་བ་ལས་ལུས་ཤིན་ཏུ་སྦྱངས་པར་འགྱུར་རོ། །ལུས་ཤིན་ཏུ་སྦྱངས་པ་ལས་བདེ་བ་མྱོང་བར་འགྱུར་རོ། །བདེ་བ་ལས་སེམས་རྩེ་གཅིག་ཏུ་འགྱུར་རོ། །སེམས་རྩེ་གཅིག་པ་ལས་ཡང་དག་པ་ཇི་ལྟ་བ་བཞིན་དུ་རབ་ཏུ་ཤེས་པར་འགྱུར་རོ། །ཡང་དག་པ་ཇི་ལྟ་བ་བཞིན་དུ་རབ་ཏུ་མཐོང་བར་འགྱུར་རོ། [«ཅོ་» 5a.1] །ཡང་དག་པ་ཇི་ལྟ་བ་བཞིན་རབ་ཏུ་ཤེས། །ཡང་དག་པ་ཇི་ལྟ་བ་བཞིན་རབ་ཏུ་མཐོང་ན [«སྣར་» 6b.1] ཡིད་འབྱུང་བར་འགྱུར་རོ། །ཡིད་བྱུང་ན་མི་ཆགས་པར་འགྱུར་རོ། །མ་ཆགས་ན་རྣམ་པར་གྲོལ་བར་འགྱུར་ཏེ།[69]

།དེ་ལྟར་ན་ཡང་དག་པ་ཇི་ལྟ་བ་[70] བཞིན་དུ་རབ་ཏུ་མཐོང་ནས་སེམས་རྣམ་པར་གྲོལ་བར་རྣམ་པར་གཞག་[71] གོ།

---

69 This passage is also quoted in Yaśomitra's *Explanation* (AKV) in which the Sanskrit is preserved (Wogihara, *Sphuṭârthā*, I, 54): *tasyārtha-pratisaṁvedino dharma-pratisaṁvedinaś cotpadyate prāmodhyaṁ / pramuditasya prītir jāyate / prīta-manasaḥ kāyaḥ praśrabhyate / praśrabdha-kāyaḥ sukhaṁ vedayate / sukhitasya cittaṁ samādhīyate / samāhita-citto yathābhūtaṁ prajānāti yathābhūtaṁ paśyati / yathābhūtaṁ prajānan yathābhūtaṁ paśyan nirvidyate / nirviṇṇo virajyate / virakto vimucyate //* although the Tibetan differs superficially from this in the AKV.

70 «པེ་»«སྣར་»: -བ་

((1) །དང་པོ་ནི། ཐལ་འགྱུར་དང་རྒྱུད་དུ་སྨྲ་བའི་དབུ་མ་པའི་ཁྱད་པར་བཤད་པར་བྱ།)

།གལ་ཏེ་དོན་དམ་པ་མ་རྟོགས་པ་དག་གིས་སྔོན་པོ་ལ་སོགས་པའི་དོན་དེ་དག་ཡོངས་སུ་གཅོད་པའི་རང་གི་ངོ་བོ་གང་ཡིན་པ་དེ་ཉིད་ཀྱིས་ཕྱིན་ཅི་མ་ལོག་པར་གྱུར་ན་ [《པེ་》 6a.1] ནི་དེའི་ཚེ་དེ་ཇི་ལྟར་སྣང་བའི་དངོས་པོའི་ངོ་བོ་ཉིད་ཀྱི་དེ་ཁོ་ན་མཐོང་བའི་ཕྱིར་དགྲ་བཅོམ་པ་དག་བཞིན་དུ་དེ་དག་དངོས་པོ་མེད་པའི་[72] མི་སྐྱེ་བས་ལེན་པ་མེད་པའི་ཡོངས་སུ་མྱ་ངན་ལས་འདས་པས་ཐར་པར་འགྱུར་ཏེ། །ཇི་ལྟར་

གང་ན་ལུས་ཀྱང་ཞིག་པ་དང་།
།འདུ་ཤེས་འགགས་ཤིང་ཚོར་བྲལ་བ།
།འདུ་བྱེད་སྦྱོར་བ་ཀུན་སྲུན་འཕྲིན།
།རྣམ་པར་ཤེས་པ་ནུབ་གྱུར་པ།[73]

།ཞེས་གསུངས་པ་དང་། །དེ་བཞིན་དུ།

---

[71] 《པེ་》《སྣར་》: བཞག 《དཔེ་ 942 n. 5》 notes that ཆོས་ཅན་འདིའི་ནང་དུ་གཞག་རྣམས་ 《པེ་》 《སྣར་》: ལ་བཞག་ཅེས་འཁོད་ཀྱང་བསྡུར་མཆན་དུ་བཀོད་མེད།

[72] 《པེ་》《སྣར་》{SS}: པ་ཕྱིས་

[73] The *Udānavarga* (26.16: Bernhard, *Udānavarga*, I, 322; f. 233a.4–.5) reads: *bhitvā kāyaṁ ca saṁjñāṁ ca vedanāṁ vyupaśāmya ca // vijñānāstagamaṁ labdhvā duḥkhasyânto nirucyate //*; *lus zhig tshor ba bsil bar gyur / 'du shes 'gags zhing 'du byed zhi / rnam par shes pa nub gyur pa / 'di dra 'di ni sdug sngal mtha' //*. Chandrakīrti's PPMMV (La Vallée Poussin, *Madhyamakavṛttiḥ*, 520 n. 1; f. 173b.5–.6) reads: *abhedhi kāyo nirodhi samvedanāpaṇṭhai [pathai] rahinsu [itsu] sahinsu [itsu] saccadhima samo sasvarāṇām vijānam arthagamed //*; *gang na lus zhig 'du shes 'gags / tshor ba thams cad bral gyur zhing / 'du byed nye bar zhi ba dang / rnam par shes pa nub gyur pa //*. A Pāli equivalent of a passage matching the one cited in PPMMV in the UV (8.9: Steinthal, *Udāna*, 93; tr. Woodward, *Minor Anthologies*, II, 113) reads: *abhedi kāyo nirodhi saññā, vedanā pi 'tidahaṁsu sabbā, vūpasamiṁsu saṅkhārā, viññāṇam attham agamā 'ti.*

མ་ཞུམ་པ་ཡི་ལུས་ཀྱིས་ནི།
།ཚོར་བ་དང་དུ་ལེན་པ་ན།
།དེ་ཡི་སེམས་ཀྱི་རྣམ་པར་ཐར།
།མྱ་ངན་འདས་པ་མར་མེ་བཞིན།[74]

།ཞེས་འབྱུང་བ་ལྟ་བུའོ། །དེ་ལྟར་བྱིས་པ་རྣམས་ཀྱང་ཡང་དག་པ་མཐོང་བའི་ཕྱིར་དགྲ་བཅོམ་པ་བཞིན་དུ་དེ་དག་ཐམས་ཅད་བཏང་བས་མྱ་ངན་ལས་འདས་པར་འདོད་པར་གྱིས་ཤིག །འོན་ཏེ་དེ་དག་དགྲ་བཅོམ་པ་བཞིན་དུ་ཐམས་ཅད་མེད་པས་རྣམ་པར་གྲོལ་བར་མི་འདོད་ན། །བྱིས་པ་མ་རིག་པ་[75] ཕྱིན་ཅི་ལོག་པ་དག་གང་ལ་ཇི་ལྟར་རྟོག་པ་དེ་བཞིན་དུ་ངེས་པར་མི་འགྱུར་ཏེ། །དེ་བས་ན་དེ་དག་གི་ཡོད་པར་ལྟ་བ་ནི་དེ་ཁོ་ན་མཐོང་བར་མི་འགྱུར་རོ།

((2) །གཉིས་པ། འཐད་ཕྱོགས་ངོས་བཟུང་བ།)

།དེའི་ཕྱིར་བཅོམ་ལྡན་འདས་ཀྱིས།

མིག་དང་རྣ་བ་སྣ་ཡང་ཚད་མ་མིན།[76]
།ལྕེ་དང་ལུས་དང་སེམས་ [《སྡེ་》 5b.1] ཀྱང་ཚད་མ་མིན།[77]

---

[74] The PPMMV (La Vallée Poussin, *Madhyamakavṛttiḥ*, 520; f. 173b.6) reads: *asaṁlīnena kāyena vedanām adhyavāsayat / pradyotasyeva nirvāṇaṁ vimokṣas tasya cetasaḥ //*. While the *Avadāna-śataka*, (Speyer, *Avadānaçataka*, II, 199.8–.9) reads, with some differences: *asaṁlīnena cittena vedanā adhivāsayan / pradyotasyeva nirvāṇaṁ vimokṣas tasya cetasa iti //*

[75] 《པེ་》《སྣར་》{SS}: པས་

[76] 《པེ་》《སྣར་》{SS}: ཡིན་

[77] 《པེ་》《སྣར་》{SS}: ཡིན་

།གལ་ཏེ་དབང་པོ་འདི་དག་ཚད་ཡིན་ན།
།འཕགས་པའི་ལམ་གྱིས་སུ་ལ་ཅི་ཞིག་བྱ།

།འདི་ལྟར་དབང་པོ་འདི་དག་ཚད་མིན་ཏེ།
།ངོ་བོ་ཉིད་ཀྱི་བེམས་[78] པོ་ལུང་མ་བསྟན།
།དེ་ཕྱིར་མྱ་ངན་འདས་པའི་ལམ་འདོད་གང་།
།དེས་ནི་ [«སྣར་» 7a.1] འཕགས་པའི་ལམ་གྱིས་[79] བྱ་བ་བྱོས།[80]

།ཞེས་གསུངས་སོ། །དེ་སྐད་དུ་

འདི་དག་འདུ་བྱེད་ལོག་པས་[81] བརྟགས་པ་སྟེ།
ཡང་དག་མིན་ལ་ཡང་དག་ཡོད་ལ་མེད།
།མ་བྱུང་བ་དང་མ་སྐྱེས་ཆོས་རྣམས་ལ།
།ཡང་དག་ཉིད་དང་འབྱུང་བ་ལོག་པར་བརྟགས།[82]

---

78 «པེ་»«སྣར་»: ཀྱིས་བེམ་ {SS}: ཀྱིས་བེམས་

79 «པེ་»«སྣར་»{SS}: གྱིས་ «སྡེ་»«ཅོ་»: གྱི་

80 The Sanskrit of this passage (9.23–24: Vaidya, *Samādhi-rāja-sūtra*, 47–48) reads: *na cakṣuḥ pramāṇaṁ na śrotra ghrāṇaṁ na jihva pramāṇaṁ na kāya-cittam / pramāṇa yady eta bhaveyur indriyā kasyārya-mārgeṇa bhaveta kāryam // yasmād ime indriya apramāṇā jaḍāḥ svabhāvena avyākṛtāś ca / tasmād ya nirvāṇa-pathaiva arthikaḥ sa ārya-mārgeṇa karotu kāryam //*. Cf. Scherrer-Schaub (*Yuktiṣaṣṭikāvṛtti*, 130 n. 77) for text critical notes.

81 «པེ་»«སྣར་»{SS}: ཤེས་ལོག་པ་

82 The Sanskrit is preserved (13.20: Wogihara and Tsuchida, *Saddharmapuṇḍarīka-sūtram*, 239.22–240.3): *viparīta saṁjñī hi ime vikalpitā asanta-santā hi abhūta-bhūtataḥ // anucchitāś câpi ajāta-dharmā jātā tha bhūtā* [S-S: *bhūta*] *viparīta-kalpitāḥ*. Vaidya (138–139) reads *anutthitāś* for *anucchitāś*, while Scherrer-Schaub (*Yuktiṣaṣṭikāvṛtti*, 130 n. 78) notes Kern and

(cont'd)

[«ཅོ་» 5b.1] ཞེའོ། །དེ་དག་ཇི་ལྟར་ཡང་དག་པར་མཐོང་བ་མ་ཡིན་ཞེ་ན། །ཡང་དེ་ཉིད་ལས།

གང་ཚེ་འདུས་བྱས་འདུས་མ་བྱས།
།ཡང་དག་ཡང་དག་མ་ཡིན་དང་།   [«པེ་» 6b.1]
།རབ་འབྲིང་ཐ་མའི་ཆོས་རྣམས་ལ།
།རྣམ་པ་ཀུན་ཏུ་སྤྱོད་པ་མེད།

།བརྟན་པ་བུད་མེད་ཅེས་མི་སྤྱོད།
།སྐྱེས་པ་ཞེས་ཀྱང་མི་རྟོག་སྟེ།
།ཆོས་སོ་ཅོག་ནི་མ་སྐྱེས་ཕྱིར།
།བཙལ་བར་བྱས་ཀྱང་མ་མཐོང་ངོ་།

།ཆོས་འདི་ཐམས་ཅད་མེད་པ་སྟེ།
།སྐྱེ་བ་མེད་ཅིང་འབྱུང་བའང་མེད།
།རྟག་ཏུ་སྟོང་པ་བྱེད་མེད་གནས།
།འདི་ནི་མཁས་པའི་སྤྱོད་ཡུལ་ཡིན།[83]

Nanjio's reading (*Saddharma-puṇḍarīka-sūtra*, 281.11–12) of the manuscript variant *anuśtitāś* for *anucchitāś*, referring to Simonsson's analysis of its Tibetan rendering with *ma skyes* rather than *langs ma yin* (the usual equivalent of *anutthita*). Scherrer-Schaub (*Yuktiṣaṣṭikā-vṛtti*, 130 n. 77) cites the closest of two Tib. versions edited by Simonsson, *Indo-Tibetische Studien*, 65: *'di dag 'dus shes log par brtags pa ste // yang dag min la yang dag yod la med // ma byung ba dang ma skyes chos rnams la // yang dag nyid dang 'byung bar log par brtags //*. Cf. Simonsson, *Indo-Tibetische Studien*, 65, 67–68.

83 The Sanskrit, preserved in *Saddharma-puṇḍarika-sūtra* (13.16–17, 19: Wogihara and Tsuchida, 239) reads: *yadā na carate dharme hīna-utkṛṣṭa-madhyame / saṁskṛtâsaṁskṛte câpi bhūtâbhūte ca sarvaśaḥ // strīti nâcarate dhīro puruṣeti na kalpayet / sarva-dharmān ajātatvād gaveṣanto na paśyati // …asantakā dharma ime prakāśitā aprādurbhūtāś ca ajāta sarve / śūnyā*

(cont'd)

།ཞེས་གསུངས་སོ། །དེ་ལྟར་མཐོང་བ་ནི་དེ་[84] ཁོ་ན་མཐོང་བ་སྟེ། །དེ་ཡང་བྱིས་པ་རྣམས་ལ་མེད་དོ། །དེའི་ཕྱིར་དེ་ཁོ་ན་མཐོང་བ་མ་ཡིན་པས་དེ་དག་རྣམ་པརཿ ཐར་པར་[85] མི་གཞུག་གོ།

(ii. །གཉིས་པ། ཞར་བྱུང་།)

((1) །དང་པོ། གཉིས་སུ་ལྟ་བས་མི་གྲོལ་བར་བསྟན་པ།)

།གང་གི་ཕྱིར་དེ་ལྟར་མེད་པར་ལྟ་བ་དེ་ཉེས་པ་ཐམས་ཅད་ཀྱི་འབྱུང་གནས་[86] ཏེ། །ངན་པར་འགྲོ་བའི་འབྲས་བུ་དང་མི་བདེ་བ་མྱོང་བའི་འབྲས་བུ་ཡང་ཡིན་པ་ལྟར། །ཡོད་པར་ལྟ་བ་ཡང་སྐྱེ་བོ་བྱིས་པ་རྣམས་དང་འདྲིས་པ་བདེ་འགྲོའི་འབྲས་བུ་དང་། །ཚེ་རབས་ཐམས་ཅད་བདེ་བ་མྱོང་བའི་འབྲས་བུ་སྟེ།[87] །དེ་ལྟ་བས་ན་ལྟ་བ་གཉིས་འཁོར་བའི་འབྲས་བུ་ཡིན་པས་རིགས་པ་དང་འགལ་ལོ།

ཡོད་པས་རྣམ་པར་མི་གྲོལ་[88] ཏེ།

།མེད་པས་སྲིད་པ་འདི་ལས་མིན། || **4ab** ||

།གང་གི་ཕྱིར་མི་གཙང་བས་མི་གཙང་བ་བཀྲུ་བར་མི་འགྱུར་བ་དེའི་ཕྱིར་འཁོར་བའི་མི་གཙང་བ་འབྱུང་བར་འགྱུར་བའི་རྒྱུ་ལྟ་བ་འདི་གཉིས་ཀྱིས་སྲིད་པ་ལས་འདའ་བའི་མཚན་ཉིད་རྣམ་པར་གྲོལ་བ་ཐོབ་པར་

---

nirīhā sthita nitya-kālaṁ ayaṁ gocaro ucyati paṇḍitānām //, as noted by Scherrer-Schaub (*Yuktiṣaṣṭikāvṛtti*, 131 n. 79). The Tibetan, from Simonsson, *Indo-Tibetische Studien*, 63, is: *chos 'di dag ni yod pa ma yin bstan // thams cad 'byung ba med cing skye ba med // rtag tu mi g.yo stong pa nyid du gnas // de ni mkhas pa rnams kyi pyod yul yin //.*

[84] 《པེ་》《སྣར་》{SS}: དེ་ 《སྡེ་》《ཅོ་》: -དེ་

[85] 《པེ་》《སྣར་》: -ཐར་པར་

[86] 《པེ་》《སྣར་》: +ཡིན་

[87] 《ཏྣི་》 comments: རིན་ཐེང་དུ། ཡོད་པ་པ་དེ་བདེ་འགྲོར་འགྲོ། མེད་པ་པ་དེ་ངན་འགྲོར་འགྲོ་ཞེས་གསུངས་སོ།

The canonical quote reads (《སྡེ་》): མེད་པ་པ་ནི་ངན་འགྲོར་འགྲོ། ཡོད་པ་པ་ནི་བདེ་འགྲོར་འགྲོ།

[88] {SS}: འགྲོལ་

མི་ནུས་སོ། །གལ་ཏེ་དེ་ལྟར་ཡོད་པ་དང་མེད་པར་ལྟ་བ་ནི་ཕུང་པོ་ཁམས་དང་སྐྱེ་མཆེད་ལས་རྣམ་པར་ [«སྣར་» 7b.1] གྲོལ་བར་མི་འགྱུར་ན། །རྣལ་འབྱོར་པ་དག་[89] ལྟ་བ་གང་གིས་ [«སྡེ་» 6a.1] རྣམ་པར་གྲོལ་བར་འགྱུར་ཞེ་ན།

((2) །གཉིས་པ། གཉིས་མེད་རྟོགས་པས་གྲོལ་བར་བསྟན་པ།[90])

དངོས་དང་དངོས་མེད་ཡོངས་ཤེས་པས།
།བདག་ཉིད་ཆེན་པོ་རྣམ་པར་གྲོལ། ‖ **4cd** ‖

།ཞེས་བྱ་བ་སྨོས་པ་ཡིན་ཏེ། །དངོས་པོ་ལ་མ་བརྟེན་པར་དངོས་པོ་མེད་པར་མི་འགྲུབ།[91] །དངོས་པོ་དང་དངོས་པོ་མེད་པར་[92] གཉིས་ཀ་རང་གི་ངོ་བོར་གྲུབ་པ་མེད་པར་གནས་སོ། །དེ་གཉིས་དངོས་པོ་མེད་པར་ཡོངས་སུ་ [«པེ་» 7a.1] ཤེས་པཿ དངོས་པོ་དང་[93] དངོས་པོ་མེད་པའི་རང་གི་ངོ་བོ་ལ་སོགས་[94] ཡོངས་སུ་མི་རྟོག་[95] པའི་རང་བཞིན་གང་ཡིན་པ་དེ་ནི་དེ་ལྟར་དངོས་པོ་དང་དངོས་པོ་མེད་པ་ཕྱིན་ཅི་མ་ལོག་པར་ཡོངས་སུ་ཤེས་པ་སྟེ། །དེ་ལྟར་ཡོངས་སུ་ཤེས་པ་ [«ཅོ་» 6a.1] དེས་

[89] «སྣར་»: བདག

[90] «ཏཱི་» comments: རིན་ཕྲེང་དུ། གཉིས་ལ་མི་བརྟེན་ཐར་པར་འགྱུར་ཞེས་པའི་དོན། The full quote reads («སྡེ་»): ཡང་དག་ཇི་བཞིན་ཡོངས་ཤེས་ཕྱིར། གཉིས་ལ་མི་བརྟེན་ཐར་པར་འགྱུར།

[91] «པེ་» «སྣར་»: +།དངོས་པོ་མེད་པ་ལ་མ་བརྟེན་པར་ཡང་དངོས་པོར་མི་འགྲུབ་སྟེ།

[92] «པེ་» «སྣར་» {SS}: པ་

[93] «པེ་» «སྣར་»: -དངོས་པོ་དང་།

[94] {SS}: +པ་

[95] «པེ་» «སྣར་»: རྟོགས་

བདག་ཉིད་ཆེན་པོ་རྣམས་ཀྱིས་[96] རྣམ་པར་གཞག་གོ། །དེའི་ཕྱིར་དེ་དག་སྐྱེ་བོ་བྱིས་པ་རྣམས་ལས་ཤིན་ཏུ་འདས་པ་དམིགས་པ་མེད་པའི་ཡེ་ཤེས་ལ་གནས་པས་དེ་དག་ཉིད་ཆེ་བའི་ཕྱིར་བདག་ཉིད་ཆེན་པོ་ཞེས་བྱ་སྟེ། །འཕགས་པ་ཞེས་བརྗོད་དོ།

།དངོས་པོ་དང་དངོས་པོ་མེད་པའི་མཚན་མ་ལ་རྟོག་པ་ལས་བྱུང་བའི་འདོད་ཆགས་ལ་སོགས་པ་ནི་[97] ཁམས་གསུམ་ལས་མི་འདའ་བའི་རྒྱུར་གྱུར་པས་བྱིས་པ་རྣམས་ནི་འཆིང་བ་སྟེ། །དེས་བྱིས་པ་དག་འཇུག་པ་ལ་རང་དབང་མེད་པར་བྱས་ནས་འགྲོ་བ་ལྔར་འཁོར་བ་ན་འཁོར་རོ། །དངོས་པོ་དང་དངོས་པོ་མེད་པ་མི་དམིགས་པ་ནི་དེའི་མཚན་མ་རྟོག་[98] པ་མེད་པའི་ཕྱིར་[99] མི་སྐྱེ་བས་ངེས་པར་འདོད་ཆགས་ལ་སོགས་པའི་རྒྱུན་ཆད་དོ། །དེ་དག་རྒྱུན་ཆད་པས་རྣམ་པར་གྲོལ་བར་འགྱུར་བས་ན།[100] །འདི་ཉིད་རྣམ་པར་གྲོལ་བའི་ཐབས་སུ་རིགས།[101]

(2. །གཉིས་པ། མཐའ་གཉིས་ཀྱི་སྒྲུབ་བྱེད་དགག་པ།)

(a. །དང་པོ། ལུང་གི་སྒྲུབ་བྱེད་མི་འཐད་པ།)

(i. །དང་པོ། བྱིས་པ་ལ་མ་ངེས་པ།)

།འདིར་སྨྲས་པ། །དངོས་པོ་དང་དངོས་པོ་མེད་པ་དག་ནི་ཡོད་དོ། །གལ་ཏེ་དེ་དག་མེད་དུ་ཟིན་ན་དེའི་ཚེ་ཁྱོད་ཀྱི་འཁོར་བ་དང་མྱ་ངན་ལས་འདས་པ་ཡང་མེད་པར་འགྱུར་རོ། །འཁོར་བ་ནི་ཉེ་བར་ལེན་པའི་ཕུང་པོ་ལྔའི་རང་ [《སྣར་》 8a.1] གི་ངོ་བོ་ཡིན་པས་དངོས་པོའི་ངོ་བོ་སྟེ། །ཉེ་

96 《པེ་》《སྣར་》{SS}: ཀྱི་རྣམ་པར་གྲོལ་བ་

97 《པེ་》《སྣར་》{SS}: -ནི་

98 《པེ་》《སྣར་》: ལ་རྟོགས་ {SS}: ལ་རྟོག་

99 《པེ་》《སྣར་》{SS}: +ཕྱིས་

100 《སྣར་》: ནས།

101 《པེ་》《སྣར་》{SS}: -། +སོ།

བར་ལེན་པའི་ཕུང་པོ་ལྔ་པོ་དེ་དག་ཉིད་ལས་[102] ཉོན་མོངས་པས་འཕངས་ནས། །འགྲོ་བ་རྣམས་སུ་འགྲོ་བ་ནས་འགྲོ་བ་གཞན་དུ་འགྲོ་བའི་ཕྱིར། །འཁོར་བ་ཞེས་བྱ་བས་ན་དེ་ཡང་ཡོད་དོ། །དེ་ཡོད་པས་ན་དངོས་པོ་ཡོད་པ་ཉིད་དོ། །མྱ་ངན་ལས་འདས་པ་ཐར་པ་ནི་འཁོར་བ་ཟད་པའི་རང་བཞིན་ཏེ། །སྡུག་བསྔལ་ [«སྡེ་» 6b.1] ཕྱིས་[103] མི་སྐྱེ་བས་དེའི་[104] དངོས་པོ་མེད་པའོ། །དེ་བས་ན་འཁོར་བ་མེད་པའི་དངོས་པོ་མྱ་ངན་ལས་འདས་པ་ཡང་སྲིད་དེ་ཡོད་དོ།

།ཆཤད་པ་གལ་ཏེ་འཁོར་བ་དང་མྱ་ངན་ལས་འདས་པ་དེ་གཉིས་ཡོད་ན་ནི་དངོས་པོ་[«པེ་» 7b.1] དང་དངོས་པོ་མེད་པ་གཉིས་ཀྱང་ཡོད་པར་འགྱུར་བ་ཞིག་ན། །དེ་གཉིས་ནི་མེད་དོ།

།འོ་ན་དེ་གཉིས་ཡོད་ཅེས་[105] བཅོམ་ལྡན་འདས་ཀྱིས་མ་གསུངས་སམ། འདི་ལྟར་འཁོར་བ་ཡོངས་སུ་ཟད་པར་བྱ་བ་དང་། །མྱ་ངན་ལས་འདས་པ་ཐོབ་པར་བྱ་བའི་ཕྱིར་ཡང་ཆོས་བསྟན་ཏོ། །གལ་ཏེ་དེ་དག་མེད་ན་དེའི་ཚེ་སངས་རྒྱས་བཅོམ་ལྡན་འདས་རྣམས་ཀྱི་ཆོས་བསྟན་པ་ཡང་དོན་མེད་པར་འགྱུར་བ་ཞིག་ན་དོན་མེད་པ་ནི་མ་ཡིན་ནོ། །དེ་བས་ན་འཁོར་བ་དང་ [«ཅོ་» 6b.1] མྱ་ངན་ལས་འདས་པ་ཡོད་པས་དངོས་པོ་དང་དངོས་པོ་མེད་པ་གཉིས་ཀྱང་གྲུབ་པོ།

།ཆཤད་པ་འཁོར་བ་དང་མྱ་ངན་ལས་འདས་པ་གཉིས་སུ་[106] ཆཤད། །སྨྲས་པ་འཕགས་པ་རྣམས་ལའོ། །གལ་ཏེ་འཕགས་པ་རྣམས་ལ་ནི། །གལ་ཏེ་འཕགས་པར་གྱུར་ཟིན་པ་རྣམས་ལ་དེ་ཆཤད་པར་སེམས་ན་ནི་དེ་དག་དེ་[107] ཆཤད་པ་གང་གིས་འཕགས་པ་རྣམས་སུ་འགྱུར། །དེ་ལྟར་ན

[102] «པེ་» «སྣར་» {SS}: +དང་

[103] «སྣར་» : ཕྱིན་

[104] «པེ་» «སྣར་» {SS}: དེ་ནི་

[105] «པེ་» «སྣར་» {SS}: དོ། །ཞེས་

[106] «པེ་» «སྣར་» {SS}: +ལ་

[107] «པེ་» «སྣར་» : -དེ་

འོ་ན་ནི་འཕགས་པར་འགྱུར་བའི་ཕྱིར་དེ་བསྟན་ཏོ། །གལ་ཏེ་དེ་ལྟ[108] ན་དེ་ཐོས་པ་དང་སེམས་པ་ལ་སོགས་པའི་རིམ་གྱིས་འཕགས་པར་འགྱུར་བས་འདི་ནི་འཕགས་པ་མ་ཡིན་པ་རྣམས་ཀྱི་ཆེད་དུ་གྱུར་ཏོ། །འཕགས་པ་མ་ཡིན་པ་དེ་དག་ནི་ཐོག་མ་མེད་པ་ཅན་གྱི་འཁོར་བ་ན་དངོས་པོར་ལྟ་བ་ལ་གོམས་པས་དེའི་གཉེན་པོར་འཁོར་བ་ལྡོག་པའི་མཚན་ཉིད་ཆོས་ཤིན་ [«སྣར་» 8b.1] ཏུ་བཟང་པོ་མྱ་ངན་ལས་འདས་པ་མ་བསྟན་ན། །དངོས་པོར་ཆགས་པ་ལས་བཟློག་པར་མི་ནུས་སོ། །འཇིག་རྟེན་ནི་བདེ་བ་རྒྱ་ཆེན་པོ་དང་ལྡན་པར་འདོད་པས་དེ་ལ་དེ་ཉེ་བར་བསྟན་ན་བདེ་བ་ལས་ཀྱང་བཟློག་པར་ནུས་ན། །རབ་ཏུ་སྡུག་བསྔལ་ལ་སོགས་པ་ལྟ[109] སྨོས་ཀྱང་ཅི་དགོས་ཏེ།

།དེ་བས་ན་མྱ་ངན་ལས་འདས་པ་དེ་བསྟན་ཏེ། །དེ་སྐྱེ་བོ་བྱིས་པ་རྣམས་ཀྱི་ཆེད་དུ་གྱུར་པ་ཉིད་ཡིན་པར་བསྟན་པའི་ཕྱིར།

ཿཡང་དག[110] མ་མཐོང་འཇིག་རྟེན་དང་།
།མྱ་ངན་འདས་པར་རློམ་སེམས་ཏེ།[111] || **5ab** ||

།ཞེས་སྨོས་སོ། །དེ་ལོ་ན་མ་མཐོང་བ་ནི་འཁོར་བ་ཞེས་བརྗོད་པ། །འཇིག་རྟེན་ [«སྡེ་» 7a.1] དང་དེ་ལྡོག་པ་ཞེས་བརྗོད་པ་མྱ་ངན་ལས་འདས་པ་འདི་གཉིས་ལ་མི་མཐུན་པའི་ཕྱོགས་དང་ [«པེ་» 8a.1] གཉེན་པོའི་དངོས་པོར་གནས་ཤིང་གཅིག་ནི་བླང་གཅིག་ནི་དོར་བར་སེམས། །དེ[112] དེའི་ཕྱིར་ཏེ་སྐྱེ་བོ་འཁོར་བ་ལ་རྒྱབ་ཀྱིས་ལྟ་བར་འགྱུར་ཞིང་[113] དེ་ལྡོག་པ་ལ་མོས་པ་སྐྱེས་པ་

---

108 «པེ་»«སྣར་»{SS}: ལྟར་

109 «པེ་»«སྣར་»: +ལ་

110 «ཏྲི་»: དེ་ཉིད་

111 Skt. preserved in Āryadeva's *Cittaviśuddhiprakaraṇa*, cited in Lindtner (*Nāgārjuniana*, 104): *saṁsāraṁ caiva nirvāṇaṁ manyante 'tattvadarśinaḥ* /

112 «པེ་»«སྣར་»: སེམས་ཏེ་ {SS}: སེམས་ཏེ། །

དག་ལ་རྟེན་ཅིང་འབྲེལ་པར་འབྱུང་བ་བསྟན་པས་སྐྱང་བར་བྱ་བའི་སྐྱེ་བ་མེད་པ་བདེ་བར་རྟོགས་པར་ནུས་སོ། །དངོས་པོ་སྐྱེ་བ་མེད་པར་རྟོགས་ན་དངོས་པོ་མེད་པ་ལ་ཅི་ཞིག་གི་དངོས་པོ་མེད་པ་མྱ་ངན་ལས་འདས་པར་བརྟག་ཅེས་མྱ་ངན་ལས་འདས་པ་ལ་མངོན་པར་ཆགས་པ་ཡང་བདེ་བར་སྤོང་ནུས་སོ། །དེ་ལྟར་དེ་ཁོ་ན་ཉིད་མཐོང་[114] ལ་ཞུགས་ནས་འཕགས་པར་གྱུར་པ་དེ་ནི།

(ii. །གཉིས་པ། འཕགས་པ་ལ་བསྟན་པ་མ་གྲུབ་པ།)

((1) །དང་པོ། འཕགས་པས་མ་གཟིགས་པ།)

:ཡང་དག་[115] མཐོང་བས་[116] འཇིག་རྟེན་དང་།

།མྱ་ངན་[117] འདས་པར་རློམ་སེམས་མེད།[118] || **5cd** ||

།འཕགས་པ་ངོ་བོ་ཉིད་མི་དམིགས་པའི་ [«ཅོ་» 7a.1] ཆོས་རྟོགས་པས་རབ་ཏུ་ཕྱེ་བ་རྣམས་ནི་དེ་གཉི་ག་མི་དམིགས་ཤིང་མི་རྟོག་གོ་ཞེས་བྱ་བར་དགོངས་སོ། །དེ་བས་ན་བྱིས་པའི་སྐྱེ་བོའི་རྟོག་པའི་དབང་དུ་འཁོར་བ་དང་མྱ་ངན་ལས་འདས་པ་གཉིས་ཡོད་དོ་ཞེས་བསྟན་པས་དངོས་པོ་དང་དངོས་པོ་མེད་པ་གཉིས་ཡོད་དོ་ཞེས་གང་སྨྲས་པ་དེ་རིགས་པ་མ་ཡིན་ནོ།

།གལ་ཏེ་འཁོར་བ་དང་མྱ་ངན་ལས་འདས་པ་གཉིས་འཕགས་པ་ལ་བསྟན་པ་མ་ཡིན་ [«སྣར་» 9a.1] ན། །འཕགས་པའི་བདེན་པ་བཞི་པོ་དེ་དག་བསྟན་པ་དེ་ཇི་ལྟར་རུང་བར་འགྱུར།

---

113 «པེ་» «སྣར་»: གྱུར་ཅིང་ {SS}: གྱུར་ཞིང་

114 «པེ་» «སྣར་» {SS}: +བ་

115 «ཏྲི་»: དེ་ཉིད་

116 {SS}: བ་

117 «པེ་» «སྣར་»: +ལས་

118 Skt. preserved in Āryadeva's *Cittaviśuddhiprakaraṇa*, cited in Lindtner (*Nāgārjuniana*, 104): *na saṁsāraṁ na nirvāṇaṁ manyante tattvadarśinaḥ* //.

།གལ་ཏེ་འདི་དག་འཕགས་པ་རྣམས་ལ་བདེན་པ་ཡིན་ན་ནི་དེའི་ཚེ་འཕགས་པའི་བདེན་པ་རྣམས་ཞེས་[119] བྱར་རུང་ངོ་། །གལ་ཏེ་དེ་དག་འཕགས་པ་པ་མ་[120] ཡིན་པ་དང་སྦྱར་ན་ནི་དེའི་ཚེ་འཕགས་པའི་བདེན་པ་ཞེས་བྱར་མི་རུང་ངོ་།

།གལ་ཏེ་དེ་ལྟ་ན་འཕགས་པའི་ཐ་སྙད་བརྒྱུད་ཀྱང་ཇི་ལྟར་རུང་བར་འགྱུར། །དེ་དག་ནི་འཕགས་པ་ཉིད་ཀྱི་མ་ཡིན་གྱི། །ཐ་སྙད་དེ་དག་ཟག་པ་[121] དང་བཅས་པས་[122] འཇིག་རྟེན་གྱི་ཡིན་ནོ། །དེ་བས་ན་འཇིག་རྟེན་གྱི་དངོས་པོ་ལ་ཡང་གང་ཇི་ལྟར་གནས་པ་བཞིན་དུ་རང་གི་ངོ་བོ་ལས་མི་བསྒྱུར་བར་རྣམ་པར་གཞག་པ་དེ་ཡང་འཕགས་པ་ཞེས་བརྗོད་དུ་རུང་ངོ་།

།ཡང་ན་འཕགས་པར་འགྱུར་བའི་བདེན་པ་རྣམས་ནི་འཕགས་པའི་ [《པེ་》 8b.1] བདེན་པ་རྣམས་སོ།[123] །གང་ལ་དམིགས་ [《སྡེ་》 7b.1] པ་ཡོད་པ་ཡང་དམིགས་པ་དེ་ནི་རྣམ་པ་གཉིས་ཏེ། །དེ་ལ་ཕྱིན་ཅི་ལོག་དང་ཕྱིན་ཅི་མ་ལོག་པའོ། །དེ་ལ་ཕྱིན་ཅི་ལོག་ནི་བདེ་བ་ལ་སོགས་པར་འཛིན་པ་[124] སྟེ། །ཀུན་རྫོབ་ཏུ་ཡང་དེའི་བདག་ཉིད་དུ་དངོས་པོ་རྣམ་པར་མི་གནས་པའི་ཕྱིར་རོ། །ཕྱིན་ཅི་མ་ལོག་པ་ནི་སྡུག་བསྔལ་བ་ལ་སོགས་པ་སྟེ།[125] དངོས་པོ་ཀུན་རྫོབ་ཏུ་དེའི་བདག་ཉིད་དུ

---

119 《པེ་》《སྣར་》{SS}: ༶ཞེས་

120 《སྣར་》: -མ་

121 《ཅོ་》 appears to contain a dittographic error at this point: +པ་

122 《པེ་》: -པས་

123 《པེ་》《སྣར་》{SS}: + ཡང་ན་འཕགས་པས་བསྟེན་པའི་བདེན་པ་རྣམས་ནི་འཕགས་པའི་བདེན་པ་རྣམས་སོ།

124 《པེ་》《སྣར་》 appear to contain a dittographic error at this point: +སོགས་པར་འཛིན་པ་

125 《སྡེ་》《ཅོ་》 appear to contain a dittographic error at this point, repeating the previous two phrases preceded by དངོས་པོ་, that is: +དངོས་པོ་ཀུན་རྫོབ་ཏུ་ཡང་དེའི་བདག་ཉིད་དུ་དངོས་པོ་རྣམ་པར་མི་གནས་པའི་ཕྱིར་རོ། །ཕྱིན་ཅི་མ་ལོག་པ་ནི་སྡུག་བསྔལ་བ་ལ་སོགས་པ་སྟེ།

ཡོད་པའི་ཕྱིར་རོ། །དེ་ཙམ་ཞིག་དང་སྦྲུར་ནས་འཕགས་པའི་ཐ་སྙད་ཅེས་བྱ་བ་བཞིན་དུ་འཕགས་པའི་བདེན་པ་རྣམས་ཞེས་བྱའོ།

།ཅི་མྱ་ངན་ལས་འདས་པ་ཡང་ཀུན་རྫོབ་ཀྱི་བདེན་པ་ཡིན་ནམ།

།དེ་དེ་བཞིན་ཏེ། །འཁོར་བར་ཡོངས་སུ་རྟོག་པ་ཡོད་ན་མྱ་ངན་ལས་འདས་པར་ཡོངས་སུ་རྟོག་སྟེ།[126] །དེ་གཉི་ག་ཡང་འཇིག་རྟེན་གྱི་ཐ་སྙད་ཡིན་པའི་ཕྱིར་རོ། [«ཙོ་» 7b.1] །དེ་བས་ན་བཅོམ་ལྡན་འདས་མ་ལས་གསུངས་པ།

> །ཚེ་[127] དང་ལྡན་པ་རབ་འབྱོར་མྱ་ངན་ལས་འདས་པ་ཡང་སྒྱུ་མ་ལྟ་བུ་རྨི་ལམ་ལྟ་བུའོ་ཞེས་སྨྲའམ། །ཤཱ་རིའི་བུ་[128] མྱ་ངན་ལས་འདས་པ་བས་ [«སྣར་» 9b.1] ཆེས་ལྷག་པའི་ཆོས་ཤིག་ཡོད་ན་ཡང་སྒྱུ་མ་ལྟ་བུའོ་ཞེས་ཁོ་བོ་སྨྲའོ་[129]

ཞེས་འབྱུང་ངོ་། །གལ་ཏེ་དེ་[130] འཁོར་བར་རྟོག་པ་ལ་ལྟོས་པ་མ་ཡིན་ན་དེ་སྒྱུ་མ་ལྟ་བུར་མི་འགྱུར་རོ། །དེ་བས་ན་མྱ་ངན་ལས་འདས་པ་ཡང་ཀུན་རྫོབ་ཀྱི་བདེན་པར་ཡོངས་སུ་བརྟགས་པ་ཡིན་ནོ།

---

126 «ཙོ་»: ཏེ།

127 «སྣར་»: དེ་

128 «པེ་» «སྣར་» {SS}: +གལ་ཏེ་

129 Although a comparable passage appears in the ASPP, AA, and PPMMV, the response in the second statement is addressed to a devaputra in the ASPP, AA and PPMMV, rather than to Śāriputra as given here. The Tibetan in ASPP reads: ལྷའི་བུ་དེ་དག་གིས་སྨྲས་པ། འཕགས་པ་རབ་འབྱོར་མྱ་ངན་ལས་འདས་པ་ཡང་སྒྱུ་མ་ལྟ་བུ་རྨི་ལམ་ལྟ་བུའོ་ཞེས་ཟེར་རམ། ཚེ་དང་ལྡན་པ་རབ་འབྱོར་གྱིས་སྨྲས་པ། ལྷའི་བུ་དག་བདག་ནི་གལ་ཏེ་མྱ་ངན་ལས་འདས་པ་ལས་ཁྱད་པར་དུ་འཕགས་པའི་ཆོས་གཞན་ཞིག་ཡོད་ཀྱང་དེ་ཡང་སྒྱུ་མ་ལྟ་བུ་རྨི་ལམ་ལྟ་བུའོ་ཞེས་སྨྲའོ། while the Skt., preserved in ASPP (Vaidya, *Aṣṭasāhasrikā*, 20) reads: *nirvāṇam apy ārya subhūte māyopamaṁ svapnopamam iti vadasi // āyuṣmān subhūtirāha tadyadi devaputrā nirvāṇād apy anyaḥ kaścid dharmo viśiṣṭataraḥ syāt tam apy ahaṁ māyopamaṁ svapnopamam iti vadeyam /*

།གལ་ཏེ་དེ་ལྟར་ན་མྱ་ངན་ལས་འདས་པ་དོན་དམ་པའི་བདེན་པའོ་ཞེས་ཇི་སྐད་དུ་བཤད།

།དེའི་བདག་ཉིད་དུ་འཇིག་རྟེན་ལ་མི་སླུ[131]་བའི་ཕྱིར་འཇིག་རྟེན་གྱི་ཐ་སྙད་ཀྱིས་དོན་དམ་པའི་བདེན་པ་ཞེས་བཤད་དོ། །སླུ[132]་བ་འདུས་བྱས་གང་ཡིན་པ་དེ་ནི་དོན་དམ་པའི་བདེན་པ་མ་ཡིན་ནོ། །བདེན་པ་གསུམ་ནི་འདུས་བྱས་ཀྱི་མཚན་ཉིད་དེ་ངོ་བོ་ཉིད་ཡོད་པར་སྣང་བས་བྱིས་པ་རྣམས་ལ་སླུ[133]་བའི་ཕྱིར་ཀུན་རྫོབ་ཀྱི་བདེན་པར་རྣམ་པར་གཞག་གོ། །འོ་ན་བཅོམ་ལྡན་འདས་ཀྱིས་དགེ་སློང་དག་འདི་ལྟ་སྟེ། །མི་ [«པེ་» 9a.1] སླུ་བའི་ཆོས་ཅན་མྱ་ངན་ལས་འདས་པ་འདི་ནི་བདེན་པའི་མཆོག་གཅིག་པུའོ་ཞེས་གསུངས་པ་དེ་ཇི་ལྟ་བུ། །ཇི་ལྟར་འདུས་བྱས་ལོག་པར་སྣང་བས་བྱིས་པ་རྣམས་ལ་སླུ[134]་བ་དེ་བཞིན་དུ་མྱ་ངན་ [«སྣེ་» 8a.1] ལས་འདས་པ་ནི་དེ་ལྟ་མ་ཡིན་ཏེ། །རྟག་པར་སྐྱེ་བ་མེད་པའི་རང་གི་ངོ་བོར་གནས་པའི་ཕྱིར་དེ་ནི་བྱིས་པ་རྣམས་ལ་འདུས་བྱས་ལྟར་སྐྱེ་བའི་ངོ་བོར་ནམ་ཡང་མི་སྣང་ངོ་། །དེ་བས་ན་མྱ་ངན་ལས་འདས་པ་ནི་རྟག་ཏུ་མྱ་ངན་ལས་འདས་པ་ཉིད་དུ་གནས་པས་འཇིག་རྟེན་གྱི་ཐ་སྙད་ཀྱིས་དོན་དམ་པའི་བདེན་པ་ཞེས་བཤད་དོ།

།འཕགས་པ་དོན་དམ་པ་གཟིགས་པ་ལ་གནས་པ་རྣམས་ནི་འཁོར་བའམ་མྱ་ངན་ལས་འདས་པ་མི་དམིགས་ཏེ་དེའི་ཕྱིར་ཡང་དག[135] མཐོང་བ་འཇིག་རྟེན་དང་མྱ་ངན་ལས་འདས་པར་རློམ་སེམས་མེད་ཅེས་བྱ་བ་གྲུབ་པོ།

---

130 «པེ་»«སྣར་»: -དེ་

131 «པེ་»«སྣར་»{SS}: བསླུ་

132 «པེ་»«སྣར་»{SS}: བསླུ་

133 «པེ་»«སྣར་»{SS}: བསླུ་

134 «སྣར་»: བསླུ་

135 «པེ་»«སྣར་»: +པ་

((2) །གཉིས་པ། དེའི་འཐད་པ།)

།ཅིའི་ཕྱིར་འཕགས་པ་དོན་དམ་པ་གཟིགས་པ་ལ་གནས་པ་དག་འཁོར་བའམ་[136] དོན་དམ་པ་དམིགས་པར་མི་འགྱུར་ཞེ་ན། །འདི་ལྟར།

སྲིད་པ་དང་ནི་མྱ་ངན་འདས།
།དེ་གཉིས་ཡོད་པ་མ་ཡིན་ནོ། || **6ab** ||

།སྲིད་པ་ནི་ཉེ་བར་ལེན་པའི་ཕུང་པོ་ལྔ་རྣམས་ཏེ། དེ་དག་ཀྱང་རྟེན་ཅིང་འབྲེལ་པར་འབྱུང་བའི་ཕྱིར་གཟུགས་བརྙན་བཞིན་ [《སྣར་》 10a.1] དུ་ངོ་བོ་ཉིད་ཀྱིས་མེད་པའོ། །དེ་དག་མེད་ན་ [《ཅོ་》 8a.1] དེའི་དངོས་པོ་མེད་པ་ཡང་ཤིན་ཏུ་མེད་པའི་ཕྱིར་དེ་གཉིས་ཡོད་པ་མ་ཡིན་ནོ་ཞེས་བཤད་དོ། །མེད་པ་མཐོང་བ་ནི་དེ་ཁོ་ན་མཐོང་བ་མ་ཡིན་ཏེ་རབ་རིབ་ཅན་ལ་སོགས་པས་ཀྱང་དེ་ཁོ་ན་མཐོང་བར་ཐལ་བར་འགྱུར་བའི་ཕྱིར་རོ། །འཕགས་པ་རྣམས་ནི་དེ་ཁོ་ན་གཟིགས་པ་ཡིན་ཏེ། མེད་པའི་རང་གི་ངོ་བོ་[137] གཟིགས་[138] པས་མི་འོས་སོ།

(b. །གཉིས་པ། དེ་དག་ལ་མྱང་འདས་མི་འཐད་པ།)

(i. །དང་པོ། རང་གི་མྱང་འདས་ངོས་བཟུང་བ།)

((1) །དང་པོ། མདོར་བསྟན།)

།གལ་ཏེ་མྱ་ངན་ལས་འདས་པ་ཅི་ཡང་མེད་པ་ཞིག་ཡིན་ན། །འཕགས་པ་རྣམས་མྱ་ངན་ལས་འདས་པ་ཐོབ་པོ་ཞེས་རྣམ་པར་གཞག་པ་དེ་ཇི་ལྟ་བུ་ཞེ་ན།

---

136 《པེ་》《སྣར་》: བའང་།

137 《པེ་》 contains a haplographic error at this point: -གཟིགས་པ་ཡིན་ཏེ། མེད་པའི་རང་གི་ངོ་བོ་

138 {SS} questions this reading as a possible mistake for གཟུགས་

སྲིད་པ་ཡོངས་སུ་ཤེས་པ་ནི།

།མྱ་ངན་འདས་ཞེས་[139] བརྗོད་པ་ཡིན།[140] || **6cd** ||

།ཞེས་བྱ་བ་སྨོས་[141] སོ། །སྲིད་པ་དེ་ཉིད་ཀྱི་ངོ་བོ་ཉིད་སྐྱེ་བ་མེད་པ་ཡོངས་སུ་མི་ཤེས་པའི་ཚུལ་གྱིས་ཡོངས་སུ་ཤེས་པ་གང་ཡིན་པ་[142] དེ་ཉིད་མཚན་མ་ཐམས་ཅད་རབ་ཏུ་ཞི་ [«པེ་» 9b.1] བའི་ངོ་བོ་ཡིན་པས་ཐ་སྙད་ཀྱི་བདེན་པ་དང་སྦྱར་ནས་མྱ་ངན་ལས་འདས་པ་ཞེས་བྱ་བ་རང་གི་ངོ་བོར་གྲུབ་པ་ནི་གང་ཡང་མེད་པར་ཤེས་པར་བྱའོ། །ཇི་ལྟར་མི་རྟག་པ་ཉིད་དངོས་པོ་མེད་པའི་ངོ་བོ་རང་བཞིན་གྱིས་ཡོངས་སུ་གྲུབ་པ་མེད་པ་དེ་དངོས་པོ་ལ་མ་ལྟོས་པར་ངོ་བོ་ཉིད་ཀྱིས་ཡོངས་སུ་གྲུབ་པར་རྣམ་པར་ [«སྡེ་» 8b.1] གཞག་མི་ནུས་པ་དེ་བཞིན་དུ་མཁས་པ་ཡང་སྒྱུ་མ་བྱས་པ་ལྟ་བུའི་དངོས་པོ་ལ་མ་ལྟོས་པར་མྱ་ངན་ལས་འདས་པ་ཞེས་བྱ་བ་རང་བཞིན་གྱིས་གྲུབ་པ་གང་ཡང་ཡོངས་སུ་བརྟག་པར་མི་ནུས་སོ་ཞེས་བསྟན་པའི་ཕྱིར།

((2) །གཉིས་པ། རྒྱས་བཤད།)

དངོས་[143] པོ་སྐྱེས་པ་ཞིག་པ་ལ།

།ཇི་ལྟར་འགོག་པ་བརྟག་[144] པ་བཞིན།

---

139 {SS} citing {Dh} reads: ཤེས་

140 The Sanskrit of the complete verse, identified by Lindtner (*Nāgārjuniana*, 104–105) reads: *nirvāṇaṁ ca bhavaś caiva dvayam etan na vidyate / parijñānaṁ bhavasyaiva nirvāṇam iti kathyate //* Scherrer-Schaub (*Yuktiṣaṣṭikāvṛtti*, 144 n. 125) lists the three complete and four partial citations of k.6 identified by Lindtner (*Nāgārjuniana*, 104–105).

141 «པེ་»«སྣར་»: སྨས་

142 «ཅོ་» contains a dittographic error: +གང་ཡིན་པ་

143 «པེ་»«སྣར་»{SS}: དངོས་ «སྡེ་»«ཅོ་»: དང་

144 «པེ་»«སྣར་»: རྟག་

།དེ་བཞིན་སྒྱུ་མ་བྱས་པ་ལྟར།
།མཁས་པ་དག་གིས་འགོག་[145] པར་དགོངས། || 7 ||

།ཞེས་བྱ་བ་སྨོས་སོ། །ཇི་ལྟར་དངོས་པོ་སྐྱེས་པའི་མི་རྟག་པ་ཉིད་དེ་མེད་པར་གྱུར་པས་རྣམ་པར་གཞག་པས་རང་གི་ངོ་བོར་གྲུབ་པ་མེད་དོ། །ཡོད་པ་ཞིག་ཡིན་ན་ནི་དངོས་པོ་ལ་མི་ལྟོས་པར་རང་གི་ངོ་བོ་མཐོང་བར་འགྱུར་རོ། །དེ་བཞིན་དུ་འཕགས་པ་ཡང་འགོག་པ་ [《སྣར་》 10b.1] ཞེས་བྱ་བ་རང་གི་ངོ་བོར་གྲུབ་པ་གང་ཡང་མི་དམིགས་ཏེ། །ཤེས་རབ་ཀྱིས་རྣམ་པར་དཔྱད་ན། །སྒྱུ་མ་བྱས་པའི་གླང་པོ་ཆེ་ལྟར་ངོ་བོ་ཉིད་མེད་པ་རང་བཞིན་གྱིས་མ་སྐྱེས་པ་གང་ཡིན་པ་དེ་མྱ་ངན་ལས་འདས་པའོ། །དེ་ཡང་སྒྱུ་མ་བྱས་པ་ལྟ་བུ་ཞེས་བྱ་བ་དེ་ཉིད་ལ་བརྟེན་ནས་མྱ་ངན་ལས་འདས་པར་རྣམ་པར་གཞག་[146] པ་ན། [《ཅོ་》 8b.1] །འཇིག་རྟེན་གྱི་ཐ་སྙད་ཀྱིས་མི་རྟག་པ་ཉིད་[147] རྣམ་པར་འཇོག་གོ། །དེས་ན་འཁོར་བ་དང་མྱ་ངན་ལས་འདས་པ་ཞེས་བྱ་བ་ངོ་བོ་ཉིད་མེད་པར་གྲུབ་པོ། །དེ་ལྟར་ན་དངོས་པོའི་ངོ་བོ་ཉིད་ཡོངས་སུ་ཤེས་ནས་མི་དམིགས་པ་གང་ཡིན་པ་དེ་ཉིད་མྱ་ངན་ལས་འདས་པར་གདོན་མི་ཟ་བར་ཤེས་པར་བྱའོ།

(ii. །གཉིས་པ། གཞན་ལ་མྱང་འདས་འཐོབ་པ་མི་འཐད་པ།)

((1) །དང་པོ། མདོར་བསྟན་པ།)

།དེ་བཞིན་[148] དུ་ན།

---

145 《སྣར་》: འགོགས་

146 《པེ་》《སྣར་》: བཞོག་

147 {SS}: +དུ་

148 《པེ་》{SS}: གཞན་

རྣམ་པར་འཇིག་པས་འགོག་འགྱུར་གྱི།[149]
།འདུས་བྱས་ཤེས་པས་མ་ཡིན་ནོ།[150]
།དེ་ནི་སུ་ལ་མངོན་སུམ་འགྱུར།
།ཞིག་ཅེས་པ་དེ་ཇི་ལྟ་བུ། **|| 8 ||**

།གལ་ཏེ་སྒྱུ་མ་བྱས་པ་བཞིན་དུ་ཆོས་ཐམས་ཅད་མི་དམིགས་ [《པེ་》 10a.1] པའི་དུས་ན་སྐྱེ་བ་མེད་པ་གང་ཡིན་པ་དེ་མྱ་ངན་ལས་འདས་པ་མ་ཡིན་གྱི། །གཟུགས་ལ་སོགས་པའི་རང་གི་ངོ་བོའི་མཚན་ཉིད་དངོས་པོའི་རང་བཞིན་རྒྱུ་རྐྱེན་ལས་དང་ཉོན་མོངས་པ་དང་མི་ལྡན་པས[151] ཕྱིས་མི་སྐྱེ་བ་གང་ཡིན་པ་དེ་མྱ་ངན་ལས་འདས་པ་སྙམ་དུ་སེམས་ན[152] གལ་ཏེ་དེ་ལྟར་གྱུར་ན་དངོས་པོའི་རང་གི་ངོ་བོའི་མཚན་ཉིད་ཞིག་ནས་རྒྱུན་ཆད་པའི་ཚུལ་གྱིས་མྱ་ངན་ལས་འདས་པར་གྱུར་ཏེ། །འདུས་བྱས་ཡོངས་སུ་ཤེས་པས་ནི་མ་ཡིན་པར་འགྱུར་རོ།

།གལ་ཏེ་འདི་ཉིད་འདོད་པ་ཡིན་པས་ན་ཉེས་པ་ [《སྡེ་》 9a.1] མེད་དོ་ཞེ་ན་ཡང་འདི་འཐད་པ་མ་ཡིན་ཏེ།

།འདི་ལྟར་དེ་ཁོ་ན་མཐོང་བས་འགོག་པ་མངོན་སུམ་དུ་བྱ་དགོས་ན་འགོག་པ་དེ་ལྟ་བུ་དེ་ནི་ཕུང་པོ་མ་འགགས[153] པའི་ཚེ་ནི་མེད་པ། །འགགས་ནས་ནི་སུ་ཡང་མེད་ན་འགོག་པ་དེ་སུ་ལ་མངོན་སུམ་དུ་འགྱུར། །ཕུང་པོའི་རྒྱུན་ཡོད་པའི་དུས་ན་ནི་དེ་ཁོ་ན་མཐོང་བའི་དུས་གང་ཟག་འཕགས་པ་ཤཱ་རིའི་

---

149 《པེ་》《སྣར་》: གྱིས་

150 《པེ་》《སྣར་》{SS}: ན།

151 《ཅོ་》: པའི་

152 《པེ་》《སྣར་》: +ནི་

153 《པེ་》《སྣར་》: འགག་

བྱ་ལ་སོགས་པ་ཡོད་པས་འགོག་[154] པ་དེ་མངོན་སུམ་ [《སྣར་》 11a.1] ཞེས་བྱ་བ་དེ་རིགས་སོ།

།གལ་ཏེ་དེའི་ཚེ་དེས་ཅི་མཐོང་ན་དེའི་ཚེ་ཅི་ཞིག་དེ་ལ་མངོན་སུམ་དུ་འགྱུར།

བཤད་པ། མ་མཐོང་དུ་ཟིན་ཀྱང་རྣམ་པར་ཤེས་པས་དེའི་རྣམ་པར་རིག་པས་[155] མངོན་སུམ་དུ་ཞེས་གདགས་སོ། །གཞན་དག་གིས་ཀྱང་ཡུལ་རང་གི་མཚན་ཉིད་ཀྱི་རྣམ་པ་དང་མཐུན་པས་སྔོན་པོ་ལ་སོགས་པར་སྣང་བའི་རྣམ་པར་ཤེས་པ་གཞན་ཡང་མངོན་སུམ་དུ་བསྟན་ཏོ། །འདི་ལ་ཡང་དེ་དང་མཐུན་པ་ཡོད་པས་དེ་མངོན་སུམ་ཞེས་བྱ་བ་དེ་འགལ་བ་མེད་དོ།

།སྡུག་བསྔལ་འགོག་པ་མངོན་སུམ་དུ་འགྱུར་ཞེས་བྱ་བར་དངོས་པོའི་རང་གི་མཚན་ཉིད་ནི་མངོན་སུམ་གྱི་[156] ཡུལ་ཡིན་པར་ཁས་བླངས་པས་དངོས་པོ་མེད་པ་ [《ཅོ་》 9a.1] ནི་མངོན་སུམ་གྱི་ཤེས་པས་རིག་པར་[157] མི་རུང་སྟེ། །སྡུག་བསྔལ་འགོག་པ་ནི་མངོན་སུམ་དུ་མི་འདོད་ན་འགོག་པ་ཤེས་པས་འགོག་པའི་བདེན་པ་[158] ཇི་ལྟར་མངོན་སུམ་དུ་བྱ། །སྡུག་བསྔལ་མི་སྐྱེ་[159] ཙམ་ཡང་ [《པེ་》 10b.1] དངོས་པོའི་ངོ་བོར་མི་རུང་ངོ་།

---

154 《སྣར་》: འགོགས་

155 The definition of a consciousness given by Vasubandhu in the AK ad k. 1.16a (Pradhan, 11; La Vallée Poussin, *L'Abhidharmakośa*, I, 30–31) is: *vijñānaṁ prativijñaptiḥ // viṣayaṁ viṣayaṁ prativijñaptir upalabdhir vijñānaskandha ity ucyate*; །རྣམ་ཤེས་སོ་སོར་རྣམ་རིག་པ། །ཡུལ་དང་ཡུལ་ལ་སོ་སོར་རྣམ་པར་རིག་ཅིང་དམིགས་པ་ནི་རྣམ་པར་ཤེས་པའི་ཕུང་པོ་ཞེས་བྱའོ།

156 《པེ་》: ཀྱི་

157 《པེ་》《སྣར་》{SS}: +ཡང་།

158 《པེ་》《སྣར་》{SS}: པ་ 《ཅོ་》《སྡེ་》: པར་

159 《པེ་》《སྣར་》{SS}: +བ་

།གང་སྡུག་བསྔལ་མི་སྐྱེ་[160] ཙམ་འགོག་པ་ཡིན་པར་མི་འདོད་[161] ཀྱང་སྡུག་བསྔལ་མི་སྐྱེ་[162] ཙམ་ལས་དོན་གཞན་དུ་གྱུར་པའི་འགོག་པ་རང་གི་ངོ་བོས་[163] གྲུབ་པ་བསྟན་པར་མི་ནུས་སོ། །འགོག་པ་ཞེས་པ་ཟག་པ་མེད་པ་ནི་མངོན་སུམ་དུ་འདོད་ན། །དེ་ཡང་དེ་ལྟར་གྱུར་པས་དེ་ནི་མངོན་སུམ་དུ་མི་འགྱུར་རོ། །གལ་ཏེ་འགོག་པ་ཞེས་པ་མངོན་སུམ་དུ་གྱུར་ན་ནི་དེའི་ཚེ་དེས་ཡོངས་སུ་བཅད་པའི་འགོག་པ་ཡང་འགགས་པས་མངོན་སུམ་ཉིད་དུ་ཁྱོད་ཀྱི་གཞུང་ལྟར་ན་ཀོ་བུམ་པ་ཞེས་པ་མངོན་སུམ་དུ་མི་འདོད་ན་སྔོན་པོ་ལ་སོགས་པ་ལྟར་བུམ་པ་མངོན་སུམ་དུ་མི་རུང་བ་དེ་བཞིན་དུ་འགོག་པ་ཡང་མི་འགྱུར་རོ། །རྣལ་འབྱོར་པ་རྣམས་ཀྱི་བླ་མས་བསྟན་པ་ལས་སྐྱེས་པ་རྣམ་པར་རྟོག་པ་དང་མ་འདྲེས་པ་[《སྡེ་》 9b.1] གཅིག་ཏུ་ཡུལ་སྒྲོ་བཏགས་པ་མེད་པ་དོན་ཙམ་མཐོང་བ་གང་ཡིན་པ་དེ་ཡང་འགག་[164] པ་ལ་མི་སྲིད་དོ།[165]

།རང་གི་མཚན་ཉིད་དངོས་པོར་ཡོད་པ་གང་ཡིན་པ་དེ་ཉིད་སྤྱིའི་མཚན་ཉིད་ཀྱིས་གོམས་[《སྣར་》 11b.1] པར་བྱས་ན་ནི་རིམ་གྱིས་བསྒོམས་པ་ལས་བྱུང་བའི་ཡེ་ཤེས་སྐྱེ་ཞེས་གྲགས་ཏེ།[166] །རྣམ་པར་མི་རྟོག་པའི་ཡེ་ཤེས་དེའི་གཟུང་[167] བའི་དངོས་པོ་གང་ཡིན་པ་དེ་ཡང་སྒྲོ་བཏགས་

160 《པེ་》《སྣར་》{SS}: +བ་

161 《པེ་》《སྣར་》{SS}: +པ་དེས་

162 《པེ་》《སྣར་》{SS}: +བ་

163 《པེ་》《སྣར་》{SS}: བོར་

164 《པེ་》《སྣར་》{SS}: འགོག་

165 《ཏཱི་ 13a.5–.6》: །བོ་བོ་ཅག་ལ་ཉེས་པ་མེད་དེ། འཕགས་པ་ཤཱ་རིའ་བུ་ལ་སོགས་པས་རང་བཞིན་སྐྱེ་མེད་ཀྱི་འགོག་པ་དེ་མངོན་སུམ་དུ་བྱས་པའི་ཕྱིར། གཞན་ཡང་འགོག་པ་མངོན་སུམ་དུ་མི་འཐད་དེ། དགག་གཞི་ཕུང་པོ་མངོན་སུམ་དུ་རྟོགས་ནས་འགོག་པ་ཤུགས་ལ་རྟོགས་པར་མི་འཐད་དེ་གནས་སྐབས་དེར་ཕུང་པོ་ཁྱོད་མི་འདོད་པའི་ཕྱིར། དངོས་སུ་རྟོགས་པར་མི་འཐད་དེ། མངོན་སུམ་གྱི་ཤེས་པ་རང་མཚན་གྱི་དངོས་ཡུལ་ཅན་དུ་ཁས་བླངས་པའི་ཕྱིར་རོ།

166 《པེ་》《སྣར་》: གྲག་སྟེ།

པ་མེད་པའི་ངོ་བོ་[168] ཡིན་པས་ན་རང་གི་མཚན་ཉིད་ཁོ་ནའོ། །འདི་ལྟར་མི་རྟག་པ་ཉིད་ཁོང་དུ་ཆུད་ན་ཐོག་མ་དང་ཐ་མའི་ཕྱོགས་ཀྱིས་སྟོང་པ་དངོས་པོ་ཙམ་ཁོང་དུ་ཆུད་དོ། །དེ་བས་ན་དེ་ཡང་ཡུལ་གྱི་རང་གི་མཚན་ཉིད་ཡིན་པས་སྔོན་པོ་ལ་སོགས་པ་ཙམ་ལ་དམིགས་པའི་རྣམ་པར་ཤེས་པ་བཞིན་དུ་མངོན་སུམ་ཉིད་དོ་ཞེ་ན། །འོན་ཀྱང་དཔྱོད་ན་རང་དང་སྤྱིའི་མཚན་ཉིད་ཐ་དད་པར་ཁས་བླངས་པས་སྤྱིའི་མཚན་ཉིད་ཀྱི་རྣམ་པ་ལ་སྒོམ་པའི་སྦྱོར་བ་གྲུབ་པའི་ངོ་བོའི་ཡུལ་རང་གི་མཚན་ཉིད་དུ་མི་འཐད་དེ། །ཧ་ཅང་ཐལ་བར་འགྱུར་བའི་ཕྱིར་དེའི་ཚིག་དེ་འབྲེལ་པ་ མེད་དོ།

།དེ་ལྟར་ཡིན་གྱིས་ཀྱང་འགོག་པ་ལ་ནི་སྡུག་བསྔལ་ལྡོག་ [«པེ་» 11a.1] པའི་ངོ་བོའི་དངོས་པོའི་བག་ཙམ་ཡང་མེད་པས་འགོག་པ་ཞེས་པའི་མངོན་སུམ་དུ་ག་ལ་འགྱུར་ཏེ། །དེ་ལྟ་བས་ [«ཅོ་» 9b.1] ན་གསུང་རབ་ལས་སྡུག་བསྔལ་མི་སྐྱེ་བར་ཤེས་པ་ནི་མངོན་སུམ་མོ་ཞེས་འབྱུང་བས་སྐྱེ་བ་མེད་པའི་ངོ་བོ་དེ་ལ་ཤེས་པས་སྐྱེས་པར་བྱེད་མི་སྲིད་དེ། །གདོན་མི་ཟ་བར་སྐྱེ་བ་མེད་པའི་ཚུལ་དུ་བྱེད་པར་འགྱུར་རོ། །དེ་ལྟར་ན་གལ་ཏེ་དམིགས་པ་བཞིན་དུ་ཤེས་པ་ཡང་སྐྱེ་བ་མེད་པའི་ངོ་བོ་ཡིན་ན་ནི་ཤེས་པ་དེ་དམིགས་པ་ཇི་ལྟ་བ་བཞིན་པས་ཞུགས་པར་རུང་ངོ།

།འཇིག་རྟེན་ན་ཡང་རྣམ་པ་དེ་ལྟ་བུས་མངོན་སུམ་ཞེས་བརྗོད་དོ། །འདི་ལྟར་མགྲོན་[169] པོ་ཞིག་གིས་རང་གི་མདུན་འོངས་ན་ཡུལ་ཆུ་རབ་ཏུ་དྭངས་པ་[170] ཆེན་པོས་གང་བ་འདྲ་བ་ཞིག་རྒྱང་རིང་པོ་ནས་མཐོང་བ་དང་། །དེ་རྒྱལ་[171] བར་འདོད་ལ་[172] ཉམས་ཀྱིས་མི་ནུས་ཤིང་སྐྲག་པས་ཡུལ་[173]

---

167 «པེ་» «སྣར་» : བཟུང་

168 «པེ་» «སྣར་» {SS}: +ཉིད་

169 «པེ་» «སྣར་» {SS}: འགྲོན་ «ཅོ་» appears to have been corrected to read འགྲོན་ from the more archaic spelling of མགྲོན་

170 «དཔེ་» : དྭངས་པ་ «སྡེ་» «ཅོ་» : དངས་པ་ «པེ་» «སྣར་» {SS}: དང་བ་

171 «པེ་» «སྣར་» : བརྒྱལ་

ནས་འོངས་པའི་ཞིང་ [≪སྣར་≫ 12a.1] པ་ཞིག་ལ་རྒྱུ་འདི་ཇི་[174] ཙམ་ཞེས་སྨྲས་པ་དང་། དེས་དེ་ལ་འདི་ན་རྒྱུ་ག་ལ་ཡོད་རྒྱུ་འདྲ་[175] འདི་ནི་སྒྲིག་རྒྱུའོ། །དེ་སྟེ་ངའི་ཚིག་ལ་ཡིད་མི་ཆེས་ན་དེར་སོང་ལ་ལྟོས་ཤིག་དང་ངའི་ཚིག་ནི་[176] མངོན་སུམ་དུ་འགྱུར་རོ་ཞེས་སྨྲས་པ་ན། །དེ་རྒྱུ་མེད་པར་ [≪སྡེ་≫ 10a.1] བསྟན་པས་རང་གི་ཚིག་ཀྱང་མགྲོན་པོ་[177] ལ་མངོན་སུམ་དུ་འགྱུར་རོ་ཞེས་སྨྲས་པ་དེ་བཞིན་དུ་མེད་པ་དང་མི་དམིགས་པ་ཡང་འཇིག་རྟེན་[178] མངོན་སུམ་ཞེས་ཐ་སྙད་འདོགས་ཏེ་དེའི་ཕྱིར་འཇིག་རྟེན་གྱི་ཀུན་རྫོབ་ཀྱི་བདེན་པས་མི་དམིགས་པའི་ཤེས་པ་ལ་མངོན་སུམ་ཞེས་བྱ་བ་འགལ་བ་མེད་དོ། །ཤེས་པ་བྱེད་པར་གྱུར་པ་གང་གིས་དངོས་པོ་གང་གི་དོན་ཇི་ལྟ་བ་བཞིན་དུ་ཡོངས་སུ་གཅོད་པ་དེ་དེའི་མངོན་སུམ་ཞེས་བྱ་བས་[179] ན་ལུང་དེ་རིགས་[180] པ་ཡིན་ནོ།

---

172 ≪པེ་≫: པ་

173 ≪པེ་≫ ≪སྣར་≫: +དེ་

174 ≪པེ་≫ ≪སྣར་≫ {SS}: ཅི་

175 ≪པེ་≫ ≪སྣར་≫ {SS}: +བ་

176 ≪པེ་≫ ≪སྣར་≫ {SS}: དེ་

177 ≪པེ་≫ ≪སྣར་≫ {SS}: འགྲོན་པོ་ ≪ཅོ་≫: མགྲོན་བུ་

178 {SS}: +ན་

179 ≪པེ་≫ ≪སྣར་≫: བ་

180 ≪པེ་≫ ≪སྣར་≫: རིག་

((2) །གཉིས་པ། རྒྱས་བཤད།)

((a) །དང་པོ། ལྷག་བཅས་མི་འཐད་པ།)

།དེ་ལ་ཕུང་པོའི་རྒྱུན་ཆད་པའི་ངོ་བོ་ལ་ནི་གང་ཡང་མེད་ན་འགོག་པ་དེ་སུ་ལ་མངོན་སུམ་དུ་འགྱུར་རོ། །གང་སྐྱེ་བ་ཟད་དོ་ཚངས་པར་སྤྱོད་པ་[181] བསྟེན་ཏོ། །བྱ་བ་བྱས་སོ། །འདི་ལས་སྲིད་པ་གཞན་མི་ཤེས་སོ་[182]ཞེས་བྱ་བ་འདི་ལ་སྐྱེ་བ་ཟད་ [«པེ་» 11b.1] པའི་ཤེས་པ་གང་ཡིན་པ་དེ་ཡང་མི་རུང་སྟེ། །དངོས་པོ་འགའ་ཞིག་སྐྱེ་བ་མེད་ན་དངོས་པོ་ཟད་དོ་ཞིག་གོ། །ཡང་མི་སྐྱེའོ་ཞེས་བྱ་བར་ཡང་འགྱུར་ན། །ཇི་སྲིད་དུ་དེའི་རྒྱུ་དང་རྐྱེན་གྱིས་འཕངས་པའི་ཕུང་པོའི་རྒྱུན་འབྱུང་བ་དེ་སྲིད་དུ་དེ་ལ་སྐྱེ་བ་ཡོད་པས་ན་དེ་ཟད་པར་ཁོང་དུ་ཆུད་པར་མི་ནུས་སོ།

།འདི་ལས་སྲིད་པ་གཞན་མི་ཤེས་སོ་ཞེས་བྱ་བའི་ཚིག་ལས་དྲངས་[183] ཏེ། །གལ་ཏེ་མ་འོངས་པའི་སྐྱེ་བ་མ་མཐོང་བས་དེ་སྐད་ཅེས་བྱའོ་ཞེ་ན། །ཡང་དེ་ལྟ་ཡིན་དུ་ཟིན་ན་དེའི་དུས་ན་དེའི།[184]

གལ་ཏེ་ཕུང་པོ་མ་འགགས་ན།
།ཉོན་མོངས་ཟད་ཀྱང་འདས་མི་ [«ཅོ་» 10a.1] འགྱུར། || **9ab** ||

།མདོ་ལས་ནི་ཕུང་པོ་འགགས་ན་མྱ་ངན་ལས་འདས་ [«སྣར་» 12b.1] པ་ཞེས་གསུངས་ཏེ།

།སྡུག་བསྔལ་འདི་མ་ལུས་པར་སྤངས་པ་རབ་ཏུ་བཏང་བ་བྱང་བར་གྱུར་པ་ཟད་པ་འདོད་ཆགས་དང་བྲལ་བ་འགོག་པ་ཉེ་བར་ཞི་བ་ནུབ་པ་སྡུག་བསྔལ་གཞན་གྱིས་[185] མཚམས་མི་

---

181 «པེ་»«སྣར་»{SS}: པ་ «སྡེ་»«ཅོ་»: པར་

182 A comparable passage occurs in the *Lalitavistara*: *kṣīṇā me jātiḥ, uṣitaṁ brahmacaryam, kṛtaṁ karaṇīyam, nāparasmād bhavaṁ prajānāmīti*. Cf. Vaidya, *Lalitavistara*, 304, according to Scherrer-Schaub, *Yuktiṣaṣṭikāvṛtti*, 160 n. 181.

183 «པེ་»«སྣར་»: གྲངས་

184 «པེ་»: དེ།

སྦྱོར་ཞིང་ཕྱིས་མི་སྐྱེ་བ་གང་ཡིན་པ་དེ་ཉིད་ཞི་བ། །དེ་ཉིད་གྱ་ནོམ་པ་སྟེ། །འདི་ལྟ་སྟེ། །ཕུང་པོ་ཐམས་ཅད་རབ་ཏུ་བཏང་བ་སྲིད་[186] པ་ཟད་པ་འདོད་ཆགས་དང་བྲལ་བ་འགོག་པ་མྱ་ངན་ལས་འདས་པའོ་[187]

ཞེས་འབྱུང་བ་ཡིན་ཏེ། །དེ་ལ་མདོ་སྡེ་ལས་སྡུག་བསྔལ་འདི་ཞེས་བྱ་བའི་ཚིག་གིས་ནི་ད་ལྟར་ཉིད་ཀྱི་སྡུག་བསྔལ་[188] དབང་དུ་བྱས་ཏེ། །མ་ལུས་པར་སྤངས་པ་ནས་ཉུབ་པར་གྱུར་པའི་བར་དུ་གསུངས་སོ། །མ་འོངས་པའི་སྡུག་བསྔལ་གྱི་དབང་དུ་བྱས་ཏེ། །སྡུག་བསྔལ་ [«སྡེ་» 10b.1] གཞན་གྱིས་[189] མཚམས་མི་སྦྱོར་ཞེས་བྱ་བ་ནས་མྱ་ངན་ལས་འདས་པ་ཞེས་བྱ་བའི་བར་དུ་བསྟན་ཏོ། །དེ་བས་ན་འདིར་ཡང་སྐྱེ་བ་[190] ཟད་དོ་ཞེས་བྱ་བའི་ཚིག་ནི་ད་ལྟར་ཉིད་ཀྱི་མི་སྐྱེ་བར་བསྟན་པའོ། །འདི་ལས་སྲིད་པ་གཞན་མི་ཤེས་སོ་ཞེས་བྱ་བའི་ཚིག་ནི་མ་འོངས་པའི་སྡུག་བསྔལ་དང་སྦྱར་བར་རེས་སོ། །ད་ལྟར་གྱི་དུས་ན་ཡང་དེའི་ཕུང་པོ་དེ་དགག་པ་མེད་ན་ནི་དེ་མྱ་ངན་ལས་འདས་པ་ཡང་མི་མཐོང་།[191] །གལ་ཏེ་སྡུག་བསྔལ་གྱི་ངོ་བོ་ཉིད་སྐྱེ་བ་མེད་པ་མཐོང་བ་དེའི་ཚེ་ན་སྐྱེ་བ་དེ་མི་དམིགས་

---

185 «པེ་» «སྣར་» {SS}: གྱི་

186 «པེ་»: བཏང་བ་སྲིད་ «སྣར་»: བཏང་བ་བསྲིད་ «སྡེ་»: བཏུང་བ་སྲིད་ {SS}: བཏང་བ་སྲེད་

187 May ("Āryadeva et Candrakīrti IV," 58–59 n. 61) gives this version of the Skt.: *yat svalpasya duḥkhasyāsheṣaprahāṇaṁ pratiniḥsargo vyantībhāvaḥ kṣayo virāgo nirodho vyupaśamo 'staṁgamaḥ anyasya ca duḥkhasyāpratisaṁdhir anutpādo 'prādurbhāvaḥ / etac chāntam etat praṇītam yad uta sarvopadhipratiniḥsargas tṛṣṇā-kṣayo virāgo nirodho nirvāṇaṁ* Cf. Scherrer-Schaub, *Yuktiṣaṣṭikāvṛtti*, 162 n. 183.

188 «པེ་» «སྣར་{SS}»: +གྱི་

189 «པེ་» «སྣར་» {SS}: གྱི་

190 «སྡེ་» «ཅོ་»: -ཞེས་བྱ་བའི་བར་དུ་བསྟན་ཏོ། །དེ་བས་ན་འདིར་ཡང་སྐྱེ་བ་

191 «པེ་» «སྣར་» {SS}: འཐད་དོ།

[«པེ་» 12a.1] པས་སྡུག་བསྔལ་ཟད་པ་ཉིད་དུ་འགྱུར་ན། །གཞན་དེ་དག་ནི་དེ་ལྟར་མི་འདོད་པས་དེའི་ཚེ་མྱ་ངན་ལས་འདས་པར་མི་འགྱུར་རོ།

((b) །གཉིས་པ། ལྷག་མེད་མི་འཐད་པ།)

།ཅི་སྟེ་བཅོམ་ལྡན་འདས་ཀྱིས་མྱ་ངན་ལས་འདས་པ་ནི་གཉིས་སུ་གསུངས་ཏེ་ཕུང་པོའི་ལྷག་མ་དང་བཅས་པ་དང་། །ཕུང་པོའི་ལྷག་མ་མེད་པ་ཡིན་ཏེ་དེའི་ཕུང་པོའི་ལྷག་མ་དང་བཅས་པ་ནི་ཕུང་པོ་ཙམ་དུ་ཟད་དོ། །ཉོན་མོངས་པའི་འཆིང་བ་[192] ལས་གྲོལ་བ་ཡིན། །ཕུང་པོ་ལྷག་མ་མེད་པ་ནི་ཕུང་པོའི་རྒྱུན་ཆད་པའི་མཚན་ཉིད་ཡིན་[193] པས་ཕུང་པོ་དང་ [«སྣར་» 13a.1] བཅས་པའི་མྱ་ངན་ལས་འདས་པ་ལ་འདོད་ཆགས་ལ་སོགས་པའི་འཆིང་[194] བ་སྤངས་ཀྱང་མྱ་ངན་ལས་འདས་པར་མི་འདོད་དོ་སྙམ་དུ་སེམས་ན་ནི་འོ་ན་མདོ་སྡེ་ལས་རྗེས་བཟླས་ཞེས་བྱ་བའི་མདོ་སྡེ་འདི་ནི། ཤཱ་རིའི་བུ་ཡིས་མྱ་ངན་འདས། །མངོན་སུམ་བྱས་ནས་ཆཤད་པ་ཡིན། །ཞེས་འབྱུང་བ་ཇི་ལྟར་ཆཤད། །དེ་ནི་ཉོན་མོངས་པ་མེད་པ་མངོན་སུམ་དུ་བྱ་བའི་དབང་དུ་བྱས་ནས་གསུངས་པར་ངེས་ཀྱི་ཕུང་པོ་དང་བྲལ་བ་ནི་མ་ཡིན་ནོ་ [«ཅོ་» 10b.1] ཞེས་བྱ་བ་ན་[195] ཡང་གལ་ཏེ་དེ་ལྟ་ཡིན་དུ་ཟིན་ན་གང་སྡུག་བསྔལ་འདི་མ་ལུས་པར་སྤངས་ཤིང་རབ་ཏུ་བཏང་ཞེས་བྱ་བ་ལ་སོགས་པ་འདི་དག་ཆཤད་པར་མི་འགྱུར་གྱི།

192 «པེ་» «སྣར་» {SS}: བཅིངས་པ་

193 {SS}: -ཡིན་

194 «པེ་» «སྣར་»: བཅིང་

195 «པེ་» «སྣར་» {SS}: -ན་

།གལ་ཏེ་ཉོན་མོངས་པ་དེ་དག་མ་ལུས་པར་སྤངས་པ་ནས་ཐུབ་པར་འགྱུར་[196] ཞེས་བྱ་བའི་བར་དུ་དེ་སྐད་གསུངས་པའི་རིགས་སོ། །སྡུག་བསྔལ་ཞེས་སྨོས་པ་ནི་ཉེ་བར་ལེན་པའི་ཕུང་པོ་ལྔ་རྣམས་བསྡུས་པར་མངོན་ཏེ། །འདིར་སྡུག་བསྔལ་དང་ཀུན་འབྱུང་བ་དང་། འཇིག་རྟེན་ཞེས་བྱ་བ་ལ་སོགས་པ་ནི་ཉེ་བར་ལེན་པའི་ཕུང་པོ་ལྔ་རྣམས་ཀྱི་རྣམཿགྲངས་སུ་[197] གཞག་[198] པའོ། །གལ་ཏེ་དེ་སྐད་བྱུང་དུ་ཟིན་ཀྱང་སྤྱིར་སྨོས་པའི་སྒྲ་ཕྱོགས་གཅིག་ལ་བྱ་བའང་ [«སྡེ་» 11a.1] ཡོད་དེ། །འདི་ལྟར་ཉོན་མོངས་པ་རྣམས་ཉིད་ལ་[199] སྡུག་བསྔལ་ཞེས་བྱའོ་ཞེས་ཟེར་ན་ཡང་ཅིའི་[200] དོན་དང་སྦྱར་དུ་རུང་བ་མེད་ན་ནི་དེ་དེ་ལྟར་འགྱུར་བ་ཞིག་ན་ནམ་ཉེ་བར་ལེན་པའི་ཕུང་པོ་ལྔ་རྣམས་ [«པེ་» 12b.1] ཀྱི་ངོ་བོ་ཉིད་སྐྱེ་བ་མེད་པར་མཐོང་བ་སྲིད་པ་དེ་ན་སྤྱིའི་སྒྲ་ཕྱོགས་གཅིག་ལ་འཇུག་ཅེས་བྱར་མི་རུང་ངོ་།

།དེ་སྟེ་ཡང་ཕུང་པོ་ལ་མངོན་པར་ཞེན་པ་མི་གཏོང་ལ་དོན་འདི་ཁས་མི་ལེན་ན་དེ་ལྟ་[201] ན་ཡང་དེའི་ཉོན་མོངས་པ་སྐྱེ་བ་མེད་པའི་མཚན་ཉིད་ཀྱང་མྱ་ངན་ལས་འདས་པར་མི་འགྱུར་རོ། །གལ་ཏེ་དེའི་ཚེ་སྡུག་བསྔལ་སྐྱེ་བ་མེད་པའི་ངོ་བོ་མྱ་ངན་ལས་འདས་པར་མི་འདོད་ན་དེའི་ཚེ་འདོད་ཆགས་ལ་སོགས་པའི་བཅིང་བ་བཅད་པས་ཉོན་མོངས་པ་མེད་པར་གྱུར་ཀྱང་དེའི་ཚེ་ [«སྣར་» 13b.1] འཇིག་ཚོགས་ལ་ལྟ་བ་ལ་སོགས་པའི་རྒྱུ་ཡོད་པར་དམིགས་པ་དང་། །དེ་ལ་དམིགས་པས་འདོད་

---

196 «པེ་» «སྣར་» {SS}: གྱུར་

197 «སྣར་»: གྲངསུ་ [= གྲངས་སུ་]

198 «པེ་» {SS}: བཞག་ «སྣར་»: ཞག་

199 «པེ་» «སྣར་»: ལས་

200 «པེ་» «སྣར་» {SS}: སྤྱིའི་

201 «པེ་» «སྣར་» {SS}: ལྟར་

ཆགས་ལ་སོགས་པ་བསྐྱེད་[202] པའི་ཕྱིར་ངེས་རྣམ་པར་གྲོལ་བ་གང་ཡིན་པ་དེ་ཡང་འཐོབ་[203] པར་མི་འགྱུར་ཏེ། །དེ་བས་ན་དེའི་དུས་ན་གྲོལ་བར་ཁས་བླང་དུ་མི་རུང་ངོ།

།ཕུང་པོ་རྣམས།

གང་ཚེ་དེ་ཡི་དེ་འགགས་[204] པ།

།དེ་ཡི་ཚེ་ན་གྲོལ་བར་འགྱུར། || **9cd** ||

།ཞེས་བྱར་མི་རུང་ངོ། །ཕུང་པོ་དམིགས་པས་རྒྱུ་དེ་ལས་བྱུང་བ་[205] ཉོན་མོངས་པ་རྒྱུན་མི་འཆད་པའི་ཕྱིར་དེའི་ཕུང་པོ་རྣམས་འགག་པ་དེ་ཡང་མི་སྲིད་དོ། །ཉོན་མོངས་པ་རྣམས་ཀྱང་ཡོད་ལ། །རྒྱུ་དེ་ལས་བྱུང་བའི་ལས་ཀྱིས་འཕངས་པ་ཡང་ཡོད་ན། །རྒྱུ་ཉོན་མོངས་པ་དང་ལས་ལས་བྱུང་བའི་སྐྱེ་བའི་རྒྱུན་མཐར་ཐུག་པ་མེད་པར་འགྱུར་བའི་ཕྱིར་དེའི་ཕུང་པོ་རྣམ་[206] པར་ཆད་པའི་མཚན་ཉིད་ཐར་པ་མི་སྲིད་དོ།

།དེ་བས་ན་སྐྱེ་བ་ཟད་དོ་ཞེས་པ་[207] མ་འོངས་པའི་ཕུང་པོ་དང་སྦྱར་བའི་ཞེས་པ་དེ་ཡང་མི་སྲིད་པས་ཞིག་ཅེས་པ་དེ་ཇི་ལྟ་བུ་ཞེས་བྱ་བ་སྨོས་སོ། [«ཅོ་» 11a.1]

---

202 «པེ་» «སྣར་» {SS}: སྐྱེད་

203 «པེ་» «སྣར་» {SS}: ཐོབ་

204 «པེ་»: ཡི་དེ་འགག་ «སྣར་»: ཡིད་འགག་

205 {SS}: བའི་

206 «པེ་» «སྣར་»: རྣམས་

207 «པེ་» «སྣར་» {SS}: བྱ་བ་

(iii. །གསུམ་པ། རང་ལ་འཐད་པ།)

((1) །དང་པོ། འདུས་བྱས་འཕགས་པའི་མཉམ་གཞག་གིས་མི་གཟིགས་པའི་རྒྱུ་མཚན།)

།དེའི་ཕྱིར་དེ་[208] དེ་ལྟར་ཇི་སྐད་སྨྲས་པ་རིགས་པས་ངོ་བོ་ཉིད་ཡོད་པར་སྨྲ་བ་ལ་རྣམ་པར་གྲོལ་བ་ཡེ་མི་སྲིད་པར་[209] བསྟན་ནས་སྟོང་པ་ཉིད་དུ་སྨྲ་བ་ལ་རྣམ་པར་གྲོལ་བ་སྲིད་པ་[210] བསྟན་པའི་ཕྱིར།

མ་རིག་རྐྱེན་གྱིས་བྱུང་བ་ལ།
།ཡང་དག་ཤེས་པས་[211] རྣམ་བརྟགས་ན།
།སྐྱེ་བ་དང་ནི་འགག་པའང་རུང་།
།གང་ཡང་དམིགས་པར་མི་འགྱུར་རོ། ‖ 10 ‖

།ཞེས་བྱ་བ་སྨོས་སོ། །མ་རིག་པ་ཡི་[212] [«སྡེ་» 11b.1] རྐྱེན་གྱིས་ [«པེ་» 13a.1] བྱུང་། །ཞེས་བྱ་བ་ལ་མ་རིག་པ་ནི་འདུ་བྱེད་དང་རྣམ་པར་ཤེས་པ་ལ་སོགས་པའི་དོན་གྱི་[213] མདོན་སུམ་དང་གཅིག་ནས་གཅིག་ཏུ་བརྒྱུད་པའི་[214] རྐྱེན་ཏོ།[215]

---

[208] «པེ་»«སྣར་»{SS}: -དེ་

[209] Tib. *ye mi srid pa*, Skt. *sarvathābhāva* [Mvy 6407].

[210] «པེ་»«སྣར་»{SS}: པར་

[211] ཡང་དག་ཡེ་ཤེས་ = *samyagjñāna* [Mvy 4469].

[212] «པེ་»«སྣར་»: པའི་

[213] «པེ་»«སྣར་»{SS}: གྱི་ «སྡེ་»«ཅོ་»: གྱིས་

[214] Tib. *gcig nas gcig tu brgyud pa*, Skt. *paraṁparātantra.

[215] «ཏྭི་»: །འདུ་བྱེད་ལ་སོགས་པ་བཅུ་གཅིག་ལ་མ་རིག་པ་དངོས་པོ་དང་བརྒྱུད་ཅི་རིགས་པར་རྐྱེན་དུ་ཡོད་པས་ན་མ་རིག་རྐྱེན་ཅན་ཏེ་དེ་ལས་བྱུང་བ་ལ་ཡང་དག་པའི་འཕགས་པའི་ཡེ་ཤེས་ཀྱིས་གཟིགས་པའི་ངོ་ན་འདུས་བྱས་ཐོག་མར་སྐྱེ་བ་དང་མཐར་འགག་པ་ཡང་རུང་སྟེ་སྤྲོས་པ་འགའ་ཡང་དམིགས་པར་མི་འགྱུར་རོ།

།མ་རིག་པའི་རྐྱེན་ལས་བྱུང་བ་འདུ་བྱེད་ལ་སོགས་པའི་དོན་གལ་ཏེ་རང་གི་མཚན་ཉིད་དུ་གྲུབ་པར་གྱུར་ན་དེ་རང་གི་མཚན་ཉིད་དུ་གྲུབ་པའི་ཕྱིར་མ་རིག་པ་ལ་མི་ལྟོས་སོ། །རང་གི་མཚན་ཉིད་དུ་གྲུབ་པ་བུམ་པ་ལ་སོགས་པ་ནི་རང་གི་ངོ་བོ་ལ་སྒྲིབ་པ་མུན་པ་མེད་ན་ཤིན་ཏུ་གསལ་བར་དམིགས་སོ། །རྐྱེན་གྱི་བྱེ་བྲག་དག་[216] དང་ལྡན་པས་རབ་རིབ་ཅན་གྱིས་ཡོངས་སུ་བརྟགས་པ་ [《སྣར་》 14a.1] པ་སྒྲ་ལ་སོགས་པའི་དངོས་པོར་ཤེས་པ་ནི་ཇི་ལྟ་ཇི་ལྟར་རང་གི་ངོ་བོ་མེད་པར་འགྱུར་ཏེ། །རྣམ་པར་བྱང་བའི་མིག་ཅན་དག་ལ་ནི་སྣང་བར་མི་འགྱུར་རོ། །དེ་ལྟར་རྣམ་པར་བརྟགས་པའི་མཚན་ཉིད་དུ་གྲུབ་པ་ནི་སྒྲ་[217] ཡང་དག་པ་ལ་སོགས་པ་བཞིན་དུ་ཡོད་པར་གཞག་མི་ནུས་སོ།

།དེ་བཞིན་དུ་འདུ་བྱེད་ལ་སོགས་པ་འདི་དག་ཀྱང་གལ་ཏེ་རང་གི་མཚན་ཉིད་དུ་གྲུབ་པར་གྱུར་ན་དེའི་ཚེ་བདེན་པའི་དོན་གཏན་ལ་ཕབ་པ་ལས་སྐྱེས་པ་འཕགས་པ་ཡང་དག་པའི་ཡེ་ཤེས་ཅན་རྣམས་ཀྱིས་ཀྱང་རང་གི་མཚན་ཉིད་གཞིག་ཏུ་མི་[218] རུང་བ་[219] གཟིགས་པས་བུམ་པ་ལ་སོགས་པ་སྣང་བ་དང་བཅས་པ་བཞིན་དུ་དམིགས་ཤིང་ཡུལ་དུ་འགྱུར་བའི་རིགས་ན་མ་རིག་པ་འགགས་པས་འདུ་བྱེད་འགག་གོ་ཞེས་བྱ་བའི་ཚིག་གིས་དེ་ལྟར་ཡང་མི་འགྱུར་རོ། །དེའི་ཕྱིར་ཡང་དག་པའི་ཡེ་ཤེས་ཤར་བ་ན་རབ་རིབ་ཅན་གྱིས་དམིགས་པའི་སྒྲ་ལ་སོགས་པ་འདི་དག་ལྟར་རང་གི་མཚན་ཉིད་མི་སྣང་བས་རང་གི་མཚན་ཉིད་ཡོད་པ་[220] གཞག་མི་ནུས་སོ།

།ནམ་ཞིག་འདི་ལྟར་མ་རིག་པའི་རྐྱེན་ལས་བྱུང་བ་འདུ་བྱེད་ལ་སོགས་པ་ལ་རབ་རིབ་མེད་པ་ཅན་རྣམས་ལྟར་ཡང་དག་པའི་ཡེ་ཤེས་ཀྱིས་བརྟགས་ན་དེ་རབ་རིབ་ཅན་གྱིས་དམིགས་པའི་སྒྲ་ལ་སོགས་པ

---

216 《པེ་》《སྣར་》: -དག་

217 《པེ་》《སྣར་》{SS}: སྒྲ་ 《སྡེ་》《ཅོ་》: སྦྲ་

218 《སྣར་》: མ་

219 {SS}: བར་

220 《པེ་》《སྣར་》{SS}: པར་

བཞིན་དུ་ཡང་དག་པའི་ཡེ་ཤེས་ཀྱི་དུས་ན་འདུ་བྱེད་ལ་ [«ཅོ་» 11b.1] སོགས་པའི་སྐྱེ་བ་[221] འགག་པ་གང་ཡང་ངེས་[222] པར་ [«པེ་» 13b.1] མི་དམིགས་སོ།

((2) །གཉིས་པ། དེ་ཉིད་གོམས་པ་བྱ་བ་བྱས་སོ་ཞེས་པའི་ཐ་སྙད་ཀྱི་ཡུལ་དུ་བསྟན་པ།)

((a) །དང་པོ། དངོས།)

།རྟེན་ཅིང་འབྲེལ་པར་འབྱུང་བ་གང་ཡིན་པ་འདི་ཡི་སྐྱེ་བ་དང་འགག་པ་མི་དམིགས་པའི་ཡེ་ཤེས་ཀྱི་དུས་ན།

མཐོང་བའི་ཆོས་ལ་མྱ་ངན་འདས།
།བྱ་བ་བྱས་པའང་དེ་ཉིད་དོ། || **11ab** ||

།ཚེ་འདི་ཉིད་ [«སྡེ་» 12a.1] ལ་རྣལ་འབྱོར་པ་དེའི་ཆོས་ཐམས་ཅད་མི་དམིགས་པའི་ཡེ་ཤེས་ཀྱི་དུས་གང་ཡིན་པ་དེ་ཉིད་མཐོང་བའི་ཆོས་ལ་མྱ་ངན་ལས་[223] འདས་པའོ། །བྱ་བ་བྱས་པ་ཉིད་[224] ཀྱོན་བྱ་བ་བྱས་པ་ཉིད་ཅེས་བྱའོ། །སྐྱེ་བ་དང་འགག་པ་མི་དམིགས་པའི་ཡེ་ཤེས་ཀྱི་དུས་གང་ཡིན་པ་དེ་ཉིད་མཐོང་བའི་ཆོས་ལ་མྱ་ [«སྣར་» 14b.1] ངན་ལས་འདས༔པ་དང་[225] བྱ་བ་བྱས་པ་ཞེས་བྱ་བར་ཤེས་པར་བྱ་སྟེ། །ལུང་དག་ལས་དགེ་སློང་མཐོང་བའི་ཆོས་ལ་མྱ་ངན་ལས་འདས་པ་ཞེས་གསུངས་པ་དང་འཕགས་པ་ཤཱ་རིའི་བུས་མྱ་ངན་ལས་འདས་པ་མངོན་སུམ་དུ་བྱས་ཏེ། །མདོ་འདི་ཙཤད་དོ་ཞེས་འབྱུང་བ་དེ་ཉིད་དེའི་མཐོང་བའི་ཆོས་ལ་མྱ་ངན་ལས་འདས་པ་ཡིན་པར་བལྟའོ། །སྐྱེ་

221 «པེ་»«སྣར་»: བའམ་

222 «པེ་»: ངོས་

223 «པེ་»«སྣར་»: ་ལས་

224 «པེ་»«སྣར་»{SS}: +མཐོང་བའི་ཆོས་ལ་

225 «སྣར་»: པའོ་

བ་ཟད་དོ། །ཚངས་པར་སྤྱོད་པ་བསྙེན་ཏོ། །བྱ་བ་བྱས་སོ། །འདི་ལས་སྲིད་པ་གཞན་མི་ཤེས་སོ་ཞེས་གང་གསུངས་པ་དེ་ཡང་བྱ་བ་བྱས་པ་འདི་ཉིད་ཡིན་པར་རིག་པར་བྱ་སྟེ། །དེ་ནི་རྟེན་ཅིང་འབྲེལ་པར་འབྱུང་བའི་སྐྱེ་བཿ མེད་པ་དང་འགག་པ་[226] མེད་པའོ།

།ཅི་སྟེ་ཞེས་པ་འདི་[227] རྟེན་ཅིང་འབྲེལ་པར་འབྱུང་བའི་སྐྱེ་བ་དང་འགག་པ་མི་དམིགས་པའི་མཚན་ཉིད་དེ་ཁོ་ན་བོར་ཏེ། །དམིགས་པའི་དངོས་པོ་རང་གི་མཚན་ཉིད་ཀྱི་ངོ་བོ་ཞིག་ཡོད་པར་ཡོངས་སུ་རྟོག་ན་དངོས་པོ་རྣམས་ནི་ཕན་ཚུན་ཐ་དད་པའི་རང་གི་ངོ་བོ་[228] ཡིན་པས་དེ་ངེས་པར་དེས་བྱེ་བྲག་ཏུ་ཡོངས་སུ་གཅད་[229] དགོས་པར་འགྱུར་ཏེ། །ངོ་བོ་གཞན་ཡོངས་སུ་ཤེས་པས་དངོས་པོའི་ངོ་བོ་གཞན་ཡོངས་སུ་གཅད་[230] པར་མི་ནུས་སོ། །སྔོན་པོའི་ངོ་བོ་ཤེས་པས་སེར་པོ་ཡོངས་སུ་གཅོད་མི་ནུས་པ་དེ་བཞིན་དུ་འདི་ལ་ཡང་།

((b) །གཉིས་པ། རྟོགས་བྱ་ཆོས་དབྱིངས་ལ་རྣམ་པ་མི་འདྲ་བ་མེད་པར་བསྟན་པ།)

ཆོས་ཤེས་དེ་ཡི་འོག་ཏུ་ནི།
།འདི་ལ་བྱེ་བྲག་དབྱེ་ [«པེ་» 14a.1] ཡོད་ན། **|| 11cd ||**

།ཤིན་ཏུ་ཕྲ་བའི་དངོས་ལ་ཡང་།
།གང་གིས་སྐྱེ་བར་རྣམ་བརྟགས་པ།

---

226 «པེ་»«སྣར་»{SS}: མེད་པ་དང་འགག་པ་ «སྡེ་»«ཅོ་»: -མེད་པ་དང་འགག་པ་

227 {SS} questions the reading of the beginning of this passage.

228 Skt. reconstructed by Scherrer-Schaub as *anyonyabhinna-svabhāva*.

229 «པེ་»«སྣར་»{SS}: བཅད་

230 «པེ་»«སྣར་»{SS}: བཅད་

།རྣམ་པར་མི་མཁས་དེ་ཡིས་ནི།
།རྐྱེན་ལས་བྱུང་བའི་དོན་མ་མཐོང་། || **12** ||

།དེ་ལ་ཆོས་ཞེས་[231] བྱ་བའི་སྒྲ་ནི་མྱ་ངན་ལས་འདས་པ་ལ་བྱའོ། །དེ་ཡང་རྟེན་ཅིང་འབྲེལ་པར་འབྱུང་བའི་ངོ་བོ་ཉིད་ལས་གཞན་མ་ཡིན་ཏེ། །མདོ་སྡེ་ལས་ཀྱང་གསུས་རྟེན་ཅིང་འབྲེལ་པར་འབྱུང་བ་མཐོང་བ་དེས་ཆོས་མཐོང་ངོ་ཞེས་[232] ཇི་སྐད་འབྱུང་བ་ཡིན་ནོ། །རྟེན་ཅིང་འབྲེལ་པར་འབྱུང་བ་དེ་དང་མྱ་ངན་ལས་འདས་པ་ཐ་མི་དད་ [«སྡེ་» 12b.1] པའི་རང་བཞིན་དུ་གྱུར་པར་ཡོངས་སུ་གཅོད་པའི་ [«ཅོ་» 12a.1] ཤེས་པ་གང་ཡིན་པ་དེ་ཆོས་ཤེས་པའོ། །ཆོས་ཤེས་པས་རྟེན་ཅིང་ [«སྣར་» 15a.1] འབྲེལ་པར་འབྱུང་བའི་དོན་ཁོང་དུ་ཆུད་པར་བྱ་སྟེ། །དེ་ཡང་བསྟན་བཅོས་ལས།

གང་དང་གང་དག་རྟེན་འབྱུང་བ།
།དེ་དག་ངོ་བོ་ཉིད་ཀྱིས་ཞི།
།དེ་ལྟ་བས་ན་སྐྱེ་བ་དང་།
།སྐྱེས་པ་ཉིད་ནི་ཞི་བའོ།[233]

[231] «པེ་» «སྣར་» {SS}: ཤེས་

[232] The *Śālistambha-sūtra*, (Shastri, *Nālandā*, 1) reads: *yo bhikṣavaḥ pratītyasamutpādaṁ paśyati, sa dharmaṁ paśyati sa buddhaṁ paśyati.* For Pāli and other citations, see Scherrer-Schaub, *Yuktiṣaṣṭikāvṛtti*, 173 n. 231.

[233] MMK 7.16 (Scherrer-Schaub, "*Yuktiṣaṣṭikāvṛtti,*" 173 n. 233): *pratītya yad yad bhavati tat tac chāntaṁ svabhāvataḥ / tasmād utpadyamānaṁ ca śāntam utpattireva* ca //; «སྡེ་»: །རྟེན་ཅིང་འབྱུང་བ་གང་ཡིན་པ། །དེ་ནི་ངོ་བོ་ཉིད་ཀྱིས་ནི། །དེ་ཕྱིར་སྐྱེ་བཞིན་ཉིད་དང་ནི། །སྐྱེ་བ་ཡང་ནི་ཞི་བ་ཉིད།

།ཞེས་འབྱུང་བ་ཡིན་ནོ། །འདི་ལ་སྐྱེས་པར་གྱུར་པ་དང་། །སྐྱེ་བ་ངོ་བོ་ཉིད་ཀྱིས་སྐྱེ་བ་མེད་པ་གང་ཡིན་པ་[234] རྟེན་ཅིང་འབྲེལ་པར་འབྱུང་བའི་དོན་དུ་གསུངས་སོ། །སྡུག་བསྔལ་ཡང་རྟེན་ཅིང་འབྲེལ་པར་འབྱུང་བ་ཡིན་པས་རང་བཞིན་གྱིས་མ་སྐྱེས་པའོ། །གང་གིས་[235] ངོ་བོ་ཉིད་ཀྱིས་སྐྱེ་བ་མེད་པ་དེ་ཉིད་མྱ་ངན་ལས་འདས་པ་སྟེ། །གཉི་ག་ཡང་མ་སྐྱེས་པའི་ཕྱིར་རོ། །འདི་ལྟར་ཡང་

འཁོར་བ་ལས་ནི་མྱ་ངན་འདས།
།ཁྱེ་བྲག་དབྱེ་བ་ཅུང་ཟད་མེད།
།མྱ་ངན་འདས་ལས་འཁོར་བ་ཡང་།
།ཁྱེ་བྲག་དབྱེ་བ་ཅི་ཡང་མེད།

།མྱ་ངན་འདས་ཀྱི་མཐའ་འདི་ནི།
།འཁོར་བའི་མཐའ་ཡང་དེ་ཡིན་ཏེ།
།དེ་གཉིས་ལ་ནི་ཅུང་ཟད་ཀྱང་།
།ཁྱེ་བྲག་ཤིན་ཏུ་ཕྲ་བའང་མེད།[236]

---

234 «པེ་»«སྣར་»{SS}: +དེ་

235 «པེ་»«སྣར་»{SS}: གི་

236 MMK 25.19–.20 reads: *na saṁsārasya nirvāṇāt kiṁ cidasti viśeṣaṇaṁ / na nirvāṇasya saṁsārāt kiṁ cidasti viśeṣaṇaṁ // nirvāṇasya ca yā koṭiḥ saṁsārasya ca / na tayor antaraṁ kiṁ cit susūkṣmam api vidyate //*; «སྡེ་»: །འཁོར་བ་མྱ་ངན་འདས་པ་ལས། །ཁྱད་པར་ཅུང་ཟད་ཡོད་མ་ཡིན། །མྱ་ངན་འདས་པ་འཁོར་བ་ལས། །ཁྱད་པར་ཅུང་ཟད་ཡོད་མ་ཡིན། །མྱ་ངན་འདས་མཐའ་གང་ཡིན་པ། །དེ་ནི་འཁོར་བའི་མཐའ་ཡིན་ཏེ། །དེ་གཉིས་ཁྱད་པར་ཅུང་ཟད་ནི། །ཤིན་ཏུ་ཕྲ་བའང་ཡོད་མ་ཡིན།

།ཅེས་བྱ་བ་བསྟན་པ་ཡིན་ནོ། །མཐའ་ཞེས་བྱ་བའི་སྒྲ་ནི་མཆོག་ཏུ་བྱུང་[237] བའོ། །མཆོག་ཏུ་བྱུང་བ་ཞེས་བྱ་བ་ནི་ཕུལ་དུ་ཕྱིན་པ་ཞེས་བྱ་སྟེ། །ཕྲིས་པའི་སྐྱེ་བོ་རྣམས་ཀྱི་སྤྱོད་ཡུལ་དུ་མ་[238] གྱུར་པའི་མཐའི་རང་བཞིན་ནི་གཉི་ག་ཡང་མ་སྐྱེས་པའི་ཕྱིར་ [«པེ་» 14b.1] ངོ་བོ་ཉིད་ཀྱིས་སྐྱེ་བ་མེད་པས་འཁོར་བ་དང་མྱ་ངན་ལས་འདས་པ་གཉིས་གཅིག་གོ།

།དེ་བས་ན་མྱ་ངན་ལས་འདས་པ་དང་ཁྱད་པར་མེད་པའི་ཕྱིར་རྟེན་ཅིང་འབྲེལ་པར་འབྱུང་བ་ལ་ཡང་ཆོས་ཞེས་[239] བྱ་སྟེ། །དེ་མཐོང་བས་མྱ་ངན་ལས་འདས་པ་ཡང་མཐོང་བས་ན་སུས་རྟེན་ཅིང་འབྲེལ་པར་འབྱུང་བ་མཐོང་བ་དེས་ཆོས་མཐོང་ངོ་། །ཆོས་ཀྱི་ངོ་བོ་ཉིད་དང་སངས་རྒྱས་བཅོམ་ལྡན་འདས་ཐ་མི་དད་པས་ན་[240] མཐོང་བས་སངས་རྒྱས་མཐོང་བ་ཡིན་ནོ།

།དེ་ལྟར་ན་རྟེན་ཅིང་འབྲེལ་པར་འབྱུང་བའི་སྐྱེ་བ་[241] མེད་པ་ལ་དམིགས་ [«སྣར་» 15b.1] པའི་ཆོས་ཤེས་པས་རྟེན་བདེན་པ་གསུམ་རྟེན་ཅིང་འབྲེལ་པར་འབྱུང་བ་ངོ་བོ་ཉིད་ཀྱིས་མ་སྐྱེས་ལ། །མྱ་ངན་ལས་འདས་པ་ཡང་དེའི་ངོ་བོ་ཉིད་ཡིན་པར་མཐོང་བས་མངོན་པར་རྟོགས་པ་གཅིག་ཏུ་ཟད་དོ། །དེ་ལ་རྟེན་ཅིང་འབྲེལ་པར་འབྱུང་བ་ལ་དམིགས་པའི་ [«སྡེ་» 13a.1] ཆོས་ཤེས་པ་སྡུག་བསྔལ་གྱི་སྐྱེ་བ་མེད་པ་དང་འགག་པ་མེད་པ་ཡོངས་སུ་གཅོད་པ་གང་ཡིན་པའི་བདག་ཉིད་དེ་སྡུག་བསྔལ་ཡོངས་སུ་ཤེས་སོ། །ལས་དང་ཉོན་མོངས་པའི་སྐྱེ་ [«ཅོ་» 12b.1] བ་དང་འགག་པ་མེད་པ་ཡོངས་སུ་གཅོད་པ་གང་ཡིན་པ་དེ་ནི་ཀུན་འབྱུང་བ་ཤེས་པའོ། །རྟེན་ཅིང་འབྲེལ་པར་འབྱུང་

237 «པེ་»«སྣར་»: འབྱུང་།

238 «པེ་»«སྣར་»{SS}: f- «སྡེ་»«ཅོ་»: -མ་

239 «པེ་»«སྣར་»{SS}: ཤེས་

240 «པེ་»{SS}: པས་ན་དེ་ «སྣར་»: པ་ན་དེ་

241 «པེ་»«སྣར་»{SS}: +མེད་པ་དང་འགག་པ་

བའི་སྐྱེ་བ་མེད་པ་དང་འགག་པ་མེད་པ་ཡོངས་སུ་གཅོད་པ་མ་[242] ཡིན་པ་འདི་ནི་འགོག་པ་ཞེས་པའོ། །ལམ་གྱི་བདེན་པ་ཡང་རྟེན་ཅིང་འབྲེལ་པར་འབྱུང་བ་ཡིན་པས་ངོ་བོ་ཉིད་ཀྱིས་སྐྱེ་བ་མེད་པ་དང་འགག་པ་མེད་པ་ཡོངས་སུ་གཅོད་པ་གང་ཡིན་པ་དེ་ནི་ལམ་ཞེས་པའོ། །དེ་ལྟར་ན་ཆོས་ཞེས་པས་སྐད་ཅིག་གཅིག་ལ་རྟེན་ཅིང་འབྲེལ་པར་འབྱུང་བ་མཐོང་བས་སྟོན་མ་མཐོང་བའི་བལྟ་[243] བར་བྱ་བ་གཞན་མི་སྲིད་དོ།

།གལ་ཏེ་དེ་ལྟར་ན་[244] མཐོང་བའི་ལམ་སྐད་ཅིག་མ་བཅོ་ལྔར་ཇི་ལྟར་གཞག

།སྡེ་པ་ཁ་ཅིག་ནི་མཐོང་བའི་ལམ་སྐད་ཅིག་མ་བཅོ་ལྔར་མི་འདོད་ཀྱི། །མངོན་པར་རྟོགས་པ་གཅིག་ཏུ་ཟད་པར་འདོད་དོ། །དེ་དག་གི་འདོད་པ་དང་ [《པེ་》 15a.1] སྙད་[245] པ་འདི་[246] མི་འགལ་ལོ། །གང་དག་སྐད་ཅིག་མ་བཅོ་ལྔར་འདོད་པ་དེ་དག་གི་ལྟར་[247] ཡང་དེ་ལྟ་བུས་གདུལ་བའི་སྐྱེ་བོ་ལ་དེ་བསྟན་པས་ཕན་གདགས་པའི་ཕྱིར་ཞེས་པ་ངོ་བོ་གཅིག་ལ་[248] ཆར་ཕྱེ་སྟེ། །ཆ་བཅོ་ལྔར་རྣམ་པར་གཞག་གོ།

།གལ་ཏེ་དེ་ལྟར་ན་ལམ་སྒོམ་པ་རྣམ་པ་བཅུ་དྲུག་པ་དེ་ཅི་ལྟ་བུར་ཐར་པར་[249] འདོད་པ་རྣམས་ལམ་རྣམ་པ་གཞན་དག་གིས་དེ་ཁོ་ན་ཞེས་པ་ལ་འཇུག་པ་གོམས་པར་བྱ་བའི་ཕྱིར་ [《སྣར་》

242 《པེ་》《སྣར་》{SS}: གང་

243 《པེ་》《སྣར་》{SS}: ལྟ་

244 《ཏྣེ་》: ཉན་ཐོས་ཀྱི་སྡེ་སྣོད་ཁ་ཅིག་ལས"'

245 《པེ་》: བཅད་

246 《པེ་》: འདིའི་

247 《པེ་》《སྣར་》{SS}: +ན་

248 《སྣར་》: ལས་

249 《པེ་》《སྣར་》: པ་

16a.1] འདི་ཡང་ཡོངས་སུ་བརྟགས་ནས་རྣམ་པར་གཞག་པ་ཉིད་དེ། །དེ་ཁོ་ན་ནི་ངོ་བོ་གཅིག་པུར་ཟད་དོ།

།ཅི་སྟེ་ཁྱད་པར་དུ་དབྱེ་བའི་རྣམ་པ་དངོས་པོ་གཞན་ཤེས་པ་གཞན་གྱིས་[250] གཟུང་བ་ཞིག་ཡོད་ན་ནི། །དེའི་ཚེ་རྣམ་པ་ཡོངས་སུ་མ་བཅད་པ་[251] ཡོངས་སུ་བཅད་དགོས་པར་འགྱུར་ཏེ། །ཆོས་ཤེས་པ་དེའི་འོག་ཏུ་བྱེ་བྲག་ཏུ་ཡོངས་སུ་གཅོད་པར་བྱ་བ་བྱེ་བྲག་དབྱེ་བ་ཞིག་ཡོད་ན་ནི་དེའི་དམིགས་པ་གཞན་དུ་བརྟགས་པས་དེས་དེའི་ངོ་བོ་བྱེ་བྲག་ཏུ་ཡོངས་སུ་གཅད་[252] དགོས་པས་མི་མཁས་པ་སུས་དངོས་པོ་ཤིན་ཏུ་ཕྲ་བ་ལ་རང་གི་ངོ་བོར་སྐྱེ་བར་རྣམ་པར་བརྟགས་པས་ཀྱང་རྟེན་ [«སྡེ་» 13b.1] ཅིང་འབྲེལ་པར་འབྱུང་བའི་དོན་ངོ་བོ་ཉིད་ཀྱིས་སྐྱེ་བ་མེད་ཅིང་རོ་གཅིག་པའི་དོན་མི་ཤེས་པ་ཡིན་ན་རགས་[253] པ་ས་ལ་སོགས་པ་ལྟ་ཅི་སྨོས།

།དེ་[254] ལྟར་རྟེན་ཅིང་འབྲེལ་པར་འབྱུང་བའི་དོན་དེ་མཚན་ཉིད་གཅིག་ཏུ་མཐོང་སྟེ། །རིམ་གྱིས་གོམས་པར་བྱས་ནས་མ་རིག་པ་མ་ལུས་པར་འགགས་ཏེ། །རྟེན་ཅིང་འབྲེལ་པར་འབྱུང་བའི་ངོ་བོ་ཉིད་ལ་དམིགས་པའི་ཤེས་པ་ལ་གནས་པ་ནི་མཐོང་བའི་ཆོས་ལ་མྱ་ངན་ལས་ [«ཅོ་» 13a.1] འདས་པ་དང་བྱ་བ་བྱས་པ་ཞེས་བྱ་བར་རྣམ་པར་གཞག་སྟེ་གཞན་དུ་མ་ཡིན་ནོ།

---

250 «པེ་»«སྣར་»: ཀྱི་

251 «པེ་»: -པ་

252 «པེ་»«སྣར་»{SS}: བཅད་

253 «པེ་»«སྣར་»{SS}: རག་

254 «པེ་»«སྣར་»: ཇི་

((c) |གསུམ་པ། གཞན་གྱིས་བརྟགས་པ་བྱ་བ་བྱས་པའི་ཐ་སྙད་ཀྱི་ཡུལ་དུ་མི་རུང་བ།)

((i) |དང་པོ། གཞན་ཕྱོགས་ཉེས་པ་དང་བཅས་པ།)

((x) |དང་པོ། ཐོག་མ་ཡོད་པར་ཐལ་བ།)

|ཅི་སྟེ་ཁྱོད་ཀྱི་གཞུང་ལྟར་ན།

ཉོན་མོངས་ཟད་པའི་དགེ་སློང་གི།
|འཁོར་བ་གལ་ཏེ་རྣམ་བཟློག་[255] ན།
|རྫོགས་པའི་སངས་རྒྱས་རྣམས་ཀྱིས་ཀྱང་།
|ཅི་ཕྱིར་དེ་ཡི་རྩོམ་མི་བཟད།[256] **|| 13 ||**

|གལ་ཏེ་ཡེ་ཤེས་ཀྱིས་ཉོན་མོངས་པ་བཟློག་ན་ལས་ལྡོག་སྟེ། |རྒྱུ་དང་རྐྱེན་དུ་མི་ [«པེ་» 15b.1] ལྡན་པའི་ཕྱིར་ཐོག་མ་མེད་པ་ནས་འཁོར་བར་འཇུག་པ་དང་སྐྱེ་བ་དང་འཆི་བ་གཅིག་ནས་གཅིག་ཏུ་བརྒྱུད་པ་རང་གི་མཚན་ཉིད་ཀྱིས་གྲུབ་པའི་ངོ་བོ་གཟུགས་ལ་སོགས་པའི་རྒྱུན་ལྡོག་ན་དེ་ལྟ་ན་ནི་དེ་རྩོམ་པ་རྫོགས་པའི་སངས་རྒྱས་རྣམས་ཀྱིས་མ་གསུངས་པ་ནི་གཏན་ཚིགས་འདི་ལྟ་བུ་ཞིག་གིས་བཅོམ་ལྡན་འདས་ཀྱིས་རྩོམ་པ་མ་གསུངས་སོ། |ཞེས་འདི་ལ་ཁྱོད་ཀྱི་ཕུང་པོའི་རྒྱུན་དེའི་རྩོམ་པ་ཐ་མ་བཞིན་དུ་བརྗོད་དགོས་པར་འགྱུར་རོ།

|མི་མཁྱེན་ཏེ་[257] མ་གསུངས་སམ་ [«སྣར་» 16b.1] གཞན་ཞིག་གི་ཕྱིར་མ་གསུངས་ཞེས་བྱ། |འདི་ལ་བཅོམ་ལྡན་འདས་ནི་ཐམས་ཅད་མཁྱེན་པར་[258] ཁས་ལེན་པའི་ཕྱིར་མི་མཁྱེན་ནི་མི་

---

255 «པེ་» «སྣར་» : བཟློག་ {SS}: ལྡོག་ following {Dh}

256 «པེ་» «སྣར་» {SS}: བཤད་

257 «པེ་ P.» : དེ་

258 «པེ་» «སྣར་» : པ་

སྲིད་དོ། །གཞན་ཞིག་གི་ཕྱིར་མ་གསུངས་ཞེས་བྱར་ན་དེ་ཡང་མི་རིགས་སོ། །ཟོ་ཆུན་བརྒྱད་མོའི་འཁྲུལ་འཁོར་ལྟར་ཐོག་[259] མ་མེད་པའི་ཕྱིར་མ་གསུངས་ཞེས་བྱར་ན་ནི་གལ་ཏེ་དེ་ལྟར་ན་ཟོ་ཆུན་བརྒྱད་མོའི་འཁྲུལ་འཁོར་ལྟར་ཐོག་མ་མེད་པ་དེ་བཞིན་དུ་དེའི་ཐ་མ་ཡང་མེད་པར་འགྱུར་ཏེ། །འཁོར་ལོ་ལ་སོགས་པའི་དཔེ་ལ་ཡང་དེ་སྐད་ཅེས་བརྗོད་པར་བྱའོ།

།ཟད་པར་འགྱུར་རོ་ཞེས་བཤད་པས་ཐ་མ་ཡོད་པ་སྐད་བྱ་ན་ནི་དེའི་ཕྱིར་སངས་རྒྱས་བཅོམ་ལྡན་འདས་ལ་མི་མཁྱེན་པ་ཡོད་པར་འགྱུར་ཏེ། །མི་མཁྱེན་མི་སྲིད་པས་ཐོམ་པ་ཡང་བསྟན་དགོས་སོ། །མ་བསྟན་ན་ཡང་རིགས་པ་འདི་དང་སྦྱར་[260] ན་མེད་དུ་མི་རུང་སྟེ [《སྡེ་》 14a.1] དེ་བས་ན།

((y) །གཉིས་པ། འདོད་པ་ལ་བསལ་བ་དགོད་པ།)

ཐོམ་པ་ཡོད་ན་ངེས་པར་ཡང་།[261]

།ལྟ་བར་གྱུར་པ་ཡོངས་སུ་འཛིན། **|| 14ab ||**

།ཐོམ་པ་ཡོད་པར་བརྟགས་ན་ནི། །འཁོར་བ་ཐོག་མ་ཅན་དུ་འགྱུར་རོ། །ཐོག་མ་ཡོད་པ་ཅན་དུ་གྱུར་ན་ནི་རྒྱུ་མེད་པར་སྐྱེ་བ་ཁས་བླངས་པས་ལོག་པར་ལྟ་བ་ཉིད་དུ་འགྱུར་རོ།

((ii) །གཉིས་པ། རང་ཕྱོགས་ལ་ཉེས་པ་མེད་པ།)
((x) །དང་པོ། རྟེན་འབྱུང་མཐའ་བྲལ་དུ་བསྟན་པ།)

།རྟེན་ཅིང་འབྲེལ་པར་འབྱུང་བ་སྨྲ་བ་ལ་ནི་ཉེས་པ་འདི་མེད་དོ། །སུ་དངོས་པོ་རྣམས་རྟེན་ཅིང་འབྲེལ་པར་འབྱུང་བའི་འདོད་པ་དེ་ནི་དེ་དག་ངོ་བོ་ཉིད་ཀྱིས་མ་སྐྱེས་པར་འདོད་པས་དེ་དག་གི་ཐོག་མ་

---

[259] 《པེ་》《སྣར་》: ཐོགས་

[260] 《ཅོ་》: སྦྱིར་

[261] 《པེ་》《སྣར་》《ཏྲི་》{SS}: ཡང་། 《སྡེ་》: ཡོང་། 《ཅོ་》: ཡོད།

འམ་ཐ་མ་མེད་པས་ཡོངས་སུ་བརྟག་པ་མི་ནུས་པར་བསྟན་ [«ཅོ་» 13b.1] པའི་ཕྱིར། [«པེ་» 16a.1]

རྟེན་ཅིང་འབྲེལ་པར་གང་འབྱུང་བ།
།དེ་ལ་སྔོན་དང་ཐ་མ་ཅི། || **14cd** ||

།ཞེས་བྱ་བ་སྨོས་ཏེ་གདོན་མི་ཟ་བར་འདི་ཉིད་ཁས་བླངས་དགོས་སོ།

((y) །གཉིས་པ། རང་བཞིན་ཡོད་ན་རྟག་པར་ཐལ་བ།)

།གཞན་དུ་ན་ནི་འཁོར་བ་ཐོག་མ་ཅན་དུ་འགྱུར་བར་ཡང་མ་ཟད་དེ། །ངོ་བོ་ཉིད་ཀྱིས་སྐྱེས་པ་ན་[262] གཞན་དུ་འགྱུར་མི་སྲིད་པས་རྟག་པ་ཁོ་ནརཿ གྱུར་པར་[263] བསྟན་པའི་ཕྱིར།

སྔོན་སྐྱེས་པ་ནི་ཇི་ལྟ་བུར།
།ཕྱི་ནས་རབ་ཏུ་ལྡོག་པར་འགྱུར། || **15ab** ||

།ཞེས་བྱ་བ་སྨོས་སོ། །ངོ་བོ་ཉིད་མི་འགྱུར་བས་རྟག་གོ་ཞེས་བྱ་བའི་ཐ་ཚིག་གོ། །དངོས་པོ་སྐྱེ་བ་དེའི་རང་བཞིན་མེད་པ་ལས་འབྱུང་བ་ཁས་ལེན་ན་ནི། །རྫོམ་པ་ཡོད་ན་ངེས་པར་ཡང་། །ལྟ་བར་གྱུར་ [«སྣར་» 17a.1] པ་ཡོངས་སུ་འཛིན། །མེད་པ་ལས་དངོས་པོ་རྣམསཿ རྒྱུན་མི་[264] རྒྱུ་མེད་པ་ཁོ་ན་ལས་སྐྱེ་བར་འགྱུར་རོ། །དེ་བས་ན་རྒྱུ་མེད་པར་ལྟ་བ་དེ་ཡང་དེ་བཞིན་དུ་ཡོད་ལ་དེ་ཡང་འབྲེལ་ན་ནི་ཆད་པར་ལྟ་བའི་སྐྱོན་དུ་ཡང་འགྱུར་རོ། །ནམ་ཞིག་འདི་ལ། །རྟེན་ཅིང་འབྲེལ་པར་

---

262 «པེ་»«སྣར་»{SS}: ནི་

263 «པེ་»«སྣར་»{SS}: འགྱུར་བར་

264 «པེ་»«སྣར་»{SS}: སྐྱེ་ན་ནི་

གང་འབྱུང་བ། །དེ་ལ་སྔོན་དང་ཕ་མ་ཅི། །ངོ་བོ་ཉིད་ཀྱིས་མ་སྐྱེས་པའི་ཕྱིར་ཏེ། །འདི་ལྟར་རྟེན་ཅིང་འབྲེལ་པར་འབྱུང་བས་འདི་ནི་ངོ་བོ་ཉིད་ཀྱིས་མ་སྐྱེས་པའོ།

((z) །གསུམ་པ། རང་བཞིན་མེད་པའི་དཔེ་བསྟན་པ།)

((1") །དང་པོ། དཔེའི་སྒྲོ་ནས་མདོར་བསྟན་པ།)

།དེས་ན་ཐེ་ཚོམ་མེད་པར།

སྔོན་དང་ཕྱི་མའི་[265] མཐའ་སྤངས་པས།[266]
།འགྲོ་བ་སྒྱུ་མ་བཞིན་དུ་སྣང་། ‖ **15cd** ‖

།ཇི་ལྟར་སྒྱུ་མ་མཁན་གྱིས་སྒྱུ་མ་སྤྲུལ་པའི་སྔགས་ཀྱི་སྦྱོར་བ་ལས་[267] གླང་པོ་ཆེ་དང་རྟ་དང་མི་ལ་སོགས་པ་བྱུང་བ་རྣམས་ངོ་བོ་ཉིད་ཀྱིས་མ་སྐྱེས་ན་གླང་པོ་ཆེ་ལ་སོགས་པར་སྣང་སྟེ། །དེ་དག་ལ་གླང་པོ་ཆེ་ཡང་དག་པ་ལ་སོགས་པ་ལྟར་སྔོན་དང་ཕ་མའི་[268] རྟོག་པ་མི་འབྱུང་བ་དེ་བཞིན་དུ་གླང་པོ་ཆེ་ཡང་དག་པ་ལ་སོགས་པར་འདོད་པ་རྣམས་ཀྱང་རྟེན་ཅིང་ [《སྟེ་》 14b.1] འབྲེལ་པར་འབྱུང་བས་སྔོན་དང་ཕྱི་མའི་མཐར་བརྟག་[269] པ་མི་རིགས་ཏེ་དེ་ལྟར་ན། །སྔོན་དང་ཕྱི་མའི་མཐའ་སྤངས་པ། །འགྲོ་བ་སྒྱུ་མ་བཞིན་དུ་སྣང་། །སྐྱེས་ནས་སྐད་ཅིག་ཀྱང་མི་སྡོད་པར་འགྲོ་བས་འགྲོ་བར་

265 《སྣར་》: མིའི་

266 {SS}: པ་ following {Dh}

267 《པེ་》《སྣར་》{SS}: ལ་

268 《ཅོ་》: མིའི་

269 《སྣར་》: བཏག་

བྱའོ།[270] །སླུ་[271] བའི་བདག་ཉིད་པས་སྒྱུ་མ་སྟེ། །དེའི་ངོ་བོ་ཉིད་ལ་རྨོངས་[272] པ་རྣམས་ལ་[273] ལོག་པར་སྣང་བས་སླུ་[274] བ་ཡིན་ [«པེ་» 16b.1] ནོ།

((2") །གཉིས་པ། དངོས་བཤད་པ།)

།དེའི་སླུ་[275] བ་ཉིད་བསྟན་པའི་ཕྱིར།

གང་ཚེ་སྒྱུ་མ་བྱུང་[276] ཞེ་འམ།
།གང་གི་ཚེ་ན་འཇིག་འགྱུར་ཞེས།
།སྒྱུ་མ་ཤེས་པ་དེར་མི་རྨོངས།
།སྒྱུ་མ་མི་ཤེས་ཡོངས་སུ་སྒོམ། || **16** ||

།ཞེས་བྱ་བ་སྨོས་སོ། །ཇི་ལྟར་སྒྱུ་མ་མཁན་གྱི་སྔགས་ཀྱི་རྐྱེན་ལས་བྱུང་བའི་བུད་མེད་ན་ཆུང་སྒྱུ་ཐབས་རྣམས་ལེགས་པར་ [«ཅོ་» 14a.1] བསླབས་པ་ལྷ་བུ་དབྱིབས་དང་སྤྱོད་ལམ་ཤིན་ཏུ་མཛེས་པ་ཚུལ་ཤིན་ཏུ་[277] མཛེས་ཤིང་གཞོགས་སྟེགས་[278] ལ་མཁས་པ་ཕུན་སུམ་ཚོགས་པ་ཡིད་

---

270 «པེ་»«སྣར་»: བའོ།

271 «པེ་»«སྣར་»{SS}: །བསླུ་

272 «པེ་»: རྨོངས་

273 «པེ་»: མ་

274 «པེ་»«སྣར་»{SS}: བསླུ་

275 «པེ་»«སྣར་»{SS}: བསླུ་

276 {SS}: འབྱུང་

277 «སྣར་»: དུ་

278 «པེ་»«སྣར་»: གཞོག་སྟེག་

འཕྲོག་པ་དག་ནི་དེའི་ངོ་བོ་ཉིད་ལ་མི་མཁས་པ་འདོད་པ་ལ་ཞེན་པ་རྣམས་ལ་ན་ [«སྣར་» 17b.1] ཆུང་ཡང་དག་པ་བཞིན་དུ་མཆོག་ཏུ་དགའ་བའི་གནས་སུ་འགྱུར་ཏེ། །དེ་ལ་ཇི་ལྟར་མི་མཁས་པ་དག་རྣམ་པར་རྟོག་པ་ལྟར་རང་བཞིན་མེད་དེ་དེའི་ངོ་བོ་ཉིད་ལ་མཁས་པ་སྒྱུ་མ་མཁན་ནི་སྒྱུ་མ་ཡང་དག་པ་མ་ཡིན་པར་སྣང་བ་ཁོང་དུ་ཆུད་པས་དེ་ལྟར་ཡང་རྨོངས་པའི་སེམས་མི་འབྱུང་ངོ་།

((3") །གསུམ་པ། དོན་བཤད་པ།)

།དེ་བཞིན་དུ་འདིར་ཡང་སྒྱུ་མ་མཁན་ལྟ་བུའི་རྣལ་འབྱོར་པ་མཁས་པ་རྣམས་ཀྱིས།

སྲིད་པ་སྨིག་རྒྱུ་སྒྱུ་[279] འདྲ་བར།
།བློ་ཡིས་མཐོང་བར་གྱུར་ན་ནི།
།སྔོན་གྱི་མཐའ་འམ་ཕྱི་མའི་མཐར།[280]
།ལྟ་བས་ཡོངས་སུ་བསླད་མི་འགྱུར། || 17 ||

།རྣལ་འབྱོར་པས་སྲིད་པ་འདུས་བྱས་མ་ལུས་པ་སྒྱུ་མ་དང་སྨིག་རྒྱུ་བ་[281] ལྟ་བུར་བློ་ཡང་དག་པའི་བསམ་པ་སོ་སོ་[282] རང་གི་ཤེས་རབ་ཀྱིས་[283] མཐོང་ན་དོན་དམ་[284] པའི་ངོ་བོ་ཉིད་དུ་གང་ཡང་མི་དམིགས་པས་དངོས་པོའི་རང་བཞིན་གང་ཡིན་པ་དེ་ལ་སྔོན་གྱི་མཐའ་འམ། །ཕྱི་མའི་མཐར་ཡོངས་

---

279 «པེ་»: - སྒྱུ་; appears to be due to a deficiency in the printing block.

280 «སྣར་»: མཐའ།

281 {SS}: -བ་

282 «སྣར་» {SS}: སོར་

283 «པེ་» «སྣར་»: ཀྱི་

284 «སྣར་»: དོམ་

སུ་བསྙད་པར་མི་འགྱུར་ཏེ། །བློ་ཕྱིན་ཅི་ལོག་པར་མི་འགྱུར་རོ། །དེ་བས་ན་འཕགས་པའི་སྐྱེ་བོར་[285] ཐམས་ཅད་གཞིགས་ཤིང་རྗེས་སུ་གཞིགས་པ་ངོ་བོ་ཉིད་མེད་པའི་ལམ་འདི་བོར་ནས་བདག་[286] ནི་སྒྱུ་མའི་བུད་མེད་ལ་མི་མཁས་པ་དག་བཞིན་དུ།

(3. །གསུམ་པ། མཐའ་གཉིས་ཀྱི་ངོ་བོ་དགག་པ།)

(a. །དང་པོ། འཐད་པ་དགོད་པ།)

(i. །དང་པོ། སྐབས་འགོད་པ།)

གང་དག་གིས་ནི་འདུས་བྱས་ལ།
།སྐྱེ་དང་འགག་པར་རྣམ་བརྟག་[287] པ།
།དེ་དག་རྟེན་འབྱུང་ [«སྡེ་» 15a.1] འཁོར་ལོ་ཡི།
།འགྲོ་བ་ཤིན་ཏུ་མི་ཤེས་སོ། **|| 18 ||**

།རང་གི་མཚན་ཉིད་སྐྱེ། །རང་གི་མཚན་ཉིད་ [«པེ་» 17a.1] འགག་གོ་ཞེས་དེ་ལྟར་གང་དག་རང་གི་མཚན་ཉིད་སྐྱེ་ཞིང་འགག་པའི་ཚུལ་གྱིས་འདུས་བྱས་ཀྱི་[288] སྐྱེ་བ་[289] དང་འགག་པ་

---

285 {SS}: བ་

286 «པེ་» «སྣར་» {SS}: བ་དག་

287 «པེ་» «སྣར་» {SS}: བརྟགས་

288 «པེ་»: བྱ་སྐྱེ་

289 «སྣར་»: བོ་

ཡོངས་སུ་བརྟགས་པ་དག་གིས་[290] ནི་རྟེན་ཅིང་འབྲེལ་པར་འབྱུང་བའི་འཁོར་ལོ་ལ་ཐོག་མ་དང་དབུས་དང་། །ཐ་མ་དང་བྲལ་བ་མགལ་མེ་བསྐོར་བ་ལྟ་བུའི་འགྲོ་བ་འཇུག་[291] པ་ཤིན་ཏུ་མི་ཤེས་ཏེ།[292]

(ii. །གཉིས་པ། འཐད་པ་དངོས།)

((1) །དང་པོ། སྤྱིའི་དོན།)

།འདུས་བྱས་རང་བཞིན་ཡོད་པ་སྐྱེ་ཞིང་འཇིག་མི་སྲིད་པ་ལ་སྐྱེ་བ་དང་འཇིག་པ་རྟོག་པས་དེ་དག་གིས་རྟེན་ཅིང་འབྲེལ་པར་འབྱུང་བའི་འཁོར་ལོ་ཁོང་དུ་ཆུད་ཅེས་བྱའོ།

((2) །གཉིས་པ། ཡན་ལག་གི་དོན་ཏོ།)

((a) །དང་པོ། སྐྱེ་བའི་མཐའ་དགག་པ།)

།རང་གི་མཚན་ཉིད་དུ་སྐྱེ་བར་ཁས་བླངས་ན་ཅིའི་ཕྱིར་རྟེན་ཅིང་འབྲེལ་ [《ཅོ་》 14b.1] པར་འབྱུང་བའི་དོན་ཁོང་དུ་ཆུད་པ་མ་ཡིན་ཞེས་ཟེར་བ་དེ་ལ།

དེ་དང་དེ་བརྟེན་གང་བྱུང་[293] བ།
།རང་བཞིན་དུ་ནི་[294] དེ་མ་[295] སྐྱེས།

---

[290] 《ཏྲི་》 glosses this as: མི་མཁས་པ་གང་དག་

[291] 《སྣར་》: འཇིག་

[292] 《སྣར་》: ཤེ་སྟེ།

[293] 《པེ་》《སྣར་》: བརྟེན་གང་འབྱུང་ MABh: རྟེན་གང་འབྱུང་

[294] MABh: གི་ངོ་བོར་

[295] 《སྣར་》: ན་

།རང་བཞིན་དུ་ནི་ [«སྣར་» 18a.1] གང་མ་སྐྱེས།[296]
།དེ་ནི་སྐྱེས་[297] ཞེས་[298] ཇི་སྐད་བྱ།[299] **|| 19 ||**

།ཞེས་བྱ་བ་སྨོས་སོ། །དེ་དང་དེ་བརྟེན་ཞེས་བྱ་བ་ནི་དེ་དང་དེ་ལ་ལྟོས་ཞེས་བྱ་བའི་ཐ་ཚིག་གོ།[300] །དེ་དང་དེ་ཞེས་བྱ་བ་སྤྱིར་བསླུག་པ་ཐམས་ཅད་བསྡུ་བའི་ཕྱིར་[301] ཚིག་འདིས་ནང་གི་མ་རིག་པ་ལ་སོགས་པ་དང་ཕྱིའི་རླུང་གི་དཀྱིལ་འཁོར་ལ་སོགས་པ་མ་ལུས་པ་དག་འདུ་བྱེད་ལ་སོགས་པ་དང་ཆུའི་དཀྱིལ་འཁོར་ལ་སོགས་པ་སྐྱེ་བ་ལ་རྒྱུའི་དངོས་པོར་གནས་པར་གྱུར་ཏེ།

།རྒྱུ་དེ་དང་དེ་ལ་བརྟེན་ནས་གང་སྐྱེ་བ་དེ་གལ་ཏེ་རང་གི་ངོ་བོས་[302] གྲུབ་པ་ཞིག་ཡིན་ན་ནི་དེ་ཡོད་པར་གྱུར་པས་གྲུབ་པའི་ངོ་བོའི་དུས་བཞིན་དུ་སྐྱེ་བའི་རྒྱུ་ལ་མི་ལྟོས་པར་འགྱུར་རོ། །ཇི་སྟེ་སྐྱེ་བ་དེ་སྔོན་རང་གི་ངོ་བོ་[303] མེད་ན་ནི་སྐྱེས་པ་དེ་ཡང་གཟུགས་བརྙན་བཞིན་དུ་ངོ་བོ་ཉིད་ཀྱིས་ཡོད་པ་མ་ཡིན་པར་མངོན་པས། །དེ་དང་དེ་བརྟེན་གང་བྱུང་བ། །རང་བཞིན་དུ་ནི་དེ་མ་སྐྱེས། །ཞེས་བྱ་བ་སྨོས་སོ།

---

296 MABh: གི་ངོ་བོར་མ་སྐྱེས་གང་།

297 «པེ་» «སྣར་» : སྐྱེ་

298 {SS}: ཞེས་ after {Dh}

299 The Skt. preserved in various sources (cf. Scherrer-Schaub, *Yuktiṣaṣṭikāvṛtti*, 188 n. 290) and given by Lindtner (*Nāgārjuniana*, 108–109, and n. 19) reads: *tat tat prāpya yad utpannaṁ nôtpannaṁ tat svabhāvataḥ | svabhāvena yan nôtpannam utpannaṁ nāma tat katham ||*.

300 «ཏྣི་» glosses this as: རྒྱུ་དང་རྐྱེན་དེ་དང་དེ་ལ་བརྟེན་

301 «པེ་» «སྣར་» «ཅོ་» : ཕྱིའི་

302 «པེ་» «སྣར་» {SS}: བོར་

303 «པེ་» «སྣར་» {SS}: བོར་

།ཅི་སྐྱེ་བ་ངོ་བོ་ཉིད་ཀྱིས་མེད་ཀྱང་སླ་[304] སྟེ་ཐ་སྙད་དུ་གཟུགས་སྐྱེས་སོ། །ཚོར་བ་སྐྱེས་སོ་ཞེས་བྱ་བས་སྐྱེ་བ་ཡོད་དོ་སྙམ་དུ་སེམས་ན་ནི་

ཀྱེ་མ་ལམ་ལོག་པར་སོང་དུ་གདོན་མི་ཟའོ། །མཁས་པས་ནི་གཟུ་[305] བོ་ལྟ་བུའི་བློས་རྣམ་[«པེ་» 17b.1] པར་དཔྱད་པའི་རིགས་པ་སྙམ། །རང་བཞིན་དུ་ནི་གང་མ་སྐྱེས། །དེ་ནི་སྐྱེས་ཞེས་ཇི་སྐད་བྱ།

།སའི་རང་གི་མཚན་ཉིད་ནི་སྲ་[306] བ་སྟེ། །གལ་ཏེ་དེ་རང་གི་མཚན་ཉིད་དུ་ [«སྡེ་» 15b.1] མ་སྐྱེས་པར་སེམས་ན་དེ་གཤེར་བའི་མཚན་ཉིད་དུ་སྐྱེས་སོ་[307] ཞེས་བརྟག་ཏུ་ནི་མི་རུང་ན། །དེ་གཞན་གང་ཅི་ཞིག་ཏུ་སྐྱེ་བར་བརྟག

།དེ་བས་ན་བདག་དང་གཞན་ལས་སྐྱེ་མི་སྲིད་པས་སྐྱེ་བ་མེད་[308] གྲུབ་བོ།[309]

((b) །གཉིས་པ། འཇིག་པའི་མཐའ་དགག་པ།)

།དེ་ལྟར་རྟེན་ཅིང་འབྲེལ་པར་འབྱུང་བ་ལ་སྐྱེ་བ་མི་སྲིད་པ་ཅི་བསྟན་ནས།[310] །ད་ནི་འགག་པ་མི་སྲིད་པར་བསྟན་པར་བཞེད་ནས།

---

304 «པེ་» {SS}: སླ་ «སྣར་» «སྡེ་» «ཅོ་»: ཟླ་

305 «སྣར་»: གཟོ་

306 «པེ་» «སྣར་» {SS}: སྲ་ «སྡེ་» «ཅོ་»: ཕྲ་

307 «པེ་» «སྣར་» {SS}: སོ། «སྡེ་» «ཅོ་»: ས་

308 «པེ་» «སྣར་» {SS}: +པར་

309 {SS}: པོ།

310 «པེ་» «སྣར་»: ན།

རྒྱུ་ཟད་པ་ཡིས་[311] ཞི་བ་ནི།
།ཟད་ཅེས་བྱ་བར་མངོན་པ་སྟེ།
།རང་བཞིན་དུ་[312] ནི་གང་མ་ཟད།
།དེ་ལ་ཟད་ཅེས་ཇི་སྐད་བརྗོད། ‖ **20** ‖

།ཅེས་བྱ་བ་སྨོས་སོ། །སྐྱེས་པའི་དངོས་པོ་སྐྱེ་བ་ཡོད་ན་འཇིག་ལ་དངོས་པོའི་གནས་པ་ཡང་རྐྱེན་གྱི་ཁ་ན་ལས་ཏེ་གནས་པའི་རྐྱེན་མེད་ན་འཇིག་པར་འགྱུར་བས་དེ་ལྟར་[313] ན་འཇིག་རྟེན་ན་རྒྱུ་ཟད་ནས་ཞི་བ་དང་མྱ་ངན་ལས་འདས་[314] པ་གང་ཡིན་པ་དེ་ཉིད་ [«སྣར་» 18b.1] ཞི་བ་ཞེས་བྱ་བར་དམིགས་ཏེ། [«ཅོ་» 15a.1] །གང་ཡང་གནས་པའི་རྐྱེན་མེད་ན་ཟད་པར་འགྱུར་བ་དེ་གནས་པའི་རྐྱེན་མེད་པ་ལ་རག་ལས་པས་རང་གི་ངོ་བོར་གྲུབ་པ་མེད་པར་ཁོང་དུ་ཆུད་ནས། །རང་བཞིན་གྱིས་ནི་གང་མ་ཟད། །དེ་ལ་ཟད་ཅེས་ཇི་སྐད་བརྗོད། །ཅེས་བྱ་བ་སྨོས་སོ།

།གལ་ཏེ་རང་བཞིན་གྱིས་ཟད་པ་ཞིག་ཡོད་ན་ནི་དེ་[315] རྐྱེན་ལ་ལྟོས་པར་མི་འགྱུར་རོ།[316] །དེ་རྒྱུ་ཡོངས་སུ་ཟད་པ་ལས་མ་ཡིན་པར་འགྱུར་རོ། །དེའི་ཕྱིར་ལས་དང་ཉོན་མོངས་པའི་དངོས་པོ་མེད་པར་མ་གྱུར་ཀྱང་མྱ་ངན་ལས་འདས་པར་འགྱུར་ཏེ། །དེ་བས་ན་འབད་མི་དགོས་པར་ཐར་བར་འགྱུར་

311 «པེ་»«སྣར་»: ཡི་

312 {SS}: གྱིས་

313 «པེ་»«སྣར་»: ལྟ་

314 «པེ་»: -འདས་

315 «ཅོ་»: -དེ་; appears to have been edited out.

316 «པེ་»«སྣར་»{SS}: ཏེ།

རོ། །མར་དང་རས་ཡོངས་སུ་མ་ཟད་པར་མར་མེ་འཆི་བར་འགྱུར་བའི་རིགས་ན་དེ་ཡང་དེ་ལྟ་མ་ཡིན་པས་རང་གི་ངོ་བོར་གྲུབ་པའི་འགག་པ་མེད་དོ།

།ཅི་སྟེ་མར་དང་རས་ཡོངས་སུ་ཟད་པ་ནི་མར་མེའི་འཆི་བའི་རྒྱུ་མ་ཡིན་ཏེ། །ཇི་ལྟ་[317] ཞེ་ན།

མར་དང་རས་ལྷན་ཅིག་ཏུ་འགགས་ལ་མར་མེའི་སྐད་ཅིག་མ་ཐ་མ་དེའི་ [«པེ་» 18a.1] རིགས་ཀྱི་མར་མེ་སྐད་ཅིག་མ་མ་འོངས་པའི་ལྷན་ཅིག་བྱེད་པའི་རྒྱུ་མེད་པས་སྐྱེ་བའི་ཡན་ལག་གི་དངོས་པོར་མ་གྱུར་པ་མ་འགགས་སོ། །མ་འོངས་པ་ཡང་སྐྱེ་བའི་རྐྱེན་མེད་པས་མ་སྐྱེས་ཏེ། །དེ་ལྟ་བས་ན་མ་འོངས་པའི་རྐྱེན་མེད་པས་འདི་ལ་སྐྱེ་བ་མེད་ཅེས་བྱའོ།

།སྙམ་དུ་སེམས་ན་ཡང་དེ་ལྟར་མ་འོངས་པའི་རྐྱེན་མེད་པ་མི་སྐྱེ་བའི་རྒྱུར་འགྱུར་ན་ནི་གལ་ཏེ་རྐྱེན་མེད་པར་མ་གྱུར་ [«སྡེ་» 16a.1] ན་གདོན་མི་ཟ་བར་སྐྱེ་བར་འགྱུར་རོ། །དེ་ལྟར་ན་མི་སྐྱེ་བ་ཡང་རྒྱུ་ཉིད་དུ་ཁས་བླངས་པ་ཡིན་ནོ་དེ་ལྟར་ཁས་ལེན་ན་རྒྱུ་ཟད་ནས་ཞི་བ་གང་ཡིན་པ་དེ་ཟད་པ་ཞེས་བྱ་བར་ཁས་བླངས་པ་ཡིན་ནོ།

།གང་དག་དངོས་པོ་རྣམས་ཀྱི་འགག་པ་རྒྱུ་མེད་པ་[318] ཡིན་པར་འཛིན་པ་དེ་དག་གི་འགག་པ་དེ་དངོས་པོ་[319] ལ་བརྟེན་པར་མི་འགྱུར་ཏེ། །ནམ་མཁའི་མེ་ཏོག་ལ་སོགས་པ་བཞིན་དུ་རྒྱུ་མེད་པའི་ཕྱིར་རོ།

།གལ་ཏེ་དངོས་པོ་མེད་པའི་ཕྱིར་རྫ་མ་ལ་སོགས་པ་ཡང་རྟེན་ཅིང་འབྲེལ་པར་འབྱུང་བ་མ་ཡིན་ན་དེ་དག་ཀྱང་དངོས་པོ་ལ་བརྟེན་པས་དེ་བས་ན་དེ་དག་གཅིག་ཏུ་ངེས་པ་མེད་དོ་ཞེ་ན་ཡང་།

འཇིག་རྟེན་ན་རྒྱུ་དང་བཅས་པ་གྲགས་པས་དེ་དག་[320] ལྟར་མ་ཡིན་ནོ། །ཡང་ན་དེ་དག་ཀྱང་འགག་པ་བཞིན་དུ་དངོས་པོ་ལ་བརྟེན་པ་མེད་པའི་སྐྱོན་དུ་འགྱུར་ [«ཅོ་» 15b.1] རོ།

---

[317] «པེ་»«སྣར་» {SS}: ལྟར་

[318] «ཅོ་»: པར་

[319] «སྣར་»: -པོ་

།གལ་ཏེ་མེད་པ་ལ་རྒྱུ་ཞེས་ཇི་སྐད་དུ་བྱ་ཞེ་ན།

།ཡོད་པ་ལས་[321] ཡང་རྒྱུ་ཞེས་ཇི་སྐད་དུ་བྱ། །ས་བོན་ [«སྣར་» 19a.1] ཡོད་པའི་དུས་ཉིད་ན། །མྱུ་གུའི་རྒྱུའི་དངོས་པོར་ནི་ཤེས་པར་མི་རུང་སྟེ། །མེད་པར་འགྱུར་བའི་ཚེ་རྒྱུར་འགྱུར་རོ། །དཔེར་ན་མེད་པར་འགྱུར་བའི་རྣམ་པར་ཤེས་པ་ཉིད་རྣམ་པར་ཤེས་པ་གཞན་གྱི་དེ་མ་ཐག་པའི་རྐྱེན་དུ་ཁས་བླངས་པ་[322] ལྟ་བུ་སྟེ། །རྣམ་པར་ཤེས་པ་དེ་ཡོད་པའི་དུས་ན་རྣམ་པར་ཤེས་པ་གཞན་གྱི་རྒྱུ་ཡིན་ནོ་ཞེས་ནི་བརྗོད་པར་མི་ནུས་སོ། །རྣམ་པར་ཤེས་པ་གཉིས་ཅིག་ཅར་དུ་མི་འབྱུང་བའི་ཕྱིར་རོ། །ཡོད་པ་དང་མེད་པ་གཉིས་ཀྱི་གནས་པ་རྟོགས་[323] པའི་རྣམ་པར་ཤེས་པ་གཞན་ནི་[324] མི་སྲིད་དོ།

།ཡ་ལ་རྒྱུ་འགགས་མ་ [«པེ་» 18b.1] ཐག་པ་ནི་འབྲས་བུ་སྐྱེ་བའི་[325] རྐྱེན་ཡིན་ནོ་ཞེས་བྱ་བར་[326] མི་རིགས་སོ་ཟེར་བ་ཡང་ཡོད།

།དེ་བས་ན་མེད་པ་ཡང་རྒྱུར་སྲིད་པས་མེད་པ་རྒྱུར་མི་རུང་ངོ་ཞེས་བྱ་བར་མི་རིགས་སོ།

།གལ་ཏེ་རིགས་པས་རྣམ་པར་དཔྱད་ན་རྒྱུར་མི་སྲིད་དོ་ཞེ་ན་ཡང་དེ་ནི་དེ་ལྟ་མ་ཡིན་ཏེ། །འཇིག་རྟེན་གྱི་དངོས་པོ་རྣམས་ནི་རྣམ་པར་བརྟག་ཅིང་ཁས་བླང་བར་མི་བྱ་སྟེ། །འཇིག་རྟེན་ཇི་ལྟ་བ་བཞིན་

---

320 {SS}: +དེ་

321 «པེ་» «སྣར་» {SS}: ལ་

322 «པེ་» «སྣར་»: བླང་བ་

323 «པེ་» «སྣར་»: མ་རྟོགས་ {SS}: མ་གཏོགས་

324 «པེ་» «སྣར་»: ན་

325 «ཅོ་»: སྐྱེས་པའི་

326 «པེ་» «སྣར་»: བ་

དུའོ། །འཇིག་རྟེན་ན་ཡང་མེད་པ་ལ་རྒྱུ་ཞེས་བྱ་བར་[327] ཡོད་དེ། །འདི་ལྟར་ཆུ་མེད་པས་འབྲུ་མ་རུང་བརཿའགྱུར་རོ།[328] །ཟན་མེད་པས་ངའི་བུ་ཤིའོ། །ཞེས་དེ་སྐད་དུ་ཆུ་དང་ཟན་མེད་པས་འབྲུ་དང་བུ་མཿརུང་བར་[329] བྱས་སོ་ཞེས་ཟེར་རོ། །འཇིག་ [«སྡེ་» 16b.1] རྟེན་པའི་ཐ་སྙད་ཐམས་ཅད་ལ་འཐད་པ་མེད་པས། །འཇིག་རྟེན་ན་གྲགས་པའི་དོན་རྣམས་ཀྱང་འཇིག་རྟེན་ན་གྲགས་པས་རྣམ་པར་གཞག་པར་བྱ་སྟེ། །འཐད་པས་ནི་མ་ཡིན་ནོ། །ཆུ་ལ་སོགས་པ་མེད་པ་ནི་འཇིག་པའི་རྒྱུ་ཞེས་བྱ་བ་ཡོད་དེ། །དེ་བས་ན། །རྒྱུ་ཟདཿཔ་ཡིས་[330] ཞི་བ་ནི། །ཟད་ཅེས་བྱ་བར་མངོན་པ་སྟེ། །ཞེས་བྱ་བ་གྲུབ་པོ།

།རྒྱུ་ཟད་པ་ཉིད་ཉེ་བར་བཟུང་ནས་ཟད་པ་ཞེས་བྱ་བར་རྣམ་པར་གཞག་སྟེ། །ཟད་པ་དེ་ནི་རྒྱུ་ཟད་པའི་སྔ་རོལ་གྱི་གནས་ན་མི་སྲིད་ལ་ཟད་ནས་ཡོད་པས་རང་གིས་གྲུབ་པའི་ངོ་བོ་ཉིད་མེད་དོ། །གང་རང་བཞིན་གྱིས་མ་ཟད་དེ་[331] རྒྱུ་ལ་མི་[332] ལྟོས་པར་ངོ་བོ་ཉིད་ཀྱིས་ཟད་པ་ཡང་མ་ཡིན་པ་དེ་དག་གཞན་གྱི་ངོ་བོ་གང་གིས་ཟད་ཅེས་བྱ་བར་རྣམ་པར་གཞག །ཟད་པ་མ་ཡིན་པའི་ངོ་བོའི་ཆོས་ནི་ཟདཿཔའི་ངོ་བོ་ཉིད་[333] མི་མཐུན་པས་ཟད་པའི་ངོ་བོར་རྣམ་པར་གཞག་ [«ཅོ་» 16a.1] པར་མི་ནུས་སོ། [«སྣར་» 19b.1]

---

327 «པེ་»«སྣར་»: བ་

328 «པེ་»«སྣར་»{SS}: འགྱུར་ཏོ།

329 «པེ་»«སྣར་»{SS}: རུངས་པར་

330 «པེ་»«སྣར་»: པའི་

331 «པེ་»«སྣར་»: ཏེ་

332 {SS}: མ་

333 «པེ་»«སྣར་»: ངོ་བོ་ཉིད་དང་། «ཅོ་»: ངོ་བོར་ཉིད་

(iii. །གསུམ་པ། །མཇུག་བསྡུ་བ།)

།གང་གི་ཕྱིར་དེ་ལྟར་སྐྱེ་བ་དང་འགག་པ་འདི་རང་གི་དངོས་པོས་ཀྱང་སྲིད་པ་མ་ཡིན་ལ། །གཞན་གྱི་དངོས་པོས་ཀྱང་མ་ཡིན་པ་དེའི་ཕྱིར་རྣལ་འབྱོར་པས་རྟེན་ཅིང་འབྲེལ་པར་འབྱུང་བ་ཇི་ལྟ་བ་བཞིན་དུ་མཐོང་སྟེ་འཐད་པས་རྣམ་པར་དཔྱད་ན།

དེ་ལྟར་གང་ཡང་སྐྱེ་བ་མེད།
།གང་ཡང་འགག་ [《པེ་》 19a.1] པར་མི་འགྱུར་རོ། **|| 21ab ||**

((b) །གཉིས་པ། ལུང་འགལ་སྤང་བ།)

((i) །དང་པོ། སྐྱེ་འཇིག་གསུངས་པ་དྲང་དོན་དུ་བསྟན།)

།ཁམ་པོ་གཉིས་པའོ།

།གལ་ཏེ་དེ་ལྟར་སྐྱེ་བ་དང་འཇིག་པ་གཉིས་མི་སྲིད་ན་བཅོམ་ལྡན་འདས་ཀྱིས།

ཀྱེ་མ་འདུ་བྱེད་རྟག་པ་[334] མེད།
།སྐྱེ་ཞིང་འཇིག་པའི་ཆོས་ཅན་ཡིན།
།སྐྱེས་ནས་འགག་པར་འགྱུར་བ་སྟེ།
།དེ་དག་ཉེ་བར་ཞི་བ་བདེ།

།ཞེས་དེ་སྐད་གསུངས་པ་ཇི་ལྟ་བུ། །གལ་ཏེ་སྐྱེ་བ་དང་འཇིག་པ་གཉིས་མེད་དུ་ཟིན་ན་དེའི་ཚེ་སྐྱེ་བ་དང་འཇིག་པའི་ལམ་སྨྱ་ངན་ལས་འདས་པར་འགྲོ་བའི་མན་ངག་བསྟན་པར་མི་འགྱུར་བ་ཞིག་ན། བསྟན་པས་དེ་བས་ན། །སྐྱེ་བ་དང་འཇིག་པ་གཉིས་ཡོད་དོ་ཞེ་ན

---

[334] 《སྣར་》: -པ་

ཡང་བཅོམ་ལྡན་འདས་ཀྱིས་དེ་སྐད་གསུངས་མོད་ཀྱི།[335] །དེ་གཉིས་རང་གི་ངོ་བོར་གྲུབ་པ་ལ་ལྟོས་ནས་གསུངས་[336] པ་ནི་མ་ཡིན་ནོ། །དེ་མེད་ཀྱང་འཇིག་རྟེན་འདི་རྟེན་ཅིང་འབྲེལ་པར་འབྱུང་བས་སྒྲུབ་པ་མཛད་དེ།

སྐྱེ་བ་དང་ནི་འཇིག་པའི་ལམ།
།དགོས་པའི་དོན་དུ་བསྟན་པའོ། || **21cd** ||

།དེ་བསྟན་པའི་སྒོ་ནས་དགོས་པ་འབབ་[337] ཞིག་སྒྲུབ་དགོས་ [《སྡེ་》 17a.1] པས་བཅོམ་ལྡན་འདས་ཀྱིས་སྐྱེ་བ་དང་འཇིག་པའི་ལམ་བསྟན་ཏོ། །སྐྱེ་བ་དང་འཇིག་པའི་ལམ་གྱིས་བསྟན་པའི་དགོས་པ་གང་ཞེ་ན།

(ii. །གཉིས་པ། སྐྱེ་འཇིག་ལ་བརྟེན་ནས་རང་བཞིན་མེད་པར་རྟོགས་ཚུལ།)
((1) །དང་པོ། དགོས།)

།དེ་བསྟན་པའི་ཕྱིར།

སྐྱེ་བ་ཞེས་པས་འཇིག་པ་ཞེས།
།འཇིག་པ་ཞེས་པས་མི་རྟག་ཞེས།
།མི་རྟག་ཉིད་ལ་འཇུག་ཞེས་པས།
།དེས་ནི་ཆོས་ཀྱང་རྟོགས་པར་འགྱུར། || **22** ||

[335] 《པེ་ P.》: གྱི།

[336] 《པེ་》: གསུམས་

[337] 《པེ་》《སྣར་》{SS}: འགའ་

།ཞེས་བྱ་བ་སྨོས་སོ། །འདུ་བྱེད་རྣམས་ལ་ཆགས་པ་ནི་མྱ་ངན་ལས་འདས་པའི་གྲོང་ཁྱེར་དུ་འགྲོ་བའི་ལམ་བསྒྲིབས་ཤིང་འདུག་པས་བཅོམ་ལྡན་འདས་ཀྱིས་དེའི་གཉེན་པོར་རེ་ཞིག་སྐྱེ་བ་དང་འཇིག་པའི་ལམ་ཨཤད་དོ། །ཇི་ལྟ[338] ཞེ་ན། །འདི་ལྟར་སྐྱེ་བ་ཤེས་པས་འཇིག་པ་ཤེས་ཞེས་བྱ་བ་སྟེ། །སྐྱེ་བ[339] འཇིག་པའི་རྒྱུ་བར་གྱུར་པའི་ཕྱིར་རོ། །འཇིག་པ་ཤེས་པ་ལ་འཇིག་པ་དང་མི་རྟག་པ་གཉིས་དོན་གཅིག་ཏུ [«སྣར་» 20a.1] ཁོང་དུ་ཆུད་པའོ། །ས་གསུམ་གྱི་མི་རྟག་པ་ཉིད་ཀྱི་མེ་རབ་ཏུ་འབར་བའི་ནང་དུ[340] འདུག་པ་ཁྱིམ་རབ་ཏུ [«པེ་» 19b.1] འབར་བར་ཆུད [«ཅོ་» 16b.1] པ་བཞིན་དུ་གདོན་མི་ཟ་བར་དེ་ལས་འདའ་བར་འདོད་ན་རྟེན་ཅིང་འབྲེལ་པར་འབྱུང་བའི་ཆོས་ཉིད་ངེས་པར་འཕྲིནཿ་པར་འགྱུར[341] པ་མ་སྐྱེས་པ་མ་འགགས་པ་ཁོང་དུ་ཆུད་ན་ངེས་མཆོག་ཏུ་ཟབ་པ་མྱ་ངན་ལས་འདས་པ་ཞེས་བྱ་བའི་ཆོས་ཁོང་དུ་ཆུད་དོ།

།དེའི་ཕྱིར་དེ་ལྟར་བློ་མཆོག་དང་ལྡན་པའི[342] རིམ་གྱིས་སྐྱེ་བ་དང་འཇིག་པའི་རྗེས་སུ་འབྲངས[343] ནས།

((2) །གཉིས་པ། ཕན་ཡོན།)

:གང་དག་རྟེན[344] ཅིང་འབྲེལཿ་པར་འབྱུང་།[345]
།སྐྱེ་དང་འཇིག་པ་རྣམ་སྤངས་པ།[346]

---

338 «པེ་» «སྣར་» {SS}: ལྟར་

339 «པེ་» «སྣར་» {SS}: +ནི་

340 «པེ་» «སྣར་» : ན་

341 «པེ་» {SS}: པར་གྱུར་ «སྣར་» : པ་གྱུར་ «སྡེ་» «ཅོ་» : པ་འགྱུར་

342 «པེ་» «སྣར་» : པ་

343 «སྣར་» : འབྲང་།

།ཞེས་པར་གྱུར་པ་དེ་དག་ནི།
།ལྟ་གྱུར་སྲིད་པའི་རྒྱ་མཚོ་རྒྱལ།[347] || 23 ||

།སྐྱེ་བ་མེད་པས་དངོས་པོར་ལྟ་བ་མེད། །འཇིག་པ་མེད་པས་ཆད་པར་ལྟ་བ་མེད་དོ། །སྐྱེ་བ་དང་འཇིག་པ་མེད་ན་རང་གི་མཚན་ཉིད་མེད་པས་[348] རྟག་པར་ལྟ་བ་མི་འབྱུང་ངོ་། །དེ་ལྟར་རྟེན་ཅིང་འབྲེལ་པར་འབྱུང་བའི་སྐྱེ་བ་དང་འཇིག་པ་མི་དམིགས་ན་ལྟ་བར་གྱུར་པའི་སྲིད་པའི་རྒྱ་མཚོ་ལས་རྒྱལ་[349] བ་ཡིན་ནོ། །ལྟ་བར་གྱུར་པ་ཉིད་སྲིད་པའི་རྒྱ་མཚོའོ། །ལྟ་བའི་ཆུ་བོ་ཉིད་ལྟ་བར་གྱུར་པའི་སྲིད་པའི་རྒྱ་མཚོ་ཡིན་ནོ། །སྟོང་པ་ཉིད་ལ་བརྟེན་པ་དག་ནི་སྟོང་པ་ཉིད་མཐོང་བའི་གྲུ་ཆེན་པོས་གདོན་མི་ཟ་བར་དེ་ལས་རྒྱལ་[350] བར་འགྱུར་རོ།

(iii. །གསུམ་པ། མངོན་ཞེན་ཅན་གྱིས་མི་རྟོགས་པར་བསྟན།)

།གང་དག་སྟོང་པ་ཉིད་དུ་ལྟ་བས་ [«སྡེ་» 17b.1] འཇིག་པ་དེ་དག་ནི་རྟེན་ཅིང་འབྲེལ་པར་འབྱུང་བ་སྐྱེ་བ་དང་འཇིག་པའི་མཐའ་གཉིས་སུ་ལྟུང་བ་དང་བྲལ་[351] བར་ཁོང་དུ་ཆུད་པར་མི་ནུས་ཏེ་དེ་དག་གདོན་མི་ཟ་བར།

---

344 «ཟིན་»: གང་ཟག་བསྟེན་

345 {SS}: འབྱུང་བ། following {Dh}

346 {SS}: པར། following {Dh}

347 «པེ་» {SS}: བརྒྱལ།

348 «པེ་» «སྣར་»: པར་

349 «པེ་» «སྣར་» {SS}: བརྒྱལ་

350 «པེ་» «སྣར་» {SS}: བརྒྱལ་

351 «ཅོ་»: བྲེལ་

སོ་སོའི་སྐྱེ་བོ་དངོས་བདག་ཅན།
།ཡོད་དང་མེད་པར་ཕྱིན་ཅི་ལོག
།ཉེས་པས་ཉོན་མོངས་དབང་གྱུར་པ།
།རང་གི་སེམས་ཀྱིས་བསླུས་པར་འགྱུར། ‖ **24** ‖

།ལས་ཇི་ལྟ་བ་དང་ཉོན་མོངས་པ་ཇི་ལྟ་བ་བཞིན་དུ་སོ་སོར་སྐྱེ་བས་སོ་སོའི་སྐྱེ་བོའོ། །གང་དངོས་པོ་རྣམས་ལ་བདག་ཉིད་དུ་གནས་པར་འཛིན་པ་དེ་དག་དངོས་བདག་གམ།[352] དངོས་པོ་ལ་བདག་ཏུ་འཛིན་པ་གང་ཡིན་པ་དེ་དག་དངོས་བདག་ཅན་ཏེ། །བདག་ཏུ་འཛིན་པས་དེ་ལ་དམིགས་པའི་ཕྱིར་རོ། །ཡང་ན་ནི་དངོས་པོ་ལ་མངོན་པར་ཞེན་ [«པེ་» 20a.1] པས་དངོས་བདག་ཅན་ཏེ། །དེ་དག་དངོས་པོ་ [«སྣར་» 20b.1] དང་དངོས་པོ་མེད་པ་ལ་ཕྱིན་ཅི་ལོག་པའི་ཉེས་པ་རང་གིས་ཡོངས་སུ་རྟོག་པས་བསྐྱེད་པས་ཉོན་མོངས་པ་རྣམས་ཀྱི་དབང་དུ་འགྱུར་རོ། །དེ་དག་དངོས་པོ་ཡིད་དུ་འོང་བའི་གནས་སུ་གྱུར་པ་ལ་ནི་རྗེས་སུ་ཆགས་པར་འགྱུར། །དེ་མེད་པ་ལ་ནི་ཁོང་ཁྲོ་བར་འགྱུར་རོ་ཞེས་བྱ་བ་ལ་སོགས་པ་དང་སྦྱར་[353] རོ།

།ཉོན་མོངས་པའི་ [«ཅོ་» 17a.1] དབང་དུ་གྱུར་པས་འཇུག་སྟེ། གང་དགེ་བ་དང་མི་དགེ་བའི་ལས་ཉེ་བར་ལེན་པ་ཡོད་ན་[354] འཁོར་བས་དེ་ལྟར་སོ་སོའི་སྐྱེ་བོ་དངོས་པོ་ལ་མངོན་པར་ཞེན་པ་རྣམས་རང་གི་སེམས་ཀྱིས་བསླུས་སོ། །དངོས་པོ་ལ་མངོན་པར་ཞེན་པ་རང་གི་སེམས་ཀྱིས་ཡོངས་སུ་བརྟགས་པ་དང་། །དངོས་པོའི་རང་གི་ངོ་བོ་རང་བཞིན་གྱིས་གྲུབ་པ་མེད་པའི་ཕྱིར་དངོས་

---

352 «པེ་» «སྣར་» {SS}: ཅན་ནམ།

353 «པེ་ P.»: སྦྱོར་

354 «པེ་» «སྣར་»: +འཁོར་བ་ན་

པོ་རྣམས་ཀྱི་དེ་བཞིན་ཉིད་མཐོང་བ་བསྒྲིབས་ཏེ་ཕྱིན་ཅི་ལོག་ཏུ་སྒྲོ་བཏགས་[355] པས་རང་གི་སེམས་ཀྱིས་བསླུས་ཏེ་བྲིད་ཅེས་བྱ་བའི་ཐ་ཚིག་གོ།

(iv. །བཞི་པ། མོས་པ་རྣམས་ཀྱིས་རྟོགས་ཚུལ།)

((1) །དང་པོ། མཛད་པ་མཐར་ཕྱིན་པ་རྣམས་ཀྱིས་རྟོགས་ཚུལ།)

།སྲུ་དག་དགེ་བའི་བཤེས་གཉེན་གྱིས་སྟོང་པ་ཉིད་བསྟན་པ་ལ་གཡངས་[356] ལྷ་བུར་མི་སེམས་ཞིང་། །འདི་ནི་ཆོས་རྣམས་ཀྱི་དོན་དམ་པ། །འདི་ནི་མྱ་ངན་ལས་འདས་པའི་གྲོང་ཁྱེར་དུ་འགྲོ་བ་ཡིན་པར་ཤེས་པ་བསླུ་[357] བའི་སེམས་ལ་བསླུ་[358] བ་ཉིད་དུ་ཡང་དག་པར་རྟོགས་ནས་སྐད་ཅིག་ཙམ་ཡང་ཡིད་མི་རྟོན་པ་དེ་དག་ནི་ངེས་པར་འཕགས་པར་གྱུར་པར་བལྟ་སྟེ།

དངོས་ལ་མཁས་པ་རྣམས་ཀྱིས་ནི།[359] [«སྡེ་» 18a.1]
།དངོས་པོ་མི་རྟག་སླུ་[360] བའི་ཆོས།
།གསོག་དང་སྟོང་པ་བདག་མེད་པ།
།རྣམ་པར་དབེན་པར་རབ་ཏུ་མཐོང་། ॥ 25 ॥

---

355 «སྣར་»: བཏགས་

356 «པེ་» «སྡེ་» «ཅོ་» {SS}: གཡངས་ «སྣར་» «ཏྲི་»: གཡང་ས་

357 «པེ་» «སྣར་» {SS}: བསླུ་

358 «པེ་» «སྣར་» {SS}: བསླུ་

359 «ཏྲི་»: མྱ་ངན་ལས་འདས་པར་འགྲོ་བའི་ལམ་དུ་རྟོགས་པའི་དངོས་པོ་ལ་མཁས་པ་རྣམས་

360 «པེ་» «སྣར་» {SS}: བསླུ་

།བྱུང་བས་དངོས་པོ་ཞེས་བྱ་སྟེ། །དངོས་པོ་ཞེས་བྱ་བའི་སྒྲ་ནི་འདུས་པ་[361] ལ་བྱའོ། །དངོས་པོ་དེ་ཡང་སྐད་ཅིག་རེ་རེ་ལ་འཇིག་པའི་ངང་ཅན་ཡིན་པས་མི་རྟག་པའོ། །དངོས་པོའི་རང་བཞིན་ནི་ངོ་བོ་ཉིད་མེད་པ་ཡིན་ན་གང་གི་[362] ཕྱིར་བྱིས་པ་རྣམས་ལ་ངོ་བོ་ཉིད་ཡོད་པར་སྣང་བ་དེའི་ཕྱིར་སྒྱུ་མ་ལ་སོགས་པ་བཞིན་དུ་སླུ་བས་ན་ [«པེ་» 20b.1] དངོས་པོ་དེ་ཉིད་སླུ་བའི་ཆོས་སོ། །རིང་དུ་གནས་པའི་མཐུ་མེད་ལ་[363] རང་བཞིན་གྱིས་ཉམ་[364] ཆུང་བས་གསོག་[365] གོ། །ངོ་བོ་ཉིད་མེད་པའི་ཕྱིར་སྟོང་པའོ། །བདག་གིས་སྟོང་པའི་ཕྱིར་བདག་མེད་པ་སྟེ། །མི་རྟག་པ་ལ་སོགས་པས་དངོས་པོའི་ངང་[366] གི་ངོ་བོ་བསྟན་ཏོ།

།དེ་བས་ན་དངོས་པོ་འདི་དེ་ལྟར་མཐོང་བས་མཁས་པ་དེ་དག་གིས་དབེན་པར་ [«སྣར་» 21a.1] མཐོང་ངོ་། །དབེན་ཞེས་བྱ་བ་ནི་སྟོང་པའོ། །དེ་ལྟར་ན་དབེན་པ་[367] མཐུན་པའི་ཕྱིར་སྐྱེ་བ་མེད་པའི་དགོན་པ་རྣམས་ལ་དབེན་པ་ཞེས་བྱ་སྟེ། །དེ་བཞིན་དུ་འདིར་ཡང་རྣལ་འབྱོར་པས་དངོས་པོ་དབེན་པར་མཐོང་ཞེས་བྱ་བ་ནི་སྟོང་པར་མཐོང་བའི་བར་ལ་བྱའོ། །དེ་དག་དངོས་པོ་ཉིད་སྐྱུར་ཏེ་དབེན་པར: མཐོང་བ་ནི་[368] མཐོང་བ་མ་ཡིན་གྱི། །དངོས་པོ་སྟོང་པར་གྱུར་པ་ལ་སྟོང་པར་མཐོང་ངོ་།

---

[361] «པེ་» «སྣར་» {SS}: བྱས་

[362] «པེ་» «སྣར་»: གིས་

[363] «ཅོ་»: པ་

[364] «པེ་»: ཉམས་

[365] «པེ་» «སྣར་»: བསོག་ Skt. **rikta.*

[366] {SS}: ངང་གང་ «པེ་» «སྣར་»: +གང་

[367] «པེ་» «སྣར་» {SS}: +དང་

[368] «པེ་» «སྣར་» {SS}: མཐོང་བ་ནི་ «སྡེ་» «ཅོ་»: -མཐོང་བ་ནི་

།སྟོང་པ་ཉིད་བསྟན་[369] པའི་ [《ཅོ་》 17b.1] ཕྱིར་མི་རྟག་པ་ལ་སོགས་པ་བྱེ་བྲག་རྣམས་སྨོས་སོ།

།ཡང་ན་དབེན་པ་ནི་དྲི་མ་མེད་པ་ཡིན་ན་འདི་ལྟར་སོ་སོའི་སྐྱེ་བོ་རྣམས་ཕྱིན་ཅི་ལོག་ཏུ་གྱུར་པ་རང་བཞིན་གྱིས་ཡོངས་སུ་དག་པའི་དངོས་པོ་ཡང་རང་གི་རྟོག་པའི་དྲི་མས་སྦགས་པའི་ཕྱིར་ཕྱིན་ཅི་ལོག་ཏུ་ཁོང་དུ་ཆུད་ཀྱི་འཕགས་པ་རྣམས་ནི་དེ་ལྟ་མ་ཡིན་ཏེ། །དེ་དག་ནི་མེད་པ་ལ་སྒྲོ་མི་འདོགས་པར་དབེན་པར་དྲི་མ་མེད་པ་ཉིད་དུ་གཟིགས་སོ།

།ཡང་ན་འཕགས་པ་རྣམས་དེ་ཁོ་ནའི་ཡེ་ཤེས་ལས་བཞེངས་ནས་དངོས་པོ་ལ་གཟིགས་ན་དབེན་པར་གཟིགས་སོ་ཞེས་བྱ་བའི་ཐ་ཚིག་གོ། །འཕགས་པ་མཛད་པ་མཐར་ཕྱིན་པ་ཉི་ཚོས་འདི་ལྟར་གཟིགས་པར་ཡང་མ་ཟད་དེ།

((2) །གཉིས་པ། སློབ་དཔོན་རང་ཉིད་ཀྱིས་གཟིགས་ཚུལ།)

།སློབ་དཔོན་ཡང་རང་གི་ཞེས་པ་ལ་བརྟེན་ནས། །རིགས་[370] པ་དང་བཅས་པའི་ཆོས་ཉིད་རབ་ཏུ་རྟོགས་པས་ཆོས་ཉིད་ལ་གཅེས་ [《སྡེ་》 18b.1] པར་འཛིན་པ་ཡང་དག་པར་སྐྱེས་ཏེ།

།རང་གིས་རིགས་པ་སྟོན་པ་ན།

གནས་མེད་དམིགས་པ་ཡོད་མ་ཡིན།
།རྩ་བ་མེད་ཅིང་གནས་པ་མེད།

---

[369] 《ཅོ་》: བསར་

[370] 《པེ་》《སྣར་》: རིག་

།མ་རིག་རྒྱུ་ལས་[371] ཤིན་ཏུ་བྱུང་།
།ཐོག་མ་དབུས་ [«པེ་» 21a.1] མཐའ་རྣམ་པར་སྤྲངས། || **26** ||

།ཆུ་ཤིང་བཞིན་དུ་སྙིང་པོ་མེད།
།དྲི་ཟའི་གྲོང་[372] ཁྱེར་འདྲ་བ་སྟེ།
།རྨོངས་པའི་གྲོང་ཁྱེར་མི་བཟད་[373] པ།
།འགྲོ་བ་སྒྱུ་མ་བཞིན་དུ་སྣང་། || **27** ||

།ཞེས་བྱ་བ་སྨོས་སོ། [374] །འདི་ལ་བརྟེན་པས་གནས་ཏེ།[375] །ལོ་ཏོག་རྣམས་ཀྱི་རྒྱུར་གྱུར་པ། །ས་གཞི་བཞིན་དུ་གཞི་བྱེད་པའོ། །འདིའི་གནས་མེད་པས་གནས་མེད་པའོ། །བརྟེན་པར་བྱ་བས་དམིགས་པ་སྟེ། །ལྷུང་མི་ནུས་པ་རྣམས་ལྷུང་བར་བྱེད་པའི་འཁར་[376] བ་བཞིན་ནོ། །འདིའི་དམིགས་པ་ཡོད་པ་མ་ཡིན་ནོ། །རྩ་བ་ནི་རྒྱུའི་གཙོ་བོ་སྟེ་དེ་ཡང་དེ་ལས་འབྱུང་བ་རྣམས་ཀྱི་སྐྱེ་བ་དང་། །འདས་པ་དང་འཕེལ་བའི་རྒྱུ་སྟེ། །དཔེར་ན། །ཤིང་རྣམས་ཀྱི་རྩ་བ་ལྟ་བུའོ། [«སྣར་»

371 «པེ་» «སྣར་»: ལ་

372 «སྣར་»: ཀྲོང་

373 «པེ་» «སྣར་»: ཟད་

374 «ཏྲི་» notes: འཐད་པ་བཞི་སྟོན་པ་ནི་འགལ་རྐྱེན་གྱི་སྒོ་ནས''' while «ཟིན་» remarks: རྐྱེན་གསུམ་གྱི་དབང་གིས''''བདག་རྐྱེན། དམིགས་རྐྱེན། དེ་མ་ཐག་རྐྱེན་རིམ་པ་བཞིན་དུ་གནས་མེད་དམིགས་མེད་རྩ་བ་གསུམ་གྱིས་བདག་མེད་དུ་སྟོན་ཏོ།

375 «པེ་» «སྣར་»: པ་སྟེ།

376 «པེ་» {SS}: འཁར་ «སྣར་» «སྣེ་» «ཅོ་»: འཁོར་

21b.1] །གནས་པ་ཡོད་པ་མ་ཡིན་པས་གནས་པ་མེད་པའོ། །གནས་པ་[377] དང་དམིགས་པ་དང་སྐྱེ་བའི་རྒྱུ་དང་གནས་པ་མེད་པ་འདིས་འགྲོ་བ་མ་གྲུབ་པ་ཉིད་དུ་བརྗོད་དོ། །དེ་དག་ནི་དངོས་པོ་རྣམས་འགྲུབ་པའི་རྒྱུ་ཡིན་ན་དེ་དག་ཀྱང་འགྲོ་བ་[378] མེད་པས། །དེའི་ཕྱིར་འགྲོ་བ་ནི་ལོག་པའོ། །དེ་ལ་གནས་ནི་སྐྱེ་མཆེད་དྲུག་གོ། །དམིགས་པ་ནི་ཆོས་ཐམས་ཅད་དེ་མཐུན་[379] མཐུན་དུ་སྦྱོར་རོ། །རྩ་བ་ནི་ས་བོན་གྱི་ཆོས་ཀྱི་ཚུལ་གྱིས་རྒྱུའི་རྐྱེན་ཏོ། །འདིས་གནས་ [《ཅོ་》 18a.1] པར་བྱེད་པས་གནས་པ་སྟེ། །དེས་སྐྱེས་[380] པ་གནས་པའི་ཕྱིར་རོ། །དེ་དག་ཐམས་ཅད་ནི་རྟེན་ཅིང་འབྲེལ་པར་འབྱུང་བས་ངོ་བོ་ཉིད་མེད་དེ། །དེ་དང་དེ་བརྟེན་གང་བྱུང་བ། །རང་གི་དངོས་པོར་དེ་མ་སྐྱེས། །ཞེས་གོང་དུ་བསྟན་པ་ཡིན་ནོ། །དེའི་ཕྱིར་གནས་ལ་སོགས་པ་དང་བྲལ་བའི་འགྲོ་བ་ནི་ཡོད་པར་མི་རུང་ངོ།

།གལ་ཏེ་དེ་ལྟར་འགྲོ་བ་མེད་ན་ཇི་ལྟར་དེའི་རང་གི་ངོ་བོ་རྣམ་པ་སྣ་ཚོགས་སུ་དམིགས་ཞེ་ན།[381]

།འཕགས་པ་རྣམས་ནི་འགྲོ་བ་རྣམ་པ་སྣ་ཚོགས་སུ་མི་[382] དམིགས་ཏེ། །དེ་དག་ལ་འགྲོ་བ་སྟོང་པ་ཉིད་དུ་རོ་གཅིག་པས་སྟོང་པ་ཉིད་ལ་རྣམ་པ་སྣ་ཚོགས་ཡོད་པ་མ་ཡིན་ནོ། །དེ་བས་ན་བྱིས་པ་མ་རིག་པའི་གཉིད་[383] ཀྱིས་ལོག་པ་ཕྱིན་ཅི་ལོག་ཏུ་གྱུར་པ་དག་ནི་ [《པེ་》 21b.1] མ་སད་དེ་རྨི་

377 《པེ་》《སྣར་》{SS}: -པ་

378 《པེ་》《སྣར་》{SS}: +ལ་

379 《པེ་》《སྣར་》: -མཐུན་

380 《ཅོ་》: སྐྱེས་

381 《པེ་》《སྣར་》: -ཞེ་ན་

382 《པེ་》: མ་

383 《སྣར་》: གཉིས་

ལམ་སྐྱི་[384] [《སྡེ་》 19a.1] བ་བཞིན་དུ་སྣ་ཚོགས་སུ་དམིགས་པར་བསྟན་པའི་ཕྱིར། །མ་རིག་རྒྱུ་ལས་ཤིན་ཏུ་བྱུང་། །ཞེས་བྱ་བ་སྨོས་ཏེ། །ངོ་བོ་ཉིད་ཀྱིས་གྲུབ་པ་མེད་པ་དང་། །མ་རིག་པ་ཡོད་པས་འགྲོ་བ་ངོ་བོ་ཉིད་ཀྱིས་མ་གྲུབ་སྟེ། །མ་རིག་པའི་ས་བོན་གྱི་རྒྱུ་ལས་གྱུར་པ་[385] ངེས་སོ།

།ཇི་ལྟར་ངོ་བོ་ཉིད་ཀྱིས་གྲུབ་པ་མེད་པ་དེ་ལྟར་བསྟན་པའི་ཕྱིར། །ཐོག་མ་དབུས་མཐའ་རྣམ་པར་སྤངས། །ཞེས་བྱ་བ་སྨོན་ཏེ་སྐྱེ་བ་དང་གནས་པ་དང་འཇིག་པ་དང་བྲལ་བ་ཞེས་བྱ་བའི་ཐ་ཚིག་གོ། །འདིའི་ཕྱིར་ཡང་མ་རིག་པའི་ས་བོན་ལས་བྱུང་བ་སྟེ། །འདི་ལྟར་ཆུ་ཤིང་བཞིན་དུ་སྙིང་པོ་མེད་པའོ། །གལ་ཏེ་མ་རིག་པའི་ས་བོན་ལས་བྱུང་བ་མ་ཡིན་ན། །དེའི་ཚེ་བརྟགས་ན་སྙིང་པོ་དམིགས་པར་འགྱུར་བའི་རིགས་ན་[386] འདུས་བྱས་ནི་བརྟགས་ན་ཆུ་ཤིང་གི་ཕུང་པོ་བཞིན་དུ་སྙིང་པོ་མེད་དོ། །གང་སྙིང་པོ་མེད་ཀྱང་སྙིང་པོ་ཅན་དུ་སྣང་བ་དེ་གཏི་མུག་གི་མཐུ་ལས་ [《སྣར་》 22a.1] བྱུང་བ་སྟེ། །དེ་ལྟར་ན་འགྲོ་བ་ནི་མ་རིག་པའི་ས་བོན་ལས་བྱུང་བའོ།

།འདིའི་ཕྱིར་ཡང་མ་རིག་པའི་ས་བོན་ལས་བྱུང་བ་སྟེ། །འདི་ལྟར་དྲི་ཟའི་གྲོང་ཁྱེར་ལྟ་བུ་ཡིན་པའི་ཕྱིར་ཏེ། །འདི་ལྟར་དྲི་ཟའི་གྲོང་ཁྱེར་ཡང་དག་པ་[387] བཞིན་དུ་སྣང་ཡང་བརྟགས་ན་དེ་བཞིན་མ་ཡིན་པས་གྲོང་[388] ཁྱེར་ཡང་དག་པ་མ་ཡིན་ནོ། །གང་གི་ཕྱིར་དེ་ལྟར་བརྟགས་ན་མ་རིག་པའི་ས་བོན་གྱི་རྒྱུ་ལས་བྱུང་བའི་འགྲོ་བ་ངོ་བོ་ཉིད་ཀྱིས་མ་གྲུབ་པ་དེའི་ཕྱིར་འདི་ནི་ངེས་པར་རྨོངས་པའི་གྲོང་ཁྱེར་མི་བཟད་པ། །འགྲོ་བ་སྒྱུ་མ་བཞིན་དུ་སྣང་། [《ཅོ་》 18b.1] །གནོད་པར་བྱེད་པ་བཟློག་པར་དཀའ་བ་དང་། །མུན་པས་བསྒྲིབས་པས་རང་གི་ངོ་བོ་རྟོགས་པར་དཀའ་བའི་ཕྱིར། །འགྲོ་བ

[384] 《པེ་》《སྣར་》: སྨི་

[385] 《པེ་》《སྣར་》{SS}: པར་

[386] 《སྣར་》: ནི་

[387] 《ཅོ་》: པར་

[388] 《སྣར་》: གྲོངས་

མི་བཟད་པ་ཞེས་བྱ་བ་[389] སྟེ། །མ་རུངས་[390] པ་དང་དབུགས་འབྱིན་པ་མེད་པའི་གནས་དང་འཇིགས་པར་བྱེད་ཅེས་བྱ་བའི་ཐ་ཚིག་གོ། །དེའི་ཕྱིར་འདི་ནི་ཕྱིན་ཅི་མ་ལོག་པ་རྣམས་ཀྱིས་[391] སྒྱུ་མ་བཞིན་དུ་གཟིགས་སོ། །བྱིས་པ་རྣམས་ཀྱི་རྨོངས་ [«པེ་» 22a.1] པའི་གྲོང་ཁྱེར་གང་ཡིན་པ་དེ་[392] འཕགས་པ་རྣམས་ཀྱིས་སྒྱུ་མ་བཞིན་དུ་གཟིགས་ཏེ། །མ་རིག་པའི་མུན་པ་དང་བྲལ་བའི་ཕྱིར་རོ།

((3) །གསུམ་པ། དེའི་འཐད་པ།)

((a) །དང་པོ། ལུང་།)

།འདིའི་ཕྱིར་ཡང་འདི་ལྟར་འགྲོ་བ་དེ་དངོས་པོ་མེད་དེ་འདི་ལྟར།

ཚངས་པ་[393] ལ་སོགས་[394] འཇིག་རྟེན་འདི།
།བདེན་པར་[395] རབ་ཏུ་གང་བརྗོད་པ།
།འཕགས་ལ་ [«སྡེ་» 19b.1] དེ་ཡང་བརྫུན་ཞེས་གསུངས།
།དེ་ལས་གཞན་ན་[396] ཅི་ཞིག་ལུས། ॥ **28** ॥

---

389 «པེ་»«སྣར་»: -བ་

390 «པེ་»«སྣར་»: རུང་

391 «སྣར་»: རྣམ་གྱིས་

392 «པེ་»«སྣར་»{SS}: +ནི་

393 «པེ་»«སྣར་»: -པ་

394 «པེ་»: +པ་

395 «པེ་»«སྣར་»: པ་

396 «པེ་»«སྣར་»{SS}: ནི་

སྒྱུ་མ་ལྟ་བུར་མ་གྱུར་པ་གང་ཡང་ཡོད་དམ་ཞེས་བྱ་བ་ཚིག་གི་ལྷག་མའོ།

།དབང་པོ་ཡུལ་[397] ལས་འདས་པའི་དོན་ཡོངས་སུ་གཅོད་པ་ནི་[398] འཇིག་རྟེན་ན་[399] ཚངས་པ་ནི་ཚད་མའོ། །དེ་ལྟར་ཚད་མར་གྱུར་པ་དེ་ལ་དངོས་པོ་རྣམས་ཀྱི་རང་གི་ངོ་བོ་བདེན་པར་སྣང་བ་གང་ཡིན་པ་དེ་ཡང་འཕགས་པ་རྣམས་ལ་བརྫུན་ནོ་ཞེས་བཅོམ་ལྡན་འདས་ཀྱིས་མྱ་ངན་ལས་འདས་པ་ཉིད་བདེན་པ་གཅིག་པུའོ། །ཞེས་བསྟན་པ་ནི་གསུངས་ཏེ། །འདུས་བྱས་ནི་བརྫུན་པ་སླུ་[400] བའི་ཆོས་ཅན་ཡིན་ན་གཞན་དག་ལ་སྣང་བ་གང་ཡིན་པ་དེ་བརྫུན་པར་ཅིའི་ཕྱིར་མི་འགྱུར། །གང་ལ་བརྫུན་པ་ཉིད་དུ་ཐེ་ཚོམ་མེད་པ་དེ་ལས་གཞན་[401] ཅི་ཞིག་ལུས་ཞེས་བྱ་བ་ནི་ [《སྣར་》 22b.1] སྒྱུ་མ་ལྟ་བུར་མ་གྱུར་པ་གང་ཡང་མེད་ཅེས་བྱ་བའི་ཐ་ཚིག་གོ། །འདི་ནི་གདོན་མི་ཟ་བར་ཁས་བླང་བར་བྱའོ།

((b) །གཉིས་པ། རིགས་པ།)

།གཞན་དུ་ན་གལ་ཏེ་ཚངས་པ་ལ་སོགས་པ་དང་། །འཕགས་པ་རྣམས་འཇིག་རྟེན་འདི་ལ་ལྟ་བ་མཚུངས་པར་གྱུར་ན་ནི་དེའི་ཚེ་འཕགས་པ་རྣམས་དང་འཕགས་པ་མ་ཡིན་པ་རྣམས་མཚུངས་པ་ཉིད་དུ་འགྱུར་རོ། །དེ་དག་མཚུངས་པར་མི་སྲིད་པར་བསྟན་པའི་ཕྱིར།

འཇིག་རྟེན་མ་རིག་ལྡོངས་གྱུར་པ།
།སྲིད་[402] པའི་རྒྱུན་གྱི་རྗེས་འབྲང་[403] དང་།

---

397 {SS}: -ཡུལ་

398 {SS}: ན་

399 《པེ་》: -ན་

400 《པེ་》《སྣར་》{SS}: བསླུ་

401 {SS}: +ནི་

402 《ཏྲི་》{SS}: སྲེད་

།མཁས་པ་སྤྱོད་དང་བྲལ་བ་ཡི།

།དགེ་བ་རྣམས་ལྷ་ག་ལ་མཉམ། || 29 ||

།ཞེས་བྱ་བ་སྨོས་ཏེ་མ་རིག་པའི་ལིང་ཏོག་གིས་ཁེབས་ནས། །བློའི་མིག་ལྡོངས་པར་གྱུར་པ་ཚངས་པ་ལ་སོགས་པ་འགྲོ་བ་མ་ལུས་པ་ཡང་དག་པར་ [«ཅོ་» 19a.1] མཐོང་བ་དང་བྲལ་བའི་ཕྱིར། །རང་དབང་མེད་པར་འགྲོ་བ་ཐོག[404] མ་མེད་པའི་ [«པེ་» 22b.1] འཁོར་བས་འཁོར་བར་འཕངས་པས་བྲུབ་པ[405] ན་ཤུགས་ཀྱིས་ལྷུ་བ་འཁོར་བ་ལྷ་བུའི་འཁོར་བའི་འཁོར་ལོ་རྒྱ་ཀླུང་ཆེན་པོར་ཕྱིན་ཅི་ལོག་གི་རླུང་གིས་དཀྲུགས[406] ཏེ། །འབྲུགས་པས་དགེ་བའི་ཕྱོགས་ཀྱི[407] གྲུ་ཆག[408] པ་དགེ་བའི་ལས་ཀྱི་རྣམ་པར་སྨིན་པའི་འབྲས་བུ་མཐར་ཐུག་པའི་ལྡོང[409] ཅན་སྤྱོད་པའི་རྒྱུན་གྱི་རྗེས་སུ་འགྲོ་བ་སོ་སོའི་སྐྱེ་བོ་དང་། །མཁས་པ་ཤེས་རབ་ཀྱིས་དག་པ་བློའི་མིག[410] ཅན་དམ་པའི་ཆོས་བདུད་རྩིའི་ཁ་བའི་རྒྱུན་གྱི་བཏུང་བས་ངོམས་པ་གཅིག་ཏུ་ཆོས་ཀྱི་དང་ཚུལ་ཅན་གྱི་དགེ་བ་རྣམས་དང་། [«སྡེ་» 20a.1] །གང་དུ་སྨོས་པའི་འཇིག་རྟེན་དུ་མཚུངས་པར་བརྟག་ཏུ་ག་ལ་རུང་སྟེ།

---

403 «ཟིན་» glosses this as: སྤྱོད་པའི་རྒྱ་ཀླུང་གི་རྒྱུན་ཕྱོགས་སུ་རྗེས་སུ་གཞོལ་བའི་ཚངས་པ་སོགས་ while «ཏཱི་» unpacks these two lines as: ཚངས་པ་ལ་སོགས་པའི་འཇིག་རྟེན་པ་བློའི་མིག་མ་རིག་པའི་རབ་རིབ་ཀྱིས་ལྡོངས་ཤིང་ཁེགས་པར་གྱུར་པ་ཕྱིན་ཅི་ལོག་གི་སྤྱོད་པའི་རྒྱ་བོའི་རྒྱུན་གྱི་རྗེས་སུ་འབྲངས་པའི་སོ་སོའི་སྐྱེ་བོ

404 «པེ་»«སྣར་»: ཐོགས་

405 «ཅོ་»: བྲུ་

406 «པེ་»«སྣར་»: བཀྲུགས་

407 «པེ་»: གྲི་

408 «པེ་»: ཆགས་

409 «པེ་»«སྣར་»{SS}: ལྡོང་ «སྡེ་»«ཅོ་»: ལྟོང་

410 «པེ་»«སྣར་»: མིག་ «སྡེ་»«ཅོ་»: མིང་

།སྣང་བ་དང་། །སྨུན་པ་དང་། །འཁོར་བ་དང་། །མྱ་ངན་ལས་འདས་པ་མཚུངས་པར་བརྟག་[411] པ་ནི་མི་རིགས་སོ།

།དེ་བས་ན་ཚངས་པ་ལ་སོགས་པའི་འཇིག་རྟེན་འཁོར་བའི་རྗེས་སུ་མཐུན་པར་འགྱུར་བ་འདི་ནི་བདེན་པ་གང་ཡིན་པ་དེ་ནི་གདོན་མི་ཟ་བར་འཕགས་པ་རྣམས་ལ་བརྫུན་པ་ཡིན་ནོ། །གང་གི་ཕྱིར་དེ་[412] དེ་ལྟར་འཕགས་པ་རྣམས་ཀྱིས་འདི་སྐད་ཅེས། །རྨོངས་པའི་གྲོང་ཁྱེར་མི་བཟད་པ། །འགྲོ་བ་སྒྱུ་མ་བཞིན་དུ་སྣང་། །ཞེས་སྨོས་པ་གང་ཡིན་པ་དེ་ལ་མཁས་པ་རྣམས་དོགས་པ་སྤྱངས་ཏེ་མོས་པར་བྱའོ།

(B. །གཉིས་པ། ཕུང་སོགས་གསུངས་པ་དྲང་དོན་དུ་བསྒྲུབ་པ།)

(1. །དང་པོ། དེ་ཁོ་ན་ཉིད་བསྟན་པའི་རིམ་པ།)

(a. །དང་པོ། རིམ་པ་དངོས།)

།འདིར་སྨྲས་པ། [《སྣར་》 23a.1] །གལ་ཏེ་འགྲོ་བ་སྒྱུ་མ་བཞིན་དུ་རང་བཞིན་གྱིས་སྟོང་ན་འདི་ལ་བཅོམ་ལྡན་འདས་ཀྱིས་དེ་ཁོ་ན་གང་ཡིན་པ་དེ་མི་བསྟན་པར་ཕུང་པོ་དང་ཁམས་དང་སྐྱེ་མཆེད་ཡོད་དོ་ཞེས་བསྟན་པ་བདེན་པ་མ་ཡིན་པ་འདིས་ཅི་ཞིག་བྱ།

།ཆཤད་པ། །བདེན་པ་ཉིད་ནི་བསྟན་གྱི་བརྫུན་པ་ནི་མ་ཡིན་ནོ་ཞེས་བྱ་བ་འདི་[413] ག་ལས་འོངས། །འཇིག་རྟེན་[414] བདེན་ཡང་མི་དགོས་ན་ནི་ཁ་ཅིག་མི་བསྟན་ཏོ། །བརྫུན་ཡང་དགོས་པ་ཡོད་ན་ནི་ལ་ལ་བསྟན་དགོས་ཏེ་འདི་ལ་ནི་དོན་དམ་པ་ལ་འཇུག་པའི་ཐབས་སུ་དགོས་པ་ཡོད་པས་ཕུང་པོ་དང་ཁམས་ལ་སོགས་པ་བདེན་པ་མ་ཡིན་ཡང་ཡོད་དོ། །ཞེས་ཐོག་མ་ཉིད་དུ་བསྟན་པའི་དབང་དུ་བྱས་ཀྱི། །དེ་ཁོ་ན་ཡང་དག་པ་སྟོང་པ་ཉིད་ནི་མ་ཡིན་ཏེ། དེ་ལ་ཐོག་མར་བསྟན་ན་དོན་ [《པེ་》

---

411 《པེ་》《སྣར་》{SS}: བརྟགས་

412 《པེ་》《སྣར་》: -དེ་

413 《པེ་》《སྣར་》{SS}: +ནི་

414 《པེ་》《སྣར་》{SS}: +ན་

23a.1] མེད་པར་འགྱུར་བའི་ཕྱིར་རོ། [«ཅོ་» 19b.1] །མཐའ་གཉིས་ཀྱི་གཡང་ས་མེད་པའི་ཆོས་འདི་སྐྱེ་བོ་བློ་གྲོས་མ་བྱང་བ་ལ་ཐོག་མ་ཉིད་དུ་བསྟན་མི་བཟོད་དེ།[415] །དེ་བས་འགྲོ་བའི་དོན་སྒྲུབ་པ་ལ་མཁས་པ་ཐབས་ལ་ཁོང་བཟོ་བས།

དེ་ཉིད་ཚུལ་[416] ལ་ཐོག་མར་ནི།
།ཐམས་ཅད་ཡོད་ཅེས་བརྗོད་པར་བྱ།
།དོན་རྣམས་རྟོགས་ཤིང་ཆགས་པ་[417] ནས།
།དེ་ཡི་འོག་ཏུ་དབེན་པའོ།[418] **|| 30 ||**

།སྐྱེ་བོ་བློ་གྲོས་མ་བྱང་བ་དག་ཐོག་མ་ཁོ་ནར་སྟོང་པ་ཉིད་དུ་ལྟ་བ་ལ་བཙུད་ན་ཤིན་ཏུ་མགོ་རྨོངས་པར་འགྱུར་ཏེ། །དེ་བས་ན་འཕགས་པ་རྣམས་སྟོང་པ་ཉིད་ཐོག་མ་ཁོ་ནར་མི་སྟོན་ཏེ། །དངོས་པོ་ལ་ཆགས་པ་དང་ལྡན་པ་དངོས་པོའི་ངོ་བོ་ [«སྣེ་» 20b.1] ཉིད་རབ་ཏུ་དབྱེ་བ་ལ་དགའ་བ་རྣམས་ཀྱི་འདོད་པའི་དོན་ཡང་དག་པར་བརྗོད་པས་བདག་ལ་གཅེས་པར་འཛིན་པར་བྱ་བའི་ཕྱིར་དེ་ཁོ་ན་ཚོལ་བ་ལ་ཐོག་མར་ཐམས་ཅད་ཡོད་དོ་ཞེས་བརྗོད་པར་བྱའོ།

།དེའི་དངོས་པོ་ནི་དེ་ཉིད་དོ། །བརྗོད་པར་འདོད་པའི་དོན་སྤྱིའི་དངོས་པོ་དང་འབྲེལ་བ་ཅན་དེའི་ཞེས་བྱ་བ་འདི་དང་སྦྱར་རོ། །དངོས་པོ་ནི་རང་གི་ངོ་བོ་སྟེ། །གང་གི་རང་གི་ངོ་བོ་གང་ཡིན་པ་དེ་ནི་

---

415 «ཅོ་»: དོ།

416 «ཏྲི་» «པེ་» «སྣར་» {SS}: ཚོལ་ «ཟིན་»: འཚོལ་

417 «པེ་» «སྣར་»: མེད་

418 Skt. of this verse preserved in SBS (ed. Bendall, Part I, 385), cited by Lindtner (*Nāgārjuniana*, 110): *sarvam astīti vaktavyam ādau tattvagaveṣiṇaḥ // paścād avagatārthasya niḥsaṅgasya viviktatā //*

དེའི་དངོས་པོ་སྟེ། དེ་ཁོ་ནའོ། །རང་གི་ངོ་བོའོ། །ངོ་བོ་ཉིད་དོ། །དེ་བཞིན་ [《སྣར་》 23b.1] ཉིད་དོ། །གཞན་མ་ཡིན་པ་ཉིད་དོ་ཞེས་བྱ་བའི་ཐ་ཚིག་གོ།

།དེ་ཁོ་ན་ཚོལ་བའི་ངང་ཚུལ་ཅན་ཡིན་པས་ན་དེ་ཁོ་ན་ཚོལ་བའོ། །དེ་ཁོ་ན་ཚོལ་བར་འདོད་པ་དེ་ལ་བླ་མ་ཕན་པར་འདོད་པས་ཇི་སྐད་བརྗོད་པར་བྱ་ཞེ་ན། །ཐམས་ཅད་ཡོད་དོ་ཞེས་བརྗོད་པར་བྱའོ། །བྲམ་ཟེ་[419] ཐམས་ཅད་ཅེས་བྱ་བ་ནི་ཕུང་པོ་ལྔ་དང་། །སྐྱེ་མཆེད་བཅུ་གཉིས་དང་། །ཁམས་བཅོ་བརྒྱད་ཀྱི་བར་དག་གོ་ཞེས་གསུངས་སོ། །དེའི་ཤེས་པ་དང་སྦྱར་ཏེ་ཕུང་པོ་ལ་སོགས་པ་དེ་དང་འདི་ཡོད་པར་བརྗོད་པར་བྱའོ། །ཕུང་པོ་ལ་སོགས་པ་དེ་དག་ཀྱང་ཉེ་བར་བཟུང་སྟེ་དེ་དང་འདིའི་ཡོད་པ་གང་ཡིན་པ་དེ་ཉེ་བར་བཟུང་ནས་རིང་པོ་དང་། །ཐུང་དུ་བཞིན་དུའམ། །མར་མེའི་འོད་བཞིན་དུ་བསྟན་[420] ཏེ་གྱུར་པ་དེ་ལས་གཞན་དུ་མ་ཡིན་ཏེ། །དེ་ལྟར་ན་ཉེ་བར་བཟུང་བའམ་བརྟེན་པར་ [《པེ་》 23b.1] ཟད་དོ།

།དོན་རྟོགས་ཞེས་བྱ་བ་ཇི་ལྟ་བུ་ཞེ་ན།

འབྲས་བུ་རྣམས་ཀྱི་མཐའ་མེད་པའི་ཕྱིར་དང་། །འབྲས་བུ་རེ་རེའི་རྐྱེན་ཀྱང་དུ་མ་ཡོད་པའི་ཕྱིར་དང་། །རྐྱེན་རེ་རེ་ལ་ཡང་བརྟགས་ན་ཐོག་མ་མེད་པའི་འཁོར་བ་བཞིན་དུ་རྒྱུའི་ཚོགས་པ་གཅིག་ནས་གཅིག་ཏུ་བརྒྱུད་པའི་མཐའ་མི་མཐོང་བའི་ཕྱིར་ [《ཅོ་》 20a.1] འབྲས་བུའི་རྩོམ་པ་ལ་འཇིག་[421] པར་ལྟ་བས་རྒྱུའི་ཚོགས་པ་གཅིག་[422] བརྒྱུད་པས་བསྒྲུབས་པའི་འབྲས་བུ་རྐྱེན་དུ་མ་ལས་བྱུང་བ་གྲུབ་མ་ཐག་ཏུ་འཇིག་པར་རྟོགས་ཤིང་། །སྐྱེ་བ་ནི་ཤིན་ཏུ་འབད་པས་བསྒྲུབ་པར་བྱ་བ་ཡིན་ལ། །ཤིན་ཏུ་འབད་པས་བསྒྲུབས་པ་འཇིག་པ་ནི་འབད་པ་མེད་པར་ཡང་འབྱུང་བར་རྟོགས་ནས་འདུས་བྱས་

---

[419] 《པེ་》: +ཐམས་ཅད་ 《སྣར་》: +ཐོད་

[420] 《པེ་》《སྣར་》{SS}: བརྟེན་

[421] 《པེ་》《སྣར་》: འཇིགས་

[422] 《པེ་》《སྣར་》{SS}: +ནས་གཅིག་ཏུ་

ཀྱི་ཆོས་ཉིད་ལ་སྒྲིད་ལུག་པ། །བྱིས་པ་སྐྱེ་བོའི་སྤྱོད་པ་ལ་མངོན་པར་མི་བསྟོད་པ། །སྐྱེ་བ་ལ་མངོན་པར་མི་དགའ་བ། །འཇིག་པ་ལ་མི་འཕྲོད་པར་འཛིན་པ། །འཁོར་ [«སྡེ་» 21a.1] བ་རྣམས་ལ་ཆགས་པ་འདོར་བར་འདོད་པ། །འཁོར་བ་སྤོང་བར་འདོད་པ། །བདག་ལ་ཆགས་པ་ལྡོག་པར་གྱུར་པས་དེ་ལྟར་དོན་ཁོང་དུ་ཆུད་པ་ལ་དེའི་འོག་ཏུ་དབེན་པ་ནི་རིགས་ཀྱི་སྤ་རོལ་དུ་[423] ནི་མ་ཡིན་ནོ། །དེ་ལྟར་བྱས་ན་སློབ་དཔོན་གྱིས་སྟོང་པ་ཉིད་བསྟན་པ་ཡང་འབྲས་བུ་མེད་པར་མི་འགྱུར།

།སློབ་མ་རྣམས་ཀྱང་སྟོང་བ་དང་། [«སྣར་» 24a.1] །ཕྱིན་ཅི་ལོག་ཏུ་འཛིན་པས་ལོག་པར་ལྟུང་བར་མི་འགྱུར་རོ། །དེ་ལྟར་མ་བྱས་ན་ཀུན་རྫོབ་དང་དོན་དམ་པའི་བདེན་པ་གཉིས་རྣམ་པར་གནས་[424] པ་དང་། །མི་མཐུན་པར་གྱུར་པའི་ཕྱིར་སྟོང་པ་ཉིད་བསྟན་པས་ལོག་པར་ལྟུང་བར་འགྱུར་རོ།[425] །དེ་ལྟར་གྱུར་ན་མི་དགེ་བ་སྤང་[426] མི་ནུས་སོ། །མི་མཁས་པའི་བློ་ཅན་དག་འགྲོ་བ་འདིའི་སྟོང་པའོ། །སྙམ་དུ་འཛིན་ཞིང་[427] འདི་ནི་སྟོང་པ་ཉིད་ན་འདིས་ཅི་ཞིག་བྱ་ཞེས་ངེས་པར་བསྒྲུབ་པར་བྱ་བའི་དགེ་བའི་ལས་ལ་མི་སྤྲོ་བར་འགྱུར་ཏེ། །དེ་བས་ན་འདི་ཡང་སྦྲུ་གཞོག་མ་སྐྱེས་པའི་བུ་རང་གི་ཚང་བོར་ནས་འཕུར་བ་བཞིན་དུ་བརླག་པར་འགྱུར་ཏེ།

(b. །གཉིས་པ། དེ་ལས་འདས་པའི་ཉེས་དམིགས།)

།འདི་ལྟར་སོ་སོ་རང་གིས་རྟོགས་པ་དང་བྲལ་བའི་ཕྱིར།

---

423 «པེ་» «སྣར་» {SS}: ཏུ་

424 «ཅོ་»: གནོས་

425 «པེ་»: -རོ་

426 «པེ་» {SS}: སྤོང་ «སྣར་»: སྤང་

427 «པེ་» «སྣར་»: ཅིང་

རྣམ་པར་དབེན་དོན་མི་ཤེས་ལ།
།ཐོས་པ་ཙམ་ལ་ [«པེ་» 24a.1] འཇུག་བྱེད་ཅིང་།
།གང་རྣམས་བསོད་ནམས་[428] མི་བྱེད་པ།
།སྐྱེས་བུ་ཐ་ཤལ་དེ་དག་བརླག || **31** ||

།འཇིག་རྟེན་པ་ཉིད་ཀྱི་དོན་དམ་པ་ལ་གནས་ཏེ་ཕྱིན་ཅི་མ་ལོག་པ་རྣམ་པར་བྱང་བའི་ཕྱོགས་ཕུན་སུམ་ཚོགས་ཤིང་སྟོང་པ་ཉིད་ཀྱི་དེ་ཁོ་ན་སོ་སོ་རང་གིས་རྟོགས་པ་ན་བསོད་ནམས་དང་བསོད་ནམས་མ་ཡིན་པ་མི་བྱ་བ་ནི་རིགས་སོ། །གང་དག་སྟོང་པ་ཉིད་སོ་སོ་རང་གིས་རྟོགས་པ་[429] མེད་པར་སྟོང་པ་ཉིད་ཀྱི་སྒྲ་ཐོས་པ་ཙམ་གྱིས་བྱ་བ་བྱས་པ་རྣམས་ཀྱི་སྤྱོད་ [«ཅོ་» 20b.1] པ་ལྷུར་རྗེས་སུ་འཚོས་པ་ནི་མི་དགེ་བའི་ལས་ཉིད་ལ་ཞུགས་པ་ཡིན་གྱི། །དགེ་བ་ལ་ནི་མ་ཡིན་ཏེ། །དེ་དག་གདོན་མི་ཟ་བར་སྒྲོ་གཞོག་རྫོགས་པའི་བྱའི་རྒྱལ་བྱིའུ་ཕྲུག་སྒྲོ་གཞོག་མ་སྐྱེས་པས་བྱ་བ་བཞིན་དུ་ཉོན་མོངས་པའི་མཐར་འགྱུར་རོ། །ཆུ་ཐོས་པ་ཙམ་གྱིས་སྐོམ་[430] པ་མི་ཕྱེད་[431] ལ། །ཟས་ཐོས་པ་ཙམ་གྱིས་ཀྱང་བཀྲེས་པ་མི་ཕྱེད་[432] དེ། །དེ་བསྟན་[433] ན་དེ་དག་ཕྱེད་[434] པ་བཞིན་དུ་འདི་རྟོགས་ནས་སྐྱེས་བུ་ཐ་ཤལ་དེ་

---

428 «ཅོ་»: རྣམས་

429 «སྣར་»: -པ་

430 «པེ་» «སྣར་»: སྒོམ་

431 «པེ་» {SS}: ཕྱིད་

432 «པེ་» «སྣར་» {SS}: ཕྱིད་

433 «པེ་» «སྣར་»: བསྟེན་

434 «པེ་» «སྣར་» {SS}: ཕྱིད་

དག་བརྟག་གོ་ཞེས་བརྗོད་དོ། །གཅིག་ཏུ་མི་དགེ་བ་ [«སྡེ་» 21b.1] ལ་འཇུག་པས་དེ་དག་ནི་སྐྱེས་བུ་ཐ་ཤལ་ལོ།

(c. །གསུམ་པ། དེའི་གཉེན་པོ།)

།དེ་ལྟར་དེའི་ཉེས་པ་ཡོངས་སུ་སྤྱང་བར་བཞེད་ནས། །བཅོམ་ལྡན་འདས་ཀྱིས་ཉན་[435] པ་རྣམས་ལ་ཀུན་རྫོབ་ཀྱི་བདེན་པ་ལས་ཡོངས་སུ་མ་ཉམས་པའི་དོན་རེ་ཞིག་ཐོག་མ་ཉིད་དུ།

ལས་[436] ཀྱི་འབྲས་ [«སྣར་» 24b.1] བུ་ཡོད་པ་དང་།
།འགྲོ་བ་རྣམས་ཀྱང་ཤིན་ཏུ་[437] བརྗོད།[438] || **32ab** ||

།སེམས་ཅན་རྣམས་གང་ལ་གནས་ནས་ལས་རྣམས་བྱེད་ཅིང་དེའི་འབྲས་བུ་ཡང་ཟ་བའི་འགྲོ་བ་ལྷ་བཅོམ་ལྡན་འདས་ཀྱིས་གསུངས་སོ། །དེའི་འོག་ཏུ་དེ་དག་གི་འདི་བདེན་ནོ་སྙམ་དུ་མངོན་པར་ཞེན་པ་མཆོག་ཏུ་འཛིན་པ་ལུས་ཀྱི་མདུད་པ་འདིའི་གཉེན་པོར།

།དེ་ཡི་རང་བཞིན་ཡོངས་ཤེས་དང་།
།སྐྱེ་བ་མེད་པ་དག་ཀྱང་བསྟན། || **32cd** ||

---

435 «ཅོ་»: ཉེན་

436 «ཏྷི་» «པེ་» «སྣར་» {SS}: ལས་ «སྡེ་» «ཅོ་»: ལུས་ «ཟིན་» appears to have skipped this verse.

437 «པེ་» «སྣར་»: དུ་

438 «ཏྷི་» rewords these two lines as: ལས་རྣམས་འབྲས་བུར་བཅས་ཉིད་དང་། །འགྲོ་བ་དག་ཀྱང་ཡང་དག་བཤད།

།འགྲོ་བ་ལ་སོགས་པ་ཡང་རྟེན་ཅིང་འབྲེལ་པར་འབྱུང་བ་ཡིན་པས་ངོ་བོ་ཉིད་ཀྱིས་མ་སྐྱེས་པའོ། །དེའི་རང་བཞིན་ཡོངས་སུ་ཤེས་པ་ལམ་དང་འགྲོ་བ་ལ་སོགས་པ་རྣམས་ཀྱི་སྐྱེ་བ་མེད་པ་ལམ་གྱི་ཡེ་[439] ཤེས་ཐོབ་པར་བྱ་བ་ཡང་བསྟན་ཏོ།

(2. །གཉིས་པ། ཕུང་སོགས་གསུངས་པ་དགོངས་པ།)

(a. །དང་པོ། དངོས།)

།དེ་བས་ན་འདི་ལྟར་གཉི་གའི་བདག་ཉིད་བསྟན་པ་རྣམ་པར་གཞག་པ་འདི་ལ་དགོས་པའི་ཆེད་དུ་བསྟན་པ་ནི༑ [《པེ་》 24b.1] གང་དོན་གྱི་ཆེད་དུ་བསྟན་པ་ནི་[440] གང་ཞེ་ན། །འདི་ལ་དཔྱད་ན་གཏན་ལ་དབབ་ཏུ་རུང་སྟེ།

དགོས་[441] པའི་དབང་དུ་[442] རྒྱལ་བ་རྣམས།
།ང་དང་ང་ཡི་ཞེས་གསུངས་ལྟར།
།ཕུང་པོ་ཁམས་དང་སྐྱེ་མཆེད་རྣམས།
།དེ་བཞིན་དགོས་[443] པའི་དབང་གིས་གསུངས།[444] || **33** ||

---

439 《ཅོ་》: ཡི་

440 《པེ་》《སྣར་》{SS}: -གང་དོན་གྱི་ཆེད་དུ་བསྟན་པ་ནི་

441 《ཏྰེ་》: དགོངས་

442 《ཏྰེ་》: གིས་

443 《ཏྰེ་》: དགོངས་

444 Skt. preserved in *Bodhicaryāvatārapañjikā* (Vaidya, 181) given by Lindtner (*Nāgārjuniana*, 110–111) as: *mamety aham iti proktaṁ yathā kāryavaśāj jinaiḥ / tathā kāryavaśāt proktāḥ skandhāyatanadhātavaḥ //*. See Scherrer-Schaub (*Yuktiṣaṣṭikāvṛtti*, 251 n. 487) for citations and comparisons of this verse with others.

།སངས་རྒྱས་བཅོམ་ལྡན་འདས་ནི་ང་དང་ང་ཡིར་འཛིན་པ་སྤངས་པ་ཡིན། །ཡང་བརྗོད་པར་བཞེད་པའི་དོན་གྱི་[445] སྒོ་ནས་བསྟན་པའི་ཕྱིར་འཇིག་རྟེན་གྱི་ཆེད་དུ་ང་དང་ངའི་ཞེས་གསུངས་པ་དེ་བཞིན་དུ་དགོས་པའི་དབང་གིས་ཕུང་པོ་དང་སྐྱེ་མཆེད་དང་ཁམས་རྣམས་གསུངས་ཏེ། །དེའི་རྣམ་པར་དབྱེ་བ་བསྟན་པ་མེད་པར་འཇིག་རྟེན་དེ་ཁོ་ན་ལ་ཞུགས་པའི་ཐབས་མེད་པའི་ཕྱིར་རོ། [《ཅོ་》 21a.1]

(b. །གཉིས་པ། ཤེས་བྱེད།)

།ཇི་ལྟར་དགོས་པའི་དབང་དུ་ཕུང་པོ་དང་། །སྐྱེ་མཆེད་དང་། །ཁམས་རྣམས་བཤད་ཀྱི་དེ་ཁོ་ནའི་དོན་དུ་ནི་མ་ཡིན་པར་འདི་ཇི་ལྟར་ཤེས་པར་ནུས་པ་[446] འདི་ནི་འཐད་པ་དང་ལུང་གིས་ངེས་པར་ཟུང་སྟེ།

(i. །དང་པོ། རིགས་པ།)

།དེ་ལ་རེ་ཞིག་འཐད་པའི་དབང་དུ་བྱས་ནས།

འབྱུང་བ་ཆེ་ལ་སོགས་བཤད་པ།
།རྣམ་པར་ཤེས་སུ་ཡང་དག་འདུ།
།དེ་ཤེས་པས་ནི་འབྲལ་[447] འགྱུར་ན།
།ལོག་པར་རྣམ་ [《སྡེ་》 22a.1] བརྟགས་མ་ཡིན་ནམ།[448] || 34 ||

---

[445] 《པེ་》《སྣར་》{SS}: ཀྱི་ 《སྡེ་》《ཅོ་》: གྱི་

[446] {SS}: -པ་ +། །

[447] 《ཉི་》: འབྲས་ although 《ཟིན་》 appears to read it as འབྲལ་

[448] The Skt. of this verse is preserved in the *Sākāra-siddhi-śāstra* (see *Jñānaśrīmitranibandhāvalī*, ed. Thakur, *Buddhist Cities*, 405) as noted by Lindtner (*Nāgārjuniana*, 111 n. 34): *mahābhūtādi vijñāne proktaṁ samavarudhyate // tajjñāne vigamaṁ yāti nanu mithyā vikalpi-*
(cont'd)

།ཞེས་བྱ་བ་སྨོས་སོ། །རྣམ་པར་ཤེས་པས་དམིགས་པ་གང་གི་རྣམ་པ་འཛིན་ཅིང་སྐྱེ་བའི་དམིགས་པ་དེ། །རྣམ་པར་ཤེས་པ་ [《སྣར་》 25a.1] ལ་རྣམ་པ་ཉེ་བར་བསྒྲུབས་པའི་རང་གི་དངོས་པོ་ཐོབ་ནས་དངོས་པོའི་དོན་གྱི་ངོ་བོ་ཉིད་ཀྱིས་འབྱུང་བ་ཆེན་པོ་ལ་སོགས་པར་ཡོངས་སུ་བརྟགས་སོ། །རྣམ་པར་ཤེས་པ་ལ་འགའ་ཞིག་གི་རྣམ་པར་མ་བཞག་པ་ལ་ནི་འཇིག་རྟེན་གྱིས་ཡོད་པ་ཉིད་དུ་རྣམ་པར་གཞག་མི་ནུས་ཏེ། །མོ་གཤམ་གྱི་བུ་ལ་སོགས་པ་ཡང་ཡོད་པར་ཐལ་བར་འགྱུར་བའི་ཕྱིར་རོ། །དེ་བས་ན་འབྱུང་བ་དང་འབྱུང་བ་ལས་གྱུར་པ་དང་། །སེམས་དང་སེམས་ལས་བྱུང་བ་དང་། །སེམས་དང་ལྡན་པ་མ་ཡིན་པ་རྣམས་ནི་རྣམ་པར་ཤེས་པའི་རྣམ་པའི་རྒྱུ་ཅན་ཡིན་པའི་ཕྱིར་འབྱུང་བ་ཆེན་པོ་ལ་སོགས་པ་གང་དང་གང་བཤད་པ་ཅི་ཡང་རུང་བ་དེ་དག་ཐམས་ཅད་ནི་རྣམ་པར་ཤེས་པར་ཡང་དག་པར་འདུ་ཞིང་ཁོངས་སུ་ཆུད་དོ།[449]

།གང་གི་ཚེ་རྣལ་འབྱོར་པས་ཡོད་པ་མེད་པ་ཡིན་པའི་དོན་སྒྲོ་འདོགས་པའི་རྣམ་ [《པེ་》 25a.1] པར་ཤེས་པའི་ཚངས་པ་དེ་བརྫུན་པ་སླུ་[450] བའི་ཆོས་ཅན་དུ་མཐོང་ཞིང་རང་བཞིན་གྱིས་སྐྱེ་བ་མེད་པར་མཐོང་བ་དེའི་ཚེ་ངེས་པར་དེ་ཤེས་ཏེ། །ཇི་ལྟར་གནས་པའི་སེམས་རང་གི་ངོ་བོས་སྐྱེ་བ་མེད་པར་ཤེས་པས་ངེས་བསྐྱེད་པ་འབྱུང་བ་ཆེན་པོ་ལ་སོགས་པ་མ་ལུས་པ་དག་ཀྱང་གཟུགས་འགགས་[451]

---

tam // Following an Idealist interpretation of this verse, Śāntarakṣita comments: སེམས་ཙམ་ལ་ནི་བརྟེན་ནས་སུ། །ཕྱི་རོལ་དངོས་མེད་ཤེས་པར་བྱ། །ཚུལ་འདིར་བརྟེན་ནས་དེ་ལ་ཡང་། །ཤིན་ཏུ་བདག་མེད་ཤེས་པར་བྱ།

449 《ཟིན་》 summarizes this as: འབྱུང་བ་བཞི་དང་སེམས་སེམས་འབྱུང་ལྡན་མིན་འདུ་བྱེད་སོགས་ཆོས་ཅན། ཁྱོད་ཕྱིན་ཅི་ལོག་གི་བློས་ལོག་པར་བརྟགས་པ་ཡིན་པར་ཐལ། ཁྱོད་འདོད་བྱེད་ཀྱི་ཤེས་པ་རང་བཞིན་མེད་པར་རྟོགས་པའི་སྟོབས་ཀྱིས་ཁྱོད་ལ་བདེན་འཛིན་དང་བྲལ་བར་འགྱུར་བའི་ཕྱིར། དེ་ཐལ། ཁྱོད་ཀྱི་རྣམ་ཤེས་ལ་རྣམ་པ་བཞག་ཅིང་རྣམ་ཤེས་ཀྱི་ཁྱོད་ལ་བརྟགས་ནས་བཞག་པའི་ཕྱིར།

450 《པེ་》《སྣར་》{SS}: བསླུ་

451 《པེ་》《སྣར་》: འགག་པ་

ན་གཟུགས་བརྙན་འགགས་[452] པ་བཞིན་དུ་འབྲལ་བར་འགྱུར་ན། །དེ་ལྟ་བུ་གང་ཡིན་པ་དེ་གཟུགས་བརྙན་བཞིན་དུ་ལོག་པར་རྣམ་པར་བརྟགས་པ་ཉིད་མ་ཡིན་ནམ།

།དེའི་ཕྱིར་དེ་ལྟར་ཕུང་པོ་ལ་སོགས་པ་དེ་དག་ནི་རྣམ་པར་ཤེས་པའི་རྒྱུས་ཡོད་པ་ཉིད་དེ་[453] མེད་ན་ཡོད་[454] པས་ངོ་བོ་ཉིད་དུ་གྲུབ་པ་མེད་པ་ཁོ་ན་ཡིན་པ་ལ་ངར་འཛིན་པ་དང་ང་ཡིར་འཛིན་པའི་ [«ཅོ་» 21b.1] མངོན་པའི་ང་རྒྱལ་ཅན་གྱི་དབང་དུ་བསྟན་པར་རིགས་སོ།

(ii. །གཉིས་པ། ལུང་།)

།རེ་ཞིག་དེ་ལྟར་རིགས་པས་ཕུང་པོ་ལ་སོགས་པ་དགོས་པའི་དབང་དུ་བསྟན་པར་ཤེས་པར་བྱས་ནས། །ད་[455] ནི་ལུང་གིས་ཕུང་པོ་ལ་སོགས་པ་བརྟུན་པ་ཉིད་དུ་བསྟན་པས་དགོས་པའི་ཆེད་དུ་བརྗོད་པར་བསྟན་པའི་ཕྱིར།

མྱ་ངན་འདས་པ་བདེན་གཅིག་པུ། [«སྣར་» 25b.1]
།རྒྱལ་བ་རྣམས་ཀྱིས་གང་[456] [«སྡེ་» 22b.1] གསུངས་པ།
།དེའི་ཚེ་ལྷག་མ་ལོག་པ་ཞེས།
།མཁས་པ་སུ་ཞིག་རྟོགས་མི་བྱེད།[457] || 35 ||

452 «པེ་» «སྣར་» {SS}: འགག་

453 «པེ་» «སྣར་» {SS}: +དེ་

454 «པེ་» «སྣར་» {SS}: +པ་མེད་

455 «ཅོ་»: དེ་

456 «ཏཱི་»: གང་ «པེ་» «སྣར་»: རྣམ་ «སྡེ་» «ཅོ་»: རྣམས་ {SS}: ནམ་ (following {Dh})

457 «ཏཱི་» rewords these last two lines as: །དེ་ཚེ་ལྷག་མ་ལོག་མིན་ཞེས། །མཁས་པ་སུ་ཞིག་རྟོག་པར་བྱེད།

།ཅེས་བྱ་བ་སྨོས་སོ། །བཅོམ་ལྡན་འདས་ཀྱིས་དགེ་སློང་དག་འདི་ལྟ་སྟེ། །མི་སླུ་[458] བའི་ཆོས་ཅན་མྱ་ངན་ལས་འདས་པ་འདི་ནི་བདེན་པའི་མཆོག་གཅིག་ཏུའོ་[459] ཞེས་གསུངས་པ་ཏེ་ལུང་འདིས་[460] དོན་གྱིས་ན་ཤེས་རབ་ཅན་སུ་ཞིག་ཕུང་པོ་ལ་སོགས་པ་བརྟེན་པའི་དོན་ཁོང་དུ་ཆུད་པར་མི་འགྱུར།

(3. །གསུམ་པ། སྐྱེ་མེད་གསུངས་པ་ངེས་དོན་ཡིན་པར་བསྟན་པ།)

(a. །དང་པོ། མ་རིག་པ་ལ་སྣང་བས་རང་བཞིན་མེད་པ།)

།གང་གི་ཕྱིར་ཕུང་པོ་དང་། །སྐྱེ་མཆེད་དང་། །ཁམས་དེ་དག་རྣམ་པ་དེ་ལྟར་རིགས་[461] པ་དང་། །ལུང་གིས་རྣམ་པར་དཔྱད་ན་ངོ་བོ་ཉིད་ཀྱིས་[462] གྲུབ་པ་མེད་པ་དེའི་ཕྱིར་ངེས་པར།

ཇི་སྲིད་ཡིད་ཀྱིས་[463] རྣམ་གཡོ་བ།
།དེ་སྲིད་བདུད་ཀྱི་སྤྱོད་ཡུལ་ཏེ། || **36ab** ||

།འཕགས་པའི་ཤེས་རབ་ཀྱི་དབང་པོའི་སྲོག་གི་བར་ཆད་བྱེད་པས་བདུད་དེ་དེ་ཡང་ཁམས་གསུམ་གྱི་ས་ཆེན་པོ་པ་ཕྱིན་ཅི་ལོག་བཞིའི་བློན་པོ་ཆེན་པོ་དང་ལྡན་པ་འདོད་ཆགས་ལ་སོགས་པ་ཉོན་མོངས་པའི་འཁོར་གྱིས་རྟག་ཏུ་ [《པེ་》 25b.1] འཁོར་བ། །འཕགས་པ་མ་ཡིན་པ་སྐྱེ་བོ་མཐའ་དག་

458 《པེ་》《སྣར་》{SS}: བསླུ་

459 《པེ་》《སྣར་》{SS}: པུའོ།

460 《པེ་》《སྣར་》{SS}: འདིའི་

461 《པེ་》《སྣར་》: རིག་

462 《པེ་》《སྣར་》: ཀྱི་

463 《ཏྲཻ་》《པེ་》《སྣར་》{SS}: ཀྱི་

གིས་སྨྲ་[464] མ་ཕབ་པ། །སྤྱོད་པ་བཟང་པོ་མ་ཡིན་པ་[465] ཞུགས་[466] པའི་རྗེས་སུ་སོང་བ། །འཁོར་བ་པའི་སེམས་ཅན་མ་ལུས་པ་[467] འཕེལ་བར་བྱེད་པ་མ་རིག་པ་ཞེས་བྱ་བ་ཡིན་ཏེ་ཚུལ་བཞིན་མ་ཡིན་པས་དངོས་པོ་ལ་རྣམ་པར་རྟོག་ན་མ་རིག་པའི་ཡུལ་ལས་མི་འདའ་བ་ཉིད་དུ་མངོན་ནོ། །གང་གི་ཚེ་དེ་བདུད་ཀྱི་སྤྱོད་ཡུལ་ཡིན་པ་དེའི་ཚེ་དེ་སྐྱེ་བ་མེད་ན་ཡིད་[468] འཇུག་པ་མི་འབྱུང་བའི་ཕྱིར་བདུད་ཀྱི་ཡུལ་ཉིད་མེད་པར་འགྱུར་བས།[469] [470]

དེ་ལྟ་ཡིན་ན་འདི་ལ་ཡང་།[471]
།ཉེས་པ་མེད་པར་ཅིས་[472] མི་འཐད།[473] **|| 36cd ||**

---

464 «པེ་»: སྨྱ་

465 «པེ་» «སྣར་» {SS}: +ལ་

466 «ཅོ་»: ཞུབས་

467 «པེ་» «སྣར་» {SS}: པར་

468 «པེ་» «སྣར་» {SS}: +ཀྱི་ This appears to be a correction / interpolation in the «པེ་» blocks.

469 «ཅོ་»: འམ་ or རམ་, ms. unclear.

470 «ཟིན་» comments: ཇི་སྲིད་ཚུལ་མིན་ཡིད་བྱེད་ཀྱིས་གཡོ་བ་ཡོད་པ་དེ་སྲིད་དུ་འཕགས་པའི་ཤེས་རབ་ཀྱི་སྲོག་གི་དབང་པོ་འགག་པར་བྱེད་པའི་བདུད་ཀྱི་སྤྱོད་ཡུལ་ལས་མ་འདས་པ།

471 «ཏཱི་»: ནི།

472 «པེ་» «སྣར་»: ཅི་

473 «ཏཱི་» unpacks this as: སྐྱེ་མེད་མངོན་དུ་གྱུར་པ་དེ་ལྟ་ཡིན་ན་སྐྱེ་མེད་མངོན་སུམ་དུ་རྟོགས་པའི་འདི་ལ་ཇི་སྐད་བཤད་པའི་ཉེས་པ་མེད་པར་ཅིའི་ཕྱིར་མི་འཐད་བདུད་ཡུལ་དང་བྲལ་བའི་ཕྱིར།

།འདི་ཞེས་བྱ་བ་ནི་དེའི་ངོ་བོ་ཉིད་སྐྱེ་བ་མེད་པ་ཡོངས་སུ་ཤེས་པ་ཡིན་པར་སྟོན་ཏེ། །དེའི་དབང་དུ་བྱས་པའི་ཕྱིར་ཉེ་བར་གྱུར་པས་ཉེ་བ་མངོན་སུམ་གྱི་ཚིག་འདིས་འདི་ལ་ཞེས་བྱ་བ་བསྟན་ཏོ།

།འདིའི་ཕྱིར་ཡང་ངོ་བོ་ཉིད་སྐྱེ་བ་མེད་པ་ཡོངས་སུ་ཤེས་པ་ན་[474] ངོ་བོ་ཉིད་ཡོངས་སུ་ཤེས་པ་ནི་མ་ཡིན་ནོ།

(b. །གཉིས་པ། མ་རིག་པའི་རྗེས་སུ་འགྲོ་ལྡོག་བྱེད་པས་རང་བཞིན་མེད་པ།)

(i. །དང་པོ། མ་རིག་པའི་རྗེས་སུ་བྱེད་པར་བསྟན་པ།)

།དེའི་ཕྱིན་ཅི་ལོག་ཡོད་ན་ནི་ཡོད་ལ་མེད་ན་ནི་མེད་པའི་ [《ཅོ་》 22a.1] ཕྱིར་རོ། [《སྣར་》 26a.1] །དེ་ལྟར་བསྟན་པའི་ཕྱིར།

མ་རིག་རྐྱེན་གྱིས་འཇིག་རྟེན་ཞེས།
།འདི་ལྟར་རྫོགས་པའི་སངས་རྒྱས་གསུང་།[475]
།དེའི་[476] ཕྱིར་འཇིག་རྟེན་འདི་དག་ཀྱང་།
།རྣམ་པར་རྟོག་པ་[477] ཅེས་མི་འཐད། ‖ 37 ‖[478]

---

474 《པེ་》《སྣར་》{SS}: +རིགས་ཀྱི་

475 {SS}: གསུངས། following {Dh}

476 《པེ་》《སྣར་》: དེ་

477 《པེ་》《སྣར་》{SS}: པར་

478 Following Tsong Khapa's lead (《ཟིན་》 8a.6), Gyaltsap (《ཏཱི་》 27b.1) rewords the entire verse as follows: འཇིག་རྟེན་མ་རིག་རྐྱེན་ཅན་དུ། །གང་ཕྱིར་སངས་རྒྱས་རྣམས་གསུངས་པ། །དེ་ཡི་ཕྱིར་ན་འཇིག་རྟེན་འདི། །རྣམ་རྟོག་ཡིན་ཞེས་ཅིས་མི་འཐད།

།ཅེས་བྱ་བ་སྨོས་སོ། །གང་གི་རྐྱེན་མ་རིག་པ་ཡིན་པ་དེ་མ་རིག་པའི་རྐྱེན་ [《སྡེ་》 23a.1] ལས་བྱུང་བ་སྟེ་འཇིག་རྟེན་ནོ། །འཇིག་རྟེན་ནི་ཉེ་བར་ལེན་པའི་ཕུང་པོ་ལྔ་རྣམས་སོ། །དེ་ལ་མ་རིག་པའི་རྐྱེན་གྱིས་འདུ་བྱེད་རྣམས། །འདུ་བྱེད་ཀྱི་རྐྱེན་གྱིས་རྣམ་པར་ཤེས་པ་ཞེས་བྱ་བ་ལ་སོགས་པ་འདིས་འདི་ལྟར་བཅོམ་ལྡན་འདས་ཀྱིས་འཇིག་རྟེན་འདིའི་རྐྱེན་ནི་མ་རིག་པའོ་ཞེས་བསྟན་པ་དེའི་ཕྱིར། །རང་གི་ངོ་བོ་གྲུབ་པ་མེད།[479] །རང་གི་ངོ་བོ་གྲུབ་པ་རྫས་ལ་སོགས་པའི་རྐྱེན་ནི་མུན་པ་མ་ཡིན་ནོ། །དེ་བས་ན་མ་རིག་པ་རྐྱེན་དུ་གྱུར་པའི་ཕྱིར། །འཇིག་རྟེན་རྣམ་པར་རྟོག་པ་ཅིའི་ཕྱིར་འཐད་དེ།[480] །འཇིག་རྟེན་རྣམ་པར་རྟོག་པ་ཙམ་དུ་འཐད་པ་ཉིད་དོ་ཞེས་བྱ་བར་དགོངས་སོ།

།རྣམ་པར་རྟོག་པ་ནི་རྣམ་པར་རྟོག་པའོ། །རྣམ་པར་རྟོག་པ་ཙམ་དུ་ཟད་པས་ན་རྣམ་པར་རྟོག་པ་སྟེ། །རྣམ་པར་རྟོག་པ་ཙམ་དུ་ཟད་དོ་ [《པེ་》 26a.1] ཞེས་བྱ་[481] བའི་ཐ་ཚིག་གོ། །རང་གི་ངོ་བོ་གྲུབ་པ་མེད་པས་མུན་ཁུང་ན་མེའི་[482] ཚུལ་དུ་ཡོངས་སུ་རྟོག་པ་འབྱུང་བ་ལྟར་འཇིག་རྟེན་ཡང་རྣམ་པར་རྟོག་པ་ཙམ་དུ་རྣམ་པར་གཞག་གོ།

(ii. །གཉིས་པ། མ་རིག་པ་ལོག་ན་ལྡོག་པ།)

།དེ་ལྟར་ཕྱིན་ཅི་ལོག་ཡོད་ན་འཇིག་རྟེན་ཡོད་པར་ཅི་བསྟན་ནས། །ད་ནི་ཕྱིན་ཅི་ལོག་མེད་ན་མེད་པར་བསྟན་པའི་ཕྱིར།

---

[479] {SS}: +དེ།

[480] {SS}: -དེ་ We read མི་འཐད་ here.

[481] 《ཅོ་》: བྱེད་

[482] 《པེ་》《སྣར་》{SS}: མིའི་

མ་རིག་འགགས་པར་གྱུར་ན་ནི།
།གང་རྣམས་འགག་པར་འགྱུར་བ་རྣམས།
།དེ་དག་མི་ཤེས་ཀུན་བརྟགས་པར།
།ཅི་ཡི་ཕྱིར་ན་གསལ་མི་འགྱུར། || **38** ||

།ཞེས་བྱ་བ་སྨོས་སོ། །སྣང་བ་བྱུང་ན་མུན་ཁུང་ན་མེའི་[483] ཚུལ་དུ་སྣང་བ་མི་དམིགས་པ་བཞིན་དུ་རིག་པ་བྱུང་ན། །གང་ལོག་པ་དེ་ངེས་པར་མི་ཤེས་པས་ཡོངས་སུ་བརྟགས་པའི་ཕྱིར་ངོ་བོ་ཉིད་དུ་གྲུབ་པ་མེད་པར་གནས་སོ།

(c. །གསུམ་པ། སྐྱེ་འཇིག་གནས་གསུམ་རྒྱུ་ལ་ལྟོས་པས་རང་བཞིན་མེད་པ།)

།འདིའི་ཕྱིར་ཡང་འཇིག་རྟེན་དངོས་པོ་མེད་དེ། །གཟུགས་བརྙན་བཞིན་ [«སྣར་»
26b.1] དུ་རྒྱུ་དང་རྐྱེན་ལས་བྱུང་བའི་ཕྱིར་རོ། །དེ་ཉིད་བསྟན་པའི་ཕྱིར།

རྒྱུ་ཡོད་པ་ལས་གང་བྱུང་[484] ཞིང་།
།རྐྱེན་མེད་པར་ནི་གནས་པ་མེད།
།རྐྱེན་མེད་ཕྱིར་ཡང་འཇིག་འགྱུར་བ།
།དེ་ནི་ཡོད་པར་ཇི་ལྟར་ཤེས།[485] || **39** ||

---

[483] «པེ་» «སྣར་» {SS}: མིའི་

[484] {SS}: འབྱུང་ following {Dh}

[485] The Skt. of this verse, preserved in *Bodhicāryāvatāra-pañjikā*, ad. IX, 85, (Vaidya, 234), reads: *hetutaḥ saṁbhavo yasya sthitir na pratyayair vinā / vigamaḥ pratyayābhāvāt so 'stīty avagataḥ kathaṁ //*

།ཞེས་བྱ་བ་སྨོས་སོ། །གལ་ཏེ་འཇིག་རྟེན་ངོ་བོ་ཉིད་དུ་གྲུབ་ན་ནི་དེའི་ཚེ་[486] རང་བཞིན་གྱི་ངོ་བོར་གྲུབ་པ་ཡོད་པས་རྒྱུ་དང་རྐྱེན་ལ་ལྟོས་ [«ཅོ་» 22b.1] ཏེ་འབྱུང་བར་[487] མི་འགྱུར་ཞིང་། །རྒྱུ་དང་བཅས་[488] ལས་འབྱུང་བར་ཡང་མི་འགྱུར་ཏེ། །ངོ་བོ་ཉིད་ནི་བྱས་པ་མེད་པའི་ [«སྡེ་» 23b.1] ཕྱིར་རོ། །གནས་པ་ཡང་རྐྱེན་ལ་རག་ལས་པར་མི་འགྱུར་རོ། །ངོ་བོ་ཉིད་ཀྱིས་གྲུབ་པ་ཡོད་ན་གཞན་དུ་འགྱུར་མི་སྲིད་དེ། །འདི་ལྟར་གཞན་དུ་འགྱུར་བ་སྨྲང་བའི་ཕྱིར་གནས་པའི་རྐྱེན་བཙལ་བ་ནི་རིགས་[489] པར་འགྱུར་རོ། །གང་གནས་པའི་རྐྱེན་ལ་རག་ལས་པ་དེ་གཟུགས་བརྙན་བཞིན་དུ་ངོ་བོ་ཉིད་མེད་པར་གྲུབ་པ་ཡང་རིགས་སོ། །གང་ངོ་བོ་ཉིད་དུ་གྲུབ་པ་དེ་ནི་རང་བཞིན་གྱིས་མི་འགྱུར་བས་གནས་པའི་རྐྱེན་མེད་ཀྱང་ལྡོག་པ་[490] མི་རིགས་སོ། །གང་གནས་པའི་རྐྱེན་མེད་ན་ལྡོག་པ་དེ་ནི་གཟུགས་བརྙན་བཞིན་དུ་ངོ་བོ་ཉིད་ཀྱིས་གྲུབ་པ་མེད་པར་འོས་སོ། །གང་དེ་ལྟར་ངོ་བོ་ཉིད་ཀྱིས་གྲུབ་པ་མེད་པ་དེ་གཞན་གྱིས་ཇི་ལྟར་ཡོད་པར་ཁོང་དུ་ཆུད་པའི་རྒྱུ་མེད་པས་དེ་ཡོད་པ་ཉིད་དུ་མི་རིགས་སོ་ཞེས་བྱ་བར་དགོངས་སོ། [«པེ་» 26b.1]

---

486 «པེ་» «སྣར་» {SS}: +དེའི་

487 «པེ་» «སྣར་»: བ་

488 «པེ་» «སྣར་» {SS}: +པ་

489 «པེ་» «སྣར་»: རིག་

490 «སྣར་» {SS}: པར་

(C. །གསུམ་པ། ཕུང་པོར་ཞེན་པའི་ཉེས་དམིགས།)

(1. །དང་པོ། སྐབས་དགོད་པ།)

(a. །དང་པོ། གཞན་སྡེ་རང་བཞིན་ཡོད་པར་སྨྲ་བ་དེ་ཙམ་ཡ་མཚན་མེད་པ།)

།མུ་སྟེགས་ཅན་རྟེན་ཅིང་འབྲེལ་པར་འབྱུང་བ་མི་སྨྲ་བ་རྣམས་ཀྱི་དངོས་པོ་རྣམས་ལ་ངོ་བོ་ཉིད་ཡོད་པར་མངོན་པར་ཞེན་པ་གང་ཡིན་པ་དེ་ནི་རང་གི་གྲུབ་པའི་མཐའ་ལས་བྱུང་[491] བ་དང་མི་འགལ་བས།

གལ་[492] ཏེ་ཡོད་པར་སྨྲ་བ་[493] རྣམས།
།དངོས་ལ་ཞེན་པར་གནས་པ་ནི།
།ལམ་དེ་ཉིད་ལ་གནས་པ་སྟེ།
།དེ་ལ་ངོ་མཚར་ཅུང་ཟད་མེད། **|| 40 ||**

།གྲངས་ཅན་གྱིས་རང་གི་གྲུབ་པའི་མཐའ་ལས་ཡོན་ཏན་སྙིང་སྟོབས་དང་། །རྡུལ་དང་མུན་པ་གསུམ་རྟག་པར་ལོབས་ལ། །བྱེ་བྲག་པས་ཀྱང་རང་གི་གྲུབ་པའི་མཐའ་ལས་ས་དང་། །ཆུ་དང་མེ་དང་རླུང་གི་རྡུལ་ཕྲ་རབ་ཡན་ལག་ཅན་མ་ལུས་པའི་དངོས་པོ་རྩོམ་པ་རྟག་པ་ཉིད་དུ་ལོབས་ནས་རྟག་པའི་དངོས་པོར་སྨྲ་བའི་ཕྱིར་གལ་ཏེ་དངོས་པོ་ལ་ཞེན་པར་ [«སྣར་» 27a.1] གནས་པ་དང་ངོ་བོ་ཉིད་བཟུང་ནས་གནས་པ་དེ་ལ་ནི་བློ་མཆོག་དང་ལྡན་པ་དག་ངོ་མཚར་དུ་འཛིན་པ་ཅུང་ཟད་ཀྱང་མེད་དེ་ཡ་མཚན་དུ་བྱ་བ་ཅུང་ཟད་ཀྱང་མེད་པ་ཡིན་ནོ།

།དེ་ཅིའི་ཕྱིར་ཞེ་ན། །འདི་ལྟར་མི་སྲིད་པའི་དངོས་པོ་ལ་བརྟེན་པ་ནི་འཇིག་རྟེན་ན་ངོ་མཚར་གྱི་རྒྱུ་ཡིན་ནོ། །སྲིད་པའི་དངོས་པོ་ལ་བརྟེན་པ་ནི་དེ་ལྟ་མ་ཡིན་ཏེ། །དེ་རིགས་པའི་ཕྱིར་རོ། །རང་གི་

---

491 «པེ་»«སྣར་»{SS}: འབྱུང་

492 «ཟིན་»: གང་

493 «ཅོ་»: བར་

གྲུབ་པའི་མཐའ་ལས་ཡོད་པར་བསྟན་པ་སྟོན་ཞིང་ཁོང་དུ་ཆུད་པ་ལ་ནི་ངོ་མཚར་གྱི་རྒྱུ་མེད་པས་ངོ་མཚར་ཅུང་ཟད་ཀྱང་མེད་པར་རིགས་སོ།

།བྱེ་བྲག་ཏུ་ [《སྡེ་》 24a.1] སྨྲ་བ་དང་། མདོ་སྡེ་པ་དང་། །རྣམ་པར་ཤེས་པ་ཙམ་དུ་སྨྲ་བ་གྲུབ་པས་[494] མཐའ་ལས་ [《ཅོ་》 23a.1] ཡོད་པ་མི་སྲིད་པ་ཡོངས་སུ་སྟོན་པ་ནི་བློ་མཆོག་དང་ལྡན་པ་དག་ལ་མཆོག་ཏུ་ངོ་མཚར་བསྐྱེད་པ་ཡིན་ནོ།

(b. །གཉིས་པ། རང་སྡེ་རང་བཞིན་ཡོད་པར་སྨྲ་བ་ཆེས་མི་རིགས་པ།)

།དེ་དག་ལ།[495]

སངས་རྒྱས་ལམ་ལ་བརྟེན་ནས་ནི།
།ཐམས་ཅད་མི་རྟག་སྨྲ་བ་རྣམས།
།རྩོད་པ་ཡིས་ནི་དངོས་པོ་ལ།
།ཆགས་གནས་གང་ཡིན་དེ་རྨད་[496] དོ། || **41** ||

།རྟེན་ཅིང་འབྲེལ་པར་འབྱུང་བ་ནི་སངས་རྒྱས་པའི་ལམ་ཡིན་ཏེ། །དེ་ལ་བརྟེན་ནས་འདུ་བྱེད་དེ་དག་ཐམས་ཅད་རྟེན་ཅིང་འབྲེལ་པར་འབྱུང་བའི་ཕྱིར་མི་རྟག་པའོ།[497] །ཞེས་དེ་སྐད་ཁས་ལེན་ཀྱང་དངོས་པོ་རྣམས་ཀྱི་རང་གི་ངོ་བོ་གྲུབ་པར་སྟོན་པར་འདོད་པ་དེ་སྟོང་པ་ཉིད་དུ་སྨྲ་བ་ལ་རྩོད་པར་བྱེད་ཅིང་

---

494 《པེ་》《སྣར་》{SS}: པའི་

495 《པེ་》《སྣར་》: -ལ་

496 《སྡེ་》《ཅོ་》: སྨད་ 《ཏྲི་》《པེ་》《སྣར་》{SS}: རྨད་ apparently following the gloss of this line in 《ཏྲི་》 as: རྨད་དུ་བྱུང་ངོ།

497 《པེ་》: པའི་

དེ་མི་སྲིད་པའི་དངོས་པོ་ལ་བརྟེན་པ་ནི་ངོ་མཚར་ཆེ་བས་དེ་རྨད་དུ་གྱུར་པའོ། །ངོ་མཚར་ཆེ་བ་དེ་ཡང་འཇིག་རྟེན་ན་ཡ་མཚན་དུ་ [《པེ་》 27a.1] གྱུར་པས་རྨད་དུ་བྱུང་བ་ཞེས་བྱའོ།

།དེ་ལྟར་ཐམས་ཅད་ཀྱང་མི་རྟག་པར་སྨྲ་བ་[498] ལ་རྟེན་ཅིང་འབྲེལ་པར་འབྱུང་བའི་ལམ་ཁས་[499] ལེན་པར་གྱུར་ཀྱང་དངོས་པོའི་ངོ་བོ་ཉིད་སྟོན་ཅིང་[500] རྣམ་པར་གནས་པ་ནི་ཧྲ་དམུ་[501] རྐྱོད་པོང་[502] བུའི་སྤྱོད་པ་ལྟར་བཙོས་པ་བཞིན་དུ་མཁས་པ་དག་ལ་རབ་ཏུ་ངོ་མཚར་དུ་འགྱུར་རོ། །ཕྱག་བྱ་བར་འོས་པ་[503] མ་ཡིན་པ་ལ་ཕྱག་འཚལ་ལོ་ཞེས་བྱ་བའི་ཚིག་བཞིན་དུ་རྨད་དུ་བྱུང་བའི་སྒྲ་བསྟོད་པའི་ [《སྣར་》 27b.1] ཚིག་འདི་ཡང་[504] བསྟིང་བ་ཡིན་ནོ།

(c. །གསུམ་པ། དེའི་འཐད་པ།)

།རྟེན་ཅིང་འབྲེལ་པར་འབྱུང་བ་ཁས་ལེན་པ་སངས་རྒྱས་པའི་ལམ་ལ་བརྟེན་པ་དག

དེ་ནི་འདི་ཞེས་གང་དག་ལ།
།བརྟགས་ན་རབ་ཏུ་མི་དམིགས་ན།

---

498 《པེ་》《སྣར་》: -བ་

499 《པེ་》《སྣར་》: མཁས་

500 《པེ་》《སྣར་》{SS}: ཞིང་

501 《པེ་》《སྣར་》: རྨུ་

502 《པེ་》: བུང་

503 《པེ་》《སྣར་》{SS}: པར་

504 《སྣར་》: དག་

།བདེན་པ་དེ་ནི་འདིའོ་[505] ཞེས།

།རྩོད་པས་མཁས་པ་སུ་ཞིག་སྨྲ།[506] **|| 42 ||**

།འདི་ལྟར་གཟུགས་དང་ཚོར་བ་དང་། །རྣམ་པར་ཤེས་པ་དང་། །འདུས་བྱས་གཞན་ཐམས་ཅད་རྟེན་ཅིང་འབྲེལ་པར་འབྱུང་བའི་ཕྱིར་ངོ་བོ་ཉིད་ཀྱིས་མ་སྐྱེས་པའོ། །གང་ངོ་བོ་ཉིད་ཀྱིས་མ་སྐྱེས་པ་དེའི་མཚན་མ་དམིགས་སུ་མེད་པའི་ཕྱིར་གཟུགས་དེ་ནི་འདིའོ། །ཚོར་བ་དེ་ནི་འདིའོ། །རྣམ་པར་ཤེས་པ་དེ་ནི་འདིའོ། །འདུས་བྱས་གཞན་དེ་ནི་འདིའོ་ཞེས་བློ་ལ་རྣམ་པ་ཐམས་ཅད་དུ་མི་སྣང་སྟེ། །དེ་ལྟར་གང་གིས་ཀྱང་བྱེ་བྲག་ཏུ་མི་སྣང་བ་གང་ཡིན་པ་[507] དེ་ནི་འདིའོ་ཞེས་གཞན་ལ་བསྟན་ [«སྡེ་» 24b.1] པར་མི་ནུས་སོ། །གང་བསྟན་པར་མི་ནུས་པ་དེ་ལ་ཤེས་རབ་ཅན་དག་རྩོད་པ་སྨྲ་བ་ནི་མི་རིགས་སོ། །རྩོད་པ་ཞེས་བྱ་བ་ནི་གང་ལ་བདག་གི་ཕྱོགས་སྒྲུབ་པ་དང་། །གཞན་གྱི་ཕྱོགས་གཞིག་པའོ། །དེ་ལྟར་དངོས་པོ་གང་ཡང་མི་དམིགས་ན་ [«ཅོ་» 23b.1] རང་གིས་ཁས་བླངས་པ་དངོས་པོ་བདེན་པ་གང་ཡིན་པ་དེ་ནི་འདིའོ་ཞེས་བསྟན་[508] པར་བྱ་བ་དེ་ཅུང་ཟད་ཀྱང་ཡོད་པར་ག་ལ་འགྱུར། །གཞན་གྱིས་ཁས་བླངས་པའི་དངོས་པོ་བརྫུན་པ་གང་ཡིན་པ་དེ་ནི་འདིའོ་ཞེས་བསྟན་པར་བྱ་བ་དེ་ཡང་ཅུང་ཟད་ཀྱང་ཡོད་པར་ག་ལ་འགྱུར།

---

505 {SS}: འདི་འོ་

506 Gyaltsap («ཊཱི་» 28b.1–.2) follows Pa-tshab's translation, with some variation, giving it as: འདིའམ་དེའོ་ཞེས་གང་དུ། །རྣམ་པར་དཔྱད་ན་མི་དམིགས་ན། །རྩོད་པས་འདིའམ་དེ་བདེན་ཞེས། །མཁས་པ་སུ་ཞིག་སྨྲ་བར་འགྱུར།

507 «པེ་» «སྣར་» {SS}: +དེ་

508 «པེ་» «སྣར་» : བསྟེན་

(2. །གཉིས་པ། ཉེས་དམིགས་དངོས།)

(a. །དང་པོ། དངོས་པོར་སྨྲ་བ་ཐར་ལམ་ལས་གྲོལ་བར་ལྟ་བའི་ཆུས་ཁྱེར་བར་བསྟན་པ།)

(i. །དང་པོ། གཞན་སྡེ་ལྟ་བས་ཕྱོགས་པར་བསྟན་པ།)

།དེ་ལྟར་རྟེན་ཅིང་འབྲེལ་པར་འབྱུང་བའི་དོན་རང་བཞིན་གྱིས་སྐྱེ་བ་མེད་པའི་དོན་དུ་ཁོང་དུ་མ་ཆུད་པ་ཤིན་ཏུ་ཕྱིན་ཅི་ལོག་ཏུ་གྱུར་པ་དག་གིས།

མ་བརྟན་[509] པར་ནི་གང་དག་གིས།
།བདག་གམ་འཇིག་རྟེན་མངོན་ཆགས་པ།
།རྟག་དང་མི་རྟག་སོགས་ལྟ་བས།
།ཀྱེ་མ་དེ་དག་འཕྲོགས་[510] པ་ཡིན། **|| 43 ||**

།གང་དག་ཕུང་པོ་ལྔ་ [《པེ་》 27b.1] གཟུགས་བརྙན་ལྟ་བུ་རང་བཞིན་མེད་པ་ལ་བརྟེན་ནས་བདག་ཏུ་མི་འདོགས་ཀྱི། །སེམས་རང་གི་མཚན་ཉིད་དུ་གྲུབ་པ་ལ་བདག་གོ་ཞེས་རྣམ་པར་འཇོག་པ་དེ་དག་གདོན་མི་ཟ་བར་ལྟ་བའི་ཆུ་བོ་ཆེན་པོས་མྱ་ངན་ལས་འདས་པའི་ལམ་ལས་དེད་ཅིང་ཁྱེར་བར་འགྱུར་རོ།

།ཇི་ལྟ་[511] ཞེ་ན། །དེ་ལ་[512] སེམས་ངོ་བོ་ཉིད་དུ་གྲུབ་པར་ [《སྣར་》 28a.1] འདོད་ན་ཡང་ན་ནི་རྟག་པར་འགྱུར། །ཡང་ན་ནི་མི་རྟག་པར་འགྱུར་རོ། །གལ་ཏེ་རྟག་པར་འགྱུར་ན་དེའི་ཚེ་ཐེར་ཟུག་ཏུ་སྨྲ་བ་ཡིན་ནོ། །འོན་ཏེ་མི་རྟག་ན་དེའི་ཚེ་ཆད་པར་སྨྲ་བ་ཡིན་ཏེ། །བྱུང་ནས་མེད་པར་

---

509 《ཏྲི་》《པེ་》《སྣར་》{SS}: བརྟེན་

510 《པེ་》《སྣར་》: ཕྲོགས་

511 《པེ་》《སྣར་》{SS}: ལྟར་

512 《སྣར་》: ལས་

གྱུར་པ་ནི་ཆད་པར་ལྟ་བ་ཡིན་ནོ། །དེ་ལྟར་དེ་དག་ཀྱེ་མ་ལྟ་བས་འཁྲུགས་པ་ཡིན་ནོ། །ཀྱེ་མ་ཞེས་བྱ་བའི་སྒྲ་ནི་སྐྱེ་སྡུགས་འདོན་པའམ་[513] ངེས་པར་རིག་པར་བྱའོ། །དེ་ལྟར་འཇིག་རྟེན་ཞེས་བྱ་བ་ཕུང་པོ་ལྔ་པོ་རང་གི་མཚན་ཉིད་ཀྱིས་གྲུབ་པར་འདོད་ན་ཡང་མཐུན་པར་སྐྱོན་དུ་འགྱུར་བར་སྨྲར་རོ།

།ཡང་ན་འདི་ནི་དོན་གཞན་ཏེ། །གྲངས་ཅན་ལ་སོགས་པ་[514] གང་དག་མ་བརྟེན་པར་བདག་རྟག་པ་དང་། །ངོ་བོ་ཉིད་ཀྱིས་གྲུབ་པ་དང་། །རྟེན་ཅིང་འབྲེལ་པར་འབྱུང་བ་མ་ཡིན་པ་དང་། །འཇིག་རྟེན་ཡང་རང་བཞིན་གྱི་བདག་ཉིད་དང་། །རང་བཞིན་ཡང་འགྱུར་བ་མེད་པའི་ཕྱིར་ངོ་བོ་ཉིད་ཀྱིས་གྲུབ་[515] པར་ཞེན་ལ་འགྱུར་བའི་ཚོགས་ནི་ [«སྡེ་» 25a.1] ལྡོག་པར་འདོད་དོ། །གཞན་དག་ནི་གཞན་དུ་འདོད། །ཀྱེ་མ་དེ་དག་ནི་གདོན་མི་ཟ་བར་རྟག་པ་དང་མི་རྟག་པ་ལ་སོགས་པའི་ལྟ་བ་རྣམས་ཀྱིས་འཁྲུགས་པར་འགྱུར་རོ།

(ii. །གཉིས་པ། རང་སྐྱེ་ལྟ་བས་འཁྲུགས་པར་བསྟན་པ།)

།རང་གི་སྐྱེ་བ་གང་དག་ཕུང་པོ་ལྔ་དང་བདག་བརྟེན་[516] པར་ཁས་ལེན་ཀྱང་རྫས་སུ་ཡོད་པ་ཉིད་དུ་ཞུགས་པ་དང་གང་དག་མ་རིག་པ་དང་འདུ་བྱེད་ལ་སོགས་པ་རྒྱུ་དང་རྐྱེན་ཚོགས་པ་ [«ཅོ་» 24a.1] ལས་བྱུང་བ་ཡིན་ཡང་[517] རྣམ་པར་ཤེས་པ་ལ་སོགས་པ་རྫས་སུ་ཡོད་པ་ཉིད་དུ་བརྗོད་པ་དེ་དག་ཀྱང་དེ་བཞིན་དུ་ལྟ་བ་ལོག་པར་ཞུགས་པ་ཡིན་པར་བསྟན་པའི་ཕྱིར།

---

513 «ཅོ་»: པར་མ་

514 «པེ་»: -པ་

515 «པེ་» «སྣར་» {SS}: +པོ་ཞེས་མངོན་

516 «པེ་»: རྟེན་

517 «ཅོ་»: ལང་

གང་དག་བརྟེན་ནས་དངོས་པོ་[518] རྣམས།
།ཡང་དག་ཉིད་དུ་འགྲུབ་འདོད་པ།
།དེ་དག་ལ་ཡང་རྟག་སྐྱོགས་[519] ཀྱི།
།སྐྱོན་དེ་ཇི་ལྟར་འབྱུང་མི་འགྱུར། ॥ **44** ॥

།ཞེས་བྱ་བ་སྨོས་སོ། །ཇི་ལྟར་བདག་དང་ཆོས་ཀྱི་ངོ་བོ་ཉིད་ཀྱི་དོན་ཡོད་པ་དང་། །མེད་པར་ཁས་བླངས་པ་ལ་རྟག་པ་དང་། །ཆད་པའི་སྐྱོན་དུ་འགྱུར་བ་དང་མཚུངས་པའི་ཕྱིར་རོ།

(iii. །གསུམ་པ། སྟོང་པར་སྨྲ་བ་དེ་ལས་ལྡོག་པར་བསྟན་པ།)

།ཇི་སྐད་སྨོས་པའི་ལྟ་བ་དག་བསལ་ནས་རྟེན་ཅིང་ [«པེ་» 28a.1] འབྲེལ་པར་འབྱུང་བ་ཇི་ལྟར་གནས་པའི་དོན་ཁོང་དུ་ཆུད་ན། [«སྣར་» 28b.1]

གང་དག་བརྟེན་ནས་དངོས་པོ་རྣམས།
།ཆུ་ཡི་ཟླ་བ་ལྟ་བུར་ནི།
།ཡང་དག་མ་ཡིན་ལོག་མིན་པར།
།འདོད་པ་དེ་དག་ལྟས་མི་འཕྲོགས། ॥ **45** ॥

།གལ་ཏེ་གཟུགས་ལ་སོགས་པ་ངོ་བོ་ཉིད་ཀྱིས་མེད་པ་ཡིན་ན། །དེ་དག་ངོ་བོ་ཉིད་ཀྱིས་མེད་པས་ངོ་བོ་ཉིད་གཞན་དུ་འགྱུར་མི་སྲིད་དེ། །ངོ་བོ་ཉིད་ཀྱིས་མེད་པ་ནི་ཕྱིས་ཡོད་པར་མི་རུང་ངོ་། །རྒྱུ་དང་རྐྱེན་ཡོད་དུ་ཟིན་ཀྱང་གང་ཡང་སྐྱེ་མི་སྲིད་པ་དང་རྒྱུ་དང་རྐྱེན་རྣམས་ཀྱང་དེ་ལྟ་བུའི་རང་བཞིན་ཡིན་པས་མི་སྲིད་པའི་ཕྱིར་རྟེན་ཅིང་འབྲེལ་པར་འབྱུང་བ་དང་འགལ་བར་འགྱུར་རོ།

---

518 «པེ་»: པ་

519 «པེ་» «སྣར་» {SS}: སོགས་

།འོན་ཏེ་ཉེས་པ་དེ་ཡོངས་སུ་སྤང་བར་འདོད་དེ། །ངོ་བོ་ཉིད་ཀྱིས་ཡོད་པར་ཁས་ལེན་[520] ན་ཡང་དེའི་ཚེ་དེ་ལྟར་བྱུང་བ་བཞིན་དུ་རྒྱུ་དང་རྐྱེན་རྣམས་ཀྱིས་ཀྱང་འབྱུང་བར་མི་འགྱུར་ཏེ། །ཿརྒྱུ་དང་[521] རྐྱེན་རྣམས་ཀྱང་དགོས་པ་མེད་པས་ཡོད་པར་མི་འགྱུར་རོ། །དེ་ལྟ་ན་ཡང་རྟེན་ཅིང་འབྲེལ་པར་འབྱུང་བ་དང་འགལ་བར་འགྱུར་རོ།

།རྟེན་ཅིང་འབྲེལ་པར་འབྱུང་བ་དང་འགལ་ན་རྣམ་པར་གཞག་པ་ཐམས་ཅད་ཞིག [《སྡེ་》 25b.1] པར་འགྱུར་རོ།[522] །བོང་བུའི་རྭ་ལ་སོགས་པ་བཞིན་དུ་འགྲོ་བ་ཡང་མི་དམིགས་པར་འགྱུར་རོ། །དེ་བས་ན་ཁམས་དང་འགྲོ་བ་དང་། །སྐྱེ་གནས་དང་། རིགས་དང་། །རུས་དང་། །ཚེ་རིགས་དང་། །ཁ་དོག་དང་། །གཟུགས་དང་། །སྟོབས་དང་། །བློ་དང་། །དབང་པོ་སོ་སོ་ཐ་དད་པའི་འགྲོ་བ་དང་། །འགྲོ་བ་མ་ལུས་པའི་རྟེན་ཕྱི་རོལ་གྱི་རླུང་[523] གི་དཀྱིལ་འཁོར་ལ་སོགས་པ་དང་། །གསེར་དང་། །དངུལ་དང་། །ཿཨནྡྲ་ནཱི་ལ་[524] དང་། །ཤེལ་[525] དང་། །པདྨ་རཱ་ག་ལ་སོགས་པ་དང་། །ཿཀུ་མུ་ད་དང་། །པདྨ་དང་།[526] །ཤིང་དང་། །རི་དང་། །སྨན་དང་། །བུམ་པ་དང་། [《ཅོ་》 24b.1] །ཤིང་རྟ་ལ་སོགས་པ་དམིགས་སུ་མེད་པ

---

[520] 《པེ་》: ལན་

[521] 《པེ་》《སྣར་》: -རྒྱུ་དང་

[522] 《པེ་》《སྣར་》{SS}: ཏེ།

[523] 《པེ་》: ཀླུང་

[524] {SS}: ཨིནྡྲ་ནི་ལ་

[525] 《པེ་》《ཅོ་》: ཤལ་

[526] 《པེ་》《སྣར་》{SS}: །པདྨ་དང་། །ཀུ་མུ་ད་དང་།

སྣ་ཚོགས་ཀྱང་མེད་པ་ཉིད་དུ་འགྱུར་རོ། །དེ་དམིགས་སུ་ཡོད་བཞིན་དུ་མེད་པར་ཁས་བླང་བ་[527] ནི་མི་རིགས་སོ།

།དེ་བས་ན་གང་བརྟེན་ཏེ་འབྱུང་བའི་ངོ་བོ་ཉིད་ཀྱིས་ཡོད་པ་དང་མེད་པ་སྤངས་པ་སྟེ། །རྐྱེན་འདི་ཙམ་གྱིས་གྲུབ་པས་གཟུགས་བརྙན་བཞིན་དུ་དེ་ངོ་བོ་ཉིད་ཀྱིས་གྲུབ་པ་མེད་པར་ཁས་བླང་བར་བྱ་སྟེ། །ཇི་ལྟར་འཕགས་པ་ལྷས།

།འབྲས་བུ་ཡོད་པར་གང་འདོད་དང་།
།འབྲས་བུ་མེད་ [«སྣར་» 29a.1] པར་གང་འདོད་ལ།
།ཀ་བ་ལ་སོགས་ཁྱིམ་ [«པེ་» 28b.1] དོན་དུ།
།བརྒྱན་[528] པའི་དོན་ཀྱང་མེད་པར་འགྱུར།

།ཞེས་སྨོས་པ་ལྟ་བུའོ། །དེ་ལྟར་རྟག་པ་དང་ཆད་པ་སྤངས་ནས་རྟེན་ཅིང་འབྲེལ་པར་འབྱུང་བ་གཟུགས་བརྙན་ལྟ་བུ་བློ་ཕྱིན་ཅི་[529] ལོག་གི་[530] སྤྱོད་ཡུལ་དུ་གྱུར་པ་དང་འགལ་བ་མེད་པས་ཇི་སྐད་སྨོས་པའི་འགྲོ་བ་སྣ་ཚོགས་མི་སྲིད་པ་མ་ཡིན་ནོ།

།འཕགས་པ་རྣམས་ཀྱང་ཕྱིན་ཅི་ལོག་སྤངས་ཏེ། །བརྫུན་དུ་སྒྲོ་མི་འདོགས་པས་རྣམ་པར་གྲོལ་བ་མི་སྲིད་པ་མ་ཡིན་ནོ། །གང་གི་ཕྱིར་རྟེན་ཅིང་འབྲེལ་པར་འབྱུང་བ་འདི་ལྟར་ངོ་བོ་ཉིད་ཀྱིས་སྐྱེ་བ་མེད་པ་དེའི་ཕྱིར་རིགས་པ་འདིས་དངོས་པོ་རྣམས་ལ་གང་དག་བརྟེན་ནས་དངོས་པོ་རྣམས་ཆུའི་ཟླ་བ་ལྟ་བུར་ནི་འདོད་པ་དེ་དག་རང་གི་ངོ་བོར་གྲུབ་པ་མེད་པས་གཟུགས་བརྙན་བཞིན་དུ་རང་གི་ངོ་བོ་ཉིད་ཀྱི་

---

527 «པེ་» «སྣར་» {SS}: བླང་བར་ «ཅོ་» : བླངས་པ་

528 «པེ་» «སྣར་» {SS}: རྒྱུན་

529 {SS}: +མ་

530 «པེ་» «སྣར་» {SS}: རྒྱུན་

བདེན་པ་ཡང་མ་ཡིན་བརྫུན་པ་ཡང་མ་ཡིན་པར་འདོད་དེ། །འདི་ལྟར་བསམ་པ་འདི་ནི་དངོས་པོར་གྱུར་པ་ལ་བརྟེན་པ་སྟེ། །རྟེན་ཅིང་འབྲེལ་པར་འབྱུང་བ་ནི་དངོས་པོ་ཡོད་པ་མ་ཡིན་ལ། །གཟུགས་བརྙན་ལྟ་བུར་གྱུར་པ་དེའི་ཕྱིར་དེ་ཡང་དག་པ་མ་ཡིན་ནོ། །ཡང་དག་པར་ཡོད་ན་གཞན་དུ་འགྱུར་ [«སྡེ་» 26a.1] མི་སྲིད་པར་ཐལ་བར་འགྱུར་རོ། །འཇིག་རྟེན་ན་[531] ཡང་དག་པ་དང་འདྲ་བར་སྣང་བས་ལོག་པ་ཡང་མ་ཡིན་ནོ། །ཡང་དག་པ་མ་ཡིན་པ་ཞེས་བྱ་བ་ཡང་ལ་ལ་ལ་བསྟན་པ་དང་དགོས་པ་འགྲུབ་པའི་ཕྱིར་རོ། །གང་གི་ཕྱིར་ཡང་དག་པ་མ་ཡིན་པ་དེའི་ཕྱིར་རྟག་པར་སྨྲ་བ་མ་ཡིན་ནོ། །གང་གི་[532] ཡང་དག་པ་མ་ཡིན་པ་ཡང་མ་ཡིན་པ་དེའི་ཕྱིར་ཆད་པར་སྨྲ་[533] བའམ་ལོག་པར་སྨྲ་བ་མ་ཡིན་ནོ།

།དེ་ལྟར་གཟུགས་བརྙན་བཞིན་དུ་རྟེན་ཅིང་འབྲེལ་པར་འབྱུང་བ་རང་བཞིན་མེད་པར་ཁོང་དུ་ཆུད་ན་གདོན་མི་ཟ་བར་རྩོལ་བཞིན་མ་ཡིན་པར་རྣམ་པའི་རླུང་གིས་དཀྲུགས་ཏེ་འཁྲུགས་པར་གྱུར་པའི་རྦ་རླབས་ཆེན་པོ་བརྟག་པ་དང་མི་རྟག་པ་ལ་སོགས་པའི་ལྟ་བའི་ཆུ་ [«སྣར་» 29b.1] བོ་ལས་རྟེན་ཅིང་འབྲེལ་པར་འབྱུང་བ་ [«ཅོ་» 25a.1] ཞེས་པའི་གྲུས་བཀྲལ་ནས་མྱ་ངན་ལས་འདས་པའི་སྐྱེད་[534] མོས་ཚལ་གྱི་ཐང་སངས་རྒྱས་ཀྱི་ཆོས་མ་འདྲེས་པའི་ཞིང་གི་ཚལ་གྱིས་མཛེས་པར་བྱས་པ། །བྱང་ཆུབ་ཀྱི་ཡན་ལག་གི་རིན་པོ་ཆེ་སྣ་ཚོགས་ཡིད་འཕྲོག་[535] པ་ཡོད་པ། །སྟོབས་བཅུ་དང་ལྡན་པས་ [«པེ་» 29a.1] དྲི་མ་མེད་པ། །ཟད་པ་དང་མི་སྐྱེ་བ་ཞེས་པས་དབེན་པར་བདེ་བར་ཕྱིན་ཏེ། །གཞན་དག་ལ་ཡང་དེའི་རྗེས་སུ་འགྲོ་བ་རྟེན་ཅིང་འབྲེལ་པར་འབྱུང་བའི་གཏམ་གསང

531 «པེ་»«སྣར་»{SS}: +ཡང་

532 {SS}: +ཕྱིར་

533 «པེ་»: སྨུ་

534 «པེ་»: སྐྱེས་

535 «པེ་»: འཕྲོགས་

བསྟོད་དེ་[536] སྟོན་པས་བསྒྲོ་བ་དེ་བསྒྲུབ་[537] པ་ལ་བརྩོན་པ་[538] འཁོར་བའི་[539] རྒྱ་མཚོ་ཆེན་པོའི་ནང་ན་འདུག་པ་རྟག་པ་ལ་སོགས་པའི་ལྟ་བའི་ཆུ་བོ་རྣམས་ཀྱིས་མགོ་རྨོངས་པ་དེ་དག་ངེས་པར་སྒྲོལ་ལོ།

(b. །གཉིས་པ། ལྟ་བ་དེ་ཉིད་དོན་མིན་པའི་རྒྱུར་བསྟན་པ།)

(i. །དང་པོ། དངོས།)

།གང་དག་རྟེན་ཅིང་འབྲེལ་པར་འབྱུང་བའི་ཆོས་ཉིད་འདི་ཁོང་དུ་མ་[540] ཆུད་དེ། །དངོས་པོ་རྣམས་ཀྱི་རང་གི་མཚན་ཉིད་[541] ཡོངས་སུ་རྟོག་པ་དེ་དག་ནི་གདོན་མི་ཟ་བར་

དངོས་པོར་ཁས་ལེན་ཡོད་ན་ནི།
།འདོད་ཆགས་ཞེ་སྡང་འབྱུང་བ་ཡི།
།ལྟ་བ་མི་བཟད་མ་རུངས་འཛིན།
།དེ་ལས་བྱུང་བའི་རྩོད་པར་འགྱུར།[542] **|| 46 ||**

།དེ་ལ་འདོད་ཆགས་ནི་རང་གི་ཕྱོགས་ལ་མངོན་པར་ཞེན་པའི་མཚན་ཉིད་དོ། །ཞེ་སྡང་ནི་གཞན་གྱི་ཕྱོགས་ལ་རྒྱབ་ཀྱིས་བལྟས་པའི་མཚན་ཉིད་དོ། །འདོད་ཆགས་དང་ཞེ་སྡང་གང་ལས་འབྱུང་བ་དེ་

---

536 «པེ་» «སྣར་»: ཏེ་

537 «པེ་» «སྣར་» {SS}: སྒྲུབ་

538 «པེ་» «སྣར་» {SS}: +ལ་

539 «པེ་»: བར་

540 «པེ་» «སྣར་»: -མ་

541 «པེ་» «སྣར་» {SS}: +ལ་

542 The Skt. is preserved in Haribhadra's *Abhisamayālaṁkārāloka* (Wogihara, 161) and is given by Lindtner (*Nāgārjuniana*, 114–115) as: *rāga-dveṣodbhavas tīvra-duṣṭa-dṛṣṭi-parigrahaḥ / vivādās tat-samutthāś ca bhāvābhyupagame sati //*

འདོད་ཆགས་དང་ཞེ་སྡང་འབྱུང་བའོ། །རྣམ་པར་སྨིན་པ་ཤིན་ཏུ་མི་བདེ་བ་དང་ཤིན་ཏུ་བཟོད་པར་དཀའ་བའི་ཕྱིར་མི་བཟོད་པའོ། །སེམས་ཀྱི་རྒྱུད་ [《སྡེ་》 26b.1] ལ་གནོད་པ་སྐྱེད་པར་བྱེད་པ་དང་། །འདའ་བར་དཀའ་བའི་ཕྱིར་མ་རུངས་པ་སྟེ། །དེ་ཡང་གང་ཞེ་ན། །ལྟ་བ་ཡོངས་སུ་འཛིན་པའོ།

།ལྟ་བ་ལ་གནས་པ་འདི་ལྟ་བུ་འདི་ཡང་དངོས་པོར་[543] ལེན་པ་ལས་སྐྱེའོ། །ལྟ་བ་ཡོངས་སུ་འཛིན་པ་ཡོད་ན་རང་གིས་ཁས་བླངས་པའི་དོན་བསྟན་པར་འདོད་པ་དང་། །གཞན་གྱིས་ཁས་བླངས་པ་ཞིག་འདོད་པའི་ཕྱིར་ལྟ་བ་ཁས་ལེན་པ་ལས་བྱུང་བའི་རྩོད་པ་དངོས་པོ་[544] ལ་མངོན་པར་ཞེན་པའི་རྩ་བ་ལས་བྱུང་བ་གཞན་དག་ཀྱང་འབྱུང་ངོ་།

(ii. །གཉིས་པ། དེ་ལྡོག་ཚུལ།)

((1) །དང་པོ། མདོར་བསྟན།)

།གང་གི་ཕྱིར་དེ་དེ་ལྟར་གྱུར་པའི་ཕྱིར།

དེ་ནི་ལྟ་བ་ཀུན་གྱི་རྒྱུ།
།དེ་མེད་ཉོན་མོངས་མི་སྐྱེ་སྟེ།
།དེ་བས་དེ་ནི་ཡོངས་ཤེས་ན།
།ལྟ་དང་ཉོན་མོངས་ཡོངས་སུ་འབྱང་།[545] ॥ 47 ॥

---

[543] 《པེ་》《སྣར་》{SS}: +ཁས་

[544] 《སྣར་》: -པོ་

[545] The Skt. is preserved in *Abhisamayālaṁkārāloka* (Wogihara, 161) and is given by Lindtner (*Nāgārjuniana*, 114–115) as: *sa hetuḥ sarva-dṛṣṭīnāṁ kleśotpattir na taṁ vinā / tasmāt tasmin parijñāte dṛṣṭi-kleśa-parikṣayaḥ //*

[《སྣར་》 30a.1] །དངོས་པོར་ཁས་ལེན་པ་ཡོད་ན་དེ་ནི་སྔོན་གྱི་མཐའ་དང་ཕྱི་མའི་མཐའ་དང་དབུས་ཡོངས་སུ་རྟོག་[546] པས་དེ་ལ་དམིགས་པ་ལྟ་བར་གྱུར་པ་རྣམས་སུ་ལྟུང་བ་ཡོད་པས་ན་དངོས་[《ཅོ་》 25b.1] པོར་འཛིན་པ་དེ་ལྟ་བར་གྱུར་པ་ཐམས་ཅད་ཀྱི་རྒྱུ་ཡིན་ནོ། །ལྟ་བར་གྱུར་པ་ཡོད་ན་རྒྱུ་དེ་ལས་བྱུང་བའི་ཉོན་མོངས་པ་འབྱུང་[547] སྟེ། །རང་གི་ [《པེ་》 29b.1] ལྟ་བ་ལ་འདོད་ཆགས་འབྱུང་བ་དང་། །དེས་ང་རྒྱལ་དུ་འགྱུར་བ་དང་། །གཞན་གྱི་ལྟ་བ་ལ་ཞེ་སྡང་འབྱུང་བའི་ཕྱིར་དང་། །ཐམས་ཅད་དུ་གཏི་མུག་འབྱུང་བས་ལྟ་བར་གྱུར་པ་ལས་ཉོན་མོངས་པ་རྣམས་འབྱུང་ངོ་།

།གང་གི་ཕྱིར་དེ་ལྟར་ལྟ་བ་དང་། །ཉོན་མོངས་པ་ཐམས་ཅད་དངོས་པོར་དམིགས་པའི་རྒྱུ་ལས་བྱུང་བ་དེའི་ཕྱིར་དངོས་པོ་དེ་ཡོངས་སུ་ཤེས་ཏེ། །དངོས་པོའི་རང་གི་ངོ་བོ་ཇི་ལྟ་བ་བཞིན་དུ་ཁོང་དུ་ཆུད་ན་དམིགས་པ་མེད་པས་ལྟ་བ་རྣམས་ལྡོག་གོ། །དེ་ལོག་ན་ཉོན་མོངས་པ་རྣམས་སྤོང་ངོ་།

((2) །གཉིས་པ། རྒྱས་བཤད།)

((a) །དང་པོ། ཤེས་བྱའི་གནས་ཚུལ།)

((i) །དང་པོ། བརྟེན་ནས་སྐྱེས་པ་དང་། རང་བཞིན་མེད་པ་མི་འགལ་བ།)

།གལ་ཏེ་འདི་སྙམ་དུ།

གང་གིས་དེ་ཤེས་འགྱུར་ཞེ་ན།
།རྟེན་ཅིང་འབྱུང་བ་མཐོང་བ་སྟེ།

[546] 《པེ་》《སྣར་》: རྟོགས

[547] 《པེ་》: བྱུང

།ྃརྟེན་ཅིང་[548] སྐྱེས་པ་མ་སྐྱེས་ཞེས།[549]
།ཡང་དག་[550] མཁྱེན་པ་མཆོག་གིས་གསུངས།[551] **|| 48 ||**

།རྟེན་ཅིང་འབྲེལ་པར་འབྱུང་བ་མཐོང་ནས་དངོས་པོ་རྣམས་ལ་ངོ་བོ་ཉིད་དུ་དམིགས་པར་མི་འགྱུར།[552] །གང་བརྟེན་[553] ནས་སྐྱེས་པ་[554] དེ་ནི་གཟུགས་བརྙན་བཞིན་དུ་ངོ་བོ་ཉིད་ཀྱིས་མ་སྐྱེས་པའི་ཕྱིར་རོ།

།བརྟེན་ནས་བྱུང་བ་གང་ཡིན་པ་དེ་ནི་བྱུང་བ་ཉིད་དུ་ངེས་ཏེ། །དེ་ལ་མ་བྱུང་ཞེས་བྱ་བའི་སྒྲར་ཇི་སྐད་དུ་གདགས། །གལ་ཏེ་མ་སྐྱེས་པ་ཞེས་བྱ་བ་ན་[555] ནི་དེ་ [«སྡེ་» 27a.1] བརྟེན་ནས་སྐྱེས་པ་ཞེས་བྱར་མི་རུང་སྟེ། །དེ་བས་ན་ནང་འགལ་བའི་ཕྱིར་དེ་རིགས་[556] པ་མ་ཡིན་ནོ་ཞེས་ཟེར་ན།

།ཀྱེ་མ་ཀྱི་ཧུད་རྣ་བ་དང་སྙིང་མེད་པས་ཀྱང་བདག་ལ་ཀླན་ཀ་བཙལ་བ་གང་ཡིན་པ་དེ་ནི་བདག་མ་རུངས་པ་ཞེས་བབ་བོ།[557] །གང་བརྟེན་ནས་སྐྱེས་པ་དེ་གཟུགས་བརྙན་བཞིན་དུ་ངོ་བོ་ཉིད་ཀྱིས་སྐྱེས་

548 {SS}: བརྟེན་ནས་ following the root text.

549 «པེ་»«སྣར་»: ཞེས།

550 «ཏྣི་ 30a.4»: ཐམས་ཅད་

551 The Skt. of this verse is preserved in *Abhisamayālaṁkārāloka* (Wogihara, 161) and is given by Lindtner (*Nāgārjuniana*, 114–115) as: *parijñā tasya keneti pratītyotpāda-darśanāt / pratītya jātaṁ câjātam āha tattva-vidāṁ varaḥ //*

552 {SS}: +ཏེ།

553 «པེ་»«སྣར་»: རྟེན་

554 «ཅོ་»: སྐྱེ་བ་

555 «པེ་»«སྣར་»: -ན་

556 «པེ་»«སྣར་»: རིག་

557 {SS}: བོ།

པ་མ་ཡིན་ནོ་ཞེས་ཁོ་བོས་གང་གི་ཚེ་སྨྲས་པ་དེའི་ཚེ་དེ་ལ་ཀླན་ཀ་ [«སྣར་» 30b.1] བརྩལ་བའི་སྐབས་ག་ལ་ཡོད།

།བརྟེན་ནས་འབྱུང་བའི་རྣམ་པ་གང་གི་གཟུགས་བརྙན་དམིགས་པ་དེའི་བརྫུན་པར་གྱུར་པ་དམིགས་པ་ཁོ་བོ་མ་སྐྱེས་པའོ་ཞེས་སྨྲའི། །བདག་ཉིད་གང་གིས་དེའི་བྱུང་[558] བ་མེད་པ་རྣམ་པར་གཞག་པ་དེ་ཉིད་ཀྱིས་དེའི་སྐྱེ་བ་མེད་པར་བརྗོད་དོ།

།བདག་ཉིད་གང་གིས་དེའི་སྐྱེ་བ་མེད་པར་རྣམ་པར་གཞག་ཅེ་ན།

།ཡང་དག་པར་འདོད་པའི་ངོ་བོ་ཉིད་ཀྱིས་འདོད་ཀྱི། །བརྫུན་པའི་ངོ་བོས་ནི་མ་ཡིན་ཏེ། །དེ་ནི་ངོ་བོ་དེས་རྟེན་ཅིང་འབྲེལ་པར་འབྱུང་ [«པེ་» 30a.1] བ་ཁས་བླངས་པའི་ཕྱིར་རོ། །དེའི་ཕྱིར་དེ་ལྟར་སྐྱེ་བ་དང་མི་སྐྱེ་བ་འདི་གཉིས་ཡུལ་མ་ཡིན་པའི་ཕྱིར་གཅིག་གི་ཡུལ་དུ་[559] ག་ལ་འགྱུར། [«ཅོ་» 26a.1]

།གལ་ཏེ: རྟེན་ཅིང་[560] འབྲེལ་པར་འབྱུང་བ་ཇི་ལྟར་དམིགས་པ་དེ་ལ་སྐྱེ་བ་མེད་པ་ཞེས་མི་སྟོན་གྱི། །ངོ་བོ་ཉིད་ལ་སྐྱེ་བ་མེད་པ་ཞེས་སྟོན་ན་འདི་ལ་ཁྱོད་ཀྱིས་དེ་སྐད་སྨྲས་པ་ལྟ་བུ་སྟོན་མ་ཐོས་པ་ཅི་ཞིག་བསྟན་པར་འགྱུར།

།ཁོ་བོ་ནི་སྟོན་མ་ཐོས་པ་ཅུང་ཟད་ཀྱང་མི་སྟོན་ཏེ། །འོན་ཀྱང་བསྟན་བཅོས་ནི་ཇི་ལྟར་གནས་པའི་ཆོས་ཉིད་བསྟན་པ་ཆེད་ཆེ་བར་བྱ་བ་ཡིན་ན་ཇི་ལྟར་གནས་པའི་ཆོས་ཉིད་དེ་ལ་ཡང་ཕྱིན་ཅི་ལོག་གི་རྗེས་སུ་འབྲང་བ་འདྲེན་[561] པོ་ཕྱོགས་བསླད་པ་ལྟ་བུ་དག་རྣམ་པ་[562] གཞན་དུ་ཡོངས་སུ་རྟོག་གོ།

---

558 «པེ་»«ཅོ་»: འབྱུང་ 559 «པེ་»«སྣར་»: +གཅིག་

560 «པེ་»«སྣར་»: -རྟེན་ཅིང་

561 «པེ་»«སྣར་»{SS}: འགྲོན་

562 «ཅོ་»: པར་

།རྟེན་ཅིང་འབྲེལ་པར་འབྱུང་བ་ངོ་བོ་ཉིད་ཀྱིས་མ་སྐྱེས་པ་སྟེ། །ཕྱིན་ཅི་ལོག་པའི་བདག་ཉིད་དུ་མ་བྱུང་བ་ཡིན་ན་སོ་སོའི་སྐྱེ་བོ་དག་དེ་ལ་ངོ་བོ་ཉིད་ཀྱིས་སྐྱེ་བར་ཡོངས་སུ་རྟོག་སྟེ། །དེ་ལ་མངོན་པར་ཞེན་ནས་ཀུན་ནས་ཉོན་མོངས་སོ། །ཀུན་ནས་ཉོན་མོངས་[563] དེ་སྐད་བའི་ཕྱིར་ཉན་ཐོས་དང་། །རང་སངས་རྒྱས་དང་བྱང་ཆུབ་སེམས་དཔའ་ཡང་དག་པར་རིག་པ་རྣམས་ཀྱི་མཆོག་སངས་རྒྱས་བཅོམ་ལྡན་འདས་ཀྱིས་གསུངས་པ། །བརྟེན་ནས་སྐྱེས་པ་མ་ [《སྡེ་》 27b.1] སྐྱེས་ཤེའོ། །སྒྱུ་མ་མཁན་ནི་སྒྱུ་མའི་[564] ན་ཆུང་ཡང་དག་པ་[565] སྙམ་དུ་མངོན་པར་ཞེན་ནས་ཀུན་ནས་ཉོན་མོངས་པར་མི་འགྱུར་གྱི། །ན་ཆུང་ཡང་དག་པ་སྙམ་དུ་མངོན་པའི་ངཀྱལ་ཅན་ཕྱིན་ཅི་ལོག་ཏུ་གྱུར་པ་དེ་ལ་ནི་ཀུན་ནས་ཉོན་མོངས་པ་འབྱུང་ངོ་། །དེ་བཞིན་དུ་འདི་ལ་ཡང་བརྟེན་ནས་བྱུང་བ་ངོ་བོ་ཉིད་ [《སྣར་》 31a.1] ཀྱིས་མ་སྐྱེས་སོ་ཞེས་བཅོམ་ལྡན་འདས་གསུངས་པས་[566] དངོས་པོ་རྣམས་ལ་ངོ་བོ་ཉིད་དུ་མངོན་པར་ཞེན་པ་བཟློག་པ་ཡིན་ནོ།

((ii) །གཉིས་པ། འགལ་བར་གཟུང་བས་ཉེས་པ་ཀུན་འབྱུང་བར་བསྟན་པ།)

།འདི་ལྟར།

ལོག་པའི་ཤེས་པས་ཟིལ་གནོན་[567] པ།
།བདེན་པ་མིན་ལ་བདེན་འཛིན་པའི།

[563] 《པེ་》《སྣར་》{SS}: +པ་

[564] 《པེ་》《སྣར་》{SS}: +ན་ཆུང་ལ་

[565] 《པེ་》《སྣར་》{SS}: ཟིན་ནོན་

[566] 《པེ་》《སྣར་》: གསུང་བས་

[567] 《པེ་》《སྣར་》: ཟིན་ནོན་

།ཡོངས་སུ་འཛིན་དང་རྩོད་སོགས་[568] ཀྱི།
།རིམ་པ་ཆགས་ལས་ཤིན་ཏུ་བྱུང་། **|| 49 ||**

།དེ་ལྟ་བས་ན་དངོས་པོ་བདེན་པ་མ་ཡིན་པ་[569] བདེན་པར་འདུ་ཤེས་པ་དེ་བཟློག་པའི་ཕྱིར་བཅོམ་ལྡན་འདས་ཀྱིས་རྟེན་ཅིང་འབྲེལ་པར་འབྱུང་བ་བསྟན་ཏོ། །རྟེན་ཅིང་འབྲེལ་པར་འབྱུང་བ་ནི་སླུ་[570] བའི་ཕྱིར་བདེན་པ་མ་ཡིན་ནོ། །དེ་བདེན་པ་མ་ཡིན་ [«པེ་» 30b.1] པར་རྟོགས་ན་དངོས་པོ་ལ་ཆགས་པ་ལྡོག་གོ། །དངོས་པོ་ལ་ཆགས་པ་ལོག་[571] ན་དངོས་པོ་ཡོངས་སུ་འཛིན་པ་ལྡོག་གོ། །ཡོངས་སུ་འཛིན་པ་ནི་བདག་གིར་བྱེད་པ་སྟེ། །དེ་ནི་དེ་ལྟར་ལྡོག་གོ། །དེ་ལོག་ལ་[572] འདོད་པ་ལ་ཆགས་པར་གྱུར་པ་དང་། །ལྟ་བ་ལ་ [«ཅོ་» 26b.1] ཆགས་པར་འགྱུར་བའི་[573] རྩོད་པ་ཡང་ལྡོག་གོ། །རྩོད་པ་ལོག་ན་འཐབ་པ་ལ་སོགས་པ་ཡང་ལྡོག་གོ།

((b) །གཉིས་པ། བློས་རྟོགས་ཚུལ།)

((i) །དང་པོ། དངོས།)

།དེ་བས་ན་དངོས་པོ་བརྟེན་ནས་གྲུབ་པ་གང་ཡང་མི་དམིགས་ན་གདོན་མི་ཟ་བར།

རྩོད་མེད་ཆེ་བའི་བདག་ཉིད་ཅན།
།དེ་དག་ལ་ནི་ཕྱོགས་མེད་དོ། **|| 50ab ||**

---

568 «པེ་»: སེགས་ «སྣར་»: སོཏ་

569 «པེ་» «སྣར་» {SS}: +ལ་

570 «སྣར་»: བསླུ་

571 «པེ་»: ལོགས་

572 «པེ་» «སྣར་» {SS}: ན་

573 «པེ་»: འགྱུར་བའི་ {SS}: གྱུར་པའི་

།རང་གི་ཕྱོགས་ཁས་ལེན་པ་ཡོད་ན་ནི་དེའི་ཚེ་དེ་གཟུགས་པའི་ཕྱིར་གཞན་རྣམས་དང་རྩོད་པར་གྱུར་ན་དེ་དག་ལ་ནི་དེ་ལྟ་བུ་ཡང་མེད་པས་དེ་བས་ན་རྩོད་མེད་ཆེ་བའི་བདག་ཉིད་ཅན་ནོ། །གལ་ཏེ་དེ་དག་ལ་རང་གི་ཕྱོགས་མེད་དུ་ཟིན་ཀྱང་གཞན་གྱི་ཕྱོགས་གཞིག་པ་མེད་མི་སྲིད་དེ། །དེ་བས་ན་གཞན་གྱི་ཕྱོགས་ཡོད་དང་། །བདག་གི་ཕྱོགས་ཀྱང་མེད་དུ་མི་རུང་ངོ་། །ཕྱོགས་ཤིག་ཡོད་ན་ནི་བདག་གི་[574] ཕྱོགས་སམ་གཞན་གྱི་ཕྱོགས་མེད་[575] པར་ཡང་འགྱུར་ན། །གང་གི་ཚེ་ཕྱོགས་ཡེ་མེད་[576] དེའི་ཚེ།

།གང་རྣམས་ལ་ནི་ཕྱོགས་མེད་པ།
།དེ་ལ་གཞན་ཕྱོགས་ག་ལ་ཡོད། ‖ **50cd** ‖

།གང་གི་ཚེ་དེ་ལྟར་དངོས་པོ་མེད་པས་བདག་དང་ [《སྡེ་》 28a.1] གཞན་གྱི་ཕྱོགས་མེད་པ་དེའི་ཚེ་དེ་ལྟར་མཐོང་བ་རྣམས་ཀྱི་ཉོན་མོངས་པ་རྣམས་ངེས་པར་འགག་ [《སྣར་》 31b.1] པར་འགྱུར་རོ།

((ii) །གཉིས་པ། དེའི་འཐད་པ།)

།ཇི་ལྟ་[577] ཞེ་ན། །དེ་དག་འདི་ལྟར།

གང་ཡང་རུང་བའི་གནས་རྙེད་ནས།
།ཉོན་མོངས་སྦྲུལ་གདུག་[578] གཡོན་ཅན་གྱིས།

---

[574] 《པེ་》《སྣར་》: གིས་

[575] 《པེ་》《སྣར་》{SS}: ཡོད་

[576] 《པེ་》《སྣར་》{SS}: +པ་

[577] {SS}: ལྟར་

[578] 《པེ་》: གདུགས་

།ཟིན་པར་འགྱུར་རོ་གང་གི་སེམས།

།གནས་མེད་དེ་དག་ཟིན་མི་འགྱུར། ‖ **51** ‖

།འདོད་ཆགས་ལ་སོགས་པ་ནི་རང་བཞིན་གྱིས་འདུ་བྱེད་ཀྱི་ནགས་ཐིབས་པོ་ན་རྒྱུ་བ་དགེ་བའི་ཕྱོགས་ཀྱི་སྲོག་གི་བར་ཆད་བྱེད་པ་ལྟ་བ་ལ་སོགས་པའི་མིག་གི་དབང་པོའི་ཕུག་ཏུ་གནས་བཅས་པ་ཡུལ་གྱི་རླུང་ལ་ཡིད་ཆགས་པ་ཡུན་རིང་པོ་ནས་རྗེས་སུ་འབྲང་བའོ། །གཡོན་ཅན་ནི་སྦྲུལ་ལྟར་འགྲོ་བ་སྟེ། །འཛིན་པ་ལ་བརྩོན་པས་དེ་དག་ནི[579] སྦྲུལ་ལོ། །གནས་བརྟེན་པར་བྱ་བ་རྒྱུ་འགའ་ཞིག་ཆེད་ནས་འགའ་ཞིག་ལ་འཛིན་ཏོ། །གང་དག་དངོས་པོ་ཐམས་ཅད་དུ་མི་དམིགས་པས་ཉོན་མོངས་པའི་སྦྲུལ་གྱིས[580] གནས་པའི་ [《པེ་》 31a.1] རྒྱུ་མ་ལུས་པར་བསྒྲིགས་ཤིང་དྲན་པ་དང་ཤེས་བཞིན་གྱི[581] དབང་པོའི་ཕུག་རྣམས་བཀག་པ་དེ་དག་ཉོན་མོངས་པའི་སྦྲུལ་གྱིས་ཟིན་པར་འགྱུར་བའི་གནས་མེད་པར་བྱས་པས་གང་དག་གི་སེམས་ལ་གནས་པ་མེད་པ་ནི་ཟིན་པར་མི[582] འགྱུར་ཏེ། །དངོས་པོར་དམིགས་པ་མེད་ན་སེམས་ཀྱི[583] ཕྱོགས་ཡོངས་སུ་མི་འཛིན་པའི་ཕྱིར་རོ། །དེའི་ཕྱིར་དེ་ལྟར་གང་དག་གིས[584] སེམས་ལ་དམིགས་པ་མེད་པ་དེ་དག་ཉོན་མོངས་ [《ཅོ་》 27a.1] པའི་སྦྲུལ་གདུག་པ་གཡོན་ཅན་གྱིས་ཀྱང་མི་ཚུགས་ཤིང་ཟིན་པར་མི་འགྱུར་རོ།

---

579 《པེ་》: ན་

580 《པེ་》《སྣར་》{SS}: གྱི་

581 《པེ་》《སྣར་》{SS}: གྱིས་

582 《ཏྲི་》{SS}: མི་ 《པེ་》《སྣར་》《སྡེ་》《ཅོ་》: -མི་

583 《པེ་》《སྣར་》{SS}: ཀྱིས་བདག་དང་གཞན་གྱི་

584 {SS}: གི་

(c. །གསུམ་པ། དངོས་ཞེན་ཡོད་ནས་ཉོན་མོངས་སྤོང་མི་ནུས་པར་བསྟན་པ།)

(i. །དང་པོ། དངོས།)

།གང་དག་གཟུགས་ལ་སོགས་པའི་[585] རང་བཞིན་དམིགས་ཀྱང་ཉོན་མོངས་པ་རྣམས་སྤང་དུ་རུང་[586] བར་འདོད་པ་དེ་དག་ལ་ནི་ཉོན་མོངས་པ་རྣམས་སྤང་བར་འགྱུར་བ་མེད་[587] དོ་ཞེས་བསྟན་པའི་ཕྱིར།

གནས་དང་བཅས་པའི་སེམས་ཡོད་ལ།

།ཉོན་མོངས་དུག་ཆེན་ཅིས་མི་འབྱུང་། || **52ab** ||

།ཞེས་བྱ་བ་སྨོས་སོ། །དངོས་པོར་དམིགས་ན་ནི་[588] འདོད་ཆགས་ལ་སོགས་པ་ཉོན་མོངས་པ་རྣམས་ཀྱི་འབྱུང་བ་གདོན་མི་ཟ་བར་མི་ལྡོག་སྟེ་[589] འབྱུང་ངོ་།

།ཇི་ལྟ་[590] ཞེ་ན། །གལ་ཏེ་དངོས་པོ་དེ་ཡིད་དང་མཐུན་པར་གནས་ན་ནི་དེའི་ཚེ་དེ་ལ་རྗེས་སུ་ཆགས་པ་བཟློག་པར་[591] དཀའ་བར་འགྱུར་རོ། [«སྡེ་» 28b.1] །ཅི་སྟེ་མི་མཐུན་ན་ཡང་དེའི་[«སྣར་» 32a.1] ཚེ་དེ་ལ་ཁོང་ཁྲོ་བ་དང་། །ཞིག་པ་ཟ་བ་བཟློག་དཀའ་བར་འགྱུར་རོ།

585 «སྡིང་ 71b.5»: པ་རྣམས་ཀྱི་

586 «སྡིང་ 71b.5»: སྤོང་

587 «པེ་» «སྣར་»: སྤོང་བར་འགྱུར་བ་མེད་ «སྡིང་»: སྤོང་བ་མི་སྲིད་པ་ཉིད་

588 «ཅོ་»: པའི་

589 «པེ་» «སྣར་»: ཏེ་

590 «པེ་» «སྣར་» {SS}: ལྟར་

591 «པེ་» «སྣར་» {SS}: -པར་

།འོན་ཏེ་རྟོག་པ་དེ་གཉིས་ཀ་བསྩལ་[592] ཀྱང་དེའི་ཚེ་[593] རང་གི་ངོ་བོ་ལ་སྒྲོ་འདོགས་ཤིང་དམིགས་པ་ལས་བྱུང་བ་བཏང་སྙོམས་སུ་འགྱུར་བའི་ཡུལ་ལ་མ་རིག་པའི་བག་ལ་ཉལ་བ་བཟློག་དཀའ་བར་འགྱུར་རོ། །ཐ་མལ་པར་འདུག་པའི་གནས་ན་[594] ཀུན་ཏུ་འབྱུང་བའི་མ་རིག་པའི་བག་ལ་ཉལ་འཁོར་བའི་སྡུག་བསྔལ་འབྱུང་བ་དང་མཐུན་པ་གནོད་པའི་བདག་ཉིད་ཉོན་མོངས་པའི་སྦྲུལ་འབྱུང་བར་དམིགས་ནས།

(ii. །གཉིས་པ། དེ་དང་ལྡན་པ་ལ་བརྩེ་བ་བྱ་བར་བསྟན་པ།)

གང་ཚེ་ཐ་མལ་[595] འདུག་པ་ཡང་།
།ཉོན་མོངས་སྦྲུལ་གྱིས་ཟིན་པར་འགྱུར། || **52cd** ||

།ཞེས་བྱ་བ་སྨོས་སོ། །གང་གི་ཚེ་གཏི་མུག་དེ་རྟག་ཏུ་འབྱུང་བར་གྱུར་པ་དེ་ནི་ཀུན་ཏུ་རྨོངས་པ་[596] དེ་ཁོ་ན་མཐོང་བ་བསྒྲིབས་པའི་སོ་སོའི་སྐྱེ་བོ་དག་གཏི་མུག་གི་མཐུས་གྲུབ་པའི་དངོས་པོའི་རང་གི་མཚན་ཉིད་ལ་གནོད་མི་ཟ་བར།

བྱིས་པ་བདེན་པར་འདུ་ཤེས་པས།
།གཟུགས་བརྙན་ལ་ནི་ཆགས་པ་བཞིན། [《པེ་》 31b.1]

---

592 《པེ་》{SS}: བསལ་ 《སྣར་》: བསམ་

593 《པེ་》《སྣར་》{SS}: +དེའི་

594 《སྣར་》: ནས་

595 《ཏྭི་》《སྡིང་ 71b.6》: བར་མར་ 《ཏྭི་》 glosses this as: གང་གི་ཚེ་ཆགས་སྡང་མེད་པའི་བར་མ་ལ་བཏང་སྙོམས་པར་འདུག་པ་’’

596 《པེ་》《སྣར་》{SS}: པས་

།དེ་ལྟར་འཇིག་རྟེན་རྨོངས་པའི་ཕྱིར།
།ཡུལ་གྱི་གཟེབ་ལ་ཐོགས་པར་འགྱུར། ‖ **53** ‖

།ཇི་ལྟར་བྱིས་པ་འཇིག་རྟེན་གྱི་ཐ་སྙད་མི་ཤེས་པ་རང་བཞིན་གྱིས་རྣམ་པར་ཤེས་པ་བླུན་པ་དག་གཟུགས་བརྙན་དམིགས་པ་ན་དེ་ལ་དངོས་པོ་ཡོད་པར་འཛིན་ཞིང་ཆགས་པར་འགྱུར་ཏེ་[597] ཅི་ཡང་བྱེད་ཅིང་དེ་དང་རྩེ་བ་དེ་བཞིན་དུ་བྱིས་པ་མ་རིག་པ་དང་ལྡན་པ་གཏི་མུག་གི་མཐུས་སྐྱེས་པ་ལ། །དངོས་པོ་ཡོད་པ་ཡང་དག་པར་རྟོག་པ་ལ་མངོན་པར་ཞེན་པ་ལུས་དང་ངག་ཡིད་ཀྱིས་[598] འཇུག་པས། །དེ་དང་དེ་ལ་མངོན་པར་ཞེན་པས། །རྗེས་སུ་ཆགས་པ་དང་། །ཁོང་ [《ཅོ་》 27b.1] ཁྲོ་བ་དང་། །ང་རྒྱལ་ལ་སོགས་པས་རང་དབང་མེད་པར་འཇུག་པ་བྱིས་པ་བཞིན་དུ་ཅི་དང་ཅི་ཡང་བྱེད་ཅིང་འཁོར་བའི་གཟེབ་ལ་ཐོགས་པ་འཁོར་བའི་ངོ་བོ་ཉིད་མི་ཤེས་པ་དག་ནི་[599] འཕགས་པ་རྣམས་ལ་སྙིང་བརྩེ་བའི་ཡུལ་དུ་སྣང་ངོ་། །ཤེས་རབ་ཀྱི་དྲག་[600] པའི་སྤྱན་དང་ལྡན་པ་འཕགས་པ་དག་ནི་ངོ་བོ་ཉིད་ཡང་དག་པ་ཇི་ལྟ་བ་བཞིན་དུ་གཟིགས་པས།

(iii. །གསུམ་པ། གཞན་དེ་ལས་ལྡོག་པ།)

དངོས་པོ་གཟུགས་བརྙན་ལྟ་བུར་ནི།
།ཡེ་ཤེས་མིག་ [《སྣར་》 32b.1] གིས་རབ་མཐོང་ན།
།བདག་ཉིད་ཆེན་པོ་དེ་དག་ནི།
།ཡུལ་གྱི་འདམ་ལ་མི་ཆགས་སོ། ‖ **54** ‖

---

[597] 《པེ་》《སྣར་》{SS}: +ཅི་དང་

[598] 《པེ་》《སྣར་》{SS}: དང་ཡིད་ཀྱི་

[599] 《པེ་》《སྣར་》{SS}: ནི་ 《སྡེ་》《ཅོ་》: མི་

[600] 《པེ་》《སྣར་》{SS}: ཀྱིས་དག་

།ཆགས་པ་མེད་ན་དངོས་པོ་རྣམས་ལ་ [《སྡེ་》 29a.1] དེའི་བདག་ཉིད་དུ་ཆགས་ཤིང་འཇུག་པ་མེད་པས་ཡུལ་གྱི་འདམ་ལ་ཆགས་པར་མི་འགྱུར་ཏེ།

(d. །བཞི་པ། ཡུལ་གྱི་གཟེབ་ལ་ཐོགས་པ་དང་མི་ཐོགས་པའི་དབྱེ་བ་བསྟན་པ།)

(i. །དང་པོ། མདོར་བསྟན།)

།འཕགས་པ་རྣམས་ནི་གཟུགས་བརྙན་ལ་བློ་བྱུང་བ་དང་འདྲ་ཞིང་[601] ཞེས་བྱ་བའི་ཐ་ཚིག་[602] གོ། །དེའི་ཕྱིར་དེ་ལྟར་ཤིན་ཏུ་བྱིས་པའི་བློ་ཅན་དག་ནི་གཟུགས་བརྙན་ལ་བྱིས་པ་བཞིན་དུ་གདོན་མི་ཟ་བར།

བྱིས་པ་རྣམས་ནི་གཟུགས་ལ་ཆགས།
།བར་མ་དག་ནི་འདོད་ཆགས་བྲལ།
།གཟུགས་ཀྱི་རང་བཞིན་ཤེས་པ་ཡི།[603]
།བློ་མཆོག་དག་ནི་རྣམ་པར་གྲོལ།[604] || 55 ||

།དེ་ལ་བྱིས་པའི་མཚན་ཉིད་དང་ལྡན་པ་ནི་བྱིས་པ་སྟེ། །དེ་ཡང་ཉེས་པར་[605] སེམས་པ་སེམས་པ་དང་། །ཉེས་པར་སྨྲ་བ་སྨྲ་བ་དང་། །ཉེས་པར་བྱེད་པའི་ལས་བྱེད་པའོ། །དེ་ལ་ཉེས་པར་སེམས་པ་སེམས་པ་ནི་གང་དག་ལུས་མི་གཙང་བ་དང་སྐད་ཅིག་ཅིང་འཇིག་[606] པའི་ངང་ཅན་ལ་གཙང་བ་དང་།

---

601 《པེ་》《སྣར་》{SS}: -ཞིང་

602 《པེ་》: ཚིགས་

603 《པེ་》《སྣར་》: ཡིས།

604 The Skt. is preserved in the *Cittaviśuddhiprakaraṇa* (Patel, 2), given by Lindtner (*Nāgārjuniana*, 116–117) as: *bālā rajyanti rūpeṣu vairāgyaṁ yānti madhyamāḥ / svabhāva-jñā vimucyante rūpasyottama-buddhayaḥ //*

605 《པེ་》《སྣར་》: པ་

606 《པེ་》: འཇིགས་

།མི་འཛིག་པའི་ང་ང་ཅན་དུ་སེམས་པའོ། །ཉེས་པར་སྨྲ་བ་སྨྲ་བ་ཞེས་བྱ་བ་ནི་བསྔགས་[607] པར་མི་འོས་པ་རྟག་ཏུ་ཕན་གདགས་དགོས་པ་སྡུག་བསྔལ་གྱི་བདག་ཉིད་ཅན་གྱི་ལུས་ལ་ [«པེ་» 32a.1] མིང་དང་ཚིག་དང་ཡི་གེའི་ཚོགས་སྣ་ཚོགས་ཀྱིས་བསྔགས་པ་བརྗོད་པའོ། །ཉེས་པར་བྱེད་པའི་ལས་བྱེད་པ་ཞེས་བྱ་བ་ནི་མི་དགེ་བའི་རྣམ་པར་སྨིན་པ་སྡུག་བསྔལ་དུ་འགྱུར་བའི་ལས་རྩོམ་པའོ། །དེ་ལྟར་བྱིས་པ་དེ་དག་[608] མི་གཙང་བཞིན་དུ་གཟུགས་ལ་ཆགས་སོ། །བར་མ་ནི་གང་དག་མི་གཙང་བ་ལ་ཇི་ལྟར་གནས་པ་བཞིན་དུ་སྨོད་ཅིང་གཟུགས་ལ་སྡུག་བསྔལ་བརྒྱ་ཕྲག་དུ་མ་བསྔགས་[609] པར་མཐོང་སྟེ། །གཟུགས་ལ་འདོད་ཆགས་དང་བྲལ་བར་འགྱུར་ནས་བསམ་གཏན་དང་གཟུགས་མེད་པའི་སྙོམས་པར་འཇུག་པ་འཐོབ་སྟེ། །འདོད་པའི་ཁམས་ལས་ཤིན་ཏུ་འདས་པ་དེ་དག་ནི་ [«ཅོ་» 28a.1] བར་མའོ། །གང་དག་གཟུགས་ཀྱང་ངོ་བོ་ཉིད་ཀྱིས་མེད་དེ། །གཟུགས་བརྙན་བཞིན་དུ་ཁོང་དུ་ཆུད་པ་དེ་དག་ནི་གཟུགས་ལཿ སོགས་པའི་[610] རྣམ་པར་རྟོག་པ་རྣམས་ལས་གདོན་མི་ [«སྣར་» 33a.1] ཟ་བར། །གཟུགས་ཀྱི་རང་བཞིན་ཤེས་པ་ཡིས།[611] །བློ་མཆོག་རྣམས་ནི་རྣམ་པར་གྲོལ།

(ii. །གཉིས་པ། རྒྱས་བཤད།)

།དོན་དེ་ཉིད་རྣམ་པར་དབྱེ་བ་བསྟན་པའི་ཕྱིར།

---

607 «ཅོ་»: སྔགས་

608 «པེ་» «སྣར་» {SS}: +ནི་

609 «པེ་» «སྣར་» {SS}: བསགས་

610 «པེ་» «སྣར་»: སོང་བའི་

611 {SS}: ཡི།

སྡུག་ཆེས་པ་[612] ལ་ཆགས་པར་འགྱུར།[613]
།དེ་ལས་ལྡོག་པས་འདོད་ [《སྡེ་》 29b.1] ཆགས་བྲལ།
།སྒྱུ་མའི་སྐྱེས་བུ་ལྟར་དབེན་པར།
།མཐོང་བས་[614] མྱ་ངན་འདས་པར་འགྱུར། **|| 56 ||**

།ཞེས་བྱ་བ་སྨོས་སོ། །སྒྱུ་མའི་སྐྱེས་བུ་བཞིན་དུ་འགྲོ་བ་དབེན་ཞིང་སྟོང་སྟེ། །མྱ་ངན་ལས་འདས་པ་མཐོང་ནས་གང་དག་མྱ་ངན་ལས་འདས་པར་གྱུར་པ་དེ་དག་ནི་བློའི་མཆོག་དང་ལྡན་པ་སྟེ། །དེ་དག་ཀྱང་ཉན་ཐོས་དང་རང་སངས་རྒྱས་དང་བཅོམ་ལྡན་འདས་སུ་ཤེས་པར་བྱའོ། །ཕར་མ་དག་ནི་འཇིག་རྟེན་པ་རྣམས་ཏེ། འདོད་པའི་འདོད་ཆགས་དང་བྲལ་བའོ། །བྱིས་པ་རྣམས་ནི་འདོད་པ་ལ་ཆགས་པར་ཤེས་པར་བྱའོ།

(D. །བཞི་པ། ཐར་པའི་ཕན་ཡོན།)

(1. །དང་པོ། སོ་སོར་བཤད་པ།)

(a. །དང་པོ། སྤྲངས་པའི་ཡོན་ཏན།)

།སྒྱུ་མའི་སྐྱེས་བུ་བཞིན་དུ་འགྲོ་བ་དབེན་པར་མཐོང་ནས་མྱ་ངན་ལས་འདས་པ་ཇི་ལྟར་འགྱུར་ཞེ་ན།

ལོག་པའི་ཤེས་པས་མངོན་གདུང་བའི།
།ཉོན་མོངས་སྐྱོན་རྣམས་གང་ཡིན་ཏེ།

---

612 《ཊཱི་》 explains: །འདོད་པ་ཁམས་པ་རྣམས་ནི་གཟུགས་ལ་སོགས་པ་ལ་སྡུག་སྙམ་དུ་ཚུལ་བཞིན་མ་ཡིན་པར་ཡིད་ལ་བྱས་པས་ཆགས་པ་སྐྱེ་བར་འགྱུར་ལ།

613 《པེ་》《སྣར་》: གྱུར་

614 {SS}: ནས་ following {Dh}

།དངོས་དང་དངོས་མེད་རྣམ་[615] རྟོག་པ།
།དོན་ཤེས་གྱུར་ལ་མི་འབྱུང་ངོ་། ॥ 57 ॥

།ཞེས་བྱ་བ་སྨོས་སོ། །གང་གིས་འགྲོ་བ་སྒྱུ་མ་བཞིན་དུ་དམིགས་པ་དེས་དངོས་པོ་དང་དངོས་པོ་མེད་པའི་རང་གི་མཚན་ཉིད་ངོ་བོར་མི་དམིགས་པས་དངོས་པོ་དང་ [«པེ་» 32b.1] དངོས་པོ་མེད་པར་ཡོངས་སུ་ཤེས་ཏེ། །དེ་གཉིས་ལ་ཡོངས་སུ་མི་རྟོག་[616] པའི་ཕྱིར་རྣམ་པར་མི་རྟོག་པ་ཡིན་ནོ། །དངོས་པོ་དང་དངོས་པོ་མེད་པ་རྣམས་རྣམ་པར་རྟོག་པ་དོན་ཤེས་པ་དེ་ལ་འདོད་ཆགས་ལ་སོགས་པ་ཉོན་མོངས་པ་གང་ཡིན་པ་དེ་དག་གདོན་མི་ཟ་བར་འཁོར་བའི་རྒྱུར་མི་འགྱུར་རོ།

།ཉོན་མོངས་པ་དེ་དག་ནི་ལོག་པའི་ཤེས་པས་མངོན་པར་གདུང་བ་རྣམས་ལ་འབྱུང་ངོ་། །མངོན་དུ་[617] གདུང་བའི་ངང་ཚུལ་ཅན་ནི་མངོན་པར་གདུང་བ་ཅན་ནོ། །ལོག་པའི་ཤེས་པས་མངོན་པར་གདུང་བས་ལོག་པའི་ཤེས་པས་མངོན་པར་གདུང་བའོ། །ཕྱིན་ཅི་ལོག་པ་དག་ཡུལ་ལ་དམིགས་ [«སྣར་» 33b.1] པ་རྐྱེན་ནས་ཉོན་མོངས་པ་རྣམས་ཀྱིས་གདུང་བར་[618] བྱེད་དོ།

།དོན་རྟོགས་པ་ལ་ནི་དེ་དག་མེད་པས་[619] [«ཅོ་» 28b.1] གདོན་མི་ཟ་བར་མྱ་ངན་ལས་འདའོ། །བྱིས་པ་རྣམས་ནི་ཕྱིན་ཅི་ལོག་ཏུ་གྱུར་པས་མྱ་ངན་ལས་འདས་པར་མི་འཐད་དོ། །དེ་དག་

615 «པེ་»: རྣམས་

616 «སྣར་»: རྟག་

617 «པེ་» «སྣར་»: -དུ་

618 «པེ་» «སྣར་»: ཀྱི་གདུངས་པར་ {SS}: ཀྱིས་གདུངས་པར་

619 «སྣར་»: པར་

ནི་འདོད་ཆགས་དང་འདོད་ཆགས་དང་བྲལ་བའི་གནས་ལ་ཡོངས་སུ་རྟོག་པས་ཇི་ལྟར་དམིགས་པའི་ཡུལ་ལ་ཆགས་པ་དང་། །མི་ཆགས་པ་ཡོད་པར་འགྱུར།[620]

(b. །གཉིས་པ། རྟོགས་པའི་ཡོན་ཏན།)

།འཕགས་པ་དག་ནི་འཁོར་བ་འདི་ལ། [«སྡེ་» 30a.1]

གནས་ཡོད་ན་ནི་འདོད་ཆགས་དང་།
།འདོད་ཆགས་བྲལ་བ་དམིགས་འགྱུར་ན།
།གནས་མེད་བདག་ཉིད་ཆེན་པོ་རྣམས།
།ཆགས་པ་མེད་ཅིང་ཆགས་བྲལ་མིན། **|| 58 ||**

།གང་ལ་ཆགས་པ་དེ་ཡང་དམིགས་ལ་གང་ལ་མི་ཆགས་པ་དེ་ཡང་དམིགས་ན་ནི་ཆགས་པ་དང་མི་ཆགས་པ་གཉིས་སུ་རུང་ངོ་། །དངོས་པོ་ལ་རང་གི་ངོ་བོར་སྒྲོ་མི་འདོགས་[621] ནཿའདོད་ཆགས་དང་[622] འདོད་ཆགས་དང་བྲལ་བ་དག་[623] མི་འབྱུང་ངོ་། །འཕགས་པ་རྣམས་ནི་དངོས་པོའི་རང་གི་ངོ་བོ་མི་དམིགས་པས་དེ་བས་ན་དེ་དག་གནས་མེད་དེ། །དམིགས་པ་མེདཿཔས་ངེས་པར་སྨྲ་[624] ལས་འདའོ།

620 {SS}: +རོ།

621 «པེ་»«སྣར་»: འདོག་

622 «པེ་»«སྣར་»{SS}: འདོད་ཆགས་དང་ «སྡེ་»«ཅོ་»: -འདོད་ཆགས་དང་

623 «པེ་»«སྣར་»: -དག་

624 «པེ་»«སྣར་»: པར་སྨྲ་ངན་ {SS}: པས་ངེས་པར་སྨྲ་ངན་

(2. །གཉིས་པ། མཇུག་སྡུད།)

།དེའི་ཕྱིར་དེ་ལྟར་རྣམ་པར་དཔྱད་ན།

གང་དག་རྣམ་པར་དབེན་[625] པ་ལ།
།གཡོ་བའི་ཡིད་ཀྱང་མི་གཡོ་སྟེ།
།ཉོན་མོངས་སྦྲུལ་གྱིས་དཀྲུགས་[626] པ་ཡི།
།མི་བཟད་སྲིད་པའི་རྒྱ་མཚོ་རྒལ།[627] ‖ 59 ‖

།རང་བཞིན་གྱིས་རྒོད་པའི་ཕྱིར་སེམས་སྤྲེའུ་ལྟ་བུ་དབེན་པ་འགྲོ་བ་སྟོང་པ་ཞེས་དམིགས་པ་འདི་ལ་གང་དག་བསྟན་[628] པར་ [«པེ་» 33a.1] གནས་པ་དག་ནི་སྲིད་པའི་རྒྱ་མཚོ་ཉོན་མོངས་པའི་སྦྲུལ་གྱིས་གང་བ་དམིགས་པ་རྒལ་[629] བའོ།

(III. །གསུམ་པ། བརྩམས་པའི་དགེ་བ་བསྔོ་བ།)

།དེ་ནི་རབ་ཏུ་བྱེད་པའི་དགེ་བ་ཡོངས་སུ་བསྔོ་བའི་ཕྱིར།

དགེ་བ་འདི་ཡིས་སྐྱེ་བོ་ཀུན།
།བསོད་ནམས་ཡེ་ཤེས་ཚོགས་བསགས་ཏེ།

---

625 «སྣར་»: དབྱེན་

626 «པེ་» «སྣར་»: བཀྲུགས་

627 «པེ་» «སྣར་» {SS}: བརྒལ།

628 {SS}: བརྟན་

629 «པེ་» «སྣར་» {SS}: བརྒལ་

།བསོད་ནམས་ཡེ་ཤེས་ལས་བྱུང་བ།[630]

།དམ་པ་གཉིས་ནི་ཐོབ་པར་ཤོག **|| 60 ||**

།ཅེས་བྱ་བ་སྨོས་སོ། །ཤེས་རབ་མ་གཏོགས་པ་དང་ཤེས་རབ་ཀྱི་རྒྱུ་མ་གཏོགས་པ་སེམས་ཅན་གྱི་[631] ཁམས་མཐའ་དག་ཡོངས་སུ་ཤེས་པར་བྱ་བའི་ཕྱིར་བསྒྲུབས་པ་དགེ་བ་དཔག་ཏུ་མེད་པ་ཐམས་ [«སྣར་» 34a.1] ཅད་ནི་བསོད་ནམས་ཀྱི་[632] ཚོགས་ཞེས་པ་བསྟན་ཏོ།[633] །ཤེས་རབ་དང་ཤེས་རབ་ཀྱི་རྒྱུ་སངས་རྒྱས་སུ་འགྱུར་པར་ཡོངས་སུ་བསྔོ་བ་ཐམས་ཅད་ནི་ཡེ་ཤེས་ཀྱི་ཚོགས་སོ།

སྐྱེ་བོ་ཐམས་ཅད་ཀྱིས་ཚོགས་དེ་གཉིས་བསགས་ཏེ་ཉེ་བར་བསྒྲུབས་ནས་བསོད་ནམས་ཡེ་ཤེས་ལས་བྱུང་བའི་དམ་པ་བླ་ན་མེད་པ་ཐོབ་པར་ཤོག་ཤིག[634] །བྱུང་བ་ནི་སྐྱེས་པའོ། །བསོད་ [«ཅོ་» 29a.1] ནམས་དང་ཡེ་ཤེས་ལས་བྱུང་བ་དེ་དག་ནི་བསོད་ནམས་དང་ཡེ་ཤེས་ལས་བྱུང་བ་སྟེ། །དེ་གཉིས་གང་ཞེ་ན། །གཟུགས་ཀྱི་སྐུ་དང་ཆོས་ཀྱི་སྐུའོ།

།དགེ་བ་ [«སྡེ་» 30b.1] འདིས་དེ་གཉིས་ཐོབ་པར་ཤོག་ཤིག[635]

།ཀླུ་ཡི་རྒྱན་ཡིན་འཇིགས་དང་བཅས་པས་ཡོངས་སྤངས་པ།
།རིགས་པའི་ཀུ་མུ་ད་འདི་ཁ་འབྱེད་ཟླ་བ་ནི།

---

630 {SS}: བའི་ following {Dh}

631 «པེ་»«སྣར་»: གྱིས་

632 «པེ་»«སྣར་»: གྱི་

633 «པེ་»«སྣར་»: ཞེས་བསྟན་ཏོ། «ཅོ་»: ཞེས་པ་བསྟན་ཏོ། «སྡེ་»: ཤེས་པ་བསྟན་ཏོ།

634 «པེ་»«སྣར་»{SS}: ཅིག

635 «པེ་»«སྣར་»{SS}: ཅིག

།ཉེས་པའི་འབྱུང་གནས་རབ་རིབ་རྣམ་པ་རབ་བཅོམ་ནས།
།བློ་གྲོས་མི་ལྡན་སྐྱེ་བོ་རྣམས་ལ་གྲགས་པས་མཛེས།

།ཆོས་ཉིད་དང་ནི་མི་འགལ་གང་འཇུག་པ།
།དོན་དེ་གལ་ཏེ་ཇི་སྐད་ཅེས་བརྗོད་ཀྱང་།
།དེ་ལ་ཉེས་ཞེས་[636] སངས་རྒྱས་མི་གསུང་ཕྱིར།
།བདག་གིས་ཡང་དག་རྟོགས་ལ་དོགས་པ་མེད།

།དེ་ཕྱིར་བདག་གིས་འཇོམ་སྤྲངས་གུས་བྱས་ཏེ།
།རིགས་[637] པ་དྲུག་ཅུ་པ་འདི་རྣམ་པར་ཕྱེ།
།རྣམ་པར་ཕྱེ་བའི་བསོད་ནམས་གང་ཡིན་འདིས།
།འགྲོ་བ་མ་ལུས་[638] ཐུབ་དབང་སྒྱུར་གྱུར་ཅིག

།རིགས་[639] པ་དྲུག་ཅུ་པའི་འགྲེལ་པ་འདི་ནི་སློབ་དཔོན་ཟླ་བ་གྲགས་པ་[640] ཞེས་བྱ་བ་ཐེག་པ་ཆེན་པོ་དབུ་མའི་སློབ་དཔོན་ཡུལ་ས་མ་ཏ་ནས་སྐྱེས་ [«པེ་» 33b.1] པ། །སྨྲ་སྟེགས་ཅན་རྟོག་གེ་ངན་པར་སྨྲ་བའི་ཚོགས་ཐམས་ཅད་ཀྱི་མུན་པ་མང་པོ་རྣམ་པར་འཇོམས་པ། དེ་བཞིན་གཤེགས་པ་

636 «པེ་» «སྣར་» {SS}: ཞེས་

637 «སྣར་»: རིག་

638 «པེ་» «སྣར་» {SS}: ལུས་ «སྡེ་» «ཅོ་»: ལས་

639 «པེ་» «སྣར་»: རིག་

640 «པེ་» «སྣར་»: གྲགས་

བཀའ་[641] མཐའ་གཉིས་རྣམ་པར་སྤྲངས་པའི་ནམ་མཁའི་དཀྱིལ་ཐོས་པ་དང་བསམ་[642] པ་ལས་བྱུང་བའི་ཡེ་ཤེས་ཀྱིས་སྣང་བར་གྱུར་ན། །གནས་པ་ཡང་དག་པ་མ་ཡིན་པའི་ཕྱིན་ཅི་ལོག་རྣམ་པ་སྣ་ཚོགས་ཀྱི་ཚ་བས་གདུངས་པའི་འགྲོ་བ་མཐའ་དག་བསིལ་བར་མཛད་པའི་ཟླ་བ་འོད་ཟེར་དྲི་མ་མེད་པ་དཔག་ཏུ་མེད་པར་[643] གྲགས་པ་ཡིན་ཏེ། །དེས་མཛད་པའི་རིགས་[644] པ་དྲུག་ཅུ་ [《སྣར་》 34b.1] པའི་འགྲེལ་པ་རྫོགས་སོ།།

།རྒྱ་གར་གྱི་མཁན་པོ་ཛི་ན་མི་ཏྲ་དང་། དཱ་ན་ཤཱི་ལ་དང་། ཤཱི་[645] ལེན་དྲ་བོ་དྷི་དང་། ཞུ་ཆེན་གྱི་ལོ་ཙྪ་[646] བ་བནྡེ་ཡེ་ཤེས་སྡེས་བསྒྱུར་ཅིང་ཞུས་ཏེ་གཏན་ལ་ཕབ་པའོ།།

---

641 《ཅོ་》{SS}: བཀའ་

642 《པེ་》《སྣར་》{SS}: བསམས་

643 《པེ་》《སྣར་》{SS}: པས་

644 《པེ་》《སྣར་》: རིག་

645 《སྣར་》: ཤཱོ་

646 《པེ་》: ཙ་

APPENDICES

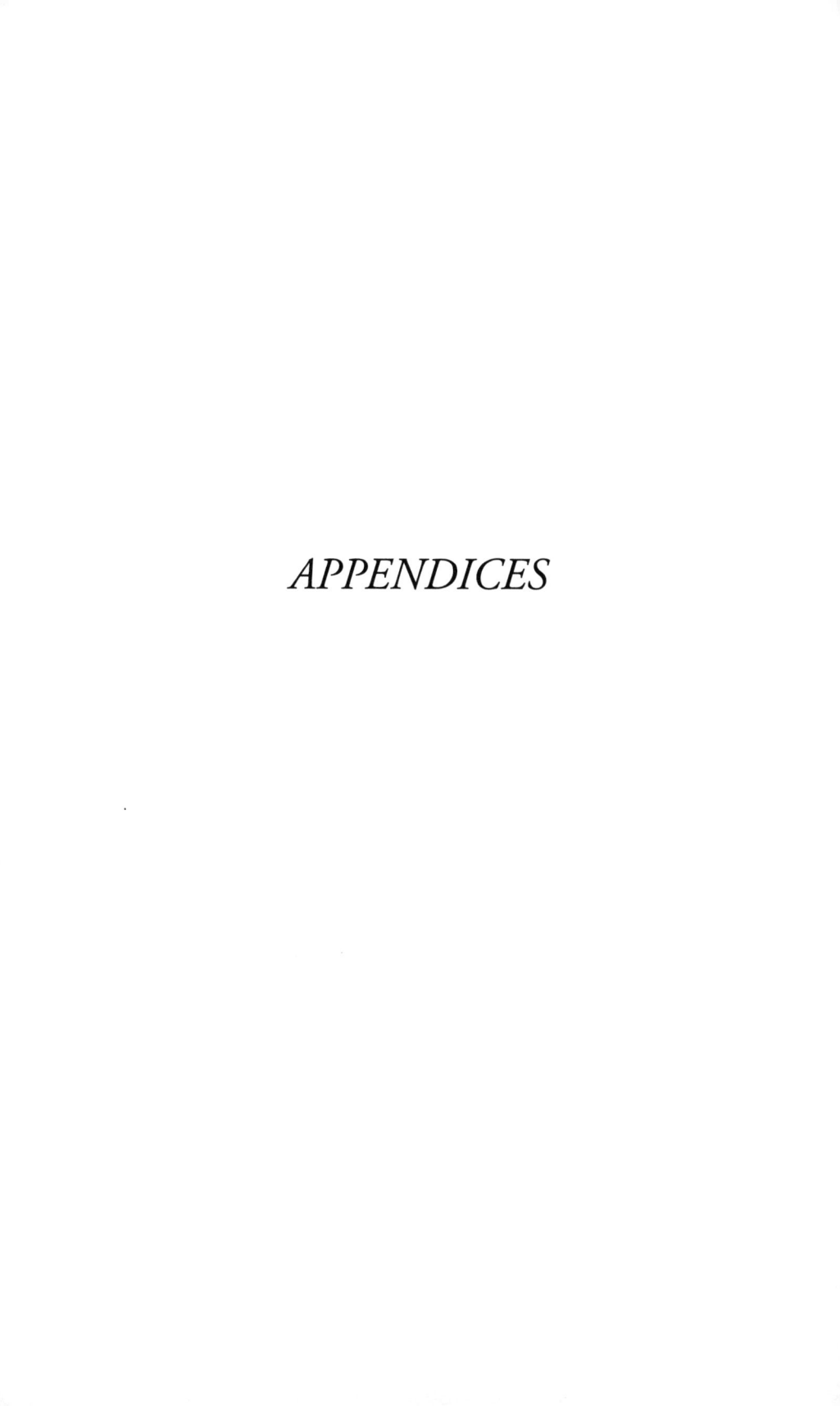

Topical Outline of the Reason Sixty (English)

From Gyaltsap Darma Rinchen's *rigs pa drug cu pa'i ṭīkka*

I. Author's preliminary homage
- A. Purpose [of the homage]
- B. The concise meaning [of the homage]
- C. The meaning of the individual words of the homage
  - 1. The actual meaning of the words
  - 2. Dispelling objections

II. The actual text which is the object of composition
- A. Teaching relativity as free from the two extremes
  - 1. Refuting the extreme of permanence
    - a. The realization of relativity as free of elaborations
      - i. The actual explanation
      - ii. Advice on the teaching of the profound
        - (1) Conjoining this with the refutation of nihilism
        - (2) Advice to listen to the refutation of the view of absolutism
    - b. The reasonings that refute the extreme of absolutism
      - i. A consequence of the appropriateness of the occasion
        - (1) The difference between Dialecticist and Dogmaticist Centrists
        - (2) Identifying the correct thesis
      - ii. Addenda
        - (1) There is no liberation through the two views
        - (2) Liberation [comes only] from a non-dual realization
  - 2. Refuting that [lack of intrinsic identifiability] establishes the two extremes
    - a. [Objection:] [Lack of intrinsic identifiability] is not scripturally established
      - i. [Objecting to the statement:] The naïve will not ascertain it
      - ii. [Response:] It is not taught for the noble ones
        - (1) [The life-cycle and nirvana] are not seen by the noble ones
        - (2) The correctness of that
    - b. It is not correct to posit nirvana with respect to the two [extremes]
      - i. It is not correct that one obtains nirvana by grasping at it
        - (1) The brief indication
        - (2) The extensive explanation
      - ii. It is not correct that one obtains nirvana by any other means
        - (1) In brief

(2) Extensive explanation

(a) That it is not correct for [nirvana] with remainder

(b) That it is not correct for [nirvana] without remainder

iii. Correctness with respect to our own [position]

(1) Why created things are not seen by a noble's meditative equipoise

(2) Thatness as the referent of the conventional expression "the object of meditation is accomplished"

(a) The actual presentation

(b) Showing that the realized truth realm lacks variety of forms

(c) Others' notions untenable in the functionally conventional realm

(i) That others' positions have faults

(x) The consequence that [the life-cycle] would have a beginning

(y) Establishing clarity with regard to the assertion

(ii) That our own position lacks faults

(x) The teaching of relativity as free from the extremes

(y) That if [the life-cycle] were intrinsically real it would be permanent

(z) Giving examples of a lack of intrinsic reality

(1") In brief, through examples

(2") The actual explanation

(3") The explanation of the meaning

3. Refuting the reality of the two extremes

a. Stating what is correct

i. Stating the context

ii. What is actually correct

(1) The general meaning

(2) The secondary meanings

(a) Refuting the extreme of [intrinsic] creation

(b) Refuting the extreme of destruction

iii. Conclusion

b. Eliminating [charges of] contradiction with scripture

i. [Buddha's] mention of creation and destruction as interpretable meaning

ii. How to understand intrinsic unreality through creation and destruction

(1) The purpose

(2) The benefits

iii. Showing how the fanatical will not understand [the truth]

iv. How the positively oriented can understand

(1) How those who have fulfilled their duties can understand

(2) How the master [Nagarjuna] himself saw [things]

(3) The reasoning for that

(a) [In accordance with] scriptural statements

(b) [In accordance with] reasoning

B. Proving that mention of the aggregates, and so forth, is of interpretable meaning

1. The stage of teaching reality

a. The actual stages

b. Perceiving the faults of transgressing that

c. The antidotes to that

2. The intention behind the statements on the aggregates

a. Actual intention

b. How to know the intention

i. [Through] reasoning

ii. [Through] scripture

3. Indicating that statements on non-production are of definitive meaning

a. Intrinsic unreality [of things] present [only] to misknowledge

b. Intrinsic unreality according to the pattern of misknowledge

i. Showing its conformity with misknowledge

ii. Stopping misknowledge and eliminating [the life-cycle]

c. Intrinsic unreality, looking at the causes of birth, duration, and destruction

C. The problems of clinging to the aggregates

1. Establishing the context

a. No wonder just that other philosophers advocate intrinsic realities

b. Buddhist philosophers are highly irrational to advocate intrinsic existence

c. The correctness of that

2. The actual perception of faults

a. Showing naïve realists swept off the liberation path by streams of views

i. Showing Vedist philosophers being deprived by the addictive view

ii. Showing some Buddhists to be deprived by the addictive view

iii. Showing the assertion of voidness to be the opposite

b. Teaching that very view to be the cause of everything useless

i. The actual teaching

ii. The procedure for reversing that

(1) The teaching in brief

(2) The extensive explanation

(a) The status of objects of knowledge

(i) Relative creation is not incompatible with intrinsic unreality

(ii) Showing all faults arising from holding them to be incompatible

(b) The procedure for realization by awareness

(i) The actual procedure

(ii) The reasoning for that

c. Showing that you cannot abandon addictions if you have the reality-habit

i. The actual teaching

ii. Showing loving concern for those endowed [with the reality-habit]

iii. How others are the opposite

d. The difference between being and not being stuck in the object trap

i. Summary

ii. Detailed explanation

D. The benefits of liberation

1. The individual explanations

a. The good qualities of abandonment

b. The good qualities of realization

2. The conclusion

III. Dedicating the virtues arising from composition

Topical Outline of the Reason Sixty (*Tibetan*)

From Gyaltsap Darma Rinchen's *rigs pa drug cu pa'i ṭīkka*

I. །དང་པོ། རྩོམ་པའི་སྔོན་འགྲོ་མཆོད་བརྗོད།

  A. །དང་པོ། དགོས་པའི་དོན།

  B. །གཉིས་པ། བསྡུས་དོན།

  C. །གསུམ་པ། ཚིག་དོན།

    1. །དང་པོ། དངོས།

    2. །གཉིས་པ། རྩོད་སྤང་།

II. །གཉིས་པ། བརྩམས་པར་བྱ་བའི་གཞུང་དངོས།

  A. །དང་པོ། རྟེན་འབྲེལ་མཐའ་བྲལ་དུ་བསྟན་པ།

    1. །དང་པོ། ཡོད་མཐའ་དགག་པ།

      a. །དང་པོ། རྟེན་འབྱུང་སྤྲོས་བྲལ་དུ་གང་གིས་རྟོགས་པ།

        i. །དང་པོ། དངོས།

        ii. །གཉིས་པ། ཟབ་མོ་བསྟན་པར་གདམས་པ།

          (1) །དང་པོ། མེད་ལྟ་དགག་པ་བཤད་ཟིན་དྲན་པ་ལ་སྦྱར་བ།

          (2) །གཉིས་པ། ཡོད་ལྟ་དགག་པ་ལ་མཉན་པར་གདམས་པ།

      b. །གཉིས་པ། ཡོད་མཐའ་འགོག་པའི་རིགས་པ།

        i. །དང་པོ། སྐབས་སུ་བབས་པའི་ཐལ་བ།

          (1) །དང་པོ་ནི། ཐལ་འགྱུར་དང་རྒྱུད་དུ་སྨྲ་བའི་དབུ་མ་པའི་ཁྱད་པར་བཤད་པར་བྱ།

          (2) །གཉིས་པ། འཐད་ཕྱོགས་ངོས་བཟུང་བ།

        ii. །གཉིས་པ། ཞར་བྱུང་།

          (1) །དང་པོ། གཉིས་སུ་ལྟ་བས་མི་གྲོལ་བར་བསྟན་པ།

          (2) །གཉིས་པ། གཉིས་མེད་རྟོགས་པས་གྲོལ་བར་བསྟན་པ།

    2. །གཉིས་པ། མཐའ་གཉིས་ཀྱི་སྒྲུབ་བྱེད་དགག་པ།

      a. །དང་པོ། ལུང་གི་སྒྲུབ་བྱེད་མི་འཐད་པ།

        i. །དང་པོ། བྱིས་པ་ལ་མ་ངེས་པ།

        ii. །གཉིས་པ། འཕགས་པ་ལ་བསྟན་པ་མ་གྲུབ་པ།

          (1) །དང་པོ། འཕགས་པས་མ་གཟིགས་པ།

(2) །གཉིས་པ། དེའི་འཐད་པ།

b. །གཉིས་པ། དེ་དག་ལ་མྱང་འདས་མི་འཐད་པ།

i. །དང་པོ། རང་གི་མྱང་འདས་ངོས་བཟུང་བ།

(1) །དང་པོ། མདོར་བསྟན།

(2) །གཉིས་པ། རྒྱས་བཤད།

ii. །གཉིས་པ། གཞན་ལ་མྱང་འདས་འཐོབ་པ་མི་འཐད་པ།

(1) །དང་པོ། མདོར་བསྟན་པ།

(2) །གཉིས་པ། རྒྱས་བཤད།

(a) །དང་པོ། ལྷག་བཅས་མི་འཐད་པ།

(b) །གཉིས་པ། ལྷག་མེད་མི་འཐད་པ།

iii. །གསུམ་པ། རང་ལ་འཐད་པ།

(1) །དང་པོ། འདུས་བྱས་འཕགས་པའི་མཉམ་གཞག་གིས་མི་གཟིགས་པའི་རྒྱུ་མཚན།

(2) །གཉིས་པ། དེ་ཉིད་གོམས་པ་བྱ་བ་བྱས་སོ་ཞེས་པའི་ཐ་སྙད་ཀྱི་ཡུལ་དུ་བསྟན་པ།

(a) །དང་པོ། དངོས།

(b) །གཉིས་པ། རྟོགས་བྱ་ཆོས་དབྱིངས་ལ་རྣམ་པ་མི་འདྲ་བ་མེད་པར་བསྟན་པ།

(c) །གསུམ་པ། གཞན་གྱིས་བརྟགས་པ་བྱ་བ་བྱས་པའི་ཐ་སྙད་ཀྱི་ཡུལ་དུ་མི་རུང་བ།

(i) །དང་པོ། གཞན་ཕྱོགས་ཉེས་པ་དང་བཅས་པ།

(x) །དང་པོ། ཐོག་མ་ཡོད་པར་ཐལ་བ།

(y) །གཉིས་པ། འདོད་པ་ལ་བསལ་བ་དགོད་པ།

(ii) །གཉིས་པ། རང་ཕྱོགས་ལ་ཉེས་པ་མེད་པ།

(x) །དང་པོ། རྟེན་འབྱུང་མཐའ་བྲལ་དུ་བསྟན་པ།

(y) །གཉིས་པ། རང་བཞིན་ཡོད་ན་རྟག་པར་ཐལ་བ།

(z) །གསུམ་པ། རང་བཞིན་མེད་པའི་དཔེ་བསྟན་པ།

(1") །དང་པོ། དཔེའི་སྒོ་ནས་མདོར་བསྟན་པ།

(2") །གཉིས་པ། དངོས་བཤད་པ།

(3") །གསུམ་པ། དོན་བཤད་པ།

3. །གསུམ་པ། མཐའ་གཉིས་ཀྱི་ངོ་བོ་དགག་པ།

a. །དང་པོ། འཐད་པ་དགོད་པ།

i. །དང་པོ། སྐབས་འགོད་པ།

ii. །གཉིས་པ། འཐད་པ་དངོས།

(1) །དང་པོ། སྤྱིའི་དོན།

(2) །གཉིས་པ། ཡན་ལག་གི་དོན་ཏོ།

(a) །དང་པོ། སྐྱེ་བའི་མཐའ་དགག་པ།

(b) །གཉིས་པ། འཇིག་པའི་མཐའ་དགག་པ།

iii. །གསུམ་པ། །མཇུག་བསྡུ་བ།

(b) །གཉིས་པ། ལུང་འགལ་སྤང་བ།

(i) །དང་པོ། སྐྱེ་འཇིག་གསུངས་པ་དྲང་དོན་དུ་བསྟན།

ii. །གཉིས་པ། སྐྱེ་འཇིག་ལ་བརྟེན་ནས་རང་བཞིན་མེད་པར་རྟོགས་ཚུལ།

(1) །དང་པོ། དགོས།

(2) །གཉིས་པ། ཕན་ཡོན།

iii. །གསུམ་པ། མངོན་ཞེན་ཅན་གྱིས་མི་རྟོགས་པར་བསྟན།

iv. །བཞི་པ། མོས་པ་རྣམས་ཀྱིས་རྟོགས་ཚུལ།

(1) །དང་པོ། མཛད་པ་མཐར་ཕྱིན་པ་རྣམས་ཀྱིས་རྟོགས་ཚུལ།

(2) །གཉིས་པ། སློབ་དཔོན་རང་ཉིད་ཀྱིས་གཟིགས་ཚུལ།

(3) །གསུམ་པ། དེའི་འཐད་པ།

(a) །དང་པོ། ལུང་།

(b) །གཉིས་པ། རིགས་པ།

B. །གཉིས་པ། ཕུང་སོགས་གསུངས་པ་དྲང་དོན་དུ་བསྒྲུབ་པ།

1. །དང་པོ། དེ་ཁོ་ན་ཉིད་བསྟན་པའི་རིམ་པ།

a. །དང་པོ། རིམ་པ་དངོས།

b. །གཉིས་པ། དེ་ལས་འདས་པའི་ཉེས་དམིགས།

c. །གསུམ་པ། དེའི་གཉེན་པོ།

2. །གཉིས་པ། ཕུང་སོགས་གསུངས་པ་དགོངས་པ།

a. །དང་པོ། དངོས།

b. །གཉིས་པ། ཤེས་བྱེད།

i. །དང་པོ། རིགས་པ།

ii. །གཉིས་པ། ལུང་།

3. །གསུམ་པ། སྐྱེ་མེད་གསུངས་པ་ངེས་དོན་ཡིན་པར་བསྟན་པ།

a. །དང་པོ། མ་རིག་པ་ལ་སྣང་བས་རང་བཞིན་མེད་པ།

b. །གཉིས་པ། མ་རིག་པའི་རྗེས་སུ་འགྲོ་ལྡོག་བྱེད་པས་རང་བཞིན་མེད་པ།

i. །དང་པོ། མ་རིག་པའི་རྗེས་སུ་བྱེད་པར་བསྟན་པ།

ii. །གཉིས་པ། མ་རིག་པ་ལོག་ན་ལྡོག་པ།

c. །གསུམ་པ། སྐྱེ་འཇིག་གནས་གསུམ་རྒྱུ་ལ་ལྟོས་པས་རང་བཞིན་མེད་པ།

C. །གསུམ་པ། ཕུང་པོར་ཞེན་པའི་ཉེས་དམིགས།

1. །དང་པོ། སྐབས་དགོད་པ།

a. །དང་པོ། གཞན་སྡེ་རང་བཞིན་ཡོད་པར་སྨྲ་བ་དེ་ཙམ་ཡ་མཚན་མེད་པ།

b. །གཉིས་པ། རང་སྡེ་རང་བཞིན་ཡོད་པར་སྨྲ་བ་ཆེས་མི་རིགས་པ།

c. །གསུམ་པ། དེའི་འཐད་པ།

2. །གཉིས་པ། ཉེས་དམིགས་དངོས།

a. །དང་པོ། དངོས་པོར་སྨྲ་བ་ཐར་ལམ་ལས་གྱོལ་བར་ལྟ་བའི་རྒྱུས་ཁྲེར་བར་བསྟན་པ།

i. །དང་པོ། གཞན་སྡེ་ལྟ་བས་ཕྱོགས་པར་བསྟན་པ།

ii. །གཉིས་པ། རང་སྡེ་ལྟ་བས་ཕྱོགས་པར་བསྟན་པ།

iii. །གསུམ་པ། སྟོང་པར་སྨྲ་བ་དེ་ལས་ལྡོག་པར་བསྟན་པ།

b. །གཉིས་པ། ལྟ་བ་དེ་ཉིད་དོན་མིན་པའི་རྒྱུར་བསྟན་པ།

i. །དང་པོ། དངོས།

ii. །གཉིས་པ། དེ་ལྡོག་ཚུལ།

(1) །དང་པོ། མདོར་བསྟན།

(2) །གཉིས་པ། རྒྱས་བཤད།

(a) །དང་པོ། ཤེས་བྱའི་གནས་ཚུལ།

(i) །དང་པོ། བརྟེན་ནས་སྐྱེས་པ་དང་། རང་བཞིན་མེད་པ་མི་འགལ་བ།

(ii) །གཉིས་པ། འགལ་བར་གཟུང་བས་ཉེས་པ་ཀུན་འབྱུང་བར་བསྟན་པ།

(b) །གཉིས་པ། བློས་རྟོགས་ཚུལ།

(i) །དང་པོ། དངོས།

(ii) །གཉིས་པ། དེའི་འཐད་པ།

c. །གསུམ་པ། དངོས་ཞེན་ཡོད་ནས་ཉོན་མོངས་སྤོང་མི་ནུས་པར་བསྟན་པ།

i. །དང་པོ། དངོས།

ii. །གཉིས་པ། དེ་དང་ལྡན་པ་ལ་བརྩེ་བ་བྱ་བར་བསྟན་པ།

- iii. །གསུམ་པ། གཞན་དེ་ལས་ལྡོག་པ།
- d. །བཞི་པ། ཡུལ་གྱི་གཟེབ་ལ་ཐོགས་པ་དང་མི་ཐོགས་པའི་དབྱེ་བ་བསྟན་པ།
  - i. །དང་པོ། མདོར་བསྟན།
  - ii. །གཉིས་པ། རྒྱས་བཤད།

D. །བཞི་པ། ཐར་པའི་ཕན་ཡོན།

1. །དང་པོ། སོ་སོར་བཤད་པ།
   - a. །དང་པོ། སྤྱངས་པའི་ཡོན་ཏན།
   - b. །གཉིས་པ། རྟོགས་པའི་ཡོན་ཏན།
2. །གཉིས་པ། མཇུག་སྡུད།

III. །གསུམ་པ། བརྩམས་པའི་དགེ་བ་བསྔོ་བ།

Trilingual Glossary

English	Sanskrit	Tibetan
absolute (ultimate)	paramārtha	don dam pa
absolutism	astivāda, śāśvatavāda	yod par smra ba, rtag par smra ba
absorption (equipoise, trance)	samāpatti	snyoms par 'jug pa
action (evolution)	karma	las
addiction	kleśa	nyon mongs
addicted mentality	kliṣṭamanas	nyon mongs pa'i yid
affect (feeling)	vedanā	tshor ba
affective obscuration	kleśāvaraṇa	nyon mongs pa'i sgrub pa
aftermath insight	pṛṣṭalabdhajñāna	rjes thob ye shes
aggregate (life-process)	skandha	phung po
physical	rūpa-	gzugs kyi-
sensory	vedanā-	tshor ba'i-
perceptual	saṁjñā-	'du shes kyi-
emotional	saṁskāra-	'du byed kyi-
cognitive	vijñāna-	rnam par shes pa'i-
alienated individual	pṛthagjana	so so'i skyes bo
altruism (love)	adhyāśaya (maitri)	lhag bsam, byams pa
analysis	vitarka, vicāra	brtag pa, dpyod pa
Analyst	Vaibhāṣika	bye brag smra ba
analytic insight	vipaśyanā	lhag mthong
anger (aggression)	krodha, dveṣa	khong khro, she sdang
archetypal deity	iṣṭadevatā	yi dam
attention	manaskāra	yid la byed pa
bias (position)	pakṣa	phyogs
birth (life, creation)	jāti, utpatti	skyes pa, 'byung ba
birthless (unborn, uncreated)	ajāti, anutpāda	skyes med, ma 'byung ba
physical aggregate	rūpaskandha	gzugs kyi phung po
body	kāya	sku
causality	karmaphala	las bras
cause	hetu	rgyu

English	**Sanskrit**	**Tibetan**
Central Way	Madhyamaka	dbU ma
Centrism	Mādhyamika	dbU ma
Centrist	Mādhyamika	dbU ma pa
cognition	vijñāpti	yongs su shes pa
cognitive obscuration (resistance)	jñeyāvaraṇa	shes bya'i sgrib pa
concentration	samādhi	ting nge 'dzin
condition	pratyāya	rkyen
consciousness	vijñāna	rnam par shes pa
consciousness aggregate	vijñānaskandha	rnam shes phung po
consensus	lokayaśa	'jigs rten gyi grags
consequence (effect)	phala	'bras bu
constructed	vikalpita, parikalpita	rnam par brtags pa, kun tu brtags pa
construction	kalpanā	brtags pa
mental	vikalpanā	rnam par brtags pa
contemplation	dhyāna	bsam gtan
continuum	saṁtāna	rgyun
convention	vyavahāra	tha snyad
conventional (consensual)	vyāvahārika	tha snyad pa
conventional usage	upādāyaprajñapti	brten nas gdags pa
creation (created)	saṁskāra, jāti (saṁskṛta)	'du byed, skye ba ('dus byas)
cyclic life (life-cycle)	saṁsāra	'khor ba
denial (repudiation)	apavāda	skur ba 'debs pa
dependent origination (relativity)	pratītyasamutpāda	rten cing 'brel bar 'byung ba (rten 'brel)
desire	kāma, rāga	'dod pa, chags pa
Dialecticist Centrist	prāsaṅgikamādhyamika	thal bar dbus ma pa
direct experience (perception)	pratyakṣa	mngon sum
discipline	vinaya	'dul ba
discrimination	paricchinna	yongs su gcod pa

English	**Sanskrit**	**Tibetan**
Dogmaticist Centrist	svātantrikamādhyamika	rang rgyud dbus ma pa
doubt	vicikitsā	the tshom
dualism	dvayavāda	gnyis su smra ba
education	sikṣā	bslab pa
effort (enthusiasm)	vīrya	brtson 'grus
egoism	ahaṁkāra	ngar 'dzin
egocentrism	ātmagraha	bdag 'dzin
element	dharma	chos
emotion (creation)	saṁskāra	'du byed
emotional aggregate	saṁskāraskandha	'du byed phung po
empathy (compassion)	karuṇā	nying rje
enlightened	buddha	sangs rgyas pa
enlightened altruist	bodhisattva	byang chub sems pa
entity (fact)	bhāva	dngos po
equanimity	upekṣā	btang snyom
equipoised insight	samāhitajñāna	mnyam bzhags ye shes
eternalism	śāśvatavāda	rtag par smra ba
ethics (justice)	śīla	tshul khrims
evolution (action)	karma	las
evolutionary		
causality	karmaphala	las 'bras
conservation	karmāvipraṇaśa	las chud mi za ba
maturity	karmavipāka	las rnam par smin pa
existent	sat	yod pa
experience	anubhava	myong ba
Experientialist	yogācāra	rnal 'byor spyod pa
extinction	nirodha	'gog pa
extreme	anta	mtha
fabrication	prapañca	spros pa
fact (entity, being)	bhāva, satya	dngos po, bden pa
faith (confidence)	śraddhā	dad pa
false (fictive)	viparīta, mithyā	log pa, rdzun ba
form (matter)	rūpa	gzugs
formless	ārūpya	gzugs med
freedom (liberation)	mokṣa, viveka	thar pa, dben pa
genius	bodhi, buddha	blo, sangs rgyas

English	Sanskrit	Tibetan
great soul	mahātmā	bdag nyid chen po
ground (basis)	āśraya, ādhāra	gzhi, gnas
habit	graha	'dzin pa
habituation	abhiniveśa	mngon par zhen pa
Idealist	vijñānavādin	sems tsam pa
identity (nature)	lakṣaṇa	mtshan nyid
illusion	māyā	rgyu ma
illusory	māyopama	rgyu ma ltar
impermanence	anityatā	mi rtag nyid
Individual Vehicle	Hīnayāna	theg dman
Individualist	hinayānika	theg dman pa
inference	anumāna	rjes dpag
insight (intuition)	jñāna	ye shes
aftermath	pṛṣṭalabdha-	rjes thob ye shes
equipoise	samāhita-	mnyam bzhag ye shes
instinct	vāsanā	bag chags
interdependence	parasparāpekṣa	phan thsun ltos pa
interpretable meaning	neyārtha	drang don
intrinsic	sva-	rang
identity	svalakṣaṇa	rang gi msthan nyid
objectivity	svarūpa	rang gi ngo bo
reality	svabhāva	rang bzhin
intuition (insight)	jñāna	ye shes
life (being)	utpāda (gati)	skye ba ('gro ba)
life-cycle (cyclic life)	saṁsāra	'khor ba
(living) being	jaṅgama	'gro ba
meditation	bhāvanā	sgoms pa
mental factors	caitasika	sems 'byung
mental perception	mānasapratyakṣa	yid kyi mngon sum
method (art)	upāya	thabs
mind (mentality)	citta (manas)	sems (yid)
mindfulness	smṛti	drangs nges
misknowledge	avidyā	ma rig pa
mistaken	viparīta	phyin ci log pa
naïve	bāla	byis pa
nature	lakṣaṇa, svabhāva	mtshan nyid, rang bzhin

English	**Sanskrit**	**Tibetan**
negandum	pratiṣedhavya	dgag bya
negation	pratiṣedha	dgag pa
pure	prasajya-	med dgag
implicative	paryudāsa-	ma yin dgag
nihilism	abhāvavāda	med par smra ba
nihilistic view	ucchedadṛṣṭi	chad par lta ba
noble	ārya	'phags pa
individual	āryapudgala	'phags pa'i gang zag
truth	āryasatya	'phags pa'i bden pa
non-analytic	avicāra	dpyod med
non-perception	anupalabdhi	dmigs pa med pa
nothingness	abhāva	dngos med, med pa
object	artha, ālambana	don, dmigs pa
objectification	upālambha	nye bar dmigs pa
objectivity	svarūpatā	rang gi ngos bo nyid
obscuration	āvaraṇa	sgrib pa
perception (direct experience)	pratyakṣa	mngon sum
perceptual aggregate	saṁjñāskandha	'du shes phung po
person	pudgala	gang zag
philosophy	yukti, vāda	rigs pa, smra ba
position	pakṣa	phyogs bzang
practitioner	yogin/ī	rnal 'byor
primary element	mahābhūta	'byung ba chen po
privacy	svātantryā	rang rgyud
profound	gambhīra	zab mo
pure science	abhidharma	mngon chos
quiescence	śamatha	zhi gnas
real	sat	yang dag pa
reality	satya, tattva, svabhāva	bden pa, de nyid, rang bzhin
superficial	saṁvṛtisatya	kun rdzob bden pa
conventional	vyāvahārikasatya	tha snyad bden pa
ultimate	paramārthasatya	don dam pa'i bden pa
realization	adhigama	rtogs pa

English	**Sanskrit**	**Tibetan**
realm	dhātu	khams
of desire	kāmadhātu	'dod pa'i khams
of form	rūpadhātu	gzugs gyi khams
of formless	ārūpyadhātu	gzugs med pa'i khams
reason	yukti, hetu	rigs pa, rtags
recognition	parijñāna	yons su shes pa
referent	artha, vastu	don, gzhi
reflection (image)	pratibimba	gzugs brnyan
reification	samāropa, adhyāropa	sgro 'dogs pa
relativity (dependent origination)	pratītyasamutpāda	rten cing 'brel bar 'byung ba
remedy	pratipakṣa	gnyen po
resistance (obscuration)	āvaraṇa	sgrib pa
cognitive	jñeyāvaraṇa	shes bya'i-
affective	kleśāvaraṇa	nyon mongs pa'i-
science	vidyāsthāna	rig gnas
self	ātma	bdag
personal (subjective)	pudgalātma	gang zag bdag
phenomenal (objective)	dharmātma	chos kyi bdag
self-centeredness	ātmasneha	bdag ches 'dzin
self-habit	ātmagraha	bdag 'dzin
selflessness	anātmatā (nairātmyā)	bdag med pa
sense faculty	indriya	dbang po
element	dhātu	khams
medium	āyātana	skye mched
skill	kauśalya	mkhas pa
social (mundane)	laukika	'jig rten pa'i
status (establishment)	siddha, siddhatva	grub ba
substance	dravya	rdzas
superficial reality	saṁvṛtisatya	kun rdzob bden pa
technique (art, method)	upāya	thabs
thing	dharma, bhāva	chos, dngos po
tolerance	kṣanti	bzod pa

English	**Sanskrit**	**Tibetan**
Traditionist	Sautrāntika	mdo sde pa
transcendence	nirvāṇa, pāramitā	mya ngan 'das, pha rol tu phyin pa
transcendent insight	vipaśyanā	lhag mthong
(ultimate) particular	svalakṣaṇa	rang gi mtsan nyid
ultimate reality (truth)	paramārthasatya	don dam bden pa
unconscious egocentrism	sahaja-ātmagraha	lhan skyes-bdag 'dzin
uncreated	asaṁskṛta, anutpāda	'dus ma byed pa, ma skyes pa
Universal Vehicle	mahāyāna	theg pa chen po
Universalist	mahāyānika	theg pa chen po pa
vacant (isolation)	viveka	dben pa
validating cognition	pramāṇa	tshad ma
Victor	jina	rgyal ba
view (addictive view)	dṛṣṭi (dṛṣṭigata)	lta ba (lta bar 'gyur ba)
voidness (emptiness)	śūnyatā	stong pa nyid
wisdom	prajñā	shes rab
world	jagat, loka	'jig rten

Intellectual-Historical Timeline of Indian Buddhism

Pāṇini (c. 550 BCE) Shākyamuni (c. 550 BCE) Upaniṣads

Theravadins at Pāṭaliputra (Ashoka c.250 BCE) Mahāsaṁghikas at Nālandā

Patañjali's Grammar (c. 200 BCE) (c. 150 BCE) Patañjali's Yoga

Mahāsaṁghikas favored in Taxila & Andhra (c. 78–144 CE)

Nāgārjuna (c. 150–250 CE)

Nālandā expanded, Dhānyakaṭaka (c. 200 CE)

Āryadeva (c. 200–300 CE)

Vasubandhu (c. 385–480) Asaṅga (c. 370–450)

Vātsyāyana (4th–5th CE) (4th CE) Vyāsa

Shrī Nālandā Mahāvihāra founded
by Kumāragupta I (r. 413–455) and his heirs

Chandra the Grammarian (c. 400–460)

Dignāga (c. 480–540) (c. 440–510) Bhartṛhari

Buddhapālita (c. 470–550) (c. 500) Gauḍapāda

Sthiramati (c. 470–560)

Bhāvaviveka (c.500–600) Dharmapāla (c. 550–620)

Uddyotakāra (550–610) Kamalabuddhi (c. 550–620) (v. 629–645) Xuan zang

Kumārila (6th–7th CE) Chandrakīrti (c. 590–670) (v. 671–689) Yi jing

Dharmakīrti (c. 610–680) Chandragomin (c. 600–670)

Shāntideva (c. 700)

Jñānagarbha & Haribhadra (8th CE) (c. 700–780) Shaṅkara

Shāntarakṣita (740–810)

Kamalashīla (760–815)

Odantapurī (730–1199) & Vikramashīla (c. 750–1300)

Udāyana (10th CE) Atīsha (982–1054) (c. 1050) Abhinavagupta

Abhayākaragupta (c. 1100) (d. 1137) Rāmānuja

Chag-lotsawa visits Nālandā (1234–1236)

Invaders raid Nālandā-Vikramashīla (c. 1250–1300)

Speculative Reconstruction of Chandrakīrti's Biography

590 Chandrakīrti born in Samātha (Sanathi?), South India

596 Chandrakīrti ordained, begins monastic grammar school

600 Bhāvaviveka rebuffed by Dharmapāla, retires to Dhānyakaṭaka

604 Chandrakīrti begins study of basic sciences, Mahāsaṁghika canon

606 Harṣavardana (Shīladitya I) ascends to throne in Kanauj

608 Harṣavardana starts construction of 7th Vihāra at Nālandā

610 Chandrakīrti travels north to Nālandā, begins Mādhyamika Studies

615 Chandrakīrti writes *Madhyamakāvatāra*

620 Chandrakīrti succeeds Kamalabuddhi as Chair of Mādhyamika Studies

621 Chandrakīrti writes *Pransannapadā*

622 Chandrakīrti writes *Śūnyatāsāptativṛtti*

623 Chandrakīrti appointed superintendent of Nālandā farm

624 Shashāṅka destroys Buddhist monasteries and shrines in Magadha

625 Harṣavardana defeats Shashāṅka, erects Nālandā perimeter wall

626 Chandrakīrti writes *Catuḥśatakaṭīkā*, Dharmapāla dies

631 Xuan zang arrives to study with Shīlabhadra at Nālandā

633 Chandrakīrti writes *Yuktiśaṣṭikavṛtti*, Harṣa's Vihāra completed

640 Chandrakīrti writes *Pañcaskandhaprakaraṇa*

643 Xuan zang leaves Nālandā, Dharmakīrti rises to prominence

644 Chandragomin arrives at Nālandā, debate with Chandrakīrti begins

648 King Shīla succeeds his father, Harṣavardana

650 Chandrakīrti succeeds Shīlabhadra as Abbot, counsels B. Vimuktisena

652 Chandragomin leaves Nālandā, Chandrakīrti-Chandragomin debate ends

653 Chandrakīrti writes *Triśaraṇasāptati*, teaches Jayadeva

658 Chandrakīrti retires to Koṅkana, Ratnasiṁha succeeds him as Abbot

661 Chandrakīrti practices/teaches *Guhyasamāja*, dictates *Pradīpodyottana*

675 Chandrakīrti dies, Yi jing arrives at Nālandā

685 Yi jing cites Dharmakīrti as a "recent" luminary, leaves Nālandā

686 Jayadeva succeeds Ratnasiṁha as Abbot, teaches Shāntideva

Abbreviations

AA *Abhisamayālaṁkāra, Ornament of Realizations*

Conze, E. *Abhisamayālaṁkāra.* Rome: Serie Orientale Roma, 1954.

AAV *Abhisamayālaṁkāravṛtti, Ornament of Realizations Commentary*

Pensa, C. *Abhisamayālaṁkāravṛtti.* Rome: Serie Orientale Roma, 1967.

AD *Vyākaraṇasūtra-Aṣṭādhyāyī, Grammar Scripture*

Shastri, S. ed. *Aṣṭādhyāyī-sūtra-pāṭha.* Mylapore: Bālarāma Series 2.

ad k. commentary on kārikā(s)

AK *Abhidharmakośa, Treasury of Pure Science*

Pradhan, P. (ed.) *Abhidharmakośabhāṣya of Vasubandhu.* Patna: K.P. Jayaswal Research Institute (1967).

AKV *Abhidharmakośavyākhyā, Explanation of the Treasury of Pure Science*

Wogihara, U. (ed.) *Spuṭārthā Abhidharmakośavyākhyā by Yaśomitra.* 7 fasc. Tōkyō, 1932–1936.

AN *Akṣayamatinirdeśa, Teaching of Aksyayamati*

ASPP *Aṣṭasāhasrikāprajñāpāramitā, Eight Thousand Line Transcendent Wisdom Sūtra*

BA *Deb ter sṅon po, Blue Annals*

Roerich, G.N. *The Blue Annals.* 2 vols. Calcutta, 1949, 1953. English translation.

BBB *The Blue and Brown Books*

Wittgenstein, L. *The Blue and Brown Books.* New York, 1958.

BSBh *Brahmasūtrabhāṣya, Brahma Scripture Commentary*

Brahmasūtra with Śaṅkarabhāṣya. Delhi: Works of Śankarācārya, 3, 1964.

BST *Buddhist Sanskrit Text Series*

BSV *Bodhisattvasaṁvaraviṁśaka, Twenty Verses on the Bodhisattva Vows*

Tatz, M. *Difficult Beginnings: Three Works on the Bodhisattva Path*. Boston, Shambhala,1985. English Translation.

BT *rGya-gar Chos-'byung, History of Indian Buddhism*

Obermiller, E. *Buston's History of Buddhism*. London, 1935. English translation.

c. circa

C Chone Tengyur (*Chos-gnas bsTan-'gyur*)

Institute for the Advanced Studies of World Religions. Stony Brook, 1976. Microfiche edition.

Ch. Chapter

CŚ *Yogācāracatuḥśataka, Experientialist Four Hundred*

CŚṬ *Yogācāracatuḥśatakaṭīkā, Commentary on the Four Hundred*

Tillemans, T.J.F. *Materials for the Study of Āyradeva, Dharmapāla and Candrakīrti*. Wien: Arbeitskreis fur Tibetische und Buddhistische Studien, 1990.

CV *Culture and Value*

Wittgenstein, L. *Culture and Value*. New York: Harper, 1970.

CVy *Candravyākaraṇa, Chandra's Grammar*

Doshi, B.J. *Candravyākaraṇam*. Jodhpur: Rajasthan Research Institute, 1967.

D Derge Tengyur

Yamaguchi, Z., Takasaki, J., Ejima, Y. *sDe dge Tibetan Tripiṭaka bstan hgyur*: dbU ma Section (14 vols.). Tokyo, 1977–1982. Critical edition and reprint. Asian Classics Input Project, Release IV. Compact Disc edition.

DBS *Daśabhūmikasūtra, Ten Stages Scripture*

Rahder, J. *Daśabhūmikasūtra*. Louvain, 1926.

Dh *Yuktiśaṣṭikakārikā*

Ye shes sde, trans. *Rigs pa drug cu pa tshig le'ur byed pa.* Dunhuang MS.

DS *Deśanastava, Confessional Praise*

Tatz, M. *Difficult Beginnings: Three Works on the Bodhisattva Path.* Boston: Shambhala,1985. English translation.

f. folio (Tibetan books)

ff. following; folios (Tibetan books)

GST *Guhyasamājatantra, Esoteric Communion*

Bagchi, S. ed. *Guhyasamāja Tantra or Tathāgataguhyaka.* Mithila: BST 9, 1965. Sanskrit edition.

HL *Da tang ci en si sān zang fa shī zhuan, The Life of Xuan zang*

Beal, S. *The Life of Hiuan Tsiang by the Shaman Hui li.* London, 1888/1914. English translation.

k.(ks.) kārikā(s) (Sanskrit verses)

L *Yuktiṣaṣṭikākārikā*

Lindtner, C. *Nāgārjuniana.* The Hague, 1982. Critical edition of extant Sanskrit verses and the Tibetan text.

LAS *Laṅkāvatārasūtra, Mission to Lanka Scripture*

Suzuki, D.T. *Laṅkāvatāra Sūtra.* 2 vols. London, 1956. Sanskrit edition and English translation.

LSNP *Drang-nges legs bshad snying po, The Essence of True Eloquence*

Thurman, R.A.F. *Tsong Khapa's Speech of Gold in the Essence of True Eloquence* (*Essence*). Princeton, 1984. English translation.

MA *Madhyamakāvatāra, Central Way Introduction*

La Vallée Poussin, L. de. *Madhyamakāvatāra de Candrakīrti.* St. Petersburg, 1926. Critical edition of the Tibetan text and autocommentary.

MABh *Madhyamakāvatārabhāṣya, Central Way Introduction Commentary*

See MA.

MAL *Madhyamakāloka, Central Way Illumination*

MAV *Madhyāntavibhāga, Discrimination Between Center and Extremes*

Pandeya, R.C. *Madhyāntavibhāgaśāstra*. Delhi, 1971. Sanskrit edition.

MCB *Mélanges Chinois et Bouddhiques*

MH *Madhyamakahṛdaya, Heart of the Central Way*

Sanskrit manuscript rediscovered by R. Saṁkṛtyāyāna has been partially published; see Eckel, M., *To See the Buddha*. New York, 1992.

MK *Māṇḍūkyakārikā-Āgamaśāstra, Tradition Scripture*

Bhattacharya, V. *The Āgamaśāstra of Gauḍapāda*. Calcutta, 1943.

MMK *Prajñānāma-Mūlamadhyamakakārikā, Wisdom, Fundamental Verses of the Central Way.*

Inada, K. *The Mūlamadhyamakakārikās of Nāgārjuna*. Tokyo, 1970.

MS *Mīmāṁsakasūtra, Scholastic Scripture*

Jha, G. *Śabara-Bhāṣya*. Gaekwad's Oriental Series, LXVI, LXX, LXXIII, Baroda, 1933, 1934, 1936.

MSA *Mahāyānasūtrālaṁkāra, Universal Vehicle Discourse Literature*

Levi, S. *Mahāyāna-Sūtrālaṁkāra*. 2 vols. Paris, 1907, 1911. Sanskrit edition and French translation.

Mvy *Mahāvyutpatti.*

Sakaki, R., ed. *Mahāvyutpatti*. Tokyo: Suzuki Research Foundation, 1962.

n. note

N Narthang Tengyur

NS *Nyāyasūtra, Logic Scripture*

Vidyābhuṣaṇa, S.C. *Nyāya Sūtras of Gautama. Sacred Books of the Hindus*. Allahabad, 1930.

OC *On Certainty*

Wittgenstein, L. *On Certainty*. New York: 1969. English translation.

p. (pp.) page(s)

P Peking Tengyur

The Tibetan Tripiṭaka: Peking Edition. Tibetan Tripiṭaka Research Foundation: Tokyo and Kyoto, 1956.

PI *Philosophical Investigations*

Wittgenstein, L. *Philosophical Investigations*. New York: 1953. English translation.

PPMMV *Mūlamadhyamakavṛtti-Prasannapadā-nāma, Lucid Exposition*

Dbu ma rtsa ba'i 'grel pa tshig gsal ba. Tōh. 3860.

PS *Pramāṇasamuccaya, Compendium on Valid Knowledge*

PSP *Pañcaskandhaprakaraṇa, Elucidation of the Five Aggregates*

Lindtner, C., ed. *Pañcaskandhaprakaraṇa*. Acta Orientalia 40, 1979.

RA *Ratnāvali, Jewel Rosary*

Rin chen 'phreng ba. Tōh. 4158.

RGV *Ratnagotravibhāga, Analysis of the Jewel Matrix*

Johnston, E. *Ratnagotravibhāga-mahāyānottaraśāstra*. Patna, 1950. Sanskrit edition.

S(SS) Scherrer-Schaub, C. *Yuktiṣaṣṭikāvṛtti*.

Critical edition of the Tibetan text.

Skt. Sanskrit

SN *Saṁdhinirmocanasūtra, Elucidation of the Intention Scripture*

Lamotte, E. *Explication des Mysteres*. Louvain and Paris, 1935. Tibetan edition and French translation.

ŚS *Śūnyatāsāptatī, Voidness Seventy*

Komito, D. *Nāgārjuna's Śūnyatāsāptatī*. Ithaca, 1982.

ŚSV *Śūnyatāsāptativṛtti, Voidness Seventy Commentary*

Erb, F. *Śūnyatāsāptativṛtti*. Stuttgart, 1997. Tibetan text and German translation of Chandrakīrti's commentary on ŚS, ks. 1–14.

T *Yuktiṣaṣṭikākārikā*

Tola and Dragonetti. "The 'Yuktiṣaṣṭikā' of Nāgārjuna," 1983. Tibetan edition and English translation.

TN *rGya-gar chos-'byung, History of Indian Buddhism*

Chattopadhyaya A., and Chimpa, L. *Tāranātha's History of Buddhism in India*. Simla, 1970. English translation.

TG Tengyur (*bsTan-'gyur*)

TJ *Madhyamakahṛdaya-Tarkajvāla, Blaze of Argument*

Tōh. Yensho Kanakura, ed. *A Catalogue of the Tohoku University Collection of Tibetan Works on Buddhism*. Sendai, 1953.

tr. translation

TŚS *Triśaraṇasāptati, Three Refuge Seventy*

Sorenson, P. *Triśaraṇasāptati of Candrakīrti*. Tibetan edition and English translation. 1986.

UV *Udānavarga, Categorical Sayings*

Ched du brjod pa'i tshoms. Tōh. 326.

V *Yuktiṣaṣṭikāvṛtti*

Pa tshab nyi ma grag, trans. *Rigs pa drug cu pa'i 'grel pa*. P, No. 5265, Vol. 98.

VP *Vākyapadīya, On Words and Statements*

Shastri, Pt. C. *Vākyapadīya with the Commentary of Vṛṣabhadeva*. Lahore, 1934.

VV *Vigrahavyāvartanī, Rebuttal of Objections*

In Vaidya, P.L. *Prasannapadamūlamadhyakavṛtti*. Darbhanga, 1960. Includes Sanskrit edition.

XZ *Si Yu Ki, Records of the Western World*

Beal, S. *Si-Yu-Ki: Buddhist Records of the Western World, Translated from the Chinese of Hiuen Tsang*. London, 1884/1969.

Y *Yuktiṣaṣṭikāvṛtti*

Yamaguchi, S. *Yuktiṣaṣṭikāvṛtti*. Tokyo, 1965. Critical edition of the Tibetan and Chinese texts with Japanese translation.

YJ *Nan hai ji gui nei fa zhuan, Record of the Buddhist Religion in India and Malasia*

Takakusu, J. *A Record of the Buddhist Religion as Practiced in India and the Malay Archipelago*. Oxford, 1896. English Translation from the Chinese of I-Tsing (Yi jing).

YṢ *Yuktiṣaṣṭikā, Reason Sixty*

Loizzo, J. See herein for English translation and Tibetan edition.

YSu *Yogasūtra, Integration Scripture*

Prasada, R. *Yoga Sūtras of Patañjali with Yoga Bhāṣya of Vyāsa*. Sacred Books of the Hindus, Allahabad, 1924.

YṢV *Yuktiṣaṣṭikāvṛtti, Reason Sixty Commentary*

Loizzo, J. See herein for English translation and Tibetan edition.

Z *Yuktiṣaṣṭikākārikā*

Pa tshab nyi ma grags, trans. *Rigs pa drug cu pa tshig leu'r byed pa. Zhol par khang edition* (MS).

Ze *Zettel*

Wittgenstein, L. *Zettel*. Oxford, 1967. English translation.

Bibliography

Reference Works

Chone Tanjur Microfiche Edition. Stony Brook, NY: Institute for Advanced Study of World Religions, 1976.

Mahāvyutpatti. (Sakaki, R., ed.) Tokyo: Suzuki Research Foundation, 1962.

Oxford Latin Dictionary. Oxford: Clarendon Press, 1982.

sDe dge Tibetan Tripitaka bstan hgyur, dbU ma section. (Yamaguchi, Z.; J. Takasaki; and E. Yasunori, eds.) 14 Vols. Tokyo: Tokyo, 1977.

The Tibetan Tripitaka: Peking Edition. (P) Tibetan Tripiṭaka Research Foundation: Tokyo and Kyoto, 1956.

Hakuju Ui, et al., eds. *Chibetto Daizōkyō Sōmokuroku / A Complete Catalogue of the Tibetan Buddhist Canons (Bkaḥ-ḥgyur and Bstan-ḥgyur).* Sendai: Tōhoku Imperial University, 1934.

Canonical Sources

"P" and "Tōh." refer to the Catologues of the Tibetan Tripitaka Research Institute (Peking), and Ui and Kanakura (Tōhoku), respectively

Scriptures

Akṣayamatinirdeśasūtra, Blo gros mi zad pa'i bstan pa'i mdo, Teaching of Aksayamati (AN). P, No. 842, Vol. 34.

Aṣṭasāhasrikā-prajñāpāramitā-sūtra, Shes rab brgyad stong pa, Eight Thousand Line Transcendent Wisdom Sutra. P, No. 734, Vol. 21; Tōh. 12.

Buddhāvataṁsakanāmamahāvaipulyasūtra, Sangs rgyas phal po che zhes bya ba shin tu rgyas pa chen po'i mdo, Garland Scripture. P, No. 761, Vols. 25–26.

Daśabhūmikāsūtra, Mdo sde sa bcu pa, Ten Stages Scripture (DBS) (Part of the Garland Scripture). P, No. 761, Vol. 25.

Gandavyūhasūtra, Stug por bkod pa'i mdo, Dense Array Scripture. P, No. 778, Vol. 29; Tōh. 110.

Guhyasamājatantra, gSang ba 'dus pa'i brgyud, Esoteric Communion Scripture (GST). Tōh. 442.

Kaśyapaparivarta, 'Od srung gi le'u, Kashyapa Chapter (Section of Ratnakuta). P, No. 760, Vol. 24; Tōh. 87.

Kātyāyana-sūtra, Saṁyutta II, Kaccāyanagotto. Saṁyutta-Nikāya. London: PTS, 1884–1898.

Lankāvatārasūtra, Lang kar gshegs pa'i mdo, Mission to Lanka Scripture (LAS). P, No. 775, Vol. 29; Tōh. 107.

Mahā-saṁnipāta-ratnaketu-dhāraṇī-sūtra. Sūtra of the Great Collection of Dhāraṇīs of [the bodhisattva] Ratnaketu. Tōh. 138.

Prajñāpāramitāhṛdayasūtra, Shes rab snying po'i mdo, Heart of Transcendent Wisdom Scripture. P, No. 160, Vol. 6; Tōh. 21.

Prajñāpāramitāśatasāhasrikāsūtra, Shes rab 'bum, Transcendent Wisdom One Hundred Thousand, Mother Scripture. P, No. 730, Vol. 29; Tōh. 106.

Saddharmapuṇḍarīkasūtra, Dam chos pad ma'i dkar po'i mdo, Lotus of the True Dharma Scripture. Tōh. 113; P 781, Vol. 30.

Saṁdhinirmocanasūtra, dGongs pa nges par 'grel pa'i mdo, Elucidation of the Intention Scripture (SN). P, No.774, Vol. 29; Tōh. 106.

Samādhi-rāja-sūtra, Ārya-sarva-dharma-svabhāva-samatā-vipañcita-samādhi-rāja-nāma-mahāyāna-sūtra, 'phags pa chos thams cad kyi rang bzhin mnyam pa nyid rnam par spros pa ting nge 'dzin gyi rgyal po, King of Samādhis Scripture. Tōh. 127.

Udānavarga, Categorical Sayings. Publications of the Pali Text Society, vol. 12.

Vajracchedikasūtra, rDor rje gcod pa, Diamond Cutter Scripture. Tōh. 16.

Vimalakīrtinirdeśa. Tōh. 176.

Other Sanskrit and Tibetan Works

Āryadeva

Yogācāracatuḥśataka, rNal 'byor sphyod pa'i bzhi brgya pa, Self-Regulation Four Hundred, Four Hundred (CŚ). P, 5246, Vol. 95; Tōh. 3846.

Asaṅga

Abhidharmasamuccaya, mNgon pa kun las btus pa, Pure Science Compendium. Tōh. 4049.

Bodhisattvabhūmi, Byang chub sems pa'i sa, Enlightened Altruist Stages. P, No. 5538, Vol. 110.

Avalokitavrata

Prajñāpradīpaṭīkā, Shes rab sgron me'i rgya cher 'grel pa, Wisdom Lamp Commentary. P, No. 5259, Vols. 96–97; Tōh. 3859.

Bhāvaviveka

Mādhyamikahṛdaya, dbU ma'i snying po, Heart of the Central Way, Heart (MHK). P, No. 5255, Vol. 96; Tōh. 3855.

Mādhyamikahṛdayavṛttitarkajvāla, rTog ge 'bar ba, Blaze of Argument (TJ). P, No. 5256, Vol. 96; Tōh. 3856.

Buddhapālita

Buddhapālitamūlamadhyamakavṛtti, bdU ma rtsa ba'i 'grel pa bud dha pa li ta, Buddhapālita Commentary (BMMV). P, No. 5242, Vol. 96; Tōh. 3856.

Bu-ston

rGya gar chos 'byung, History of Indian Buddhism (BT). See: Obermiller, *History*.

Chandragomin

Bodhisattvasaṁvaraviṁśaka, Byang chub sems dpa'i sdom pa nyis shu pa, Twenty Verses on the Enlightened Altruist's Vow (BV). Tōh. 4081.

Cāndravyākaraṇasūtra, Chandra's Grammar (CVy). Tōh. 4069.

Deśanastava, bShags pa'i bstod pa, Confessional Praise (DS). Tōh. 1159.

Chandrakīrti

Catuḥśatakaṭīkā, bZhi brgya cher 'grel pa, Commentary on [Āryadeva's] Four Hundred (CŚṬ). P 5266; Tōh. 3865.

Madhyamakāvatāra, dbU ma la 'jug pa, Introduction to the Central Way (MA). P 5261; Tōh. 3861.

Madhyamakāvatārabhāṣya, dbU ma la 'jug pa grel pa, Commentary on the Introduction to the Central Way (MABh). P 5262; Tōh. 3862.

Mūlamadhyamakavṛttiprasannapadā, dbU ma rtsa ba'i 'grel pa tshig gsal, Lucid Exposition (PPMMV). P 5260; Tōh. 3860.

Yuktiṣaṣṭikāvṛtti, Rigs pa drug cu pa'i 'grel pa, Reason Sixty Commentary (YṢV). P 5265; Tōh. 3864.

Śūnyatāsāptativṛtti, sTong pa nyid bdun bcu pa, Voidness Seventy Commentary (ŚSV). P 5268; Tōh. 3867.

Triśaraṇasāptati, gSum la skyabs su 'gro ba bdun bcu pa, Seventy [Stanzas on] the Three Refuges. P 5366/5478; Tōh. 3971.

Pañcaskandhaprakaraṇa, Phung po lnga'i rab tu byed pa, Elucidation of the Five Aggregatess. P 5267; Tōh. 3866.

Dharmakīrti

Pramāṇaviniścaya, Tshad ma rnam par nges pa, Ascertainment of Validating Cognitions. P 5710; Tōh. 4211.

Dharmapāla

Catuḥśatakavṛtti, Guang ba'i lun shi lun, Four Hundred Commentary. Taisho No. 1571.

Dignāga

Pramāṇasamuccaya, tshad ma kun las btus pa, Compendium of Valid Knowledge (PS). P, No. 5700, Vol. 130; Tōh. 4203.

Gö Lotsawa ('Gos lo tsa ba)

Deb ter sngon po, Blue Annals (BA). See Roerich.

Gyaltsap Darma Rinchen (rGyal-tshab Dar-ma-rin-chen)

dBu ma rin chen 'phreng ba'i snying po'i don gsal bar byed pa. Collected Works (*gsung 'bum*) vol. KA; Tōh. 5427.

Rigs pa drug cu pa'i ṭīkka, Commentary on [Nāgārjuna's] "Sixty Stanzas of Reasonings." Collected Works (*gsung 'bum*). New Zhol redaction, vol. CA; Tōh. 5443.

Jamyang Shepa ('Jam dbyangs bzhad pa)

dbu ma 'jug pa'i mtha' dpyod, Decisive Analysis of the Introduction to the Central Way.

Jñānagarbha

Satyadvayavibhaṅga, bden gnyis rnam 'byed, Analysis of the Two Realities. Tōh. 3881.

Kamalaśīla

Bhāvanākrama, sgom pa'i rim pa, Meditation Stages. P, No. 5310–12, Vol. 102; Tōh. 3915–17.

Madhyamakāloka, dbu ma snang ba, Central Way Illumination. P, No. 5287, Vol. 101; Tōh. 3887.

Losang Dorjey (Blo-bzang-rdo-rje)

byang chub lam gyi rim pa'i mtha' dpyod gsung rab rgya mtshor 'jug pa'i gru gzings, Ship for entering into the Ocean of Textual Systems, the Decisive Analysis of [Tsong Khapa's] "Stages of the Path to Enlightenment." New Delhi: Mongolian Lama Guru Deva (1980).

Maitreya

Abhisamayālaṁkāra, mngon rtogs rgyan, Ornament of Realizations (AA). P, No. 5184, Vol. 88; Tōh. 3786.

Dharmādharmatāvibhaṅga, Chos dang chos nyid rnam par 'byed pa, Discrimination between Phenomenon and Noumenon (DDV). P, No. 5523, Vol. 108; Tōh. 4022.

Madhyāntavibhāga, bdUs mtha rnam 'byed, Discrimination between Center and Extremes (MAV). P, No. 5522, Vol. 108; Tōh. 4021.

Mahāyānasūtrālaṁkāra, mDo sde rgyan, Universal Vehicle Discourse Literature (MSA). P, No. 5521, Vol. 108; Tōh. 4020.

Ratnagotravibhāgamahāyānottaratantraśāstra, rGyud bla ma, Analysis of the Jewel Matrix (RGV). P, No. 5525, Vol. 108; Tōh. 4024.

Nāgārjuna

Bodhicittavivaraṇa, Byang chub sems 'grel, Disclosure of the Spirit of Enlightenment. Tōh. 1800–1801.

Lokātītastava, 'Jig rten las 'das par bstod pa, Transcendental Praise. P, No. 2012, Vol. 46; Tōh. 1120.

Prajñānāmamūlamadhyamakakārikā, dbU ma rtsa ba shes rab, Wisdom, Fundamental Verses of the Central Way (MMK). P, No. 5224, Vol. 95; Tōh. 3824.

Rājaparikātharatnāvalī, Rin chen 'phreng ba, Jewel Rosary (RA). P, No. 5658, Vol. 129; Tōh. 4158.

Śūnyatāsāptati, sTong nyid bdun cu pa, Voidness Seventy (ŚS). Tōh. 3827.

Vigrahavyāvartanī, rTsod pa bzlog pa, Rebuttal of Objections (VV). P, No. 5228, Vol. 95; Tōh. 3828.

Yuktiṣaṣṭikā, Rigs pa drug bcu pa, Reason Sixty (YṢ). P, 5225, Vol. 95; Tōh. 3825.

Śāntarakṣita

Madhyamakālaṁkāra, dbU ma'i rgyan, Central Way Ornament. P, No. 5284, Vol. 101; Tōh. 3884.

Tattvasaṁgraha, De kho na nyid bsdus pa, Compendium of Principles. P, Vol. 113; Tōh. 4266.

Śāntideva

Bodhisattvacāryāvatāra, Byang chub sems pa'i sphyod pa la 'jug pa, Introduction to the Practice of the Enlightened Altruist. Tōh. 3871.

Sthiramati

Madhyāntavibhāgaṭīkā, dbUs mtha'i 'grel pa, Discrimination Commentary (MVT). P, Vol. 48; Tōh. 4032.

Triṁśikāvṛtti, Sum cu pa'i bshad pa, Thirty Commentary. P, Vol. 58; Tōh. 4064.

Tāranātha

rGya gar chos 'byung, History of Indian Buddhism (T). See Chattopadhyaya and Chimpa.

***Tsong Khapa Losang Drakpa* (*Tsong kha pa blo bzang grags pa*)**

gsung 'bum (*Collected Works*). Peking Edition. Tokyo: Suzuki Research Foundation, 1956.

ston pa bla na med pa la zab mo rten cing 'brel bar 'byung ba gsung pa'i sgo nas bstod pa legs par bshad pa'i snying po, Short Essence of True Eloquence. Collected Works (*gsung 'bum*) KHA, Thor bu, ff. 15a4–18b4.

byang chub lam gyi rim pa chen mo, Great Stages of the Path. Collected Works (*gsung 'bum*) PA, 481ff.

gsung rab kyi drang ba dang gnas pa'i don rnam par phye ba gsal bar byed pa legs par bshad pa'i snying po, Essence of True Eloquence. Collected Works (*gsung 'bum*) PHA, 91ff.

dbu ma rtsa ba'i tshig leur byas pa'i rnam bshad rigs pa'i rgya mtsho, Ocean of Reason. Collected Works (*gsung 'bum*) BA, 281ff.; P 6143.

rigs pa drug cu pa'i zin bris, Notes on [Tsong Khapa's Lecture on Nāgārjuna's] the "Reason Sixty." Transcribed by Rgyal-tsab Dar-ma-rin-chen. Collected Works (*gsung 'bum*) of Tsong-kha-pa, vol. BA, Tōh. 5404 = Collected Works (*gsung 'bum*) of Rgyal-tsab Dar-ma-rin-chen, New Zhol redaction, vol. CA; Tōh. 5444.

dbu ma 'jug pa'i rnam bshad dgongs pa rab gsal, Illumination of the Intention. Collected Works (*gsung 'bum*) MA, 267ff.

Vasubandhu

Abhidharmakośa, Chos mngon pa'i mdzod, Treasury of Pure Science (AK). P, No. 5590, Vol. 115; Tōh. 4089.

Viṁśatika, Nyi shu pa, Twenty Stanzas (VS). P, Vol. 58; Tōh. 4056.

Vimuktisena

Abhisamayālaṁkāravṛtti, mNgon rtogs rgyan 'grel pa, Ornament of Realizations Commentary. P, No. 5185, Vol. 88.

General Bibliography

Arnaud, J.P. *Freud, Wittgenstein et la Musique*. Paris: Presses Universitaires de France, 1990.

Arnold, D. "Candrakīrti on Dignāga on *Svalakṣaṇas*." *Journal of the International Association of Buddhist Studies* 26, no. 1 (2003): 139–174.

Austin, J.L. *How to Do Things with Words*. Oxford: Oxford University Press, 1962.

Bagchi, S., ed. *Śrīguhyasamājatantram*. Buddhist Sanskrit Texts, no. 9. Darbhanga: Mithila Institute, 1965.

Biardeau, M. *Théorie de la Connaissance et Philosophie de la Parole dans le Brahmanisme Classique*. Paris: Mouton, 1964.

Basham, A. *A Cultural History of India*. Oxford: Oxford University Press, 1975.

Batchelor, S., trans. and ed. *Śāntideva: A Guide to the Bodhisattva's Way of Life*. Dharamsala: Library of Tibetan Works and Archives, 1979.

Baura, D.K. *Viharas in Ancient India*. Calcutta: Indian Publications, 1969.

Beal, S. *The Life of Hiuen Tsiang, by the Shaman Hwui Li*. 1888. New edition, London: K. Paul, Trench, Trübner, 1911.

———. *Si-Yu-Ki: Buddhist Records of the Western World, Translated from the Chinese of Hiuen Tsang (A.D. 629) by Samuel Beal*. 1884. Reprint (2 vols. in 1), Delhi: Oriental Books Reprint Corp. (dist. by Munshiram Manoharlal), 1969.

Bendall, C., ed. *Śikṣāsamuccaya*. The Hague: Mouton, 1957.

Benhabib, S., and F. Dallmayr, eds. *The Communicative Ethics Controversy*. Cambridge: Massachusetts Institute of Technology Press, 1990.

Berger, P., and T. Luckman. *The Social Construction of Reality*. New York: Anchor, 1967.

Bernhard, F., ed. *Udānavarga*. 2 Vols. Sanskrittexte aus den Turfunden, 10. Gottingen: Vandenhoeck & Ruprecht, 1965, 1968.

Berzin, A. "Lam Rim Man Ngag." Ph.D. dissertation, Harvard University, 1972.

Bhattacharya, B., ed. *Sādhanamālā*. 2 Vols. Baroda: Oriental Institute, 1968.

Bhattacharya, K., trans. and ed. *The Dialectical Method of Nāgārjuna* (*Vigrahavyāvartanī*). Delhi: Motilal Banarsidass, 1978.

Bhattacharya, V., ed. and trans. *The Āgamaśāstra of Gauḍapāda*. Calcutta: University of Calcutta, 1943.

Bhattacharya, V., ed. *The Catuḥśataka of Āryadeva*. Calcutta: Visvabharati, 1931.

Bouveresse, J. *Wittgenstein Reads Freud*. Princeton: Princeton University Press, 1995.

Boyd, J. *Satan and Māra*. Leiden: Brill, 1975.

Broido, M. "*bshad thabs*: Some Tibetan Methods of Explaining the Tantras." In *Proceedings of the Csoma de Körös Symposium: Held at Velm-Vienna, Austria, 13–19 September 1981*, vol. 2, ed. by E. Steinkellner and H. Tauscher. *Wiener Studien zur Tibetologie und Buddhismuskunde*, heft 10–11. Wien: Arbeitskreis für Tibetische und Buddhistische Studien, Universität Wien, 1983.

Canfield, J.V., ed. *The Philosophy of Wittgenstein*. 15 vols. New York: Garland Publishing, 1986.

Carelli, Mario E., *Sekoddeśaṭīkā of Nadapada (Naropa): Being a commentary of the Sekkodeśa of the Kalacakra Tantra*. Baroda, 1941.

Cavell, S. "The Availability of Wittgenstein's Later Philosophy." 1962. In *Wittgenstein: The Philosophical Investigations*, ed. by G. Pitcher, 151–185. Notre Dame: The University of Notre Dame Press, 1968.

———. "Aesthetic Problems of Modern Philosophy." 1969. In *The Philosophy of Wittgenstein*, ed. by J.V. Canfield. Vol. 14: 1–24. New York: Garland Publishing, 1986.

———. "Criteria and Judgement." 1979. In *The Philosophy of Wittgenstein*, ed. by J.V. Canfield. Vol. 7: 283–317. New York: Garland Publishing, 1986.

Chakravarti, C., ed. *Guhyasamājatantrapradīpodyotanaṭīkāṣadkoṭivyākhyā*. Patna: Kashi Prasad Jayaswal Research Institute, 1984.

Chandra, L. *Tibetan-Sanskrit Dictionary.* Delhi: International Academy of Indian Culture, 1959.

Chang, G.C.C. *The Buddhist Teaching of Totality.* University Park: University of Pennsylvania, 1974.

Chattopadhyaya, A., and L. Chimpa. *Tāranātha's History of Buddhism in India.* Simla: Indian Institute for Advanced Study, 1970.

Chihara, S., and J. Fodor. "Operationalism and Ordinary Language." 1965. In *Wittgenstein: The Philosophical Investigations,* ed. by G. Pitcher, 384–419. Notre Dame: The University of Notre Dame Press, 1968.

Chomsky, N. *Aspects of the Theory of Syntax.* Cambridge: Massachusetts Institute of Technology Press, 1965.

Cioffi, F. "Wittgenstein's Freud." In *Studies in the Philosophy of Wittgenstein,* ed. P. Winch, 184–210. London: Routledge & Kegan Paul, 1969.

Cleary, J.C., and T. Cleary. *The Blue Cliff Record.* Boulder: Shambhala Press, 1977.

Conze, E., trans. and ed. *Abhisamayālaṁkāra.* Serie Orientale Roma, no. 6. Rome: Istituto Italiano per il Medio ed Estremo Oriente, 1954.

Coulson, M. *Three Sanskrit Plays.* New York: Penguin, 1981.

Cowell, E.B., and F.W. Thomas. *The Harṣa-Carita of Baṇa.* Delhi: Motilal Banarsidass, 1968.

Cozort, Daniel, *Unique Tenets of the Middle Way Consequence School.* Ithaca: Snow Lion Publications, 1998.

Das, S.C. *Tibetan-English Dictionary.* Calcutta: 1902.

Dash, B. *Tibetan Medicine, with Special Reference to Yoga Śataka.* Dharamsala: Library of Tibetan Works and Archives, 1976.

Davidson, R., and J. Davidson. *The Psychobiology of Consciousness.* New York: Plenum Press, 1980.

de Jong, J.W. *Cinq Chapitres de la Prasannapadā.* Paris: Paul Geuthner, 1949.

———. "La Madhyamakaśāstrastuti de Candrakīrti." *Oriens Extremus* 9 (1962): 47–56

———. "Les Sūtrapiṭaka des Sarvāstivādin et des Mūlasarvāstivādin." In *Mélanges d'Indianisme à la mémoire de Louis Renou*, 395–402. Paris: De Boccard, 1968.

———. "Notes à propos des colophons du Kanjur." In *Zentralasiatische Studien*, vol. 6, 505–559. Wiesbaden, 1972.

———. "The Study of Buddhism: Problems and Perspectives." *Studies in Indo-Asian Art and Culture* 4 (1975): 13–26.

———. "Textcritical Notes on the Prasannapadā," *Indo-Iranian Journal* 20 (1978): 25–59, 217–252.

Deleuze, G., and F. Guattari. *What is Philosophy?* Trans. by H. Tomlinson and G. Burchell. New York: Columbia University Press, 1994.

Della Santina, P. *Causality and Emptiness: The Wisdom of Nagarjuna*. Singapore: Buddhist Research Society, 2002. (Available as a free PDF at various online web sites.)

Demiéville, P. *Le Concile de Lhasa*. Paris: Écoles des Hautes Études, 1963.

Dhargyay, G.N. *The Tibetan Tradition of Mental Development*. Dharamsala: Library of Tibetan Works and Archives, 1978.

Dietz, S. "Der Autor des Suhṛllekha." In *Proceedings of the Csoma de Körös Symposium: Held at Velm-Vienna, Austria, 13–19 September 1981*, vol. 2, ed. by E. Steinkellner and H. Tauscher. *Wiener Studien zur Tibetologie und Buddhismuskunde*, heft 10–11. Wien: Arbeitskreis für Tibetische und Buddhistische Studien, Universität Wien, 1983.

Dirks, N. *The Hollow Crown: Ethnohistory of an Indian Kingdom*. Cambridge: Cambridge University Press, 1987.

Doshi, B.J., ed. *Ācāryacandragomipranītam Cāndravyākaraṇam*. Jodhpur: Rajasthan Research Institute, 1967.

Dreyfus, G. *Recognizing Reality: Dharmakīrti's Philosophy and its Tibetan Interpretations*. Albany: State University of New York Press, 1997.

Dumont, L. *Homo Hierarchicus*. Paris: Gallimard, 1966.

Dutt, N. *Gilgit Manuscripts*. Calcutta: Calcutta Oriental Press, 1959.

———, ed. *Bodhisattvabhūmi [Being the XVth Section of Asaṅgapāda's Yogācārabhūmiḥ]*. Patna: K.P. Jayaswal Research Institute, 1966.

Dutt, S. *Buddhist Monks and Monasteries of India*. London: Wisdom, 1962.

Dweyer, P. *Sense and Subjectvity: A Study of Wittgenstein and Merleau-Ponty*. Leiden: Brill, 1990.

Eckel, M. *To See the Buddha: A Philosopher's Quest for the Meaning of Emptiness*. Princeton: Princeton University Press, 1992.

Erb, F. *Śūnyatāsāptativṛtti: Candrakīrti's Kommentar zu den "Siebzig Versen über die Leerheit" des Nāgārjuna (Kārikas 1–14)*. Tibetan text and German translation of Chandrakīrti's commentary on ŚS, ks. 1–14. *Tibetan and Indo-Tibetan Studies* 6. Stuttgart: Franz Steiner Verlag Wiesbaden, 1997.

Esnoul, A.M. *Les Strophes de Sāṁkhya (Sāṁkhya-Kārikā) avec le Commentaire de Gaudapāda; Texte Sanskrit et Traduction Annotée par Anne-Marie Esnoul*. Paris: Les Belles Lettres, 1964.

Farmer, E., et al. *Comparative History of Civilizations in Asia*. Reading, Mass.: Addison-Wesley Pub. Co., 1977.

Fenner, P. "A Therapeutic Contextualization of Buddhist Mādhyamika Consequential Analysis." In *Religious and Comparative Thought*, ed. by P. Bilimoria and P. Fenner, 319–352. Delhi: Śrī Satgūru, 1988.

———. *The Ontology of the Middle Way*. Dordrecht: Kluwer Academic Publishers, 1990.

Filliozat, J. *Yogaśataka: Texte Medical Attribue a Nāgārjuna*. Pondicherry, 1979.

Franco, E. *Dharmakīrti on Compassion and Rebirth*. Wien: Arbeitskreis fur Tibetische und Buddhistische Studien Universität, 1997.

Freud, S. *The Interpretation of Dreams*. 1900. In *The Standard Edition of the Complete Psychological Works of Sigmund Freud*, trans. and ed. by J. Strachey, vol. 4. London, Hogarth Press, 1953–74.

———. "Recommendations to Physicians Practising Psychoanalysis." 1913. In *The Standard Edition of the Complete Psychological Works of*

Sigmund Freud, trans. and ed. by J. Strachey, 12: 111–120. London, Hogarth Press, 1953–74.

———. "The Unconscious." 1915. In *The Standard Edition of the Complete Psychological Works of Sigmund Freud*, trans. and ed. by J. Strachey, 14: 166–196. London, Hogarth Press, 1953–74.

———. "Further Difficulties on the Path of Analysis." 1917. In *The Standard Edition of the Complete Psychological Works of Sigmund Freud*, trans. and ed. by J. Strachey, 17: 137–44. London, Hogarth Press, 1953–74.

———. "The Ego and the Id." 1923. In *The Standard Edition of the Complete Psychological Works of Sigmund Freud*, trans. and ed. by J. Strachey, 19: 12–66. London, Hogarth Press, 1953–74.

———. *Civilization and its Discontents*. 1931. In *The Standard Edition of the Complete Psychological Works of Sigmund Freud*, trans. and ed. by J. Strachey, 21: 104–184. London, Hogarth Press, 1953–74.

Gadamer, H.G. *Truth and Method*. New York: Seabury Press, 1975.

Gangadean, A. "Formal Ontology and the Dialectical Transformation of Consciousness." *Philosophy East and West* 29 (January 1979): 21–48.

Geertz, C. *The Interpretation of Cultures: Selected Essays*. New York: Basic Books, 1973.

Gerow, E. *Indian Poetics*. Wiesbaden: Otto Harrassowitz, 1977.

Gier, N. *Wittgenstein and Phenomenology*. Albany: State University of New York Press, 1981.

Gokhale, V.V. "The Vedānta-Philosophy described by Bhavya in his Madhyamakahṛdayakārikā." *Indo-Iranian Journal* 2 (1958): 165–180.

Govinda, A.B. *The Psychological Attitude of Early Buddhist Philosophy and its Systematic Representation according to Abhidhamma Tradition*. New York: Weiser, 1974.

Greenberg, J.R., and S.A. Mitchell. *Object Relations in Psychoanalytic Theory*. Cambridge: Harvard University Press, 1983.

Gudmunsen, C. *Wittgenstein and Buddhism*. London: Macmillan, 1977.

Gyatso, G.K. *Clear Light of Bliss*. London: Wisdom, 1982.

———. *Ocean of Nectar: Wisdom and Compassion in Mahayana Buddhism.* London: Tharpa Press, 1995.

Habermas, J. *Knowledge and Human Interests.* Trans. by J. Shapiro. Boston: Beacon Press, 1971.

———. *Moral Consciousness and Communicative Action.* Cambridge: Massachusetts Institute of Technology Press, 1990.

Hacker, P.M.S. "The Refutation of Solipsism." In *The Philosophy of Wittgenstein*, ed. by J.V. Canfield. Vol. 12: 121–151. New York: Garland Publishing, 1986.

Hahn, M. *Nāgārjuna's Ratnāvalī: Vol. 1, Basic Texts (Sanskrit, Tibetan, Chinese).* Bonn: Indica et Tibetica Verlag, 1982.

Hamilton, B. *Religion in the Medieval West.* London: Edward Arnold, 1986.

Harre, R., and G. Gillett. *The Discursive Mind.* Thousand Oaks: Sage Publications, 1994.

Hattori, M. *Dignāga on Perception.* Cambridge: Harvard University Press, 1968.

Hillman, J. *Revisioning Psychology.* New York: Harper, 1977.

Hoffman, H. *Tibet: A Handbook.* Bloomington: Indiana University Press, 1975.

Hopkins, P.J. *Meditation on Emptiness.* London: Wisdom Publications, 1983.

———. *Buddhist Advice for Living and Liberation.* Ithaca, NY: Snow Lion Publications, 1998.

Hopkins, P.J., Kensur Lekden, and Tsong-ka-pa. *Compassion in Tibetan Buddhism.* Ithaca: Snow Lion, 1980.

Huntington, J. *The Emptiness of Emptiness.* Chicago: University of Chicago Press, 1992.

Ichigo, M. *Madhyamakālaṁkāra of Śāntarakṣita with his Own Commentary or Vṛtti and with the Subcommentary or Pañjika of Kamalaśīla.* Kyoto: Kyoto Sangyo University, 1995.

Inada, K. *Nāgārjuna: a Translation of his Mūlamadhyamakakārikā with an Introductory Essay of Kenneth K. Inada.* Tokyo: Hokeseido Press, 1970.

Ingalls, D. *Sanskrit Poetry.* Cambridge: Harvard University Press, 1965.

———. *The Dhvanyāloka.* Cambridge: Harvard University Press, 1977.

Isayeva, N. *Shankara and Indian Philosophy.* Albany: State University of New York Press, 1993.

———. *From Early Vedanta to Kashmir Shaivism: Gaudapada, Bhartrhari, and Abhinavagupta.* Albany: State University of New York Press, 1995.

Jacobson, N.P. *Buddhism and the Contemporary World: Change and Self-Correction.* Carbondale: Southern Illinois University Press, 1983.

Jamspal, L.; S. Chophel; and P. Della Santina. *Nāgārjuna's Letter to King Gautamīputra.* Delhi: Motilal Banarsidass, 1978.

Jamspal, L., et al. *The Universal Vehicle Discourse Literature.* New York: American Institute of Buddhist Studies, 2004.

Jha, G., ed. *Śabara-Bhāṣya.* Gaekwad's Oriental Series, nos. LXVI, LXX, LXXIII. Baroda: Oriental Institute, 1933, 1934, 1936.

Johnston, E., ed. *Ratnagotravibhāga-mahāyānottaraśāstra.* Patna: K.P. Jayaswal Institute, 1950.

Joshi, L. *Studies in the Buddhistic Culture of India.* Delhi: Motilal Banarsidass, 1967.

Kajiyama, Y. "Later Mādhyamika on Epistemology and Meditation." In *Buddhist Thought and Asian Civilization*, ed. M. Kiyota. Honolulu: University of Hawaii Press, 1978.

Kalupahana, D. *Causality: The Central Philosophy of Buddhism.* Honolulu: University of Hawaii Press, 1982.

———. *Nāgārjuna: The Philosophy of the Middle Way.* Albany: State University of New York Press, 1986.

Kanakura, Y., ed. *A Catalogue of the Tōhoku University Collection of Tibetan Works on Buddhism.* (Tōh. numbers 5,001–7,083). Sendai: Tōhoku Imperial University, 1953.

Kenny, Anthony J.P., et al. *Wittgenstein and his Times*. Ed. by Brian McGuinness. Chicago: University of Chicago Press, 1982.

Kern, H. and B. Nanjio, eds. *Saddharma-puṇḍarīka-sūtram*. St. Petersburg, 1908–1912.

Kielhorn, F., ed. *Mahābhāṣya de Patañjali*. 3 vols. Poona: Bhandarkar Oriental Research Institute, 1962–1972.

King, R. *Early Advaita Vedānta and Buddhism: The Mahāyāna Context of the Gaudapādīya-kārikā*. Albany: State University of New York Press, 1995.

Kitcher, P. *The Advancement of Science: Science Without Legend, Objectivity without Illusions*. Oxford: Oxford University Press, 1993.

———. *Freud's Dream: A Complete Multidisciplinary Science of Mind*. Cambridge: Massachusetts Institute of Technology Press, 1998.

Kohut, H. *The Restoration of the Self*. New York: Psychoanalytic Press, 1972.

Komito, D., trans. and ed. *Nagarjuna's Seventy Stanzas: A Buddhist Psychology of Emptiness*. Ithaca: Snow Lion Press, 1987.

KOUDA Ryōshū, *Vimalakīrtinirdeśa: Transliterated Sanskrit Text Collated with Tibetan and Chinese Translations*. Tokyo: Taisho University Press, 2004.

Krasser, Helmut, "On Dharmakīrti's Understanding of pramāṇabhuta and His Definition of pramāṇa," *Wiener Zeitschrift für die Kunde Südasiens* 45 (2001): 173–199.

Krishna Murthy, K. *Nāgārjunkoṇḍa: A Cultural Study*. Delhi: Concept Publication Company, 1977.

Kristeva, J. *Revolution in Poetic Language*. Trans. by M. Waller. New York: Columbia University Press, 1984.

Kuhn, T. *The Structure of Scientific Revolutions*. Chicago: Chicago University Press, 1962.

La Vallée Poussin, L. de, ed. *Madhyamakāvatāra de Candrakīrti*. Paris: Muséon, 1907–1911.

———, *Bouddhisme: Études et Matériaux*. London: Luzac & Co., 1898.

———, ed. *Douze Causes*. Gand: Université de Gand, 1913.

———, "Documents d'Abhidharma (II et III)," *Mélanges Chinois et Bouddhiques*, 1 (1931–32): 65–125.

———, "Documents d'Abhidharma," *Mélanges Chinois et Bouddhiques*, 5 (1936–37): 1–187.

———, *L'Abhidharmakośa de Vasubandhu*. 6 vols. Paris and Louvain: Société Belge d'Études Orientales, 1923–1931; reprinted: "L'Abhidharmakośa de Vasubandhu," *Mélanges Chinois et Bouddhiques*, 16, nos. 1–6 (1971).

———, ed. *Madhyamakavṛttiḥ: Mūlamadhyamakakārikās (Mādhyamikasūtras) de Nāgārjuna avec la Prasannapadā Commentaire de Candrakīrti*. 1903–1913. Reprint, Osnabrück: Biblio Verlag, 1970.

Lalou, M. *Répertoire du Tanjur: d'après le Catalogue de P. Cordier [Catalogue du Fonds Tibétain de la Bibliothèque Nationale par P. Cordier]*. 3 vols. Paris: Bibliothèque Nationale, 1909–1933.

———. *Inventaire des Manuscrits Tibétains de Touen-houang Conservés à la Bibliothèque Nationale*. 3 vols. Paris: Maisonneuve, 1939, 1950, 1961.

———. "Les Textes Bouddhique au Temps de Khri-srong-lde-btsan." *Journale Asiatique* (1953): 313–553.

Lamotte, É. *Samdhinirmocana Sūtra: l'explication des Mystères*. Louvain: Bibliothèque de l'Université, 1935.

———. "Madhyamakavṛtti, XVIIe Chapitre." *Mélanges Chinois et Bouddhiques*, 4 (1936): 265–288.

———. *Histoire du Bouddhisme Indien*. Louvain: Institut Orientaliste, 1958, 1976.

———. *Le Traité de la Grande Vertu de Sagesse (Mahāprajñāpāramitāśāstra)*. 5 vols. Louvain: Bureaux du Muséon, 1944–1980.

———. *La Somme du Grande Véhicule d'Asaṅga (Mahāyānasaṃgraha)*. 2 vols. Louvain: Bureaux du Muséon, 1938–1939.

Lang, K. *Āryadeva's Catuḥśataka*. Copenhagen: Akademisk Forlag, 1986.

Laṭi Rinbochay, and P.J. Hopkins, *Death, Intermediate State and Rebirth in Tibetan Buddhism*. Ithaca: Snow Lion, 1980.

Lenoir, T., ed. *Inscribing Science: Scientific Texts and the Materiality of Communication*. Stanford: Stanford University Press, 1998.

Lévi, S., ed. *Mahāyāna-Sūtrālaṁkāra: Exposé de la Doctrine du Grande Véhicule*. Paris: Librarie Honoré Champion, 1907 (Sanskrit); 1911 (French).

Lindtner, C. "Den rette laeres tres vers." In *Nāgārjuna Juvelkoeden og Andre Skrifter*, 85–92. Copenhagen: Sankt Angskars Forlag, 1980.

———, "Atīśa's Introduction to the Two Truths, and Its Sources." *Journal of Indian Philosophy* 9, 1981, 161–214.

———, *Nāgārjuniana: Studies in the Writings and Philosophy of Nāgārjuna*. Copenhagen: Akademisk Forlag, 1982.

———, "Candrakīrti's *Pañcaskandhaprakaraṇa* I: Tibetan Text." *Acta Orientalia* 40 (1979): 87–145.

Loizzo, J. "Wittgenstein and the Mādhyamika." Senior Independent Study Thesis, Amherst College, 1977.

———. "Intersubjectivity in Wittgenstein and Freud: Other Minds and the Foundations of Psychiatry." *Journal of Theoretical Medicine* 12, no. 3 (1997): 111–129.

Lopez, D. *A Study of Svātantrika*. Ithaca: Snow Lion, 1987.

Makransky, J. *Buddhahood Embodied*. Albany: State University of New York Press, 1997.

Margulies, A. *The Empathic Imagination*. New York: W.W. Norton, 1989.

Matilal, B.K. *Epistemology, Logic and Grammar in Indian Philosophical Analysis*. The Hague: Mouton, 1971.

May, Jacques, trans. and ed. *Candrakīrti Prasannapadā Madhyamakavṛtti: Douze Chapitres*. Paris: Adrien-Maisonneuve, 1959.

———. "Āryadeva et Candrakīrti sur la Permanence (IV)." *Études de Lettres* 195, no. 3 (1982): 45–76.

McGuinness, B. "Freud and Wittgenstein." In *Wittgenstein and his Times*, ed by B. McGuinness, 27–43. Oxford: Basil Blackwell, 1982.

Meyendorff, J. *Byzantine Theology: Historical Trends and Doctrinal Themes*. New York: Fordham University Press, 1974.

Monk, R. *Ludwig Wittgenstein: The Duty of Genius*. New York: Free Press: Maxwell Macmillan International, 1990.

Morick, H., ed. *Wittgenstein and the Problem of Other Minds*. New York, McGraw-Hill, 1967.

Murti, T.R.V. *The Central Philosophy of Buddhism*. London: Allen & Unwin, 1955.

Murty, K.S. *Nāgārjuna*. Delhi: Motilal Banarsidass, 1978.

Muthuswami, N.E., ed. *Rasavaiśeṣikasūtram: Bhadanta Nāgārjunaviracitam; Narasiṁhakṛtabhāṣyopetam*. Trivandrum: Publication Division, Govt. Ayurveda College, 1976.

Nagatomi, M. "The Pramāṇavārtika of Dharmakīrti." Unpublished manuscript, Harvard University, 1979.

Nagel, T. *The View From Nowhere*. Oxford: Oxford University Press, 1986.

Naudou, J. *Les Bouddhistes Kaśmīriens au Moyen Age*. Paris: Presses Universitaires de France, 1968

Needham, J. *Science and Civilization in Ancient China*. Oxford: Oxford University Press, 1964.

Nietzsche, F. *Twilight of the Idols; and the Anti-Christ*. Baltimore: Penguin, 1972/1990.

Nikam, N.A., and R. McKeon, eds. *Edicts of Asoka*. Chicago: Chicago University Press, 1958.

Oberlies, T. *Studie zum Cāndravyākaraṇa: Eine Kritische Bearbeitung von Candra IV.4.52–148 und V.2*. Stuttgart: Franz Steiner Verlag Wiesbaden, 1989.

Obermiller, E. *Analysis of the Abhisamayālaṁkāra*. London: Luzac, 1936.

———, trans. *History of Buddhism [by Bu-ston]*. 2 vols. Heidelberg: O. Harrassowitz, 1931–1932.

Pandeya, R.C., ed. *Madhyāntavibhāgaśāstra*. Delhi: Motilal Banarsidass, 1971.

Patel, P.B., ed. *Cittaviśuddhiprakaraṇa of Āryadeva: Sanskrit and Tibetan Texts*. [Calcutta]: Visva-Bhāratī, 1949.

Pensa, C., ed. *Abhisamayālaṁkāravṛtti di Ārya-Vimuktisena*. Serie Orientale Roma, no. 37. Rome: Istituto Italiano per il Medio ed Estremo Oriente, 1967.

Perdue, Daniel E., *Debate in Tibetan Buddhism*. Ithaca: Snow Lion Publications, 1992.

Phillips, D.L. *Wittgenstein and Scientific Knowledge*. London: MacMillan Press, 1977.

Piaget, J. *Genetic Epistemology*. New York: Cambridge University Press, 1970.

Pitcher, G., ed. *Wittgenstein: The Philosophical Investigations*. Notre Dame: The University of Notre Dame Press, 1968.

Popper, K. *The Logic of Scientific Discovery*. New York: Harper & Row, 1965.

Potter, K. *Presuppositions of India's Philosophies*. Westport, Conn.: Greenwood Press, 1972.

Pradhan, P. (ed.) *Abhidharmakośabhāṣya of Vasubandhu*. Patna: K.P. Jayaswal Research Institute (1967).

Prasāda, R., trans. and ed. *Patanjali's Yoga Sutras, with the Commentary of Vyāsa and the Gloss of Vāchaspati Miśra*. 1912. Sacred Books of the Hindus, no. 4. Reprint, New York: AMS Press, 1974.

Pribram, K. *Languages of the Brain: Experimental Paradoxes and Principles in Neuropsychology*. Englewood Cliffs, N.J.: Prentice-Hall, 1971.

Radhakrishnan, S., and C. Moore. *Sourcebook in Indian Philosophy*. Princeton: Princeton University Press, 1957.

Rahder, J. *Dashabhūmikasūtra*. Leuven: J.-B. Istas, 1926.

Raju, P.T. *Philosophical Traditions of India*. London: Allen & Unwin, 1971.

Ricoeur, P. *Freud and Philosophy*. Trans. by D. Savage. New Haven: Yale University Press, 1970.

———. *Hermeneutics and the Human Sciences*. Trans. by J. Thompson. Cambridge: Cambridge University Press, 1982.

———. *Oneself as Another*. Trans. by K. Blamey. Chicago: University of Chicago Press, 1992.

Rieff, P. *Freud: The Mind of the Moralist*. New York: Viking, 1959.

Rizzi, C. *Candrakīrti*. Delhi: Motilal Banarsidass, 1988.

Roberts, R.C. "The Grammar of a Virtue." In *The Grammar of the Heart*. Ed. by R. Bell, 149–170. San Francisco: Harper and Row, 1988.

Robinson, J.B., trans. *Buddha's Lions: The Lives of the Eighty-Four Siddhas [by Abhayadatta]*. Tibetan Translation Series, no. 10. Berkeley: Dharma Publishing, 1979.

Roerich, G.N. *The Blue Annals*. 2 vols. Calcutta: Royal Asiatic Society of Bengal, 1949, 1953.

Rorty, R. *Philosophy and the Mirror of Nature*. Princeton: Princeton University Press, 1979.

———. "Criteria and Necessity." 1973. In *The Philosophy of Wittgenstein*, ed. by J.V. Canfield. Vol. 7: 217–233. New York: Garland Publishing, 1986.

———. "Wittgenstein, Privileged Access, and Incommunicability." 1970. In *The Philosophy of Wittgenstein*, ed. by J.V. Canfield. Vol. 9: 152–166. New York: Garland Publishing, 1986.

Rotman, B. *Signifying Nothing: The Semiotics of Zero*. San Jose: Stanford University Press, 1987.

Ruegg, D.S. *The Life of Bu ston Rin po che, with the Tibetan Text of the Bu ston rNam thar.* Serie Orientale Roma, no. 34. Rome: Istituto Italiano per il Medio ed Estremo Oriente, 1966.

———. *La Théorie du Tathāgatagarbha et du Gotra*. Paris: École Française d'Extrême-Orient, 1969.

———. "Le Dharmadhātustava de Nāgārjuna." In *Études Tibétaines Dédiées à la Mémoire de Marcelle Lalou*, 448–471. Paris: Librairie d'Amérique et d'Orient, 1971.

———. "The Uses of the Four Positions of the Catuṣkoṭi and the Problem of the Description of Reality in Mahāyāna Buddhism." *Journal of Indian Philosophy* 5 (1977): 1–71.

———. "Mathematical and Linguistic Models in Indian Thought: The Case of Zero and Śūnyatā." *Wiener Zeitschrift für die Kunde Südasiens* 22 (1978): 171–181.

———. *The Literature of the Madhyamaka School of Philosophy in India.* Wiesbaden: Otto Harrassowitz, 1981.

———. "Autour du lTa ba'i khyad par de Ye śes sde." *Journal Asiatique* (1981): 207–229.

———. "Towards a Chronology of the Madhyamaka School." In *Indological and Buddhist Studies: Volume in Honor of Prof. J.W. de Jong on his Sixtieth Birthday*, ed. by L.A. Hercus, et al., 505–530. Canberra: Faculty of Asian Studies (Australian National University), 1982.

———. "Purport, Implicature and Presupposition: Sanskrit *abhiprāya* and Tibetan *dgoṅs pa / dgoṅs gźi* as Hermeneutical Concepts." *Journal of Indian Philosophy* 13 (1985): 309–325.

Sakya Drakpa Gyaltsan. *Candragomin's Twenty Verses on the Bodhisattva Vow and its Commentary.* Dharamsala: Library of Tibetan Works and Archives, 1982.

Sāṁkṛtyāyana, R. "Second Search of Sanskrit Palm-leaf Mss. in Tibet." *Journal of the Bihar and Orissa Research Society* 23, no. 1 (1937): 1–57.

Śaṅkara. *Brahmasūtra with Śaṅkarabhāṣya.* Works of Śaṅkarācārya, 3. Delhi: Sri Satguru, 1964.

Sarton, G. *Introduction to the History of Science.* 1927–1948. Baltimore: Williams & Wilkins, 1948.

Saunders, J.T., and D.F. Henze. *The Private-Language Problem: A Philosophical Dialogue.* New York: Random House, 1976.

Schaeffer, Philipp. *Yukti-ṣaṣṭikā: Die 60 Sätze des Negativismus nach der Chinesischen Version Übersetzt.* Materialien zur Kunde des Buddhismus 3. Heidelberg, 1923.

Schafer, R. *A New Language for Psychoanalysis.* New Haven: Yale University Press, 1976.

———. *Language and Insight.* New Haven: Yale University Press, 1978.

Schayer, Stanislaw. *Ausgewählte Kapitel aus der Prasannapadā: (V, XII, XIII, XIV, XV, XVI).* Polska Akademja Umiejetnosci 14. W Krakowie: Nakładem Polskiej Akademji Umiejetności, 1931.

Scherrer-Schaub, C., *Yuktiṣaṣṭikāvṛtti: Commentaire à la Soixantaine sur le Raisonnement.* Mélanges Chinois et Bouddhiques 25. Bruxelles: Institut Belge des Hautes Études Chinoises, 1991.

———, "*Yuktiṣaṣṭikāvṛtti* of Candrakīrti." In K. Potter, ed., *Encyclopedia of Indian Philosophy*, Delhi, Motilal Banarsidass, 1995.

Scholem, G. *Major Trends in Jewish Mysticism.* New York: Schoken, 1995.

Shankalia, H.D. *Nālandā University.* Delhi: Oriental Press, 1972.

Sharma, R.K., and B. Dash, eds. and trans. *Agniveśa's Carakasaṁhitā.* 7 vols. Chowkhamba Sanskrit Studies, vol. 94. Varanasi: Chowkhamba Sanskrit Series Office, 1976–2002.

Shastri, H.N. *Nālandā and its Epigraphic Material.* Delhi: Śrī Satgūru, 1942.

Silk, Jonathan, "Possible Indian Sources for the Term *tshad ma'i skyes bu* as *pramāṇabhūta.*" *Journal of Indian Philosophy* 30 (2002): 111–160.

Simonsson, N. *Indo-Tibetische Studien: Die Methoden der Tibetischen.* Uppsala: Almqvist & Wiksells, 1957.

Sorenson, P., ed. and trans. *Triṣaraṇasāptati: the Septuagint on the Three Refuges [by Candrakīrti].* Wien: Arbeitskreis für Tibetische und Buddhistische Studien, Universität Wien, 1986.

Spence, D. *Narrative Truth and Historical Truth: Meaning and Interpretation in Psychoanalysis.* New York: W.W. Norton, 1982.

Speyer, J.S. *Avadānaçataka: A Century of Edifying Tales.* 2 vols. St. Petersbourg, 1902–1909.

Sprung, M., ed. *The Problem of Two Truths in Buddhism and Vedānta.* Boston: Reidel, 1973.

———, trans. *Lucid Exposition of the Middle Way*. Boulder: Prajñā Press, 1979.

Srivastava, B. *Harṣa and His Times: A Glimpse of Political History During the Seventh Century A.D.* Chowkhamba Sanskrit Studies, vol. 86. Varanasi: Chowkhamba Sanskrit Series Office, 1976.

Stcherbatsky, Th. *The Conception of Buddhist Nirvāṇa.* Leningrad: Pub. Office of the Academy of Sciences of the USSR, 1927.

———. *Madhyānta-vibhāga: Discrimination Between Middle and Extremes.* Delhi: Sri Satguru Publications, 1992.

———. *Buddhist Logic.* 2 vols. New York: Dover, 1962. (Originally published 1930–32.)

Steinkellner, E. "Remarks on Tantristic Hermeneutics." In *Proceedings of the Csoma de Körös Memorial Symposium: Held at Mátrafüred, Hungary, 24–30 September, 1976*, ed. by L. Ligeti. Biblioteca Oriental Hungarica, no. 23. Budapest: Akadémiai Kiadó, 1978.

Steinkellner, E., and H. Tauscher, eds. *Proceedings of the Csoma de Körös Symposium: Held at Velm-Vienna, Austria, 13–19 September 1981*, vol. 2. *Wiener Studien zur Tibetologie und Buddhismuskunde.* Wien: Arbeitskreis für Tibetische und Buddhistische Studien, Universität Wien, 1983.

Stolorow, R., and G. Atwood. *Contexts of Being: The Intersubjective Foundations of Psychological Life.* Hillsdale: The Analytic Press, 1992.

Strachey, J., trans. and ed. *The Standard Edition of the Complete Psychological Works of Sigmund Freud.* 24 vols. London, Hogarth Press, 1953–74.

Streng, F.J. *Emptiness: A Study in Religious Meaning.* Nashville: Abingdon, 1967.

Suzuki, D.T., trans. *The Lankāvatāra Sūtra.* 2 vols. London: Routledge & K. Paul, 1956.Takakusu, J. *A Record of the Buddhist Religion as Practiced in India and the Malay Archipelago.* Oxford: Clarendon Press, 1896.

Takasaki, J. *A Study of the Ratnagotravibhāga*. Rome: Istituto Italiano per il Medio ed Estremo Oriente, 1966.

Tambiah, S. *World Conqueror and World Renouncer: A Study of Buddhism and Polity in Thailand against a Historical Background.* Oxford: Oxford University Press, 1976.

Tat, W. *Ch'eng Wei-Shih Lun: Doctine of Mere-Consciousness.* Hong Kong: Dai Nippon, 1973.

Tatz, M. *Difficult Beginnings: Three Works on the Bodhisattva Path.* Boston: Shambhala Press, 1985.

Thakur, U. *Buddhist Cities in Early India.* Delhi: Sundeep Prakashan, 1995.

Thapar, R. *Recent Perspectives in Indian History.* Delhi: Sangham, 1995.

Thibaut, G. *The Vedānta Sūtras of Bādarāyaṇa with Śaṅkara's Commentary.* Sacred Books of the East, nos. 34 & 38. Delhi: Motilal Banarsidass, 1968.

Thurman, R.A.F. "Non-egocentrism in Candrakīrti and Wittgenstein." *Philosophy East and West* 30 (July, 1980).

———. "Vajra Hermeneutics." In *Buddhist Hermeneutics*, ed. by D. Lopez. Honolulu: University of Hawaii Press, 1988.

———. *Inner Revolution: Life, Liberty, and the Pursuit of Real Happiness.* New York: Riverhead Books, 1998.

———, ed. *Life and Teachings of Tsong Khapa.* Dharamsala: Library of Tibetan Works and Archives, 1982.

———, trans. *The Holy Teaching of Vimalakīrti.* University Park: Pennsylvania State University Press, 1976.

———, trans. *Tsong Khapa's Speech of Gold in the Essence of True Eloquence: Reason and Enlightenment in the Central Philosophy of Tibet.* Princeton: Princeton University Press, 1984.

Tilghman, B.R. *Wittgenstein, Ethics, and Aesthetics: The View from Eternity.* Albany: State University of New York Press, 1991.

Tillemans, T. *Materials for the Study of Āryadeva, Dharmapāla and Candrakīrti.* Wien: Arbeitskreis fur Tibetische und Buddhistische Studien Universität Wien, 1990.

———. *Persons of Authority*. Stuttgart: Franz Steiner Verlag, 1993.

Tilmann, V. *Buddha und Seine Lehre in Dharmakīrti's Pramāṇavārttika*. Vienna: Universität Wien, 1984.

Tola, F., and C. Dragonetti. "The 'Yuktiṣaṣṭikā' of Nāgārjuna." *Journal of the International Association of Buddhist Studies* 6, no. 2 (1983): 94–123.

Toynbee, A. *A Study of History*. Oxford: Oxford University Press, 1957.

Tsong-ka-pa. *Tantra in Tibet*. London: Allen & Unwin, 1977.

Tucci, G. "Two Hymns of the Catuḥstava of Nāgārjuna." *Journal of the Royal Asiatic Society* (1932): 309–325.

———. *Tibetan Painted Scrolls*. 2 vols. and portfolio. Rome: Libreria dello Stato, 1949.

———. *Minor Buddhist Texts*. Serie Orientale Roma, no. 9. Rome: Istituto Italiano per il Medio ed Estremo Oriente, 1956–1958.

Ui, H. *A Complete Catalogue of the Tibetan Buddhist Cannons*. Sendai: Tōhoku Imperial University, 1934.

URYŪZU Ryūshin. "Nāgārjuna kenkyū (1): Kūsho to Engi ni tsuite." *Meijo Daigaku Jimbun Kiyo* 14 (October 1973): 23–40.

———. "Nāgārjuna kenkyū (2)." *Kyoto Daigaku Jimbun Ronso* 23 (1974): 134–160.

———. *Rokujūju Nyoriron (Rokujūshiju no seirron oyobi chūshaku)*. Daijo Butten, vol. 14. Tōkyō: Chūō Kōronsha, 1974.

———. "Nāgārjuna kenkyū (3)." *Kyoto Daigaku Jimbun Ronso* 29 (1981): 34–59.

———. "Rokujūju Nyoriron ni okeru Nāgārjuna no shiso." *Bukkyogaku* 12 (October 1981): 1–24.

Vaidya, P.L. *Études sur Āryadeva et son Catuḥśataka*. Paris: Geuthner, 1923.

———, *Aṣṭasāhasrikā Prajñāpāramitā*. Darbhanga: Mithila Institute, 1960.

———, *Lalitavistara*. Darbhanga: Mithila Institute, 1958.

———, *Prasannapadāmūlamadhyamakavṛtti*. Darbhanga: Mithila Institute, 1960.

———. *Bodhicaryāvatāra of Śāntideva with the Commentary Pañjikā of Prajñākaramati.* Buddhist Sanskrit Texts, no. 12. Darbhangha, Mithila Institute, 1960.

———, *Samādhi-rāja-sūtra.* Darbhanga: Mithila Institute, 1961.

Vidyābhuṣaṇa, S.C., trans. *Nyāya Sūtras of Gautama.* 2nd ed., rev. and enl. by Nandalal Sinha. Allahabad: Panini Office, 1930.

Walleser, M. *The Life of Nāgārjuna from Tibetan and Chinese Sources.* Delhi: Nag Publishers, 1979.

Wangyal, G. *The Door of Liberation.* New York: Lotsawa, 1978.

Wayman, A. *Yoga of the Guhyasamājatantra: The Arcane Lore of Forty Verses.* Delhi: Motilal Banarsidass, 1977.

———, trans. *Calming the Mind and Discerning the Real.* New York: Columbia University Press, 1978.

Wayman, A., and F. Lessing. *Mkhas-grub rje's Fundamentals of the Buddhist Tantras.* The Hague: Mouton, 1968.

Weber, M. *The Religion of India: The Sociology of Hinduism and Buddhism.* 1958 (English trans.). Reprint, Delhi: Munshiram Monoharlal, 1996.

Wedemeyer, C. "Vajrayāna and its Doubles: The Tantric Works of Āryadeva." Ph.D. dissertation, Columbia University, 2000.

Willemen, Charles, *Dharmapada: A Concordance to Udānavarga, Dhammapada, and the Chinese Dharmapada Literature.* Bruxelles: L'Institut Belge des Hautes Études Bouddhiques, 1974.

Winch, P., ed. *Studies in the Philosophy of Wittgenstein.* London: Routledge & Kegan Paul, 1969.

Wittgenstein, L. *Philosophical Investigations.* New York: Macmillan, 1953.

———. *The Blue and Brown Books.* New York: Harper, 1958.

———. *On Certainty.* New York: Harper, 1969.

———. *Culture and Value.* New York: Harper, 1970.

———. *Zettel.* Berkeley: University of California Press, 1970.

———. *Philosophical Grammar.* Oxford: Blackwell, 1975.

———. *Tractatus Logico-Philosophicus*. New York: Humanities, 1976.

———. *Lectures and Conversations on Ethics, Aesthetics and Religious Belief.* Berkeley: University of California Press, 1979.

———. *Last Writings on the Philosophy of Psychology.* 2 Vols., Oxford: Blackwell, 1982/1992.

Wogihara, U., ed. *Abhisamāyālaṃkārāloka Prajñāpāramitāvyakhya*. Tōkyō: Toyo Bunko, 1932–1935.

———. *Sphuṭârthā Abhidharmakośavyākhyā: The Work of Yaśomitra.* 7 vols. Tōkyō: Publishing Association of the Abhidharmakośavyākhyā, 1932–1936.

Wogihara, U., and C. Tsuchida, eds. *Saddharmapuṇḍarīka-sūtram*. Tōkyō, 1934–1935.

Wujtasik, D. *The Roots of Āyurveda*. New York: Penguin, 1998.

Yamaguchi, Susumu. "Japanese Translation with Critical Edition of *Yuktiṣaṣṭikā*. In *Chūgan Bukkyō Ronkō*. Tōkyō: Sankibō Busshorin, 1944/1965, 29–110.

———. *Index to the Prasannapadā Madhyamaka-vṛtti*. 2 vols. Kyoto: Heirakuji, 1974.

———. "Nāgārjuna's Mahāyānaviṁśaka," *The Eastern Buddhist* IV (1926): 56–72.

Yangchen Gawai Lodoe. *Paths and Grounds of Guhyasamaja According to Arya Nagarjuna*. Commentary by L. Tsephel; trans. by T. Dorjee and J. Russell; ed. by D. Komito and A. Fagan. Dharamsala: Library of Tibetan Works and Archives, 1995.

Yates, F. *Giordano Bruno and the Hermetic Tradition*. Chicago: Chicago University Press, 1964.

Index

C

L

O